ORGANIZED CRIME

A Worldwide Perspective

Sean Grennan

Long Island University—C.W. Post Campus

Marjie T. Britz

Clemson University

PEARSON
Prentice
Hall

Upper Saddle River, New Jersey 07458

Library of Congress Cataloging-in-Publication Data

Grennan, Sean.
    Organized crime: a worldwide perspective/Sean Grennan, Marjie T. Britz.
      p. cm.
    Includes bibliographical references and index.
    ISBN 0-13-171094-X
    1. Organized crime.   2. Gangs.   I. Britz, Marjie.   II. Title.

HV6441.G74 2006
364.1'06—dc22

                                        2005049172

Executive Editor: Frank Mortimer, Jr.
Associate Editor: Sarah Holle
Production Editor: Milford Publishing Services
Production Liaison: Brian Hyland
Director of Manufacturing and Production: Bruce Johnson
Manufacturing Manager: Ilene Sanford
Managing Editor: Mary Carnis

Manufacturing Buyer: Cathleen Pertersen
Cover Design Coordinator: Miguel Ortiz
Cover Designer: Joseph DePinho, DePinho Design
Cover Image: Matthew Antrobus, Stone/Getty Images
Marketing Manager: Adam Kloza
Formatting: Integra
Printing and Binding: R.R. Donnelly, Harrisonburg

Pearson Education LTD.
Pearson Education Singapore, Pte. Ltd
Pearson Education, Canada, Ltd
Pearson Education–Japan
Pearson Education Australia PTY, Limited
Pearson Education North Asia Ltd
Pearson Educación de Mexico, S.A. de C.V.
Pearson Education Malaysia, Pte. Ltd
Pearson Education Upper Saddle River, New Jersey

10 9 8 7 6 5 4 3 2 1
ISBN 0-13-171094-X

Dedication

Sean Grennan dedicates the work he did in this book to some very important people who will always be in his life: Mollie, Megan, Carmine C., Lauren, and Linda F. Last, but not least, all the wonderful students I have had the pleasure of meeting and teaching over the past 20 years.

As always, Marjie T. Britz dedicates this work in loving memory of her dad, Theodore Albert Britz. She further dedicates this book to two other special men who have touched her life: Dennis M. Payne, who took her under his wing, welcomed her into his family, and always shared a cocktail with his "lovely bride, Jan"—she'll remember you always; and Joe W. Morgan, Jr., who consistently amazes her with his compassion for his fellow human beings and with his legal acumen.

Contents

Preface

Traditionally, the term *organized crime* has been very narrowly defined. Based on the government's characterization, criminal groups were included only if they demonstrated commonalities of structure, regulations and criminal activities and lacked ideological foundations. Without exception, such a characterization tended to be exclusive, and disparate groups were largely ignored. As a result, research in the area has focused on the phenomenon of organized crime, not the criminal syndicates themselves.

A number of college textbooks exist in the marketplace that concentrate almost exclusively on the methods of organized crime while failing to provide adequate attention to those groups outside traditional definitions, definitions which were formulated around a single group (Italian-Americans). This book approaches the study of organized crime in an entirely different way. The first two chapters evaluate theories and definitions of organized crime, while the remainder of the book provides a comprehensive discussion of traditional, nontraditional, and emerging criminal syndicates.

Each criminal group included in the book is viewed historically, territorially, economically, and politically in an effort to provide a complete package of all international criminal groups. This informational package includes historical background on the formation of each group, including when and how the group was created. The ethnic, racial, or ideological makeup of each gang is discussed, along with each group's rules, regulations, rituals, hierarchy, and criminal enterprises. Each chapter also explores law enforcement initiatives, including history, legislation, and success rate, as well as a discussion of the corruption of authority where applicable.

This book provides students with an in-depth perspective on organized criminal syndicates that no other book on the market offers. With this text, students gain knowledge concerning the development of organized groups not only in the United States but also internationally. Written with the college student in mind, this book contains meaningful information that provides the reader with greater knowledge and understanding of organized criminal gangs. Such information assists students during their coursework and gives them a comprehensive understanding of the operations of global crime groups.

CRIMINAL GANGS AND ORGANIZED CRIME

The Preface introduced the basic idea that what an organized criminal group is and does has not changed significantly over the years. How gang members carry out their activities, the tools they use, the organizational sophistication they display, and the criminal activity they engage in may change, but the composition of the gang itself does not. Having said this, it is important to note that the natural process of maturation has often been overlooked by scholars and law enforcement officials alike. As a result, definitional characterizations of criminal gangs, improperly focusing on generational characteristics, have proven to be somewhat lacking. Thus, it is essential to establish a working definition of criminal gangs and their progenies.

Academic and practitioner definitions of *street gangs* and *organized crime groups* have traditionally appeared to be irreconcilable—treated as completely independent entities. However, historical analysis of both has revealed that the development of such groups is anything but independent. *Criminal gangs*, in fact, are simply a less complex, less sophisticated precursor to *organized crime groups*. Thus, while all organized crime groups may be characterized as criminal gangs, the reverse is not always the case. The following chapter will evaluate traditional definitions of both, identify their similarities, and establish a working definition for use throughout the text.

CRIMINAL GANGS

An evaluation of the literature reveals a marked level of definitional inconsistency among, and within, the academic and law enforcement communities. Goldstein (1991), for example, offers 14 different definitions of a gang. These range from 1912 to 1990 and include definitions offered by academics and professionals. Conly et al. (1993) offer 6 definitions, again using those provided by academics and professionals. Neither the

14 definitions in one study nor the 6 in the other are the same. So what? The community's response and the resources it provides for combating the "gang problem" will rely heavily (if not completely) on how gangs and the "gang problem" are defined. Thus, being able to define the problem leads one to the response and the available resources. If we cannot define the problem, we cannot address it. The absence of a common definition is surprising given that interest in gangs goes as far back as the 1890s, if not earlier. In fact, it could also be argued that the Capulets and Montagues of Shakespeare's *Romeo and Juliet* could be considered gangs.

The professional community, in looking for advice and direction in this area, would probably find yet another reason to see academia as not being useful, because we cannot agree among ourselves about what a gang is. Miller (1980) sees this problem as significant and calls on the "social scientists to define what a gang is to counteract the manipulation of the term by people outside the social science research community" (in Horowitz, 1990: 43). Miller goes on to argue that law enforcement and the media (you could add corrections, juvenile justice, etc.) broaden or narrow their definition as it suits their own particular cause. One of the problems that arises is the inability to compare information about gangs across cities or times. Decker and Kempf (1991) note that even within the same jurisdiction, different parts of "the system" define the problem differently. This lack of a clear definition forces public officials to respond to an ill-defined problem and could make them look as if they do not know what is going on in their own community. It often results in a denial that a gang problem exists and/or in the overidentification of gangs, gang members, and the gang problem (Huff, 1990). The search for a definition may also overshadow our purpose in looking at gangs and in solving the gang problem. Ryan (1998) makes the point that we may be spending too much time defining gangs rather than addressing strategies to deal with, prevent, and intervene with them.

It may, however, be beneficial that a firm definition does not exist. Each group involved in working with gangs has its own interests and assumptions and would probably never agree on a specific definition in the first place. Second, a firm definition might restrict research on gangs and the topics studied. With a firm definition in place, new questions or foci could be discouraged. As it is, every study of gangs and the gang problem offers its own definition of what a gang is. Typically these definitions rely on the definitions imposed on gangs by those from whom the information is sought (e.g., law enforcement, gangsters themselves). While these variations make cross-jurisdictional comparisons difficult, knowing the definitions assigned by those involved assists in understanding the interplay between the justice system personnel, the community, and the gang. It also affects the publicity (or lack of it) afforded the problem, the distribution of resources, and the gangster's treatment by the system. Zatz (1985) notes that issues of definition do affect the way a suspected gangster is identified and treated by the justice system.

Clearly, as gangs have evolved, so too have the definitions. Can we identify some commonalities, some characteristics that are common to the Hole in the Wall Gang and the Rolling 60s? Miller (1974) surveyed more than 100 criminal justice and youth services agencies about their respective definitions of what makes up a gang. In terms of consensus, he identifies six major elements:

1. Being organized
2. Having identifiable leadership
3. Identifying with a territory
4. Having continual association
5. Having a specific purpose
6. Engaging in illegal activities

Within many of the definitions one encounters, these six general elements will appear. They also make evident how the character of gangs has changed. While we believe that each of Miller's six elements is characteristic of all gangs, whether juvenile or adult, clearly other elements must also be considered. One element is the increase in violent behavior. Noted gang researcher Irving Spergel in testimony before the Senate's juvenile justice subcommittee commented that the gang problem is "amorphous and complex, . . . that we seem to know what to do rather than what not to do, but that violence is a major consideration" (December 19, 1994). While Spergel made this comment in December 1994, Miller in 1975 noted, "Contemporary youth gangs pose a greater threat to public order and a greater danger to the safety of the citizenry than at any other time during the past" (in Goldstein, 1991: 7). Given that we have made little current progress in addressing the gang problem, one can only speculate about what this twenty-first century will bring. It is also important to note that in his same testimony, Spergel commented that he did not believe the savagery itself had radically changed but that the instruments of violence certainly had. Newer and more deadly instruments of violence result in a more certain end for those involved in the violence.

Besides more serious firepower, these new instruments are often used impersonally. The escalation of violence also appears to have an intergenerational dynamic to it. In those gangs that contain an intergenerational connection, primarily Hispanic and some Chicago gangs, younger gangsters seem to want to match or outdo their predecessors. Still others want to live up to their moniker. Spergel identifies some other nonbehavioral reasons: Gangs today have more weapons; they are more sophisticated; they have a greater ability to "hit and run" (e.g., drive-bys); and membership may have grown (Goldstein, 1991). Also, gangs appear more willing to use weapons and see them as signs of power (Conly et al., 1993). It must also be remembered that violence has in many ways become an acceptable response to life's obstacles.

The other new element is drugs. Many gangs are involved in the drug trade, and some appear to exist exclusively for that purpose. Some are involved in selling drugs, others in doing drugs; drugs are a defining element in many (if not all) current gang activities. Any current gang definition needs to consider, in some form, the increase in violence and drug activity. It should be noted, however, that if drugs were to be removed from society or legalized, gangs would still exist. They would simply find another illegal outlet for making money.

Returning to the idea of violence, it must be understood that violence is not the primary activity of most gangs. "Hanging out" and partying (certainly not criminal activities) are still staple gang activities, as is participation in many truly conventional activities, most notably athletics. In fact, most gang activity is not violent; however, violence permeates gang life and gang activity. A gang cannot be territorial without the willingness to use violence to exert and maintain control of their territory. Violent events do much to provide cohesion for the gang, and as Klein has commented, violence has a mythic quality (in Decker, 1995). Gang members talk about it, retell the story, and use it as a focal point for the next violent episode. Even though very little gang time is taken up with violence, as Sanders notes, "It is the willingness to do violence that makes a gang a gang" (1994: 12; emphasis in the original). For those who interact with the gang, the knowledge that the group will use violence is what sets it apart from other groups—gang or nongang, juvenile or adult, criminal or noncriminal. Using violence is proof positive of the ongoing willingness to do violence. Violence, even if used sparingly, then plays a key role in defining a gang and gang behavior.

What, then, makes a gang a gang, at least as most people think of a gang? It is violence. Even Miller (1975), who did not want to overemphasize violence, used it to differentiate street groups from gangs. So, if it is violence that defines a gang, what kind of violence, and how does it work with respect to the gang? Sanders (1994) provides us with some answers. First, a gang must use deadly force. They must use or be prepared to use enough force to kill someone. This killing can occur in a defensive or offensive posture, but death is the key.

Second, the violence must be used in the name of the gang. The members, when engaging in a violent crime, recognize that it is done for or with the gang. This intent is most evident with drive-by shootings. As Davis notes in his study of drive-bys, those involved in the shootings "dressed in ways that marked them as gang members" (1995: 17). The gang members in his study saw any sign of disrespect as an affront that warranted attack, and the members "accepted the implied responsibility of being willing to commit a violent crime for the organization" (1995: 18). For Garfinkel (1967), the violence and the gang are mutually enforcing: Violence defines the event as gang related, and the gang is seen as causing the violence.

The third aspect involves gang solidarity. Violence serves as a solidifying force for the gang. Group solidarity increases in the face of external threats to the group. Because gangs have few sources of internal cohesion, the external threats posed by the police and rival gangs serve to maintain group cohesion (Klein, 1968). Whether viewed as appropriate or not, the violence serves as a solidifying force. This cohesion, however, is a unique balancing act for gangs. Too much external pressure, usually in the form of a law enforcement response or several deaths, can have the opposite effect. If the belief is "[W]e're getting shot at or arrested everywhere we go, the gang can become viewed as a source of problems and disunity" (Sanders, 1994: 18). Thus, it must be "the right amount of violence" at the "right time" against the "right people" to maintain group cohesiveness. Violence therefore is generally not the gang's all-consuming passion; it must be balanced with other activities, legitimate and illegitimate.

The fourth part involves territoriality. Many gang definitions talk about territory or turf. Although this aspect is changing somewhat, gangs are identified by their turf. Implied in this notion is, again, the use of violence. A gang cannot keep territory without being willing to use violence in keeping it. Thus violence is necessary to maintain territorial integrity (Sanders, 1994).

While violence is a defining behavior for gangs, it is not and does not need to be constant or engaged in by all members. As a group, a gang is composed of a variety of individuals, many of whom will prove their loyalty to the gang in ways other than violence (e.g., stealing, pimping). The frequency and intensity of the gang's violence may also vary. Many gangs may go years without a violent act; it is their reputation for violence that keeps them a gang. Indeed, when a gang feels its reputation is in jeopardy, gang members are likely to resort to violence to renew their gang status, to let everyone around know they are still here and, more important, still violent.

As important as violence is in defining a gang, it is not the sole determinant. Also important is the transpersonal nature of membership. A gang is defined not by its specific members at any given point in time but as a phenomenon transcending its membership. The gang exists no matter who its members are. The gang as a unit, as a force to be reckoned with, remains. This idea is important for identifying a gang, for it differentiates a gang from what Yablonsky (1962) calls a "near group," ad hoc, impermanent, and transitory.

What then is a gang? Not wanting to reinvent the wheel and recognizing the merit present in each state's criminal justice agencies' own definitions, Sanders's definition (with some qualifications) may be utilized:

> A youth gang is any transpersonal group of youths that shows a willingness to use deadly violence to claim and defend territory, and attack rival gangs, extort or rob money, or engage in other criminal behavior as an activity associated with its group, and is recognized by itself and its immediate community as a distinct dangerous entity. The basic structure of gangs is one of age and gender differentiation, and leadership is informal and multiple (1994: 20).

However, there appear to be two deficiencies in Sanders's model. One is that age differentiation does not seem relevant when evaluating youth or adult gangs. A youth gang, by definition, is no different from an adult gang. Adult gangs are also defined by transpersonality, a willingness to use violence, and acts of criminal behavior with and for the gang. Because of benefits associated with gang membership, many gangsters are remaining in the gang longer or even for life. In addition, the maturation of youth gangs into organized crime syndicates is all but inevitable in most cases. Thus, the tag "youth" should be removed. A gang is a gang is a gang, no matter the age of its members.

Our other deficiency has to do with Sanders's point about leadership. Not one gang but rather a multiplicity of gangs and gang types exists, each with the "basics": a willingness to use deadly violence to claim and defend territory, attack rival gangs, extort or rob money, or engage in other criminal behavior as an activity associated with its group, recognized by itself and its immediate community as a distinct dangerous entity but each having unique qualities as well. For many, this uniqueness is its leadership. The importance of leadership is certainly true of organized crime, many Asian gangs, some Hispanic gangs, and the Disciples and Vice Lords. Many of these have a well-defined leadership structure, with policies in place for replacement, succession, etc. Clearly this structure is formal and singular rather than informal and multiple. The same can be said of many early-twentieth-century gangs. It can be argued, then, that most gangs whose leadership is informal and multiple are probably not transpersonal and cease to exist when their leadership is arrested or dead. Such groups are more consistent with Asbury's (1928) definition of a *mob* and are not appropriate for discussions involving criminal gangs. Although these groups do emerge periodically, their lack of longevity coupled with their relative spontaneity makes them inappropriate in a discussion of criminal gangs. Thus, a new definition emerges, borrowing much from Sanders but having a more contemporary flair:

> A criminal gang is any transpersonal group of individuals that shows a willingness to use deadly violence to claim and defend territory, and attack rival gangs, extort or rob money, or engage in other criminal behavior as an activity associated with its group, and is recognized by itself and its immediate community as a distinct dangerous entity. The basic structure of gangs is one of gender and leadership differentiation unique to its particular location and history. In addition, all criminal gangs maintain organizational rules and regulations including, but not limited to, secrecy. Such characteristics create the potential for organizational longevity.

For many, knowing what a gang is, is important for deciding what a gang-related crime is. Unfortunately, not all agencies define a gang-related incident in the same way, and just because the police call an incident gang-related (or non-gang-related) does not necessarily make that definition correct. Often, this definition occurs because the individual involved has been identified as a gangster; however, as Katz (1993) argues, even though a criminal has been identified as a gangster, it does not mean that the crime was caused by gang involvement. Spergel, et al. suggest that "a gang crime incident is an incident in which there was gang motivation, not mere participation by a gang member" (1990: 23). They believe that a gangster's nongang crime should be recorded but should be differentiated from his gang crime. For example, Sanders notes the shooting of a rival lover by a gangster. Even though the rival was not a gangster and the violent act was not one in the name of the gang but rather in the name of love, because the shooter was a gangster, the police identified the crime as gang-related.

Being in a gang will result in criminality. Often it will be direct and at other times indirect, but it will be criminal nevertheless. In fact, it is the criminality that directs our attention to the gang. A gang itself is not illegal; being in a gang is not illegal. What is illegal is gang members' criminal behavior. Is it necessary—other than as an academic exercise—to really know the difference, to categorize the difference? Does knowing the difference assist us in dealing with gangs? In many gangs, a gangster cannot commit a crime on his or her own; the gang will get its cut somehow. Thus the gangster who goes into the local "stop and rob," empties the cash register, and uses the money for his personal good and who is subsequently disciplined by the gang members either for bringing too much pressure on them or for not giving them their cut, did he not commit a gang-related crime? In other instances, the individual gangster may engage in criminal behavior that he could not pull off were it not for his gangster status. Is this not also gang-related? We believe the gang- and non-gang-related crime distinction is an artificial one that does nothing but cloud the issues here. If an identified hard-core gangster commits a crime, it is gang-related and should be recorded as such.

A criminal gang, then, is a group of individuals who are willing to use violence in pursuit of their goals, who engage in criminal behavior individually or collectively, and who have a specific structure defining themselves. A street group is not, then, a gang because it is not willing to use violence in pursuit of its objectives. Yablonsky's near groups are not gangs because they are transitory. With some exceptions, any group that is not willing to use violence, is transitory, or does not claim territory is, therefore, not a gang. The fact that these groups are not gangs does not make them any less worthy of study or less dangerous; it does, however, make them different from a gang and generally does require a different response.

ORGANIZED CRIME

As noted previously, all *organized crime groups* began as criminal gangs. Organized crime groups do not spontaneously appear. In fact, all organized crime groups discussed in this text were traditionally treated as street gangs. For the most part, the vast majority of organized crime groups originated as a result of perceived oppression and discrimination or perceptions of restrictive governments. Throughout history, the emergence of criminal groups and subsequent violence has been greatest during periods of economic depression. The deprivation experienced in the mid-1800s, for example, was characterized by a dramatic increase in gang affiliation in New York City (Asbury, 1928). However, economic deprivation is not the sole determinant in gang development. Indeed, the convergence of a variety of variables bears greater weight than any single causative agent and may enhance the potentiality for organization within street gangs. A cultural emphasis on masculinity, historical territorial rivalries, and the advent of mass unemployment all serve to increase the primacy of group affiliation and to decrease the likelihood of antigang maturation of members. Thus, the evolution of common street gangs into organized criminal syndicates involves a variety of factors; however, the majority of definitions associated with both fail to address this issue. In fact, definitions of *organized crime* are as diverse, as inaccurate, and as numerous as those traditionally associated with criminal gangs. Law enforcement gatherings, senatorial committees, academic consortiums, and even Hollywood studios have created definitions based largely on anecdotal accounts by mob informants. For the most part, these definitions have focused primarily on Italian organized crime, denying the existence of criminal syndicates among other ethnicities.

The first attempts to formally define organized crime were undertaken by two different government commissions. While both of them uncovered a network of sophisticated multijurisdictional criminal entrepreneurs, they proved to be largely ineffectual at the time. The first definition of organized crime in the United States was created in 1915 by the Chicago Crime Commission. In an attempt to define what they considered *institutionalized crime*, the commission was the first of its kind to recognize differences between traditional crimes and criminals and the emerging pattern of criminal behavior perpetrated by organized criminal groups. They found that such entities were unique in that they resembled an independent society of sorts, with systemized tasks and practices, unique traditions and rituals, and distinctive jargon. These findings were expanded on by the Wickersham Commission of 1929. This commission, designed to evaluate the impact of Prohibition, found that the organization of criminal activity surrounding Prohibition was actually created by it. (Unfortunately, the structure that was created during and that flourished throughout the period did not end with the repeal of the Eighteenth Amendment, as profits from bootlegging had been utilized to create additional criminal markets.) As with the recommendations of its predecessor, the admonitions put forth by the Wickersham Commission were largely ignored until the 1950s, and organized crime continued on its path of organizational sophistication and criminal maturation.

In 1957, a string of gangland murders and the discovery of a meeting of top-echelon underworld figures in Apalachin, New York, propelled the Italian mafia into the national spotlight. Such events served as an impetus for government scrutiny and law enforcement activity. At that time, the Kefauver Committee, which had been in existence since 1950, increased its efforts to evaluate the connection of organized crime to gambling. In addition, the committee expanded its original focus to include a plethora of other organized criminal activities. Headed by Senator Estes Kefauver, the committee transfixed the American public as it televised the testimony of over 600 witnesses. The national appeal was twofold: (1) The invention of the television was relatively new, and (2) the witnesses included movie stars, politicians, and prominent organized crime figures. The committee concluded that an international conspiracy to traffic in narcotics and other contraband had deep roots in immigrant communities across the United States and that an organized criminal syndicate with a sophisticated hierarchy was directly responsible for the proliferation of vice-related activities. Unfortunately, these assertions were largely predicated on assumptions and hyperbole, as virtually no testimony alluded to a vast criminal network. As Bell (1953: 139) notes, "[N]either the Senate Crime Committee in its testimony nor Kefauver in his book presented any real evidence that the Mafia exists as a functioning organization." Thus, the findings were viewed with skepticism by the public and law enforcement alike. Although an historical evaluation indicates that these statements were largely accurate, the overstatements and generalizations distanced the very audience they were intended to impress.

The McClellan Committee formed in the early 1960s was more successful in proving the existence of the Italian mafia. The committee, formally known as the Senate Permanent Subcommittee on Investigations, was largely assisted by the testimony of mob turncoat Joe Valachi. For the first time, the government had access to an organizational insider privy to the group's structure, customs, and criminal activities.[1] Valachi's account, like most anecdotal accounts of life in the mob, indicated that the majority of his youth was spent in various street gangs (including the "Minute Men") and that he engaged in a variety of disorganized criminal activity such as burglarizing and fencing stolen goods. He testified that he and others of his street gang joined an organized group of criminals called La Cosa Nostra (LCN), which when literally translated means "this thing of ours." He outlined the organizational structure of the entity, identifying layers of leadership and the roles and responsibilities of each. He additionally testified to the existence of a formal commission of leaders and the identities of current players in organized crime. Finally, he fully discussed methods of racketeering and the infiltration of legitimate marketplaces by Italian organized crime. Although the committee failed to outline a specific definition of organized crime, Valachi's testimony added the element of racketeering, which was previously absent in articulated models of organized crime.

POST VALACHI

Since Valachi's ousting of numerous bosses in the 1960s, death, both natural and not, has claimed many of them including (but not limited to) the following:

Anthony Accardo	Chicago	died of natural causes
Joseph Bonanno	New York	died of natural causes
Angelo Bruno	Philadelphia	was murdered
Joe Colombo	New York	was murdered
Frank DeSimone	Los Angeles	died of natural causes
Carlo Gambino	New York	died of natural causes
Vito Genovese	New York	died in prison
Sam Giancana	Chicago	was murdered
Stephen Magaddino	Buffalo	died of natural causes
Ray Patriarcha	New England	died of natural causes
Joseph Zerilli	Detroit	died of natural causes

In 1967, the President's Commission on Law Enforcement and the Administration of Justice offered an extremely vague, overly inclusive definition of the phenomenon, stating that organized crime involved "a society that seeks to operate outside the control of the American people and their government. It involves thousands of criminals, working within structures as large as those of any corporation." Under this definition other ethnic groups that were heavily involved in syndicated criminal activity were excluded. However, the Omnibus Crime Control and Safe Streets Act of 1968 remedied this oversight, declaring that organized crime included "the unlawful activities of the members of a highly organized, disciplined association engaged in supplying illegal goods and services including, but not limited to, gambling, prostitution, loan-sharking, narcotics, labor racketeering, and other lawful activities."

Although the act's definition proved to be more inclusive than its predecessors, it failed to address issues of political corruption—a variable necessary for the continuation of criminal groups. Perhaps by design, the language included therein excluded individuals who were not card-carrying members of an organized crime family. In addition, it disregarded the motivation behind such activities, making no mention of pecuniary gain. In fact, these two characteristics of organized crime were not addressed until 1980, when the Pennsylvania Crime Commission, focusing primarily on organized crime activities in Philadelphia and Pittsburgh, expanded the definition put forth by the Omnibus Crime Control and Safe Streets Act of 1968, stating:

> The unlawful activity of an association trafficking in illegal goods or services, including but not limited to gambling, prostitution, loansharking, controlled substances, labor racketeering, or other unlawful activities or any continuing criminal conspiracy or other unlawful practice which has as its objective large economic gain through the fraudulent or coercive practices or improper governmental influence.

Covering all the bases, the commission also expanded on the original definition put forth by the President's Commission on Law Enforcement and the Administration of Justice:

> [Organized crime is a] society that seeks to operate outside the control of the American people and their governments. It involves thousands of individuals working within structures as complex as any large corporation, subject to laws more rigidly enforced than those of legitimate governments. Its actions are not impulsive but rather the result of intricate conspiracies, carried on over many years and aimed at gaining control of whole fields of activity in order to amass huge profits.

Ironically, the definition most used by law enforcement entities is the one that originated with the Pennsylvania Crime Commission, a state rather than a federal entity. For all intents and purposes, this characterization was the most comprehensive

A WORD ABOUT IDEOLOGY

Traditionally, definitions of organized crime specifically precluded groups or organizations with articulated ideology or those lacking geographic demarcations. However, the premise that gangs and organized crime groups are nonideological is badly flawed. To suggest that terrorist and racist organizations must be excluded due to their underlying dogma all but suggests that these groups are less insidious or less criminal than their economically motivated counterparts. In fact, historical accounts of gang formation reveal many political and religious cliques whose ideologies manifested themselves in traditional street crime activities. In Davies's (1998) historical analysis of gang development in Glasgow, Scotland, he found both territorial and sectarian alliances. Indeed, family-based or socially perpetuated ideologies coupled with existing apathy to others actually serve to solidify organizational members, creating greater resiliency and organizational longevity. Thus, this text does not disqualify those sorts of entities.

A WORD ABOUT POLITICAL CORRUPTION

Criminal gangs have long relied on their connections to practice criminal activity and to avoid prosecution. Beginning with Tammany Hall, criminal gangs were often used as muscle by politicians, forcing people to vote a certain way and preventing the opposition from voting. This allowed gangs to control both the politicians and the local police. The corruption was so bad, in fact, that the state legislature abolished the municipal police and the police board originally developed under the 1853 act, an act designed to prevent corruption. The legislation resulted in the creation of a Metropolitan Police District, which four governor-appointed commissioners would supervise. However, the original police, with the support of the mayor, refused to relinquish their positions, and a battle erupted between the municipal police and the newly appointed metropolitan police. When the National Guard finally quelled the battle, 52 policemen were injured.

Over the next several months, police presence and accompanying law and order were nonexistent as the police fought among themselves, often countermanding one another. The National Guard became a regular presence, and it was forced to step in and stop the rioting among criminal gangs while the police brutalized one another. Thus, law enforcement of the era was an oxymoron. As Asbury notes, "[S]o demoralized were the police by political chicanery and by widespread corruption within their own ranks that they were unable to enforce even a semblance of respect for the law" (1928: 174).

of the period; however, it too suffered from some deficiencies, most notably the omission of territoriality and monopolization. Thus, any definition of organized crime must include the following interdependent elements:

1. *Structure and hierarchy.* Virtually all organized crime groups are characterized by recognition of responsibility, task assignment, and leadership. Each organized crime group has a system of interrelated positions, whether formally appointed or elected, that are specifically designed to facilitate task accomplishment. The people in these positions, who are recognized by organizational members, assign responsibilities, dictate policy and procedures, and ensure compliance.

2. *Violence.* The threat or the utilization of violence is necessary for both task efficacy and organizational longevity. It is an essential component of criminal activities such as extortion, loan-sharking, and racketeering. It is also important in maintaining control over organizational members. Ironically, the potential for violence may be more important than the actual violence itself, as reputations for violence often negate the need to employ it.

3. *Recognizability.* Organized crime groups are recognized not only by law enforcement authorities but by their communities as well. This is necessary for the extortion of funds, as they rely on the specter of a mass criminal organization to intimidate potential victims. It is also necessary for the corruption of political figures. Such recognizability may be likened to the threat of violence, violence which is not employed but which causes targets to realize their own vulnerability against an army of criminals.

4. *Longevity.* Whether guided by religious zeal or motivated by pecuniary gain, goals must include the organization's preservation. Members must recognize the continuity of group ideology and the organization itself. Such recognition necessarily includes their own impermanency and vulnerability.

5. *Recruitment.* To further ensure organizational longevity, criminal groups must maintain the ability to replenish their ranks as positions become available. Traditionally, ethnically based organized crime groups recruited youngsters from the neighborhood, evaluating the youngsters' criminal prowess and organizational loyalty by assigning them small tasks. While recent immigrant criminal groups have continued this practice, traditional groups such as the LCN are increasingly forced to replenish their personnel with family members or longtime associates. (Throughout the text, the authors will discuss the various methods of recruitment employed by individual organizations.)

6. *Entrepreneurial activities.* All organized crime groups are characterized by elevated levels of innovative and opportunistic entrepreneurial criminal activity.

Such innovation is necessary as changes in legislation and law enforcement efforts combine to reduce the cost-benefit ratio of various activities. The repeal of the Eighteenth Amendment, for example, forced organized crime groups to develop new markets to replace revenue lost by the legalization of alcohol. Many groups turned to narcotics to refill depleted coffers. The use of technology by contemporary groups is illustrative of innovation. Organized crime groups are also extremely opportunistic, engaging in virtually any activity that results in pecuniary gain. The use of stolen credit cards for personal purchases is a perfect example.

7. *Exclusive membership.* Entrance into the criminal group requires some commonality with organizational members. As Asbury (1928) discovered in his evaluation of criminal gangs in early-twentieth-century New York, those groups that came together for the sole purpose of committing criminal activity but that lacked ethnic solidarity also lacked organizational longevity. Culture, shared experiences, traditions, and religion often play a role in the solidification of norms and expectations of the group prior to criminal activity. Such commonalities may include, but are not limited to, race, ethnicity, criminal background, or ideology. However, such common traits do not ensure organizational admittance. Just as money is not the sole factor in entrance to exclusive country clubs, incumbent members closely scrutinize a potential member's background. In fact, the level of inspection employed by these groups is often greater than that found in law enforcement agencies. Organizational fit, individual loyalty, and criminal ability are but a few of the factors that determine an individual's acceptance.

8. *Strict rules and regulations.* Organized crime groups are characterized by elevated levels of rules and regulations. Paramount in each is the rule of silence. Individuals violating organizational secrecy are almost always killed. While rules vary between individual groups, all are established to ensure organizational longevity and task efficacy. Rules of conduct between members, for example, are necessary to negate potential friction within the group. Noncompliance results in organizational discipline ranging from loss of respect to loss of life.

9. *Ritualism.* Just like noncriminal societies, aberrant groups also display a tendency for ritualism. Induction ceremonies, organizational meetings, and the like are all characterized by ceremonial trappings. The development of jargon and customary displays of respect solidify members and further sanctify the organization itself.

10. *Profitability.* All members of organized crime syndicates are expected to enhance organizational coffers through criminal enterprise. The practice of tithing to organizational leaders or elders furthers the interests of the organization in the form of political bribery or, in some cases, the support

of criminal defense. Even ideologically based groups must maintain a positive cash flow to support their dogmatic platform.

11. *Racketeering and infiltration of legitimate businesses.* Although traditionally associated with the LCN, the practice of racketeering and the infiltration of legitimate businesses have permeated all corners of organized crime. With the increasing amount of legislation designed to identify illegal profits, the laundering of money through legitimate sources has become increasingly common. In addition, a facade of legitimacy furthers organizational goals and increases organizational longevity, as the business of crime becomes more palatable to an American public desensitized to white-collar crime.

12. *Corruption of political officials.* The organized corruption of political officials, including police officers, politicians, and jurists, has a long history in the United States. Criminal gangs have long colluded with these entities, beginning with Tammany Hall in the early 1800s. In fact, early systems of policing, which included the practice of appointments by aldermen and then the Board of Police Commissioners in New York City, established an incestuous relationship among politicians, police, and criminal gangs (the police owed the politicians who appointed them, the politicians owed the criminal gangs that fixed their elections, and the criminal gangs owned them both).

13. *Monopolization.* Like their legitimate counterparts, organized crime groups enhance their profitability through monopolization. Such efforts are not solely restricted to criminal activities such as narcotics, gambling, and prostitution; criminal groups seek to monopolize legitimate industries as well. In New York and Atlantic City, for example, the Italian mafia's involvement in organized labor resulted in a construction monopoly, and builders were forced to pay a street tax for every building erected. In addition, the garbage industry in New York was long controlled by the LCN, which received monies from every "independent" collector in the city. Such monopolies are possible through the use of violence and labor racketeering.

14. *Criminal activity.* It goes without saying that all organized crime groups engage in criminal activity. Such activity ranges from the relative simplistic crimes of gambling, prostitution, loan-sharking, extortion, burglary, murder, assault, and arson to more complex endeavors such as racketeering, stock fraud, narcotics trafficking, alien smuggling, money laundering, and casino skimming. The level of each is largely determined by organizational culture and individual capability. While some groups may specialize in one type of criminal activity such as narcotics, others engage in a variety of activities.

DISTINGUISHING CRIMINAL GANGS FROM ORGANIZED CRIME

Although much ado is made in the popular media and the academic literature about the differences between gangs and organized crime, a careful evaluation of the topic indicates that gangs may simply be a less evolved criminal group, because the vast majority of organized crime members trace their criminal history to youth gangs. While the primary purpose of either may vary from the political to the ideological to the pecuniary, both engage in criminal activity to support the membership and group platform. Thus, lines of demarcation between gangs and organized crime are increasingly blurred; just as LCN crews meet traditional definitions of gangs, Chicago-based street gangs clearly fit within the parameters of the definition of organized crime. However, three differences must be noted between the two:

1. Geographic territory and boundaries are more salient to gangs than to organized crime.

2. While many street gangs are propagated primarily by juveniles and young adults, organized crime groups, due to elevated levels of criminal maturity, tend to be dominated by middle-aged or elder adults.

3. Not all gangs have the potential to become organized crime groups, but all organized crime groups were previously gangs.

Thus, the following definition emerges:

Organized crime is a recognizable, monopolistic, self-perpetuating, hierarchical organization willing to use violence and the corruption of public officials to engage in both traditional vice-related activities and complex criminal enterprises, and it ensures its organizational longevity through ritualistic practices, rules and regulations, organizational tithing, and investment in legitimate businesses. Because the majority of groups discussed in the text meet the above description, the terms *organized crime, criminal gang(s)*, and *gangs* will be used interchangeably throughout the text unless otherwise noted. It is important to mention that the few groups not meeting the organized crime definition above have demonstrated the potential to do so through natural maturation.

ENDNOTE

1. It must be noted that Valachi's testimony has been discredited by various sources due to its self-serving nature. In addition, Valachi's account is peppered with inaccuracies promoted by the popular media of the time. Thus, it is unclear as to which portions of his testimony actually reflect his independent recollections and which portions are patently false.

CHAPTER 2

THEORIES OF CRIMINAL SUBCULTURES AND ORGANIZED CRIME

As it is with any organization, group members go a long way in defining a criminal gang's structure and organization. Given that criminality, especially violent criminality, is key in defining organized crime groups and their activity, why would an individual want to join one? Keep in mind that while members are of all ages, it is rare that one joins or begins criminal associations as an adult. Clearly some individuals learn about criminal gangs while in prison and upon their release form associations with the local gang, but for the most part, gang membership begins during youth and adolescence. Additionally, some evidence suggests that gang formation and one's entry into a gang vary with the location or context of the criminal organization. In New York, for example, ethnic street gangs developed within neighborhood tenements. In Los Angeles, city and suburban gangs developed differently, with violence being the flashpoint for gang formation in the city, followed by drug dealing. In the suburbs of Los Angeles, drug dealing came first, followed by gang formation and recruitment and then violence. In Milwaukee, Wisconsin, gangs developed out of dance groups when fights broke out after the dance competitions; in addition, traditional corner groups also coalesced around the fighting. Without exception, such groups respond with and are solidified by violence when threatened by outsiders. Thus, criminal organizations form and individuals join them for a variety of reasons associated with the individuals and with the community where they reside. While gangs are not exclusively ethnic or racial, the contexts associated with being an ethnic or racial minority provide an impetus for gang formation. Throughout history, when any ethnic group (e.g., Jews, Irish, Italian) was at the bottom, gangs were formed. Certainly one explanation that is frequently offered is that the gang fills a void in the individual's life. Typically, for this type of individual, the traditional family does not exist, leaving the individual to believe she or he is alone and must cope with her or his problems alone. The gang, then, becomes a surrogate family providing the individual with personal attention and a sense of identity.

Johnston (1983) identifies several factors that increased the chance that one might choose gangsterism: community characteristics, social and institutional attachments, and a definition of self. Many of the gangsters in Johnston's study tended to be from communities where the perception of racial tension was high. Most of the gangsters did, in fact, come from single-parent families with little parental control. These gangsters also tended to have problems in school as well as low self-esteem and relatively low self-confidence in any setting. The gang, then, could provide these youth with the status, a sense of self-worth, and a place of acceptance that they at least perceived they did not have in their family life; again, this scenario is not unusual for disenfranchised ethnic groups.

Individuals join gangs for a variety of reasons, including individual needs for identity, recognition, protection, love and understanding, status, money, and opportunity. Wade (1993) identifies the following reasons for joining a gang: acceptance, recognition, a sense of belonging, status, power, discipline (or consistency), structure, unconditional love, shelter, food, clothing, nurturing, activities, economic support, and respect. She goes on to comment that many gang members tell her that their families only provide three or four of these.

Despite the criminality and violence associated with being in a gang, joining up may be viewed as normal and respectable. The criminality and violence may be seen as secondary to the excitement, fun and frolic, and association with peers of similar class, interest, need, and persuasion (Sarnecki, 1986). Deukmajian (1981) and Rosenbaum and Grant (1983) suggest that the consequences of being a gangster may not be recognized by adolescents and young adults; however, others disagree. While youths generally do not have the same maturity as adults, they do know right from wrong and know—or should know—that criminality and violence are wrong. That they do not know the consequences provides them a way out or an excuse for their behavior. Others posit that they do know the consequences of their behavior and that either they do not care or their need for status, recognition, etc., overwhelms their rationality. Still others argue that the police and juvenile courts do not do a sufficient job of attaching punishment and accountability to adolescents' behavior when they are caught, particularly the first time.

Not only may joining a gang be viewed as normal by the individual, but it may also be seen as desirable and expected in certain communities. Particularly in lower-class ethnic (white) and Hispanic communities, honor, loyalty, and fellowship are viewed as compelling reasons for joining gangs. The gang is seen as the vehicle for preserving the neighborhood and protecting its honor (Horowitz, 1983; Torres, 1979). In these communities and for these residents, the gang is an extension of rather than a substitute for the family and aids the development of the clan. For many individuals, especially Hispanics, multigenerational gang membership is the norm rather than the exception.

Gang membership may also be seen as a way of providing protection from real or perceived threats, perhaps even from the gang itself. This reason may be especially true for the new kid in school or in town. Members of the family may be harassed, intimidated, or attacked, so he or she joins the gang to be protected. While the gang member may feel safer within the gang, Savitz, Rosen, and Lalli (1980) point out that being a gangster increases the likelihood of attack, at least by another gangster. So while the individual may believe his or her safety is tenuous, joining a gang ironically increases his or her chances of becoming a victim.

In addition to the social and psychological reasons espoused for joining a gang, many individuals join a gang for financial reasons. The gang becomes a vehicle for the individual to develop contacts and the know-how for further criminality. In addition, the gangster attracts the attention of older gangsters, including those involved in traditional organized crime; many become protégés and go on to an adult criminal life. This pattern is well depicted in *The Godfather* movies. Most recently, the gang has become a place for contact with drug dealers and to prepare for a career as a dealer, hit man, or enforcer (Miller, 1975).

Summarily, various rationales for individual criminal association have been asserted throughout the years. These justifications range from hedonism to blocked opportunity to coercion. However, most have concentrated on the decision to join a criminal organization, failing to evaluate the juxtaposition of criminal behavior and criminal association. Thus, traditional theories of delinquency may be more appropriate for understanding the development of criminal organizations; below are the most common explanations and theories.

PSYCHOLOGICAL EXPLANATIONS

In a quest to understand the development of criminal gangs, theories across disciplines have abounded. While some of these theories have been specifically developed to address the phenomenon of gangs, the majority of those applied have been far less germane to the phenomenon. Unfortunately, many such theories have failed in their attempt to explain the development of organized deviance within certain ethnic and socioeconomic groups; such is the case with many psychological explanations.

Antisocial Personalities

Originally known as *sociopathy* or *psychopathy*, antisocial reactions are those impulsive behaviors that reflect an insensitivity to the needs of others and a lack of remorse or guilt on the part of the actor. Individuals with antisocial personalities are not deterred by punishments and are incapable of self-behavioral modification. They often display personable demeanors and may be admired by others for the ability to achieve need satisfaction. At the same time, they exhibit an inability to develop nurturing relationships and lack emotional depth. Thus, antisocial personalities exhibit a pathological egocentricity. On the surface, their hedonistic composition appears consistent with individuals involved in organized crime, a lifestyle which maximizes the potential for pleasure while requiring a sublime indifference to pain and suffering. The practice of murdering close associates or longtime companions is illustrative of the inability to develop bonds of loyalty beyond self-centeredness. At the same time, historical accounts of organized crime groups reveal a pattern of organizational solidarity inconsistent with this assertion. Although violated periodically, organizational rules of *omerta* are in direct contradiction to the characteristics displayed by these individuals. In addition, the applicability of this psychological disorder to those involved in organized criminal groups must assume that this condition is overrepresented in certain ethnic or socioeconomic groups. Since there is no empirical evidence to support such a presumption, its credibility remains in question.

Dependent Personalities

According to the DSM-III-R (American Psychiatric Association, 1987), a dependent personality reflects "a pervasive pattern of dependent and submissive behavior beginning by early adulthood and present in a variety of contexts." Such individuals are characterized by excessive weakness and passivity. They are incapable of leadership positions and are generally reliant on significant others throughout their life; such dependency, however, results in suppressed resentment toward others. These individuals may be dangerous because their volatility is unpredictable, but, their propensity for violence does not necessarily enhance their attractiveness to organized crime groups. Indeed, unpredictability and passivity appear to be detrimental to the organizational longevity desired by criminal gangs. As such, it is unlikely that such entities make up a majority of such gang members. While it may be a useful term to describe certain individuals who have peppered the criminal landscape, its applicability to organized crime is tenuous at best.

SOCIOLOGICAL EXPLANATIONS

While psychological explanations may be useful for certain patterns of deviant behavior, the same is not the case in the study of organized crime. Historical accounts and empirical evaluations of the phenomenon have revealed certain commonalities among criminal syndicates regardless of ethnicity; these include but are not limited to marginalization, economic deprivation, and discrimination. Such constants have been either ignored by psychological theories or dismissed as extraneous. However, it is inconceivable to suggest that certain ethnic groups that just happen to be poor and just happen to be discriminated against and just happen to be targeted by law enforcement share a common pathology, one which is coincidentally absent in the majority of the population. Thus, most experts agree that sociological explanations are more plausible.

Learning Theories

Learning theories, perhaps the most widely accepted for explaining deviant behavior, attribute deviance to the presence of criminal reinforcements external to the individual. They argue that criminal acts are largely facilitated by significant others who reinforce nonconforming behavior. In addition, they assert that such behavior and its techniques are actually *learned*, as are the definitions associated with such acts. Thus, organized crime is created in a milieu that fosters illegal activity. We consider two learning theories: Sutherland's theory of differential association and the subculture theory.

Sutherland's Theory of Differential Association. According to Sutherland (1973), criminal behavior is learned through associations with significant others. While not all individuals placed in criminal environments will engage in aberrant behavior, the likelihood of their involvement is directly related to the strength of such associations. Sutherland argues that criminal behavior results when reinforcements for criminal behavior exceed reinforcements to obey the law. In marginalized and/or economically disadvantaged communities where deviance is normative, individuals are more susceptible to illegitimate success models. Such individuals, socialized within an environment supportive of criminal activity, may turn to criminal gangs or organized crime groups to achieve socially defined measures of success. Lyman and Potter (2000: 75–76) cite nine principles of Sutherland's theory:

1. Criminal behavior is learned.
2. The fundamental basis of criminal behavior is learned in intimate personal groups.
3. Criminal behavior is acquired through interaction with other persons in a process of communication.
4. The learning process includes the techniques of committing the crime and specific rationalizations and attitudes for criminal activity.
5. General attitudes regarding the respect of laws are reflected in attitudes toward criminal behavior.
6. A person becomes delinquent/criminal because of an excess of definitions favorable to violation of the law over definitions unfavorable to violation of the law.
7. Differential association may vary in duration, frequency, and intensity.
8. The processes for learning criminal behavior parallel those of any other learning process.
9. Criminal behavior is an expression of general needs and values but is not explained by those needs and values.

Although Sutherland's theory was not directly intended to explain the development of organized crime groups, the espoused principles consistently apply to such a phenomenon. From the Italians to the Russians to the Bikers, all of these groups reinforce a criminal lifestyle by teaching techniques and (more importantly) a criminal ethos.

Subculture Theory. Like Sutherland's theory of differential association, subculture theory posits that individual behaviors vary due to subcultural constants within an individual's environment. Thus, individual behaviors are determined by differential reinforcements. To wit:

> The specific process by which deviant behavior becomes dominant over conforming behavior in specified situations is differential reinforcement. In the simplest terms, differential reinforcement means that given two alternative acts, both of which produce and are reinforced by the same or similar consequences, the one which does so in the greatest amount, more frequently, and with the higher probability will be maintained. In a sense the one that has been more successful in obtaining the desired payoffs will become dominant (Akers, 1973: 52).

Thus, the fact that the majority of criminal gangs or organized crime groups have developed in economically disadvantaged communities may be attributed to the unique norms that develop in areas conflicting with upper-class society and, in turn, their laws. The creation of such subcultures is actually a by-product of shared economic deprivations and cultural norms eschewing cooperation with government authorities. Limited by their ability to effectively communicate with nativists in their own language, these groups are actually further insulated from society at large. Thus, deviant behavior is not a deliberate attempt to violate societal expectations; rather, it is a rational response, supported by their community, to the restrictions forced on these groups.

While it is remarkable that organized crime groups have remained largely absent from empowered classes, subculture theory fails to address continuing criminal enterprises within groups long accepted in American society. The lack of language barriers and overt discrimination toward Italians, for example, has significantly reduced, if not eliminated, the Italian subculture of old. Thus, subculture theory fails to explain the continuation of organized crime syndicates.

Social Disorganization Theories

Although learning theories have dominated much of the research on gang development, social disorganization theories are gaining in popularity. Such theories posit that a combination of social conditions found within impoverished urban areas is responsible for the elevated crime rate within these neighborhoods. They suggest that the deterioration of family and social bonds, poverty, and general decay of urban centers have created an environment conducive to criminal activity. The lack of social programs designed to alleviate the effects of such deterioration has only aggravated the situation.

Thrasher, anticipating many current explanations for and explorations of gangs, attempted to look for a combination of factors involving the youth and the community in which he resided. Thrasher saw the gangster as "a rather healthy, well-adjusted, red-blooded American boy seeking an outlet for normal adolescent drives for adventure and expression" (Hardman, 1967: 7). The youth, however, was also influenced by his environment, where inadequacies in the family, housing, jobs, vocational skills, schools, etc., all combined to motivate the youth to look elsewhere for life satisfaction and rewards (Goldstein, 1991). That elsewhere was the gang.

Since Thrasher, social causation has persisted as a major determinant for gang formation. As we entered the 1980s era of gangs, more inclusive perspectives on gang formation appeared. Miller (1980), for example, observes that youth gangs persist because they are a product of conditions basic to our social order. Among these are a division of labor between the family and the peer group in the socialization of adolescents; an emphasis on masculinity and collective action in the male subculture; a stress on excitement, congregation, and mating in the adolescent subculture; the importance of toughness and smartness in the subcultures of lower-status populations; and the density conditions and territoriality patterns affecting the subcultures of urban and urbanized locales.

Similarly, Edgerton proposes a causative explanation focusing on the idea of multiple marginality:

> Contributing to the formation of gangs is residential segregation in low-income areas, poverty, poor school performance, little parental supervision, discrimination, and distrust of law enforcement. In these conditions, young people spent much of their lives together on the streets where a gang served them...as surrogate family, school, and police. We also hear from gang members...about the appeal that gang membership has for them—friendship, pride, prestige, belongingness, identity, self-esteem, and a desire to emulate their uncles and older brothers who were gang members before them (1988: x).

More recently, Hagedorn (1991) has suggested that, at least in Milwaukee, Thrasher was right. He goes further, suggesting that gang formation follows a pattern parallel to the economic and social trends in American society, most importantly, the changes in the American economy. This idea is supported by Jackson (1991), who found that as American society moves from a manufacturing economy to a service one, gang formation appears to be a natural consequence, although an unintended one. Gangs flourish in such an environment because the more moderating influences of successful adults and stable families decline. It is more than just economics. Spergel says, "The social order in gang communities is further disturbed by population movement and the disorganization created when there are rapid ethnic or racial changes in an area" (cited in Conly, 1993: 8).

Increasing multiculturalism is not the only challenge facing urban residents. Neighborhood regentrification and urban revitalization have dramatically changed the landscape in many areas, beautifying the city while sending real estate prices skyrocketing. According to some theorists, this juxtaposition of wealth and poverty has also generated feelings of anger, social injustice, and hostility among inner-city natives. This resentment is largely attributed to perceptions of discrimination in which inner-city inhabitants bear the brunt of government scrutiny without the luxury of equality of opportunity. Instead, deviant behavior is considered an acceptable adaptation to the gated walls that deny them access to American riches.

Such approaches are consistent with Merton's theory of anomie. According to Merton (1938), criminal activity is a natural by-product of the disassociation between culturally defined goals and socially structured means. In fact, it is inevitable in any society in which individuals are taught to want material things but are denied access to the means to achieve them. As a result, marginalized classes may adopt one of four adaptations: (1) *innovation*, the commitment to economic success but the rejection of legitimate means; (2) *ritualism*, the rejection of economic success but the commitment to legitimate means; (3) *retreatism*, the rejection of both legitimate goals and means; and (4) *rebellion*, the creation of new goals and the means to supplant traditional ones. Merton's adaption of innovation is quite appropriate in the explanation of organized criminal behavior among certain groups. In capitalist societies in which success is strictly measured by the accumulation of material goods, the mechanisms through which they are obtained become secondary. Thus, marginalized groups embrace illicit practices to achieve legitimate success. In other words, poverty surrounded by wealth, not poverty in and of itself, is a precursor to levels of criminal activity within a society.

Social Process Theories

Unlike the theories just discussed that were directed at understanding criminal behavior, social process theories are concerned with the process by which behavior is defined as criminal. Social process theorists argue that deviance is not exclusive to the urban poor but that middle- and upper-class deviance is largely ignored by government agencies. Social process theories gained prominence during the 1960s and 1970s when social inequality was formally recognized. In a nutshell, they suggest that the potentiality of criminal behavior exists irrespective of social status and that criminality is a direct result of social-psychological interactions of people with the institutions, organizations, and processes of society.

Conflict Theory.   Generally speaking, conflict theory posits that inequitable governments discriminatorily enact and enforce legislation to prevent upward mobility of marginalized groups. Conflict theorists argue that criminal law and the criminal justice system are used by the majority class to control the nation's underprivileged. According to them, criminal behavior is consistent across classes, but the lower class is more likely to be punished for their transgressions because they are politically, socially, and economically powerless. This is accomplished by upper-class citizens through the creation of criminal laws specifically targeting behaviors common among the lower classes while decriminalizing their own actions. By defining such lower-class behaviors as wrong, the ruling class necessarily creates an illusion of disproportionate deviance, which is quite useful in justifying exploitation. At the same time, the ruling class creates legislation that supports their own deviant behaviors, ensuring the status quo. In addition, they successfully create perceptions of righteousness for their own self-serving policies through control of information via the media. Ironically, their actions are far more costly to the public that embraces them.

In the 1970s, Ford Motor Company manufactured one of the first economy cars. The Ford Pinto was largely marketed to low- and middle-income families. Unfortunately, a defect in the design caused the cars to explode in low-impact rear-end collisions when a turn signal was in use. Although company executives did not intend to design a structurally dangerous vehicle, they were enlightened regarding the defect after several deaths occurred. After a careful analysis of the cost-benefit ratio of public disclosure versus civil litigation, the company determined that a recall would result in a lack of consumer confidence, thereby decreasing future sales. (The actual cost of installing a safety plate between the gas tank and the signal fuse was miniscule.) This determination that it was cheaper to compensate future victims who *may* file suit caused countless injuries and numerous deaths. The fact that the executives commissioning the study were never even charged with or tried for a crime is illustrative of the conflict theorists' argument that the ruling class's behavior is decriminalized—even in the case of premeditated murder.

Social Control Theory.   Like conflict theory, social control theory posits that all members of society have the potential to engage in criminal behavior; however, social control theorists do not argue that the ruling class is disproportionately under-represented in criminal courts due to their control of the social processes. They suggest that an individual's predisposition for such activity is moderated by ties to social institutions such as family, church, school, work, and/or peer groups. According to Hirschi (1969), the strengths and numbers of these associations are directly related to individual criminality, so the reduction of primary bonds results in an elevated likelihood for deviance. This theory suggests a level of sensitivity to other people absent in previous theories.

According to Moore (in Conly, 1993), most people join criminal groups by their own volition. For the most part, these individuals are characterized by a lack of social commitment and associations. In fact, gang members share nine commonalities that may be useful in applying Hirschi's theory to criminal gangs:

1. They are part of a single-parent family.
2. They have a need for social acceptance.
3. They lack a positive role model at home or school.
4. They are having difficulty in school.
5. They have dropped out of school.
6. They are generally part of a lower socioeconomic status (SES) group.
7. They are not able to become gainfully employed.
8. They lack access to community recreational facilities.
9. They have little exposure to religion.

As stated, the fact that many members of organized crime have come from dysfunctional families, have lacked legitimate employment, and are often disassociated with educational pursuits may indicate an applicability of this theory to the phenomenon in question; however, empirical research specifically evaluating this has not been conducted.

Social Psychology and Symbolic Interactionism.   Unlike behaviorists who most often categorize individual behavior as a dependent variable, social psychologists tend to view deviance in terms of mutual or circular causality (i.e., traditional variables of cause and effect are also causative and effective in reverse). An individual is neither the cause nor the effect of his or her environment; rather, each entity actively participates in the other's creation simultaneously. Thus, deviance, both theoretical and behavioral, is simply perceptual. In other words, an individual's (or group's) perceptions, whether consistent with or varying from the norm, represent the reality in which the individual (or group) lives. Simply put, the social construction of reality is based on one's understanding or experience rather than on universal expectations.

According to symbolic interactionism, individuals develop a constellation of attitudes about themselves (i.e., self) through interactions with others:

> At birth, consciousness is undifferentiated and there is no clear separation between self and others. When the baby hurts, his or her world hurts...with time, however, this union of one with all disappears as an island of self-consciousness appears. As children learn that they can cause things to happen...they begin to form a sense of self. Now, instead of the more inclusive feeling "it is happy (or sad)," there is an awakening sensation of me—"I am happy."...And as socialization becomes more intense, evaluations of self begin. "I am a good person (or a bad person)" (Lillyquist, 1982: 122).

These symbolic interactionist theorists posit that an individual's self-concept is directly related to messages that they receive through others. They argue that individuals will develop a *looking-glass self* in which perceptions of self are consistent with the way they are perceived by external agents. For example, a child who is aesthetically beautiful may actually perceive herself to be unattractive if the cues that she receives from significant others support this latter belief. Accordingly, individuals who are treated as deviant will see themselves as deviant. The manifestations of such perceptions are known as *self-fulfilling prophecies.* Thus, individuals who perceive themselves to be criminal in the eyes of others will in turn become criminal. Because newly immigrated peoples are often stereotyped in this manner, this theory suggests that the prevalence of organized crime within marginalized communities is all but inevitable for those individuals lacking positive interactions. Perversely, their criminal behavior actually reinforces negative messages, permanently creating an environment conducive to criminal behavior.

Other micro approaches are consistent with the ideology espoused in symbolic interactionism. Kurt Lewin's field theory, for example, suggests that an individual is one aspect of a total field, that behavior is the joint function of the person *and* his or her environment, and that the person and the environment partially define one another. This is also consistent with the dramaturgical perspective, which argues that behavior is determined by self-perceptions of expectations. While each of these theories appears logical on its face, they all have been widely criticized as reductionistic.

CONCLUSIONS

Throughout the years, various theories have been presented to explain deviance in society. Such explanations have been posited from individuals across disciplines ranging from psychiatry to criminology. Many of these theories have been applied to the phenomenon of organized crime, some with more success than others. Some theorists suggest that individual deviance is caused by deficiencies found within individual personalities and that organized crime groups are a compilation of such individuals, while others have argued that deviance is simply the manifestation of self-perception and that organized crime syndicates or criminal gangs comprise groups of individuals who have simply realized the inadequacies recognized by others. Unfortunately, neither of the two approaches attempts to explain the overrepresentation of marginalized populations in criminal gangs—unless, of course, it is the first approach's assertion that such subrogated peoples are disproportionately afflicted by personality disorders or the second approach's assertion that subrogated people disproportionately perceive themselves as aberrant.

Sociological explanations are more appropriate in explaining group deviance. While they vary in specificities, there are several common elements among them. With few exceptions, sociological theories of deviance recognize the social effects of minority (not necessarily race) marginalization. The lack of educational opportunities, low standards of living, elevated levels of discrimination, and blocked access to economic mobility increase the likelihood of deviant behavior among certain groups. Whether by design or coincidence, it is apparent that certain groups in every society are deprived of theoretical equality. In Western societies in which an emphasis is placed on materialism, it appears logical to assume that all groups, regardless of status, would desire the markings of capitalist success. Some theories posit that the irreconcilability of such desires with limited opportunities necessarily creates an environment in which subcultural ideologies may supplant those of the majority. Others suggest that criminal behavior is learned within a social group made up of deviant-minded individuals. Whatever the case may be, it seems unlikely that a universal consensus among social scientists will be achieved; at the same time, it appears extremely likely that criminal gangs will continue to flourish.

CHAPTER 3

ITALIAN ORGANIZED CRIME

> Slum-area youngsters joined gangs and turned to delinquent behavior at an early age. Unlike most of their contemporaries, who also belonged to corner gangs and were involved in occasional mischief-making, the criminal-in-the-making had little or nothing to do with legitimate labor, which they believed was only for "suckers," men who worked long hours for low pay and lived in overcrowded tenements with their families. It appears that all the prohibition-era racketeers, whether born in the United States or brought here as infants or children, started their careers in one or another gang. The corner gang became their school (Nelli, 1976: 107).

Perhaps the most feared criminal organization within U.S. boundaries—the Sicilian mafia—is also the least understood. Surrounded by hyperbole and mystique, historical accounts of Italian organized crime are peppered with gross inconsistencies and inaccuracies to such an extent that their repetition has obliterated all but the sensational, and the romanticized depictions of leading mob figures are so prevalent that their viciousness is often obscured. Indeed, all sources of information on the topic can be criticized. Government accounts are often clouded by agency rhetoric, while the proliferation of autobiographical accounts written by organization participants contain veracity tempered by self-promotion and personalized agendas. Empirical studies, traditionally the knowledge of choice, are virtually nonexistent due to the subversive and territorial nature of the behavior in question (Asbury, 1928; Cressey, 1969). Thus, key characters, events, activities, and even dates vary across sources and mediums, making an accurate or academic accounting an almost insurmountable task.

HISTORY

The amplification of La Cosa Nostra ("This thing of ours"), in fact, has been so great that it is unclear as to which came first—the mafia or its myth. (Some ethnic succession theorists, for example, argue that such obfuscation initiated a social contempt, which actually resulted in its existence.) Even the origins of its name are in dispute, although many claim that the word "mafia" is an acronym for *Morte Alla Francia Italia Anela* ("Death to the French is Italy's cry"). Mischaracterizations and misrepresentations aside, a careful analysis and a compilation of the various sources may help to clarify historical events and to develop a basic understanding of the underpinnings of the organizational structure, ideology, and similarities.

Contrary to popular belief and Hollywood depictions, the Italians did not invent organized crime, nor were they the first ethnicity involved in organized crime in the United States. While they are largely responsible for perfecting racketeering activity and organizational sophistication, the humble beginnings of La Cosa Nostra (LCN) are remarkably similar to organized crime groups formed before and after their introduction. Like contemporary street gangs that prey on their own communities, early LCN activities may be characterized as predatory. Relying primarily on income gained through strong-armed robberies and extortion, young Italians concentrated on the most vulnerable and available targets—members of their own communities. In fact, without the proceeds from these predatory activities, it is highly unlikely that the transition from street thuggery to sophisticated criminal activity would have been possible.

It was not until the passage of the Volstead Act in 1919 that a sophisticated hierarchical organization emerged. Prohibition not only enabled the Sicilian branch of the American underworld to capitalize on the public's lust for liquor but also provided them with working capital to enter legitimate enterprises. Contemporary groups have carefully masqueraded as legitimate corporations and have monopolized a variety of regulated industries. This facade has successfully masked the violence inherent in such organizations and has unfairly affected the playing field on which law-abiding citizens and businesses compete. Though law enforcement efforts have become increasingly successful in criminal prosecutions, the ranks of the Italian mafia have remained resilient due to their ability to recruit young males and to replenish the mafia with organizational legacies.

AMERICAN MOBSTERS

Although some incidents in the history of the American mafia remain disputed, the success and longevity of the American mafia are not. Their propensity for violence coupled with their ability to corrupt governmental structures has enabled them to

VOLSTEAD ACT OF 1919 AND THE EIGHTEENTH AMENDMENT

The Eighteenth Amendment was ratified on January 16, 1919. Its contents clearly forbade the manufacture, sale, import, or export of intoxicating beverage. However, the amendment proved to be useless prior to passage of the Volstead Act. The Volstead Act of 1919, which was passed by Congress on October 27, 1919, but which went into effect on the one-year anniversary of the Eighteenth Amendment, was actually more significant because it defined the language of the amendment. "Intoxicant," for example, was defined as any beverage containing more than 0.5 percent alcohol by volume. It also authorized federal agents to enforce any and all provisions of the amendment. Further, it specified rather harsh penalties for individuals convicted of booze trafficking. Ironically, it did not provide for criminal acts deriving from the actual imbibement of such intoxicants; as it is with today's drug laws, it was not a crime to drink or to feel alcohol's intoxicating effects. As a result, mainstream America had little to lose by enjoying the product, while at the same time they actually were directly responsible for all of the violence surrounding its existence.

The period between the ratification of the Eighteenth Amendment and the enactment of the Volstead Act enabled enterprising young criminals to stockpile homemade liquor. In addition, warehouses that housed unconsumed legitimate alcohol were raided and burglarized by these criminals. Also, the "legitimate" alcohol produced for medicinal or industrial purposes was manipulated by gangsters for consumption purposes. Speakeasies replaced bars and saloons; because they were illegal in and of themselves, they were well stocked with a virtual smorgasbord of other vice-related activities (e.g., gambling and prostitution), which allowed mainstream America to enjoy their favorite pastimes while actually supporting the criminal underworld.

Repeal of the Eighteenth Amendment, which had been designed to reduce criminal behavior, was actually a moot point. Some individuals who had once been socially undesirable (e.g., Joe Kennedy, father of John and Bobby Kennedy) channeled their illicit profits into legitimate enterprises, buying their way into society's favor. Others who foresaw the end of Prohibition had already channeled their resources elsewhere. The era of Prohibition and the laws governing it abjectly failed in their efforts to reduce criminal behavior; in fact, Americans had never stopped drinking, and an economic foundation had been laid for a criminal syndicate that continues to flourish to this day.

remain at the forefront of the criminal underworld. These characteristics, somewhat alien to earlier criminal gangs, are deeply rooted in their unique cultural and ethnic history and are throwbacks to their Italian heritage, where lines between illegitimate organizations and governmental institutions were not clearly drawn and criminal societies flourished.

The Camorra

Historical accounts of the development of organized crime in Italy traditionally trichotomized criminal groupings according to their geographic origin. The mafia, by far the most recognized grouping in this country, primarily comprised individuals from Sicily, the N'Drangheta from Calabria, and the camorra from Naples. While all groups represented criminal societies, the Sicilian mafia and the Neopolitan camorra had the greatest impact on the development of Italian organized crime in the United States. Like many contemporary prison gangs, the camorra was developed as a form of self-defense for Italian inmates incarcerated in institutions with large Spanish populations in the early 1800s. Upon release, these inmates expanded their criminal activities to the urban sprawl of Naples, perfecting extortion rackets and engaging in vice-related activity. This group was largely responsible for the organizational structure of many American groups. Although such structure is often attributed to the Sicilian mafia, the early camorra was characterized by its complex structure and its initiation procedures. Probationary status was required of all newcomers, and their dedication to the group was proven through their actions. All men had to engage in some sort of violent activity, and all probationers were required to surrender their possessions to the group. In return, the families of successful initiates were financially provided for when the initiates were incarcerated. A formal hierarchy, very similar to the American model which would emerge much later, existed; it included bosses and captains. The camorra thrived in Italy for almost a century. Corrupt politicians and law enforcement administrators allowed them to engage in a wide array of criminal activities, often placing members in official positions. Such support, coupled with the regulatory oversight provided by the family, enabled the camorra to develop new international markets, including the United States where they engaged in alien smuggling. Members of the camorra and others with Neopolitan roots flourished in the American criminal underworld, identifiable through their flamboyant styles of dress and mannerisms (e.g., Al Capone, Vito Genovese, John Gotti). However, the onset of Facism in Italy proved to be devastating to all of Italy's criminal societies, especially the camorra. Their southern counterpart, the mafia, fared much better, maintaining a consistent, albeit weakened, presence throughout Mussolini's reign and establishing a powerful criminal syndicate in the United States. Although the camorra has surfaced in Italy post-Facism, it appears relatively powerless in the face of mafia-controlled government institutions.

The Sicilian Mafia

As stated, many authors have credited the Sicilian mafia with the current organizational models displayed by the American contingent of the LCN. This assumption is sorely misplaced, as the Sicilian mafia emerged primarily as a disorganized rural phenomenon resulting from an immobile class system in the 1880s. According to Blok (1974), the mafia developed through the marriage of violent peasant entrepreneurs, the *gabelloti*, and Sicilian thieves. Acting as estate managers for absentee landlords, the *gabelloti*, fulfilled a variety of roles in feudal Sicily. First and foremost, they represented a pseudo-judiciary, mediators of disputes and arbitrators of "justice." In addition, they provided employment for the lower classes while lining the coffers of the landed aristocracy and serving as an unofficial agency of social control. In a country lacking adequate government resources, such juxtaposition inevitably led to unprecedented power—economically, socially, and politically—as the mafia extorted tithes and demanded fines from peasant and aristocrat alike. However, the tradtional mafia was not ruled by a single entity and may instead be characterized as individual groups of opportunistic criminals who had the propensity and capability of organized violence.

Although Mussolini claimed to have eliminated all Italian criminal societies (especially the mafia) by prosecution (or persecution) of mafia members, he failed to provide strong government policy and social order. Consequently, most criminal societies resurfaced after his fall for the same reasons they had originally developed. Thus, Mussolini's impact on the mafia was not as significant in Italy as it was in the United States, which was flooded with an influx of displaced mafiosi. In fact, expansionist tendencies since Mussolini's "purge" increased the group's visibility across the entire country. While thriving in traditional criminal endeavors such as extortion and drugs, the group also entered legitimate marketplaces. Such criminal diversification increased the need for cooperation (albeit grudgingly), regulation, and organization

---

PALERMO'S MAXI TRIAL
Crackdown on the Sicilian Mafia

In the early 1980s, competition for the heroin market in Sicily became quite deadly. Politicians, justice officials, and even mafia dons were targeted for extinction by the mafia power structure. Tommaso Buscetta (aka Don Masino) was one of the latter, marked for death by Corleone bosses Salvatore Riina and Bernardo Provenzano. Hoping to escape assassination, Buscetta fled to Brazil, where he was promptly arrested pending extradition back to Italy.

Learning of his inevitable deportation, Buscetta attempted suicide but was unsuccessful, so Buscetta took the only avenue left available to him—he sang like a canary, identifying players, outlining family structures, and reconstructing criminal events. Upon his testimonial evidence, 474 indictments were issued. These indictments, totaling over 8,000 pages, required the construction of a new maximum-security courtroom, including 30 steel cages with bulletproof glass. Although many individuals were tried in absentia, those present proved extremely hostile to journalists and court officials. Such hostility held little sway as 254 convictions totaling almost 1,600 years in prison were handed down. Buscetta's personal vendetta was complete as all 12 members of the Cupola (the Palermo Commission) received life sentences. Unfortunately, two of the prosecutorial crusaders involved in the coup, Giovanni Falcone and Paolo Borsellino, were later murdered.

among the competing criminal societies. This structure was laid out by mafia informant Antonio Calderone:

> Cosa Nostra is the society of men of honor. According to estimates, these men num-
> ber more than 1500, divided among 67 families in the province of Palermo alone. The
> families are the basic units each holding sway over a recognized territory. Each family
> has a chief, its capofamigila, chosen by its members. He is aided by a hand-picked con-
> siglieri or counselor. Below come a number of deputies, and below them what could
> be called sergeants of the organization—each one known as the copodecina (head
> of ten) in charge of five, ten, 20 or even 30 soldati, the rank-and-file soldiers. Above
> the families lies the high command. The capomandamento is the colonel responsible
> for three families. He, in turn, answers to a provincial committee. Above that lies a
> regional committee, the government of the Cosa Nostra. Not even the Mafia claims
> national power. Instead, it has given affiliate membership to the heads of both the
> Calabrian 'Ndrangheta and the Neapolitan Camorra (cited in Lyman et al., 2000: 338).

Such organization was designed to serve as a pseudo United Nations, governing
members and maintaining peace between the factions. However, the heroin wars of
the past four decades have decried the group's effectiveness. In fact, the period
between 1960 and 1990 was marked by unprecedented levels of violence. Virtually
every segment of the population experienced losses, with justice officials and politicians often targeted, as Salvatore "Toto" Riina waged a bloody war against Tommaso
Buscetta. Riina's volatile approach resulted in more than 800 murders and unprecedented cooperation between his soldiers and the public, who were fearful of his
unchecked violence. It also resulted in the infamous Palermo maxi trial in which
Buscetta was the ultimate victor—responsible for the permanent incarceration of all of
his former rivals. However, the mafia, in concert with other criminal societies, continues to be so insidious and self-perpetuating that the convictions of the entire hierarchy
in the 1980s barely slowed it down. Currently at its helm is Bernardo Provenzano,
a lifetime friend of Riina and a fugitive since 1963.

Bernardo Provenzano began his career as a hit man for longtime Corleone
boss Luciano Liggio. Although on the lam for assorted murder charges since 1963,
Provenzano acted as a silent partner to Riina. However, his operational approach
and management style directly contradict Riina's mercurial tendencies. Quite simply,
Provenzano revitalized the decaying organization by returning the group to its humble
roots—encouraging members to live modestly, maintain family values, and swear fealty
to the group (Cullen, 2001). He regained the public's empathy by stopping much of the
random violence, especially violence directed at respected figures. Additionally, he
created an atmosphere of corruption reminiscent of the 1800s through the careful solicitation of politicians and officials. Such complicity is so complete that reports indicate
that Prime Minister Berlusconi has all but encouraged the mafia's revitalization
(Cullen, 2001). Thus, the Sicilian mafia remains extremely powerful and intrinsically
institutionalized in many of the island's current political and social agencies.

American factions of Italian organized crime have not routinely assassinated federal judges, prosecutors, or politicians and are not as intrinsically interwoven in national politics. This apparent distance is not to suggest, however, that their more subtle approach has not affected governmental policy, prosecution efforts, and local politics. Indeed, past experience indicates that much of the success and continuing longevity enjoyed by the American mafia lies in their ability to manipulate governmental institutions, policies, and interests. Thus, the difference in the two is not the outcome but the approach. American mobsters, perhaps recognizing the futility of armed conflict in a militarily strong environment, rely on the power of economic persuasion through corruption of poorly paid street-level officers and local politicians. While both approaches have advantages, the American approach traditionally allowed mobsters to limit occupational fatalities from outsiders. By limiting violence to insiders only, they also successfully achieved a facade of respectability within their communities and beyond, allowing them to enjoy tolerance and even outright acceptance among the American public. On the surface, then, it may appear that the American criminals are far removed from their Sicilian counterparts, but in actuality Sicilian ideals of loyalty and tradition permeate the U.S. mafia subculture and both provide a blueprint for organizational consistency and lay the foundation for organizational structure.

MEMBERSHIP REQUIREMENTS AND INITIATION

Unlike some contemporary gangs, which seem to lack formalized structures and hierarchy, the American mafia is a highly organized, formally structured, and well-oiled criminal machine. Strictly patriarchal, the American mafia has never been an equal opportunity employer. Traditionally, only card-carrying Sicilian males were eligible for membership. Homeland prejudices and ethnic stereotypes, brought over by immigrants, separated some Italian communities and subsequent organized crime families. Cultural differences in dress, style, and language that were undetectable to non-Italians were, in some cases, as divisive as race or religion. Although the increasing lack of ethnic purity has moderated these hostilities and blurred ethnic lines, cultural manifestations often hint at individual lineage. For example, Sicilian gangsters such as Carlo Gambino and Paul Castellano are subdued and somber by nature, disdaining the flamboyance exhibited by Neapolitan John Gotti (Jamieson, 1989). Currently, entrance requirements mandate an Italian surname and a paternal lineage.

Similar to other ethnicities, Italian individuals traditionally attracted to LCN shared an impoverished or working-class background. Sonny Franzese, for example, was one of 18 children born to a baker. Many were also products of immigrant families or immigrants themselves. Anecdotal evidence suggests that their family's, in particular their father's, marginality motivated their criminal pursuits. Currently, members are often products of mafia families, second- and third-generation mobsters (e.g., Michael Franzese and John Gotti, Jr.). Ancestry notwithstanding, paternal marginality and ethnic

WISEGUYS
Neighborhood Icons

Everybody worked, and worked hard. They just never got paid much. Sure, they were better off than our grandparents who got stuffed into disease-infested rat holes as soon as they stepped off the boat and were expected to be grateful for any dirty job…our fathers would take anything they could get. They were construction workers, factory workers, bricklayers, storekeepers, truck drivers, waiters, janitors, stevedores. A few of the really lucky ones had civil service jobs. No one had any real money, except, of course, the wiseguys (Fopiano and Harvey, 1993: 7–9).

consistency do not, by themselves, guarantee entrance into this criminal subculture. Prospective members are often recruited in childhood or adolescence, acting as runners or valets for neighborhood "wiseguys" (i.e., "made" members or those formally recognized as family members), while other individuals, drawn to the mystique and apparent wealth of neighborhood mobsters, actively pursue mafia membership. As William Fopiano remembers:

> Tony [the "Canadian" Sandrelli] always looked like a million dollars. Me and the other kids used to watch him stepping out of his shiny new Cadillac in cashmere coats and two-hundred-dollar mohair suits with lapels sharper than our dads' razors. The man who had me go get Tony's suit was his friend, Henry Salvitella. . . . You could always find Henry and Tony at a table in the Florentine with a frail, quiet man with a thick Sicilian accent. His name was Frank Cucchiara [boss of Boston family], and he was known as the "Cheeseman" for a cheese importing business he owned a few blocks away on Endicott Street.
>
> We all knew that these men were mobsters. We knew it from street talk and what we read in the papers, even if we were too young to have any idea exactly what they did or where their power came from. That was something we couldn't see. There were no machine guns or tough-guy bodyguards or bulletproof limousines around. All we knew was that they were better off than everybody else and people treated them as if they were important. They seemed to move in some exciting, secret world that was invisible to anyone who wasn't one of them (Fopiano and Harvey, 1993, 7–8).

As young adults, these individuals are expected to exhibit criminal entrepreneurship, contribute to family coffers, and pay homage to local wiseguys. Often these youngsters develop their own gangs or "crews" with one youth acting as leader. Moneymaking enterprises traditionally include credit card scams, merchandise hijacking, and residential burglary. Entire groups and individual leaders passing muster are quickly recognized and recruited by local mafiosi, signifying the initial step toward organizational entry. These prospective recruits must be sponsored by at least one family member and successfully demonstrate their organizational worthiness. (Although some deny the existence of a formal probationary period, arguing that the extended period between introduction and initiation negates such a formalized practice, anecdotal retellings, including Valachi's, describe a formal probationary period when members must do anything that is asked of them prior to "being straightened out.") Accordimg to Franzese (1992: 91), "[This] pledge period last[s] nearly a year. The family [takes] this time to train the recruits in discipline and carefully measure their character, all the while waiting for the right low-level 'work' to present itself."[1] Once organizational loyalty has been proven, the names of prospective members are circulated among the surrounding components of LCN. At this time, objections may be raised by other families; this prevents potential conflicts with other groups claiming that individual. It further ensures that the potential member is a "stand-up" guy and is not associated with law enforcement.

Those successfully being "called up" or "straightened out" are then formally inducted into their respective family with as much solemnity as High Mass. Post-Valachi recollections of induction ceremonies are remarkably similar to the one related in the 1960s (e.g., burning of a saint's image, shedding of blood, dagger and gun, good food). Members are led to a private location where they are greeted by the entire hierarchy of their chosen family. (Such individuals are seated in a horseshoe-type shape with the boss, underboss, and consigliere in the middle. Many accounts suggest that proximity to the center indicates the organizational power of a particular individual.) At the trial of Gambino crime boss and longtime friend John Gotti, Salvatore "Sammy the Bull" Gravano testified:

> [Paul Castellano] asked me if I liked everybody there. I told him yes. He asked me a few questions. One of the last questions he asked me was would I kill if he asked me to. I told him yes.... He told me what was my trigger finger. I pointed to my trigger finger. He pinched it, blood came out. He put it on the saint, and started to burn the saint in my hand. He said, honor the oath. He said to me, that if I divulge any of the secrets of this organization that my soul should burn like the saint.... I kissed him on both cheeks. I kissed everybody. I went around the table and kissed everybody. I sat down. They got up. They locked hands. They unlocked hands. They made me get in the middle of it.... They locked hands again and told me, at that point, I was part of the brotherhood. I was a made member and I belonged (Maas, 1968).

This formal recognition represents an important milestone in the recipient's criminal career. As one wiseguy related to undercover special agent Joseph Pistone, "[G]etting made is the greatest thing that could ever happen to me . . . I've been looking forward to this day ever since I was a kid" (Pistone and Woodley, 1987). Indeed, formal organizational membership is immediately recognized by insiders and outsiders alike. Organizational jargon recognizes family affiliation and graduation from associate status, as new members are introduced as "friends of ours." These

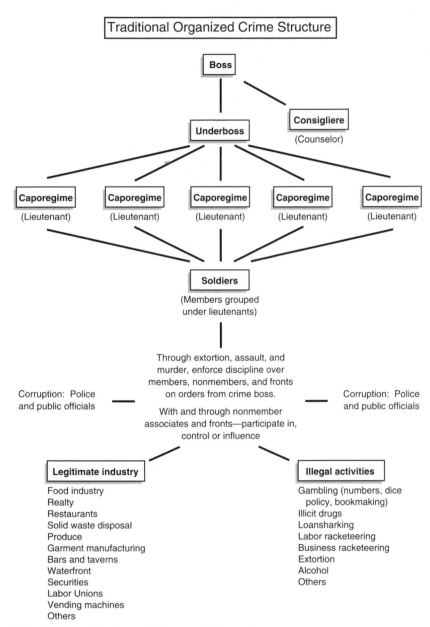

Figure 3–1   Traditional Organized Crime Structure

newly recognized "soldiers" are assigned to a capo or *caporegime*. Usually, this individual is one with whom they have previous criminal association. Entering on the bottom rung of the organizational hierarchy, new soldiers must again prove their worth through moneymaking criminal enterprise and "tithing" a predetermined percentage of their profit to their captain. Capos in turn direct group profits to the higher-ups, paying homage directly to the family boss. Underbosses and consiglieres (i.e., family advisors) receive their portion from the head of the family (Bonavolonta and Duffy, 1996; Cressey, 1969; Fopiano, 1993; Pistone and Woodley, 1987).

ORGANIZATIONAL STRUCTURE

Joe Valachi was the first to document the hierarchical structure of La Cosa Nostra, stating that the LCN was tightly organized with independent (yet sovereign) units (e.g., Boston, Buffalo, Chicago, Cleveland, Detroit, Kansas City, Los Angeles, Newark, New Orleans, Philadelphia, Pittsburgh, San Francisco, and five New York families).[2] He also indicated that resort areas such as Miami and Las Vegas were considered open territory in which all families could operate, but they were overseen by a commission comprising 9 to 12 bosses across the country. Since his testimony, other families have emerged, including some in Canada. For the most part, these newer families are sponsored or supervised by traditional families that are proximally located (Frank Balistrieri, longtime boss of the Milwaukee family, for example, answered to Chicago). However, recent accounts confirm that the organizational structure has remained consistent over time in all 24 families.

The Commission

Independent as they may appear, individual families are supervised by an executive board. The creation of "the commission" directly followed the end of the Castellammarese War and was designed to eliminate the violence of the 1920s and early 1930s. Originally, the commission was made up of bosses from Buffalo (Stephen Magaddino), Chicago (Al Capone), and Cleveland (Frank Milano) and from the five New York families (Lucky Luciano, Vincent Mangano, Joseph Profaci, Joseph Bonanno, and Gaetano Gagliano) (Talese, 1971). However, some commission members occupying "permanent seats" have been temporarily unseated during times of disgrace (e.g., Gotti, Bonanno, Colombo), while new seats have been established for families such as Kansas City and Detroit. The commission may be characterized as a cross between the Supreme Court and the United Nations. As a body, the role of the commission is primarily one of oversight, regulation, and mediation. It regulates relationships between the families, promotes and facilitates joint ventures, and resolves actual and potential disputes among families. In addition, the commission issues national policy on organizational structure, extends formal recognition to newly chosen family bosses and prospective members, and resolves leadership disputes within families (e.g., those of Nicky Scarfo, John Gotti, Carmine Persico). "Hits," or murders between warring factions, must receive the blessing of the commission. The commission members also serve as gatekeepers to the entire organization by controlling membership books.[3] The five New York families have traditionally dominated the commission because up to one-third of the entire organization is contained within that geographic area; in fact, most of the disputes erupting in New York are arbitrated among the five New York bosses alone.

The Boss

Each LCN family may be characterized as a dictatorship, with the family boss as the absolute power. Although there are some exceptions, these individuals are usually longtime members who have an air of ruthlessness and a knack for earning incontestable organizational loyalty.[4] These individuals are responsible for the actions (and necessary discipline) of all members of their family. Traditionally, these individuals remained insulated from prosecution due to the paramilitary structure of the LCN in which a strict chain of command prohibited uninitiated direct contact between a soldier and his boss.[5] Although operating out of humble abodes such as bars, restaurants, and vending companies, these individuals enjoy a kingly position and are treated with Old World respect by all members (e.g., people rising on their entrance, being silent unless spoken to, kissing their hands). They are often as heavily guarded as legitimate heads of state and maintain personal chauffeurs and lackeys. Depending on the strength of the family, these individuals may also enjoy a seat on the national commission, which dictates policy and arbitrates disputes. Individual bosses rely primarily on the earnings of their subordinates, rarely initiating new businesses. Theoretically, these individuals are the least vulnerable to mob violence, as a commission-sanctioned rule prohibits their assassination; however, several bosses, including Paul Castellano, Angelo Bruno, and Carmine Galente, have been murdered in recent years.

The Underboss

Generally speaking, the underboss acts as a vice president in charge of field operations. Responsible for the supervision of the family's income-producing ventures, he confers regularly with the captains, communicating orders from and reporting their concerns to the boss (Meskil, 1972). The underboss is also responsible for collecting tithes from the various captains. Traditionally, this person is individually selected by the acting boss and represents the heir apparent to his boss's position. In those cases when the rules of succession are ignored, intrafamily violence is often a result (e.g., the Paul Castellano family). The level of power enjoyed by the underboss is determined by the role dictated by his superior. Some underbosses, such as Tommy "Three-Finger Brown" Lucchese, have all but ruled a family, while others have merely served as lackeys (e.g., Tommy Bilotti, underboss to Castellano). The underboss also serves as acting boss when the boss is suddenly removed by illness, incarceration, or death.

The Consigliere

Contrary to Hollywood depictions, an organization's consigliere is not typically an attorney; instead, this position is usually occupied by a highly respected member of the group. According to Meskil:

> [T]he consigliere is chosen for his knowledge, wisdom and sound judgment, or perhaps because the boss trusts him more than anyone else ... the counselor advises the boss on all matters concerning the family, from personal feuds between members and petty infractions of rules to multimillion-dollar enterprises that may involve other families or legitimate people. The capo (Boss) is not obliged to accept his consigliere's advice, but he almost always does ... though the consigliere has no troops under his command except a few personal retainers, he is the brains of the family and his ideas directly affect the lives and livelihoods of all the members (1972: 82).

The *Caporegime*

Caporegimes or *capos* are self-made members who serve as organizational captains or lieutenants. They are appointed by the family boss and earn a percentage of all monies made by their subordinates. Each capo runs a small crew comprising 10 to 25 individuals, some self-made members and some not. These crews are autonomous in nature, inasmuch as they do not interfere with other family businesses. Some of these individuals specialize in certain types of criminal activity (e.g., hijacking, burglary, narcotics, gambling, murders), while others are generalists. They routinely meet at a central location, usually at a legitimate business owned by the capo or another family member—most often restaurants or bars in the heart of Italian districts. Capos must report the earnings of their crew to the underboss and must allocate a predetermined percentage to their superiors. They are under significant pressure to earn money and may apply strong-arm tactics to accomplish this goal. Capos may discipline or kill members of their own crew without permission.

RULES AND REGULATIONS

In addition to regulations formally mandated by the commission regarding organizational structure and occupational ideology (e.g., order of succession, tithing) LCN groups have traditionally shared a complex system of rules and customs deeply rooted in ethnic heritage and occupational culture. Customarily, for example, members avoided last names, supported other members regardless of their situation, and showed respect to others and deference to supervisors. They were prohibited from physically striking other members or interfering with their businesses. However, each has been forsaken at least once, and emerging trends indicate a growing disregard for traditional strictures. While many of these rules have been romanticized, one that

ZIPS AND "THE PIZZA CONNECTION"

One of the most famous cases in mafia history was dubbed "the Pizza Connection" due to the suspects' choice of cover—a pizzeria. Although the case concluded in 1987, the seeds of the narcotics conspiracy were sown 30 years earlier. In 1957, Tommaso Buscetta met with Charles "Lucky" Luciano, Joseph Bonanno, Carmine Galante, Angelo and Salvatore La Barbera (true Sicilian mafiosi based in Palermo), and Gaetano Badalamenti, then boss of the Ciucull family in Palermo. This meeting established a heroin pipeline between Sicily and the United States, which was an information bonanza for wannabe American gangsters. (These individuals, called "zips," started arriving in droves.) Eventually, however, Tommaso Buscetta turned state's evidence and was entered into the Witness Protection Program. He died recently at age 73 somewhere in the United States.

The American case, which concluded in 1987, involved Salvatore "Toto" Catalano, a Bonanno *caporegime,* and recent immigrant Gaetano Badalamenti. Badalamenti, once a prominent figure in the Sicilian mafia, was said to have transported over $1 billion in street-level heroin. This heroin was distributed through the auspices of the defendants' pizzerias. The individuals involved in this case routinely used coded language to discuss their drug transactions, thinking that it would protect them from criminal prosecution. This assumption proved to be extremely naive and short-sighted. This case was followed quickly by an additional one that involved members of the Gambino crime family. Thus, it appears that the Italian mob has not retreated from traditional criminal activity. Although many of them are involved in legitimate businesses, many others pursue traditional criminal activity. In fact, recent arrests in Charlotte, North Carolina, and Oakland, California, based on the Racketeer Influenced and Corrupt Organizations (RICO) Act, suggest that many of the Italian families have actually created relationships between themselves and other criminal organizations such as outlaw motorcycle gangs, Colombian cartels, etc.

appears to have withstood generational apathy is the prohibition against the violation of another member's wife. In fact, this offense is considered so egregious that it "means death without trial" (Maas, 1968: 96). Colombian *caporegime* Carmine "Mimi" Scialo, for example, was murdered and his testicles removed for making a play for the wife of Sonny Franzese while Franzese was incarcerated (Franzese et al., 1992). According to Valachi, this edict was a direct result of past cases when bosses murdered soldiers to marry their wives[6] (Maas, 1968).

Although most mafiosi memoirs have suggested that organizational members are prohibited from trafficking in narcotics, this is somewhat misleading. Virtually all of the most powerful LCN groups, especially the Genovese and Bonanno families, have dabbled in the trade. In fact, the mafia's involvement in narcotics can be traced as far back as Lucky Luciano. Even Joseph Bonanno, an individual who vehemently denies any involvement in that "dirty business," attended a mafia summit at the Grande Albergo edelle Palme Hotel in Palermo, which resulted in a heroin pipeline between Sicily and the United States. Indeed, the Bonanno family was all but decimated in the largest international narcotics case in history ("the Pizza Connection"). Although the commission *has* periodically issued bans on narcotics trafficking for self-preservation, it has placed the governance of drug trafficking in the hands of individual families. As such, ruling bosses have issued such prohibitions; for the most part, however, they have not investigated allegations of noncompliance and have chosen to remain ignorant of the source of individual tithes. Even Paul Castellano, the former Gambino boss who established a death penalty for offenders, accepted drug monies from other families. Thus, stringent occupational guidelines have proven situational at best, but some sociologists have argued that universal rules exist in all criminal organizations.

According to Cressey (1969: 175–178), five rules of conduct permeate every criminal organization:

1. Be loyal to members of the organization. Do not interfere with each other's interests. Do not be an informer. . . . [This rule] is a call for unity, for peace, for maintenance of the status quo, and for silence.

2. Be rational. Be a member of a team. Don't engage in battle if you can't win. [This rule demands] the corporate rationality necessary to conducting illicit businesses in a quiet, safe, profitable manner . . . violence involving other Cosa Nostra members and stealing from members is to be avoided.

3. Be a man of honor. Always do right. Respect womanhood and your elders. Don't rock the boat . . . emphasis on honor actually functions to enable despots to exploit their underlings. It is the right and duty of every member to question every other member's conduct, even that of a boss or underboss, if he suspects that the other man is not "doing right."

4. Be a stand-up guy. Keep your eyes and ears open and your mouth shut. Don't sell out . . . [you] must be able to withstand frustrating and threatening situations without complaining or resorting to subservience . . . [a man] shows [sic] courage and heart . . . does not whine or complain in the face of adversity, including punishment, because "If you can't pay, don't play."

5. Have class. Be independent. Know your way around the world. . . . To be straight is to be a victim: . . . a man who is committed to regular work and submission to duly constituted authority is a sucker . . . [be] concerned with [your] own honesty and manliness as compared with the hypocrisy of corrupt policemen and corrupt political figures.

Unfortunately, Cressey's depiction loses something in the translation. Admonitions of "Respect your elders and womanhood" fly in the face of contemporary mafia groups. Elders are respected based on the position they hold and the power they wield.

Castellano's ignominious demise on the curb outside Sparks Steak House illustrates the amount of respect extended to organizational elders. While reserving Friday night as official "wives' night out" may spare them the discomfort of an introduction of their wife to their girlfriend, it would probably not result in high marks on most morality tests. Indeed, it would appear that the proposed rules represent an earlier breed of criminal, one rarely exposed to external cultural or religious ideologies. These apparent contradictions do not suggest, however, that identifiable similarities of conduct did not exist historically. In fact, a compilation of informant accounts and government sources indicates it was the following similarities that granted early Italians the leverage to achieve the highest echelons of the criminal underworld; in fact, many authors suggest that the breakdown of these traditional norms has resulted in an increase in successful criminal prosecutions.

Other rules that have apparently been forsaken by the newer generation are as follows:

1. Economically support your community.
2. Keep street-level drugs out of your community.
3. Maintain church ties.

These patterns of behavior are directly related to the early economic success of the Italian mafia. Poverty-stricken communities, desperate for any means of economic support, unwittingly supported an institution that was most harmful to them. However, the superficiality expressed by early mafiosi regarding the activities in the preceding list enabled them to gain legitimacy and support from the communities that spawned them. Later generations, forsaking this tradition, have found that Italian communities that once embraced them and their kind would forcibly expel them if given the opportunity. Indeed, it appears that while contemporary street groups are attempting to emulate the model of the Italians, Italian youths are abandoning structural and cultural mainstays.

The most glaring and self-serving of all is, of course, *omerta*—the code of silence. While every successful criminal organization has a code of secrecy, none has been more successful than LCN groups in ensuring its compliance. Traditionally, this code of *omerta* insulated mafia families from criminal prosecutions. Indeed, mafia informants were virtually an unheard-of phenomenon prior to Valachi's 1963 appearance at the McClellan Committee (i.e., the Subcommittee on Investigations of the U.S. Senate Committee on Operations). Recent years have seen an increase in governmental informants and organizational turncoats. In fact, John Gotti, head of the Gambino crime family, and Philadelphia boss Nicky Scarfo are but two of many high-ranking mafia officials who have organizational informants to thank for their lengthy prison sentences. Though various authors have attributed the decrease in organizational loyalty to increasing prosecution efforts, the answer may lie in an overall disregard for culturally mandated conduct by fourth-generation Italians. Indeed, Cressey's (1969) identification of five universal rules of conduct is based on outdated generational constructs.

KEY HISTORICAL AND POLITICAL EVENTS AND ENTITIES

The Black Hand

Some authors suggest that Italian organized crime existed long before Prohibition and that much of the early criminality displayed by the Italians was far removed from highly industrialized areas such as New York City and Chicago. Indeed, much weight is given to an incident occurring in the late 1800s in the southern city of New Orleans. Many accounts argue that the murder of Chief David Hennessey was in retaliation for this officer's involvement in earlier mafia cases in which numerous individuals were convicted; however, one of the few academic studies of the phenomenon negates this supposition. In fact, Nelli (1976: IX) states:

> [S]o many writers have accepted and repeated myths and distortions of fact so many times that inaccuracies have become accepted as truths. Furthermore, most of the studies have concentrated on the experience in one city, New York, and have generalized from that situation about the entire country. Certainly New York has been of great importance in the emergence and growth of syndicate crime in the United States; at the same time, significant differences among cities did exist, and still exist.

In fact, it is unclear whether an "organized" criminal syndicate existed, as has often been argued. Nelli (1976) points out that revisitations of the incident alternatively blame the mafia or the camorra. This inconsistency reveals a pattern of sensationalism and inaccuracy. It appears that contemporary authors have actually perpetuated the myth of a nationwide Italian syndicate by relying on editorial comments made during the time of the trial. These editorial comments, and much of the remaining text, were inherently laden with anti-Italian/anti-immigrant sentiment based on white Anglo-Saxon protestant (WASP) distrust of Catholicism. Caricatures showing crazed Italians warned of the danger of this new "breed" of homo sapiens. In fact, a review of court transcripts and official proceedings indicates a veritable buffet of circumstantial evidence based on little more than ethnic stereotypes. In any event, the acquittal of all defendants charged in the murder of Chief Hennessy reaffirmed city residents' perceptions of a wide-scale criminal society, one that could corrupt even their most Christian neighbors. The subsequent lynching of those acquitted, which was accomplished with the assistance of prison personnel, extended the myth of "the Black Hand," a secret criminal society (Nelli, 1976). And so began the American mafia.

By the beginning of the twentieth century, ethnic criminal gangs sprouted up across the country. Metropolitan areas experiencing an influx of immigrants reported criminal activity perpetrated by bands of Southern Italian immigrants. For the most part, these groups were highly unstructured and preyed primarily on their own communities. Extortionists and common thugs abounded and quickly became known as "the Black Hand." Although the origin of such a title is debated (some authors attribute it to secret Sicilian societies, while others proclaim it to be a term used for resistance groups during the Spanish Inquisition), it seems apparent that the name was selected due to its ominous nature (Nelli, 1976). Extortion letters demanding specific sums and threatening dire consequences if ignored were sent to a variety of successful businessmen. These letters, signed La Mano Nera, proved to be a lucrative enterprise for their authors. It was a rare exception, indeed, when these letters failed to elicit the desired response. Shortsighted individuals who refused to bow to these extortion attempts quickly lost their homes and businesses to explosions set by the Black Handers. Other individuals were either assaulted or murdered. It appeared to local residents that these extortion bands were invulnerable. Schools, churches, and government institutions all bowed to the Black Handers; however, these individuals were largely unorganized and lacked the organizational longevity soon displayed by the Italian mafia. For the most part, individuals engaging in Black Hand activities were not members of the more structured mafia. In fact, some of the most powerful figures in organized crime were victimized by the Black Hand. For example, Ignazio "Lupo the Wolf" Saietta, one of the most successful counterfeiters in New York, reportedly paid $10,000 to the Black Hand when members of his family were threatened. The apparent confusion or bifurcation of the groups seems to have originated because "Italian gangs of this era used the Black Hand reputation and known techniques as covers, eliminating rivals in such a manner as to suggest Black Hand operations to the police and to the public" (Nelli, 1976: 79).

Prosecution efforts and law enforcement resources were not completely helpless against Black Hand extortionists, however. One officer in particular, Lieutenant Petrosino, was particularly effective in identifying Italian criminals. Rising quickly through the ranks, he was appointed head of the "secret service branch" of the New York City Police Department (NYPD) and was given the task of eliminating Black Hand and anarchist activity. He was gunned down in the streets of Palermo while cooperating with Italian authorities. While no one was arrested for his murder, Sicily's most powerful crime boss, Don Vito Cascio Ferro, bragged that he had personally carried out the hit (Nelli, 1976).

Several factors eventually culminated in the death of La Mano Nera. The continuation of Petrosino's secret squad, community groups such as the White Hand, and the cessation of Italian immigration all combined to reduce the feasibility of Black Hand extortion. The introduction of federal postal regulations coupled with the severity of sanctions for violations further decreased the cost-benefit ratio associated with such activity. In addition, the well-publicized retaliation from intended victim Big Jim Colosimo, in which all three extortionists were murdered by Johnny Torrio and company, illustrated the vulnerability of individual gangs. Most importantly, the passage of the Volstead Act, which prohibited the sale and manufacture of alcoholic beverages, dramatically expanded vice-related opportunities. Some Black Handers, such as Frank Uale (Yale) and the extremely volatile and violent Genna brothers, moved into the increasingly lucrative business of booze.

Chicago, Capone, and Prohibition

It must be pointed out that implanted Old World traditions were but one of many characteristics that resulted in organizational longevity for the American mafia. Emphasis on organizational loyalty, hierarchical structure, rule codification, and the like enabled Italian-Americans to rise to the top of the underworld "food chain," surpassing early Jewish and Irish rivals. However, the primary impetus for their ascension was not of their own making; rather, it was the result of two seemingly unrelated and government-initiated events—the passage of the Volstead Act in 1919 and Mussolini's purge.

The passage of the Volstead Act in 1919 opened a market ripe for criminal organizations. With the same farsightedness displayed by their homeland predecessors, criminally minded Italian-Americans saw Prohibition as a way to circumvent traditional social and economic roadblocks faced by recent immigrants. As one FBI agent put it:

> When Prohibition went into effect in 1920, well, they might have well have put up billboards all over Sicily with big arrows pointing toward America: attention thieves, smugglers, and confidence men. This way to the land of crooked deals and fat profits. Of course, criminal groups from other countries came to the United States, too, but the Italian mafia was tougher and better organized. And their consciences were less troubled, I think, by the idea of preying on their own kind (Bonavolonta and Duffy, 1996: 56–57).

Although a variety of sources, such as academic textbooks and the popular media, credit Alphonse "Scarface" Capone with bringing organized crime to Chicago, this distinction is sorely misplaced. Not only other Italians but other ethnicities preceded Capone as well. As in New York, the foundations for organized crime in Chicago must be attributed to the Irish, a group that brought a semblance of order to a chaotic underworld. Originally involved in prostitution rackets and gambling, the Irish established a foothold in both economic and political circles. In fact, it was the Irish who created a sophisticated "wire" service, which effectively cornered the market for off-track betting, preventing the "past-posting" that had been so costly to gambling operators. Indeed, it appears that the Irish criminals had a finger on the pulse of society's deviant side; however, increasing numbers of Italian immigrants coupled with the advent of Prohibition signaled the end of Irish dominance in Chicago. Their shortsightedness and the underestimation of the Italian threat resulted in the displacement of the Irish as rulers of the underworld.

Prior to the passage of the Volstead Act of 1919, Italian criminals, like their Irish predecessors, engaged in a variety of illegal activities. Bookmaking, loan-sharking, and prostitution became mainstays in American culture due primarily to the efforts of organized crime groups. The demand for such services was exaggerated in industrialized areas, and the supply was provided by a long list of criminal entrepreneurs. Arguably, Irish criminals originally satisfied these demands. Individuals from the Irish community controlled New York's Tammany Hall and Chicago's First Ward.

However, an influx of Italian immigrants into the Midwest reduced the power of Irish politicians and set the stage for one of the bloodiest conflicts in American history. Indeed, prior to World War II, Chicago's infamous organized crime figures proved to be more successful and far more recognized than their New York counterparts, who tended to keep a more low-key profile (Nelli, 1976).

One of the first individuals to capitalize politically on the growth of Italian communities was also one of the first to gain a foothold in vice activities on Chicago's South Side. Born in Calabria, Italy, James ("Big Jim" or "Diamond Jim") Colosimo came to the South Side of Chicago as a young boy. Indiscriminate in his career choices, Big Jim alternated between legitimate employment and illegal enterprise. An accomplished thief and pimp, Colosimo nevertheless was essential in garnering support in the Italian community for Michael "Hinky Dink" Kenna. Rewarded with a precinct captaincy, Colosimo capitalized on his political power to ensure that his illegitimate enterprises would be unmolested by authorities. In 1902, Colosimo married a former whore and current madam and took over the management of her flourishing prostitution business. A partnership with Maurice Van Bever in 1903 established a white slave trade that lured young girls with promises of grandeur and kept them through violence. The Mann Act of 1910 proved to be ineffective at best and did not threaten

THE EAST COAST MAFIA AND THE CHICAGO OUTFIT

Although Italian organized crime has permeated all facets of American life, the most active geographic areas have remained New York and Chicago. However, the structure and daily practices of the two are somewhat unique and may be predicated on the roots of origin of historical leaders (in Chicago, the camorra; in New York, the mafia). As there is only one "family" in Chicago, demographic territorialism, although recognized, is minimal, and individual crews are based more on criminal enterprise. One presiding boss maintains control over the entire outfit while maintaining a "board of directors" comprising territorial leaders. For the most part, the outfit is highly informal, lacking much of the ritualism found in New York, and the induction of new members is extremely limited. Accordingly, most crews are made up of a sole self-made member and his chosen associates. These crews operate more collectively, and members are compensated even during lean times. Generally speaking, narcotics trafficking is not as popular among Chicago wiseguys, who prefer to exploit traditional rackets (e.g., gambling, vending machines, prostitution, and extortion). The decentralized nature and the absence of drug peddlers have proven to be much harder to prosecute, which has enabled the Chicago outfit, with few exceptions, to operate with impunity. The practice of supporting crew members during lean times has also lessened the number of organizational turncoats, although one small-time hoodlum was responsible for the conviction of outfit boss Rocco Infelice in 1992.

Colosimo's position as king of prostitution on Chicago's South Side. Due to his expanding fortune, Colosimo became a target for Black Hand extortionists. Enter Johnny Torrio.

Like Colosimo, Johnny Torrio was brought to the United States at an early age. Settling in New York City's Lower East Side, Torrio quickly rose to prominence as leader of the James Street Boys—a band of juvenile delinquents who would ascend to the highest echelons of Italian organized crime. Boyhood friends such as Paul (Vaccarelli) Kelly, Frankie (Uale) Yale, and Alphonse "Scarface" Capone proved to be instrumental in the expansion of Italian organized crime. Brought to Chicago in 1910 by his uncle, Big Jim Colosimo, Torrio quickly rose to prominence within his uncle's business by arranging the execution of a band of Black Hand extortionists. After the pandering indictment in 1910 proved unsuccessful and public pressure called for the abolishment of brothels, Torrio expanded Colosimo's operations to neighboring Cook County suburbs. The most famous of these, the Four Deuces (due to its location at 2222 Wabash Avenue), also housed Torrio's office, full-service gambling, and a well-stocked bar. With the arrival of New York's Alphonse "Scarface" Capone and the onset of Prohibition, Torrio's rise to the pinnacle of Chicago's underworld was all but secure. The one obstacle, his Uncle Jim, was fortuitously murdered on May 11, 1920, in the entrance hall of his nationally renowned restaurant, Colosimo's Cafe. Though it is unclear as to who was responsible for his murder (conflicting accounts point to any number of possible suspects, such as Frankie Yale, Al Capone, Colosimo's estranged wife, or Torrio himself), the benefits to Torrio and the young Capone were enormous. Torrio inherited Colosimo's empire, and Capone became his second in command.

Freed from his uncle's supervision, Torrio, a brilliant organizer and criminal mastermind, put together a criminal organization while maintaining a veneer of civility. Known throughout Chicago's First Ward as a devoted husband and devout Catholic, Torrio effectively separated his personal and professional life. Dealing in white slavery, gambling, bootlegging, and, of course, violence, Torrio encouraged other criminal leaders to abandon traditional activities such as robbery and burglary, and he assigned territories for alcohol distribution. Leaders across Chicago took note, and a new era of vice was born. High levels of violence and treachery characterized this era. Rival gangs, jockeying for position in Chicago's lucrative bootlegging business (some reports estimate the profits obtained by the Torrio–Capone organization alone were as much as $240 million), were often dissatisfied with their designated area and proceeded to rub out any and all competitors (Nelli, 1976). Torrio's better-staffed organization was originally resilient to this type of violence, but conflicts between other gangs resulted in a high number of casualties on all sides.

One of the most notorious battles was waged between a group headed by Irish gangster and florist Dion O'Banion and the terrible Gennas, six Italian brothers known for their volatile tempers. While it remains unclear as to who started the conflict, the end result is not debated. On November 10, 1924, while preparing flowers for the funeral of Mike Merlo (reputed leader of Unione Siciliana), O'Banion was shot six times at close range. In retaliation, Hymie Weiss (aka Earl Wajciechowski) went after Capone and Torrio as reputed supporters of the Gennas. Capone escaped unscathed, but Torrio was not as lucky. Torrio was shot several times while walking with his wife. Though he survived the ordeal, Torrio did not return to Chicago after a nine-month prison stint arising from his involvement of a raid on one of O'Banion's breweries. Some authors report that Torrio was not actually shot by Hymie Weiss and company but was ordered murdered by none other than Al Capone himself (Giancana and Giancana, 1992).

Capone's ascension to the underworld throne was characterized by even greater levels of violence. Irish gangs, wary of Capone's increasing dominance, banded together to defeat the Neapolitan. Originally, Capone enjoyed a high level of community support, being branded a hero after paying for the physician who treated a young mother who was injured by machine-gun fire directed at Capone. However, Capone fell from grace after his gunmen murdered an assistant state's attorney. Several cease-fires were called due to waning business and public condemnation, yet peace was never long-lasting. Capone's violent rage erupted when it was reported that Frankie Yale (his onetime friend and benefactor) was hijacking shipments of Capone's liquor. Capone retaliated by killing the New York boss. In addition, Capone arranged the murder of "Bugs" Moran, a Chicago gangster who had inherited Weiss's bootlegging operation. In what became known as the St. Valentine's Day Massacre, seven Moran associates (six gangsters and a hanger-on) were cold-bloodedly murdered execution-style. Unfortunately for him, one of the victims closely resembled Moran, and some reports suggest that the gunmen believed Moran to be one of the victims. Witnesses reported seeing "policemen" enter the warehouse where the execution took place. In actuality, Capone's supporters lured their victims into the warehouse by masquerading as police inspectors.

Capone's rage was not restricted to his gangland rivals. In fact, three of Capone's leading soldiers—among them John Scalise and Albert Anselmi—were beaten to death at a banquet ostensibly held in their honor. Apparently, guests were given baseball bats and invited to join in the beating of the guests of honor. So zealous were the participants that coroners were hard-pressed (no pun intended) to find a bone intact. After serving a prison sentence designed to protect Capone and allow tempers to cool, Capone returned to Chicago and developed a system of racketeering only to be reincarcerated in 1932 for income tax evasion. His 11-year sentence was shortened significantly when it was found that Capone was suffering from advanced syphilis. The most notorious and most feared man in Chicago's history died quietly at his Miami villa, struck down not by an assassin's bullet but by his own sexual behavior.

Organized crime in Chicago continued unaffected by Capone's incarceration and subsequent death. Frank Nitti, Sam Giancana, and others developed new marketplaces while maintaining a stranglehold on the traditional activities of prostitution, gambling, etc. While revenue suffered immediately following the repeal of the Eighteenth Amendment, Chicago gangsters found an even more lucrative enterprise in racketeering and extortion. However, Chicago mafia dominance over Italian organized crime in the United States was soon supplanted by organized crime activity on the East Coast. Chicago mafiosi would never again enjoy the prominence they attained during the dry years of Prohibition. Indeed, a war that had started in

New York while Capone was still in power would continue after his downfall, and it would quickly overshadow Chicago's glory days.

Unione Siciliana and the Castellammarese War

With the advent of massive Italian immigration, increasing persecution of Roman Catholics, and passage of the Eighteenth Amendment, the stage was set for an explosion of criminal activity within poverty-stricken areas throughout New York City hit hard by discrimination. Enter Unione Siciliana. In essence, the Sicilian nation (i.e., the mafia) was transported to the United States where social discrimination necessitated the formation of Italian fraternal organizations. These organizations, originally tasked as insurance providers and neighborhood caretakers, quickly descended into illegitimate enterprise under the guidance of Ignazio Siaetta, transforming American norms of alcohol abstinence. As Inciardi puts it:

> [T]he respectability and benevolence of the Unione declined as Prohibition approached. First in New York and later in distant city branches, cadres of gangsters began to infiltrate and pervert the association. L'Unione siciliana acquired a dual character: it was open and involved in good works among needy Sicilians, yet it was hidden and malevolent, dealing in theft, murder and vice (Inciardi, 1975: 115).

After Siaetta's incarceration in 1918, the power and influence of the Unione extended across the country, and several individuals, including Al Capone, vied for the presidency. However, the leadership position brought certain dangers, most notably assassination. Those killed while serving in this capacity included: Angelo "Bloody Angelo" Genna, Samuzzo "Samoots" Amatuna, Anthony Lombardo, Pasqualine "Patsy" Lolardo, and Joseph Aiello. Most of these assassinations were ordered by Capone or his enemies. Although one of the most powerful gangsters in the country during the period, Capone was never formally recognized as the head of Unione Siciliana due to his Neopolitan heritage. Over time, the Unione faded into obscurity as individual gangs became more powerful.

Inevitably, the increasing competition among Italian groups resulted in a subsequent increase in violence. For the most part, this violence was confined to mafia families and their members, though there were some exceptions. In 1931, this competition resulted in unprecedented levels of violence between two factions. This conflict, known as the Castellammarese War, was triggered by the struggle for dominance over the territory left by Tom Reina's murder in 1930.[7] In one corner, there was Salvatore Maranzano, the reigning boss of the Italian underworld and a native Sicilian with roots in Castellammare del Golfo. Maranzano, who immigrated to the United States in 1925, was an extremely well-spoken multilinguist who had previously studied for the priesthood. His group was made up primarily of Sicilian immigrants, individuals such as Tommy "Three Fingers Brown" Lucchese, Joseph Aiello (Chicago), Joseph Profaci, and cousins Joseph "Joe Bananas" Bonanno and Stephano Magaddino (Buffalo). These mafiosi had been quite active in criminal activities in their homeland and were heavily indebted to Maranzano, who had helped them flee from Mussolini's persecution. Joe Bonanno and Stephano Magaddino, in particular, were steadfast loyalists as family affiliations extended across the ocean. In the other corner stood the contender: Giuseppe "Joe the Boss" Masseria, a squat, ambitious individual whose unflattering nicknames included "the Cork" and "1/2 Bottle." Unlike Maranzano who immigrated to the United States as a young man, Masseria grew to manhood surrounded by one of the worst public tenements in New York City where he earned a reputation for violence and thuggery. His group was a cultural hodgepodge in which Jews and Gentiles existed peacefully and Neopolitans and Sicilians overcame traditional hostility.

During the period between 1930 and 1931, over 60 killings were attributed to the war. Initially, it appeared that Masseria's troops were winning the day; however, two factors led to his demise. First, Masseria's ambitions appeared boundaryless, and members of his own organization were victimized by their boss. (Interestingly, the first known victim of Masseria's greed was Gaetano Reina, whose death ultimately triggered the war. Masseria had him murdered when Reina refused to give him his ice distribution racket, a highly lucrative business before the advent of electric refrigeration.) Second, the lack of ethnic consistency among his followers, once his greatest strength, weakened the loyalty of his followers. One by one, Masseria was deserted by his top chieftains. Some, such as Carlo Gambino, left openly while others, such as Charles "Lucky" Luciano, Vito Genovese, Francesco "Frank Costello" Castiglia, Meyer Lansky, and Benjamin "Bugsy" Siegel, changed their allegiances secretly.

On April 15, 1931, the feast day of Saint Francesco di Paola, Masseria was gunned down at Gerardo Scarpato's restaurant on Coney Island while he was enjoying a leisurely lunch with Lucky Luciano. (His top lieutenant was conveniently in the men's washroom during the shooting.) Although reports vary as to the actual killers, most agree that Luciano was the mastermind.[8] With Masseria dead, Maranzano became the undisputed king of the underworld. One of his first acts in this position was to declare himself *Capo di tutti Cappi*, boss of bosses, and he laid out the organizational structure under which the group would operate. At a meeting at Maranzano's farmhouse in the Catskills, Maas reports:

> He said that from here on we were going to be divided into new Families. Each family would have a boss and an under-boss. Beneath them there would also be lieutenants, or caporegimes. To us regular members, which were soldiers, he said, "You will each be assigned to a lieutenant. When you learn who he is, you will meet all the other men in your crew" (Maas, 1968: 106).

During this meeting, Maranzano divided the organization into five individual families and formally introduced organizational rules. These five families, originally named for their leaders, were the Luciano family (currently the Genovese family), the Gagliano family (currently the Lucchese family), the Mangano family (currently the Gambino family), the Profaci family (currently the Colombo family), and the

Bonanno family. (Of the five, only the Bonanno family has maintained its original name. The others have been renamed for longtime bosses.) New rules included both a ban on striking another self-made member and death for anyone who failed to follow a superior's order. Maranzano also reaffirmed traditional rules, including *omerta* and the prohibition against violating another member's wife or daughter. Finally, Maranzano stressed the importance of communication through a strict chain of command, emphasizing that effective communication would increase the efficiency of the organization (and insulate its leaders).[9]

This organizational structuring laid the foundation for all families operating at the time. The structure proposed by Maranzano, however, lasted far longer than his reign as mafia kingpin. Fearing the increasingly powerful relationship between Luciano, Genovese, and Jewish organized crime figures, Maranzano placed a "contract" (order to murder) on Luciano. Unfortunately for Maranzano, Luciano commissioned a similar hit, and his assassins struck first. On September 11, 1931, Maranzano was executed in his Park Avenue suite. This date came to be known as the "Night of the Sicilian Vespers" or "the Purge of the Moustache Petes" (Cressey, 1969). While these designations conjure up images of masked assassins roaming the country in search of Maranzano supporters while civilians cowered behind locked doors, no evidence supports media assertions that more than 40 mafiosi were killed; in fact, little if any evidence exists detailing even one mob-related murder other than Maranzano's.

In the wake of Maranzano's murder, other ranking members of the Italian mafia tacitly agreed to maintain peaceful relationships. Luciano convened a sit-down in Chicago, which was hosted by Capone, and members formulated an organizational board of directors, dissolving the position of "boss of bosses" and establishing territorial boundaries. This newly formed commission originally comprised the five remaining New York leaders—Lucky Luciano, Vincent Mangano, Joe Profaci, Gaetano Gagliano, and Joe Bonanno—and three others—Chicago's Al Capone, Buffalo's Stephano Magaddino, and Cleveland's Frank Milano. (The current commission also includes leaders from U.S. cities such as Detroit, Philadelphia, and Kansas City.) This meeting also saw the creation of the position of consigliere to protect soldiers from lieutenants if they had unresolved issues from the war. In addition, the commission agreed to "freeze" membership, so rival groups could not outrecruit one another (i.e., build a supreme army). Beneath the commission, 24 other families were recognized. This new approach was designed to decrease interfamily violence and provide a modicum of security for the bosses. However, the years following these summits have been characterized by comparable levels of betrayal, secret alliances, and murder, especially in New York's five families.

Five Families from New York

The formulation of the commission was supposed to put an end to interfamily fighting in New York, but periodic outbreaks still occurred. Luciano, or perhaps Torrio, saw the negative repercussions experienced in Chicago. Thus, territorial boundaries, firmly established and uncontestable, divided New York into five recognizable factions.

BOYHOOD FRIENDS, POWERFUL LEADERS

Salvatore Lucania was born to a poor family in the hillside village of Lercara Friddi. Immigrating to the United States in 1906, Lucania gained employment as a general laborer. Disdaining the poverty surrounding him, Salvatore Lucania began preying on smaller children, demanding their lunch money in return for "protection." One of Lucania's intended victims, a small boy five years younger, refused to participate. For some unknown reason, his refusal actually endeared him to Lucania, who liked his spunk. This friendship between Lucania and Meyer Lansky would become one of the first multicultural relationships in organized crime: Lansky was Jewish.

Although the two would soon go their separate ways—Lucania to reform school and Lansky to public school—they hooked up several years later. In the meantime, Lucania, leader of his own gang of ruffians, entered into an alliance with the head of the 104th Street Gang headed by Francesco "Frank Costello" Castiglia. This alliance, intended to be temporary, would last throughout Lucania's life and would ultimately lead to one of the biggest shake-ups in organized crime history. After both served short prison sentences—Lucania for drug running and Castiglia for possession of a firearm—they created their own street gang; Lansky joined them, bringing his friend Benjamin "Bugsy" Siegel. By now the two were known as Charlie Luciano (a name picked up in prison, which was more preferable to the feminized nicknames of Sal or Sally) and Frank Costello (as a joke, Luciano had changed his friend's surname to an Irish one). These names would soon reverberate within the underworld and come to symbolize both power and intelligence.

Luciano and company soon rose to prominence within the Italian underworld. Lucrative business deals during Prohibition and carefully chosen alliances ensured Luciano's position. However, the older dons were apprehensive about this upstart. Masseria and Maranzano, competing for the ultimate power position, saw the profitability of an alliance with Luciano's crew. Luciano and his advisors were not amenable to an alliance with either, recognizing the war between the two as self-defeating. They decided that both bosses had to be disposed of. But first, Luciano and his associates entertained noncompeting mobsters such as Al Capone of Chicago, Nig Rosen of Philadelphia, and Moe Dalitz of Cleveland.

Once his plan was established, Luciano "joined" forces with Masseria while carefully placing his pawns for his assassination. Captured and badly beaten by Maranzano, Luciano was released alive, if not severely scarred. (His release, after being "taken for a ride," earned him the nickname of Lucky.) Luciano arranged to have lunch with Masseria and conveniently went to relieve himself when Albert Anastasia, Genovese, and Siegel filled Masseria with lead. Shortly thereafter, Maranzano was executed on orders from Luciano, and a commission was developed to prevent future bloodshed.

Luciano, Costello, and Lansky remained steadfast friends and loyal compatriots throughout their lives. Benjamin "Bugsy" Siegel was not so lucky. In 1947, Bugsy Siegel was shot to death in the home of his mistress, Virginia Hill. The hit was ordered by his boyhood friends, Costello and Lansky, after it was reported that he was skimming money that had been loaned to him to start a casino in Las Vegas. Almost 10 years later, Frank Costello would be shot on orders from Vito Genovese. The bungled assassination attempt was carried out by Vincente "The Chin" Gigante, current boss of the Genovese crime family. Ah, to have such friends.

THE FIVE POINTS GANG

The Five Points Gang was one of the most vicious, most violent, and most recognized multicultural youth gangs in New York City at the beginning of the twentieth century. Ruling the area between the Bowery and Broadway, 14th Street and City Hall Park, the Five Points Gang specialized primarily in robbery, prostitution, and common thuggery. The following individuals were involved:

Paolo Antonio Vaccarelli (aka Paul Kelly). Leader of the Five Points Gang and at one point reputed to command the allegiance of 1,500 youths (Nelli, 1976). Unlike other Italian leaders, Vaccarelli actively pursued alliances with individuals from various ethnic backgrounds.

Frankie Uale (Yale). Person responsible for Al Capone's arrival in Chicago. Eventually the two would part ways, and Capone would order the execution of his onetime mentor.

Charles "Lucky" Luciano. Perhaps one of the biggest leaders in Italian organized crime. Luciano has been described as a youth criminal, dropping out of school in the fifth grade at the age of 14.

Johnny Torrio. Leader of his own youth gang, the James Street Boys. Torrio moved to Chicago on request from his uncle "Big Jim" Colosimo. Torrio has been credited with revolutionizing (and suburbanizing) the prostitution business in Chicago. He returned to New York after a failed assassination attempt and is often credited with the solidification of mafia leaders across the United States (i.e., the commission) through his protégé Lucky Luciano.

Alphonse "Scarface" Capone. Undisputed leader of the Chicago outfit from 1920 to 1931. Capone left school in the sixth grade shortly after he turned 14. A former bouncer for Frankie Uale (Yale), Capone received his nickname after an altercation left him with a four-inch scar across his left cheek. He was sent to Torrio under suspicion of two murders. Capone eventually placed a contract on Torrio's head, forcing him to flee to New York. On January 25, 1947, Al Capone died of pneumonia symptomatic of syphilis at his Palm Beach retreat.

The Luciano/Genovese Family.   Born in 1897, the boy christened Salvatore Lucania began his life in the United States in a rat-infested tenement in New York's Little Italy at age nine. Perceiving the lack of legitimate opportunities for those of Italian descent, Charles "Lucky" Luciano (as he would come to be known) was a chronic truant and schoolyard bully. Extorting money from children during elementary school signaled his criminal entrepreneurial nature. Along with other delinquents—most notably Meyer Lansky, Benjamin "Bugsy" Siegel, and Francesco "Frank Costello" Castiglia—he formed the Five Points Gang. It was an enterprising youth gang that relied on Luciano's uncanny criminal mind, Lansky's skill of deduction, and Siegel's and Costello's brute force. While their scams tended to be successful, no one could have anticipated the heights that the foursome would reach among New York's criminal elite.

Luciano's role in the Castellammarese War cannot be overstated. Some authors suggest that the entire conflict was actually masterminded by Luciano. They argue that Luciano cleverly played both sides against the middle, ultimately emerging as the victor (Nelli, 1976). Whether or not this argument is supported, Luciano's prominence following the conflict is indisputable. Viewed as a first among equals, Luciano's "family" was granted the largest slice of organized crime in New York City. Luciano, credited with establishing peace between warring factions, successfully prevented his own assassination but could not protect himself from criminal prosecution and subsequent deportation.

In 1936, Luciano was charged with more than 60 counts of prostitution and sentenced to 30–50 years in prison. His incarceration, however, proved to be little more than a hindrance. He continued to issue directives through underlings from his cell. His power was so absolute, in fact, that the U.S. government enlisted his aid during the early days of World War II. U.S. counterintelligence agents found it difficult to infiltrate the longshoremen's union and could not monitor "suspicious" antigovernment activity on the docks. Using "Socks" Lanza as a mouthpiece, Luciano paved the way for undercover government surveillance of anti-American activities. Furthermore, Luciano's cooperation ensured the absence of costly strikes or union problems. It was also rumored that Luciano was instrumental in the invasion of Mussolini's Fascist Italy. While these rumors are largely unsubstantiated, it would appear that Luciano and a variety of other Italian-American criminals had a compelling reason to assist the U.S. government: Mussolini's purge of Italian mafiosi had left hundreds incarcerated, homeless, or dead. It was further rumored that in exchange for his cooperation (e.g., creation of maps, deployment of personnel, and designation of "safe" areas), Luciano would receive a full pardon.

If indeed these rumors were true, Luciano was foolish to trust the U.S. government and Luciano's former nemesis-turned-governor, Thomas Dewey. Dewey did release Luciano but ordered his deportation. The role played by Luciano following his deportation is hotly debated. Some authors suggest that Luciano actually continued to receive homage from U.S. gangsters during his exile (Demaris, 1975); others suggest that Luciano and all members of the American mafia were held in contempt by their

LUCIANO AND THE YOUNG TURKS

Upon Luciano's ascension to power, it became clear that he was an organizational genius and a sophisticated entrepreneur. He aggressively developed relationships between Neopolitans and Sicilians, and he cultivated alliances with prominent non-Italians such as Dutch Schultz, Louis "Lepke" Buchalter, and Abner "Longy" Zwillman. Most importantly, Luciano maintained his closeness to childhood friends Meyer Lansky and Benjamin "Bugsy" Siegel. His arrival proved to be opportune for Italian organized crime in New York City and beyond, as it coincided with the repeal of the Eighteenth Amendment.

Now that illegal liquor rackets were no longer profitable (or even necessary), the criminal underworld was forced to develop new avenues of illicit income. Under Luciano's guidance, traditional rackets were expanded. Bookmaking, numbers running, bar keeping, extortion, hijacking, and robberies increased exponentially to meet the voracious greed created by Prohibition. Luciano also increased the prevalence of labor racketeering, successfully corrupting labor leaders through violence or guile. He also supplemented his personal coffers by drug trafficking and prostitution. Aggressively strong-arming independent operations, Luciano eventually gained control of over 1,000 brothels. Luciano, however, showed little regard or respect for the "dumb broads" he employed, often making business agreements and conducting illicit negotiations in their presence. To his chagrin, three of the women that he defamed, Nancy Presser, Cokey Flo Brown, and Mildred Harris, were directly responsible for his conviction (Lyman & Potter, 2000). Trafficking in women earned Luciano a 30- to 50-year sentence for pandering. During his incarceration, Luciano assisted the U.S. government in gathering intelligence and maintaining order among dockworkers during World War II. As a result, Luciano was deported in 1946 on the SS *Laura Keene* after serving 10 years.

Sicilian counterparts (Barzini, 1972). In reality, it is not important if the two stories cannot be reconciled. Luciano's contribution to organized crime in New York City and La Cosa Nostra far exceeds whatever humble fate he may have endured: Luciano—above all other gangsters before or since—solidified mafia factions across the country.

During much of Luciano's imprisonment, Vito Genovese oversaw family interests and acted as an intermediary for the imprisoned Luciano and the soldiers on the street. However, he was forced to flee New York in 1937 to escape a murder charge, and Luciano's boyhood friend and fellow Five Pointer assumed control. Francesco Castiglia (aka Frank Costello) was a juvenile delinquent turned power broker. Marriage and a prison stint transformed a neighborhood tough guy into a criminally astute and politically connected entrepreneur. One of the first organized crime leaders to actively pursue legitimate businesses (e.g., the Horowitz Novelty Company), Frank Costello channeled much of the revenue garnered by his criminal activity into his company. Of course, his novelty company complemented his criminal endeavors by producing and servicing punchboards and other gambling devices (Nelli, 1976). Costello was also heavily involved in the legitimate liquor business, real estate ventures, and oil prospecting, and he controlled several unions. It was this appearance of legitimacy that angered law enforcement officials, who finally achieved a conviction of contempt based on Costello's lack of cooperation during the Kefauver Committee hearings and a further conviction of income tax evasion, which was later reversed. Costello's reign ended "voluntarily" after a failed assassination attempt encouraged his "retirement."

DECEPTION AND BETRAYAL

Contrary to Hollywood depictions, Italian organized crime has long been character-ized by secret alliances and disloyalty—a lesson that almost cost Frank Costello his life. Suave, debonair, and articulate, Frank Costello had become so cosmopolitan and urbane in his legitimate pursuits that he appeared to forget the culture in which he operated. He proved to be no match for the street-fighting machinations of Vito Genovese.

Vito Genovese returned from Italy in 1946 to find that Frank Costello had become quite comfortable in his role as acting boss, so comfortable, in fact, that he refused to relinquish the title. Forging a relationship with Albert "the Executioner" Anastasia (head of the Mangano family), Costello attempted to thwart Genovese's claim to the throne. In response, Genovese enlisted the support of Joseph Profaci (Boss) and Carlo Gambino, an ambitious capo in the Mangano family. As a result, Phillip Mangano was shot to death and his brother, Vincent, disappeared (and pre-sumed murdered) in 1951, under Anastasia's direction. In retribution, Vito Genovese ordered the hit of Willie Moretti, Costello's protector, claiming that he was a liability due to his affliction of syphilis and his tendency to ramble during the Kefauver hear-ings. In the same year, Tommy Lucchese hatched a plot to kill Anastasia, but it was soon discovered. Anastasia, however, uncharacteristically forgave Lucchese—a move that would prove to be extremely shortsighted.

In 1955, Anastasia was hit while enjoying a leisurely shave. His hit, and the hit of underboss Don Scalice, was justified to the commission because they were accused of selling LCN memberships. Carlo Gambino, with the support of Lucchese and Genovese, took over the family that would eventually bear his name. Although hope-lessly outnumbered, Costello continued in his capacity, pursuing casinos in Las Vegas and driving the family into legitimate enterprises. However, in 1957, Costello was shot by Vincent "the Chin" Gigante while entering the lobby of his apartment build-ing at 115 Central Park West. Although Gigante proved to be a poor shot, Costello "voluntarily" stepped down after his recovery, and Genovese reclaimed the position that he believed he was entitled to.

Costello's successor was Vito Genovese, the individual for whom the family is now named. Genovese was a Neapolitan who had a long history of criminal activity. Prior to his ascension, Genovese had been an active proponent of narcotics trafficking, seeing it as an extension of Prohibition bootlegging. Genovese began his criminal life under the tutelage of Luciano; in fact, it has been reported that Genovese's narcotics operations were actually supported by and a product of Lucky Luciano. For the most part, Genovese's ascension to power and criminal career were characterized by long absences from New York. During World War II, for example, Genovese actually served as an interpreter for the Allied Military Government in Italy while on the lam for murder. He became a favorite of Mussolini by filling the dictator's coffers with generous "donations." This relationship actually allowed Genovese to control the black market of army supplies while in Italy. He was deported back to the United States after a dedicated Central Intelligence Division (CID) officer discovered the outstanding murder warrant. However, the chief witness against Genovese mysteriously died of an overdose while in protective custody, and Genovese was released. Upon his ascension to the top of the family that now bears his name, Genovese expanded the family's enterprises, especially those in the narcotics industry.

In 1959, Vito Genovese became the first major player in Italian organized crime to be convicted of narcotics violations. Obviously reluctant to hand the reins to one individual, Genovese continued to rule from his prison cell through his appointed bosses, Tommy Eboli, Jerry Catena, and Anthony "Tony Bender" Strollo. His power was so absolute that one of his soldiers, Joseph Valachi, sought refuge with the government to avoid being murdered while imprisoned in the same institution. Strollo subsequently lost favor and vanished in 1962, presumably murdered on the command of Genovese. Upon Genovese's death in prison in 1969, the commission formally recognized Tommy Eboli as family boss; however, he was murdered shortly thereafter. Many believe that the commission's lack of retaliation signaled their sanctioning, if not their ordering, of the hit. Coincidentally or not, a close ally of Carlo Gambino, then acting head of the commission, assumed control. Frank "Funzi" Tieri ruled in relative peace until his death in 1981.

In 1981, Anthony "Fat Tony" Salerno became the official boss of the Genovese crime family, but the real power since the early 1980s has been Vincent "the Chin" Gigante, the incompetent hit man in the Costello hit. Gigante proved to be a study in discretion, successfully avoiding prosecution for decades, even while serving as head of the commission after Gotti's incarceration. Gigante's figurehead, however, was not as lucky. In 1987, Salerno was convicted in the historic commission case and was sentenced to 100 years. Throughout the 1980s and 1990s, the Chin carefully cultivated a facade of insanity in preparation for the inevitable indictment. He wandered aimlessly about dressed in a bathrobe and slippers, being physically supported by various organizational members, including his son Andrew. In addition, the Chin scrupulously avoided being caught by even the most strategically planted devices, mumbling incoherently and communicating often through a type of sign language. Family members were forbidden to speak his name and were directed to point to their chin to signify his wishes.

Finally, Gigante thwarted law enforcement efforts by never accepting the formal position as "boss." Instead, a variety of Gigante lackeys, including Liborio "Barney" Bellomo and Frank "Farby" Serpico, served as figureheads in that position. As crazy as it seems, his antics proved to be successful in postponing court dates, generally disrupting the criminal justice system, and avoiding prosecution for over a decade. However, court-appointed psychiatrists negated his insanity plea, and he was convicted in 1997 for the unsuccessful takeover of Local 46 of the Mason Tenders along with acting boss Liborio Bellomo. Gigante was later convicted on a variety of other charges including two murder conspiracies. He is currently serving a life term, but law enforcement sources indicate that he is still issuing directives from his prison cell through various family members. His son Andrew was charged with racketeering in early 2002. He, along with six others including acting boss Ernest Muscarella, was charged with labor racketeering in the infiltration of the Internal Longshoremen's Association, Local 1804–01. Such charges indicate that the family's long practice of racketeering continues in the twenty-first century.

In 1923, Joseph "Socks" Lanza developed the United Seafood Workers Union in New York City. As such, his control over the Fulton Fish Market affected seafood prices throughout New York and the rest of the country. Fishermen who refused to pay homage (i.e., percentages per pound) watched as their catch rotted on the New York docks. His control was so absolute, in fact, that even individuals desperate for work refused to unload or deliver cargo of those not in compliance. Though he served a two-year sentence for violation of the Sherman Antitrust Act, Lanza continued to rule the waterfront until his death in 1968 (Nelli, 1976). His successors in the Genovese family have continued to reap the profits from this most lucrative racketeering market. In addition, their current enterprises include entertainment unions, a relatively new phenomenon. Much like they gained control over the Seafood Workers Union, the Genovese family (in alliance with their Chicago counterparts) has established a stranglehold on workers' unions within the entertainment field. With the exception of the Screen Actors Guild, virtually all organizations represented on movie locations are controlled through New York. It is this activity that most affects the U.S. population and was the impetus for the passage of the RICO Act (see the Criminal Prosecution and Government Efforts section in this chapter).

Although the commission case and other government efforts have resulted in the convictions of the organization's top three positions in recent years, acting street boss Dominick "Quiet Don" Cirillo is similar to Gigante in his subtle approach (minus the drooling and pajamas). Because of the release of acting boss Liborio "Barney" Bellomo in 2004, the family is expected to remain one of the most powerful, if not the most powerful, families. The family continues to be actively involved in loan-sharking, bookmaking, prostitution, hijacking, narcotics, extortion, murder, pornography, securities fraud, and racketeering in traditional fields including construction, entertainment, and service occupations; in addition, the family remains in control of the Javits Convention Center and the annual San Gennaro Festival.

CURRENT HAPPENINGS
IN THE GENOVESE CRIME FAMILY

On April 27, 2001, 33 members of the Genovese crime family were indicted on charges ranging from stock fraud to murder. These individuals, arrested in New York, Florida, and Nevada, included former acting boss Frank "Farby" Serpico; capos Alan "Baldie" Longo and Rosario Gangi; acting capos Salvatore "Sammy Meatballs" Aparo and Peter "Petey Red"; and two retired police officers, an accountant, and various members of the other four N.Y. families. Many of the charges involve a $6.8 million "pump and dump" stock scheme, in which the account used to launder the money was referred to as "the tax doctor."

The Mangano/Gambino Family.   Though what is now considered the Gambino family was actually initiated by Al Manfredi (Mineo), his short reign does not grant him a place of prominence in the annals of organized crime. A close ally of Joseph Masseria at the onset of the Castellammarese War, Mineo never lived to see its completion. Instead, Frank "Don Cheech" Scalise, a Masseria defector, was given the chieftain position after Masseria's death; however, his tenure was short-lived as he was too closely associated with slain boss Maranzano. Thus, he "voluntarily" stepped down, and Vince Mangano assumed control, appointing Albert Anastasia as underboss. Mangano's selection proved to be a poor choice, as Anastasia soon plotted the comeuppance of the Mangano brothers. With the approval of Genovese boss Frank Costello, the brothers were soon murdered, and Anastasia assumed control, selecting Scalise as his underboss.

Albert "the Executioner" Anastasia was a volatile individual who was also known as the "mad hatter" due to his ferocity and willingness to kill anyone. (He ordered a hit on the citizen who turned in Willie Sutton, a famous bank robber whom Anastasia had read about. As a coup de grace, he then ordered a hit on the soldier who had carried out the murder.) Committing his first murder prior to turning 20, Anastasia was one of the leaders of the infamous Murder, Inc. When he was not snuffing the life out of some unfortunate soul, Anastasia could be found ruling the Brooklyn waterfront via his leadership of the International Longshoremen's Union, Local 1814. Like Lanza, Anastasia virtually controlled the prices of any merchandise unloaded by his employees. In addition, Anastasia's group was responsible for millions of dollars of "hijacked" merchandise as well as other nefarious schemes including loan-sharking. In fact, some suggest that the operation was cyclical: Individuals looking for employment were "encouraged" to "borrow" money from their employers. In 1955, the "Executioner" was executed while enjoying a visit to his favorite barbershop, proving that deals made in blood often result in blood, as his alliance with Costello enabled a coup staged by Anastasia's own underboss, Carlo Gambino. Gambino, it seems, had enlisted the aid of Joseph Profaci and Vito Genovese; however, both the personnel and the justification involved in his murder remain disputed in the literature. While some authors suggest that his murder, along with that of underboss Scalise, directly resulted from the practice of "selling" memberships, others suggest that the murder was committed to prevent his gaining an interest in the highly profitable Havana gambling world dominated by notables such as Santo Trafficante and Meyer Lansky. While both explanations seem plausible, the latter appears to have more merit, as Trafficante left the hotel where Anastasia was murdered just hours before the murder. Regardless, the ever ambitious Carlo Gambino benefited the most from his death.

Carlo Gambino, the most successful organized crime boss in American history, was born in Palermo in 1902 and immigrated to the United States in 1921. He was one of the few mobsters in his day who did not immigrate with his family; Gambino came alone. His sole friend in the United States was Gaetano Lucchese, a quickly rising mobster associated with Albert Anastasia. As a soldier, Gambino started a lucrative bootlegging business

---

MURDER, INC., ALBERT ANASTASIA AND COMPANY

Murder, Inc., was the name given to one of the most notorious mercenary groups in American history. It began when the "Boys from Brooklyn"—Abe "Kid Twist" Reles, Philip "Pittsburgh Phil" Strauss, and Martin "Buggy" Goldstein—attempted to take over the pinball machine business in the East New York–Brownsville section of Brooklyn. Disregarding the proprietary interest expressed by the Shapiro brothers, the Boys from Brooklyn hired a tough crew of Italian criminals to forward their interests. The war that commenced was quite bloody, but the Boys from Brooklyn were the undisputed victors, quickly overtaking virtually all organized crime rackets in the area.

On the request of the newly formed commission and under the direction of Albert "Executioner" Anastasia, the group soon saw the profitability of murder for hire. Acting as the enforcement arm of the formal syndicate, the group was responsible for at least 100 murders across the country. Perhaps the most famous of these was the execution of Dutch Schultz. The group's prominence and notoriety grew in pace with their professionalism. Dress rehearsals, previously prepared graves, getaway cars, and the like heightened their efficiency.

The end of Murder, Inc., resulted when "Kid Twist" Reles was arrested on a variety of charges, including the murder of Alec "Red" Alpert. Unwilling to die in the electric chair, Reles became the proverbial singing canary. His testimony led to the conviction and electrocution of seven of his former partners, including Lepke Buchalter and Louis Capone. Before he could implicate Albert Anastasia, then crime boss of the current Gambino family, he became known as the canary that could sing but couldn't fly. While under police protection, he mysteriously plummeted to his death from a window on the sixth floor of a Coney Island hotel.

that flourished well after Prohibition. Gambino, along with several other gangsters, made a fortune during World War II by appropriating and distributing ration stamps with the assistance of corrupt officials of the Office of Price Administration. He further expanded his fortune by engaging in a legitimate trucking industry. Under his guidance, the Gambino crime family became the most powerful in the United States. He ruled the family, quietly and without interruption, for almost two decades, but he is most notable for the repercussions of his untimely demise in 1976.

Carlo Gambino had maintained control of his organization and remained unfettered by law enforcement initiatives due primarily to his low-key lifestyle and innate suspicion. While maintaining a modest home, Gambino controlled a large portion of New York City, and through it, the country. Gambino's determination to escape law enforcement scrutiny also resulted in an innate distrust of biological strangers, leading to his marriage of his first cousin. Subsequently, Gambino anointed his cousin (and his wife's brother) Paul Castellano as his heir apparent.

Paul "Big Paulie" Castellano remained virtually invisible to law enforcement until the 1980s. Like his cousin/brother-in-law, Castellano originally avoided government scrutiny through a low-key lifestyle. Castellano's only mistake was made as a young man when he was arrested for an armed robbery. Refusing to implicate his partners in crime, Castellano established himself as a stand-up guy. Upon his release, Castellano pursued far less violent criminal activities, increasing his presence in New York's flourishing meat market. Through traditional mafia tactics of racketeering, Castellano successfully created several legitimate butcher shops, which obtained lucrative contracts through intimidation. Although earning significant income for Gambino family coffers, Castellano remained relatively unknown even within the ranks of his family. Thus, his ascension to the family's throne was not readily accepted by the majority of organizational members, who believed that Gambino's underboss, Neil Dellacroce, was most deserving. In fact, many members felt that his appointment was a travesty—a perception that Castellano did little to change.

Castellano's appointment of the beleaguered Dellacroce as family underboss served to quell an immediate rebellion. Dellacroce, a mafia traditionalist, openly supported the new boss while quietly maintaining ironclad control of even the most unruly of crews. Thus, two factions emerged: One, headed by Dellacroce, maintained separate crews, those more traditional, and more violent, in nature; Castellano, on the other hand, allowed such separation, considering himself immune from street-level conflicts. This arrangement, supported by Castellano, increased the detachment felt by many soldiers. His purchase of a multimillion-dollar mansion, dubbed "the White House" by organizational members, solidified growing feelings of resentment.

Castellano proved to be an ineffective boss, committing several fatal mistakes. The first of these involved his hypocritical edict prohibiting narcotics trafficking within his family. This edict was questioned by many individuals within his family when it was revealed that Castellano allowed Genovese soldiers to traffic in narcotics within his demographic fiefdom if they paid him a handsome profit. While actively allowing other organizations to engage in the practice for a fee, Castellano failed to appreciate the loss of revenue experienced by his own soldiers. The indictment of various Gambino members on narcotics charges created an untenable situation for many of his most violent crews. As Dellacroce's cancer prognosis was grim, individuals recognized their eventual vulnerability (i.e., mortality). Castellano's personal life did little to ease the tensions created by his directive. Attempting to keep pace with his young lover and live-in maid, Gloria Olarte, Castellano received a penile implant, further eroding the respect of his underlings; however, Castellano remained blissfully unaware of the magnitude of dissension within his family.

In 1985, Neil Dellacroce succumbed to cancer, and Castellano made his final mistake. Castellano, then under indictment on a variety of racketeering charges, chose not to attend Dellacroce's wake, an offense so egregious that it was all but suicidal. Dellacroce, after all, had served as a faithful underboss for nearly a decade. Although shock waves reverberated throughout the entire structure of La Cosa Nostra, Dellacroce's protégé, capo John Gotti, took it the hardest. Gotti, leader of one of the most violent crews, was further affronted when Castellano chose his chauffer and bodyguard, Tommy Bilotti, as his replacement. Within two weeks, Paul Castellano and Tommy Bilotti were murdered outside Sparks Steakhouse, and John Gotti was appointed the new head of the Gambino crime family.

John "Johnny Boy" Gotti's entrance into the criminal underworld was all but predestined. One of 13 children born to poor immigrants in the South Bronx and surrounded by poverty, the young Gotti viewed wealth as only associated with those involved in mafia activities. After moving to the Brownsville East section of New York at age 12, Gotti followed his older brother, Peter, into the Fulton-Rockaway Boys. The group frequented areas populated by Italian mobsters. Hanging around social clubs, the group gained the notice of some low-level mobsters due to their ability to fence stolen property. Johnny Boy, in particular, came to the attention of Carmine Fatico, a capo for Albert Anastasia. Gotti began stealing cars and any other merchandise not tied down. Because Gotti was in and out of jails throughout the 1960s, his wife was often forced to go on welfare to support her growing family. When not incarcerated, Gotti began to hang out at the Bergin Hunt & Fish Social Club in Queens. The Bergin was owned by Fatico and was conveniently located close to the JFK International Airport. (Gotti's crew and the rest of the Gambino crime family were notorious hijackers.)

A big-time gambler and a regular loser, Gotti controlled Fatico's gambling industry until Fatico was indicted on a variety of charges. Dellacroce replaced Fatico with 31-year-old Gotti—a move that shocked gangsters and law enforcement alike. Gotti's star was on the rise. He received greater prominence after murdering James McBratney, a small-time Irish hood who reportedly had kidnapped and murdered Carlo Gambino's son. Returning from his most recent prison stint, Gotti was rewarded with a brand-new car, compliments of Carlo Gambino. It seemed that Gotti was unstoppable; he was not, however, immune to personal tragedy. In March 1980, Gotti's 12-year-old son, Frank, was struck and killed on a motorbike outside his Queens home. By all accounts, the driver of the vehicle, John Favara, a neighbor and father of Gotti playmates, was not at

LOVE AND MURDER
The Assassination of Paul Castellano

On December 16, 1985, Paul Castellano and his newly appointed underboss, Tommy Bilotti, were killed in a hail of bullets outside a popular restaurant in Midtown Manhattan. Although his murder was largely attributed to the greed of John Gotti and his followers, Castellano's death was also precipitated by his own actions.

In the early 1930s, a commission of mob leaders forbade the assassination of family bosses without the explicit permission of the commission. This rule, designed to protect organizational leaders and ensure family consistency, specified the punishment for violation—death. This is not to suggest that bosses were entirely protected from violence, but they were protected from *unsanctioned* violence. This distinction proved to be extremely important in Castellano's case.

Although many organizational members did not approve of Castellano's ascension, the commission formally sanctioned his ordination. His modest demeanor and businesslike manner, so reminiscent of his cousin/brother-in-law, were good for business. However, Castellano's gravitation toward ostentation with the purchase of "the White House" signaled an oncoming storm and slowly eroded the robust support once found among his peers, and his infatuation with his young maid all but destroyed it.

In the early 1980s, the FBI's Organized Crime Task Force received permission to place an electronic eavesdropping device in the kitchen of Castellano's palatial estate. This device proved to be one of the most successful in history and led to the indictment of the entire commission. Hours of tape revealed that Castellano routinely criticized his fellow bosses and openly discussed family business with various associates at his kitchen table. It also revealed that Castellano discussed these matters in the presence of his mistress, a major mafia faux pas. As a result, Gotti's informal petition for permission was granted by the majority of the commission. (Vincent Gigante was a notable exception, ordering the assassination of Gotti immediately following the Castellano hit.) Unfortunately for the commission, the coup was staged too late. In 1987, the structure of La Cosa Nostra was decimated in New York City. Castellano's death did not diminish the damning impact of the tapes recorded in his kitchen. Thus, Castellano's assassination saved him from both a lengthy incarceration and the embarrassment of hearing his most intimate conversations played before a live audience.

fault; Frank Gotti had darted out directly into the path of the moving car. The Gottis were devastated, but none more so than Frank's mother, Victoria. Two months after the accident, she attacked Favara with a baseball bat, but no charges were pressed. Shortly thereafter, Gotti and Victoria went to Florida on "vacation." Upon their return, they were notified of the mysterious disappearance of their neighbor John Favara.

Gotti's murder of Castellano and Thomas Bilotti in 1985 may have been motivated by power, but it was definitely a matter of self-preservation as well. Gotti and his
crew had become heavily involved in heroin trafficking. Fearing his own murder, Gotti
acted first. At age 45, he became boss of one of the most powerful organized crime
syndicates in U.S. history. For a while it appeared that Gotti would actually continue
his criminal enterprise for some time. His Armani suits and flashy lifestyle endeared
him to a community looking for heroes. His ability to outwit law enforcement authorities and evade criminal prosecution earned him the name the "Teflon Don." However, Gotti never displayed a level of intelligence comparable to his predecessors;
instead, Gotti's expensive image and sophisticated veneer were misleading. Though
Gotti achieved a position far higher than the average street thug, his organization did
not. Gotti had an Achilles' heel, and the government found it in 1991.

As stated, Gotti was arrogant—carelessly so. Believing himself invulnerable after
beating two RICO charges, Gotti ignored the lesson of recent RICO convictions
within the Lucchese and Genovese families. Electronic surveillance equipment (i.e.,
bugs) was placed in all of Gotti's hangouts—the Ravenite Social Club, his home, and

---

THE RETURN OF SAMMY THE BULL

In 1992, Salvatore Gravano's testimony resulted in the conviction of 39 mobsters,
including onetime friend John Gotti. In exchange for his testimony, Gravano served
only 5 years in prison and paid $250,000 in fines for his role in at least 19 murders.
Upon his release, Gravano (aka James Moran) promptly left the Witness Protection
Program. In 1996, he published *Underboss* (with Peter Maas), receiving $850,000 for
his efforts and appearing on national television. The choir boy image he presented
for the cameras, however, would soon be challenged.

Like the proverbial bad penny, Sammy "the Bull" Gravano returned to the front
page of the news in 2000. Instead of promoting a book, however, he was fighting new
criminal charges. It appears that Sammy had become bored (or desperate) in Arizona
and had established a very profitable ($1 million a month) Ecstasy ring. Ironically,
Gravano's latest legal troubles were directly attributed to the bravado (and stupidity)
of one of his underlings—his son. Gerard Gravano, along with his friends and fellow
criminals, had developed a white supremacist ideology and had engaged in acts of
violence against minorities and homosexuals. As is often the case in criminal prosecutions, investigators investigating one of these assaults actually stumbled across the
large-scale narcotics operation.

Gravano proved that he felt most comfortable engaging in criminal activity
within a family. This time, however, it was his biological one—Gravano's wife and
daughter were also indicted for the conspiracy. In May 2001, Gravano and his son
pleaded guilty in federal court on charges stemming from the purchase and transportation of Ecstasy from New York to Arizona. They are still awaiting trial in state court.

(most importantly) an apartment upstairs from the club "rented" by a widow of a longtime wiseguy. Federal investigators turned on their machines and heard the sweetest sound of all—John Gotti bragging about his criminal accomplishments and plans for the future. Armed with this overwhelming evidence, the feds approached Salvatore "Sammy the Bull" Gravano, who was Gotti's friend and underboss. Exposing a plot hatched by Gotti to murder Gravano, federal agents encouraged Gravano's testimony.

Gravano's testimony resulted in a multitude of convictions of the Gambino family hierarchy. (In 1992, Gotti received five life terms plus 65 years. Stricken with throat cancer, John Gotti died in a prison hospital on June 10, 2002.) As such, the organization lacked any clear guidance for a period of time. In fact, Gotti's flamboyance so angered law enforcement authorities that the leadership structure continued to be scrutinized after his incarceration, and many organizational members did not want the top position. Thus, when Gotti ordained his son Junior as his successor, little protest was raised.

Referred to as "dumbfella" by government sources, John Gotti, Jr., epitomized the twenty-first-century wiseguy. Disrespectful and embarrassingly inarticulate, Junior became an object of ridicule by many, including his father. His executive ineptitude was proven to the world in 1998 when a government raid revealed stacks of money, accompanying ledgers, and a wedding gift list that included the family affiliation, rank, and monetary gift of all individuals attending. This list confirmed law enforcement intelligence and provided vital evidence against Junior and the entire structure of LCN for racketeering.

Currently, the Gambino family's main enterprises appear to be construction, narcotics, pornography, loan-sharking, extortion, gambling, and stock fraud. Their racketeering activities ranges from cement workers unions to city hall. They are extremely active in the garment industry, controlling prices and garment production. Electronic eavesdropping devices have indicated that the commission has pressured replacement of acting bosses John Gotti, Jr., and Peter Gotti (John's brother). Initially, it was anticipated that Gotti's formal replacement was to be Nick Corozzo, longtime capo; however, Corozzo's subsequent racketeering indictment halted the succession. With Junior's conviction in late 1998, Peter Gotti remained the only viable choice. The future for the Gambinos, once one of the most powerful families, remains to be seen because without adequate leadership and consistency, their future is uncertain.

The Lucchese Family.   Gaetano "Tommy" Reina, a onetime supporter of Masseria, originally controlled the Lucchese family. Murdered in 1930, Reina did not live to see the end of the Castellammarese War. His successor, Gaetano Gagliano, served for more than two decades with Gaetano "Three Fingers Brown" Lucchese as his underboss.[10] Lucchese arrived from Sicily in 1911; he was 11 years old. First arrested at the age of 21, Lucchese would have a career that spanned nearly half a century. Formally taking over the helm upon Gagliano's death in 1953, Lucchese would prove to be an astute (if somewhat uncharismatic) leader, displaying an uncanny knack for choosing the right side of a conflict. He supported both Gambino and Genovese in their plots to become bosses of their respective families as well as the victors in the

JOHN GOTTI, JR.
The Proverbial Rocket Scientist

Like all families, LCN groups have experienced their share of intellectually challenged individuals. John Gotti, Jr., for example, is referred to as "dumbfella" by an assortment of law enforcement representatives *and* members of his own family! In fact, one of his shortsighted actions may provide critical evidence in future racketeering cases.

In April 1990, John Gotti, Jr., married his bride in a wedding fit for royalty. The hundreds of guests included representatives from every corner of the world and every branch of the LCN. The bride was beautiful, the food plentiful, and the gifts extravagant. Every attention to detail, including the traditional recording of wedding gifts, had been observed. Unfortunately, this time-honored tradition would have dire consequences for Junior and other mafiosi.

The list, used by Gotti to ascertain the level of respect from other families as well as the allegiance of soldiers, crews, and associates of his own, was well organized. It was so well organized, in fact, that it was grouped according to family affiliation and organizational position. In February 1998, this handwritten list would be utilized not for thank-you notes but for subpoenas. Interestingly, Junior's attorney would claim that the list, detailing over $250,000 worth of monetary bequests, supported his contention that the money seized in his home did not represent criminal proceeds.

Some of the most notable gifts included the following:

Bonanno Family ($6,000 Total)
Boss Joe Massino—$1,000

Underboss Salvatore Vitale and Consigliere Anthony Spero—$4,000

Joseph Chilli—$500

Joseph Chilli, Jr.—$500

Lucchese Family
The 19th Hole (former base of operations for the Lucchese family)*—$10,000

Colombo Family ($13,000 Total)
Boss (incarcerated) Carmine (Junior) Persico—$1,000

Acting Boss Victor "Little Vic" Orena—$6,000

Underboss Joseph Scopo—$5,000

Consiglieri Vincent Aloi—$1,000

Genovese Family
Boss Vincent "the Chin" Gigante—$0

Underboss Venero "Benny Eggs" Mangano—$0

*This included Boss Vic Amuso, Underboss Gaspipe Casso, and Capo Fat Pete Chiodo.

Consigliere James "The Little Guy" Ida—$0

Capo Alphonse "Allie Shades" Malangone—$5,000

Capo Salvatore "Sally Dogs" Lombardi—$1,000

Soldier Joseph "Joe Glitz" Galizia—$1,000

Gambino Family (to Name a Few)

Underboss Salvatore "Sammy the Bull" Gravano—$7,500

Consigliere Frank "Frankie Loc" Locascio—$2,000

Capo John "Jackie Nose" D'Amico and crew—$10,000

Capo Tommy Gambino and crew—$10,000

Associate Joseph Watts—$9,300

In total, 17 capos gave $5,000 each.

Colombo wars. Lucchese successfully chartered the family through the complex web of labor racketeering, beginning with the kosher poultry business in the 1930s. Lucchese also expanded the family's wealth through a sophisticated system of loan-sharking (Volkman, 1998).

During the 1930s, the center of American fashion was New York City's Garment District. Fortunes were made and lost in this clothing mecca. Nowhere was the American dream more salient. Large numbers of individuals and entities risked everything in the hopes that their lines would prove popular with the American public. Unfortunately, many of them lacked the necessary funds to mass-produce their ideas and were unable to secure legitimate loans due to their immigrant background. Instead, they turned to neighborhood lenders. These lenders, of course, were wiseguys such as Tommy Lucchese. Perfecting the "knock-down" loan, a system in which interest was charged weekly and paid prior to any application to prinicipal, Lucchese made millions. He also gained a controlling interest in a variety of businesses whose owners were unable to pay the astronomical interest. Lucchese further expanded his criminal control in the Garment District by monopolizing the trucking industry. Following this pattern in other areas, such as wholesale foods and bakeries, Lucchese established a foothold for his family in New York's criminal underworld. Lucchese also identified Kennedy Airport (formerly known as Idelwild Airport) as a prime target for the enterprising family. Implementing unions and trade associations, Lucchese successfully monopolized a variety of support systems, including trucking and warehousing, as well as created a pipeline of information necessary for shipment hijacking. (Recent indictments indicate that employees of Kennedy Airport, members of local police departments, and associates of the family are all on the payroll.) During Lucchese's reign, his family was characterized as one of the most stable. Avoiding the limelight, Lucchese lived modestly, and sent both of his children to college. Although his daughter later married the son of Carlo Gambino, there is no indication that Lucchese promoted the criminal lifestyle to his children. He died of cancer in 1967.

Although Anthony "Tony Ducks" Corallo was the early favorite to replace Lucchese, his conviction for bribery enabled Gambino ally Carmine Tramunti to ascend to Lucchese's chair. However, Tramunti's subsequent life imprisonment granted "Tony Ducks" his due. Under his tenure, the family's primary sources of revenue were a combination of traditional avenues of racketeering and the new rackets of private sanitation (i.e., garbage collection) and construction. Corallo's style was very similar to his predecessor's. He monopolized industries through traditional strong-arm tactics while living a quiet life and avoiding publicity at all costs. However, Corallo, along with his top hierarchy, was convicted in the commission case of the 1980s. He and his underboss Salvatore "Tom Mix" Santoro died in prison in 2000. His conviction and death threw the family into disarray and prompted the most violent period in the family's history.

Upon his incarceration, Corallo appointed Vittorio "Vic" Amuso and Anthony "Gaspipe" Casso as the family's boss and underboss, respectively. Engaging in a management style characteristic of Philadelphia's Nicky Scarfo, the pair were soon responsible for a variety of murders within their own family. Victims included suspected turncoats, disrespectful members, and others. In fact, no one was safe from their homicidal, and increasingly paranoid, tendencies. At one point, Amuso and Casso ordered the termination of all 30 members of the New Jersey faction headed by Tumac Acceturo. Fortunately, the soldiers selected to carry out the massacre proved to be as incompetent as hit men as Amuso and Casso were as bosses. However, two innocent individuals would die before Amuso and Casso were finally incapacitated. (Garbage collectors Robert Kubecka and Donald Barstow, refusing to relinquish their independence to the mafia, were killed due to their testimony in a former case.)

Amuso and Casso's increasing volatility encouraged organizational members to cooperate with authorities. Ironically, Casso, largely responsible for the mass exodus, cooperated with the government as well, testifying against his former partner. However, the very inconsistency and erratic behavior that made him an ineffective leader rendered him equally incompetent as an informant. Both were convicted and are currently serving life sentences. Upon his incarceration, Amuso appointed Joseph "Little Joe" DeFede as acting boss, but he was not able to enjoy his ascension for long. After assuming the reins in the mid-1990s, DeFede was soon incarcerated for a variety of racketeering charges in 1998. His replacement, Steve Crea, suffered the same fate. Currently, Louis "Louie Crossbay" Daidone is the family's acting boss. The family is actively involved in limo services, catering, nightclubs, narcotics, bookmaking, racketeering, and hijacking. The smallest of the five families, they are best known for the $8 million Lufthansa heist portrayed in the movie *Good Fellas*.

The Profaci/Colombo Family. Already an ex-convict by age 25, Joseph Profaci saw the United States as the land of opportunity and immigrated there. Profaci was one of the few active gangsters who was able to remain neutral during the

Castellammarese War. By all accounts a traditional mobster, Profaci was nevertheless one of the most successful in establishing legitimate businesses. Known as the "Olive Oil King," he was at one time the largest single importer of olive oil. Although his family remained stable and relatively free of violence during his reign, intrafamily rivalry and subordinate disloyalty marked the year prior to his death. Some members, most notably the Gallo brothers, were uncomfortable with the percentage demanded by Profaci as family boss. They were further dissatisfied with his practice of allowing blood relatives to attain positions of leadership above more deserving soldiers. Profaci, in his Old World ways, appeared to view his family as a kingdom to be inherited only through birth order. However, the final straw for the Gallo brothers (Albert, Larry, and Joseph) came after they murdered Frank "Frankie Shots" Abbatermarco, a big loan shark and gambler who either withheld money from Profaci (Jones, 1982) or was unable to pay the interest and balance due on a loan owed to Profaci (Meskil, 1976). Acting on Profaci's orders, the Gallo brothers did not believe that they were sufficiently rewarded because Profaci did not allocate any of the dead man's territory to the group. In response, the brothers kidnapped a variety of Profaci allies including: Joseph Magliocco, Profaci's underboss; Profaci's brother, Frank; and Profaci's bodyguard, John Scimone (Meskil, 1976). To secure their release, Profaci promised to meet the group's demands but reneged after the safe release of the hostages.

Profaci then lured the transgressors into vulnerable situations. Joseph "Joe Jelly" Giorelli (a Gallo supporter and alleged assassin of Anastasia), for example, disappeared on the same day that Larry Gallo narrowly escaped death. (Gallo was in the process of being murdered when an unsuspecting police officer happened upon the scene.) The war between the two soon became more violent, and within a two-year period, nine successful hits and six unsuccessful attempts occurred between the two groups. Ironically, the war's instigator, Joey Gallo, escaped most of the firefight due to his incarceration from 1962 to 1971 for attempted extortion. While the battle raged, the majority of the commission sided with the Gallos, with Joseph Bonanno representing Profaci's sole supporter. For Profaci, however, the war would have to continue without him. He died of cancer in 1957.

Upon Profaci's death, underboss Joe Magliocco assumed control. However, the commission remained opposed, so Bonanno and Magliocco plotted to have the other bosses murdered, relying on and enlisting the services of Profaci soldier and hardened killer Joe Colombo.[11] Their selection proved to be a poor choice as the power-hungry Colombo informed Gambino of the plot. Magliocco promptly threw himself on the mercy of the commission, whereupon he was stripped of his power. Bonanno, on the other hand, took the high ground, running away and placing his son in charge. As a result, the commission backed Joe Colombo as the new boss of the Profaci family and, refusing to recognize the legitimacy of Bonanno's acting boss Salvatore "Bill" Bonanno, supported Gaspar Di Gregorio.

Joseph Colombo's youth, like that of many of his criminal associates, was characterized by violence. His father and a female acquaintance were found strangled in the backseat of a car in 1938. In one of his rare legitimate pursuits, Joe Colombo joined

THE GALLO BROTHERS

Larry, Albert, and Joey ("Crazy Joe") Gallo grew up in an extremely impoverished neighborhood near the South Brooklyn waterfront. Known for their homicidal tendencies, the brothers were often enlisted in organizational murders. Originally serving with the Persico brothers under Frank "Frankie Shots" Abbatemarco, the biggest policy banker in the African-American Bedford-Stuyvesant ghetto, they eventually put together a string of small bars and restaurants, which fronted their various criminal enterprises. By all accounts, "Crazy Joe" was the leader of the three and the primary initiator of their conflict with the Profaci family leadership. Although a ruthless killer, Joey Gallo fancied himself a scholar, fond of discourse on Kafka, Balzac, and Sartre (Meskil, 1976). Ironically, this self-proclaimed scholar was officially diagnosed as a card-carrying schizophrenic with homicidal tendencies. While incarcerated at Greenhaven, Gallo befriended an array of African-American prisoners, proclaiming that they would make effective mafia soldiers. (Many argue that Colombo's assassin was related to this association.) Although his incarceration for a variety of charges spared him the violence of the war that he had started, Gallo continued to prick the ire of family leadership. Upon his release, he continued to court the favor of African-American criminals, a significant affront to his Italian heritage. In 1972, Joey Gallo was murdered in front of his family at Umberto's Clam House, a restaurant owned by Genovese capo Matty "the Horse" Ianello. The hit has been attributed to Colombo soldier Sonny Pinto (Maloney et al., 1995).

the Coast Guard during World War II but was discharged for mental problems. He promptly returned to Brooklyn and a criminal way of life, being arrested several times for gambling violations. For the most part, however, he escaped the notice of federal investigators until his ascension to his family's top seat.

With the backing of Gaetano Lucchese and Carlo Gambino, Joseph Colombo became one of the youngest mafia bosses in January 1964. The position brought him unprecedented wealth, power, and, government scrutiny. In 1966, Colombo was arrested for contempt for his refusal to answer the questions of a grand jury empaneled to investigate the mob's influence on legitimate businesses. His troubles intensified when the IRS looked into his finances, an investigation precipitated by Colombo's own actions. Posing as a real estate broker for Cantalupo Realty, Colombo applied for a license in 1966. Required to disclose financial information, Colombo revealed his luxurious lifestyle, and he was eventually indicted for income tax evasion and fraudulent documentation.

In 1970, Joe Colombo founded the Italian-American Civil Rights League, after his son was arrested for charges largely manufactured by the FBI. Holding rallies and picketing the Manhattan offices of the FBI, Colombo effectively gathered support within the Italian-American community, claiming that Italian-Americans were unfairly targeted by a prejudicial government. In fact, the League gathered so much momentum that it was soon a national phenomenon that both celebrities and politicians rushed to support. Frank Sinatra, Connie Francis, Vic Damone, and Sammy Davis, Jr., for example, lent their support for various banquets and fund-raisers, and producers of *The Godfather* agreed to strike the terms "Mafia" and "La Cosa Nostra" from the script. Colombo proved to be a most prolific speaker, characterizing himself as a civil rights leader like the fallen Martin Luther King, Jr. He also proved to be an effective administrator. Within two months, an estimated 50,000 attended a League-sponsored rally in Manhattan, and Colombo had collected hundreds of thousands of dollars in membership fees. His egomania was further satisfied when he was appointed "Man of the Year" in 1971. It seemed that Colombo was sitting on top of the world; however, within a year, Colombo would be a vegetable, and the League would be defunct.

On June 28, 1971, Colombo once again planned a Columbus Day celebration of the Italian-American Civil Rights League. This time, however, he did not enjoy the support of his fellow crime bosses, who were increasingly embarrassed by his antics. As he took the stage to greet his admirers, Colombo was shot three times at close range by Jerome Johnson, an African-American who had served time with Crazy Joe Gallo, Colombo's rival and nemesis. Johnson, of course, was immediately shot and killed by Colombo soldiers. There have been a variety of theories regarding the hit. The most widely accepted by far is that Colombo was shot at the request of the commission. Another popular theory is that Colombo's shooting was initiated by Joe Gallo, who coveted the family's top position. However, both of these theories are disputed by former Colombo boss Carmine Persico. He claims that Johnson was enlisted by the government to shoot the popular boss and frame his replacement for the murder, serving a one-two punch which would cripple the family (Meskil, 1976). Presumptions notwithstanding, Joe Colombo would linger in a vegetative state for several years before dying in 1978. His replacement was top capo Carmine "Junior" Persico.

Incarcerated at the time of Colombo's incapacitation, Persico approved the appointment of Thomas DiBella as acting boss. However, Carmine and his brother, Alphonse, remained the family leaders for all intents and purposes. By the late 1980s, both Persico brothers and underboss Gennaro Langella were facing lengthy prison terms. As a result, Carmine appointed Victor "Little Vic" Orena as acting boss with the understanding that his son, Alphonse, would assume control upon his release from prison. However, Orena became quite accustomed to his role at the top and was unwilling to relinquish it upon Alphonse's release. Preparing for war, Orena enlisted the support of Gambino boss John Gotti and various members of his organization who distrusted the college-educated yuppie. Although the commission attempted to mediate the coming storm, violence erupted within the organization. The first shots were directed at Orena himself, but the shooters were unsuccessful. Retaliatory actions by Orena loyalists were equally misguided, and an attempt on Greg Scarpa, Sr., resulted in injuries to innocents while their target escaped unscathed.

This intrafamily strife would prove quite costly to the Colombo organization. While the war ultimately claimed over a dozen lives (including two innocent bystanders), the toll on the organizational hierarchy proved more costly to the family. Almost 100 wiseguys were indicted on an assortment of charges ranging from murder to racketeering, and the majority received lengthy prison sentences. When it was over, there was no clear winner. Although Persico was the ultimate victor, 41 of his supporters were rendered ineffective through incarceration. On the other side, the Orena faction was more successful in beating the charges facing them, with only 15 of 28 being convicted, but their leader, Little Vic, was convicted and sentenced to life in prison.

By outward appearances, Alphonse Persico did make efforts to unify his tattered family by appointing Orena supporter William "Wild Bill" Cutolo as his underboss. However, such actions proved to be superficial, as Cutolo disappeared and was presumed murdered shortly thereafter. As of January 2002, Persico was awaiting trial on racketeering charges, and Cutolo's son has reported that he will testify against Persico at trial. It is anticipated that Colombo family members will continue to fight among themselves. Long characterized by internecine conflicts, it seems unlikely that a family now struggling with a lack of clear leadership will unify.

Wars within the family have depleted much of their power and moneymaking abilities. One of their main operations continues to be racketeering. The Colombo family maintains control over cement unions in the New York area. Any new construction—skyscrapers, houses, sidewalks, and even streets—is affected by the Colombo family's stranglehold of cement workers' unions. The family has proven especially vulnerable to law enforcement efforts in recent years due to the lack of loyalty and consistency of leadership within the organization. New associates are increasingly focusing on narcotics, which can only bring further violence to a family with more than its share.

The Bonanno Family. Guiseppe "Joseph" or "Don Peppino" Bonanno arrived in the United States in 1924. According to his own autobiography, Bonanno was forced out of Italy due to his anti-Fascist activities. An early supporter of Maranzano, Bonanno was disappointed by the new generation of mafia that emerged under Luciano; however, he was pleased that he was appointed head of his own family

---

FAMILY BETRAYAL

Greg Scarpa, Sr., was a pivotal player in the Colombo wars of the 1980s. In fact, he proved to be the most prolific of Colombo shooters and temporarily received organizational accolades as the epitome of the fearless hit man. (Scarpa's bravado, however, was most probably related to the fact that he was dying from AIDS—a disease he contracted through the tainted blood of a fellow crew member during a blood transfusion.) Unbeknownst to his admirers, Scarpa was also a top-echelon FBI informant for over two decades. Scarpa was denied a ceremonial funeral upon his death in prison in 1992. His exposure as a turncoat stripped him of this final respect heaped on fallen comrades—only his biological family and that of his wife attended.

(Bonanno and Lalli, 1983). Contrary to Bonanno's assertions, federal law enforcement sources indicate that one of their earliest enterprises was narcotics. Until his death in 2002, Joseph "Joe Bananas" Bonanno presented himself as a reformed mobster whose legitimate endeavors in cheese manufacturing and garment-related enterprises enabled him to survive in spite of government persecution.

Guiseppe Bonanno was born in 1905 to a powerful family in Castellammare del Golfo, a seaside town northwest of Palermo, Sicily. He first arrived in the United States in 1908 as a toddler but returned to Sicily when a war involving his family erupted. Although the conflict was quickly decided in his family's favor, his father's death left him and his mother in the care of his uncle, Giovanni Magaddino. Soon thereafter, his return to the United States was prompted by his expulsion from nautical school—an expulsion largely credited to his anti-Mussolini and anti-Facist politics. Unlike that of others in New York's underworld, Bonanno's arrival in the United States was an auspicious occasion.

Assisted by his cousin, Buffalo boss Stephano Magaddino, Bonanno quickly gained a foothold in the bootleg liquor business. He was also heavily involved in the Italian lottery and narcotics trafficking.[12] Funneling much of his illegitimate proceeds into various legitimate companies, Bonanno soon had an interest in a variety of businesses, including bakeries, clothing factories (e.g., B & D Coat Company, Morgan Coat Company, Miss Youth Clothing, Co.), cheese shops (e.g., Grande Cheese Company of Fond du Lac, Wisconsin), and laundries (e.g., Brunswick Laundry Service of Brooklyn). Bonanno used these companies to launder the proceeds from his illegitimate activities as well as using his funeral homes to dispose of mob victims.[13] In fact, Bonanno claimed to be a legitimate businessman, pointing to his vast portfolio of companies to support his claims; however, his ability to own and operate such endeavors was directly connected to extortion and labor racketeering.

BAD YEAR FOR THE BONANNOS

In 1957, Bonanno's years of impunity were at an end. At a remote farmhouse in upstate New York, Bonanno, along with many of his fellow bosses, was arrested. Although their convictions on conspiracy charges were eventually overturned, the events at Apalachin would continue to have repercussions for the ranking members of La Cosa Nostra. Bonanno would further be affected by a series of murders and attempted murders of ranking bosses, beginning with the failed assassination attempt on Frank Costello. However, the murder of Bonanno's chief ally, Albert Anastasia, and his underboss, Francesco "Don Ciccio" Scalise, would prove the most worrisome to Bonanno.* The loss of his allies would lead to Bonanno's fall from grace almost a decade later.

*Both murders, Anastasia's in a barber's chair and Scalise's at a produce stand, would be reenacted in The Godfather.

A MATCH MADE IN GANGSTER LAND

In 1956, Salvatore "Bill" Bonanno, eldest son of Joseph, married Rosalie Profaci, niece of Joseph Profaci, head of the Profaci/Colombo family. The wedding was reported to be one of the most costly of the century; guests were entertained by Tony Bennett. In fact, their wedding was said to be the inspiration for the opening scenes of *The Godfather*. Although their marriage does not appear to be a happy one, their union solidified the Bonanno and Profaci crime families, at least for the moment.

Bonanno's expansionist tendencies coupled with marked levels of egomania angered many of his criminal colleagues, including his cousin, Stephano Magaddino. Although 1957 had proven to be a bad year for the Bonannos, the year 1963 signaled the beginning of the end. In 1963, Joseph Magliocco and Joseph Bonanno reportedly put a contract on the heads of competing crime bosses Gambino and Lucchese—a charge Bonanno vehemently denied. Fleeing to Canada to escape retaliation, Bonanno allegedly left his son in charge. Unfortunately for his son, family members and the commission alike opposed his promotion. Bonanno stated that he was summoned to appear before the commission but declined because of safety concerns. He also suggested that he was abducted by armed gunmen on order of his cousin, Stephano Magaddino.[14] Soon thereafter, he claimed that he was released and fled to Tucson in fear for his life (Bonanno and Lalli, 1983). In the meantime, the commission formally deposed Bonanno, replacing him with Magaddino's brother-in-law, Gaspar Di Gregorio. However, Bonanno refused to relent, requesting family members to support his son as the legitimate leader. The "Banana War" then erupted.

Although the vast majority of family members doubted the ability of the college-educated Bill Bonanno, many still supported the edict of their founder. As a result, bullets were traded between the warring factions, and Di Gregorio, Bill's godfather, attempted to lure him to his death. Joseph Bonanno returned to New York in 1966 ostensibly to face a grand jury inquiry into the 1957 Apalachin fiasco. Within two years of his return, Bonanno finally recognized the futility of his efforts and "retired" in Tucson, where he continued to portray himself as a "Man of Honour." By that time, the Banana War had taken a heavy toll on the family, and both sides had suffered tremendous losses. Victims of the Bonanno faction included Samuel "Hank" Perrone, close friend and bodyguard to Bill, who was shot to death; and Vincent Cassese, William Gonzalez, and Vincent Garofalo, who all suffered gunshot wounds. On the other side, murder victims included Frank Mari, Tomas "Smitty" D'Angelo, Jimmy D'Angelo, Franscisco "Frank the 500" Terrelli, Michael Consolo, Michael Adamo, and Thomas Zummo. Joseph Bonanno was convicted of a minor charge in 1980 based largely on his autobiography, *Man of Honour*. By his own account, Bonanno retired after his brief prison stint and ceased all criminal activity. He died in May 2002; he was 97 years old.

Di Gregorio ruled the family until he died of cancer in 1970. The next three bosses, Paul Sciacca, Natale Evola, and Philip "Rusty" Rastelli, respectively, enjoyed very short reigns, with Sciacca and Evola dying soon after their coronation. In 1974, Carmine "Lilo" Galante assumed the reins from Rastelli, who was then facing significant legal problems.

Carmine Galante was born on February 21, 1910, to immigrants from Castellammare del Golfo. First arrested in 1924 for shoplifting, Galante had a career marked by long incarcerations. Prior to his ascension, Galante proved to be a major organized crime figure during Bonanno's tenure. In fact, it is widely believed that Galante established and supervised the Canadian/New York heroin pipeline until his arrest and imprisonment in 1962.[15] His 12-year prison sentence proved to be a blessing in disguise as it allowed him to remain neutral during the Banana War, a luxury very few enjoyed. Upon his release, Galante continued to increase the family's drug trade. Galante was not well liked by his soldiers due to his lack of generosity and his use of "zips." This unpopularity led to his assassination in 1979. Few mourned his loss, and Phillip "Rusty" Rastelli, his old nemesis, regained his throne. However, much of his reign was spent behind bars, leading to yet another war within the family.

Rastelli's incarceration resulted in a power struggle between two capos. The more powerful of the two, Dominick "Sonny Black" Napolitano, successfully ambushed his foe, "Sonny Red" Indelicato, and two supporting capos, "Philly Lucky" and "Big Trin." However, he was unable to savor his victory as it was soon revealed that one of his crew was none other than FBI Special Agent Joe "Donnie Brasco" Pistone. This revelation led to his immediate assassination. In 1985, Joseph Massino, Bonanno capo and Gotti ally, was elected as boss of the Bonanno family. Recent years have suggested that past mistakes are guiding the actions of contemporary leaders. It appears that the subtle approach is in vogue. Massino has successfully regained the family's seat on the commission, and is actively pursuing racketeering, gambling, securities fraud, loansharking, and extortion. While the family members are still heavily involved in the narcotics industry, it appears that they are attempting to shed their image as drug-dealing parasites; however, their history may prove hard to overcome.

BRINGING IT ALL TOGETHER

There were just too many stops. He made pickups from Sammy Bull, who was handling the construction business—building companies and unions—for the Family; from Jimmy Brown, who controlled the private garbage haulers through the city and their union; from Sonny Ciccone, who ran the piers and the longshoremen's union; from Tommy Gambino, who represented the Family in the Garment District; from Tony Pep, who was in the oil and gas business running a scheme for the Family that skimmed off a hefty chunk of the sales tax consumers paid on these products . . . he also visited the smaller earners like Joe Butch who had a lot of loan shark money out on the street and Tony C. who was running the Family's gambling operations up in Connecticut. Everyone paid up in cash, the money handed over in shoeboxes, plastic bags, whatever was convenient (Blum, 1993; 267).

CRIMINAL ACTIVITIES

As stated, La Cosa Nostra has proven to be extremely adaptive and entrepreneurial. Italian organized crime families have continued to prosper due to their ability to target new areas of criminal activity while maintaining a presence in traditional vices. For the most part, mafia members have done and will do anything, from selling rotten meat to manipulating Wall Street, to make a dollar. Originally, their criminal activity was largely limited to American vices of gambling, prostitution, booze, and narcotics. Currently, LCN groups are involved in stock manipulation, pornography, telecommunications fraud, counterfeiting, and more. When the traditional crimes of extortion, bribery, and murder are coupled with these emerging areas, the Italian mafia has it all. In other words, Italian organized crime groups have infiltrated any arena in which profitability is possible. They are increasingly sophisticated and are capable of exploiting any situation. Michael Franzese (dubbed the "yuppie don"), for example, was involved in everything from body shops to auto leasing companies to car dealerships to movie production to casino skimming.[16] Interestingly, their success is largely attributed to the general public—a public comprising both legitimate businessmen who walk the line between legitimate and illegitimate business practices and those individuals who covet illegal merchandise.

Racketeering

Just as Prohibition was directly responsible for the creation of an international criminal syndicate, the repeal of the Eighteenth Amendment forced organized crime to establish new sources of revenue. The easiest, most profitable, and longest lasting of those created was racketeering. Generally speaking, *racketeering* may be defined as any criminal activity based on a system of extortion. This term was originally derived from political fund-raisers (known as "rackets" due to their boisterous nature) in which individuals were forced to purchase tickets through intimidation (Maas, 1968). For the mafia, the beauty of racketeering lies in its limitless nature. In fact, racketeering is limited only by imagination. Any labor-intensive industry has proven vulnerable, a fact borne out in a 1978 report from the Chicago Organized Crime Task Force, which reported that four of the largest unions in the United States (the International Brotherhood of Teamsters, the Laborers International Union of North America, the Hotel Employees and Restaurant Employees International Union, and the International Longshoremen's Association) were controlled by Italian organized crime. Indeed, the following is a list of but a few of the marketplaces in which the LCN has gained a foothold: vending machines, bars, restaurants, liquor, trucking, cement, garbage, road, beef, chicken, and poultry.

The mafia's stranglehold over American unions began in the 1920s and continues to this day. Contrary to popular belief, the five N.Y. families continue to be involved in joint endeavors, especially in the rackets. The Colombo, Gambino, and Genovese families all get a piece of the Greater Blouse, Skirt, and Undergarment

Association. For the most part, rackets tend to be overlapping, as a variety of services are essential in any labor-intensive marketplace; however, many families do maintain individual interests. The Colombo family's interest in the entertainment business, for example, appeared to be their exclusive domain.

Italian organized crime has been involved in the movie business for several decades. However, the Colombo family during the 1960s–1980s is a good illustration of individual interests. The Colombo family, through capo Sonny Franzese, had an interest in *Deep Throat* and *The Texas Chainsaw Massacre*, while his son furthered their interest through the production of such memorable films as *Knights of the City* and *Savage Streets* (Franzese et al., 1992). Franzese's efforts also secured a foothold in the music business during rock and roll's infancy, while others stayed away from it. In fact, the Colombo family, through Franzese, owned 50 percent of the booking agency of Norby Walters, whose clients included Dionne Warwick, Janet Jackson, Rick James, Lionel Richie, the Commodores, the Spinners, the Four Tops, Luther Van Dross, Patti LaBelle, Kool and the Gang, New Edition, and Ben Vereen. They also financed Walters's sports group, World Sports and Entertainment, Inc., which signed Rob Woodson to the Pittsburgh Steelers; Reggie Rogers to the Detroit Lions; and, Tim McGee to the Cincinnati Bengals. Like other areas where the mob has infiltrated, Walters's sports company used illegal practices to attract potential clients, often paying them exorbitant sums of cash while they were still in college—a clear violation of NCAA regulations. In addition, the family provided muscle during contract negotiations, making it difficult for clients to receive a fair deal or to leave the agency. According to FBI wiretaps placed during "Operation Jockgate," physical threats were often issued to convince a recalcitrant client to remain.

Prostitution and Pornography

Without question, La Cosa Nostra has been a longtime purveyor of sin, dabbling in adult clubs, prostitution, and pornography. Prostitution, in particular, has proven to be quite profitable for the mob. While prostitution did not originate in the United States, the American branch of LCN began its involvement in the sex trade in the early 1900s. This is not to suggest that wiseguys were actively involved in street-level pimping; rather, their participation was largely limited to providing protection for established brothels. However, this has not insulated them from criminal prosecution. In fact, the Mann Act of 1910, which prohibited the transportation of women across state lines for immoral purposes, was directly attributed to the mafia's infiltration of the trade. Both Al Capone and Charles "Lucky" Luciano were convicted on charges related to prostitution.

Italian organized crime groups have furthered their interests in the sex trade in pace with technology. They are currently involved in the production and dissemination of pornography. While they do not have a monopoly of the pornography market, they have managed to engage in activities that have fueled family coffers since the 1930s when pornographic films were viewed on small coin-operated machines in

New York. Their involvement was originally revealed when Linda Lovelace, star of the infamous *Deep Throat*, revealed to the nation that she had been forced to participate in the film by armed mafia thugs. Since her revelations, others have reported similar stories. Government reports indicate that all five of the New York families have been actively involved in pornography. In the 1970s, for example, Bonanno capo Michael "Mickey Z" Zaffarano ran a national chain of adult theaters (i.e., Pussycat Cinemas), and in the 1980s, Robert "DiBi" DiBernardo was indicted for his involvement in Star Distributors of New York City, a company involved in the production and distribution of pornographic materials to adult theaters and bookstores across the country. Current reports indicate that the mafia is still actively involved in the distribution of pornography; unfortunately, they have not limited their actions to adult pornography.

Italian Lottery

Like labor racketeering, one mainstay of Italian organized crime has been the Italian lottery, a numbers racket which has reached every facet of New York society. (In 1968, it was estimated that the proceeds from such a racket were in excess of $250 million a year.) The Italian lottery is a numbers racket similar to government-sponsored lotteries in which individuals select a specified quantity of numbers. Theoretically, the numbers are unpredictable, resulting from the pari-mutuel of a specified track. (Dutch Schultz, who was extremely big in the numbers racket in Harlem, however, could manipulate this by infusing money into the system.) The numbers racket required the collusion of corrupt law enforcement authorities and the employment of outsiders. As one insider explains it:

> [C]ontrollers were vital to a successful number bank. For the most part Jewish, they were, in effect, branch office managers. As their title indicates, they also doubled as bookkeepers. This was one occupation that members of the Cosa Nostra rarely engaged in; accounting chores apparently were beneath their dignity, if not their ability . . . each controller had his own group of runners who actually collected the individual bets and returned any winnings. A controller got 35 percent of his daily gross if he was responsible for paying off the police in his area and 30 percent if the bank itself took care of this expense. The controller in turn gave his runners 20 or 25 percent of his share (Maas, 1968: 136–137).

Although state-sponsored lotteries have decreased the revenue associated with this criminal activity, it still remains a viable source of income for Italian organized crime.

Fraud

Although methods vary, fraud has long been a mainstay for Italian organized crime. Like racketeering, fraudulent activities are limited only by imagination. One of the most popular frauds involves *busted-out businesses.* America's appetite for gambling and the conservativism of financial institutions often subject "innocent" individuals to the underworld of organized crime. Thus, wiseguys often find themselves in partnership with "legitimate" businessmen who are strapped for cash. In the vast majority of these cases, mafia partners will bust out a business by purchasing large amounts of merchandise on credit, selling it on the street at wholesale prices, and forcing the company into fraudulent bankruptcy. (In addition, they may burn the shells of these busted-out businesses, collecting additional money from insurance companies.)

Wiseguys have also proven adept in the marketing of *muldoons* (i.e., stolen credit cards). Unfortunately, there are a variety of methods for securing fraudulent cards, including obtaining the cooperation of a bank employee who either makes duplicates or supplies the account number of cards being mailed out. In fact, individuals only become aware of their victimization when either their statement arrives one month later or their credit limit is reached very quickly. Muldoons are also used with the assistance of "legitimate" business owners, who knowingly allow the purchase of large amounts of merchandise with fraudulent cards. Although simplistic in nature, credit card fraud has been utilized by the mafia since their existence. Inexplicably, the advent of digital technology and computer databases has not obliterated the practice.

In the 1980s, Italian organized crime families came upon a fraud far more profitable than those they had previously committed. Their targeted victim, the government, proved to be as vulnerable as individual businessmen and insurance companies. The cash cow in this case involved government-imposed gasoline taxes.

> The key was the incompetence of the federal, state, and county governments in collecting gasoline taxes. Together, the three governing bodies demanded a twenty-seven-cent bite out of every gallon of gas sold. Demanding it and getting it were two different things. The lax collection enabled Iorizzo to stall having his owned or leased stations pay the gas taxes for as long as a year. By that time, they could close the station, the owners would vanish, and then, a month or so later, the station would reopen under new management and start again (Franzese et al., 1992: 121).

To escape detection, the conspirators registered the corporations in countries such as Panama:

> Under Panama's bearer stock law, the owner of a company was the person who had his hands on the stock. That meant the "official" owners of the stations, and of Iorizzo's umbrella operation, could be, and often were, two guys with machetes out in a Panama sugar-cane field. When the government agencies went looking for their tax money, that's who they'd have to find (Franzese et al., 1992: 121).

The scam proved to be wildly successful, and the conspirators were always careful to pay 20 percent to the family executives. In 1981, the state of New York recognized the vulnerability of the collection policies (and the tens of millions that were lost) and shifted the burden from the station owners to gasoline wholesalers, who were less numerous (and theoretically more easily supervised). However, the government granted operators a one-year grace period to make the switch, which unfortunately allowed criminals one more year to practice their scam and, more importantly, to devise new ways to beat the emerging system.

Under the new laws, wholesalers could sell to one another tax-free. Only the wholesaler who sold directly to the retailers was responsible for the taxes. This enabled organized crime figures to set up various dummy wholesale operations in which the designated company would incur all of the tax responsibility but which would default through bankruptcy prior to collection. Franzese and colleagues explain:

> Iorizzo would take a shipment of, say, a million gallons into Company A and sell it to his stations and those on his growing supply route. On paper, however, instead of the gas going to the stations, it would go to Company B, then to Company C, and finally to Company D. On paper, it would denote Company D had sold to the stations. Companies B through D were shell firms that consisted of nothing but a phone number and some stationery. Company D, the one responsible for paying the taxes, would be owned by those same guys down in the Panama sugar-cane fields. After a few hundred million gallons of invisible gasoline passed through Company D, it would declare bankruptcy. When the state and federal governments tried to collect their tens of millions in tax money, they'd have to go on the mind-numbing paper trail from Company A through Company D. At the end of this grim rainbow was no pot of tax gold but the "burnout" firm, owned by some guy named Juan in Panama, current address unknown (1992: 121–122).

On the surface, it appeared that the group was running a very successful legitimate business. In fact, one of the companies established in this scheme, Galion, became so successful that it purchased small and large independently owned suppliers across New York, New Jersey, Connecticut, and Pennsylvania. According to Michael Franzese, his take was between $5 million and $8 million a week (Franzese, 1992). Others estimated that the total amount stolen was much, much more—as much as $60–$100 million a month! Both the Colombo family and the Genovese family profited greatly from the operation. In addition, a Russian contingent, currently practicing the same sort of scheme, partnered with the Colombo family due to their lack of "influence." While each of these "legitimate" corporations proved to be wildly successful, their success was primarily due to the unfair practices of intimidation, violence, and fraud.

Securities Fraud and Stock Manipulation

The advent of technology has signaled a new dawn for increasingly sophisticated criminal entrepreneurs. One of the fastest-rising activities involves securities fraud. The most common of these involves purchasing securities at low prices, inflating their value, and then selling them at elevated prices. While this is the goal of virtually every investor, mafia families have accomplished this through deception and intimidation. One method of accomplishing this goal hinges on purchasing microcaps (i.e., low-priced securities) and then forcing brokers to sell the stock to their investors, who then hold it. This creates a false demand for the stock, pushing the price higher. They have also accomplished this through the use of fraudulent web sites and "boiler room" tactics in which sales were motivated through the use of threats (Labate, 2000). The majority of securities involved in these schemes were Internet stocks, including: RedAlert.com, Subway.com, and Powerstocks.com. One such scheme cost investors $50 million (Labate, 2000).

All five families have had representatives convicted of stock fraud, although the Bonanno and Colombo groups have been the hardest hit. For the most part, the convictions have resulted in cases where LCN groups have created their own brokerage firms. In one case, Bonanno capo Robert "Little Robert" Lino and Colombo capo Frank A. Persico established DMN Capital Investments, Inc. This company partnered brokers, lawyers, money managers, and pension fund officials with good old-fashioned wiseguys (Walsh, 2000). The scheme targeted an unsuspecting public hungry for instant wealth. This group, along with others such as White Rock Partners and Company and State Street Capital Markets Corporation, "targeted average investors . . . (who) were promised returns of as much as 100 percent on stocks that were mostly thinly traded inexpensive issues . . . in schemes involving stock manipulation, boiler room sales, and using the Internet to fraudulently hype stocks" (Walsh, 2000). Fortunately, much of this activity was uncovered by the FBI in Operation Uptick.

Black Market Goods and Narcotics

Beginning with prostitutes, gambling, and liquor, La Cosa Nostra has proven exceptionally adept in the trafficking of black market goods. Throughout history, these goods have varied over time, based on the current demand of a greedy public. In World War II, for example, Carlo Gambino made his first million through trafficking in gas ration stamps, which he either purchased from common thieves or collected through the corruption of public officials. Unbeknownst to average Americans patiently waiting for their commodities, the Office of Price Administration (OPA) estimated that approximately 2.5-million gallons of gas were purchased daily with compromised stamps.

One of the most enduring markets exploited by LCN groups has proven to be narcotics. Contrary to Hollywood versions of the American mafia, trafficking in illegal substances has long been an entrepreneurial mainstay among Italian organized crime groups. According to Anslinger and Ousler (1961: 88):

> [The mafia] has held for many years the dominant position in narcotics distribution throughout the United States. The narcotics syndicate in America came into being about the time Prohibition ended, in the early 1930s, when the gangsters were looking

TO TRAFFICK OR NOT TO TRAFFICK?

Although the mafia has long been involved in the trafficking of narcotics, individual bosses have periodically banned the practice among their families. Such prohibitions are anything but altruistic and are actually issued as a form of self-preservation. Simply put, the risks associated with the drug trade outweigh the potential profits because bosses get paid regardless. However, many soldiers do not appreciate the bosses' concern, perceiving their bosses as hypocritical and unsympathetic to their personal economic plight. In some cases, organizational prohibitions have resulted in the death of family bosses.

around for new opportunities. Dope had always been part of their operation; now it took on a bigger role. The syndicate put the operation on a businesslike basis. They hired a legal staff, set up a supervisory board, a general manager, a traveling representative and a sales force.

In fact, the first major drug case dates all the way back to the 1940s when members of the Genovese family were convicted. Lucky Luciano, along with other bosses, saw vast potential in the narcotics trade following Prohibition. Much like its approach to bootlegging, Luciano's organization carefully cultivated local politicians and police officials. This low-level corruption proved to be very successful, at least for a time; however, narcotics was not tolerated by the public or the police for long, and numerous wiseguys were sent to prison to serve extended sentences. (Vito Genovese, family boss, was convicted in the 1950s and sentenced to 15 years for a narcotics conspiracy case.) Increasingly alarmed at the potential security risk imposed by such sentences, Frank Costello issued an edict to family members to get out of drugs. While many other families paid lip service to this idea to placate Costello, others openly flouted their drug business. For a brief period, however, most did take an arm's-length approach, advising members that they were on their own if caught. In fact, many of the older bosses, such as Paul Castellano and Angelo Bruno, openly disdained narcotics endeavors by family members, yet these same bosses accepted drug proceeds from other families. Unfortunately for both, their hypocrisy led directly to their demise.

CRIMINAL PROSECUTION
AND GOVERNMENT EFFORTS

While Italian organized crime has existed since the early 1900s, law enforcement efforts, criminal prosecutions, and targeted legislation were slow in developing. While recent years have been marked by a large number of convictions of organizational elite, traditional attempts proved to be half-hearted. In fact, Hoover's FBI disavowed the very existence of the mafia for years. For the most part, any efforts were largely political in nature and were directly proportionate to government policy. In 1959, for example, 4 agents in the New York City office of the FBI were assigned to the Organized Crime Unit, while approximately 400 were assigned to domestic Communism.[17] In fact, many individuals argue that the efforts directed at combating organized crime were designed more to further political careers than to elicit the whole-scale prosecution of a criminal syndicate. However, these initiatives did prove troublesome to individual members of La Cosa Nostra, and many of them were directly responsible for the deaths of those they targeted.

Kefauver Committee

In 1950, a congressional committee was empaneled to (1) evaluate the existence of interstate wire services that transmitted the results of horse races to bookmakers; (2) tighten measures to prevent interstate crime; and (3) if necessary, secure additional funding for law enforcement agencies. However, many argue that the aim of the committee was far more expansive and that Kefauver's intent was to establish himself in the national spotlight—a goal that he certainly achieved. Led by (freshman) Senator Estes Kefauver, the Special Committee to Investigate Organized Crime in Interstate Commerce, in a two-year period, interviewed over 600 witnesses, including mobsters, business executives, movie stars, and politicians.

The committee was likened to a traveling circus, providing entertainment for the American public while visiting over a dozen cities. Mob witnesses from across the country included Carlos Marcello, New Orleans; Anthony Accardo, Chicago; and various New York bosses. Appearing before the committee proved to be fatal for several witnesses. Frank Costello's underboss, for example, was murdered after his testimony.

THE IRS—CRIME FIGHTERS EXTRAORDINAIRE

Traditionally, prosecution efforts directed at the mob were largely unsuccessful. Territorial jealousies and a general lack of cooperation within and between law enforcement agencies hampered large-scale prosecution efforts. Instead, only marginal successes occurred, directed primarily at individuals. One of the first tactics used by federal prosecutors was an effort initiated not by the Federal Bureau of Investigation but by Treasury agents. Individuals employed by the Internal Revenue Service (IRS) waded through volumes of paperwork and news accounts of mob activity, and they successfully prosecuted high-ranking mobsters such as Al Capone. The individual who had refused to pay homage to any man forgot to pay homage to the IRS. In the end, the IRS agents got what was coming to them, and so did Capone. Al "Scarface" Capone was removed permanently from the Chicago organized crime scene by slight individuals with pocket protectors. Waxey Gordon and Dutch Schultz were two other notables convicted on income tax invasion.

Although entertaining to watch, Willie Moretti's rambling testimony enabled some family dissidents to obtain the necessary permission to terminate him. Other repercussions included the attempted assassination of Costello himself. In addition, Kefauver's quest for fame resulted in dire consequences for a variety of individual politicians. These individuals, called to testify about their knowledge of organized crime, suffered irreparable damage to their political aspirations as a result. The most notable of these was Bill O'Dwyer, then U.S. ambassador to Mexico. Prior to his appearance before the committee, O'Dwyer was most famous for his successful prosecution of Murder, Inc.'s Louis "Lepke" Buchaltar. However, his inability to adequately explain his failure to prosecute Albert Anastasia completely extinguished his political lamp.

For the most part, the Kefauver Committee did not reveal any direct evidence of a national criminal conspiracy among Italian-Americans. Indeed, many of its members decried the existence of such a conspiracy, claiming that a criminal organization of such magnitude could not have existed for any period of time without identification. Thus, allusions to a national syndicate were highly suspect; however, they did recognize the corruption inherent in local political arenas.

Apalachin Incident

In 1957, representatives from the 24 families gathered in upstate New York at the remote Apalachin farmhouse of Joseph Barbara. On the agenda were several pressing matters. First, the meeting was necessary to establish peace among the New York families, who were in a state of elevated tension after the murders of Albert "the Executioner" Anastasia and Frank "Don Cheech" Scalise and the attempted murder of Frank Costello. The second order of business to be discussed included the dispensation of Anastasia's former fiefdom and the formal recognition of Carlo Gambino as his replacement. Third, the commission was to address the issue of false memberships that had been purchased from the then deceased Frank "Don Cheech" Scalise. Finally, the commission was to develop a formal policy regarding narcotics. (Although the mob had long been entrenched in narcotics trafficking, recent media attention, enhanced sentences, and the increasing power of the Federal Bureau of Narcotics [FBN] made the business less attractive to leaders. However, these issues were never discussed as the meeting was unexpectedly interrupted by a contingent of state and local police.)

Over 60 individuals were arrested by police during the raid while a comparable number successfully avoided capture by fleeing into the woods; more than $300,000 in cash was seized from those arrested. A list compiled by law enforcement indicated that mafia luminaries from all over the country were in attendance and included James Lanza from San Francisco; Frank DeSimone from Los Angeles; James Civello from Dallas; Santo Trafficante from Florida; John Scalish from Cleveland; Joseph Ida from Philadelphia; and Sam Giancana from Chicago. The New York families were also well represented. All those who were arrested were subsequently found guilty of contempt and conspiracy and sentenced to five years; however, their convictions were soon overturned as the government failed to prove any specific criminal conspiracy. Although the Apalachin arrests and convictions were soon invalidated, the information regarding the hierarchy of LCN leaders across the country was not. In fact, the intelligence gathered from the meeting resulted in the historical reconstruction and development of a framework of the organization that investigators would use thereafter.

The Apalachin incident would have far-reaching consequences for some of those involved, especially Joe Bonanno who would be indicted on conspiracy to obstruct justice in 1959. The case would also cause considerable embarrassment to the FBI, which had previously denied the existence of Italian organized crime. As a result, organized crime task forces were established across the country. In addition, the FBI launched its Top Hoodlum Program within two weeks of the incident, requiring jurisdictional offices to list the top 10 mafiosi in their area. Finally, Hoover began an aggressive (and mostly illegal) use of electronic surveillance of suspected gangsters; the surveillance would continue for several decades. The FBI's efforts, it must be noted, were directly related to the continuing conflict between J. Edgar Hoover and Harry Anslinger, head of the FBN. An evaluation of historical documents reveals that the FBN had been much more effective in tracking organized crime activities prior to Hoover's reactive policies.

McClellan Committee

In 1956, the Select Committee on Improper Activities in the Labor or Management Field was created. Chaired by Senator John McClellan (D-Ark.) and counseled by Senator Robert Kennedy (D-Mass.), the committee was empaneled to evaluate the infiltration of organized labor by Italian organized crime. In time, the committee also investigated the mafia's interests in Las Vegas. One of the committee's first actions was to investigate the actions of Teamsters president Dave Beck. Under questioning, it was alleged that Beck had embezzled more than a quarter of million dollars from the union's treasury. Under pressure, Beck resigned his position, and his very ambitious vice president, James "Jimmy" Hoffa assumed control; however, Hoffa's reign was marked by allegations of a marriage between his organization and the LCN.

Jimmy Hoffa was called before the committee in the 1960s. Owing his position to LCN supporters, Hoffa was extremely critical of Senator Robert Kennedy in the press. Such animosity was rewarded by increased government scrutiny, and Hoffa's appearance before the committee only reinforced the perception that he was a puppet of an organized crime syndicate. Eventually, Hoffa would be convicted and sentenced to prison. His attempt to reclaim his position upon his release was not well received by his former supporters, who believed that his flamboyant approach garnered too much government attention. On July 30, 1975, Jimmy Hoffa was last seen at a restaurant in suburban Detroit. It is widely speculated that his disappearance was orchestrated by members of the Detroit family and his "adopted son" Charles "Chuckie" O'Brien. While his body has never been uncovered, anecdotal accounts by mob informants indicate that his most likely resting place is beneath Giants stadium or in a New Jersey scrap yard.

In 1963, Joseph Valachi, the most famous mafia turncoat in history, appeared before the committee. Valachi, a former Genovese soldier, testified before the committee in exchange for a reduced sentence for a murder charge, which occurred while he was incarcerated for other crimes. By all reports, his testimony was the highlight of the McClellan Committee. Although the validity of his testimony would be questioned for decades by academics and law enforcement alike, his appearance riveted the American public. In the witness box, Valachi claimed to have participated in over 30 murders during his tenure. He also detailed the hierarchical organization of the LCN and the initiation process of new members while identifying the 24 families across the United States. Based on his testimony, bosses across the country, including Chicago's Anthony Accardo and Sam Giancana, were subpoenaed.

Buffered by Valachi's account, the McClellan Committee concluded that organized crime was indeed a national problem and supported the use of additional law enforcement resources. However, Valachi's testimony was extremely suspect. First and foremost, Valachi, by his own account, was a small-time hood facing very serious charges when he testified before the committee. Second, Valachi discussed in detail the hierarchical structure and subsequent chain of command (and communication) within each of the families. This directly contradicted his contention that he discussed important matters with both Lucky Luciano and Vito Genovese. Third, Valachi asserted that La Cosa Nostra was so successful due to organizational loyalty in which families of incarcerated members of good standing were supported by the members' criminal family while at the same time maintaining that his own family suffered greatly during his imprisonment. Thus, various contradictions existed within Valachi's own testimony. However, committee members never questioned his inconsistency; instead, they praised him for his veracity and told an unsuspecting public that his appearance validated independent law enforcement intelligence. Interestingly, the McClellan Committee never revealed that illegal recordings introduced during the proceedings revealed that the Kennedy family was heavily indebted to the mob members in Chicago for their assistance in the Democratic primary.

Electronic Surveillance

Throughout Prohibition, government agents routinely used electronic eavesdropping to collect evidence against those suspected of illegal activity. However, the dawning recognition of the sanctity of constitutional safeguards that emerged in the 1930s put a halt to many of these time-trusted techniques. The Federal Communications Act of 1934 prohibited the interception, analysis, and dissemination of information gathered from electronic eavesdropping (i.e., wiretaps). The constitutionality of the act was upheld in a variety of rulings by the Supreme Court, which prohibited the admittance of any evidence gathered through electronic surveillance. The act was further supported in 1939 through the actions of Attorney General Robert Jackson, who specifically prohibited the implementation of such devices by the FBI; however, such limitations were soon eroded by the efforts of J. Edgar Hoover during World War II.

Playing on national security concerns during the early 1940s, Hoover successfully petitioned President Franklin Delano Roosevelt to remove the ban on electronic surveillance of those suspected of foreign sympathy. Although original caveats specifically limited eavesdropping to such individuals and prevented the use of obtained information outside of government channels, these restrictions were expanded post–World War II to include issues of domestic security and threats to human life. Thus, legitimate electronic eavesdropping by federal agents increased exponentially. Illegitimate practices were also routine, and listening devices were placed in LCN hangouts and headquarters across the country. Information gathered in this manner was never introduced in courtroom proceedings, but it was used to create detailed profiles on a variety of American citizens, both criminals and not. (Confidential files created during Hoover's administration revealed that targets often included individuals far removed from Italian organized crime.) Such information included hierarchical structures of LCN families, personal lives of organizational members, and sexual predilections of Hollywood stars and prominent politicians. However, this activity was largely halted by President Lyndon B. Johnson due to public pressure.

Omnibus Crime Control and Safe Streets Act

In the mid-1960s, President Johnson formally denounced the illegal practices of the FBI. While recognizing the necessity for electronic surveillance, Johnson placed a six-month time limit on legitimately placed devices. Soon thereafter, a Presidential Task Force on Organized Crime recommended the formalization of legislation that would more clearly identify the limitations on law enforcement while increasing the circumstances in which wiretaps could be utilized. The result was the Omnibus Crime Control and Safe Streets Act of 1968.

Title III of the act specifically delineated the requirements for electronic eavesdropping by law enforcement officials, including those offenses which may be targeted. It stated that wiretaps were permissible only if issued upon a ruling of probable cause by a court official. Such probable cause must include the offense for which the eavesdropping is intended and the location in which the criminal evidence is to be gathered. It required that all other investigative techniques be exhausted prior to utilization and that precautions be taken to ensure that innocent conversations were excluded from analysis. It further mandated scrupulous record keeping and reporting, and it required reapplication upon expiration (i.e., permissions were only extended for a finite period of 30 days, which could only be extended based on evidence of criminal wrongdoing). Finally, it outlined punishments for violations and required disclosure of such surveillance upon cessation of activity.

The importance of Title III cannot be overstated in regard to government efforts to combat organized crime. Throughout its tenure, Title III wiretaps and electronic listening devices (e.g., bugs) have proven instrumental in a large number of cases involving both high-ranking officers and run-of-the-mill soldiers and associates. These devices have successfully been used against virtually all of the currently incarcerated bosses and proved to be the pivotal factor in the commission case of the 1980s. As previously stated, the verbosity of such characters as John Gotti, Sam Giancana, and Anthony "Fat Tony" Salerno led to their downfall. Perhaps the most notable, and most entertaining, of all devices was the one implemented in the late 1980s in the kitchen of Paul Castellano's "White House." Government agents in that case became privy to the internal machinations of not only the commission but also Castellano's convoluted love life.

Racketeer Influenced and Corrupt Organizations (RICO) Act

In 1970, Robert Blakey created the Racketeer Influenced and Corrupt Organizations Act (called the RICO statute). This particular law has been more effective in the war against organized crime than all of the other efforts combined, but the law was lost in the top-heavy government bureaucracy for many years because it was not communicated to the agents in the trenches. According to Bonavolonta and Duffy:

> [T]hat tells you something about the way Washington works ... I'm sure some bright lawyer somewhere in the Department of Justice knew all about [RICO]. But without a clear signal from someone higher up in the organizational food chain, that bright lawyer is going to keep his mouth shut, and RICO is going to sit on the books for a decade, as useless as if the law had never been passed (1996: 57).

Many believe that the acronym RICO (referring to Racketeer Influenced and Corrupt Organizations statute, 18 U.S.C. Sections 1961–1968) was a clever play on a name from the 1930 mob movie *Little Caesar* in which Edward G. Robinson played small-town hood Enrico "Rico" Bandello (Bonavolonta and Duffy, 1996). This law, overwhelmingly simple in hindsight, concentrated on the fact that La Cosa Nostra was an organization developed to pursue criminal enterprise. Created by Bob Blakey, an attorney on the U.S. Senate Subcommittee on Criminal Laws and Procedures, RICO states:

> It shall be unlawful for any person employed by or associated with any enterprise engaged in, or the activities which affect, interstate or foreign commerce, to conduct or participate, directly or indirectly, in the conduct of such enterprise's affairs through a pattern of racketeering activity or collection of unlawful debt.

In essence, RICO enabled law enforcement to use specific criminal acts such as homicide, gambling, and loan-sharking as pieces of evidence, lessening the burden of proof. In other words, state offenses, such as homicide and burglary, could now be prosecuted under federal authority without actually proving criminal culpability beyond a reasonable doubt, a feat that had traditionally been almost impossible due to the lack of witnesses. In addition, RICO broadened the spectrum of probable cause, which dramatically increased the number of successful Title III applications. It is perhaps this latter option that was more important to law enforcement in RICO cases in which the majority of evidence is actually gathered through these technological mediums.

Like Title III of the Omnibus Crime Control and Safe Streets Act of 1968, the importance of the RICO Act cannot be overstated. Now in its fourth decade of implementation, RICO has successfully been utilized against numerous members of organized crime. More importantly, it is directly responsible for the successful prosecution of entire La Cosa Nostra families. RICO prosecutions of John Gotti and the Gambino family, Anthony "Fat Tony" Salerno and the Genovese family, and Carmine "the Snake" Persico and the Colombo family are but few of the many cases that have resulted in lengthy prison sentences for the highest-ranking members of the Italian mafia. While it must be noted that these organizations still exist and continue to engage in illicit criminal enterprise, their ranks appear to be dwindling as the cost-benefit ratio increases.

Organized Crime Control Act

In the same year that the RICO statute was created, Congress passed the Organized Crime Control Act of 1970. Although a variety of provisions supporting the elimination of organized crime were included, the most important of these was the creation of the Witness Protection Program (WPP). For all intents and purposes, the WPP (operated by the U.S. Marshals Service) was designed to encourage organizational members to testify against their compatriots. Originally, the WPP was intended to provide for the protection and support of a cooperating witness and his or her family until testimony was complete. It was anticipated that providing new identities (including new Social Security numbers, occupational backgrounds, and educational records for children) for witnesses would enable them to secure gainful employment and suitable housing after a brief period of government support. While the existence of the WPP has encouraged organizational turncoats, it has been widely criticized by various sources.

Many libertarian groups openly criticize the WPP, declaring that it encourages criminals to create falsehoods to limit their own culpability and reduce punishment. Individuals such as Salvatore "Sammy the Bull" Gravano have served as their poster boys. Gravano, onetime underboss of the Gambino crime family, for example, participated in over a dozen murders and served less than one year in prison. His boss, John Gotti, received a life sentence for a fraction of the criminal behavior confessed by Gravano and died in prison in June 2002.

These same groups have also argued that the WPP has proven much more costly than originally anticipated and that the criminals that are protected are often worse than those they convict. As to the first of these arguments, they assert that the general sluggishness of the criminal justice process, coupled with the number of cases made from an individual's testimony, may require extended governmental support. In addition, they argue that many of the individuals included in the program will recidivate. Indeed, the low monthly stipend allotted to an individual accustomed to an elevated

BAD TIME FOR THE MOB

Prior to the 1970s, mob bosses and La Cosa Nostra had remained somewhat immune to the criminal justice process. Sure, there were some exceptions and much ado about isolated law enforcement successes, but for the most part, the government was at a severe disadvantage. However, the 1970s changed all that when four of the five families were badly hit by convictions of their top hierarchy. These convictions included Carmine Tramunti—Lucchese boss—5 years for perjury; Carmine Persico—Colombo boss—14 years for hijacking; Paul Sciacca—Bonanno boss—convicted of heroin trafficking; Phillip Rastelli—succeeding Bonanno boss—11 years for antitrust and extortion; Frank "Funzie" Tieri—Genovese boss—first boss convicted through RICO.

The 1980s would prove equally devastating to Italian organized crime. In February 1985, the U.S. Attorney's office in Manhattan issued indictments for the bosses of each of the five New York families: Paul Castellano—Gambino family; Carmine Persico—Colombo family; Philip Rastelli—Bonanno family; Anthony "Fat Tony" Salerno—Genovese family; and Anthony "Tony Ducks" Corallo—Lucchese family.

By the time the trial began in September 1986, Paul Castellano had been murdered and Phillip Rastelli had been severed from the case due to his indictment in a Brooklyn court. Unfortunately for the defendants, the evidence proved to be overwhelming. Strategically placed bugs and organizational turncoats unmasked the secret organization to the jury. As a result, all of the bosses were convicted of racketeering and sentenced to 100 years in prison. Of the five original bosses indicted, only one, Carmine Persico, was alive in 2002.

standard of living, coupled with his inability to forge legitimate businesses, all but guarantees his return to a life of crime. Although there is an assortment of examples that could be used to illustrate this point, the recent arrest as well as conviction of Gravano and his entire biographical family is a prime example.

CONCLUSIONS

Though many events in La Cosa Nostra history are often sensationalized to the point of absurdity, the evolution and transference of power have been well documented through government informants, electronic transmissions, and the like. Beginning with reports of the Black Hand, the concept of a formalized structure of Italian criminality has long frightened and fascinated fainthearted Americans. As early as the nineteenth century, reports of criminal secret societies permeated American folklore. Perhaps the earliest reports characterized criminal behavior among groups of Italian immigrants as embedded in a subversive ethnic society composed of young Italians referred to as the

Black Hand by apprehensive residents of New York City (Train, 1922). Indeed, incidents of strong-armed extortion were reported across the country. The murder of Police Commissioner David Hennessey in New Orleans in the late 1800s raised public hysteria to epidemic portions, and anti-Italian sentiment abounded. As stated, it is unclear whether this incident was in any way the result of an organized conspiracy. In fact, some authors argue that Italian criminality was anything but organized; rather, they suggest that pockets of illegitimate entrepreneurs were actually an exception to the hordes of Italian immigrants who successfully pursued legitimate opportunities (Train, 1922). However, this distinction is often overlooked as the beginning of the twentieth century brought a dramatic increase in organized crime within Italian-American communities, but they are not the only ethnic group that has chosen this avenue.

During the twentieth century, the majority of incoming minority ethnic groups solidified their masses in order to combat the reality of a hostile new world. Several individuals, dissatisfied with limited opportunities, banded together for the sole purpose of gaining economic independence through illicit means. Eventually, the activities of these groups became more sophisticated and expanded to international proportions. This process was marked by vicious power struggles in which many innocents and not-so-innocents were killed. After a time, the violence subsided as the Italians soon gained unequivocal domination over the criminal subculture. However, this struggle for underworld dominance has become much more pronounced as various ethnic groups clash over territorial boundaries, both materially and geographically.

The explosion of the U.S. narcotics industry, traditionally owned and operated by the Sicilian families, has resulted in the induction of various conflicting ethnicities. Although ethnic groups appear to be disparate, certain group similarities emerge regardless of ancestry. Contrary to popular media depictions that proclaim unprecedented levels of random street violence by young ethnic gangs, the early foundations of the American mafia were predicated on the same type of street-level activity. In fact, today's ethnic gangs closely resemble the humble beginnings of most recognized criminal syndicates in the country. Like their predecessors, contemporary urban gangs are primarily made up of young males from marginalized segments of society. Denied access to legitimate avenues of success, these ethnic gangs, like the Italians, rely on proceeds from illegal activities. Finding the most vulnerable targets within their own communities, these groups prey on their own kind, developing criminal networks to increase their powers of intimidation.

The Italian mafia embodies the hierarchy and autonomy prevalent in police organizations, the armed forces, and paramilitary organizations. A hierarchical structure has lent credence to the stability of La Cosa Nostra and enabled it to flourish for more than a century. This bureaucratic structure is perpetuated by the use of territorial guidelines, the provision for regulation of violence, and the mediation of disputes. However, a recent influx of contemporary youth has resulted in an increase in criminal prosecutions. Whether through careless behavior or misplaced bravado, many of today's criminals have seemed to bask in the media spotlight. Unfortunately for them, this media scrutiny is increasingly harmful to their criminal longevity. Recent organization-wide

RICO cases have decimated many of the original Italian families; however, the LCN has proven remarkably resilient to law enforcement deconstruction. Indeed, the death knell has not yet sounded for the organization founded more than a century ago. LCN's increasing use of technology and partnerships with various ethnically based organized syndicates suggest that the group will continue to prosper, albeit not quite so flamboyantly.

ENDNOTES

1. Prior to the formal initiation process, all prospective members must prove their loyalty by "putting in work" for the organization (i.e., participating in a homicide) (Franzese et al., 1992; Maas, 1968). This requirement, designed to prevent law enforcement infiltration, also serves to ensure organizational solidarity. Although many have denied that this requirement exists, Ralph Natale, former Philadelphia boss, reaffirmed this during the trial of Joseph "Skinny Joe" Merlino.

2. Valachi identified many of the main bosses; while the information was quite valuable at the time, time and violence have taken their toll on those individuals.

3. "Membership books" refer to organizational rosters. Strict control of membership is designed to discourage war by leveling power bases and to prevent law enforcement infiltration by closing the door to most individuals. These books were created and closed after the first commission meeting. They were reopened during World War II (due to the large number of mafiosi who were deported or otherwise encumbered) and for a brief period in 1954. However, the books remained closed for almost 20 years (1955–1972) due to the nefarious practices of some bosses who actually sold memberships. In 1972, the books were again reopened, and a wave of new mafiosi emerged to replace those members lost through age, death, or incarceration (Franzese et al., 1992).

4. Recent years have seen an increase in organizational nepotism, with heirs being culled from blood relations. Bill Bonanno and John Gotti, Jr., are but two examples. This practice has often encouraged dissension within the ranks, as many members are reluctant to embrace the idea of natural succession, especially in cases such as those of Bonanno and Gotti, Jr., in which both their intelligence and their courage were questioned.

5. The advent of RICO has dramatically reduced the insulation once enjoyed by LCN officers. In fact, the paramilitary structure is actually detrimental to these individuals in racketeering indictments, which focus on the existence of the structure itself, making bosses more accountable than the average soldier.

6. One of the most successful organized crime figures in American history, Vito Genovese married Anna 12 days after her husband, Gerard Vernotico, was murdered by Genovese henchmen. Years later, Anna Genovese abandoned her husband and revealed many organizational secrets during divorce proceedings. Although many thought that Genovese, a particularly vicious person, would have her killed, he did not. Anna continued to be the love of his life.

7. Interestingly, the mob's first turncoat, Joseph Valachi, married the daughter of the slain gangster. Their relationship was initiated during the heat of the Castellammarese War when Valachi and other soldiers were forced to "take to the mattresses." While Valachi was happily

ensconced with the Reina family, others moved so often that they literally took their mattresses with them.

8. Joe Valachi claimed it was Vito Genovese, Frank Livorsi, and Joe Stracci, while Luciano's autobiography named Albert Anastasia, Joe Adonis, Bugsy Siegel, and Vito Genovese as the shooters.

9. Various sources have reported additional meetings following the end of the war, including one held for the rank and file; however, the facts remain obscured. Many suggest that this meeting was actually presided over by Luciano and was designed to establish his power base. However, Valachi's account gives credit to Maranzano and argues that the 400–500 soldiers in attendance were there at the behest of the new guard.

10. Thomas "Three Fingers Brown" Lucchese obtained his nickname in 1915 when he lost his right index finger in an accident. At the time, "Three Fingers Brown" was a major league pitcher who was also missing a finger.

11. Both Bonanno and his son emphatically deny that they were involved in the plot to assassinate Gambino and Lucchese. They argue that Magliocco acted alone and that Bill was simply serving as Magliocco's chauffeur when the instructions for the assassinations were given to Colombo.

12. Although Bonanno denied trafficking in narcotics, a 1963 statement by the head of NYPD Central Intelligence Bureau estimated that one in every three members of the Bonanno family had been arrested for drug charges.

13. Although Bonanno denied this, many report that Bonanno invented the "double-decker" coffin, in which mob victims were placed underneath the bodies of legitimate customers.

14. This charge is highly questionable. While it is likely that Bonanno had reason to fear for his safety, it is absurd to think that he was kidnapped and released for no apparent reason—the mob is not characterized by high levels of forgiveness.

15. It is widely believed that Galante fathered the "black man test" in which a heroin addict would be kidnapped and injected with a double bag — if he became comatose, the drug was considered quality. In addition, many claim that Galante was the assassin of Carlo Tresca, a popular anti-Fascist journalist.

16. Although a plea agreement in 1986 required Michael Franzese to forfeit nearly $5 million in assets and pay an additional $10 million in restitution, some individuals believe that he had at least $500 million hidden away! He is currently free and living in a multimillion-dollar mansion in California.

17. Indeed, the investigation of organized crime was a very low priority, and the primary role of the handful of agents assigned in this area may be characterized as bookkeeping or, as Maas states, "collating such routine information as the whereabouts of known racketeers" (Maas, 1968: 28).

CHAPTER 4

OUTLAW MOTORCYCLE GANGS

Traditionally, organized crime groups have been predicated on similar ethnic, racial, or religious backgrounds. Created to circumvent institutional obstacles, these groups have found strength in their homogeneity and have successfully parlayed this solidarity into an increasingly global criminal syndicate. This globalization, however, has not been accomplished without sacrifice. Indeed, expansion of organized crime has resulted in concentrated efforts and increasing scrutiny from the law enforcement community. Even though this increased vigilance has negatively impacted traditional organized crime organizations, it has also obscured the threat of nontraditional criminal groups. In fact, formal definitions of organized crime groups that are based on stereotypical models have all but ignored criminal structures lacking ethnic, racial, or religious consistency. Many deviant subcultures have taken advantage of this oversight to establish themselves in the underworld superstructure and gain a foothold in the expanding vice market. Only recently recognized by some authorities as a significant threat, groups such as outlaw motorcycle gangs (OMGs) have proven particularly resilient to RICO prosecutions due largely to traditional characterizations of organized crime.

With more than 300 clubs, 5,000 members, and at least 10,000 associates, OMGs have quickly become one of the nation's largest criminal organizations (Serio, 1992). Although annual revenues of $1 billion pale in comparison to mob highs of $50 billion, OMGs have displayed a remarkable ability to adapt. This ability has enabled them to become major players in international drug markets, prostitution rackets, and arms trafficking. Unfortunately, the danger of these groups has often been overlooked because traditional stereotypes and media depictions promote images of poorly shaven, beer-swilling misfits. In fact, a sharp increase in sales of Harley-Davidsons and Hells Angels memorabilia to mainstream American males has indicated a growing cultural affinity for social outcasts and tolerance of lawlessness. However, outlaw bikers (or 1%'s, as they are called) are more than the epitome of individualism; in fact, they are blatantly antisocial and heinously criminal.

HISTORY

Calling themselves the POBOBs (Pissed Off Bastards of Berdoo), the Hells Angels motorcycle club was originally made up of disillusioned World War II veterans (SLED, 1997). Many of these returning veterans experienced feelings of disassociation and felt alienated from a society that largely expected them to resume their former lives as if their absence had been nothing more than an extended vacation. In fact, the group's original charter was little more than a fraternal organization of post-wartime camaraderie for nostalgic veterans. In this atmosphere, members were free from the strictures of polite society. Buoyed by the support of their brethren, members reveled in their newly found freedom from the traditional trappings of social conformity. Members allowed their hair and beards to grow to socially inappropriate levels to symbolize their disdain for the established order. Motorcycles, their transportation of choice, epitomized their rejection of societal expectations.

For the most part, these outward manifestations of rebellion did not indicate wide-scale criminal activity; rather, organizational ideology, if articulated, encouraged members to squeeze the largest amount of fun out of every waking moment. This carefree atmosphere, however, would prove to be short-lived, and circumstances soon forced members to choose between group association and legitimate lifestyles. Ironically, the event that propelled these former veterans into the criminal underworld occurred on Independence Day, a holiday associated with national patriotism and those people of the armed services.

Although reports differ, most authors agree that a confrontation on Independence Day in 1947 between motorcycle enthusiasts and local law enforcement signaled the beginning of outlaw motorcycle gangs. This confrontation, sensationalized in the film *The Wild One*, was instigated by the general lawlessness displayed by POBOB members. Apparently, the authorities of Hollister, California, did not appreciate the manner in which many individuals entered establishments at full throttle and responded by arresting bikers for even the smallest indiscretions. Their response and the appearance of reinforcements successfully quelled further disturbances but set in motion an antiestablishment movement far more sinister in its implications. In fact, law enforcement's actions exacerbated feelings of alienation and served as a rallying cry for future criminal behavior (Lavigne, 1987; Thompson, 2002; Wolf, 1991). Today, the same recklessness and social disregard are evidenced in the annual Fourth of July Run and others like it.

An example of OMG colors. Note the abbreviation M.C. (motorcycle club) on the front and the rockers on the back, designating location and affiliation.

Courtesy of South Carolina State Law Enforcement Division

THE BIG FOUR

Law enforcement sources list four main outlaw motorcycle gangs, each referred to as a "1%'s."[1] They are the Hells Angels, the Outlaws, the Bandidos, and the Pagans. They contain formalized bureaucracies and pose a significant threat to domestic

---

BIKERS, HIPPIES, AND POP CULTURE

A detailed analysis of popular media in the United States indicates that a true representation of the biker ethos is absent from the multitude of movies, books, and news reports focusing on outlaw motorcycle gangs. During the 1950s and 1960s, for example, newspapers detailed the most shocking of biker antics and, many say, created fictitious accounts that vilified bikers. Stories of child rape and vicious mayhem created an image of the Hells Angels as the vilest creatures alive. (Paradoxically, this negative publicity, which many decried as false, swelled membership rolls.) Popular movies of the era glamorized the biker lifestyle, portraying bikers as the last group of American individualists. Ironically, these biker films resulted in increased revenue for club coffers and individual members who participated in the filming. *Hell's Angels on Wheels* and *Hell's Angels '69*, for example, starred several Oakland Angels including Sonny Barger and John "Terry the Tramp" Tracy. In addition, Barger and the Hells Angels received compensation for serving as "consultants" on other films.

Due to the portrayal of bikers as American mavericks (and the bikers' accessibility to drugs), a somewhat harmonious relationship with the hippie movement in San Francisco developed. On the surface, both groups shared similar philosophies regarding sex, drugs, and freedom of choice; however, the relationship between the two groups was shattered due to the violence displayed by the Angels, first at antiwar protestors and then to Meredith Hunter.

In December 1969, the Hells Angels were once again thrust into the national spotlight after they were hired to provide security for the Rolling Stones during a free open-air concert in a small town 30 miles from Oakland. Like several other events of the era, the concert was the culmination of a day filled with booze, drugs, sex, and, eventually, violence. Unfortunately, poor planning on the part of event organizers all but guaranteed the latter. According to Barger et al. (2000), the first act of violence occurred when a Hells Angel named Animal punched out lead singer Marty Balin of Jefferson Airplane. Then an African-American male, Meredith Hunter, was stabbed and beaten to death by a pack of Angels. (Although Barger denies it, most writers of the period attributed the attack to racism. Hunter's date was white.) During the melee, Barger claims to have kept the music playing by pointing a loaded gun at the head of Stones' guitarist Keith Richards. Provocation notwithstanding, this event signaled the end of the relationship between the hippies and the Angels. Writers of the period dubbed it "the End of Aquarius."

security. Without exception, these groups are highly structured and increasingly volatile. Perhaps the most dangerous and certainly the most recognizable of all outlaw motorcycle gangs is the Hells Angels. This organization, originally founded immediately following World War II, is indisputably the leader of the outlaw biker subculture; however, they are not alone in their criminal pursuits. In fact, other criminal organizations pepper the North American landscape, each unique in location and criminal pursuits.

The Outlaws, best known for their bloody war with the Angels, are one of the most powerful outlaw motorcycle gangs in the world. Founded by John Davis in Chicago in 1959, the Outlaws have subsumed small groups across the country but are particularly strong from the Great Lakes to the East Coast. Their international chapters include Australia, Europe, and Canada. (Their headquarters is currently located in Detroit where it had been moved upon the Harry "Taco" Bowman's ascension to the presidency.) However, it is their presence in Canada that poses the greatest concern for law enforcement, as their war with the Angels has become an international conflict, claiming the lives of both innocents and not-so-innocents.

Outlaws' Colors

Courtesy of South Carolina State Law Enforcement Division

> ### TCB—TAKING CARE OF BUSINESS
>
> Reprisal from a Pagan consists usually of a .38-caliber double automatic Colt, two shots in the back of the head, stomping on him just like a fish wrapped up in newspaper. That is the telltale signs of a Pagan hit (unidentified Pagan informant, as quoted in Lavigne, 1987: 173).

Like the Angels, the Outlaws are heavily involved with the manufacturing and trafficking of narcotics, including methamphetamine, cocaine, and diazepam (Valium). They are also heavily involved in "white slavery" (i.e., involuntary prostitution). Victims are culled from hanger-ons, old ladies, and any female unfortunate enough to be in their path. They are extremely barbaric to women, even by outlaw motorcycle gang standards. In one case, several members assisted their brother when he punished his old lady for her failure to perform a $10 trick by nailing her to a tree. Fortunately (or not), the woman recovered after they allowed her medical attention. The absolute subservience of Outlaw old ladies is denoted by modified colors that read "Property of Outlaws." The term is taken literally, and all members are entitled to her services.

The fastest-growing group, the Bandidos are headquartered in Corpus Christi, Texas, and have over 5,000 patch-wearing members (Dimmock, 2001). Though traditionally concentrated in the southern and western regions of the United States, the Bandido nation is growing exponentially, particularly overseas. At last count, the group had over 100 chapters in 10 countries and are particularly strong in Australia (Dimmock, 2001). They are currently allied with the Outlaws and have been used as enforcers for Colombian cocaine distributors. Like the other three gangs, they are actively engaged in prostitution, narcotics, auto theft, insurance fraud, extortion, murder-for-hire, etc. Following the lead of the Hells Angels, the Bandidos once sought to establish themselves as a nonprofit fraternal organization; however, recognition of RICO extinguished their zeal. They may be recognized by their unique colors. The inspiration for their symbol was a traditional marketing mascot of Frito-Lay (i.e., the "Frito Bandido"), an overweight cartoon cowboy bearing a machete and a pistol.

The smallest of the Big Four, the Pagans (founded in 1959 in Prince George's County, Maryland) continue to dominate northeastern methamphetamine markets and are reported to have ties with other more traditional organized crime groups. (One member, Joey "Sir Lancelot" Anastasia, is reportedly the nephew of Murder, Inc.'s Albert Anastasia.) As of 1989, the Pagans claimed 900 members in 44 chapters (Lavigne, 1987). Unlike the other three, the Pagans have not successfully established themselves as an international presence, although they do have ties to smaller gangs in Canada. Due to police pressure and public outrage, the Pagans' home base has moved several times. It is currently located in Suffolk County, New York, after being ousted from Delaware County, Pennsylvania. The group is still actively involved with the Philadelphia and New York branches of the LCN. They have even participated in power struggles within the mob, particularly in Philadelphia. In addition, they have served as drug couriers, mercenaries, and extortionists for the mob. They have also contracted their murder-for-hire services in other locations to other individuals and organizations. Their symbol is a representation of an ancient fire god. Like other OMGs, the Pagans are not known for their forgiveness, and traitors are treated mercilessly:

> And in the end there was Surtyr. He had defeated Zeus, Apollo, Thor, and Ocles. In all their savagery, they could not match Surtyr's vengeance. He called his followers Pagans. So it was written in the blood of the defeated Gods that Surtyr's followers would rule the earth, and make citizens tremble at the mention of their name (anonymous Pagan as cited in Lavigne, 1987: 167).

In 1973, Ralph "Lucifer" Yanotta was targeted for death after his decision to quit the group and join the Outlaws was discovered. Under an edict issued by Pagan president John Vernon "Satan" Marron, he was taken to a rock quarry, injected with sulphuric acid, stabbed over 30 times, and shot in the head (Lavigne, 1987). Miraculously, Yanotta survived to become one of the hitters in the murders of three Angels—triggering a war between the Outlaws and the Hells Angels. Unfortunately, his family was not as lucky. His wife and brother-in-law were later murdered by the group.

Each of the Big Four motorcycle gangs poses a significant threat to U.S. society in general and the law enforcement community (Lavigne, 1996; SLED, 1997). Thus, while the Angels were the first to exhibit a formal, highly bureaucratized structure, various other organizations have displayed an amazing aptitude for criminal adaptation as well. Unfortunately, inaccurate media depictions of biker subcultures have concentrated on the Hells Angels organization. Although organized criminal behavior by bikers is almost always attributed to the Hells Angels organization, territorial boundaries observed by rival groups contradict this representation. The Angels remain the most prominent and most dangerous of all OMGs, but they are not the sole proprietors of the outlaw biker ethos. Unfortunately, competing organizations, such as the Outlaws, Bandidos, and Pagans, have only recently been recognized by law enforcement authorities as highly structured criminal organizations. This oversight has allowed a collection of bikers or outlaw motorcycle gangs to prosper throughout the continental United States.

The Hells Angels and Sonny Barger

> The Hell's Angels Motorcycle Club, once an organization dedicated to bikes, booze and boobs, is now a multi-national, multi-million dollar business that peddles drugs, pussy, and death. Yesterday's rebels have become today's pushers, pimps, and hit men. The Angels operate their criminal empires out of fortified clubhouses, not unlike the knights of old. They ride iron horses, fight holy wars with other gangs over the honor of club colors, loot and wench in their jealously guarded fiefdoms and rely in the end on protection offered by the castle—the club (Lavigne, 1987: 14).

The designation "Hells Angels" was first adopted by a group of bikers in San Bernardino in 1948. Originally made up of POBOB members, this group adopted trappings favored by World War II aviators and represented the first of many "chapters" of the now international Hells Angels Motorcycle Club (HAMC). (The winged deathhead insignia, for example, was associated with one of three squadrons of the Flying Tigers in WWII, while the Hells Angels moniker was originally coined by Commander Arvid Olsen, U.S. Air Force.) A second chapter was formed out of the former Market Street Commandos of San Francisco in 1954, and a third (and arguably the most important) chapter was added in 1957. This Oakland chapter would soon come to dominate the ever-increasing world of outlaw bikers, largely due to the efforts of a 19-year-old high school dropout. His name was Sonny Barger, and his ascension to the throne vacated by Oakland founder and president, Otto Friedli, would herald a second coming for the HAMC (Lavigne, 1987, 1996).

Although his beginnings were anything but auspicious, Barger's impact on contemporary OMGs cannot be overstated. His vision transformed a group traditionally characterized by chaos, violence, and self-destruction into a well-oiled, highly structured criminal organization. Like a general marshaling his troops, Barger successfully recruited the most intelligent Angels to serve as his administrative staff while arming them with the most vicious soldiers. Other jurisdictions, angered at his high-handedness, were quickly silenced through violence and intimidation. Subsequently, Barger created an iconoclastic empire, establishing the supremacy of the Oakland chapter over the founding Berdoo and declaring himself as the group's undisputed leader. Coupled with his para-corporate approach, his position enabled Barger to concentrate on expanding his domain.

Originally focusing on the West Coast, Barger targeted rival groups for absorption or dissolution. To accomplish Angel dominance, Barger forced competing gangs to choose between compliance and extinction—an early indication of Barger's corporate approach. According to Lavigne (1996), the majority of these takeovers were, for all practical purposes, mutually beneficial business transactions, with some groups (e.g., the Brothers from Anchorage, Alaska, and Satan's Angels from British Columbia) actually courting the HAMC. Targeted clubs, forced to abandon corporate colors and ideology for those of the new parent "company," received professional counsel, economic resources, and additional personnel when necessary. On the rare occasions when targeted groups failed to adequately appreciate the benefits of such a merger, violence ensued (e.g., the case of the Tribulators from Charleston, South Carolina). This trend continued as the Angels extended their organization across the country. In 1967, the first of dozens of East Coast chapters was formed in Lowell, Massachusetts, and in 1969 Sandy Alexander formed the Manhattan chapter. This expansionism would ignite an explosive conflict between the HAMC and the Outlaws when Alexander's wife was allegedly raped by members of the latter group. Originally, potential chapters were closely scrutinized for ideological fit as the Oakland Angels (and Barger) tried to maintain control over the growing organization; however, Barger's hyper-expansionism soon diminished this scrutiny.

The unprecedented and largely unanticipated success of this corporate approach encouraged Barger to monopolize international markets as well, beginning with the Auckland, New Zealand, chapter in 1961. To the dismay of law enforcement, Barger's Napoleonic tendencies resulted in an international criminal conglomeration, and by 1983 an estimated 56 chapters of Hells Angels existed worldwide as a result of these systematically initiated corporate takeovers. Alternately implementing public relations platforms and head-breaking strategies, the Angels successfully cornered the outlaw motorcycle gang market in locations across the globe. Increasingly sophisticated in his approach, Barger cultivated a cosmopolitan image by relying on bilingual "ambassadors" familiar with foreign customs to spread his message of group domination. This presentation, coupled with a reputation for violence, proved to be wildly successful; in fact, many international groups, like their American counterparts, actively campaigned for Angel assimilation (Lavigne, 1996).

Their success in international markets formally elevated the Hells Angels to the top of the OMG criminal hierarchy. Other groups have followed their lead, hoping to mimic the success enjoyed by the Angels organization. However, it was not sheer criminal supremacy that propelled the Angels into the forefront. Group leaders, especially Barger, aggressively sought out legitimate safeguards. Formally incorporating their organization in the 1970s, the Angels were also successful in securing tax-exempt status. Establishment of a formal nonprofit charitable organization, the Church of the Angel, negated organizational responsibilities of taxation (Lavigne, 1996). The Angels even patented their club logo (patent #926-590) in 1972! In fact, revenue garnered from copyright infringement cases has been used to fuel legal defense funds for members awaiting trial; as a result, the Angel assets swelled. Traditionally, the remaining three OMG powers in the United States scrambled behind the HAMC, hampered by individualistic members and the absence of strict hierarchical structures. However, recent international intelligence suggests that they have overcome these traditional deficiencies and are amassing personnel, assets, and sophistication at alarming rates.

SONNY BARGER—WHERE ARE YOU NOW?

Without exception, Ralph "Sonny" Barger was the most powerful and the most respected member of the Hells Angels for over four decades. As president of the Oakland chapter, he was directly responsible for the organization and criminal sophistication of the Hells Angels. His expansionism enabled the HAMC to become a global criminal syndicate and served as a model for contemporary outlaw motorcycle gangs. Although incarcerated several times, Barger had influence that never waned; however, after a bout with cancer resulted in the removal of his vocal cords, Barger slowly relinquished his power in the organization. He is currently living with his new wife and daughter, and he is a member of the Cave Creek chapter of the Hells Angels near Phoenix, Arizona.

HELLS ANGELS NORTH—A CASE STUDY OF BROTHERLY LOVE

Traditionally, the bonds of brotherhood within OMGs were sacrosanct, placed above all other interests. Pitted against law enforcement, rival gangs, and society at large, gang members had strong organizational ties forged in the fires of adversity that protected them from inside threats. However, expansionism and wealth have slowly eroded these bonds, and many outlaw motorcycle gangs, particularly the Hells Angels, have suffered significant infighting. Luckily for law enforcement, such dissension has resulted in an increase in informants and government witnesses, as members are placed in fear for their life.

Incidents that occurred in Quebec in 1985 epitomize organizational problems associated with overexpansion and globalization. In March of that year, various members of the North (Laval, Quebec) chapter arrived at the clubhouse of the Montreal chapter to discuss allegations of drug usage, improper behavior, and club policy. Primed to orally defend themselves and their actions to their fellow brothers, they arrived unarmed—an unprecedented (and extremely shortsighted) display of good faith. President Laurent "L'Anglais" Viau, along with four other North members (Michel "Willie" Mayrand, Guy-Louis "Chop" Adam, Brutus Geoffrion, Jean-Pierre "Matt le Crosseur" Mathieu) were summarily executed, wrapped in sleeping bags, weighted with chains and mortar, and unceremoniously dropped into the St. Lawrence Seaway. Another attendee spared from the original slaughter, Claude "Coco" Roy, joined his brethren in the water shortly thereafter—murdered by a fellow North member after delivering the deceased club's drug stash. Their bodies, along with at least one other, were discovered several months later. Without exception, they were buried without the fanfare typical in biker funerals. In fact, the HAMC as a group treated the deceased as nonentities.

The extermination of the North chapter is but one example of intragroup conflicts; however, this particular incident resulted in significant repercussions for the Canadian contingent of the HAMC, as members flocked to law enforcement for protection. Both Gary "Apache" Trudeau and Prospect Gerry "le Chat" Coulombe stepped forward after they were informed that they had been targeted for extermination. Of the two, Trudeau's testimony was the more compelling, as he personally confessed to committing over 40 killings himself! In exchange for his testimony, he was allowed to plead manslaughter to all, receiving a seven-year sentence.

Colors, Tattoos, and Membership Rituals

"Our tattoos were our calling cards. Everywhere the Hells Angels went we'd outdrink, outf**k, and outfight everybody" (Barger et al., 2000: 141).

Contrary to popular belief, outlaw motorcycle gangs are quite selective in their membership. The desire to ride Harley-Davidsons and engage in criminal activity does not guarantee entrance into this biker subculture; these organizations are more selective of personnel than most law enforcement agencies. Extensive background checks on all prospective members all but negate the possibility of law enforcement infiltration. Members are most often recruited by patch-wearing members, and individuals displaying too much interest in the group are often discouraged from further inquiries. Those individuals selected for introduction must often provide detailed personal histories, including the names and addresses of relatives. This practice ensures that individuals will be discouraged from supplying information to law enforcement or otherwise acting in a disloyal manner. In addition, a thorough initiation process, coupled with a complex organizational structure, has allowed many OMGs to prosper in the criminal underworld (Lavigne, 1996; SLED, 1997; Wolfe, 1991).

According to Wolfe (1991), entrance into the outlaw subculture is closely guarded. The four-step initiation process ensures compatibility and brotherhood. The majority of new members are scouted by incumbents for their general knowledge and appreciation of outlaw motorcycling values and behavior. These individuals are considered outsiders and interactions are guarded. Upon acceptance of and sponsorship by an individual member, new recruits are then introduced as "friends of the club." Unanimous approval is a prerequisite to "striking" or "prospecting," which is the next step in the initiation process. The graduation to this level is ritualized by the granting of preliminary colors—the bottom rocker designating the striker's club charter. The duration of this period may range from six months to three years. Prospects are expected to perform the most distasteful of duties without complaint. It is not uncommon for strikers to be responsible for providing entertainment, cleaning clubhouse bathrooms, and washing members' "iron" (i.e., motorcycles). Prospects are also required to serve security detail and to prove their worth by protecting established members. Most organizations even require prospects to engage in felonious assaults or murder. This requirement is one of the most effective obstacles to governmental infiltration. Currently, all of the Big Four require potential members to prospect, but in the early days, there were some exceptions (Barger et al., 2000). For example, Elliot "Cisco" Valderrama, onetime Oakland president, actually gained his membership immediately following the "recovery" of nonsanctioned patches worn by a variety of individuals falsely claiming to be Hells Angels.

Prospects or strikers who successfully complete their probationary period are then inducted into the organization as full members with all the rights and privileges

---

Biker tattoos are as numerous as, and often the complement of, ornamental patches. Nazi SS lightning bolts underneath the words "Filthy Few" represent Angel enforcers, and skulls worn by Angels often represent Outlaw hits.

HONORARY MEMBERS

There are two types of honorary members:

1. Members who have retired in good standing
2. Nonpatch-wearing individuals who have assisted the club in some way (e.g., attorneys, bail bondsmen, mechanics, entertainers)

While both groups may attend club events and parties, only the first group may wear colors. Honorary members ride behind prospects on club runs.

---

that the position implies (e.g., they are entitled to vote in weekly "church" meetings and be appointed to executive offices). This rite of passage is symbolized by the granting of full colors. *Colors* refer to the rockers and emblems worn on a member's jacket and are the most prized possession of outlaws. (In fact, colors are so important to outlaws that many individuals have them tattooed directly on their back. This "back pack" includes both the club emblem and the top and bottom rockers.) Loss of colors engenders serious repercussions, including fines and loss of membership. Traditionally, "originals" (those colors first presented to an individual upon initiation) carried various body substances of ceremony attendees; excrement, semen, urine, and the like often soiled the material permanently, as laundering is strictly prohibited. Fortunately, the cleaner, more urbane organizations no longer perform this christening ritual. Thus, soiled colors are a sign of long-time members.

The "official uniform" of outlaw motorcycle gangs is a sleeveless denim or leather jacket. Featured on the back of the jacket are the club name, location, and logo. Traditionally, this bottom rocker specifically identified a member's individual chapter affiliation; however, many of the groups have now issued generalized state rockers to circumvent law enforcement intelligence gathering. On the front of the jacket are the member's moniker, the office held, and various patches, pins, and medals. Colors are the property of the club and are to be worn only by club members, as they are regarded as sacred by outlaw motorcycle gang members. Ornamental patches and club tattoos are also prohibited for all nonmembers, including most honorary members.

Organizational Structure

Hells Angels chapters have been reported in 17 countries across the globe. This unparalleled criminal expansion of the organization may be attributed to the group's hierarchical structure and corporate ideology. Each chapter has an executive staff similar to noncriminal organizations: president, vice president, secretary, treasurer, and sergeant

COLORS

Each organization has unique emblems and jealously guard their individuality, violently assaulting copycats. In 1977, for example, two Mongols were shot to death by representatives from the Hells Angels as a sign that their choice of colors (red and white like the Angels colors) was unacceptable. To further enunciate the point, red and white carnations were delivered to their funerals moments before a car bomb explodes, injuring three more Mongols (Lavigne, 1987).

Each group has its own colors and insignias:

Hells Angels' colors are red and white and include a winged, grinning death head wearing a leather aviator's helmet. Originally, this emblem was a six-inch patch; an enlarged patch was introduced by the Oakland Angels in 1960 and remains the club's official badge.

Outlaws' colors are primarily black and white and include a white skull with red eyes over white crossed pistons trimmed in red, affectionately called "Charlie."

Pagans' colors are primarily black and white and include a representation of an ancient god of fire.

at arms (see Figures 4–1 and 4–2). Generally speaking, the responsibilities attached to these positions mirror those in traditional clubs, with one exception. The sergeant at arms, responsible for club discipline, uses violence to ensure rule compliance.

Chapter president. This person is usually elected, although some powerful members are all but self-appointed.

Chapter vice president. Selected by the president, this individual is often the heir apparent.

Chapter secretary/treasurer. This person's normal secretarial duties include taking of minutes, collection of dues, and bookkeeping (e.g., paying bills, arranging bond, and paying fines).

Sergeant at arms. This person is the president's bodyguard, enforcer, and (when the situation arises) executioner.

Road captain. He is the chapter's logistician and chief of security during annual runs. Responsibilities are exclusive to preparations and maintenance of annual runs. Planning meals, fuel stops, and routes, this individual must prepare for all contingencies, often mapping out several alternate routes. He is also responsible for informing law enforcement personnel as to the time and date the group will pass through their jurisdiction.

Unlike the Outlaws, Bandidos, and Pagans, the Hells Angels do not have formal national or international presidents; rather, the majority of the power remains with the

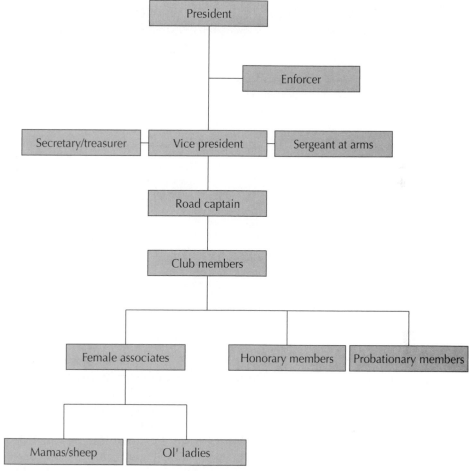

Figure 4–1   Chapter Organizational Structure

Oakland chapter. Regional officers selected by individual charters represent their club at regional meetings. The U.S. component of the Hells Angels is divided into East Coast and West Coast factions in reference to their location to Omaha, Nebraska. (The West Coast president is the designated representative for the American and Canadian locations west of Omaha as well as all of Alaska, New Zealand, and Australia. The jurisdiction of the East Coast president, on the other hand, includes everything in the United States and Canada east of Omaha as well as all other chapters not directly under the mantle of the West Coast.) Monthly meetings are held between the two factions, and each charter is expected to have representatives present. These meetings, however, are not intended to serve as governing entities; rather, chapters remain somewhat autonomous, and meetings are likened to democratic elections in which a two-thirds majority is required to pass a major resolution. Criminal activities are not discussed at these meetings. This aspect,

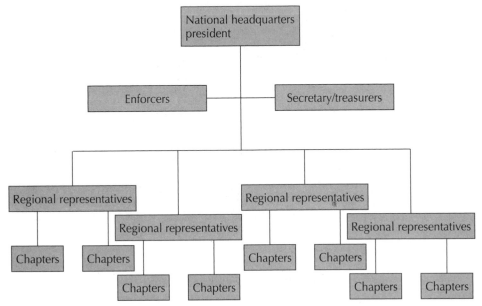

Figure 4–2 National Organizational Structure

coupled with their superficial appearance of autonomy, insulates the club from RICO prosecutions, as chapters maintain an appearance of individuality. Traditionally, however, absolute power resided with the Oakland chapter (SLED, 1997).

The annual "USA" motorcycle run is mandatory for all members and strikers not otherwise incapacitated (e.g., incarcerated, hospitalized, or dead), with sponsorship alternating between the East and West Coasts. These national runs include mandatory meetings for all national presidents. International or "world" runs, combined with the USA run when held in the United States, rotate between international and U.S. borders and enhance communication within an increasingly global organization. An agenda prepared prior to the event (usually the last week of July) includes motions submitted by individual clubs. These motions are voted on by all members. Similar to the situation in presidential elections, smaller groups are at a distinct disadvantage. Again, a motion can only be passed by a two-thirds majority. Traditionally, the Oakland chapter dominated these elections, but the semiretirement and relocation of Barger and the prosecution of the chapter's officers have somewhat leveled the playing field for other chapters.

Contrary to the setup of the Angels (who have not formalized a national presidency), the Outlaws, Bandidos, and Pagans maintain a national/international headquarters called "the mother club." The Outlaws and the Bandidos are remarkably similar in their organizational structure. Both groups have a governing board comprising the national president and four regional vice presidents. In both organizations, the national president maintains total control over club policies, bylaws, and activities. The Pagans, on the other hand, maintain officer positions that are purely figureheads, although they do receive annual salaries from club coffers. The real leadership within the Pagan organization resides in a governing body of former club presidents. Founded in 1959 in Prince George's County, Maryland, the Pagan nation does not claim a particular geographic location for its headquarters; rather, promotion to the mother club is based on criminal performance. Each member of the mother club presides over select Pagan chapters. Collectively, this governing board retains absolute power over Pagan members, and they wear the number 13 on their colors to identify them to all members (Lavigne, 1987; SLED, 1997). This mother club, reminiscent of LCN's commission, sets club policy, disciplines members, and mediates disputes. Each member of the mother club is compensated from the revenue generated by the chapters under his supervision; as such, each is directly responsible for initiating new criminal enterprises and overseeing traditional markets such as prostitution and narcotics.

All of the Big Four also maintain specialized positions to insulate themselves from law enforcement prosecution and to protect themselves from rival gangs. During runs or other club-sponsored events, road captains are appointed to coordinate security and run logistics (see Figure 4–4). These individuals are responsible for mapping out destination routes, emergency strong points, and refueling/refreshment centers. Road captains must also ensure that necessary equipment (e.g., spare motorcycle parts, guns) is included in "crash" cars. He is also responsible for maintaining run security and identifying safe locations in the event of threatening rival gangs (SLED, 1997). In addition, the Hells Angels, Outlaws, and Pagans maintain a staff of intelligence officers. These officers are responsible for gathering intelligence on law enforcement personnel, including addresses, phone numbers, financial information, and children's names. Although not a formalized position within the Bandido nation, this function is performed by the group's Nomad chapter. (This Nomad chapter is also responsible for club discipline and organizational security.) Thus, all of the Big Four maintain intelligence capabilities; this facet, which will be discussed further, insulates OMG members from criminal prosecutions (Lavigne, 1996, 1987; SLED, 1997).

Rules and Regulations

Like other criminal subcultures, outlaw motorcycle gangs have formalized rules and regulations that are violently enforced. Established to prevent law enforcement infiltration, these bylaws emphasize organizational loyalty and group solidarity. In most cases, OMGs require individuals to "befriend" incarcerated members—providing economic and emotional support upon demand. At all times, members must place group affiliation first, regardless of family or social responsibilities. Subsequently, members are expected to behave lawlessly and irresponsibly. Individual members who resist this all-encompassing lifestyle are ostracized or otherwise punished for

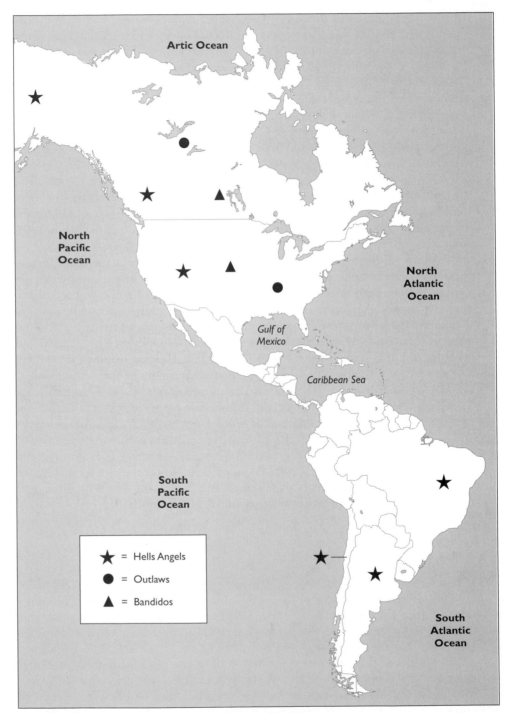

Figure 4–3   Proliferation of Outlaw Motorcycle Gangs

Figure 4-3 (continued)

111

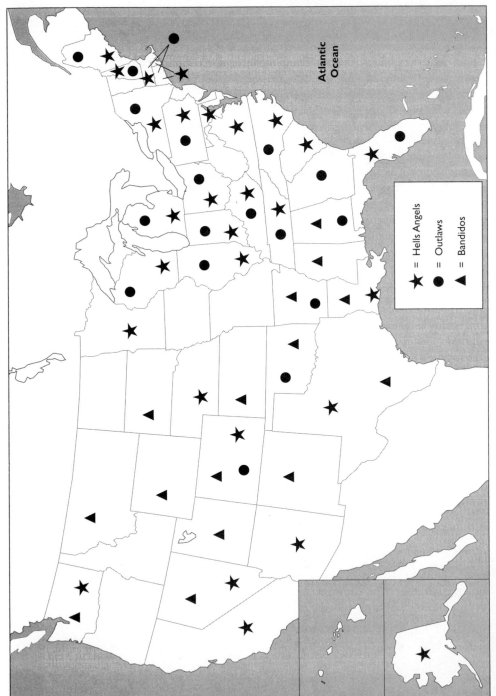

Figure 4–3 (continued)

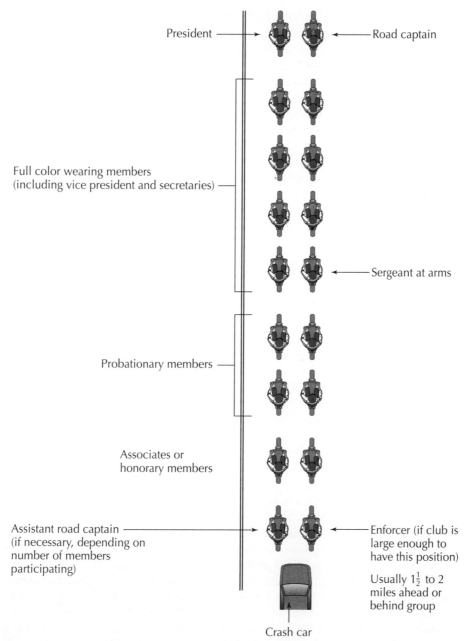

President ⟶   ⟵ Road captain

Full color wearing members
(including vice president and secretaries) ⟶

                                          ⟵ Sergeant at arms

Probationary members ⟶

Associates or
honorary members

Assistant road captain ⟶   ⟵ Enforcer (if club is
(if necessary, depending on   large enough to
number of members   have this position)
participating)
                                          Usually $1\frac{1}{2}$ to 2
                                          miles ahead or
                                          behind group

Crash car

Figure 4–4   Formation and Lineup During a Run

their shortsightedness (Lavigne, 1997). In addition, compliance with other club regulations is mandated, and merging clubs are required to adopt organizational policy. International clubs are expected to adopt English as their official language and remain cognizant of the U.S. power structure. Regular attendance at chapter "church" meetings is also required, and traveling members are expected to attend "church" while on the road. Additionally, members are expected to participate in organized runs, annual events in which members ride as a group to a designated location. These requirements ensure member accountability and organizational primacy (Lavigne, 1987, 1996; SLED, 1997).

The majority of OMGs have strict requirements regarding racial identity. Equating nonwhites with other club enemies, traditional policies of "no cops, no niggers, no snitches" pervade most outlaw bylaws (Lavigne, 1996). Prospecting clubs are often forced to expel nonwhite members.[2] This supremacist ideology permeates the outlaw subculture and extends beyond the boundaries of club membership. In fact, attacks on innocent African-Americans are encouraged by organizational ideology (Lavigne, 1996). However, exceptions to this rule do occur when exchange relationships are necessary in pursuit of criminal enterprise. One example of such complicity is the long-standing relationship between California Angels and Oakland's East Bay Dragons, a black motorcycle gang which received a 25-year Angel commemorative patch (Lavigne, 1996).

Much of the continuing success of OMGs is attributed to their strictly enforced code of silence: OMGs aggressively protect organizational secrets. However, OMGs do not restrict their violence to individual traitors. In fact, reports from law enforcement authorities indicate that OMGs extract their revenge from the most vulnerable targets—innocent women and small children. This unprecedented level of violence is of utmost concern to law enforcement agencies, because no formal limitations on violence and targeting of innocents may be identified. Unfortunately, governmental extensions of protection are disdained by those they seek to protect. Assurances of safety to significant others (primarily spouses or their informal counterparts) are met with tentative distrust and outright skepticism.

Other laws that remain in effect for the majority of outlaw biker gangs are designed to cement official bonds of brotherhood and prevent organizational chaos. Individual members, for example, are required to support (even with violence) a fellow member regardless of fault or situation. They are also prohibited from stealing from other members, and they may not use needle-injected drugs. In addition, most gangs require members to obtain club tattoos immediately following their organizational induction. Such tattoos, which include the club name, symbol, bottom rocker, and initiation date, publicly display their loyalty to the club. As such, these tattoos are for members only! Individuals forced out of the club must remove them; if they do not perform this function themselves, other members will be happy to oblige. Finally, individual chapters may have additional bylaws.

RULES ACCORDING TO BARGER

Sonny Barger, Hells Angels extraordinaire, recently revealed a list of rules that guided the Hells Angels Motorcycle Club during his tenure. Although they appear to be extremely benevolent, Barger admits that the list is far from complete and does not include those rules intended to remain private among club members. Here is Barger's list:

Members without a valid reason for missing a weekly meeting may be fined by the club.

Females are not permitted to attend regular meetings.

All new members must pay an initiation fee. The patch provided by the HAMC remains club property and must be relinquished upon request.

Club members engaged in a physical altercation with other members will be fined $5. (This would scarcely be a deterrent.)

All new members must be voted on, with any objections explained, and more than one objection results in an automatic rejection.

All members must have their own bikes.

Members in possession of extra parts must help others in need; however, they must be compensated.

No stealing is permitted among members.

Members may not belong to any other motorcycle club except the HAMC.

New members must come to three meetings on a bike before being voted on.

Prospects must abide by all the rules that bind full members.

Prospects must be proposed for a vote by a member at a meeting.

Individuals who are ejected from the club may not be readmitted. (However, there have been some exceptions.)

Individuals losing their patches must pay a fine.

On California runs, guns may be fired only between 0600 and 1600 hours.

Members may not spike the club's booze with drugs.

No live ammunition (nor any potential explosive objects) may be tossed into the bonfire.

Members may not "mess with another member's wife."

Members may not remove the chapter patch from another member.

Members may not use drugs during meetings.

PATCH DESIGNATIONS

All outlaw motorcycle gangs have their own particular system of patches. Patches are awarded for participation in runs, for official organizational designations, and most commonly for deviant sexual acts. Keep in mind that awarding of such patches often requires eyewitness testimony to substantiate the claims made. The following is a sample listing of patches awarded to various members of OMGs:

1%	This patch derives from a disclaimer by the American Motorcycle Association that stated that 99 percent of the country's motorcyclists belong to the AMA; the 1% patch designates the wearer as an outlaw.
13	It is a patch worn by an OMG member to symbolize the usage or distribution of marijuana.
22	This patch symbolizes that the wearer has previously been incarcerated.
666	This patch symbolizes the mark of Satan.
Eight ball	It is a patch worn on colors, earned by committing homosexual sodomy with witnesses present.
POBOB	This patch stands for "Pissed Off Bastards of Berdoo" (the original gang that later developed into the Hells Angels).
White-power fist	This patch, worn on colors, displays the gang's racial ideals and philosophies of white supremacy.
HAMCOE	This patch stands for "Hell's Angels Muster to Custer or Else" (originally developed to urge members to meet in Custer, South Dakota, en masse to ride to Sturgis for an anticipated showdown with their nemesis, the Outlaws).
MC	This patch stands for "Motorcycle Club."
AFFA	This patch stands for "Angels Forever, Forever Angels."
OFFO	This patch stands for "Outlaws Forever, Forever Outlaws."
Nomad	This patch, when worn as a bottom rocker on a member's colors, means that the wearer does not belong to any individual chapter. In some clubs these members are the enforcers.
White cross	It is a patch symbolizing that the wearer is wearing something he removed from a buried corpse.

Green wings	It is a patch earned when the wearer performs oral sex on a woman afflicted with some sort of venereal disease.
Purple wings	It is a patch earned when the wearer performs oral sex with a woman's corpse.
Golden wings	It is a patch earned when the wearer engages in sexual activity with a woman during a gang splash of more than 15 persons.

WOMEN AND THE OUTLAW SUBCULTURE

Like other criminal organizations, outlaw motorcycle gangs are not equal opportunity employers. OMGs are a strictly patriarchal phenomenon; females are not allowed to apply for or secure membership rights and privileges. Rather, females are relegated to marginal positions that are highly sexualized. Indeed, members vie for a variety of conquest patches—some socially deviant, some overtly criminal. This contempt for traditional notions of commitment and monogamy and the sexualization of the female gender have resulted in a highly structured stratification system within organizational boundaries. While promiscuity among males is encouraged, independent promiscuity among female companions is not tolerated. Females deviating from proscribed subservient roles are punished for their indiscretions. This rigidity is not to suggest, however, that females are not an important part of the organizational subculture. In fact, many motorcycle gangs aggressively pursue associations with certain females. Their practice of recruiting and/or seducing individuals in sensitive positions is a large part of their intelligence-gathering strategy. Reports of female associates in governmental or law enforcement occupations are increasing. Governmental intelligence reveals that some female employees of government agencies have provided counterintelligence information to OMGs. However, positions of power among female associates are nonexistent because OMGs are strictly patriarchal in nature, and females are only used to service the entrepreneurial or sexual needs of the club.

According to Wolfe (1991), three distinct classes of females permeate the outlaw subculture. "Broads," the lowest class occupied by females, refers either to individuals who have brief sexual associations with one or more members or to women in transitional stages of association who may eventually graduate to the higher levels of association— "mamas" or "old ladies." Many of these women articulate motivations similar to those of male associates. For some, the outlaw subculture embodies a spirit of social rebellion. For these women, the "heavy macho image . . . the intrigue of association . . . and the partying and excitement of the hedonistic lifestyle" act as powerful, though temporary, magnets (Wolfe, 1991: 145). On the average, the majority of these associations constitute little more than a fleeting flirtation. However, Wolfe's assertion that these encounters are entirely voluntary is somewhat misleading. Lavigne suggests that the outlaw culture's "idea of female emancipation is to take the handcuffs off a woman after they've had her" (1996: 32). Unfortunately, many females are unaware of the total lack of benevolence on the part of many OMGs, and these individuals often find that this flirtation has serious implications for their personal safety. Indeed, some individuals have reported that their participation in sexual situations was anything but voluntary and was the result of drug-induced states or threats of violence. In fact, communiqués between European and U.S. authorities report that "white slavery" and prostitution rings composed of unwilling females are increasingly becoming business favorites among outlaw motorcycle gangs (Lavigne, 1996; SLED, 1997).

For the most part, however, the majority of these females participate in the outlaw subculture quite willingly, albeit temporarily. Indeed, the bulk of these experiences represents a brief vacation to the wild side for these individuals. Most do not develop long-standing ties to specific outlaw members or the outlaw subculture in general. In fact, the same members who sample the wares of these females openly display contempt for their promiscuity. Ironically, the practice of group sex (i.e., "pulling trains") discourages members from establishing further relationships with these individuals, and it all but negates the possibility of graduation to old lady status. However, a small minority of these females do establish a somewhat permanent association with the club.

Of the three groups delineated by Wolfe (1991), the least numerically represented are "motorcycle mamas." Hierarchically, these individuals occupy a position only slightly higher than that of broads. As such, they are accorded the same level of protection accorded to organizational mascots and club animals. Jacket rockers reading "Property of _____ (organizational name)" indicate their continuing favor among club members and their willingness to perform sexual acts with any or all club members. Their primary responsibilities are twofold: (1) sexually servicing club members and their visitors, and (2) providing continuous income for club coffers. Some clubs even employ mamas in

PAGAN RULES REGARDING OLD LADIES

The following rules are listed by Lavigne (1987: 178):

1. Members are responsible for their Old Ladies.
2. Members may have more than one (1) Old Lady.
3. Members may not discuss club business with their Old Lady.
4. No Old Ladies allowed at meetings.
5. No property patch is worn on an Old Lady. So if you see a chick, you better ask before you leap.

their various sex-related enterprises, such as massage parlors and prostitution. Their position within the organization, however, remains somewhat precarious, reliant on acceptance by members and their old ladies (Lavigne, 1996; SLED, 1997; Wolfe, 1991).

The highest level of female association within outlaw motorcycle clubs is only achieved through a long-standing or monogamous relationship with one member. Females attaining such elevated status are affectionately known as "old ladies" and are accorded a measure of respect much higher than that of other female associates. This respect, however, is often hard-won, because female associates are exposed to heightened levels of scrutiny. Thus, organizational association and corresponding privileges are not extended without significant personal sacrifice.

Recognizing the compelling nature of intimate relationships, most OMGs have established informal mechanisms for ousting undesirable or nontrustworthy partners. Accordingly, indoctrination processes experienced by old ladies are more intense and demanding than those experienced by their male counterparts and serve as evaluative measures for organizational acceptance. Females seeking elevation to this grandiose status are required to display high levels of humility, submission, and obedience to respective mates. Subservient at all times, old ladies must be passive complements to displays of gendered supremacy. Indeed, a female's adherence to traditional gender roles is considered to be a reflection of her partner's masculinity and directly affects his organizational standing. As such, male members are highly encouraged—even expected—to disdain monogamy and act on their "manly urges." This expectation of sexual promiscuity is one that is not reciprocated. Indeed, extramarital (or extra-relationship, whichever the case may be) affairs by old ladies often result in immediate expulsion from the group. This practice, necessary to preserve the sanctity of the brotherhood, also ensures the privacy of club activities. In some cases, groups have actually executed former old ladies whom they felt were privy to incriminating evidence (Lavigne, 1996).

Old ladies pose the greatest threat to group solidarity, and as such, they are scrutinized more closely than organizational brethren. The significance of their role cannot be overstated; the acceptance of prospective members is often predicated on the behavior of their significant other. Members and/or strikers who are unable to adequately control the activities of their old ladies are harshly criticized and are often forced to choose between their respective mates and their "brothers." Overwhelmingly, the group's primacy is maintained, as few members choose their female companions over the group. However, old ladies receiving organizational endorsement are often used to protect club assets from governmental forfeiture. For example, Barger's motorcycle repair shop and the Oakland headquarters for the Hells Angels are "owned" by the wife of former Oakland president Sergey "Sir Gay" Walton. Linda Walton, who remained with the club after her husband became an informant, was shot four times and left permanently paralyzed after she cooperated with the Drug Enforcement Administration (DEA) on an investigation of her new husband, Hells Angel Blair Guthrie (Lavigne, 1996).

In return for their loyalty, females who successfully pass muster are entitled to display their affiliation with modified colors. The primary modification, of course, is one that clearly indicates their subservient or secondary status. "Property of" rockers accompany the club emblems. Unlike colors sported by organizational hangers-on, bottom rockers displayed by old ladies boldly proclaim individual ownership. These outward manifestations of enslavement are not without significant rewards. Additional benefits of club affiliation include club protection, extended vacations from reality, etc. In reality, biker old ladies occupy a position far below a biker's iron or colors. With few exceptions, females in these positions are physically and emotionally abused. In many cases, the absence of formal marital contracts leaves little or no legal recourse for discarded old ladies. In the rare case that legal judgments of spousal or dependent support are secured, few are satisfied because process servers are reluctant to enter OMG strongholds.

Summarily, marginalization of females appears to be a mainstay of the outlaw subculture. Sexualization of female associates serves to reinforce subcultural values and ideology while encouraging male domination and female subservience. Contrary to popular belief, working- or lower-class females are not overrepresented within these organizations; broads, mamas, and old ladies appear to be attracted to the carefree lifestyle espoused by OMGs despite their personal economic background. Almost without exception, however, these females are only slightly postpubescent. Regardless of socioeconomic status, profession, or background, the younger generation is disproportionately represented among female associates, who are used until their physical beauty has faded; then they are traded in for newer models. Finding few takers outside the outlaw subculture, many of these women are forced to remain in abusive environments.

CRIMINAL ACTIVITIES

Without exception, the informal goals of OMGs revolve around lawless lifestyles. Social institutions, including law enforcement agencies, are condemned as overly restrictive and hypocritical entities. As such, the laws they espouse are ignored; instead, rules and regulations more consistent with the outlaw ideology are adopted. This alternative system actually encourages violent behavior and victimization of others. Due to their outlaw motto and general lawlessness, OMGs are better suited than most to operate a criminal organization. Individuals who gravitate to the club, ranging from bored housewives to high-powered attorneys, protect the outlaw lifestyle that attracts them, providing safe houses and offering covers. Subsequently, outlaw motorcycle gangs have been involved in criminal activities such as murder, aggravated assault, rape, arson, robbery, prostitution, and burglary. They have also established complex criminal networks involving drugs and weapons trafficking, prostitution, and protection rackets.

Drugs

The primary source of revenue for outlaw motorcycle gangs is a compilation of illegal narcotics trafficking. Beginning in the late 1960s, the Hells Angels organization became one of the primary distributors of LSD in the San Francisco Bay area. Since that time, outlaw motorcycle gangs have been found to be active in the manufacturing, marketing, and distributing of heroin, cocaine, marijuana, seconal, STP, MDA, PCP, and amphetamines. Currently, OMGs, especially the Hells Angels, are considered to be the largest supplier of methamphetamines in the country (Lavigne, 1996; SLED, 1997). Subsequent by-products of their narcotics trade have included murder, extortion, and witness intimidation. In addition, various groups have become increasingly active in arms trafficking. Law enforcement authorities have seized from OMGs an array of sophisticated weaponry including but not limited to fully automatic weapons, silencers, explosive agents, and military antipersonnel devices (Lavigne, 1996; SLED, 1997).

Federal authorities have achieved limited success for their enforcement efforts, which have primarily concentrated on the Hells Angels organization. In the 1980s, Federal Bureau of Investigation Operations ROUGHRIDER and CACUS resulted in a number of narcotics-related convictions of Hells Angels in the northeastern and western portions of the United States. Additional enforcement efforts have resulted in a variety of arrests and seizures across the country. While the majority of these drug-related charges involve the manufacturing and distributing of methamphetamines, some governmental sources have documented links between northeastern Hells Angels chapters and the Medellin cartel of Colombia and other traditional organized groups. Links between other outlaw motorcycle gangs, such as the Bandidos, have also been established and are an increasing concern among law enforcement personnel (SLED, 1997).

As stated, the vast majority of drug-related enterprises among OMGs involve methamphetamines. Seizures of clandestine methamphetamine labs in California, Oregon, and Missouri indicate the growing demand for "ice" or "crank" within domestic markets and illustrate an OMG monopoly. Increasingly, outlaw groups are contracting with nonmember clandestine lab operators to manufacture for them. Typically, OMGs maintain ownership over required chemical products and simply pay for the "cooking" or actual manufacturing of the "ice." This practice has further insulated OMGs from criminal prosecution and law enforcement scrutiny. In addition, such activities have become so lucrative that many members have invested proceeds in legitimate businesses (Lavigne, 1996; SLED, 1997).

Outlaw motorcycle gangs are extremely protective of their drug distribution territories. Crossing territorial boundaries poses dire consequences not only for rival gangs but also for members dealing outside the confines of their individual chapters. To limit regional disputes, many OMGs have formed tenuous alliances with rival gangs. This agreement has greatly enhanced financial rewards through monopolistic jurisdictions that maintain economic regularity. In addition, strict organizational rules prohibiting "narcotics burns" (taking the goods without paying or selling substandard products) amplify product marketability.

Prostitution and Protection

Like organized crime groups of old, OMGs have also focused on vice activities to further enlarge club coffers. Surveillance reports have uncovered a complex system of prostitution rings and brothels. Members engaging in this sort of criminal activity act as pimps or procurers, earning a percentage of their prostitutes' wages. Unlike their predecessors, however, the females working in such establishments are not there of their own accord; rather, drug addiction, threats, and other intimidation tactics are employed to maintain "company personnel." These tactics have been successful in discouraging government informants or cooperative witnesses. One exception, a former prostitute in an Angels' brothel in Vallejo, California, was murdered, along with her six-year-old daughters (twins) and a male companion, for her testimony. Unfortunately for her, government assurances of protection were inadequate in the face of the group's sophisticated counterintelligence unit; her location was divulged by a postal employee on the Angel payroll (Lavigne, 1996).

Steady income is also provided by a complex web of protection rackets. Unlike traditional organized crime groups that focused on a variety of legitimate businesses, outlaw motorcycle gangs tend to target drinking establishments and social clubs. Simply stated, members promise to appear en masse in full colors unless a small monthly fee is provided. Business owners, faced with the prospect of losing legitimate business, quickly agree to such charges. To protect these arrangements, scrupulous record keeping and weekly church meetings provide "off-limits" establishments. For the most part, however, these admonitions are unnecessary because members tend to congregate in predominantly biker establishments (Lavigne, 1996).

Outlaw motorcycle gangs are increasingly establishing "legitimate" businesses to enhance money-laundering capability. While some are purchased using traditional legitimate avenues, others are acquired through violent means. This "buy out, burn out, or bomb out" is similar to methods used by Italian organized crime groups. Targeted entities may either allow a group to buy them out or face arson or explosions. Unlike the Italians, whose goal is to maximize profitability immediately by "busting out" a targeted establishment, OMGs often procure the businesses to serve as income justification or as fronts for their illegitimate activities.

Other Criminal Activities

Traditional vice-related enterprises are not the only criminal activities engaged in by outlaw motorcycle gangs. Members are also involved in nonviolent criminal activities. Over the years, outlaw motorcycle gangs have exhibited an amazing aptitude for fraudulent activities. The most well known of these, insurance fraud, involves the false reporting of injury, destruction, or disappearance of real or personal property. "Legitimate" club businesses, such as motorcycle repair shops, present an aura of respectability while providing the opportunity to traffick in stolen motorcycles, parts, and equipment. It is not uncommon for club property to burn down in the middle of the night and for club "iron" (i.e., motorcycles) to be stolen right out of club parking lots. As few individuals would venture onto OMG property and even fewer would dare to linger, such reports must be approached with a degree of skepticism. In addition, OMGs are actively involved in the theft of nonorganization property. Because members are most often expert cyclists and mechanics, members are also expert thieves. Traditional antitheft devices on motorcycles (e.g., kill switches, fuel cut-off valves) are simply nuisances to the determined biker. The theft of a motorcycle may be undertaken to obtain spare parts, to resell it, or to replace another bike. Due to the high incidence of motorcycle theft, some manufacturers such as Harley-Davidson have taken measures to prevent this by stamping vehicle identification numbers (VINs) on various parts of their motorcycle, including the engine, and by including the frame number on all registrations. However, OMGs have adapted, often purchasing, stealing, or even counterfeiting blank registration titles. Stolen motorcycle parts may be purchased at dozens of "swap meets" across the globe.

Other activities engaged in by OMGs are standard, run-of-the-mill violent felonies. The majority of these assaults, rapes, and murders are economically motivated and by-products of a moneymaking enterprise such as narcotics distribution or prostitution. However, some of these violent attacks are not fiscally motivated but are, in fact, committed in retaliation for a rival gang's actions, as punishment of a former member, or as intimidation of a government witness/informant. Still other attacks are perpetrated against innocents, further negating media depictions of fun-loving, beer-swilling misfits. Documented accounts of such viciousness include the stabbing death of a 5-year-old child. This incident, in which her parents and 17-year-old brother were also murdered, clearly illustrates the savage nature of OMGs. Indeed, it is this characteristic of outlaw motorcycle gangs that is most disturbing to law enforcement (Lavigne, 1996).

GANG WARS

Although outlaw motorcycle gangs share a common ideology, territorial disputes have arisen between organizations. In fact, gang wars are quite common in the outlaw biker culture, and each of the Big Four has been engaged in at least one. In the early 1980s, for example, disputes between the Bandidos and the Commancheros claimed numerous lives as the struggle for superiority in Sydney, Australia, heated up. In a public confrontation at a swap meet on Father's Day, 7 individuals were killed and 21 injured. Although a temporary cease-fire enabled the removal of victims, the violence continued at local hospitals (Lavigne, 1987).

Perhaps the most violent and certainly the longest-lasting feud originated in 1974 when Sandy Alexander, president of the New York Hells Angels, assaulted a member of the Outlaw organization for allegedly raping his old lady. In order to save face among his peers, the Outlaw claimed that he was blindsided by a band of Angels. Outlaw members tortured and executed three Angels in Florida in retaliation. Charlotte became the main battleground in the conflict when four Outlaws, one female associate, and the club's guard dogs were shot and killed in their clubhouse. (Some Outlaws wear the tattoo "7-4-79" to commemorate the date.) The following year the Angel clubhouse in Charlotte was blown up by rival Outlaws (Lavigne, 1996). Although the feud is still brewing, periodic cease-fires have been observed. Some law enforcement sources predict that ensuing peace talks may result in an end to the conflict; however, increased occurrences of gang disputes overseas may negate this projection (SLED, 1997).

GANGS IN CANADA

As mentioned previously, outlaw motorcycle gangs are increasingly dangerous as they extend their criminal tentacles across the world. Without exception, each of the Big Four has established either international chapters or informal connections. Leading the globalization effort are the Hells Angels, although the Outlaws and Bandidos are quickly catching up. Due to the relative "open policy" of traveling throughout North America, Canada, in particular, has been hard hit by an exponential increase in foreign-based biker gangs as well as gangs established from their constituency (e.g., Rebels, Grim Reapers, Gypsy Jokers, Rock Machine). This trend began in the late 1970s as Sonny Barger and his Angels stormed across Canada, attempting (and largely succeeding in) countrywide domination of the drug trade through a massive "patch over." Subsuming smaller groups such as the Quebec Popeyes in 1977 and the Satan's Angels in 1983, the Hells Angels successfully established chapters in all of Canada's large cities, including three in Quebec. More recently, they have launched chapters in smaller, less populated areas.

This expansion has not been accomplished without a significant amount of violence. The war between the Canadian-based Rock Machine and the Hells Angels for control of Quebec's drug market has been extremely bloody, with 160 dead and 300 injured (Boshra, 2001). As with other biker conflicts, innocents have not been spared. The conflict has escalated since 1983 when the Satan's Angels, traditionally the most powerful group in Canada, donned the colors of the HAMC, and the outgunned Rock Machine increased their use of explosives. Inevitably, the Rock Machine turned to another international power, the Bandidos, for assistance. Although law enforcement has cracked down on biker gangs, arresting 30 members in Quebec in June 2001, the war continues, as do the costs, both social and financial. In 1997, the Hells Angels Quebec president, Maurice "Mom" Boucher, ordered the execution of two prison guards, while local authorities struggled with the mounting costs associated with the war (over $100 million). (These estimates include the construction of a new courthouse specifically designed for biker trials, prosecutor salaries, prolonged detention of members, and increased costs associated with prolonged incarcerations. Additional costs have been incurred in the creation of antibiker law enforcement units.) Unfortunately, the war appears to be spreading across Canada, as three bars in Montreal were targeted for arsons within a 24-hour period in late 2001. Ironically, some politicians have refused to recognize the dangers posed by outlaw bikers. Toronto Mayor

Mel Lastman, for example, posed for photographs with the Hells Angels as he welcomed them to his city. (The Angels had come to celebrate their national "patch over.") Hells Angels Boucher, in the meantime, kept Quebec authorities busy by launching a multimillion-dollar defamation lawsuit against high-ranking officials. Perhaps Mayor Lastman should take notes.

GANGS IN AUSTRALIA

Like their Canadian counterparts, Australian authorities have struggled to contain their mounting "bikie" problem. The New South Wales (NSW) Crime Commission has reported 32 active groups and over 4,000 members nationwide, with a disproportionate number concentrated in NSW. These groups include native gangs, such as the Commancheros, the Rebels, the Coffin Cheaters, and the Gypsy Jokers, and foreign gangs, such as the Hells Angels, the Outlaws, and the Bandidos. Other groups in operation include the Nomads and the Life and Death Gang. For the most part, the Australian groups have proven more resilient to American take over than those in Canada and have, in fact, displayed levels of organizational fortitude to rival the Americans. (The Coffin Cheaters, for example, have historically legitimized their illicit goods under the guise of club-owned enterprises such as Cheetah Investments Pty. Ltd.) To protect themselves and (more importantly) their criminal supremacy, these groups have been forced into armed confrontations with the usurpers.

The Bandidos, in particular, have found few friends in the outback. They are actively at war with the Commancheros and the Gypsy Jokers, and law enforcement efforts against the group have been especially effective. They have lost members to snipers, they have been bombed out of their clubhouses by rival clubs, and they have lost millions in cash and assets to government officials armed with the Criminal Assets Recovery Act. They have even lost members through their own actions. (Rodney Partington, president of the Kurri Kurri Bandidos, was killed instantly when a bomb that he constructed to destroy the Gypsy Joker clubhouse went off prematurely.) However, the group has managed to maintain a continued presence throughout Australia and is a major supplier of methamphetamine across the country.

Another group that is heavily involved with drug trafficking, the Gypsy Jokers, is most notorious for the car-bombing murder of retired detective Dan Hancock. Hancock, a former "bikie" investigator, and a male companion were killed by an explosion outside of Hancock's house. Although clouded in mystery, Hancock was apparently targeted in retaliation for an unsolved sniper assassination of Gypsy Joker William "Billy" Grierson, who had recently insulted Hancock's daughter, a barmaid at her father's bar. Although there is no evidence to suggest that Hancock was involved, the Jokers thought differently. Unfortunately, Hancock chose to ignore repeated warnings and near misses (e.g., explosions at Hancock's hotel, the general store, and the gold battery and the arson of his home). His bravado cost him his life.

Like their American counterparts, Australian biker gangs engage in a variety of traditional organized crime activity. They are involved in prostitution rackets, drug trafficking, auto theft, and extortion. They are increasingly legitimizing their ill-gotten gains through fronts established with strong-arm tactics. Australian authorities have had some success in individual cases, recently convicting sergeant-at-arms John Tudor Williams (Western Sydney Chapter, Bandidos) of drug trafficking and eliminating 30 amphetamine labs across the country. In addition, they are considering RICO-type laws and asset forfeiture provisions as well as prohibitions on structural fortifications (for clubhouses). Such legislation would complement the Criminal Assets Recovery Act and broaden the powers of the NSW Crime Commission. However, conflicts between Australian OMGs appear to be increasing as gangs merge.

ANTIGANG LAW ENFORCEMENT

Counterintelligence

Though outlaw motorcycle gangs are now recognized as a powerful organized crime group, law enforcement efforts have seen only limited success. Individual members have been successfully targeted for prosecution, but widescale organizational prosecution has not been effective. On the surface, it may appear that their emphasis on corporate-like strategies would increase their vulnerability to RICO prosecutions, but OMGs have purposely separated the corporation and business side of the organization from the criminal activity perpetrated by its members. This functional separation does not suggest, however, that motorcycle gangs do not fit standard definitions of organized crime; rather, OMGs—beginning with Barger and the Hells Angels—have intentionally distanced themselves from officially sanctioned criminal activity. As such, OMGs as organizations have proven resilient to RICO convictions even though individuals have been convicted on a variety of charges. In fact, two of the first well-publicized cases were dismal failures for law enforcement and led to a great reluctance to seek RICO convictions. It has been suggested that the lack of prosecutorial success may be attributed to the seemingly unlimited source of funding among outlaw motorcycle gangs and the availability of corrupt officials. For example, one author reported that the Hells Angels paid $100,000 for police reports during RICO trials in 1979–1981. These documents, labeled "confidential" and "for law enforcement eyes only," were then distributed to chapters worldwide (Lavigne, 1996).

Much of the success of outlaw motorcycle gangs may be attributed to their proactive approach in avoiding criminal prosecution. Unlike traditional organized crime groups, which develop subversive tactics to avoid technically advanced surveillance equipment, OMGs exploit technology and adopt government's techniques and equipment until it is almost worthless to law enforcement efforts. OMGs employ state-of-the-art detection devices that uncover monitoring equipment such as electronic bugs and wires. They hold intelligence training sessions in which members are introduced to the latest technological advancements. Voice-stress analyzers on strikers and suspect members are used to determine the truthfulness of their responses and their loyalty to the club (Lavigne, 1996; SLED, 1997).

Further strengthening their position, OMGs rely on a loose network of informants to assist them in their counterintelligence endeavors. OMGs actively recruit associates from service occupations and have developed sources in the postal service, the electric company, the phone company, and the Department of Motor Vehicles (DMV). They have also successfully corrupted or otherwise compromised a variety of judges, prosecutors, and law enforcement officials. These associates act as intelligence-gathering agents, compiling information on government agents, judges, and potential jurors. These information sources are estimated to be far superior to ones established by governmental agencies. Not restricted by legislative mandates, these individuals obtain private addresses, cellular phone numbers, even passenger information profiles from airline manifests (Lavigne, 1996). Associates have infiltrated law enforcement agencies, a feat the government has not been able to duplicate. In essence, then, law enforcement agencies are outstaffed and outfunded.

Defense Funds and Bailbondsmen

In addition to their counterintelligence strategies, outlaw motorcycle gangs have further strengthened their organizations with in-house counsel. Keeping attorneys on retainer allows OMGs to secure the release of jailed members almost immediately. This expediency negates the possibility of jailhouse confessions and limits the power of law enforcement investigators. In addition, most OMGs have established defense funds to assist in legal expenditures. These funds are derived from mandatory donations, membership dues, and illegal revenues. Furthermore, some OMGs maintain agreements with bond companies to file individual surety. Members simply flash their club tattoo, and the bond is supplied. This "get-out-of-jail-free tattoo" is also used as a form of identification by some law enforcement agencies.

LAW ENFORCEMENT EFFORTS ABROAD

Although American law enforcement has been burdened with jurisdictional issues, sympathetic jurists, and civil challenges, Australian officials have had repeated success in their Operation Avatar. This initiative, an on-going project initiated in 1999, resulted in the seizure of 200 cars, various drugs, and 81 firearms during the period from February to November 2001. Arrests on charges ranging from prostitution to murder continue.

OPERATION CACUS

Originally, Operation CACUS was the result of a disillusioned Hells Angel. Anthony Tait, long a cop wannabe, actually initiated the investigation and solicited law enforcement interest. Paid heavily by the Federal Bureau of Investigation, Tait allowed law enforcement to accompany him on his unprecedented rise to the highest echelon of the Hells Angels organization. His cooperation and unparalleled enthusiasm were especially significant, as his credibility was unchallenged.

Unlike many criminal informants whose cooperation is secured through promises of reduced sentences, Tait voluntarily came forward without provocation. Accordingly, criminal prosecutions against the highest-ranking officers were successful. Although it did not result in RICO prosecutions, numerous individual convictions were obtained. For example:

> Ralph "Sonny" Barger. The undisputed leader of the Hells Angels, he was convicted of conspiracy to violate federal law and conversion of government property. His sentence was 31 1/2 years.

> Montgomery David "Monty" Elliott. A member of the Anchorage chapter, he was convicted of distribution of cocaine and sentenced to 41 1/2 years in custody, 3 years' special parole, and a $10,000 fine.

> John Makoto "Fuki" Fukushima. He was San Francisco chapter vice president and computer expert extraordinaire. He was convicted of possession of an unregistered firearm and received 11 1/2 years in custody, special parole with a nonassociation clause, a $25,000 fine, and forfeiture of $32,000.

> Edwin Floyd "Eddie" Hubert. President of the Anchorage chapter, he was convicted of distribution of cocaine and got 2 years in custody and 6 years' supervised release.

> Charles Daniel "Chico" Manganiello. He was convicted of distribution of methamphetamine and received a $300,000 fine, special parole for life, and forfeiture of real and personal property.

> Michael Vincent "Irish" O'Farrell. President of the Oakland chapter, he was convicted of conspiracy to violate federal law and conversion of government property; he received 31 1/2 years.

> Kenneth Jay "K.O." Owen. Touted as the world's best methamphetamine cook, he was convicted of possession and distribution of methamphetamine; he got 41 years, a $2.1 million fine, and forfeiture of over $2 million in real and personal property.

> Dennis E. "Bigfoot" Pailing. President of the Fairbanks chapter, he was convicted of possession of cocaine, distribution of cocaine, and possession of an unregistered machine gun; he was sentenced to 13 1/4 years, with 3 years' probation.

> Gerald Michael "Pee Wee" Protzman. Vice president and treasurer of the Anchorage chapter, he was convicted of conversion of government property and got probation.
>
> Richard Allen "Sleazy Ric" Rickleman. A member of the Anchorage chapter, he was convicted of possession of a firearm by a felon; he received 1 year in custody and a $3,000 fine.

Successes

As stated, the government has enjoyed only minimal success through implementation of RICO statutes. Even the most concentrated efforts by American law enforcement have fallen short of whole-scale group prosecution. In fact, a variety of cases did much to discredit the competency of law enforcement officials in their fight against outlaw bikers. The first of these, and certainly the most cost-ineffective, involved an organization-wide RICO case against Sonny Barger; his wife, Sharon; and various other members of the Hells Angels. To the dismay of the investigators, virtually all charges of attempted murder, bombings, narcotics trafficking, murder, and extortion were found without merit. Unfortunately, the public hype and media interest in the case only made the defeat more embarrassing. However, recent years have seen an increase in individual convictions, some of which involved prominent officers. The most notable victory for law enforcement was a result of a lengthy multijurisdictional task force, which relied primarily on the efforts of a top-ranking Hells Angels informant. For the first time in history, federal agents were granted access via electronic surveillance to "church meetings," annual motorcycle runs and rallies, and informal criminal discussions. Although this type of access is virtually unheard of, recent reports by law enforcement sources do indicate an increase in testimonial evidence by disgruntled members. Fortunately, such testimony has resulted in convictions of top-ranking bikers (e.g., Harry "Taco" Bowman, international president of the Outlaws; Rejean "Zig-Zag" Lessard, former president of Montreal Hells Angels; and Maurice "Mom" Boucher, president of Quebec Hells Angels).

Factors such as individual prosperity and heightened levels of intragroup violence have apparently weakened organizational bonds of loyalty and brotherhood. As such, an increasing number of turncoats have been successfully employed in prosecutorial capacities by law enforcement agencies. Though their testimonial evidence is highly self-serving, it is unclear whether their primary motivation is fear of incarceration or organizational retaliation; however, it is apparent that many individuals are frightened by intragroup violence and have turned to law enforcement for shelter. Interestingly, OMGs, which so closely resemble traditional organized crime groups and in fact mimic much of their organizational structure, have overlooked the most important lesson: Homicidal dictatorship invariably leads to organizational combustion. Thus, in many cases, the specter of group assassins may supersede the nightmare of incarceration. The Outlaws and the Hells Angels, in particular, have been hard hit by organizational informants. While the testimony of Gary "Apache" Trudeau, Hells Angels hitter extraordinaire, enlightened law enforcement to the internal conflicts among the Hells Angels, the testimony of Outlaw Wayne "Joe Black" Hicks painted a hierarchical portrait of the Outlaw organization. Hicks's testimony was directly responsible for the conviction of international president Harry "Taco" Bowman. Hicks, Bowman's confidante for 14 years, testified that Bowman gave various instructions including the murder of a number of snitches and rivals (Christian, 2001). Hicks's testimony was well received by a Florida court, which imposed a life sentence on Bowman. For his cooperation, Hicks received less than 13 years out of a possible life term. An additional snitch, Glen "Flyball" Clark, president of the Orlando chapter, fared even better for his testimony, receiving time served for a variety of charges including murder, prostitution, and racketeering. Both individuals cited the possibility of life terms and the increasing intragroup violence as justification for their actions. Motivation notwithstanding, it appears that law enforcement authorities are increasingly cognizant of subcultural structure and ideology. While much of this understanding may be attributed to the elevated numbers of organizational informants, private and public information clearinghouses are increasingly important.

Intelligence agencies that focus almost exclusively on outlaw motorcycle gangs are sprouting up across the country. Some intelligence networks are funded through state and/or federal sources, but many of these information repositories are entirely capitalistic in nature; the privatization of intelligence gathering is quite lucrative. Although the majority of public intelligence networks are regional in scope, their purpose is to gather information on narcotics, drug-related offenses, and organizations profiting from illicit substances. These nonprofit organizations compile information from a variety of jurisdictions, both local and federal, and often coordinate multijurisdictional investigations and prosecutions (Lavigne, 1996). As is the case with the Violent Criminal Apprehension Program (VICAP), information may be obtained through modus operandi, aliases, or specific locations. Unfortunately, regional repositories are grossly underutilized. As is the case in many areas of law enforcement, jurisdictional boundaries remain sacrosanct and jealousies abound, so many potential opportunities for prosecution are lost.

CONCLUSIONS

Unlike many gangs, outlaw motorcycle gangs do not share an ethnic identity, but on the average, members are white males from working-class backgrounds. Like many criminal subcultures, outlaw motorcycle gangs are primarily an American phenomenon, though many groups are extending their focus to international alliances. Originally created as fraternal organizations, biker gangs have metamorphosed from a group of vandalizing, beer-swilling hell-raisers to a highly sophisticated, increasingly mainstream organization whose sophisticated criminal structure and entrepreneurial activities rival those of corporate giants such as IBM or organized crime powerhouses such as La Costa Nostra (LCN). Their hierarchical structure and regulatory approach have resulted in unprecedented economic success, and their opportunistic approach further increases their profitability.

Long underestimated by law enforcement authorities, OMGs remain a major player in the narcotics trade. Exhibiting a remarkable aptitude for adaptation, external trappings of organizational affiliation are increasingly passé. On the decline are the leather jackets, long hair, and unkempt appearance; in their place, a more sophisticated and harder-to-identify outlaw biker is emerging. Biker "iron," necessary for membership, is seldom used except in connection with limited club events. Nissan Pathfinders and Ford Explorers are quickly becoming the transportation of choice for club officers. This suburbanite appearance enables OMGs to exist in some communities virtually unnoticed; in fact, this superficial appearance of legitimacy cloaks increasingly sophisticated criminal activities.

Like their Italian counterparts, OMGs are entering legitimate markets at unprecedented levels. Motorcycle repair shops, silk screening businesses, and drinking establishments are but a few examples. These businesses protect both club and personal assets from governmental forfeiture and are titled to club associates or old ladies. Many of these fronts are actually quite successful, due primarily to unlimited capital, low shrinkages, and intimidation tactics. In fact, law-abiding citizens find it impossible to compete in legitimate markets when these illegitimate practices are employed. When given the choice, nongang businesses are forced to choose between unholy alliances and outright extinction. Thus, the existence of OMGs has dire consequences for every segment of society, not just those practicing outside the law.

The majority of OMGs have recently forged international alliances, and all have entered illegal markets around the globe. Official chapters of the Hells Angels, indisputably the largest and most dangerous of all OMGs, have been reported in at least 17 countries, and the Outlaws and the Bandidos are quickly catching up (Lavigne, 1996; SLED, 1997). OMG activity has been reported in England, Germany, Japan, Sweden, and Russia, to name a few. Many of these chapters, perhaps influenced by pop culture, originally mirrored traditional stereotypes and primarily concentrated on street-level criminal behavior; however, recent reports indicate that these groups have quickly followed the lead of the U.S. Hells Angels. Developing elaborate criminal networks and abandoning superficial trappings of association, they are increasingly sophisticated in both their activities and their appearances. International members are also entering leadership positions within the organizational hierarchy; ultimately, however, the power structure is contained within U.S. boundaries.

The unprecedented increase in international chapters may be attributed to Barger's monopolistic approach and the group's propensity for violence. However, this international explosion has not been accomplished without significant growing pains. Increasingly, reports of interchapter fighting dominate "church meetings,"

Changing times: Two Hells Angels at Bike Week. Note the short hair and clean-cut appearance of the member on the right. Various OMG members are becoming more mainstream in their appearance, making it more difficult for law enforcement investigations. In addition, generic state rockers are replacing traditional chapter names as the bottom rocker to thwart law enforcement intelligence gathering.

Courtesy of South Carolina State Law Enforcement Division

and group leadership is struggling to maintain brotherhood among a culturally and socioeconomically diverse membership. Unfortunately for the Hells Angels, cultural and socioeconomic differences are not easily reconciled, and formal rules and regulations are not applicable in all societies. In their ethnocentrism, the U.S. Hells Angels may have sounded their own death knell in societies intolerant of intolerance. Many

TECHNOLOGY AND OUTLAW MOTORCYCLE GANGS

As discussed throughout the chapter, outlaw motorcycle gangs are increasingly sophisticated in both their criminal activity and their physical appearance. They are also more reliant on emerging technology and have computerized many of their operations. Many OMGs, including all of the Big Four, have a variety of formal web pages (although the Pagans' web site is currently "under construction")! These pages identify all of the group's recognized chapters and clearly demonstrate their capacity for globalization:

Bandidos	www.bandidosmc.com
Hells Angels	www.hellsangels.com
Outlaws	www.outlawsmc.com
Pagans	www.pagansmc.com (under construction)

Eastern European countries are so burdened by historical baggage that criminal laws remain secondary to national policy. Indeed, Hamburg and like-minded cities act as an example for U.S. law enforcement: Utilization of antisupremacist statutes grants law enforcement greater latitude in group prosecution and organizational disbandment.

Recent reports by law enforcement authorities indicate a shift in power within the Hells Angels organization. American OMGs appear to be in significant jeopardy from urban street gangs. Designed to protect them from law enforcement scrutiny, their suburbanization has increased their vulnerability to rival gangs. In fact, law enforcement authorities report that the Hells Angels are actually being forced out of areas such as Oakland. Though this hostility appears to be good news for urban authorities, gang mobilization in nonurban areas is anticipated. Many predict that formal power within the organization will move to the southeast region of the United States where competition from other criminal organizations is minimal. In addition, concentrated recruitment efforts have been initiated. Younger members, necessary to revitalize an aging organization, are increasingly targeted in prisons, schoolyards, and drinking establishments.

Presently, outlaw motorcycle gangs are recognized as a strictly organized, highly sophisticated criminal syndicate. Increasingly low key in appearance and activity, OMGs are infiltrating legitimate marketplaces, monopolizing entire industries, and corrupting political officials. Law enforcement efforts have had limited success. Personal convictions of patch-wearing members are increasingly common; however, RICO prosecutions have proven unsuccessful. Though group insularity has weakened in recent years, ties of brotherhood still abound.

ENDNOTES

1. The term "1%" was adopted by outlaw motorcycle gangs in response to a speech given by the president of the American Motorcyclist Association in which he stated that only 1 percent of all motorcycle enthusiasts were criminals. Outlaw motorcycle gangs flaunt their criminal lifestyles by wearing "1%" patches on their colors. Such designation originally served as a unifying symbol for outlaw bikers, but territorial disputes have eroded traditional camaraderie between groups.
2. Although a strict "whites only" policy is found in many organizational charters, there have been isolated exceptions. These exceptions, rare indeed, are extended only to avoid violent resistance among prospective clubs.

CHAPTER 5

SUPREMACISTS

HISTORY

A brief survey of U.S. history reveals unrivaled levels of violence and intolerance. Nepotism, a British trademark and an early foundation of American society, ensured that the prosperity enjoyed by the desirables—white male Anglo-Saxon Protestant (WASP) landowners—continued. Social regulations, legislative mandates, and even religious doctrines granted a foothold for the chosen few. Genocide, as distasteful as it sounds, was used repeatedly to ensure WASP succession. Beginning with the annihilation of Native Americans and continuing long after the abolishment of slavery, American culture reveals a pattern of intolerance inconsistent with democratic ideals. The seemingly limitless selection of white supremacist organizations is a manifestation of such bigotry. Inarguably, these organizations are the most visible and the most long-standing example of racial and religious intolerance on U.S. soil; however, they are not unique in their radical rhetoric and violent practices.

HATE CRIME

Generally speaking, a "hate crime" is a criminal act of violence, criminal mischief, trespass, arson, or intimidation that is committed because of the victim's race, color, religion, ancestry, national origin, political affiliation, gender, sexual orientation, age, and physical or mental disability; however, many states do not provide protection to all of the aforementioned groups, often eliminating gender, sexual orientation, and the disabled from their consideration.

MARTYRS OF THE WHITE SUPREMACIST/MILITIA MOVEMENT

Gordon Kahl

In 1983, Gordon Kahl was killed by Arkansas sheriff Gene Matthews in a shootout. Kahl, an ardent member of the Posse Comitatus, had previously been involved in the shooting deaths of two U.S. marshalls and the wounding of several others. Declaring that government above the county level was not only repressive but inherently unconstitutional, Kahl refused to acknowledge the legitimacy of the Internal Revenue Service. His failure to comply with taxation laws resulted in the initial confrontation with law enforcement authorities. Supremacist and militia groups have promoted the incident as an example of the abuse of the federal government. Ironically, Kahl was killed by a representative of the only level of government that he recognized.

Randy Weaver

In 1991, Randy Weaver was charged with selling two shotguns that were one-quarter-inch shorter than the legal limit. After an extensive surveillance of 18 months by the Bureau of Alcohol, Tobacco, and Firearms (BATF), U.S. Marshall William Degan, 14-year-old Samuel Weaver, and his dog were killed during a shootout. Kevin Harris, a family friend, alerted the Weavers, who collected Samuel's body. After a lengthy standoff, FBI snipers wounded Randy Weaver and Kevin Harris. During the gunfire, Randy's wife, Vicky, was shot and killed while cradling her 10-month-old infant. Weaver and Harris were eventually charged and acquitted of the murder of Degan. Weaver's family was awarded more than $3 million in a subsequent civil suit.

David Koresh

On April 19, 1993, at least 80 individuals, including 22 children, were killed at a rural retreat in Waco, Texas. The group's leader, David Koresh (formerly known as Vernon Howell), was a self-proclaimed messiah who claimed to have the answers to salvation. The incidents leading to the massacre remain questionable. Government reports indicate that 4 federal agents were killed while attempting to serve a warrant for weapons violations. After a 51-day standoff, the government, armed with CS gas and tanks, entered the compound. In the melee, Koresh and the majority of his followers were killed. Subsequently, 11 Branch Davidians were tried for the murder of the 4 agents. During the trial, the defense relied heavily on a 911 tape in which the Branch Davidians were heard pleading with the dispatcher to halt the firing because children were at risk. The anguished cries of victims and the wailing of children intermingle with the sound of gunfire. All defendants were acquitted of the most serious charges. Militias and supremacists perceive the incidents at Waco to be indicative of an increasingly secretive and violent government—one that preys on its citizens. In fact, many individuals believe that the date of the Oklahoma City bombing was carefully planned to coincide with the anniversary of the Waco massacre.

MARTYRS OF THE BLACK MILITANT MOVEMENT

Elmer "Geronimo" Pratt

In 1972, former Black Panther Geronimo Pratt was convicted of the murder of Carolyn Olsen, a 27-year-old schoolteacher in Santa Monica. Pratt's attorney, Johnny Cochran of O. J. Simpson fame, argued that prosecutors withheld key evidence in the original trial in a successful attempt by the FBI to frame Pratt. The defense contended that the government's key witness, Julius Butler, was jealous of Pratt's position within the party and joined forces with the government in order to convict an innocent man. Bolstered by the FBI's counterintelligence program (COINTELPRO), aimed at undermining radicals, Pratt's conviction was primarily based on eyewitness testimony from the slain woman's husband. This testimony, coupled with the absence of alibi witnesses (not a single Black Panther testified on Pratt's behalf), resulted in a life sentence. In 1997, Pratt was awarded a new trial due to the efforts of Cochran and Jay McCloskey, whose Centurion Ministries, based in Princeton, New Jersey, specialize in exonerating those wrongly convicted.

Mumia Abu Jamal

In 1981, Mumia Abu Jamal (aka Wesley Cook) was sentenced to death in the shooting death of Philadelphia police officer Daniel Faulkner. Jamal, a former minister of information for the Black Panther Party, has long alleged that the Philadelphia Police Department had intentionally framed him for the murder of Officer Faulkner due to his vocal condemnations regarding the city's MOVE fiasco. A radical print and radio journalist, Jamal has attracted an array of celebrities to his cause. His supporters argue that the city used intimidation tactics to coerce witnesses; they further argue that Jamal's political ideology sealed his fate. Jamal's case has mobilized individuals across the world, and protests have been staged as far away as Paris. In addition, many celebrities have vowed their support for Jamal. On October 29, 1998, the Supreme Court of Pennsylvania denied Jamal's petition for postconviction relief. As the U.S. Supreme Court has previously denied certiorari, it is anticipated that a new date will be set for Jamal's execution.

MOVE

On May 13, 1985, six adults and five children were killed and more than 50 homes were destroyed in Philadelphia after law enforcement officials used incendiary devices while effecting an arrest. These devices (reportedly containing large amounts of C-4 were dropped on the roof of the MOVE headquarters. Neighborhood houses and non-MOVE residents were devastated by the resulting fire, which was allowed to burn undeterred for several hours. Ramona Africa, widow of the group's leader, argues that their group was targeted for annihilation due to their militant posturing. She argues that the group was actually a nonviolent resistance

(continued)

(continued)

group, driven to violence by white authorities. (Nine members of the group were charged in a 1978 incident in which a Philadelphia police officer was shot and killed.) Under Ramona Africa's leadership, the group has been actively involved in the black militant movement. They have been quite vocal in their support of individuals "wrongfully convicted," such as Mumia Abu Jamal.

Contrary to media depictions, white supremacists are not the sole proprietors of racist dogma. Although their continued longevity and subversive ideology are a great concern to contemporary law enforcement, the real danger lies in overlooking their nonwhite counterparts and the increasing popularity of antiestablishment sentiment, white and black. Long characterized as a white phenomenon, supremacist ideology among nonwhite groups has often been underestimated or entirely overlooked, but membership increases in organizations such as the Black Muslims, a glorification of racist antiestablishment groups such as the Black Panthers, and a revisitation of the 1960s signal a revival of racist violence among nonwhite organizations. While the Nation of Islam may appear to have little in common with the Ku Klux Klan, their apparent differences are far outweighed by their similarities.

Both traditional and contemporary supremacist organizations have espoused anti-Semitic ideology. Bolstered by religious frameworks, these two groups share a common enemy—those of Jewish ancestry. Branding Jews as slayers of Christ or infidels, respectively, these groups are extremely successful in inciting anti-Semitic violence. In addition, contemporary supremacist organizations, race notwithstanding, effectively target governmental institutions and figures by depicting them as a product of Jewish establishments and conspiracies. Indeed, many traditional white supremacist groups have refocused their attention on what they term "Zionist-occupied government" (ZOG). Driven by hate, these groups are increasingly dangerous.[1] Their insidious nature is only intensified through their recruitment of young males.

Both white and nonwhite supremacist organizations have traditionally targeted American youths, especially economically disadvantaged youths, due to their malleable nature (see Figure 5–1). In fact, manipulation and exploitation of disillusioned generations have granted adult members the luxury of legitimization while bastardizing their young members. Free from "fund-raising" responsibilities (i.e., criminal activities), many adult members have successfully attained political positions and developed legitimate platforms that are palatable to mainstream America but are lacking in intent and substance. This superficial legitimacy is perhaps the greatest danger to U.S. society. Like their predecessors, contemporary racists minimize radical dogma while maximizing mainstream appeal. This is most easily accomplished through the promotion of derogatory stereotypes that negatively magnify cultural differences.

It must be noted that while the techniques employed by contemporary supremacists are deeply rooted in traditional organizations, their modes of communication and propaganda have advanced significantly. Relying on technological advancements, such as

Black brothers are tired of the white man in black communities.

Brothers and sisters deal with the white store owner that robs black people.

The junior Panther defends his mother.

Figure 5–1 Black Panther Coloring Book. Although the Panthers argued that theirs was a self-defense movement, many of the group's publications proved to be most proactive. The above are reproductions of images that appeared in the infamous *Black Panther Coloring Book,* which was allegedly created by the Black Panther Party to indoctrinate children with their ideology. However, the Panthers have long disavowed any knowledge of its creation, claiming that the book was published by the federal government to discredit the Panthers' movement. Interestingly, the FBI also claims no knowledge of the book's creation.

computer bulletin boards and Internet web sites, both white and black supremacists have successfully propelled their organizations into the twenty-first century, radically enhancing outdated recruitment instruments. Coupled with bleak economic and occupational projections, this strategy has resulted in an increase in youth involvement. In addition, a climate of political inconsistency, which simultaneously praises and criticizes issues such as affirmative action, has created an atmosphere conducive to supremacist ideologies on both sides. This antagonism, though not unique to contemporary society, has reached proportions similar to those of the late 1960s and early 1970s. Thus, before reviewing contemporary supremacist gangs, a discussion of the roots of such racist ideology and the precursors to current racist organizations is required.

SELECTIVE IGNORANCE—JUSTIFYING RACISM

Virtually all supremacist groups deny the contributions of other races. White supremacist ideology in the United States, for example, credits all technological inventions, literary masterpieces, and philosophical insights to white Americans. Like the majority of their ideology, this belief decries the very existence of the American fabric. As one author so eloquently puts it:

> [N]o one racial or ethic group established the United States. Mostly Scots-Irish pioneered the eastern mountains, Germans built the covered wagons that carried American pioneers of all nationalities to new homes around the continent, Swedes taught them all to build the log cabins they lived in when they got there. Mostly Chinese and Irish workers laid the tracks of the great intercontinental railroads that bound the country together in the nineteenth century. The labor of black slaves from Africa formed the basis for southern prosperity before the Civil War, and freed black men and women formed the base of the southern labor force in the century that followed. And all the while, wave after wave of immigrants from around the world were fueling American industry with their labor (Kronenwetter, 1992: 10).

MALCOLM X AND THE NATION OF ISLAM

> I've never seen a sincere white man.
> White people are born devils by nature.
> Black, brown, red, yellow, all are brothers, all are one family. The white one is a stranger. He's the odd fellow.
> Thoughtful white people know they are inferior to black people.
> The time is near when the white man will be finished. The signs are all around us.

Like Martin Luther King, Jr., Malcolm Little (aka Malik Shabazz, aka El-Hajj Malik El Shabazz, aka Malcolm X) perceived himself as a religious leader. They were both born black in a time when racial harmony did not, and could not, exist, and both were sons of Baptist ministers. Both men characterized American society as inherently racist and discriminatory. Both were extremely charismatic, and they touched thousands of lives, and both were struck down in the prime of life by assassins' bullets. These similarities, however, were superficial at best, overwhelmed by ideological differences and incompatible lifestyles. At age 26, King completed his doctorate in systematic theology, became a minister of his own congregation, and began a lifelong involvement in the civil rights movement. Malcolm, on the other hand, was completing a sentence of 8–10 years for burglary at Norfolk Prison Colony. A self-avowed atheist prior to his incarceration, Malcolm, like so many inmates, found God (in his case, Allah), and this most personal discovery proved to be monumental in its consequences.

Following the teachings of Elijah Muhammad (aka Elijah Poole, aka Elijah Karriem), the self-proclaimed divine prophet, Malcolm denounced whites as "devils," a race genetically engineered by the mad scientist, Yacub, to punish Allah and his followers. Red (Native American) and yellow (Asian) people were by-products of the engineering process. These assertions, inconsistent with traditional Islamic teachings, not only promulgated an attitude of superiority but served as a justification for any violence directed at infidels (i.e., white or Jewish Americans). Seeking to increase both individual visibility and organizational credibility, Malcolm immersed himself in the works of the world's most prominent philosophers, such as Nietzsche, Pliny, and Thoreau. His usage of their words and theories within casual and formal discourse earned him the recognition of the media, the government, and Muhammad. But most importantly, his articulate style and militant posturing gained him a most ardent following among black youth. These youth delighted when Malcolm said Kennedy's assassination was "a case of the chickens coming home to roost" and characterized the death of 120 white passengers on a flight from the United States to Paris as "good news" (X and Haley, 1964: 305). This ideology was exactly what young black males in urban poverty were seeking. Unfortunately for Malcolm, these statements, so cavalier yet consistent, signaled his exile from the Nation of Islam.[2]

Malcolm's banishment from the Nation, coupled with a pilgrimage to Mecca, appeared to soften both Malcolm's actions and his rhetoric.[3] This new Malcolm (or El-Hajj Malik El Shabazz, as he now called himself) stressed religious rather than racial brotherhood. His new organization, Organization of Afro-American Unity (OAAU), lacked consistency and was denounced by militants as too moderate and by moderates as too militant. In many circles, he was branded a hypocrite. Indeed, while arguing that his was a nonviolent, strictly self-defensive group, he stated that his followers had to "be ready to go to jail, to the hospital, and to the cemetery"; he further asserted that he would send "armed guerrillas into Mississippi," after classifying anything south of Canada as Mississippi (X and Haley, 1964: 418). On February 21, 1965, Malcolm X was shot to death in front of his family at the Audubon Ballroom by his former "brothers" of the Nation of Islam.[4] Malcolm's physical death did not result in the demise of his spiritual message; in fact, his death served as a rallying point for many young black males and initiated splinter black supremacist/antiestablishment gangs.

Current State of the Nation of Islam

As stated, the Nation of Islam was and still is particularly attractive for young black males in low-income (predominantly urban) areas. Outlining certain unrealistic expectations, its platform is consistent with many international terrorist organizations.

Like those in street gangs, members find safety in numbers and display a propensity for violence. Furthermore, this ideology eliminates individual responsibility and rationalizes economic and social failures in African-American communities. By promoting conspiracy theories and declaring white society the work of Satan, members are freed from personal responsibility. In and of themselves, these tenets are especially appealing to urban black youth who feel rejected by society. Like traditional street gang members, who perceive legitimate avenues of economic success closed, Black Muslims denounce established institutions of authority. Both groups share perceptions of governmental persecution and harassment, both groups use violence without hesitation, and both groups are extremely dangerous. Thus, both groups are a primary concern of local law enforcement; however, with its heightened focus, charismatic leaders, and definitive targets, the Nation of Islam promises to have organizational longevity, a characteristic not necessarily shared by street gangs. This variable, coupled with the ability of the Nation of Islam to disguise extremist rhetoric as political or intellectual discourse, has the greatest national implications because it creates a facade of legitimacy.

Unlike his predecessor who openly advocated guerilla-type tactics, Louis Farrakhan sends a message of racial supremacy that is neatly packaged into a social policy platform. To a casual observer, it may even appear that Farrakhan is embracing concepts of personal accountability. (After all, his Million Man March called for black males to take responsibility for their offspring.) But a more careful analysis of his teaching reveals traditional notions of government conspiracies and blue-eyed, blond devils. In essence, then, it is not the platform or even the militancy that has changed within these organizations, only their methods.

Following is a compilation of the 10 most frequently cited conciliatory requirements for Black Muslims (the Nation of Islam holiday wish list):[5]

1. We want freedom. We want a full and complete freedom.

2. We want justice. Equal justice under the law. We want justice under the law. We want justice applied equally to all, regardless of creed or class or color.

3. We want equality of opportunity. We want equal membership in society with the best in civilized society.

4. We want our people, . . . whose parents or grandparents were descendants from slaves, to be allowed to establish a separate state . . . either on this continent or elsewhere. We believe that our former slave masters are obligated to provide such land and that the area must be fertile and minerally rich . . . [and] maintain and supply our needs in this territory for 20–25 years.

5. We want freedom for all Believers of Islam now held in federal prisons . . . for all black men and women under death sentence.

6. We want an end to the police brutality and mob attacks.

7. As long as we are not allowed to establish a state or territory of our own, we demand not only equal justice under the laws of the United States, but equal employment opportunities NOW.

8. We want the government of the United States to exempt our people from ALL taxation.

9. We want equal education—separate schools up to 16 for boys and 18 for girls on the condition that the girls be sent to women's colleges and universities. We want all black children educated, taught, and trained by their own teachers.

10. We believe that intermarriage or race mixing should be prohibited.

These demands begin rather benignly and are, in fact, somewhat reasonable. Certainly few Americans wish to deny equal justice or equal employment opportunities, nor do the majority of Americans accept practices of police brutality or mob lynching. Indeed, these principles are noncontroversial on their face; however, the latter tenets are predicated on perceptions of societal persecution and smack of racism. Black Muslims advocate the release of ALL black criminals, and they argue that any criminal act perpetrated by an African-American is justifiable. They further believe that the federal government owes them land, property, and wealth as well as the choice of an independent nation and government. They also believe that African-Americans should be exempt from taxation because the existing government is neither representative nor legitimate. Ironically, they also call for legislation imposed by this illegitimate government that would outlaw interracial marriages. This antiestablishment dogma, based on religious doctrines, is essentially identical to that of other African-American hate groups, white supremacists, and a number of militia groups across the country. Unfortunately, black supremacist groups such as the Nation of Islam and the Black Panther Party are not considered to be as noteworthy of surveillance as they once were. This oversight and reallocation of government resources accord black militants the freedom to spew their hatred unchecked, inciting antiestablishment rage and seducing many African-American youths.

It may be argued that many of these young black males are not aware of or even concerned with the fundamental religious and political principles of the Nation of Islam. Economic depression, increasing threats of street violence, shrinking job market, and lack of educational opportunities promote feelings of despair among urban minorities; this sense of futility creates a need for identification and belonging and increases their vulnerability to subversive organizations and pro-violence dogma. Traditionally, criminal street gangs have filled the void in these communities. Increasingly, however, a revisitation of 1960s culture has been promoted by the popular media (e.g., movies such as *Panther* and *Malcolm X*), the legal community (e.g., the freeing of Geronimo Pratt and appellate proceedings of Mumia Abu Jamal), and individual families (i.e., today's parents are yesterday's survivors). A resurgence of black nationalism and/or militance appears to be a foregone conclusion, one that the majority of Americans appear to have missed.

BLACK PANTHERS

> I want 30 police stations blown up, one southern governor, two mayors, and 500 cops dead (James Foreman, prominent Panther leader).

The Panthers held a national attraction for the young...who had been tempered in the crucible of ghetto life (Burns, 1971: xv). Like their Black Muslim counterparts, the Black Panther Party gained national attention in the civil rights era. Founded in Oakland in 1966 by Bobby Seale and Huey Newton, the Black Panther Party for Self-Defense expanded the premises set forth by Robert Williams, leader of the North Carolina–based Deacons for Self-Defense and author of *Negroes with Guns*. Their militant approach, which focused recruitment efforts on young black males, and original platform were markedly similar to those of the Nation of Islam, with one critical distinction: The Black Panther Party held no particular religious affiliation. This divergence greatly enhanced the marketability of the Panthers among the younger generation "who were looking for someplace to channel their anger and frustration about life" (Pearson, 1994: 45). The absence of religion was especially attractive to preadults chafing under parental restraint and reluctant to denounce pleasurable activities that were finally within their reach. The Panthers also freely enjoyed the increasing tide of anger and resentment within black communities, the culmination of the Nation of Islam's tireless efforts and costly sacrifices.

Unlike their sharply dressed and increasingly articulate counterparts, the Panthers adopted uniforms consistent with their "revolutionary" movement. Garbed in black leather jackets, black berets, and dark glasses and with ammunition draped over their shoulders, they patrolled the urban streets wreaking havoc on the sensibilities of white community residents. In many respects, their tactics were similar to ones employed by an older supremacist organization, the Ku Klux Klan. Like the Klan, they randomly selected their victims based on race. Like the Klan, which recently identified the federal government as its enemy, the Panthers had a history of antigovernment dogma, openly sympathizing with North Vietnam during the conflict in Southeast Asia. Furthermore, both groups have the same interpretation of the Second Amendment. In fact, a heavily armed Panther contingent entered the California legislature in 1967 to protest the Mulford Act, an early gun-control bill, long before militia groups became popular among white supremacists.

Two further incidents in 1967 propelled the Panthers into the national spotlight and earned them the prominence in the youth community they desired. The first was inadvertently initiated by black organizations in the Bay area and black elected officials across California. Although they had not yet gained credibility in the eyes of other black groups, the Panthers were called on to serve as security detail for Malcolm X's widow, Betty Shabazz. This act, misconstrued by many, did not signal their arrival in the legitimate black community. On the contrary, the Nation of Islam's leaders, unwilling to take responsibility for Shabazz's safety, called on the most expendable and least desirable organization, the Black Panthers. In fact, these

HUEY NEWTON: THE MAN, THE MYTH, THE MONSTER

In 1966, Huey Newton and Bobby Seale founded the Black Panther Party for Self-Defense. Initially, Newton and Seale argued that the group's primary purpose was to increase the standard of living in black urban areas; to their credit, they did organize a number of community programs designed to provide basic necessities for community residents. However, many contemporary authors overlook the vicious criminal enterprises that funded the programs and the theft of legitimate contributions by its founders. Recent Hollywood interpretations, for example, glorify Newton as a defender of the disadvantaged, using violence as a last resort. Nothing could be further from the truth.

Charged with his first murder in 1967, Newton became a national hero. The murder of Oakland police officer John Frey was considered justified by many and was consistent with the antiestablishment ideology sweeping the country. Incited by images of racist police action in the South, Newton came to symbolize governmental oppression, and his release on a technicality in 1970 was touted as a victory in the war to revolutionize American institutions. This hero worship, it appears, was sorely misplaced.

After his release from prison, Newton had an escalating drug problem that was outpaced only by his murderous temper. He routinely assaulted individuals, including Party members, forcing many of them to quit. He even assaulted his lifelong friend and cofounder, Bobby Seale. In fact, "Newton dramatically beat Seale with a bullwhip and sodomized him so violently that his anus had to be surgically repaired by a physician" (Pearson, 1994: 72). Within two weeks, Newton attacked and killed Kathleen Smith, a 17-year-old prostitute who made the mistake of calling him "Baby." Unfortunately, his arrest was not soon enough to prevent three other attacks.

As stated, Newton's violence was directed at both members and nonmembers. A staff member at the Lamp Post was the recipient of a beating so severe that it knocked her glass eye right out of her head. Shortly thereafter, Newton attacked a female customer of the same establishment for "getting smart" with his bodyguard. Later the same day, Newton pistol-whipped his tailor for making the same mistake as Smith; the tailor received four skull fractures and underwent neurosurgery for his poor choice.

Newton, charged with a variety of crimes including the murder of Smith, fled to Cuba in 1974 and remained there until 1977.* Newton's reemergence was well planned. He quickly intimidated his former tailor and plotted to kill the sole witness to his murder of Kathleen Smith. Unfortunately for Newton, his selection of assassins was poor and eventually led to the Panther Party's demise.

A bungled assassination attempt left one Panther dead and one wounded. Nelson Malloy, the paramedic who treated the wound, was taken to Las Vegas,

(continued)

(continued)

where he was summarily shot and left for dead. Discovered under a pile of rocks by two tourists, Malloy, permanently paralyzed, told investigators and the media that the failed attempt signaled Newton's effort to destroy any links between the botched assassination and Newton. For the first time, the Panthers were unable to blame law enforcement sources, and even Newton's elite squad of enforcers abandoned ship.

Although Newton escaped conviction in the Kathleen Smith murder, he experienced legal problems until his death. Oddly enough, the majority of these charges were not connected with his vicious behavior; rather, they included charges of fiduciary wrongdoing, more consistent with contemporary definitions of white-collar crimes. Newton was killed in 1989 during an argument over drugs. In fact, some have argued that Newton's death was long overdue.

*In his absence, Elaine Brown assumed the helm. Unfortunately, Brown displayed a level of violence and militance only slightly lower than Newton's. In her short reign, several bodies surfaced, including that of her former bookkeeper, Betty Van Patter.

leaders, frightened by the group's militant stance and menacing appearance, were probably hoping for a most public failure. Instead, this incident propelled the Panthers into the forefront of the racial conflict and gained them a most important supporter, Eldridge Cleaver, the author of one of the nation's first radical journals (Pearson, 1994).

The second incident that had a tremendous impact on the younger generation was the arrest of Panther cofounder Huey Newton. Newton, arrested for the murder of a white police officer, soon became a symbol for American youth in general.[6] Panther chapters were developed in 48 states and many international locations. In fact, antigovernment youth gangs seemed to sprout in every community, regardless of race, economics, or religion. "Free Huey" was their motto, the Black Panther Party their model. Although the majority of these youth gangs proved to be short-lived, this unprecedented unification of American youth across racial, gender, religious, and economic lines was most significant (Pearson, 1994). The specter of omnipotence no longer immobilized the younger generation, and for the first time in history, America's youth developed a collective generational consciousness. A group realization that erupted into violence laid the foundation for contemporary antiestablishment ideology.

Many of these groups perceived the development of the Black Panthers as a long-overdue movement to demand restitution and ensure racial equality. Riding the crest of their newfound popularity, the Panther Party developed social programs in poor urban communities. These initiatives, benignly referred to as "Survival

Programs," appeared to be a straightforward attempt to increase the standard of living in minority communities. In reality, however, the militant stance of the Panthers and their proclivity for violence remained; these Survival (pending revolution) Programs were nothing if not self-serving. Educational initiatives, touted as enrichment programs, were actually more akin to platform indoctrination. The Free Breakfast for Children Program was actually initiated by a Catholic church in San Francisco and existed long before and long after the Panthers' wave of popularity. Other programs claimed by the Panthers appeared to be funded by magical fairies, because no governmental resources were allocated and few recognizable benefactors were identified. In retrospect, these programs were probably funded by the deluge of money gained through the Panthers' various criminal enterprises, activities they vehemently denied (Pearson, 1994).

Like many ethnic gangs before and since, the Panthers usually victimized businesses and residents in their own communities. Extortion and armed robbery, group favorites, appeared to have been their primary sources of income. Originally, the Panthers publicly endorsed these activities, claiming that they were the only opportunity available because of white oppression. Eventually seeking legitimacy, however, they quickly distanced themselves from members formally charged with these offenses and publicly disavowed any involvement in criminal activity. In reality, this public condemnation was superficial at best. Contrary to their public posturing, the Panthers continued their intimidation of neighborhood businesses, demanding "support" for their survivor programs, but any support other than cash advances, which were often used to support Newton's drug habit, were refused. Businesses not cooperating with Newton were quickly targeted for foreclosure. This intimidation, coupled with Newton's homicidal tendencies, resulted in the exodus of many adult members from the group. This flow was only temporarily stemmed when Newton fled to Cuba to escape prosecution for murder.

During Newton's self-imposed Cuban exile, Elaine Brown took over at the Panthers' helm. Although Brown successfully obtained mainstream political favor and governmental recognition for her efforts, her public benevolence was merely a facade. Indeed, Brown was akin to a pampered rottweiler with her propensity for viciousness hidden behind perfectly coiffed hair and painted fingernails. Brown's violence, like Newton's, was not restricted to outsiders. In fact, Brown was only slightly less violent than her predecessor. Brown's advocation of violence and lack of genteel sensibilities, however, proved futile in her quest to control the Panthers. Characterized by heightened levels of traditional gender stratification, many of the Party's younger members—especially Newton's elite squad of enforcers—rejected their female figurehead. This misogyny led to Newton's return and the Panther Party's demise (Foner 1995; Pearson, 1994).

Upon Newton's return, many of the Panther Party's most prominent leaders, such as Bobby Seale, Stokely Carmichael, and David Hilliard, abandoned the movement and developed groups of their own. Newton's elite squad, comprising primarily young black males, proved to be a bit more resilient; however, Newton's erratic behavior eventually distanced even the most ardent of his supporters. Following Newton's assassination attempt of two Panther enforcers, the remaining fanatical youths abandoned ship. The majority of these disillusioned youths joined other militant organizations, such as the Black Muslims or the Black Guerilla Family, or continued their criminal behavior unsponsored.

Many reports date the Black Panther Party's waterloo sometime in the late 1970s. This characterization obscures the continuing interest in black militancy and the Black Panther Party in the United States. In 1989, for example, more than 10,000 mourners attended the funeral of Huey Newton; many even paid their respects to the site of the drug-related murder. This resurgence also led to the republication of the Panthers' official party newspaper in 1991. Furthermore, many contemporary pop stars glorify Newton as a martyr, emulating his militance and posturing.[7] As is often the case in historical revisitations, negative characteristics are glossed over or ignored. Unfortunately, the impact of the popular media, and the revisionist accounts they promote, is often underestimated.

BLACK GUERILLA FAMILY AND BLACK PRISON GANGS

Although prison gangs have existed in U.S. correctional institutions since their inception, most are founded as defensive mechanisms, with promises of protection and insulation for their members. This basic definition does not suggest that the violent behavior they express is entirely reactionary; in fact, many of the more powerful gangs actively initiate violence toward other inmates. Much of this violence is executed as a demonstration of force. In addition, the majority of this activity appears to be racially motivated, usually targeting outsiders. However, the majority of prison gangs (e.g., the Mexican Mafia and the Nuestra Family) lack ideological consistency beyond the boundaries of racial awareness. One notable exception to this rule is the Black Guerilla Family (BGF).

Founded by former Panther George Jackson, the Black Guerilla Family originated at San Quentin in 1966. Originally, the BGF was developed as an ancillary arm of the Black Panther Party. Its ideological framework, consistent with a Maoist philosophy, encouraged political activism on the part of its members. This "activism" included assaults, rapes, and murders of nonblack inmates and prison officials. Like other prison gangs, the BGF has established partnerships with other nonideological gangs such as the Black Liberation Army. Both of these groups have aggressively recruited street gang members and have been successful in creating complex criminal networks. The recruitment of individuals from established street gangs, such as the Crips and the Bloods, has enabled the BGF to gain outside support. While this group's primary power remains ensconced within prison boundaries, the effect of supremacist indoctrination remains to be seen.

SIMILARITIES AMONG BLACK SUPREMACIST GANGS

Although popular media accounts negate the existence of racist ideology by nonwhites, the gangs already mentioned are but a few examples of nonwhite supremacist organizations in the United States. While supremacist movements appear to be sporadic and short-lived, experience suggests that the ideological frameworks guiding their actions are not. Too often, racial violence, especially violence initiated by minorities, is miscategorized as random street crime and the seriousness of its implications overlooked. Like its white counterpart, black supremacy has traditionally been characterized by intergroup conflict and competing recruitment strategies; nevertheless, underlying similarities between these organizations have resulted in ideological longevity and sporadic increases in popular support.

Inarguably, black militance is most prevalent during periods of economic depression and political persecution. Like their predecessors, contemporary militant/nationalist gangs are fortified by religious ideologies and political dogma. Subsequently, these groups remain overwhelmingly patriarchal. Without exception, these groups share platforms of equality for all men; women are not included. In keeping with religious teachings, these groups advocate a return to "traditional" family values. The most recent example, Farrakhan's Million Man March, called for black males to take responsibility for their offspring, but this seemingly benign platform masked traditional inflammatory rhetoric espoused by Farrakhan and other supremacists.

These organizations, both traditional and contemporary, are extremely hierarchical in nature. Their bureaucratic approach is responsible for both the popularity and the legitimacy these groups enjoy. Garnering political support, these groups effectively camouflage their militant posturing in ideological rhetoric. This capability is directly responsible for societal indulgence and organizational forbearance. Effectively bridging generational differences, these groups maintain economic patronage from adult groups while enhancing their appeal to disadvantaged youth.

By concentrating their recruitment efforts on those most vulnerable, both traditional and contemporary organizations have successfully amassed a group of violent individuals, seemingly expendable in nature. Proclaiming self-empowerment and equality for all, black youths are manipulated and sacrificed like pawns in a conflict for mature audiences only. Often recruited while incarcerated, criminal-minded and/or violent youths are targeted. In addition, black militant groups mimic the efforts of their white supremacist counterparts, utilizing communication and technological advancements to recruit young members. Antiwhite, anti-Semitic, and antiestablishment dogma permeates cyberspace and pervades the most innocuous of documents. Queries about black leaders, scholars, investors, or historians, for example, often result in propagandist Internet addresses or links. Unfortunately, much of this literature is passed off and interpreted as legitimate. The result is more than an avenue of revolutionary rhetoric; it is an ideological and increasingly violent battleground, one with no definitive boundaries or targets.

THE IMPACT OF 9/11

The tragedies of 9/11 are being used by racists to support their closed borders dogma and anti-Israel rhetoric by suggesting that the attacks were directly attributed to our support of Israel:

> [September 11 was a] result of the U.S. government acting on behalf of the Jews instead of on behalf of the American people (www.nationalalliance.com, accessed September 13, 2001).

Indeed, these radical groups even exhibit admiration for the terrorists:

> The enemy is, for now at least, our friends. We may not want them marrying our daughters, just as they would not want us marrying theirs. We may not want them in our societies, just as they would not want [us in] theirs. But anyone who is willing to drive a plane into a building to kill Jews is alright by me. I wish our members had half as much testicular fortitude (www.nationalalliance.com banner, accessed September 13, 2001).

WHITE SUPREMACIST GROUPS

Unlike their black counterparts, which have traditionally concentrated on antiestablishment ideologies and are a relatively new phenomenon in American society, white supremacist groups have a history of intolerance only slightly shorter than our country's existence. An evaluation of U.S. culture reveals a pattern of intolerance inconsistent with the much-espoused notion of the melting pot society. The eradication of entire tribes of Native Americans and the persecution and execution of religious dissidents are just two of many examples of such intolerance. In a society in which government expresses racially intolerant policies, it is not surprising that racist subcultures often emerge. Such dogma, however, was not originally formulated on American soil; rather, its roots may be traced back to fifteenth- and sixteenth-century Europe.

In the 1600s, racism emerged as a result of colonialism. While these great European nations were militarily equipped to handle such expansion, their homogeneous populations were not socially sophisticated enough to accept an influx of alternative cultures. Without question, European colonists proved to be militarily and scientifically more advanced than many native cultures they encountered. Such technical superiority reaffirmed their perceptions of cultural and racial superiority. Indeed, an ideology emerged within the growing European community that they were naturally and genetically superior to all other races; thus, other races were classified as subhuman. These assumptions were used as a justification for the massive exploitation that followed throughout Europe and the New World. Slavery, for example, was not caused by racism but was simply justified by it (Kronenwetter, 1992).[8] Interestingly, such perceptions were not reserved for those cultures that were militarily defeated but were directed at any non-WASP culture.

Contrary to historical reconstruction, racism in the United States has never been confined to the South. Indeed, the first wave of anti-immigrant sentiment was expressed in the 1840s as individuals from Ireland, Scandinavia, and Germany arrived en masse. Because many spoke heavily accented English and others spoke no English at all, immigrants routinely were characterized as ignorant. Such characterizations enabled the majority group to deny equality to minorities. The fact that many of these newcomers were non-Christian or non-Protestant did little to ease their plight, as they were branded as heretics. Such depictions led to increased discrimination, forcing such groups to live amid squalid conditions in abject poverty. Unfortunately, these living conditions led to disease, reaffirming the incumbent belief that these ethnicities were naturally unclean and thus more prone to medical afflictions, which then threatened the whole populace. In 1850, in an attempt to protect the status quo, nativists formed a secret society named the Supreme Order of the Star-Spangled Banner. By its own account, the group sought to "rid the United States of 'foreign' ideas and influences . . . [and] keep all 'foreigners' and Catholics from holding political offices" (Kronenwetter, 1992: 15). Since that time, cultural intolerance, often manifested in targeted violence, is often predicated on religious ideologies.

White supremacist groups proclaim that their ideology is derived from biblical teachings.

Courtesy of Charleston, South Carolina, Police Department

Like many nonracists, hatemongers often use principles of Christianity and the Bible selectively. Citing only those passages that superficially support notions of homophobia, racism, and anti-Semitism, these hate groups recite selections religiously, using God's "word" as a justification for attacks on nonbelievers. Like their antigovernment counterparts, these gangs seem to focus exclusively on the Old Testament while proclaiming themselves to be chosen by the Savior found only in the text of the New Testament. Unfortunately, these much-espoused ideologies mask the sociological factors that contribute to this type of violent fanaticism and fail to elucidate current patterns of youth involvement.

As stated, racial and religious intolerance appears to be an American mainstay; however, contemporary organizations are more likely to have large numbers of juvenile members. Sociologists argue that this trend may be attributed to the increasing uncertainty of future job opportunities, an increase in civil disorder in general, and the desensitization to violence. Throughout history, periods of economic depression have invariably resulted in elevated levels of subversive dogma. Traditionally, however, these periods of fiscal deflation impacted mature members of society while leaving teens, who often filled unskilled labor positions and menial jobs, unscathed. For the first time in U.S. history, predictions are that future generations will not achieve or even maintain the economic levels enjoyed by their parents. This bleak projection, coupled with increasingly graphic violence, racial conflict in schools, and availability of hate-oriented material on the Internet, has promulgated a sense of despair among many adolescents and increased their susceptibility to iconoclastic doctrines (Southern Poverty Law Center, 1997). This vulnerability has resulted in two significant developments in the white supremacist movement: (1) replenishment of dwindling resources in traditional hate organizations (e.g., Ku Klux Klan and Aryan Nations) hard hit by criminal prosecution and civil liability, and (2) emergence of loosely formed, increasingly violent youth gangs.

Ku Klux Klan

> [T]he success of anti-Semitism stemmed from the patness of the explanation it offered for the Klansman's anxieties: his fear of racial mixing, his financial and social insecurity, and his xenophobia (Chalmers, 1965: 352).
>
> Klaverns worked better when they could get down to local business ... members might differ in their alarm about the Jews, the international bankers ... but the pressures of Negro integration gave them a point of common concern (Chalmers, 1965: 353).

The most recognized and most flamboyant of all supremacist organizations, the Ku Klux Klan (KKK) has historically been the poster child for hate groups across the country. Inarguably, the Klan has been the most powerful of all supremacist organizations. Its tactics, both overt and covert, have ranged from business blockades to church fires to murder. Their influence on U.S. history cannot be overstated. Their history, intrinsically woven into the American fabric, has seen periods characterized by unquestionable political power interspersed with intervals of torpid infirmity. Perhaps most noted for their habit of burning crosses and wearing satin robes, the KKK has most recently been characterized by shock television as uneducated, misinformed buffoons whose greatest danger to the American public is a possible increase in dry cleaning prices. This characterization, lacking any historical overview, masks the danger of an organized group of violent individuals with only a single agenda: whole-scale extermination of all races, ethnicities, and religions, save their own.

History of the Ku Klux Klan.   Contrary to the contemporary group and its ideology, the first Ku Klux Klan (more commonly known as the KKK) was started by six disenfranchised former Confederate soldiers as a thrill-seeking fraternal organization. Perhaps the behavior exhibited by this gang of young men, forced too young into the role of adulthood, was reminiscent of shared childhood experiences. Masquerading as ghosts, they draped white sheets over themselves and their horses, and they played harmless pranks on friends and family under the cover of darkness (Chalmers, 1965; Zellner, 1995). However, this carefree behavior, lacking in malice, had an unfortunate by-product, one that would create a mean-spirited organization with far-reaching and deadly consequences, one that would continue to rise from the ashes of its previous destructions.

The Reconstruction Klan and the "Invisible Empire": Protection of the Old South (1865–1896).   The Kuklos Clan was founded on Christmas Eve, 1865, by six Confederate veterans living in Pulaski, Tennessee. Originally naming their group for the Greek word for "circle," the members developed their infamous acronym when "one member thought it would be clever to spell the name 'Ku Klux Klan,' making it almost a parody of the names of college fraternities, which are often formed out of three letters of the Greek alphabet" (Kronenwetter, 1992: 18–19). The group furthered the analogy by developing ornate rituals and fantastical terms for club offices (e.g., Grand Cyclops and Grand Scribe) and by calling individual members "ghouls." In addition, the group dressed in outlandish costumes and rode throughout the streets of Pulaski performing general mischief. Unfortunately, such sheet-clad apparitions frightened the newly released slaves, who imagined them as ghosts of deceased Confederate soldiers or otherworldly avengers bent on persecuting unruly blacks.[9] Thus, these blacks, so recently emancipated from formal institutions of slavery and visible bondage, remained captives of their own fear. Unfortunately, their exploitation only increased as a result of legislation designed to protect them.

By many accounts, the Reconstruction Acts of 1867 were designed by the Union-controlled Congress to punish the South for its rebellion. These laws, ostensibly intended to enforce the Civil Rights Bill of 1866, actually resulted in a military occupation of the South, where many white residents were denied the democratic freedom to elect their own government. In some places, former slaves were actually governing whites, an intolerable situation for a populace accustomed to equating blacks with animals. Although many believed that Southerners deserved such harsh treatment, such government action created levels of hostility that could be eased only through violence (Kronenwetter, 1992). Membership applications for the Pulaski group increased exponentially, and racist franchises were established throughout the South. Almost immediately, the Klan's fraternal and relatively benign brotherhood transformed itself into the most malevolent of entities—one in which harassment, torture, and even murder were the norm. In 1867, the growing assemblage convened in Nashville to formally elect someone to the supreme position of Grand Wizard.

As one might expect, the most notable figure to emerge during this preliminary period of Klan activity was the former slave owner and officer in the Confederate army, Nathan Bedford Forrest. Under the auspices of his office, Forrest attempted to control an organization much akin to the Hydra of Greek mythology. Random violence and unspeakable acts of terror, not sanctioned by the newly developed bureaucracy, erupted across jurisdictional boundaries and outraged blacks and whites alike. Targets were not limited to the newly emancipated but included scalawags (i.e., Southerners who became Republicans) and carpetbaggers (i.e., Northern inter-lopers who came to town with carpetbags to exploit the recently impoverished and to prey on the South's vulnerabilities). (Interestingly, Catholics were not targeted.) The violence exploded when the much-hated Ulysses S. Grant was nominated for U.S. president, a position he would eventually attain. Using fire as a weapon, KKK groups routinely burned businesses, residences, and churches belonging to the enemy. Forrest, unable to control the violence, formally disbanded the Klan in 1869, but the effectiveness of his proclamation and new government legislation were somewhat limited in scope, and violence continued among local klaverns and independent groups (e.g., the Knights of the White Camelia) for nearly 20 years.[10] In 1896, the presidential election effectively ended the Klan as Republicans and Democrats reached a compromise that granted Republican Rutherford B. Hayes the presidency while ending the radical Reconstruction of the South. For all intents and purposes, this compromise destroyed all semblance of equality for black Americans, as it returned the South to white Democrats. In fact, the passage of the infamous Jim Crow Laws (i.e., segregation laws) eliminated the need for the "invisible empire."

The Klan Resurfaces: Americanism, Anti-Immigration, and Political Corruption (1910s–1950s)

[T]he Klan also embraced a new version of nativism, and the religious bigotry that had always gone with it. . . . "Americanism" meant opposing anything "foreign" or "alien" . . . [while] favoring "Christian Civilization" meant opposing any religion that was not Christian—or, more specifically, not fundamentalist Christian, this included not only Judaism . . . but also Roman Catholicism. As the Klan saw it, the world's largest Christian faith was an alien religion, ruled by a foreign, Italian Pope (Kronenwetter, 1992: 33).

Like other illegitimate organizations that experience periodic success, the KKK once again gained prominence in 1915. Preying on the fears of the American public, the Klan successfully recruited uneducated individuals fearful of mass waves of "statue-worshipping heathens," namely Italians, Irish, and other recent immigrants. Newly arrived and fleeing from political and religious persecution, immigrants were often met with open hostility. Indeed, it would appear that intolerance and subsequent violence awaited the unwitting immigrant who stepped onto U.S. soil lost in dreams of equality and the American dream. It may be argued that these immigrants, abruptly awakened to the reality of economic competition in a capitalist society, were the lucky ones. The true victims of the KKK during this era were those who passed the threshold unscathed and not forewarned about or forearmed for institutional discrimination.

This second wave of Klan prominence was initiated in 1915 by Georgia native William J. Simmons, a disgraced Protestant minister. Initially, this rebirth was not marked by the same levels of violence as the original, nor were the targets limited to black Americans or opportunists. Indeed, Simmons, like many of his contemporary hate-mongering peers, identified various threats to WASP principles; those threats included Catholics, Jews, and immigrants. Simmons's approach appealed to a wider audience as he "championed" American principles, not just Southern norms. Unfortunately, an economic downturn and problems associated with industrialization (e.g., poverty, crime, disease) created a populace vulnerable to such posturing—a vulnerability that was exacerbated by the loss of American life in World War I. As a result, independent klaverns developed across the country, and membership rose from 5,000 in early 1920 to over 1 million in 1921!

Unlike the Reconstruction Klan, the Klan of the 1920s may be characterized as a capitalist endeavor in which Klan leaders marketed racism to build their personal fortunes. The charging of membership dues, "uniform" fees, and life insurance premiums proved a financial windfall to those in control. Simmons even hired a public relations firm in Atlanta to widen his audience. One of the firm's suggestions was that the Klan present itself as the last bastion of morality in the United States. Thus, the Klan took a formal stand against alcohol, lending its considerable support to Prohibition. Declaring Prohibition necessary to maintain a collective American morality, Simmons and company successfully promoted their individual ideology. (Coincidentally, it seems,

---

HOLLYWOOD AND THE KLAN

In the 1920s Simmons's efforts were assisted in large part by a film titled *Birth of a Nation*. The film, depicting white "gentlemen" protecting women from the sexual proclivities of depraved black males, heralded the prejudice that was to come. Although the content was absolutely erroneous, the film proved to be wildly popular, and it cemented the idea that blacks were intellectually and morally inferior to whites.

the promotion of abstinence made them all very, very wealthy.) They also enforced their dogma by expanding their violence to those they considered to be deviants, including unfaithful wives or others engaging in criminal acts. Even small transgressions were punished, and businesses choosing to remain open on Sunday were routinely vandalized by these "moral pillars." Punishments were often based on the community standards of individual klaverns, as were the levels of violence and organizational ideology. During this period, the power, prestige, and wealth of these independent groups varied by location—ranging from minor nuisances to integral parts of the political infrastructure. However, the national organization remained a political force until the actions of one of its leaders led to its demise.

The year 1925 proved to be both good and bad for the Klan. It was good because of the increase in its membership and financial support, and it was bad due to the actions of some of its members, most notably David C. Stephenson. During the same year that the Klan's power was flamboyantly displayed in the nation's capital, Stephenson, Grand Dragon and Indiana's political dictator, was tried and convicted of the torture and murder of a young woman. Stephenson, the most powerful organizational figure next to Simmons, had a fetish for biting that bordered on cannibalism. After one of his bedmates became ill from his abuse, Stephenson refused to seek prompt medical attention for her for several days. Once he released her, the victim lived just long enough to completely detail the gory event for law enforcement officials, who promptly arrested a very surprised Stephenson. Unfortunately for him, anticipated organizational or political support was not forthcoming.

Upon his conviction, allegations of mass corruption and fund misappropriation were levied by an embittered Stephenson. He also revealed the depth of political collusion, which ultimately led to the indictment of both the mayor of Indianapolis and the governor of Indiana! However, the revelation that contributions of members—many of whom were financially challenged—had been used for personal gain by Klan officers was the most damaging to the organization. In fact, the subsequent lack of donations signaled an end to this second wave of Klan prosperity. By 1930, Klan membership had fallen from its 1925 high of 5 million to 35,000. The Depression further decimated Klan membership; by 1939, when James A. Colescott assumed control, the organization was effectively bankrupt.

According to Chalmers (1965), the Klan's political influence during the 1920s was immeasurable. Representatives, senators, governors, and even a Supreme Court justice (Hugo Black), all supported by (and in some cases actually card-carrying members of) the Klan, created a governmental structure of white Protestant supremacists. During this period, the Klan extended its appeal to groups heretofore reluctant to tie their wagon to extremist organizations. This far-reaching influence enabled the Klan to invade large cross-sections of the nation, establishing chapters in all regions. However, like that of their early predecessors, the new Klan's appeal was short-lived due to its inability to control autonomous local branches that perpetrated atrocities against children and innocents, which proved too extreme for mainstream America to ignore. Once again, the Klan lost favor, and membership fell to an all-time low during the 1930s.

DIFFERENCES FROM SECOND WAVE

The Klan in this third wave had these characteristics:

1. It was primarily based in the South once again.
2. It had a smaller membership, reaching only 50,000 (as opposed to 5 million).
3. It was primarily a reactionary group that was formed in response to the civil rights movement.
4. It was much more violent, which was more consistent with the original Klan in that violence was seen as a means to an end.
5. It was single-minded in its pursuit to stop desegregation.
6. It had a broader base of targets, including anyone sympathetic to the civil rights movement. (In fact, blacks were most often targets of opportunity rather than design.)

The Third Wave: Civil Rights and Desegregation (1950s to 1970s).   The Klan resurfaced after World War II as blacks sought to secure rights promised to them after the Civil War. Dissatisfied with Jim Crow laws, which theoretically (but not in actuality) established separate but equal facilities, blacks sought to end segregation. This effort was largely spurred by President Truman's 1948 directive, which desegregated the armed forces. Six years later, the case of *Brown* v. *Board of Education* signaled the crumbling of the wall of formal segregation and the beginning of unspeakable violence.

Although the organization's previous actions had resulted in a wave of anti-Klan sentiment, the extremist ideology espoused resurfaced shortly after the Court held in *Brown* that "separate educational facilities were inherently unequal." In fact, *Brown* struck at the heart of virtually every white Southerner, rich or poor, as it threatened every facet of the Southern way of life. As Kronenwetter put it: "Wealthy whites cherished segregation because it protected their privilege. Poor whites clung to it because it gave them the only social standing they had . . . no matter how down trodden, ignorant, or otherwise disadvantaged they might be, they were at least socially superior to blacks." (1992: 42). Thus, the decision proved to be monumental in its impact, allowing previously planted seeds of discontent to bear fruit (Zellner, 1995). Almost imperceptibly, separatist ideology pervaded societal institutions, and a broader scope of intolerance took root.

Many Southern states likened the decision to the Reconstruction Acts of the 1800s and refused to acknowledge its legitimacy almost 100 years after the close of the War Between the States. Other locations across the nation responded in a similar fashion, forcing the federal government to use military force in various jurisdictions to enforce the mandate. Throughout the 1960s, Klan membership increased in pace with the eradication of Jim Crow laws. During this period, the Klan successfully widened its appeal, providing equal opportunity to all hatemongers by promising political revision and social change. This platform was widely heard, and long-smoldering embers erupted, most notably in the southern region of the United States. Violence primarily directed at blacks and Jews abounded in the South. Incidents of violence were reported in Florida, Georgia, Alabama, Mississippi, Virginia, Louisiana, and the Carolinas, while government silence gave tacit approval, if not downright legitimacy, to acts committed against nonwhite Protestants (Chalmers, 1965).

Not traditionally known for their trailblazing natures, the states of Mississippi and Alabama earned a permanent place in U.S. history as the undisputed leaders of the anti-civil rights war. Indelible images of police brutality and political corruption, captured by photographers and newsreels, were indicative of the long-simmering anger bubbling under the surface of many traditionally depressed areas in these states. Individuals faced with limited employment opportunities and economic deprivation were particularly vulnerable to inflammatory political rhetoric embraced by government officials. Examples set by Governor George Wallace, who blocked the threshold at the University of Alabama in open defiance of federal integration mandates, and Birmingham Police Chief Bull Connor, who encouraged white citizens to stamp out "insolent" black communities, promoted an atmosphere conducive to and supportive of violence. This environment resulted in the deaths of 3 people and

VIOLENCE IN THE SOUTH

In 1961, Klan groups from Mississippi and Alabama merged. Under the direction of Alabama native, Robert Shelton, the United Klans of America and the Alabama Knights of the Ku Klux Klan officially became the UKA. This group, based in Alabama, quickly became the largest and most powerful white supremacist organization of the era. This group was primarily responsible for various bombings, earning the largest city in Alabama the nickname, "Bombingham." The worst of these bombs was planted in the basement of the 16th Street Baptist Church and resulted in the deaths of three little girls. This act signaled the end of public apathy. (Almost 40 years later, the last conspirator in the case, Frank Cherry, was convicted of the crime.)

The UKA's bombing of the church effectively signaled the destruction of that part of the Klan.

Various murders committed by the Klan in Mississippi served to erode public support:

In 1963, Medger Evers was shot to death in front of his home in Jackson, Mississippi.

In 1964, three civil rights workers were shot to death on a creek bank in Philadelphia, Mississippi.

In 1965, Viola Liuzzo was shot to death on the side of a rural Mississippi road.

injuries to more than 50 when the first black student registered at the University of Mississippi.

The years following were marked by unsurpassed levels of civil unrest and disorder. While personal residences, community centers, and even religious institutions were devastated through vandalism and arson, their attackers went unpunished, acting under the tacit approval of the establishment. Some cases were even characterized by active involvement of local law enforcement.[11] Perhaps the most important act was one that brought national attention and the media spotlight to the growing turmoil in the South. In 1963, a firebomb exploded at the 16th Street Baptist Church in Birmingham, Alabama, killing three young girls. Public reaction was swift and severe. This reaction, coupled with an increase in law enforcement activity, ultimately resulted in the dismantling of Klan groups across the country (George and Wilcox, 1992).

In 1964, tactics of harassment and intimidation of known Klansmen were launched by the FBI's counterintelligence program (COINTELPRO). Threats of public exposure and sanctions for employers hiring Klansmen induced many individuals to voluntarily hang up their robes; use of informants resulted in the prosecution of some of the more steadfast members. Federal legislation was passed, and congressional investigations (i.e., the House Committee on Un-American Activities) featured hearings that exposed high-ranking Klan officials who had remained loyal to the cause and who had successfully evaded prosecution.[12] The end result was significant: In the years directly following this federal scrutiny, Klan membership decreased by 75 percent (George and Wilcox, 1992).

Today's Klan: Education, Legitimacy, and Religion (1970s to the Present).   During the 1970s, it was no longer acceptable for government to tolerate racial hatred and separatism. Due to federal desegregation legislation, state and local governments were mandated to accept a multicultural society. The Klan, which had been devastated by enforcement efforts in the 1960s, was forced to regroup and redevelop recruitment strategies. The KKK was faced with a shortage of new members, and divisive ideologies about the Klan's future direction soon developed in regional chapters (George and Wilcox, 1992).

Long characterized by internal competition, regional Klans were now openly at war with one another. The most notable of the groups, Louisiana's Knights of the Ku Klux Klan, was headed by a charismatic young man named David Duke. Duke's approach, less violent and more discreet, would prove to be the most resilient, and the most dangerous.

By creating an image of well-educated, highly intellectual organizations, David Duke successfully elevated his Klan and subsequent racist organizations to a more sophisticated level. This practice had enormous impact and insulated his members from law enforcement scrutiny. By suggesting that the Klan was a fraternal organization made up of hard-working middle-class individuals and by publicly condemning violence and criminal activity, Duke successfully recruited on college campuses, seducing a large number of

Ironically, Horace King, a well-known leader of the Klan, must receive permission from and follow the dictates of Charleston Police Chief Reuben Greenberg, an African-American Jew.

Courtesy of Charleston, South Carolina, Police Department

educated youth. Duke extended invitations to females and Catholics, two groups that had previously been denied access. Duke's allure was so strong that he successfully pursued a bid for the Louisiana State House of Representatives. Perhaps Duke's quintessential contribution to the white supremacist movement was the establishment of the National Association for the Advancement of White People (NAAWP), an organization currently gaining popularity.

While Duke was successfully increasing membership in his organization, rival klaverns were decimated by criminal prosecution and civil litigation. Overt violence and a flagrant disregard for legitimate authority proved once again to be their downfall. In fact, due primarily to the efforts of Morris Dees and the Southern Poverty Law Center (SPLC), many chapters were forced to disband and declare bankruptcy. Profits from the auction of the assets were awarded to the various victims.

It has been argued that these judgments collectively signaled the imminent demise of the KKK (George and Wilcox, 1992). Indeed, recent statistics have indicated that membership in Klan-like groups has significantly decreased (Southern Poverty Law Center, 1997). However, many of the movement's most prominent—and

JUDGMENTS AGAINST THE KLAN

In 1981, a federal court ruled against the Texas Klansmen who were "patrolling" Galveston Bay, burning boats and threatening Vietnamese fishermen, after a lawsuit was filed on behalf of the Vietnamese fishermen by Klanwatch, a branch of the Southern Poverty Law Center. The court ordered immediate termination of such activity and forced Louis Beam to disband his 2,500-member paramilitary army. (A similar ruling in 1986 forced the North Carolina–based White Patriot Party, led by Glenn Miller, to disband and resulted in a military order that prohibited servicemen from participation in such organizations.)

In 1987, Klanwatch was successful in obtaining a $7 million judgment against United Klans of America (UKA) for the murder of Michael Donald, a 19-year-old man who was found hanging from a tree. Klanwatch investigators were also responsible for much of the evidence presented at the criminal trial that resulted in the conviction of three men, including two UKA officials. One of these individuals, Henry Hays, son of the group's Grand Titan, was executed on June 6, 1997. He was the first white man executed for the murder of an African-American in Alabama since 1913.

In 1988, an Ethiopian man, Mulugeta Seraw, was beaten to death by a group of neo-Nazi skinheads. A lawsuit, filed by Klanwatch, successfully argued that the teenagers were encouraged to violence by Tom Metzger, the founder of White Aryan Resistance (WAR), and his son, John. A $12.5 million judgment effectively bankrupted Metzger, whose assets were seized and auctioned to satisfy the judgment (Dees, 1996).

In 1993, a Klanwatch lawsuit resulted in a judgment against the "invisible empire," once the largest and most violent of the Klans. The judgment called for immediate disassembly and liquidation of all assets—including its name—and payment to civil rights marchers injured in a confrontation in Forsythe County, Georgia.

In 1995, a default judgment of $1 million was awarded to the family of Harold Mansfield. The victim, an African-American sailor who had served in the Gulf War, was murdered by a member of the Church of the Creator. In an attempt to avoid payment, the church transferred ownership to William Pierce, a well-known racist and author of *The Turner Diaries*. A subsequent judgment of $85,000 was awarded, due to the fraudulent nature of the transaction.

In 1998, the Southern Poverty Law Center successfully secured the largest judgment ever awarded against the Christian Knights of the Ku Klux Klan, Grand Dragon Horace King, and four others. The judgment, $37.8 million, was secured for Macedonia Baptist Church, which was burned on June 21, 1995.

Sources: Southern Poverty Law Center, Intelligence Reports, 1996, 1997, 1998.

most deadly—leaders have emerged as powerful figures in the growing antigovernment/antiestablishment movement and have increasingly used the newly developed information superhighway to attract younger members. Individuals such as Louis Beam and Tom Metzger, minimizing overt racist rhetoric and promoting themselves as constitutional defenders, have been successful in luring disenchanted youths to their cause. This usage of uncensored Internet resources has resulted in a new wave of white supremacist/antiestablishment hatemongers. So while many have sounded the death knell for the Klan, this tolling may be both premature and dangerously misleading. In fact, the Klan's most important contribution to the legacy of intolerance is the foundation it laid for future organizations, such as the Order.[13] White Aryan Resistance, Aryan Nations, and various other neo-Nazi-type groups. Unfortunately, some experts contend that these groups are more insidious than the traditional Klan, due to their xenophobic nature. Newer groups, emphazising pan-Aryanism, are less limited in their appeal, creating the potential for international mobilization (Blee, 2002).

Youth involvement in white supremacist movements is growing.

Courtesy of Southern Poverty Law Center/Klanwatch

White Aryan Resistance

In the early 1980s, a new plague of racial intolerance reached epidemic proportions. Many of these groups maintained traditional Klan-like ideology but concentrated primarily on disassociated youth. Targeting young individuals apprehensive of shrinking job markets, these groups, primarily founded and presided over by adults, were successful in establishing a network of hate-filled teenagers with a penchant for violence. Perhaps the most influential leader to emerge during this period was former Klansman Tom Metzger. Metzger, a former Duke supporter and friend, was denounced by the Klan for his extremist ideology and passion for violence. One of the first to promote far right paramilitary structure and training, Metzger routinely distributed works such as *The Anarchist's Cookbook*, *The White Man's Bible*, and the supremacist favorite, *The Turner Diaries*. Metzger periodically found popular support for his extremist ideology, as evidenced by his winning a California congressional primary and placing fourth in a later Senate primary (Hamm, 1993). After his expulsion from the Klan, Metzger formed several organizations, each of which proved to be short-lived. His dream of a perfect hate-fueled machine of destruction went unfulfilled until he discovered the ultimate youth medium—music.

Metzger, recognizing the influence of pop culture on malleable audiences and the increasing interest of rebellious youth, abandoned traditional notions of ritualism and organization and embraced icons of the British skinhead community. Ian Stuart and his band, Skrewdriver, echoed strains of rebellion, nonconformity, and frustration resounding within the youth psyche. Their music, purely antiestablishment, stressed individuality and encouraged teens to take control. Universal in its message, the music was wildly successful in inciting passion and rage among its young listeners. This gateway to the youth subculture granted Metzger superficial legitimacy with American teens and allowed him to channel these elevated emotions into his newly formed White Aryan Resistance (WAR).

Promoting a specter of an evil establishment, Metzger preached to his targeted audience of the absence of any real future for young white males in a society controlled by Jews, minorities, and homosexuals. He justified violent acts as the means necessary to an end. He published a newspaper devoted to young people and their concerns, peppering articles with sophisticated cartoons and musical lyrics from antiestablishment rock groups. He created a television program called "Race and Reason" that cultivated his image as a highly polished, respectable businessman. He appeared as a guest on shock talk shows, portraying himself as an intellectual under attack by an antiwhite society. He developed complex computer networks and chat groups, uniting skinheads and hate groups across the country. For those not having a connection or lacking access to his WAR board, he developed a WAR hotline.

Metzger directed his message to an existing subculture of young people, the skinheads. "The skinheads are white mean machines who deliver honest casualty reports" (Tom Metzger, as quoted in Hamm, 1993: 63). Members of this subculture, initially attracted by their mutual musical preferences, distinguished themselves from other groups by their apparel of Doc Martens, military bomber-style jackets, and shaved heads. Although lacking aesthetic value, this ensemble was more mod than sinister. Indeed, the most striking aspect of this existing subculture was the absence of malice. In fact, a variety of cultures were represented in the skinhead subculture prior to Metzger's seizure of the Aryan Youth Movement (AYM)[14] (Hamm, 1993).

The takeover of AYM had widespread consequences. Appointing his son, John, as the new leader, Metzger parlayed this relationship into a successful means of recruiting high school and college students. More importantly, it allowed Metzger to repaint the canvas of the skinhead prototype. Metzger called for a decrease in visibility. By placing his son, a photogenic conservative-looking young man, in the position of leadership, Metzger was able to convince many followers to tone down their radical appearance. This toned-down outward appearance allowed members to carry out their missions covertly and hampered law enforcement efforts in adequately enumerating their strength. In fact, it has been suggested that this new approach was so successful that Metzger's soldiers infiltrated every government institution, including the military and the police (Hamm, 1993).

Skinheads

The first notable gang of unorganized skinheads appears to have been in the increasingly depressed Haight-Ashbury district. Economic depression and the musical influence of British groups such as Skrewdriver resulted in a wave of racially motivated assaults. Stereotyping minorities, Jews, and homosexuals as amoral provided an explanation for the country's decreasing economic prosperity and identified enemies to be targeted. Taking their cue from British skins, Metzger's "Resisters," and basic societal distaste, American youth gangs adopted uniforms of shaved heads, Doc Martens, and leather jackets. Unfortunately, most of these groups were incorrectly linked by law enforcement agencies, government sources, and media reports to Metzger's WAR. While Metzger's group was certainly a cause for concern, this inaccurate depiction masked unique characteristics that may have been useful in intelligence-gathering strategies of local law enforcement and federal agencies. This miscategorization, however, did have some positive by-products. In 1990, for example, Metzger, his son (John), and WAR were found to be civilly responsible in the racially motivated murder of Mulugeta Seraw, an Ethiopian immigrant.[15] This judgment ordered the Metzgers and their organization to pay $10 million to the Seraw family. The lawsuit, initiated by Morris Dees and the Southern Poverty Law Center, effectively shut down the operation of WAR (Zellner, 1995).

While the Metzgers' formalized hate institution was mortally wounded, the ideology it espoused was not. On the contrary, skinhead groups and other racist gangs emerged across the country. The primary difference between these groups and their traditional counterparts appears to be the lack of formalization, recognizable leaders, and identifiable targets. For example, in 1996 a Boston gang of racist skinheads armed with knives, chains, ax handles, and broomsticks invaded a party. The incident resulted

Apparently, this community is intolerant of skinhead activity.

Courtesy of Southern Poverty Law Center/Klanwatch

in the beating and stabbing death of Jayson Linsky, an individual who had previously asked the group to leave after they drew swastikas on their hands. This episode was particularly troubling to Massachusetts authorities, who had considered their area immune to racial violence. Unfortunately, this incident was just one of many that occurred in 1996. Many argue that incidents of skinhead violence, absent in recent years, are becoming increasingly common. In fact, Klanwatch estimates indicate that youth involvement in racially motivated assaults more than doubled between 1995 and 1996 (Southern Poverty Law Center, 1997). This estimate, disturbing in its implications, is made more so due to the lack of adequate measurement tools and the inability of traditional law enforcement agencies to closely approximate hate-crime activity.

While traditional skinhead ideologies of intolerance and racial supremacy are surfacing across the country, it is sociologically relevant to note that most of these groups are concentrated in areas rich in cultural diversity and economic deprivation. A Marxist approach might argue that the reemergence of skinhead dogma may be attributed to economic competition among sections of the lower class. Indeed, this perspective may have some merit. In a time of relative prosperity, it appears that the U.S. middle class, if there is one, is experiencing spontaneous combustion. Racial hostility among lower- and middle-class members appears to be growing, and this self-destruction is signaled not only by the growth of formalized subversive organizations, but also by the escalation of intolerance sporadically displayed by informal and largely unstructured dissident youth gangs.

Aryan Nations

In 1962, white supremacist extraordinaire Colonel William Potter Gale failed in his quest for the governorship of California. However, his campaign spawned several hate groups and greatly increased the promotion of the Christian Identity Movement through the collective networking of his protégés. One of these resulting organizations, California's Christian Defense League (CCDL), would eventually become one of the most successful of its kind. Unfortunately, this group broadened its appeal by maintaining an array of ideological foundations, including the Klan, the Skinheads, the John Birch Society, the Minutemen, the Liberty Lobby, the Posse Comitatus, the National Alliance, the American Front, and the Aryan Brotherhood (Bushart et al., 1998). Thus, membership ranged from right-wing conservatives to hard-core hate-mongers. In addition, the CCDL effectively exploited the public's fear of Communism, causing a sharp increase in membership throughout the Cold War period.

Upon the death of Wesley Swift[16] in the 1970s, the mantle of leadership was assumed by a former aerospace engineer. Richard Butler, a protégé of Colonel William Potter Gale, successfully expanded the California-based group, developing a large compound in Hayden Lake, Idaho, which became a haven of sorts for an assortment of Christian Identity believers. Notable figures in the movement, including William Pierce (author of *The Turner Diaries*), have found refuge in Hayden Lake. However, Butler has routinely denied that his organizational tenets espouse supremacist ideology; he argues that the fortress is simply the beginning of a new nation, one designed to separate whites from deviant influences. Unfortunately, Butler's assertions do not seem credible, as he has ordered the extermination of the Jewish race.

In keeping with his national approach, Butler formally changed the name of the CCDL to the Church of Jesus Christ Christian. In addition, he created the Aryan Nations—the political arm of the congregation. Both groups are largely financed through the sale of white supremacist souvenirs, while they fully support a racial holy war (RAHOWA). These efforts were greatly enhanced by the entrance of Louis Beam, an exiled Klan leader who was disgraced after a civil judgment in Texas. In the 1980s, Beam joined forces with "Reverend" Richard Butler, a vanguard of the militant right, and invited American teens to reclaim their lost heritage and take their rightful place in society (Dees, 1996). Beam's Aryan Nations quickly gained national recognition through violence and radical propaganda. Beam recognized the value of the information superhighway and was responsible for establishing the first of many hate libraries on the Internet. He was also responsible for developing a widely publicized "point" system: This point system targeted federal officials, civil rights workers, and other undesirables for assassination. In 1987, Beam, indicted for numerous counts of sedition and conspiracy, fled to Mexico. Upon his capture, he was found not guilty on all counts. Beam, increasingly antigovernment, quickly became a leader in the newly emerging Patriot movement. As publisher of *The Seditionist*, Beam outlined a new approach to a revolutionary takeover. His "leaderless resistance" platform called for the purposeful disassembly of all existing Patriot organizations, which was intended to insulate members from full-scale prosecution. This ideology, coupled with a remarkable ability to move people, has made him one of the most powerful leaders in the antigovernment movement and has ensured his ideological longevity.

In the 1990s, the Southern Poverty Law Center effectively seized the Hayden Lake compound after a civil judgment was rendered in a case in which an African-American couple was brutalized outside the gates. Since that time, August Kreis, the group's director of information and official webmaster, has publicly announced plans to relocate the group to rural Potter County, Pennsylvania; however, the move has not yet occurred, and the organization, headed by Harold Ray Redfeairn, is currently in disarray.

Neo-Nazis

During the 1930s, Adolf Hitler and the National Socialist (i.e., Nazi) Party murdered millions of people in the name of racism. By far the most successful hate group in history, Hitler's Nazis routinely tortured, maimed, and annihilated thousands monthly while gaining legitimate authority across Europe. Such success, unprecedented and never repeated, was accomplished through the bastardization of an entire race of individuals. Unfortunately, Hitler's assertion that pure Germans were direct descendants of biblical nomadic tribes was well received by a public struggling with an economic downturn. By crediting the Jews with a secret conspiracy to control national wealth, Hitler successfully created a Hydra-type entity—one which could only be controlled through extermination (Kronenwetter, 1992).

Hitler's ascension to power was largely credited to a vast army, surprising in its violence and brutality. Although his army was eventually defeated by the Allied forces in 1945, Hitler's ideology remained, periodically glorified by youth facing economic uncertainty. Current groups espousing his anti-Semitic rhetoric are commonly rooted in the American Nazi Party (ANP), founded in the 1940s by George Lincoln Rockwell. (Prior to Hitler's expansionist tendencies and heinous directives, many German immigrants supported Hitler's ideology; however, the vast majority of them soon rejected the movement, abhorring the Holocaust just like their non-German counterparts.) The members of this group (modeled after the Nazi army) were recognizable by their militaristic posturing, clothing, and rhetoric. Like Hitler, Rockwell identified an Aryan race—one divinely selected and far superior to Jews. Fortunately, Rockwell's organization did not find a niche in American society, and his message was largely ignored. His assassination in 1967 further hampered ideological dissemination, but later groups would emulate the organizational structure and model utilized by Rockwell and many of his former protégés (Kronenwetter, 1992).

After Rockwell's assassination, ardent supporter Matt Koehl renamed the group the National Socialist White People's party. Arguing that the group was simply designed as a self-defense mechanism for white Americans, Koehl promoted an "Aryan culture."

Couching his dogma in religious terms, Koehl suggested that the maintenance of Aryan culture was a sacred task entrusted to the white race (Kronenwetter, 1992). Religious underpinnings, however, did not preclude violence toward others, and Koehl's group was responsible for a variety of brutal attacks. In the 1980s, Koehl once again renamed the organization while maintaining much of the ideological tenets; fortunately, the Anti-Defamation League has reported a marked lack of interest in the group. However, other Rockwell protégés have fared much better.

In the 1960s, William Pierce developed Youth for Wallace, a youth group dedicated to the presidential election of Governor George Wallace. Although unsuccessful in its mission, Pierce soon refocused and renamed his organization. The National Youth Alliance (currently the National Alliance), still active today, was designed to be an informational clearinghouse for white supremacists. Pierce is best known for his futuristic novel *The Turner Diaries*, an apocalyptic fantasy in which a race war led by "The Order" results in the extinction of Jews. This work, considered a Bible of sorts by many white supremacist organizations, was allegedly instrumental in the Oklahoma City bombing and the formation of The Order, a particularly violent organization.

The Order

In 1983, the most violent and most criminal supremacist organization was founded. Created by former Klansman Robert Mathews, The Order argued that the decay of American society was evidenced through the increasing violence, drug use, rate of illegitimate births, and the like, all directly attributed to an insidious government administered by Jews. The Order stated that this Zionist-occupied government (ZOG) was unrepresentative of white Christian Americans. Like other white supremacist organizations before and since, Mathews's group quoted biblical scripture to justify its actions (e.g., "For we wrestle not against flesh and blood, but against principalities, against powers, against spiritual wickedness in high places," Ephesians 6:11–12). Such biblical support, a powerful tool indeed, provided a rationalization for the destruction of ZOG-controlled federal institutions and government buildings, including the Alfred P. Murrah Federal Building in Oklahoma City. In addition, it justified the attack on residences of participants and the institutions in which they worship (i.e., where they promote the destruction of America). To fund their extremist platform, group members actively engaged in an assortment of armed robberies, counterfeiting, and murder. Mathews was killed in a shootout with federal law enforcement agents in 1983; fortunately, his killing precipitated the demise of this group. Some of his more radical rhetoric may be found in other organizations, in particular, those associated with the Christian Identity movement.

Christian Identity

Originally known as Anglo-Israelism, the modern Christian Identity movement was founded by minister John Wilson in England in the mid-1800s, and brought to the United States by Reverend Edward Hines soon thereafter. This theological perspective is largely predicated on the belief that Europeans (e.g., Anglo-Saxons, Scandinavians, Celts, and Teutonic peoples) were descendants of Jacob and distant relatives of Jesus Christ. Thus, Britons were the true Israelites. Violent anti-Semitism was a natural by-product, as Jews were considered to be not only imposters but children of Satan (Kronenwetter, 1992). Such ideological extremism was further exacerbated in the post-Depression years through the efforts of Gerald L. K. Smith, editor of *The Cross and the Flag* and leader of the Christian Nationalist Crusade, and his protégé, Wesley Swift.

Christian Identity groups characterize Judaism as a race rather than a religion, which enables them to classify Jews, as well as African-Americans, Hispanics, and others as nonwhites or "mud people." Such groups, they claim, are actually representatives of a subhuman, pre-Adamic species, which was created out of the mud by Satan. In other words, they reject the notion that Adam was the first person created; they argue that other races were created along with the beasts, and that Adam and Eve were the first white people. The "Seedline Doctrine" of Identity argues that the trees, and the subsequent fruit, metaphorically referred to other races. Following this logic, they posit that Adam and Eve's fall from grace was both racial and sexual and that Cain and Abel, though twins, had different fathers.[17] The birth of Cain, of course, established a direct lineage of Satan on earth. This ideology, unpalatable to most, does appear to answer some questions regarding the biblical explanation of the human race. For example, how could two people create the entire race? If no other people existed, why was Cain marked for his sin? ("Every one that findeth me shall slay me," Genesis 4:14.)

According to Christian Identity followers, these questions are easily explained through seven covenants of the Bible:

1. *Edenic covenant.* God (i.e., Yahweh) created Eve as a life mate for Adam, for although other human forms existed, they were unsuitable "for the intermingling of blood through procreation with the light-skinned Adam, forever establishing their status in relation to the progeny of Adam" (Bushart et al., 1998: 71).

2. *Adamic covenant.* Adam and Eve, beset with the curse of mortality and immorality brought about by the fall, continued their descent through the conception of twins, one Adamic and one satanic. (Christian Identity groups argue that the "mark" of Cain was actually a recognizable characteristic visible in all of his descendants.)

3. *Noahic covenent.* Yahweh commanded Noah to build an ark to save the Adamic race. (According to Christian Identity groups, God destroyed only the portions of the earth populated by errant Adamites who were actively engaging in the mongrelization of their race. There was no need to flood the earth in its entirety, as pre-Adamic races were destined to hell as satanic children. Once again, they argue, the Adamic race was purified through the salvation of Noah; thus, white people are the direct descendants of Noah and, through him, Adam and Eve.)

4. *Abrahamic covenant.* God promised Abraham, progenitor of true Israelites, "I will make of thee a great nation and I will bless thee, and make thy name great, and thou shalt be a blessing; and I will bless them that bless thee, and curse him that curseth thee, and in thee shall all families of the earth be blessed. . . . I will make thee exceedingly fruitful, and I will make nations of thee, and kings shall come out of thee" (Genesis 12: 2–3; 17:6). Thus, the 12 tribes of Israel, claimed by virtually all supremacist organizations, were headed by each of Jacob's 12 sons. (Jacob, renamed Israel by Yahweh, was the grandson of Abraham [Bushart et al., 1998].) However, satanic forces seduced these true Israelites, resulting in their 400 years of enslavement.

5. *Mosaic covenant.* Yahweh delivered to Moses the codification of divine laws. These laws, intended only for the Adamic race, were violated almost immediately, forcing Yahweh to create yet another covenant for his chosen people.

6. *Palestinian covenant.* Yahweh patiently expressed his edict that the blessings of the land would be reserved for the Adamic race, which was to abide by the tenets originally issued in the Mosaic covenant. Those not willing would suffer dire consequences. Unfortunately for Israel, they chose to be willful and unappreciative, and Yahweh's favor was somewhat questionable until the entrance of David, the second true king of Israel.

7. *Davidic covenant.* By far the most important and long-standing covenant, the Davidic covenant foretold of a reclamation of wealth, heritage, and strength. (Christian Identity groups claim that the holy war against the infidels will result in the latter's salvation.)

Such promises assure Christian Identity believers that whites are indeed the true Israelites. Who can argue with the strength, wealth, and power of Britain and America, the new Israel? Like those of racists across the globe, these depictions provide justification for the exploitation and, ultimately, extermination of a mutant genus. Christian Identity ministers, such as Wesley Swift, deny both biblical and contemporary history, citing the above "truths" while disavowing the reality of the Holocaust. Indeed, the movement epitomizes historical revisionism, promoting anti-Semitic literature such as *The Protocols of the Learned Elders of Zion*, a political forgery produced in the nineteenth century by the Russian czar's secret police (Kronenwetter, 1992).

Variations exist among Christian Identity groups, just as they do among mainstream faiths. "Identity . . . is not a denomination such as Baptist or Methodist, but rather an article of belief that transcends doctrinal differences" (Bushart et al., 1998: 60). Without exception, these groups perceive themselves as victims of government persecution.[18] Christian Identity groups believe that the government protects every religious ideology but theirs. This reaffirms their belief that a Jewish conspiracy to destroy them through silence exists. Unfortunately, such rhetoric has not been limited to political, social, religious, and ideological outcasts. By characterizing the U.S. government as increasingly subversive and controlling, their dogma has appealed to mainstream Americans who are

POSSE COMITATUS—AN EXAMPLE OF CHRISTIAN IDENTITY

The Posse Comitatus base much of its ideology on the Posse Comitatus Act, which empowered county and local governments in rural areas and extended judicial authority to those entities. However, this group has extended the provisions of the act as intended by Congress, arguing that federal and state governments exceed the jurisdictions originally extended to them. Although not the first, one of the most successful Posse groups was founded in California by Colonel William Potter Gale (U.S. Army, retired). An associate of Wesley Swift, Gale successfully organized struggling farmers across the country. Like many organizations before and since, the Posse garnered much support by targeting a recently beleaguered group.

During the late 1970s and 1980s, American farmers were struggling with large mortgages and land devaluations. Further crippled by falling crop prices, thousands of farmers faced bankruptcy. Many of them felt betrayed by the federal government, which had subsidized or otherwise supported their loans and which was now auctioning off the very assets it had financed. Such despondency created a population ripe for religious or ideological salvation. Embracing the antiestablishment (and subsequent antitaxation) rhetoric espoused by the local Posse Comitatus, farmers were largely responsible for the astronomical growth enjoyed by the movement during this period. Ultimately, the Posse's rejection of federal sovereignty only heightened legal, financial, and social problems confronting the farmers. The movement continued to grow; unfortunately, so did its violence. Some infamous Posse murderers include the following:

> *Michael Ryan.* While executing a search warrant on the property of Michael Ryan, leader of a Posse group in rural Nebraska, state police uncovered the bodies of a 26-year-old man and a 5-year-old child, both followers of Ryan's group. Eventually convicted of both murders, Ryan was linked to the most notorious of all Posse members through the biographical literature of Gordon Kahl.

> *Gordon Kahl.* Refuting the authority of the U.S. government, Kahl killed 2 federal marshals and wounded 3 others who were attempting to arrest him for parole violations in February 1983.

tired of fighting for the right to educate their children, maintain their weapons, and promote their Christian lifestyles. In fact, these groups have been extremely successful in preying on conservative ideologies by sensationalizing incidents that strike at the core of many Christian sensibilities (e.g., abortion, pornography, narcotics, homosexuality). They argue, for example, that the satanic government is actively promoting immorality designed to weaken bonds of Christianity, promoting pornography through federally funded efforts (e.g., Maplethorpe's exhibit).

These Christian Identity groups suggest that a higher level of moral conscious-ness necessitates actions that illustrate the sanctity of divine mandates. Thus, anti-Semitism and racism still abound but are carefully couched in benign references to the overarching power of the federal government. Various groups that profess to be patriotic Americans loyal to the ideologies espoused in the original Constitution have successfully attracted many mainstream Americans who are increasingly uncomfort-able with the liberal slant of the Supreme Court. Arguing that the U.S. government in general (and the U.S. Supreme Court in particular), has eroded family values and decimated conservative principles, this patriot ideology has been accepted—if not supported—by a variety of private citizens. Although most of them have not formally joined such organizations, many deny the pathology of their existence.

SIMILARITIES AMONG WHITE SUPREMACIST GROUPS

Like their black counterparts, white supremacist groups may be characterized by ideo-logical similarities and intergroup conflicts. The majority of these organizations are predicated on far-right Christian principles, a perspective that advocates a return to tra-ditional family values and emphasizes familial responsibility and authority. Without exception, these groups are increasingly critical of governmental legislation, portraying law enforcement agencies as evil entities intent on destroying the most powerful of all institutions—the American family. Thus, white supremacist organizations are increas-ingly antiestablishment. The significance of this ideological transformation cannot be overstated when looking at their successful appeal to a cross-section of American society.

In recent years, political conservatism has become increasingly popular. Eco-nomic uncertainty, diminishing occupational opportunities, tax increases, and the ris-ing cost of health care have increased the attractiveness of right-wing politics. The once-ridiculed "religious right" has become a political force in contemporary society. The increasing vulnerability of the middle class in the United States has been success-fully targeted by traditional supremacist organizations. Downplaying their racist rhetoric and focusing on disillusioned youth, traditional groups have achieved new life, which is anticipated to be long-lasting. Without exception, these groups success-fully exploit young members, granting only superficial leadership and reserving the most unpopular and distasteful tasks for those most expendable.

SIMILARITIES BETWEEN SUPREMACIST GROUPS AND STREET GANGS

A comparison of supremacist groups and street gangs reveals a multitude of similarities often overlooked in the popular media. Like their counterparts in youth gangs, members in supremacist groups are primarily concentrated in economically deprived areas. Contrary to popular belief, the vast majority of supremacist movements originate in highly urbanized and industrialized communities and do not fit the backyard "Bubba" stereotype promoted by the media. Membership is also characterized by low educational attainment and perceptions of institutional persecution or discrimination. In addition, members of both groups tend to share common dysfunctional family situations; many of these members come from single-parent homes or physically abusive situations.

It must be noted that levels of involvement in both supremacist organizations and street gangs rise during periods of economic or social unrest; these increased levels may be attributed to an elevated sense of disassociation. Overwhelmed by community disorder, uncertain futures, and familial circumstances, low-income youths join supremacist or street gangs for a sense of belongingness and brotherhood. In essence, these groups become pseudo-families for these youths, providing structure, ideology, and, most importantly, fraternity. This sense of fellowship, however, does not come without significant expectations and responsibilities: Members of both groups are expected to sever any and all ties with outsiders (including but not limited to family members and nonconforming significant others). Subsequently, the malleability and vulnerability of these disassociated youths are often manifested in criminal and violent activities.

Like street gangs, many young hatemongers mark their territory with graffiti.

Courtesy of Southern Poverty Law Center/Klanwatch

DIFFERENCES BETWEEN SUPREMACIST GROUPS AND STREET GANGS

Like their criminal counterparts, racist groups provide explanations for economic deprivation. Both supremacist groups and street gangs perceive themselves as victims of institutionalized discrimination, but their responses to this perceived persecution differ. Whereas supremacist groups actively attack the oppression, criminal gangs engage in illicit activity to circumvent the formalized structures of oppression. These varying modes of adaptation are predicated on ideological discrepancies and signify the most compelling difference between the two.

As just stated, ideological foundations act as a dividing line between the two groups. Supremacist groups gain strength through ideological dogma and religious rhetoric. Whether spouting "Christian Identity" verbiage or pseudo-Islamic dialogue, both white and black supremacist organizations are bolstered by articulable ideals, principles, and targets. This commonality has allowed extremist ideologies to continue during periods of relative prosperity. On the other hand, criminal gangs, best known for their overt criminal activity, lack ideological consistency. Though brought together by marginalization, few members can articulate theoretical boundaries and constraints. Overlooking the ideological cohesion that exists in supremacist groups and assuming that civil litigation and criminal prosecution have neutralized supremacist groups (such as the Klan and the Panthers), some law enforcement agencies have been caught unawares by the recent resurgence of antiestablishment ideology. This oversight, coupled with the groups' subversive abilities, has enabled supremacist or antiestablishment organizations to stockpile a significant amount of hidden resources such as munitions, personnel, and literature. In actuality, victories for law enforcement have proven to be superficial at best.

Characterized by unprecedented levels of adaptability, supremacist groups have recently refocused their attention and their anger on a more vulnerable and socially acceptable target. Bowing to political correctness, both white and black supremacist groups have increasingly targeted those of Jewish ancestry. Recent accounts of anti-Semitic activity reveal an intolerance only exceeded by that of the Nazis in Germany. This redirection, more palatable to a society socialized to be wary of non-Christians, has resulted in successful membership drives in virtually all supremacist organizations. In addition, by characterizing formalized governmental structures as Jewish-owned or controlled, supremacists have effectively seduced American youth, race notwithstanding, with antiestablishment ideologies. The delusion has also reinforced traditional stereotypes and elicited a number of adult members. Unfortunately for American society, it has resulted in a cyclical pattern of antagonism and intolerance.

While both supremacists and street gang members are overwhelmingly gathered from dysfunctional familial situations, an increasing number of young supremacists are recruited from the realms of nuclear families. These nuclear families, however, are anything but traditional in nature. Unlike Norman Rockwell's depictions, these youngsters are not reared in fireside or cozy environments sprinkled with love and forgiveness; rather, elders are responsible for passing on family values that encourage

WEB OF HATE

www.natvan.com

Home page of the National Alliance, this site features the teachings of "Dr." William Pierce, author of *The Turner Diaries*. The rhetoric of this group tends to lament the discrimination directed toward whites in political, social, and economic areas. Its monthly newsletter has argued that the media is actually a Semitic tool designed to extinguish any and all racial unity among whites.

www.nidlink.com/,aryanvic

One of many Aryan Nations home pages, this site is particularly good at identifying acts the group defines as atrocities committed against whites by minorities. This site includes writings from hatemongers such as Richard Butler. The group's literature supports both separation and violence as a means to an end.

www.wpww.com

Home of White Pride World Wide, this site appeals to those individuals in need of whites-only holidays. Some of the most notable include Robert E. Lee's birthday (January 20), Stonewall Jackson Day, and Adolf Hitler's birthday (April 20). This site also details "Jewish conspiracies" within the United States. This site has periodically advocated the boycott of certain products for their antiwhite policies. These include McDonald's, for its refusal to fly the Georgia flag because it contains the Confederate battle flag; AOL and Geocites, due to their censorship of racist web pages; and Miller Brewing Company, for its support of the Thurgood Marshall Fund.

www.whitepride.net

Promoted as an entertainment site, this home page promotes various white supremacist bands such as Skrewdriver and Berserkr, bands known for their intolerant and homicidal propaganda. This site also includes sections of ethnic jokes. Like those of many supremacist organizations, this site spouts religious rhetoric to support its views of racial oppression, separation, and annihilation.

www.naawp.com

This official web page of the National Association for the Advancement of White People claims to debunk "myths" promoted by a variety of racial and religious minority groups. Viewers may, for example, view "real" crime statistics, which indicate that African-Americans tend to prey on whites. This site also provides links for those individuals searching for similar organizations.

www.stormfront.com

One of the most popular racist sites on the Net, Stormfront's home page offers a variety of options for interested parties. Hatemongers, for example, can find like-minded

(*continued*)

(continued)

partners on the new Aryan Dating Page and shop for racist artifacts in the gift shop. This site also provides a comprehensive list of links to other supremacist web pages. The authors have developed a "legal defense fund" for their founders, readers, and publications. They warn that a Jewish conspiracy is preventing Gentiles from expressing their constitutional privileges and detail an agreement between America Online and the Anti-Defamation League of B'nai B'rith and the Simon Wiesenthal Center to censor the Internet. This group also provides links to political pages, such as that of David Duke.

www.duke.org

David Duke's home page mirrors his political campaigns of old. This page espouses an intolerance for nonwhites and argues that many black politicians are actually dyed-in-the-wool criminals or are morally bankrupt. He argues that the media has fallen into the hands of antiwhite individuals who pose a significant threat to white America. Careful to distance himself from hatemongers, Duke claims to have no harsh feelings toward minority groups; to the contrary, Duke claims to be a race lover—infatuated with the notion of being white.

extremism and racism. The importance of socialization through kinship cannot be overstated. Just as youth gang members emulate community elders, young supremacists find affirmation for supremacist ideology within their families, churches, and communities. Thus, it may be argued that predestination for supremacist youths is all but guaranteed by sociological factors. Like their street-affiliated counterparts, supremacist youths are surrounded not only by support but by encouragement of their extremist ideology. However, unlike their street gang peers, who graduate from illegal group activity to illicit independent entrepreneurship, the majority of young racists do not fully evolve; in fact, racist activity is rarely, if ever, perpetrated by individuals.

Three remaining characteristics distinguish purely criminal street gangs from their supremacist counterparts. The first appears too obvious to mention: While criminal activity perpetrated by street gangs is inherently profit-driven, supremacist organizations engage in these endeavors to create revenue for the successful overthrow of ZOG and the further spreading of ideological rhetoric. Second, these supremacist organizations have utilized tools of the mass media and technological advances in communication mediums to promote their subversive dogma. These strategies, unheard of in strictly criminal street gangs, have enabled supremacist organizations to reach a cross-section of American youth. The accessibility of and the lack of censorship on the Internet have radically enhanced their traditional recruitment strategies. Third, organizational longevity of supremacist groups has been secured through successful platforms of political legitimacy and mainstream appeal. Unlike their street gang counterparts, leaders in racist groups have successfully camouflaged their proclivity for violence and subversive activities in political agendas. For the most part, street gangs are often characterized as shortsighted due to their reluctance to cultivate political patronage or associations. Thus, it is anticipated that supremacist ideology will continue to outpace and will endure far longer than criminal groups solely motivated by fiduciary gain.

CONCLUSIONS

Contrary to popular media depictions that characterize hate-motivated violence as a white phenomenon, racial violence is an equal opportunity activity. Many incidents perpetrated by nonwhites are presented as reactionary or defensive. Too often, the underlying motivations in these activities are undermined or ignored. Take, for instance, the 1993 mass murder of six commuters on a 12-car commuter train. Media accounts of this shooting suggest that Colin Ferguson, a Jamaican immigrant, simply chose to vent his rage over unrealized expectations, much like a disgruntled postal worker. These accounts frequently omit the racial singularity of those not targeted, African-Americans. This misrepresentation, likening Ferguson to a delusional misfit, negates the seriousness of racial conflict in contemporary society. Other examples of racial violence indicate a growing division in American society. Many individuals foresee a resurgence in racial supremacy that will surpass the unrest of the civil rights era. It is anticipated that youth involvement in the impending racial war will be significant; in fact, the opening salvos may have already been exchanged.

Mobilization of disassociated youth is increasingly universal in these more radical ethnocentric groups. Of particular concern is the religious and political ideology these organizations espouse. This indoctrination, whether veiled or overt in its approach, creates a complex network of like-minded individuals and legitimizes violence. Drawing on generational consciousness, adult leaders actually manipulate those individuals seeking empowerment. Utilization of mass communication interfaces further propagates racial intolerance. An unanticipated by-product is the multiplication of less formalized splinter groups. These gangs, many founded by and presided over by teens, are often the most unpredictable and the most deadly. Unfortunately, law enforcement efforts are directed at the more formalized and more traditional groups, such as the Ku Klux Klan and the Black Panthers.

The dismantling of the Black Panther Party, the assassination of Malcolm X, and the successful criminal and civil prosecution of klaverns and their leaders by the Southern Poverty Law Center are perceived by many governmental agencies as social victories, monumental in their impact. On the surface, these events (taken collectively) do appear to have reduced the desirability of hate-motivated activity, and most would agree that any progress in law enforcement efforts is deserving of applause. However, these events do not signal the demise of gang-related hatemongering, nor do they indicate widespread multicultural tolerance. On the contrary, recent exposés of the annual "good old boys" roundup epitomize the lack of social understanding or awareness. Societal divisiveness and subsequent racial violence appear to be a foregone conclusion, one that some agencies seem to have missed.

Traditionally, periods of supremacist affiliation and organizational prominence have been short-lived. Each period of prosperity enjoyed by supremacist organizations was invariably ended due to their own propensity for self-destruction, not as the result of law enforcement efforts. In fact, their emphasis on local control and lack of self-regulation created associations particularly vulnerable to the antics of individual members. Had they been able to reconcile minor ideological and jurisdictional disputes (e.g., issues of affirmative action, gay and lesbian rights, school prayer, community programs), their impact might have significantly altered the face of current social policy. Thus, it is impossible to contemplate the implications for contemporary society had they been more farsighted in their endeavors. In spite of themselves, however, they were successful in planting seeds of racism. Much like weeds, the products of such seeds are unpredictable and unbelievably resilient to the most concentrated efforts. The longevity displayed by traditional gangs must remain a major concern for law enforcement agencies. While concentrated efforts have successfully reduced supremacist membership and its mainstream appeal, the underlying foundation of racial dominance enforced by violence has not been affected. In fact, this framework has been adopted by a variety of volatile youths. These youths often mimic the ideologies and activities of traditional groups but eschew formalized institutions of hate and the superficial trappings they require (e.g., shaved heads, satin robes), thereby insulating themselves from governmental interest.

Like self-styled satanists or nondenominational churches, these gangs disavow formalization, perceiving organizations as inherently corrupt. These gangs are especially dangerous due to their ability to draft hate-filled scenarios free from law enforcement scrutiny. Inadvertently, this autonomy also allows crimes motivated by hatred to remain undetected. Unfortunately, this lack of detection reflects the gross inadequacy of current crime prevention measures and illustrates the need for a more careful perusal of incident reports. Furthermore, it is impossible to determine the depth of this new infestation of intolerance because these types of gangs are only identified if their criminal activity results in prosecution. Recent occurrences of racial violence and elevated levels of anti-Semitism have indicated a growing unrest in American society. The resurgence of racist ideology further indicates that criminal and civil proceedings against these organizations have not been successful in "curing" social intolerance. Metaphorically speaking, the venomous hatred espoused by supremacist organizations may be likened to a prevaccine epidemic. In the quest for quick-fix inoculations, root causes and the effects of short-term exposure to racist rhetoric have been overlooked, allowing pathological mutations to fester. The repercussions of such an oversight have not yet been evaluated.

ENDNOTES

1. Racism is predicated on supremacist ideology in that racists perceive themselves as superior to other races. Not all racist organizations are hate groups. Unlike other discriminatory organizations that seek to deprive other races of constitutional rights, hate groups seek to debase their very humanity (Kronenwetter, 1992). Although specific rhetoric varies, hate ideology is predicated on the belief that inferior groups pose a threat to the majority by their mere presence. Thus, the extermination of that race is essential to the preservation of society. Approved methods vary by group but include violence, forced sterilization, segregation, deportation, and even genocide.

2. Although many sources imply that Malcolm chose to leave the Nation of Islam upon discovering its leaders' penchant for adultery, a practice specifically forbidden by the Muslim faith, Malcolm stated that it was primarily due to his increasing popularity. He argued that his very public dismissal, attributed by Muhammad as a punishment for disobedience, was a calculated move by Muhammad to destroy Malcolm's credibility and isolate him from his followers. Malcolm further credited his dismissal as an attempt to conceal Muhammad's indiscretions, which he related to Malcolm prior to the split (X and Haley, 1964).

3. Space does not permit a thorough discussion of Malcolm X's (now El-Hajj Malik El Shabazz) transformation. However, in 1964, in an interview with Alex Haley, Malcolm recanted his earlier characterization of the white race as the devil race. He proposed that he had been blinded by Muhammad and that the Nation of Islam was more dissimilar than similar to the Islamic religion. He declared that all races could unite under one God, and he advocated a peaceful, nonviolent existence. This transformation, however, has been challenged, as Malcolm continued to depict the United States as a racial battleground. While the legitimacy of Malcolm's transformation remains questionable, the outcome does not: Regardless of his sincerity, Malcolm X was assassinated before the hatred and rage he created among young black males could be extinguished.

4. Betty Shabazz, Malcolm's widow, died on June 23, 1997, from burns sustained in a fire at her home. The blaze, determined to be arson, was set by her 12-year-old grandson.

5. Nation of Islam, 2005: www.noi.org.

6. Although originally convicted, Huey Newton continued to act as a rallying cry for many black organizations. He was released on bail in 1970, and all the charges concerning his involvement in the murder of Officer John Frey were dropped after two hung juries.

7. In fact, some of these pop icons inadvertently brought violence on themselves. Such was the case of actor/recording artist Tupac Shakur. The son of one of the New York 21, Shakur's lifestyle mirrored the gangsta rap that made him famous; unfortunately for Skakur, this mimicry resulted in his murder.

8. According to Kronenwetter (1992), slavery was attributed to economics, as it existed in all of the American colonies prior to its obsolescence. (It continued only in the southern region of the United States where the economic reasons for using slaves were the strongest.)

9. The Southern practice of scaring slaves into submission did not begin at the end of the Civil War; it was originally exercised by slave owners to maintain order.

10. Newly elected President Grant, along with Congress, enacted legislation designed to eradicate the Klan and other similar emerging groups (e.g., Knights of the White Camelia) and to prosecute their members. In fact, many of the original provisions were subsequently adopted by individual states, where they remain on the books; for example, most states still prohibit the wearing of masks in public places.

11. Cecil Ray Price, chief deputy sheriff of Neshoba County, was convicted with six others for the 1964 slaying of three civil rights workers (George and Wilcox, 1992).

12. It must be noted that many of the tactics employed by the FBI during this period have been harshly criticized. Some argue that COINTELPRO's main concern was not prosecution of felonious acts; rather, their activities were directed at disrupting legally protected avenues of communication and assemblage. Many also argue that these actions violated numerous constitutional rights; subversive practices of intimidation and illegal wiretaps are just two of the examples given. Many of these critics question whether the ends justify the means, citing

the case of Gary Rowe. While acting as a paid federal informant, Rowe participated in the murder of Viola Liuzzo, a civil rights worker. Encouraging Rowe to continue his participation in criminal activity, agents protected Rowe from prosecution for a collection of felonious charges, including murder. It may be argued that this knowledge, coupled with the agents' encouragement, indicated a gross disregard for the public they were allegedly protecting. Indeed these actions, consistent with many Hoover-era strategies, have been described as "cheap psychological warfare and dirty tricks" (George and Wilcox, 1992: 400).

13. Although short-lived, the importance of Robert Matthews's group, The Order (founded in 1983), cannot be overlooked in an evaluation of youth racism in the United States. Perhaps more militant than all previous organizations, The Order was responsible for several execution-style murders, including that of a government informant and Alan Berg, an outspoken Jewish radio personality. The Order was also responsible for a variety of criminal acts designed to elicit funds for future violent activities, including but not limited to several armored car heists, bank robberies, racketeering enterprises, and arms trafficking. The Order's ignominious reign of terror was concluded with the death of its founder, Robert Matthews, in a standoff with government agents. Unfortunately, the allure of The Order was only heightened by the execution of Matthews. Touted as a martyr, Matthews, in death, served to unify various factions of the militant right. Often declared the first "casualty of war" by many militant groups, Matthews accomplished something in his death that he could not have achieved had he lived—immortality.

14. Shortly after denouncing his racist past, Greg Withrow, the founder of AYM, was found near death. He had been beaten, stabbed repeatedly, and nailed to a wooden board (Hamm, 1993).

15. In 1988, Mulugeta Seraw, an Ethiopian immigrant, was beaten to death by three members of a Portland skinhead gang, East Side White Pride. Although this group had no formal ties with Metzger or WAR, racist propaganda written by Metzger (and published and distributed under the auspices of WAR) was found in the defendants' apartment. The subsequent civil lawsuit successfully argued that this publication was responsible for both the hatred expressed by the defendants and the techniques used in their attack on Seraw.

16. Swift's ideology is discussed in greater detail later in the text under the heading of "Christian Identity."

17. Some Christian Identity groups decry the sexualization and racialism of the trees of Eden and argue that the bastardization of the human race marking the entrance of a satanic lineage was created after Cain was cast out.

18. They argue that traditional Christian groups are the only ones attacked by the federal government, which lends its support to deviant groups. Their theory is strengthened by the pattern of conflagrations associated with federal agents pursuing radical white supremacists (Bushart et al., 1998). Robert Mathews—leader of the Order—was killed in a shootout with federal agents at Whidby Island, Washington, in 1983. His house (i.e., fortress) was burned to the ground. In the same year, Gordon Kahl, a flamboyant leader of the Posse Comitatus, was also shot and killed by federal agents in Arkansas. The farmhouse in which he made his last stand was also burned to the ground. Finally, the Branch Davidian Compound in Waco, Texas, along with dozens of its inhabitants, burned to the ground before evidence could be collected (Bushart et al., 1998).

CHAPTER 6

STREET GANGS

HISTORY

The Nineteenth Century

Street gangs, as we know them today, have evolved through the years from disorganized groups of street-corner hoodlums to violent yet businesslike organizations. This modification has come because of change to both inner administrative structures and gang business activities. Although there has been no decrease in their violent activities, there has been a significant increase in the types of profit-making criminal activities in which gang members participate.

Over the past 30 years, gangs have also increased their membership; many groups have expanded their territories to create nationwide (and in some cases worldwide) criminal gangs making a profit through criminal activities. There are few cities in the United States that do not have representatives from the Bloods, Crips, Latin Kings, Netas, or Mexican gangs in their vicinity. Street gangs, realizing that expansion produces an increase in the amount of their profit through drug sales, robberies, extortion, etc., are always ready to move into any locale that might produce a profit.

This increase in expansion has also brought about a drastic change in the makeup of gang membership. There no longer is any racial, ethnic, or other type of special requirement to be a member of a specific gang. This makes it easier for gangs such as the Bloods or Crips to move into and operate in areas previously described as untouchable neighborhoods because there was little or no minority population within these towns or cities. Many middle- to upper-class white areas have their own police departments, and officers in these agencies, aware of the fact that there are few minorities living in these locales, will often question and harass minority members seen hanging around or frequenting these neighborhoods. This, of course, impedes any type of criminal activity in these locations for minority gang members. Recruiting members of these communities into the gang assures gang leaders that they can carry out their business with little or no police pressure.

Historically, street gangs in the United States date back to the early to middle 1830s. A majority of these gangs and their members were from the poverty-ridden Five Points Area of New York City. The original Five Points Area encompassed the intersections of Cross, Anthony, Little Water, Orange, and Mulberry Streets. This section of the city measured approximately one acre, but over the years this acre of land produced some of the most violent gangs of the nineteenth and twentieth centuries. Most of these gangs had their beginnings in local taverns, tenements, or dance halls.

There was an increase in the number of local grocery store speakeasies that sold cheap booze, which became the watering holes for many early gang members. History indicates that the first New York City gang with some type of recognized leadership was formed in one of these local speakeasies. That gang, the Forty Thieves, went on to become one of the most notorious street gangs of its time (Asbury, 1928). Gangs such as the Shirt Tails, Roach Guards, Chichesters, Dead Rabbits, and Plug Uglies used the local speakeasies as meeting places where they planned their criminal activities.

The Plug Uglies wore huge plug hats, and they stuffed the inside of these hats with wood and leather. These hats were pulled down over their ears so that they served as helmets when members of the gang were involved in skirmishes. This gang's membership consisted of extremely large men of Irish heritage; these local tough guys were known as the most vicious gang in the Five Points Area. An appearance by a member of the Plug Uglies would cause members of other gangs to cower. A member of the Plug Uglies gang could be seen walking through the Five Points Area carrying a large club in one hand, a huge blunt instrument in the other hand, a firearm in one of his pockets, and this gigantic hat pulled down almost covering his eyes (Asbury, 1928). The sight of one of the members of this gang would put fear in the heart of an average person passing through the Five Points Area of New York City.

There were two other fairly notorious gangs that roamed the Five Points Area of New York City: the Roach Guards and the Dead Rabbits. The Roach Guards was formed and named after a local liquor sales person; it was a group of vicious thugs. The Roach Guards would victimize anyone entering their territory who would be considered weaker than the gang members and would target that person for robbery. In most instances, the members of the Roach Guards gang were identifiable by the clothing or colors they wore. All members of the Roach Guards wore pantaloons with blue stripes on the pants.

The Dead Rabbits were considered at one time to be part of the Roach Guards, but due to internal strife between different factions within the gang, a group of members broke away and formed the Dead Rabbits. They were famous as thieves and hoodlums who traveled the area of lower New York in search of a target they could assault and rob. They wore pantaloons with a red stripe on them and always carried a pike with a dead rabbit impaled on top of it (Asbury, 1928).

Bowery gangs also flourished during these times and constantly fought with the Five Point Area gangs. Both types of street gangs always found new ways to generate earnings. One way to gain easy money that was quickly discovered by the gangs was piracy. In fact, some of the New York gangs considered the most vicious and notorious of all time came out of the fourth ward of the city. Gang members roamed the docks, stealing anything that was left unprotected at night, or traveled the Hudson River in rowboats, pilfering any items left in docked boats or left unguarded on piers.

One disreputable gang was the Daybreak Boys, whose members included rogues with names such as Slobbery Jim, Sow Madden, Cow-Legged Sam McCarthy, and Patsy the Barber (Asbury, 1928). There was not a member of this gang who had not committed numerous robberies and at least one murder. At any time, gang members were ready to scuttle a vessel, crack the skull of a night watchman, or cut someone's throat (Asbury, 1928). This gang concentrated their criminal activities in both the East River and Hudson River areas and as a group were very successful thieves. In the mid-1850s, the police finally caught up with them and started hanging gang members for murders that they had been arrested and convicted for (Asbury, 1928).

In the late 1860s, a group known as the Charlton Street gang stole a sloop and cruised up and down the Hudson River from the Harlem River to Poughkeepsie, forcibly entering and robbing farmhouses and mansions along the river. This gang managed to terrorize local hamlets and, in some cases, kidnapped men, women, and children, demanding that some type of payment be made for the safe return of these hostages (Asbury, 1928).

One of the worst riots in New York City history took place in 1863, and blame for these riots was placed on conscription laws passed by Congress in March 1863. These new laws called for a draft-type procedure to increase the enrollment in the Union Army, which was being depleted due to casualties from heavy fighting in the Civil War. The cause behind this riotous behavior was gang nonsupport for conscription, but it was also a way for gangs to steal with little or no police intervention. Gangs throughout the city became deeply involved in the burning, robbing, and ravaging of the city until finally the military was brought in to suppress these insurgents (Asbury, 1928).

As many of the Irish started moving away from criminality and gang activity and into politics, new ethnic groups began to appear on the New York City gang horizon. Large groups of Eastern Europeans and Italians started immigrating to America. During the 1880s, the representation in the gangs changed to males (especially of the Jewish religion) from Eastern European countries, and these new gang members soon started appearing as gang leaders as well. One Jewish gang, the Monk Eastman gang, used the name of its leader as its moniker. Although the Jewish gangs ran a great deal of gang activity in the city, it was not long before the Italian gangs took over leadership and absorbed a great deal of the Jewish gangsters into their sphere of influence.

In the late 1890s, there was a large increase in the number of Italian immigrants arriving in New York as well as first-generation Italians participating in street gang activities. Once again, like the Jewish groups, the Italians observed the activities of the Irish street gangs and followed in their footsteps—first becoming members of existing street gangs, and then forming their own street gangs. One of the most ferocious gangs of the late 1800s was the Five Points gang. Paolo Antonini Vaccarelli (who used the street name Paul Kelly), along with his cousin Johnny Torrio, ran the gang. Members included people such as Al Capone and Lucky Luciano. Over a period of time, these Italian gangs sort of "grew up" to become the mafia/La Cosa Nostra. Street gangs as we view them today cannot be considered a unique phenomenon; they have been around for hundreds of years and will probably continue to prosper for the next hundred years.

The Twentieth Century

As a city, Chicago has had a great deal of street gang activity over the past 50 years, probably more than most cities in the United States. Within the past 40 years, California as a state has probably had more gang activity than any other state in the Union. A great deal of its gang activity started in the 1970s with the creation of the Bloods and Crips gangs in Los Angeles. New York City, on the other hand, has had at least 150 years of gang activity. Yet, up until the past 20 years, a great deal of the street gang activity in New York City has been held in check by the city's police department.

The street gang phenomenon has been greatly affected by migration. It started with the Irish street gangs, which were then followed by Eastern Europeans and Italians in the nineteenth century. The mid-twentieth century brought immigrants from Vietnam and other Asian countries. This led to an overwhelming rise in the number of Vietnamese and other Asian street gangs. Many members of these early Vietnamese street gangs served their apprenticeships with Chinese street gangs. The second wave of immigration included Salvadorians, Mexicans, and other Central American peoples. This wave resulted in the formation of both Salvadorian and Mexican street gangs, and they quickly swept across the United States.

Asian gangs have been active on the streets of New York and San Francisco for the past 40 years. They were followed by the Latin Kings, who originated in Chicago, and the Netas, who first appeared as a prison gang but who have now expanded onto the streets of New York City. The most recent street gangs to appear in the city are the Salvadorian and Mexican street gangs, but these gangs are making more of an impact on the two Long Island counties east of the city. This is especially true in Nassau County, where a great deal of street gang activity is continually kept from the public's eye by county politicians who fear that street gang activity will affect realty prices (and their tax base). With all this information in mind, we will now start detailing all you will possibly ever need to know about street gangs.

GANG IDENTIFICATION

One of the first things we must do is identify the signs that will indicate the presence of street gangs in a community. As a group, members of street gangs will leave telltale signs of their existence in a specific neighborhood. In some cases, these signs are explicit but in other cases are obscure and hidden. Overt signs by a gang or its members may be seen in graffiti, colors, clothing, symbols, and rituals, while clandestine signs can be manifested through day-to-day activities, conflicts, or frequency of specific types of criminal activity within a particular neighborhood.

Graffiti

The most obvious identifier of gang activity is the use of graffiti (see Figure 6–1). Over the years, graffiti has been seen as writing on walls; it is sometimes known as the local newspaper. Graffiti is used by gang members to mark their turf (territory), to notify other gang members of what is going on, to show disdain toward a rival gang, and to venerate a deceased member of the gang (RIP murals). Graffiti can be found in numerous locations including elevators, rooftops, public bathrooms, hallways, sides of buildings, train cars, bridges, and schools.

Gang members take pride in their turf (territory) or their area (neighborhood), a location they control and hang out in. Most gangs stake out a specific area or

Figure 6–1   Gang graffiti known as tagging is popular among street gangs.

neighborhood and claim it as their turf. At times this location can be a street corner, a specific number of city streets, a schoolyard, or a park. In any one of these areas, there will be a great deal of gang graffiti. This can be considered the staging area for the gang, and the gang's signs, colors, listing of names, and communications center will be somewhere close to this location.

For most people, graffiti looks like just a muddle of scrawling on a wall or building, but to a gang member it can contain a wealth of information. In most cases, the graffiti contains a prevalent color; this color usually represents the gang's color or colors (some gangs use more than one color). Gold and black represent the two colors used by the Latin Kings. Gang members may also use their colors within the graffiti by writing out phrases like "black and gold rule." There are times when the colors used in the graffiti are different from the gang's colors; in most cases, this is due to the fact that those are the only colors available to gang members.

Spray paint and markers are used to either write or draw informational graffiti, specific figures, or secret symbols. Another form of graffiti is known as scratchiti, which involves the scratching out of words or symbols in painted surfaces, wood, or glass with a knife. It is similar to graffiti but shorter in form because of either the effort required or the lack of space. Scratchiti is commonly seen in bus stop shelters, in public transportation locations, and on public transportation vehicles (buses or trains). Gangs such as the Bloods and Crips use different types of symbols or tags in their graffiti: The Bloods use three round circles in a triangular formation to represent a dog's paw print; the Crips use a six-pointed star (see Figure 6–2). The triangular circles and the six-pointed star are dominant in these gangs' graffiti. An example of Bloods gang graffiti would be a message such as *G-DOGNTG212*. *G-Dog* is the tag, *NTG* denotes Nine Trey Gangster (Bloods), and *212* (New York City's area code) signifies a Manhattan-based gang. See some examples in Figure 6–3.

Clothing

The latest trend in the way gang members dress has them moving away from the customary explicit display of gang colors in their clothing. We no longer see gang members wearing lots of red clothing (Bloods) or blue clothing (Crips). Styles of clothing have changed, and most of the gangs, especially East Coast groups, are now wearing designer-type clothing in place of their gang colors. Tommy Hilfiger, Calvin Klein, and FUBU (for us by us) are examples of choices for gang clothing. This doesn't mean that every one wearing certain designer clothing is a gang member, but it does mean that gang members favor a certain type of clothing. Gang members, for example, wear FUBU designer clothing because their meaning for FUBU is "Forever Us Bloods United." Bloods members prefer Calvin Klein clothing because they adapt CK to mean "Crip Killers."

Designer clothing is an in thing; gang members like being an in group and will use designer clothing and then create their own phrase(s) from the main lettering of the designer's name. Some clothing designers have created fashionable clothing with gang members in mind. Remember, clothing designers use rap music, videos, and magazines to promote their clothing. Another favorite type of clothing worn by gang members is athletic

(111th street Neighborhood Crip)   BLACK FAMILYS

Money or Murder   BLACK MUSLIMS

Figure 6–2   Crips Graffiti

team gear, and they might base their choice on an athletic team's colors. An example of this would be Bloods wearing the gear of the St. Louis Cardinals. Red is the color that Bloods relate to, so wearing Cardinal red would be a sign that you are a Bloods member.

Colors

A gang's colors are probably the thing the gang members hold as most sacred. Any defilement of their colors by another gang will immediately cause some type of violence to take place. Disregarding gang colors has caused some gangs to be involved in fights, drive-by shootings, and even murders of the other gang's disrespectful members. When a gang flies its colors, the members want to show others who they are and which gang they belong to. A bandana (known as a flag by gang members) is the

This is a warning to Blood gang members, rivals of the Folks as well as the Crips. SLOBS is a "put down" word used by Crips and Folks (who appear to be loosely aligning) to describe Blood gang members. Notice that the B is crossed out. This is another "put down" and warning for Bloods to stay away. Serious gang members will always write in a fashion to dis rival gangs. 187 is part of the California Penal Code number for homicide and 211 for armed robbery. If gang members use the word Blood or Crip instead of the dis words (Slob and Crab), a violation can be given.

East Coast represents Los Angeles gang orientation. "Cuzz" is a term of endearment used by Crips to address each other. Substituting dollar signs for the letter "S" indicates that this gang is selling narcotics.

BK stands for Blood Killer. Sometimes you will see CK which is Crip Killer.

Street names, signature of artists.

Typical Vice Lord Graffiti—the pyramid and eye of "Allah." The IVL stands for Insane Vice Lords, a Chicago group. CVL or Conservative Vice Lord graffiti is also sometimes seen. The drawing is said to represent the ancient pyramids and their black builders.

This indicates the name of the gang claiming this territory, usually a neighborhood name.

Folks is a reference to the Folk or Hoover Nation gang, which is based in Chicago but is popping up all over the South. Sometimes these gang members are also known as Shorty Folks, Shorties, and Black Gangster Disciples (BGDs).

These are the individual gang members' street names. Names are usually given based on a particular trait of the member.

The six-pointed star is the symbol of the Folks. In this example, they proudly proclaimed their affiliation and dissed (issued disrespect) the rival Vice Lords by turning the cane handle upside down (Vice Lords use the upright cane in their graffiti). The Folk Nation pitchfork is upright showing respect. The letters at the six points of the star are symbols of the concepts of the Folk Nation: life, loyalty, love, wisdom, knowledge, and understanding.

Figure 6–3   Interpretations of Gang Graffiti

customary way of showing colors by gang members. This type of flag can be carried in the back pocket, worn on the head, or spread across the face.

Gang members' clothing and accessories (bandanas, belts, shoes, and hats) will in most cases be color-coordinated according to the colors of the gang's flag. Throughout metropolitan New York City, area gang members display their colors through the beads they wear. Necklaces that are usually 24 inches in length are speckled with a series of gang colors and are worn by members. A member of the Latin Kings would wear a necklace containing yellow and black beads; the necklace would contain a string of five black beads and then a string of five yellow beads until a 24-inch necklace is completed. In some cases, a member will add a black and red symbolic bead to the sequence.

Another recently discovered method used to display gang membership was uncovered at Riker's Island jail. Corrections officers discovered that jailed gang members who tried to hide their membership in a gang colored the inside trouser pocket the color of the gang's flag. When the time came for the gang members to show their affiliation, the pocket would be turned inside out. This method makes it more difficult for corrections officials to identify prisoners with connections to street gangs.

Symbols

A person's affiliation with a gang can be expressed by the use of clothing, colors, symbols, and other accessories. Some gang members become obsessed with the gang colors and will not appear in public without some type of display of gang colors or symbols. Symbols can have their origin in the history of the gang, its culture or location, its religion or mystical beliefs. Specific jewelry, hats, patches, and tattoos are some of the ways gang members display symbols. Gang symbols are intended to be worn in the normal upward position. When a gang member captures or takes away an opposition gang's symbols, he will show disrespect for the opposition gang and for its symbols by wearing the symbols upside down or crossed out.

Rituals

Gang members use symbolic rituals that are part of their gang's culture. To attract new recruits and to help maintain the interest of their membership, gangs routinely use religion, black magic, and culture; they also use symbolic greetings, prayers, and ritualistic gatherings. Many gangs have started to imitate cults by using chants or prayers or initiation rites. Gang members might use a public park to conduct their rituals; they often stand in circular formations, with their hands clenched in the gang's hand sign. Some of these rituals are very similar to those for fraternity pledging.

Hand Signs

There are several ways gang members use hand signs or signals. To acknowledge their affiliation within the gang, gang members might use this type of nonverbal communication; in other cases, hand signals can be used to challenge another gang to partake in a skirmish. Gang members "throw signs," which means they form letters with their hands and fingers to depict gang initials or symbols. Through the use of these signs, gang members can indicate what gang they belong to (see Figure 6–4). The use of hand signals can also involve what is known as throwing down an opposing gang's signs. For example, if

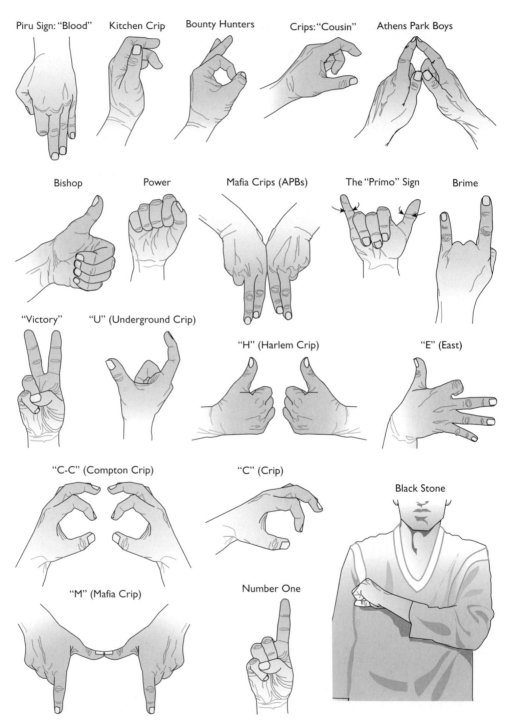

Figure 6–4   Gang Signs

a member the Chicago Vice Lords forms another gang's sign (such as a pitchfork) with his fingers and puts the sign in a downward position, this is a sign of total disrespect for the rival gang's symbol and can be considered a motive for a drive-by shooting.

Tattoos

Tattoos are an extension of gang graffiti and can show that a person is a member of a specific gang. Tattoos will normally include the name, initials, and symbols of the gang. Sometimes they may include the faction or neighborhood where the gang operates and hangs out. Gang members can have as many tattoos as they desire, and the tattoos can be of any size or detail. A great many of these tattoos are created and drawn by other gang members; the tattoos can be found on any part of the body. A recent trend involves the tattooing of a teardrop on a gang member's cheek to honor a fallen companion. Another way gang members honor a deceased gang member or leader involves tattooing his nickname, along with the initials RIP (rest in peace), on their body.

Definitions

Street gangs can be considered a group of people who align themselves with different social needs and then participate in conduct that many times requires the use of violent behavior. Gangs tend to create a great deal of havoc and fear within their areas of activity. A gang can consist of what we can consider just a rough and violent group of individuals, or it can be a group of disciplined males who plan and cleverly carry out their criminal activity.

Most of these gangs can be categorized into one of several groupings:

1. Nationwide gangs start out on a small scale in a local neighborhood and then expand throughout the United States and maybe even internationally. Bloods and Crips are examples.

2. International gangs have entered the United States to set up their criminal activities. Some examples would be the Jamaican, Russian, and Polish gangs.

3. Immigrant gangs have come to the United States to get involved in criminal activities for economic reasons. Some examples are the Chinese, Dominican, and Korean gangs.

4. Survival gangs are originally formed to provide peer support for adolescents. Some examples are the Vietnamese and Salvadorian gangs.

5. Some groups of young adults, who arrive in the United States without any other close family members, ultimately turn to violence and crime for the purpose of survival and for economic reasons. The Vietnamese and MS 13 gangs are two examples.

6. Established gangs, such as the Italians and motorcycle gangs, have been operating in the United States longer and with a higher level of competence, using both legitimate and illegitimate activities to enhance their profits.

All of these groups are similar in many ways, including their participation in drug activity, control of different areas throughout the United States, and extensive use of violence to attain their desired outcomes. Many of these gangs have formed alliances with other gangs to further enhance their criminal enterprises and to provide safer corridors for gang members to pass through while conducting business. We have to examine the reasons behind these alliances. The first reason is that organized crime/gang syndicates need the street gangs to handle street-level drug activities. Second is the need of a street gang to protect its territory; in many cases, these alliances form a protective ring around a gang's territory. Another reason for the formation of these coalitions is that drug suppliers normally provide many of these gangs with the drugs for street sales. Therefore, these gangs are aligned under a major drug syndicate (e.g., the Colombian, Nigerian, and Chinese syndicates). Because some gangs are all working for the same syndicate, the alliance is a way to ensure the safety of these gangs and their drug cohorts. Some examples of these alliances are what gangs call folk or people nations.

ORGANIZATION OF A GANG

A great deal of gang leadership is unorganized, without a true chain of command, and it can even be situational. Sometimes it is more a function of virility and reputation than of any group decision; other times there are constant changes in leadership. Leadership may also differ according to the gang's criminal activity; for example, the person running the drug operation may be different than the person who controls the gang's violent street activities. Gang leadership is usually influenced by age, time of membership in the gang, physical prowess, and influence over younger members of the gang. The longer the gang is in existence, the more established the leadership.

Membership will include hard-core members whose whole world revolves around the gang. Anything outside the gang lifestyle does not matter to them, and in most cases these members are the most violent. Most of the hard-core members are belligerently antisocial and have no use for anyone who does not agree with them. Associate gang members are usually newer members who are very visible within the gang community. Most gang members fall into this category, but a small portion of these members will follow in the footsteps of the hard-core members over time.

The third type of street gang member, known as a borderline member, is usually the youngest in the gang. These members tend to move in and out of gang activities, depending on their needs. A majority of borderline members are juvenile delinquents who grow up in the gang and are used by gang leaders to commit crimes for the gang. Activities these members participate in include drive-by shootings, robberies, burglaries, and sales of drugs. There is a fourth type of gang member that the gang depends on: a tagger. Taggers can be described as the public relations members within a gang. Most taggers avoid participation in the gang's criminal activities. What they do is focus on marking gang turf through the use of graffiti. Taggers also use graffiti to communicate with other members of the gang.

PROMINENT STREET GANGS

Mara Saldatrucha (MS 13)

During the early 1980s, El Salvador was experiencing an unbridled civil war. This war continued for over 12 years; during this time period, about 100,000 people were slain. During this same time frame, more than 1 million Salvadorians fled their country and migrated to the United States. The refugees, both legal and illegal, settled at first in California and Washington, D.C. Some of these immigrants were connected to La Mara (one of El Salvador's original violent street gangs). The Salvadorian immigrants immediately experienced cultural differences and were extremely disliked by existing American street gangs. Within a very short period of time, Mara Saldatrucha members quickly established themselves as an organized gang known for its excessive use of violence. Many of these gang members were former members of the Farabundo Marti National Liberation Front (FMLN). The FMLN was made up of peasant guerilla units that were trained to use high-tech weapons, explosives, and booby-trap techniques to engage in combat with El Salvador's affluent and influential elite, also known as the Fourteen Families.

Since the inception of MS 13 gangs in California and Washington, D.C., there has been a sizable expansion of these gangs throughout both the urban and suburban areas of at least 15 other states. The MS 13, as a street gang, can be considered somewhat different from most U.S. street gangs because members of MS 13 sustain a continuous communication network between themselves and MS 13 members in El Salvador. This affiliation between the members in both countries is a cause of great concern because the members in El Salvador have easy access to automatic weapons, hand grenades, and explosives due to the members' military backgrounds. On the streets of El Salvador, a grenade sells for about $1 and an M-16 rifle costs about $200 in U.S. currency. This coalition provides MS 13 members with access to a great deal of surplus military armaments and a network to traffic these weapons to the United States. The one weapon that is not easily accessible to MS 13 members is the semi-automatic pistol. There is a great demand for this type of weapon by gang members; in fact, MS 13 members are in such dire need of these pistols that they will actually accept this type of weapon in exchange for drugs.

Mara Saldatrucha (MS 13), like many other groups that come out of the ravages of war, has little or no fear of the police. This gang is responsible for the killing of three federal agents as well as the shootings of law enforcement officials throughout the United States and Central America. Like the Dominican gang

MARA SALVATRUCHA (MS 13)

Racial makeup. Gang members are Hispanic (predominately Salvadorian).

Gang colors. The gang uses blue and white (colors of Salvadorian flag).

Emblem. It is MSX3 (which stands for MARA SALVATRUCHA).

Criminal activities. These involve sales of narcotics and marijuana, assaults (serious physical injury to murder), thefts of vehicle parts and vehicles, robberies, criminal mischief, extortion, and intimidation.

Weapons of choice. These are machetes and knives.

History. During the 1980s, the United States experienced a large influx of immigrants from El Salvador. This mass immigration was largely attributed to the civil war that was raging in El Salvador. Many of these El Salvadorian refugees came to the Los Angeles area, with the majority settling in the Rampart section of the city. After a short time, the Mara Salvatrucha (MS 13) street gang began its criminal activities in the Los Angeles area. Although the Immigration and Naturalization Service (INS) has been successful in deporting many members of this gang, their members are now resurfacing on the East Coast. MS 13 has become one of the most violent street gangs in America, because many of its members have prior military (civil war) training.

members, MS 13 members booby-trap their stash houses. In some cases, this is done through the use of antipersonnel grenades and other dangerous explosives. There have also been cases in which individuals seeking to become full-fledged members of MS 13 are required to assault members of the law enforcement community.

MS 13 is a diverse criminal enterprise that has a number of sources of income:

1. Home invasion robberies
2. Auto thefts (The gang members then containerize the vehicles and ship them to South America, where the autos sometimes are exchanged for drugs.)
3. Extortion from legal businesses (as well as illegal businesses) operating in their territories (Gang members usually place a weekly or monthly tax on these businesses. If a business fails to comply with the gang's tax, there will be some type of retribution.)
4. Drug sales
5. Firearm and explosive sales

The original membership of MS 13 was totally Salvadorian nationals, but the gang now includes Mexicans, Guatemalans, Hondurans, and African-Americans. The MS 13 gangs are different from most traditional U.S. street gangs. It seems that each gang may not have one established leader or president; instead, senior members receive the necessary respect for their ability to survive for a number of years as an active member of the gang. The gang holds meetings on a regular basis in order to deal with incidents involving other gangs and to control all current activities being conducted by the MS 13 membership.

In the past several years, hard-core MS 13 members in El Salvador have been targeted by a death squad known as Sombra Negra (Black Shadow). The Sombra Negra has claimed responsibility for these killings in El Salvador, which has caused many MS 13 members to immigrate to the United States. Many of these are willing to take a life, if necessary, to avoid apprehension and deportation back to El Salvador.

Bloods

The Bloods street gang was set in motion at Sentinel High School in the Compton section of southeast Los Angeles in the late 1960s. The original gang name was PIRU, a name that is synonymous with the term "blood." The founders, Sylvester Scott and Vincent Owens, started this street gang as the Compton Pirus on West Piru Street in Compton; however, using the word "Piru" as a substitute for the word "blood" would not be well understood outside the Compton area. The Bloods was formed to protect its membership from rival gangs such as the Crips. Other gangs with the same motivation switched to the name Bloods or Piru to signify their alliance with the main gang.

Bloods members have become so considerable that several sets (or cliques) have developed within the gang. These particular sets often identify their group according to their place of origin, such as the Compton Bloods. Bloods wear red, and the gang color is very important to the members. The only article of blue clothing that a member of the Bloods gang will wear is jeans. Bloods are usually distinguishable by their red doo-rags (bandanas) that they wear on their heads. When communicating with each other, members of the Bloods gang avoid using the letter C in their vocabulary; in most cases, a gang member will substitute the letter B. For example, instead of saying "cigarette," a gang member would say "bigarette." Gang members do this in order to show disrespect for members of the Crips.

Since its inception in the late 1960s, the Bloods gang has grown nationwide to the point of having representative gangs in all major cities in the United States. In New York City, for example, the Bloods gang has been constantly growing and spreading to the suburbs. The infiltration into the metropolitan New York area was due the drug trade. The New York Bloods, like their counterparts throughout the United States, preach to the membership about happiness, affection, love, and peace. The gang members are told that giving their life up for the gang is the most important part of being a true Bloods. Members are recruited in schools, on the streets, and in correctional institutions throughout the metropolitan area. It is estimated by law enforcement agencies in metropolitan New York that there are more than 6,500 Bloods operating in this area.

Some specific guidelines set forth for the membership by the leaders of the Bloods gang include the following:

1. Every Bloods member should think of his brother before he thinks of drug use.
2. A brother in a higher rank should go around himself to see how his Bloods are doing.
3. Any Bloods member who may have a problem in his house that he cannot take care of can bring it to the attention of his head lieutenant or any of the lieutenants in his area.
4. Every Bloods member who holds a higher rank should never take it as means to overpower any of his brothers for any miscellaneous or biased reason.
5. Every Bloods member who holds a rank should respect his other brothers for their ranks as well as respect himself for his own rank.

The organizational structure of the Bloods gang is reasonably simple. Rank is aligned as follows:

1. *101—First Superior (Leader).* He oversees the set and is the disciplinary officer.
2. *102—Second Superior.* He assists and advises the first superior and takes command when the First Superior is not present.
3. *103—Minister of Defense.* He provides strategies and information to the First Superior for the operations of the set.
4. *104—Minister of Information.* He provides information concerning the set and its enemies.
5. *105—Head of Security.* He disciplines and provides weapons for all members of the set.
6. *106—Commanding Officer.* He dictates orders as detailed by the First Superior.
7. *107—Captain.* He distributes orders to the lieutenants.
8. *108—Head Lieutenant.* He informs and supports the Captain and performs his duties when he is not present.
9. *109—Lieutenant.* He watches over soldiers to ensure that they carry out orders given by the Captain.
10. *110—Principal Soldier.* He follows orders from lieutenants to keep banging (fighting) at all times.

Crips

The Crips was founded by Raymond Washington a short time after the 1965 riots in Watts, California, and members quickly established Crips as a very violent street gang in the early 1970s. Crips gang members have established the color blue as one of their major identifiers.

During the mid-1980s, there was a great deal of expansion by the Crips. The sale of crack/cocaine by gang members grew from a small drug operation on Central Avenue and 70th Street in Los Angeles to a nationwide venture. During the great crack/cocaine venture, many Crips started traveling to other states; some of their movement was due to a condition of their parole regulations. This led to the expansion of the Crips criminal enterprises into what was seen as virgin territory; soon there was increased violence in these new territories. Suddenly, areas that had little or no violence now had to deal with drive-by shootings during Crips turf wars with some of the already-entrenched local gangs. There was as much violence with outside gangs as there was within the Crips sets. Disputes within these sets would also lead to drive-by shootings by one Crips set against another. Crips expansion has continued to the point where they now have representation in all 50 states.

Crips expansion into New York City was first observed in 1993. The first Crips set in New York was the Harlem Crips; their members adopted the Los Angeles Crips dress style, including khaki pants, blue T-shirts, blue handkerchiefs, and blue and clear beads. It seems that many of the early members of the New York City Crips were immigrants from the Central American country of Belize. Membership in the Harlem Crips also included a group of California Crips, which had the name Harlem Crips changed to the Rolling Thirties Crips (RTC) so that this group was directly connected to a Los Angeles Crips gang of the same name. The RTC has managed to organize a rather profitable drug venture in New York City. What this lucrative business has done is to create drug wars between the Crips and other gangs, including the Bloods and the Latin Kings.

Besides the Belize members, there is also a large Hispanic population in the New York City Crips gang. Crips sets in the New York City metropolitan area are not as well structured as their brother gangs in Los Angeles. It seems that status in the New York City gang is gained through a reputation that usually relates to the amount of time a person has been a member of the gang; a senior gang member will have rank because of all the battles he has fought. In many cases, this will place gang leadership in the hands of the most senior members of the gang, who are also considered the gang's top warriors.

The Bloods and the Crips: Murders of Tupac Shakur and Biggie Smalls.   The Bloods and Crips gangs exist throughout the United States. Discussion of these street gangs would not be complete without the inclusion of the murders of Tupac Shakur and Biggie Smalls, also known as Christopher Wallace (real name) and notorious B.I.G., respectively. There was a connection between both victims and Suge Knight, and that connection will be thoroughly discussed in this section.

One of most amazing unsolved homicides in the history of the Los Angeles Police Department (LAPD) occurred on March 9, 1997: Biggie Smalls was murdered outside the Petersen Automotive Museum in Los Angeles. A very interesting aspect of both the Biggie Smalls and the Tupac Shakur homicides took place on March 18, 1997, when a black male in a Mitsubishi Montero pulled up next to a white male driving a battered Buick Regal. The black male in the Montero started a heated argument with the white male in the Regal. A gun was pulled by the black male in the Montero, and after a chase, the white male in the Regal shot and killed the black male in the Montero. It turns out that both participants in this fatal shooting were members of the LAPD. The white male, Frank Lyga, was an undercover narcotics officer, while the black male, Kevin Gaines, turned out to be a corrupt LAPD officer who was a member of the Bloods and a close associate of Suge Knight, owner of Death Row Records and a member of the Mob Piru Bloods. The assigned LAPD detective, Russell Poole, soon found himself in the middle of a controversy that involved the cover-up of Gaines's background by then LAPD Chief Bernard Parks (Sullivan, 2001). Parks requested that Internal Affairs conduct an investigation into Officer Lyga even though the shooting had been found legitimate and was within LAPD's deadly force guidelines by the shooting board and a special three-member panel of black supervisors convened by Chief Parks. Parks continued to shield Gaines even after a significant amount of documented information showed that Gaines was a notoriously corrupt officer. A short time later, Poole received information that Gaines was a participant in the Biggie Smalls murder. Then on April 9, 1997, Poole was assigned as the lead investigator in the Smalls case (Sullivan, 2001).

One of the first conclusions Poole came to was that the Smalls murder was a virtual replication of the Tupac Shakur murder in Las Vegas about six months prior to this murder. Shakur was shot and killed on September 7, 1996, while riding in a vehicle with Suge Knight. A white Cadillac pulled up alongside Knight's BMW, shots rang out, and Shakur was hit four times. He would die six days later in a Las Vegas hospital (Sullivan, 2002).

As a gangster, Suge Knight was arrested several times for assaulting people. In the early 1990s, Knight started working on forming his own record company and used his skills of exploiting people to convince rappers such as Dr Dre, DOC, and Michel'le to become his clients. This (plus an alleged threatening visit to the owner of Ruthless records, Easy E, at his studio) helped ease the transfer of personnel managers. A short time later, Snoop Dog became part of Suge's growing empire as Death Row Records grossed over $60 million at the end of its first year of business (Sullivan, 2001).

Knight and his Mob Piru Bloods gang quickly enhanced their reputation as the bad-ass gangsters through their actions with the rap singers, journalists, and other record company executives. Knight pistol-whipped Lynwood Stanley to intimidate Lynwood and his brother George. Knight was arrested and charged with felonious assault, but Suge used bribery to ease the possibility of Knight's imprisonment. Suge gave a million-dollar recording contract with his record company to Lynwood Stanley. Then, suddenly, the assistant district attorney prosecuting Suge became part of the conspiracy by suggesting that Knight receive a one-year suspended sentence. It was soon discovered that the daughter of prosecutor Lawrence Longo had signed a recording contract with Suge's record company; Longo also managed to lease his Malibu Colony home to Suge for $19,000 a month. Needless to say, Longo was forced to resign from the prosecutor's office a short time later (Sullivan, 2001).

Once his criminal case was settled, Knight sought out Tupac Shakur, who was doing time in Dannemora Prison for sexual assault, and convinced Shakur to sign with Death Row Records. This was actually the beginning of the end for Tupac, because within a year of this signing, he would be dead (Sullivan, 2001).

Shakur Tupac. The circumstances surrounding the death of Tupac are very similar to those of Biggie Smalls. Tupac was in Las Vegas on September 7, 1996, to attend a Mike Tyson fight. The fight was over in a very short period of time, and Shakur and Knight returned to the MGM Grand Hotel with their entourage of Mob Piru Bloods bodyguards. In the lobby of the MGM Grand, they saw Orlando "Baby Lane" Anderson, a Compton Southside Crips who had recently been involved in the robbery of one of Shakur's bodyguards. Shakur, Knight, and their bodyguards proceeded to pummel Anderson for more than 30 seconds, at which time hotel security broke up the beating. Shakur and his group left while a beat-up Anderson headed back to the Excalibur Hotel. Anderson changed his clothing and headed for the Treasure Island Hotel, the home base for Crips members when attending boxing matches in Las Vegas. It was decided during a meeting at Treasure Island to retaliate against Shakur by shooting him when he left the 662 Club that night in Vegas (Phillips, 2002).

After the shooting of Shakur, the allegation was denied by Biggie Smalls and P. Diddy. P. Diddy, the owner of Bad Boy records (which Biggie Smalls recorded for), showed proof that Biggie was in a recording studio in New York when this incident took place. The Crips, seeing the opportunity to make some money on the shooting of Shakur, allegedly contacted Biggie Smalls, who was staying at the MGM Grand Hotel and who disliked Shakur. Smalls supposedly agreed to pay $1 million to the Crips to kill Shakur, providing the Crips used Biggie's 40-caliber Glock pistol (Phillips, 2002; Sullivan, 2001). (After conducting research into the Shakur homicide, we have a great deal of doubt that this meeting ever took place or that Biggie Smalls has anything to do with this murder. We find it easy to believe that this whole episode surrounding the participation of Biggie in the Shakur murder could have been created by Knight to cover up his involvement in this crime. See Philips, 2002; Sullivan, 2001; Waxman, 1999.)

Knight and Shakur left the hotel in a five-car caravan of Death Row Records people/Mob Piru Bloods, with Knight driving and Shakur riding in the lead car. As the vehicles headed up the strip toward the 662 Club, Anderson and three other Crips had just left Treasure Island in a white Cadillac, with Anderson sitting in the rear left seat. As the Cadillac turned onto Flamingo Road, the Crips realized that the caravan carrying Tupac was right in front of them. An instant decision was made by the Crips to shoot Tupac as soon as possible because an opportunity like this may not occur later. The Cadillac quickly pulled alongside Shakur's car, and Anderson opened fire, with four bullets hitting Shakur and one bullet grazing Knight's head. Tupac died six days later at University Medical Center in Las Vegas (Phillips, 2002).

Two days later a gang war took place in Compton, California, between the Bloods and the Crips. As a result of this warfare, there were 12 people wounded and 3 people killed during drive-by shootings committed by members of both gangs. "Baby Lane" Anderson, the alleged shooter of Tupac, was shot and killed in 1998 in Compton without ever being properly interrogated or investigated by an inept Las Vegas Police Department. The police said the shooting of Anderson was unrelated, but anyone with knowledge of this case knows this could not be true. The 3 other Crips who were in the white Cadillac the night of the shooting are still alive and living in Compton (Phillips, 2002).

Commentary on the Shakur Murder.   It seems quite evident to anyone with investigative experience that the Las Vegas police blew this case. The police mishandled the investigation from the start: They mismanaged the crime scene, the evidence handling, and the searches of people at the scene; they did a poor job of interviewing witnesses (of which there were many still at the scene) and following up leads (especially information gathered by the Compton Police Department). This is only a sampling of how poorly the Las Vegas police messed up this investigation. What sticks out the most is the lack of care and interest in solving the murder of a male black rapper. What if the deceased had been Justin Timberlake? Would the investigation still be unsolved? It's doubtful. This case should have been solved; ask any good investigator who has read the facts surrounding this case. (The writer of this section and coauthor of the book is a retired NYPD investigator who handled numerous homicide investigations during his illustrious career in the NYPD.)

Biggie Smalls.   When we review the Biggie Smalls homicide, we will see quite a few similarities when we compare it to the Shakur murder. As mentioned in the Tupac discussion, Biggie Smalls allegedly (and it is allegedly) paid the Crips $1 million to kill Tupac. We also know that Suge Knight had an ongoing feud with both P. Diddy and Biggie Smalls of Bad Boy records plus the issue of abuse of a Crips bodyguard by Biggie Smalls.

On March 9, 1997, Biggie Smalls was shot and killed in Los Angeles after attending the Soul Train Awards. After the awards, Biggie Smalls, along with P. Diddy and other members of the Bad Boy record crew and bodyguards, attended a party at the Petersen Automotive Museum in Los Angeles. This group left the party in a five-car caravan with P. Diddy in the first car and Biggie in the second car. A black Chevrolet Impala pulled up alongside Biggie's vehicle and opened fire at the passenger's door of the car he was riding in, which resulted in the death of Biggie Smalls (who was pronounced dead upon his arrival at Cedars-Sinai Medical Center) (Sullivan, 2001).

The LAPD major case squad was assigned this case a month later, and the detective assigned was Russell Poole, the same investigator who handled the investigation of the earlier police shooting. During the investigation of this crime, Poole learned that Snoop Dog, after performing at the Los Angeles Universal Amphitheater in 1998, made statements to a Los Angeles County Sheriff's Department officer. The officer told Snoop that he knew who killed Tupac. Snoop stated to this police lieutenant that "I do too: the guy who was seated next to him." The lieutenant replied, "You mean Suge Knight?" and Snoop quickly replied "Yes" to the question (Sullivan, 2001: 93).

Poole questioned Frank Alexander, a Suge Knight bodyguard. Alexander informed Poole that Knight was in debt to Shakur for well over $6 million and that Knight refused to pay this money back to Shakur. Alexander told Poole that "Knight knew he was being videotaped while beating Orlando Anderson and staged the whole thing to give himself cover for Tupac's killing. I eventually came to believe that Anderson was paid to be there and take that beating" (Sullivan, 2001: 93).

The problem Poole had was that he never had an opportunity to interview Orlando Anderson. Anderson was shot and killed in Compton in early 1998.

Another witness, Yafeu Falu, was killed earlier in a housing project in New Jersey. Alexander and Kevin Hackie, another former Suge Knight bodyguard, further informed Poole that the killing of Biggie Smalls eliminated Death Row Records' biggest competitor and, in turn, distanced Knight from the killing of Tupac because it would look like the Smalls murder was in retaliation for the murder of Shakur (Sullivan, 2001).

During this investigation, Death Row Records' role in drug trafficking came to the surface. It seems that Suge Knight had gone back to his old role as a drug dealer. Death Row Records supplied both the Bloods and the Crips with cocaine; both gangs bought cocaine from Suge and Death Row Records people for $18,500 in Los Angeles and then sold the cocaine in New York for $26,000. Investigators turned up evidence that a number of LAPD officers, including Kevin Gaines, were not only drug couriers for Death Row Records but also counselors who advised Knight on Death Row Records' drug activities (Sullivan, 2001).

Discovering that members of Death Row Records were involved in drug trafficking also opened the door to the involvement of an LAPD officer and employees of Death Row Records in a bank robbery. David Mack was the officer involved in the bank robbery and was identified by his girlfriend, as the bank robber. There were also two unapprehended accomplices with Mack during this robbery. Money taken during the robbery was found on Mack's person as well as in his residence. While searching Mack's residence, a black Impala SS was found in his garage. Recall that the person who shot and killed Biggie Smalls was driving a black Impala SS. Detectives soon discovered that the first person to visit Mack in jail was Mack's old friend Amir Muhammed, who is a dead ringer for the shooter in the Biggie murder (Sullivan, 2001).

Commentary on the Smalls Murder.   When we view this case, we find there is very good reason to believe that the following are possibilities:

1. Suge Knight, because of his membership in the Mob Piru Bloods and because of his connections with both the Bloods and the Crips, conspired to have Tupac Shakur murdered. He then set it up to look like Biggie Smalls paid the Crips to kill Shakur. The similarities in the way these homicides were carried out are beyond coincidence.

2. Suge Knight conspired with LAPD officers Kevin Gaines, David Mack, and Ray Perez to obtain and sell the drugs, commit the bank robberies, and kill the rap singers. When the bank robbery took place, there were two other accomplices who were not apprehended.

3. The investigation of the Biggie Smalls homicide was unsolved because the hierarchy of the LAPD did not want it disclosed that members of the LAPD were involved in the Smalls murder through their association with Suge Knight. The LAPD was also aware that approximately 50 members of that department worked for Death Row Records.

4. The hierarchy of the LAPD (its chief and assistants) did everything in their power to shut down both the investigation into the Smalls murder and the allegations of corruption in the Rampart Division by detective Poole. The LAPD administration went so far as to reduce Poole's report on the Smalls homicide and the Rampart police corruption accusations from 40 to 2 pages to hide the truth from the public (Philips, 2002; Sullivan, 2001; Waxman, 1999).

All of this information is documented and factual. It shows that a minority of high-ranking police officials in the LAPD controlled the Smalls homicide in almost the same manner as the Las Vegas Police Department handled the Shakur homicide. In fact, in 2002 the estate of Biggie Smalls filed a civil suit against the LAPD in the U.S. District Court for the Central District of California. The suit states that LAPD Officer David Mack and Amir Muhammad (a friend of Mack's whose photo looks just like the artist's sketch drawn of the shooter of Biggie by witnesses after the shooting) conspired to kill Biggie. It further indicates that LAPD Chief Bernard Parks intentionally, willfully, and recklessly deferred and blocked Poole's investigation into the death of Biggie once it turned out to be evident that members of the LAPD were participants in this homicide (Bent, 2004).

The Almighty Latin Kings

The Almighty Latin Kings is an organized crime group that has continued to expand since it was created in two Hispanic communities in Chicago about 50 years ago (see Figure 6–5). One part of this gang developed in South Chicago while another group appeared around the same time in the Humbolt Park section of Chicago. The original Latin King gang had two factions: One consisted of Mexican members who followed a five-point crown; the other consisted of Puerto Ricans who at that time identified with a three-point crown. Both groups used the colors yellow and black to represent the gang. This gang has expanded throughout the United States, with their major faction now based in New York City. Today the Almighty Latin King Nation (ALKN) has joined with the Almighty Latin King Queen Nation (ALKQN), resulting in an estimated 100,000 members spread throughout the United States. A majority of the hard-core membership ranges between the ages of 15 and 40 years old.

The Latin Kings were originally a loosely knit street gang. In many ways the early Latin Kings were very similar to the original Chinese street gangs in New York in that they were formed for the same basic reasons:

1. To protect their turf from being invaded and taken over by other ethnic groups
2. To prevent unwarranted attacks on Hispanic residents because of their ethnicity and
3. To maintain the culture that the Hispanic people brought with them into this community

Thus several small Hispanic communities in Chicago ended up with their own neighborhood security force that helped maintain the safety of all Hispanic residents. They

Figure 6–5   Almighty Latin Kings graffiti. Hispanic gangs tend to be more flamboyant in their art.

also did their best to keep other ethnic groups outside this area. The ultimate outcome was that these groups, over the years, expanded into locations outside of Illinois and turned into violence-oriented street gangs that would do almost anything unlawful for a profit.

At one time, the major portion of this gang's membership was confined to correctional facilities throughout California, Connecticut, Illinois, New Mexico, and New York. It is only within the past 15 years that this gang set out on a major recruitment drive that has resulted in a very sharp increase in the number of gang members in the United States. Today, they have set up a high-caliber network of recruiters who work both inside and outside the prison walls to increase their membership. The ALKN has also managed to form an affiliation with the People Nation.

ALKN gang members appeal to the pride of young Hispanics, telling them they should know and maintain their heritage (see Figure 6–6). During their tenure as

Figure 6–6   ALKN Symbols and Grafitti

gang members, they will be able to expand their own (as well as other gang members') personal, social, and economic growth. Juveniles between the ages of 10 and 12 are recruited into the gangs and are known as Pee Wee members, while young teenagers between the ages of 12 and 14 are known as Juniors. Older adolescents between the ages of 16 and 20 are called Homeboys. Females who join the Almighty Latin King Queen Nation become gang members and must follow the same codes as male members. Females are used by the male gang members as drug dealers (see Figures 6–7, 6–8, and 6–9), gun holders, and partners in sex. New members are not informed of the consequences that they face as gang members if they step out of line. What they find out is that if they make a serious mistake or fail to perform a task properly, they will more than likely be either beaten on sight (BOS), tortured, or terminated on sight (TOS) by other gang members. Two specific instances indicate the danger faced by gang members who violate gang rules. In the first case, gang member William Cartagena was decapitated, burned, and left in the bathroom of his Bronx apartment for violating gang policy by becoming a police informer. Another member, James Gonzalez, was shot to death in Manhattan for violating gang rules related to homosexual activities (Executive Crown Authority, 1991; O'Shaughnessy, 1994; Tabor, 1994).

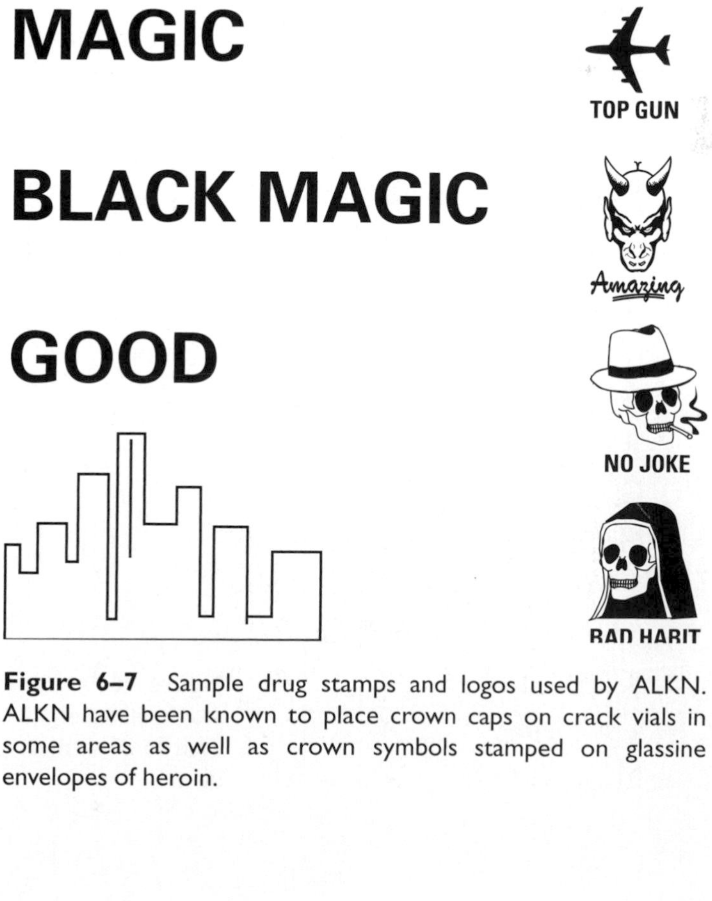

MAGIC

BLACK MAGIC

GOOD

TOP GUN

Amazing

NO JOKE

BAD HABIT

Figure 6–7 Sample drug stamps and logos used by ALKN. ALKN have been known to place crown caps on crack vials in some areas as well as crown symbols stamped on glassine envelopes of heroin.

	1	2	3	4	5
1	A	P	F	U	K
2	C	R	H	W	M
3	E	T	J	Y	O
4	D	S	I	X	N
5	B	Q	G	V	L

Sample: 55,11,32,43,45

(L A T I N)

15,43,5,53,42

(K I N G S)

Figure 6–8 Recently seized ALKN alphabet code. When choosing a letter, the ALKN member will read across and then down. Note that there is no "Z" in this code.

As an organized criminal group, the ALKN has to be considered a well-established gang that has a hierarchical structure. It also has an ever-present chain of command that demands that members strictly adhere to the group's charter. The hierarchy structure of the ALKN is described in the boxes on pages 207–209.

The Council Committee is the highest level of command within the Latin King Nation's chain of command. Leaders of the Latin King Nation are selected according to their rank to serve on the Council Committee, whose major purpose is

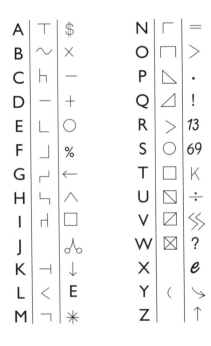

Figure 6–9 Sample of an ALKN alphabet. The alphabet is used to cloak messages to each other.

THE COUNCIL COMMITTEE STRUCTURE

Crown Chairman (also known as Padrino, meaning Father). He has total control over the gang and is the leader as well as the arranger of all the legitimate and illegitimate activities of gang members.

Executive Crown. He is second in command and runs the organization when the Crown Chairperson is not available. He reviews and analyzes planned activities of the gang membership and must also make sure that order is maintained during council meetings.

Prime Minister of Defense. He must stay on top of all security matters, provide security for all events involving the gang, and keep an updated list of all people who dislike or oppose the gang.

Crown Treasurer. He maintains all the gang's financial records, collects all back dues, and sets up budgets for all the gang's projects.

Crown Secretariat. He is the major administrative official of the gang. He must keep records relating to all gang meetings and assist the Executive Crown, Prime Minister of Defense, and Crown Treasurer. Any time records are inspected, he must be present to ensure that everything goes smoothly.

Regional First Crown of All Chapters. He maintains order in the gang and institutes social and business activities both inside and outside the gang's ranks. He must also solve any problems within each regional organization and distribute all policy changes to the membership.

Source: Executive Crown Authority, 1991.

to provide the membership with an open line of communication throughout the organization.

A second level of leadership, known as the Supreme Chapter, is responsible to make sure that all of the Council Committee's mandates and recommendations are transmitted to and executed by all members of the organization.

The third and final level of this organization is the regional chapters, whose members work for the betterment of the whole gang (Executive Crown Authority, 1991).

Rank designation is done through the use of colored beads: Black beads represent death and gold represents life. Members have five black beads followed by five gold beads, while leaders of the gang have five black beads followed by two gold beads. Black beads are worn in respect of prior members who have suffered and died for the cause of the Latin King Nation; gold beads represent the brightness of the sunlight that so gloriously illuminates the gang's crown. This emblem of the gang is a five-point

SUPREME CHAPTER STRUCTURE

Supreme First Crown. He is the highest-ranking Crown leader. Whatever rules he proposes or mandates are considered the law to be followed by all gang members. He is in total control of his region, and his major task is to make certain that everyone in the organization follows the guidelines set forth both by the Council Committee and by him.

Supreme Second Crown. He functions as second in command of the region; like the First Crown, he makes sure that all policy is adhered to by all of the membership. The Second Crown will run this organization anytime the First Crown is on leave.

Supreme Warlord. He is considered to be the gang's defense minister; he plans and implements a great deal of the strategy used by the gang during confrontations with other groups. Another assignment relegated to him is the behavior of gang members. The Supreme Warlords are responsible for the conduct of the membership, and it is their job to detect any wrongdoing within the organization. It is also their job to punish any subordinates who disobey organizational guidelines and/or standards.

Supreme Crown of Arms. He works directly for the Supreme Warlord. His main function is to manage and review all of the security strategies related to the gang's field operations. He is also responsible for both the upkeep and upgrading of all the gang's weapons, ammunition, and other defensive equipment.

Supreme Captain Crown Advisor. He has an appointed supervisory position that requires him to inform the Crowns of the history, customs, regulations, and other conditions within the organization. As a leader within the gang, he gives advice that is heavily relied on by most of the highest-ranking members of the organization.

Guardian Crown. He is one of a group of gang members that acts as a security force used to protect the Supreme First Crown and other superior officers within the organization.

crown, with each point representing one of the following five factors (Executive Crown Authority, 1991):

1. *Love.* It is carried in the hearts of the members for the Crown as well as for all other members of ALKN.
2. *Respect.* It should be shown for all other members of the Latin King Nation and the Crown. Respect for other members should coincide with the high esteem the members hold for the ALKN.
3. *Honor.* It should be shown for all other members as well as for the leaders of the ALKN. Members must always respect and honor the organization.

REGIONAL CHAPTER STRUCTURE

First Crown. He is an appointed leader who controls a specified region. He is the highest-ranking Crown in the organization and must be accorded the same respect as other high-ranking bosses.

Second Crown. He substitutes for the First Crown whenever necessary and checks the membership to assure the leaders that all members throughout the region are adhering to all gang procedures and policies.

Minister of Defense. He is placed in command of present and future strategies used by the gang to maintain its control over old or new territories, disgruntled membership, business partnerships, or threats from other gangs. He must constantly be in contact with the Supreme Warlord, who advises him on tactics and/or strategies.

Crown of Arms. He is the main advisor to the Minister of Defense and the one who maintains security throughout the gang. He controls the procuring and allocating of weapons to gang members throughout this region; he also sets up security for all field operations and keeps records on all chapter meetings.

Captain Crown Advisor. He advises gang leaders on all activities, present and future, involving members of the gang. Sometimes he is considered the gang historian because of his knowledge of gang history, customs, and procedures.

Crown Prince. He is the supervisor of all field operations who requires all members to fully comply and participate when they are assigned to field operations.

Source: Executive Crown Authority, 1991.

---

4. *Sacrifice.* It means members give up everything mentally, physically, and emotionally for the benefit of the ALKN and its membership.
5. *Obedience to ALKN.* It is shown by its members. As it is for members of a very close-knit family, it is very important that all members obey and remain loyal both to ALKN leaders and to the constitution set forth for the members of the ALKN.

A great deal of the income procured by the members of ALKN comes from their participation in drug trafficking, and most of this is done at the street level. Gang members, under the guidance of their leaders, also participate in extortion rings, weapons trafficking, and other violent activities as well as drug trafficking. Once the gang members move an operation into a neighborhood, it does not take them long to take over all the unlawful activities in that community. The ALKN has managed to do this throughout neighborhoods in Connecticut, Illinois, and New York. Federal and local law enforcement agencies have arrested numerous gang members for illegal activities involving drugs and guns. One of the most ignominious incidents took place in Staten Island in 1995. During a drug raid at the Staten Island home of ALKN leader Jose Santos, police discovered a 15-month-old baby girl lying in a crib not only wearing the traditionally colored gang beads but also having a semiautomatic pistol on each side of her head. Needless to say, four gang members were arrested for possessing drugs and weapons as well as for endangering the welfare of the child (New York City Housing Police Department, 1994; Pierre-Pierre, 1995).

Today the majority of the membership is ethnically Puerto Rican. There was little or no Mexican representation in the East Coast ALKN, and Mexican representation in Chicago faded as the Mexican community grew and formed its own Mexican gangs. The founders of the ALKN professed the need for love, respect, honor, sacrifice, and obedience in order to have unity within the gang. These five points are represented in the five points of the ALKN crown. During the mid-1980s, the Latin Kings started action for prisoners' rights, and this action actually helped bring about unification throughout the ALKN; it also brought about great expansion of the gang throughout the metropolitan New York area.

Throughout the past 15 years, membership requirements in the ALKN have become a little more modified, but a person must still have Latin blood to become a full-fledged member. Today, this includes a parent or grandparent from Spain, Portugal, France, Italy, Romania, Latvia, Virgin Islands, South or Central America, Puerto Rico, Cuba, Mexico, Dominican Republic, Antilles, or the Caribbean. Yet, with this in mind, the ALKN has over time crowned a number of non-Hispanic members who do not fit the preceding membership requirements list. Remember, as it is with all other gangs, it is power and money that count, not tradition. This gang has gone as far as to hire public relations experts to try and make the gang look good within the Puerto Rican community. In the past 5 years, the ALKN has tried to work with both New York State and New York City correctional authorities in an attempt to create its own hostel that would act as a safe house for its members recently released from prison. This hostel would provide training, education, and guidance to released members. Over the years, the ALKN has spent a great deal of time interacting with imprisoned members of other criminal organizations in an effort to become more efficient in and expand its present criminal activities. There is no door that this gang will not attempt to open in order to gain more power. Political campaigning for its chosen candidates involves the use of hundreds of gang members handing out campaign fliers and then mass voter registration drives (including the use of intimidation of voters in order to gain votes for its candidates).

Like many other gangs, ALKN has as its main source of income drug sales, but gang members are also involved in robbery, burglary, assault, auto theft, extortion, fraud, and drive-by shootings. In the late 1990s, the ALKN started to increase its presence outside the major cities. This move was due to the expanded pressure being placed on the gang members by local law enforcement. Gangs such as the ALKN have found it easier to operate in smaller cities and towns where there is an Hispanic presence in the population. This provides the ALKN with the ability to live in the Hispanic community with little or no community law enforcement action and still carry out its criminal activities in the bigger cities, which (in most cases) are not that far away.

All members are required to own a set of black and gold beads that are used in a necklace that is considered sacred. There is no set requirement to actually wear the beads. Some members wear the beads with a crucifix attached to the bottom; some

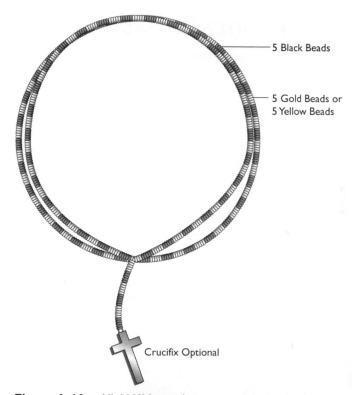

5 Black Beads

5 Gold Beads or
5 Yellow Beads

Crucifix Optional

Figure 6–10   All ALKN members must own a set of beads. The beads, which they say are sacred, are merely a sequence of strand beads worn in the fashion of a necklace. The beads will be black and gold (or yellow). Some beads are longer than others and some will have a cross (crucifix) at the bottom. Some members will always wear the beads while others refrain from wearing them.

other identifiers of gang members include black and gold clothing, black and yellow key chains, ALKN tattoos, yellow bandanas, Calvin Klein hats, beads in the rear-view mirror of a vehicle, and shaved spots in eyebrows (see Figures 6–10 and 6–11).

ALKN has gone as far as to create its own alphabet in an effort to conceal messages sent between members. The gang members hold local group meetings on a weekly basis; in most cases, they meet on Friday nights. Then they hold larger chapter, division, or state meetings on a selected Saturday each month. These meetings were always held in public parks, but due to police surveillance of outside gatherings, most of the meetings have been moved into local auditoriums or halls. The ALKN has created its own hit teams. These hit teams are used to carry out special missions and murder contracts and are known as TOS (terminate on sight). Members of these teams wear white beads with one green bead; when on a mission, they wear all-black clothing

ALKN IDENTIFIERS

Black and gold (yellow) clothing
Yellow beepers
Black and yellow keychains
Yellow bandana
A.L.K.N. tattoos
Crown insignias, jewelry, tattoos
ALKN jackets, hats, shirts, etc.
Beads hanging from rearview mirror in auto

Some members display Crown Air Fresheners on their dashboard (These are common to non-ALKN in NYC, don't jump to conclusions!)

"Crown Air Freshener"

SHAVED EYEBROWS

Right Eyebrow
Two (2) shave marks symbolize the two years that King Blood has spent away from his people.

Left Eyebrow
One (1) shave mark symbolizes their political statement against the government.

Greetings: Handshake, then hug, followed by "Amor de Rey!"

Salute: Crown hand sign, followed by hand sign across chest and back to hand salute (sign)

Conversational/Written Phrases:
"I come to you with my hand across my chest, 360 degrees..."
"Amor de Rey"
"Manito"
"B.O.S.!"
"T.O.S.!"
"The Nation!"
"The Family!"
"King _____!" "Queen _____!"

Codes: "360", "O5" (commonly used beeper codes)

Figure 6–11 Other ALKN Identifiers

and red bandanas. ALKN groups are commonly referred to as tribes and utilize Indian names for their chapters, but the variety of names they use is endless. ALKN identifies its two major enemies as the Gangster Disciple Nation (GDN) and the police.

Neta Association

The Neta Association was formed in 1979 in La Princesa prison in Puerto Rico (see Figure 6–12). An inmate known as Carlos Torres Irriarte, or Carlos "La Sombra" (the Shadow), started this group in an effort to protect the inmates from unfair practices used against them by the prison administration. During the latter part of 1979, Carlos Torres Irriarte was transferred to the Rio Piedras prison (known as Del Presidio) in Puerto Rico. As Irriarte's movement grew, other rival groups—especially Group 27— saw this as a threat to them. Then on March 30, 1981, members of Group 27 cornered Irriarte in the recreation area of the prison and shot him repeatedly with a .25-caliber handgun. Once he fell to the floor, Group 27 members stabbed Irriarte repeatedly until he died. Irriarte immediately became a martyr to the members of the Neta Association, who vowed revenge on Group 27 and the continuance of the Neta Association.

Most members of the Neta gang have prior criminal histories and joined the gang while doing time in either jail or prison. Gang members have found it easier to maintain a criminal lifestyle as members of this gang rather than to go straight. Although the Netas have a large criminal enterprise that involves their participation in a diverse number of criminal activities, their main moneymaking enterprise is drug dealing.

The Netas have formed a very tightly knit criminal organization that not only is involved in criminal activities within the prison but also carefully protects all the inmates who are members of the Neta organization. As in most other gangs, the Neta members must specifically follow 5 major points set forth by gang leaders:

1. Always show respect for Puerto Rico and its flag.
2. Know the Neta colors and understand what they mean:
   a. White—peace and harmony
   b. Red—blood shed by our members
   c. Black—reverence for our departed members
3. Swear in all new gang members.
4. Punish any member who violates gang policy.
5. Develop ever-increasing devotion to the gang and a lasting desire to fight against any attacks on it.

This gang has also put forth 27 specific rules that must be followed by all gang members (New York City Police Department, 1994).

Contemporary members of the Neta Association must all acknowledge the need for unity, respect, education, and harmony. Neta Association members have been found to be less violent than other Hispanic gangs, but there has been an increase

Figure 6–12   Neta Association Graffiti

Courtesy Florida Department of Corrections

NETA

Figure 6–13   Neta Graffiti and Tatoos

recently in their use of violence. The Neta Association has managed to form alliances with other street gangs including the Latin Kings.

Like their Latin King associates, the Netas have become heavily involved in the communities where they are active. They have become participants in community service programs and inner-city discussion groups, and they support politicians and help their campaign programs; through these actions, the gang members display a positive image. Over the past 10 years, they have gained some very positive responses from their communities. As positive community response has increased, so has the membership of this criminal group. But this is still a gang, with the majority of the members having prior criminal histories.

The structure of this organization consists of a president, vice president, secretary, treasurer, disciplinarian, and security. Local Neta groups are known as chapters or regions in most cases, and a woman member known as la primera dama (first lady) generally controls these groups. This woman is usually a senior member of the organization who maintains constant and direct contact with the correctional facilities from which the organizational commands are sent down to the chapter/region. A first lady is normally the wife, girlfriend, or mother of an imprisoned Neta leader. The use of a woman in a leadership role makes it appear that this gang has a nurturing temperament, but it is only a front put forward to try to increase community respect; the reality is that the local presidents and their staffs manage the daily operations of the Neta groups. These leaders in most cases are parolees with extensive criminal histories.

The gang colors are white, black, and red. While on probation, a gang member will wear all white beads, but once this person becomes a full-fledged member, he wears mostly white beads, with five to seven black beads and one red bead. The red bead represents the blood that gang members have shed for the family. This gang is capable of mobilizing hundreds of members in a very short period of time. They would rather meet in local schoolyards and in the colder weather move their meetings inside, usually into community centers in housing authority locations.

Women play an important role in this gang. They are the principal bearers of new members through childbirth. It is also important to remember that female members are carriers for the male gang members. The women in this gang carry drugs for sale in their backpacks; at times they also carry weapons in their backpacks.

New types of gangs have appeared in the New York City region. These gangs seem to be modeled after the gangs seen on the HBO series *The Wire*. All of the gangs were

---

NETA TERMINOLOGY

Beef. Problem or altercation with another person

De corazon. From the heart

El grito. Cry of "NETA–NETA–NETA" (usually heard at meetings)

Gas someone up. To exaggerate about something

Green light. Approval to take someone out

Hermanito. Fellow gang member

Tablasos. To beat down with a wooden board (e.g., a two-by-four)

Words not to be used for a family member include cocksucker, insect, sate, slick, snitch, son of a bitch, and son of a whore.

drug gangs, and they took up residence in the Cypress Hills housing project in the eastern New York City section of Brooklyn. It seems that in 1997 five gangs sat down together and worked out a way to evenly split up the projects so that all the gangs could jointly share hallways, public spaces, and some apartments to avoid having turf wars. The gangs are known as the Little A-Team, Rough Riders, Front Crew, Euclid Ave Boys, and Fountain and Euclid Forever. This split worked out well for all of the gangs until the police started cracking down on them. The police crackdown led to 45 arrests and a total shutdown of gang activities in these projects (E. Martinez, M. Weis, and A. Geller, 2002).

This is a prime example how gangs move into and take over neighborhoods throughout the United States. Fear was spread throughout this complex, and residents—out of fear of being killed—fail to contact the police or just feel the police will take no action to correct the gang problem. What we see in the above example is police cooperation with the community and the total elimination of gang activity by the police, but sometimes this is easier said than done.

CONCLUSIONS

Today in the United States, there are few communities that are free from gang activity. The gangs can be of any race or ethnic background; they can be organized or totally disorganized. There is no safe haven because if an outside gang recognizes the need to place gang members in a specific community, it will not be long before that community has a recognizable problem with gang activity.

Significant Numbers and Their Meaning

Number	Meaning or Gang Using Number as a Representation
OOO	Triple O; gangster blood
1	A
2	B
3	C (Folk Nation number)
4	D
5	E (People Nation, Latin Kings, and Bloods number)
6	F (Folk Nation and Crips number)
7	G
8	H
9	I
10	J
11	K
12	L
13	M
14	N
15	O
16	P
17	Q
18	R
19	S
20	T
21	U
22	V
23	W
24	X
25	Y
26	Z
31 or 031	Bloods; I have love for you, Bloods; 31 seconds = beat down
44	.44-caliber handgun
50	Police
50/50	Neutral or nongangster
78	1978 (the year Larry Hoover started Folk Nation)
88	HH or Heil Hitler (used by skinheads)
100	100 percent gangster; 100 percent Mexican gang member
101	Bloods superior; First Superior
102	Second Superior
103	Third Superior

(continued)

Significant Numbers and Their Meaning (*continued*)

Number	Meaning or Gang Using Number as a Representation
150	150 percent Neta
187	Murder (California Penal Code)
211	Robbery (California Penal Code)
212	Area code for New York City (Manhattan only)
213	Area code for Los Angeles
305	Area code for Miami
312	Area code for Chicago
360	Full circle; Universal (Latin Kings) (also used by Folk Nation)
718	Area code for New York City (except Manhattan)

Gang Phrases and Terminology

Phrase/Term/Acronym	Meaning/Translation	Gang(s)
A.B.G.	Any Body Gets It	ABG
A.D.R.	*Amor de rey* (Spanish)	Latin Kings
ALKQN	Almighty Latin King Queen Nation	Latin Kings
All is one	Greeting used by Folk Nation	Folk Nation
All is well	Greeting used by People Nation	People Nation
Amor De Rey	*Love to the king*	Latin Kings
B.F.L.	*Blood for life*	Bloods
BGDN	Black Gangster Disciple Nation	Disciples
BK	Bloods killer	Crips
BKCKLKK	Bloods killer; Crips killer; Latin King killer	Any Body Gets It
Blood in	Gang initiation in which blood of nongang member is spilled by initiating member	Bloods
Blood in, blood out	Motto of Mexican mafia	Mexican mafia Mexican gangs
Blood out	Gang member's blood spilled to get out of gang	Bloods
B's up, C's down	Disrespect of Crips by Bloods	Bloods
CFL	*Crips for life*	Crips
CK	Crips killer	Bloods
Crab	Derogatory name for Crips	Bloods
C's up, B's down	Disrespect of Bloods by Crips	Crips
De Corazon	*From the heart*	Netas

(continued)

Gang Phrases and Terminology (*continued*)

Phrase/Term/Acronym	Meaning/Translation	Gang(s)
EME	La Eme (Mexican mafia)	Mexican mafia
Five poppin, six droppin	People shooting, folk dropping (dying)	People Nation
FML	*Familia for life*	Mexican gangs
G	Gangster	All
G-ride	Gangster vehicle or stolen car	All
Hoover	Reference to Larry Hoover	Folk Nation
La Eme	Mexican mafia	Mexican gangs
Left	Left side	People Nation
LLLKWU	Love, life, loyalty, knowledge, wisdom, understanding (six principles of Folk Nation)	Folk Nation, Crips
LSRHO	Love, sacrifice, respect, honor, obedience (five principles of People Nation)	People Nation
Mi vida loca	*My crazy life*	Mexican gangs MS-13
Norte	North	Mexican gangs
Norteno	Northern California	Mexican gangs
OG (original gangster)	Originating member of a gang	All
Pee Wee	Young teen gangster	All
Perdoname Mi Madre	Forgive me, mother	Mexican gangs MS-13
Piru	Blood	Bloods
Right	Right side	Folk Nation
Shaolin	Staten Island	Bloods Crips Wu Tang
Six poppin, five droppin	Folk shooting, people dropping (dying)	Folk Nation
Slob	Derogatory name for Bloods	Crips
Sur	South	Mexican gangs
Sureno	Southern California (LA)	Mexican gangs
TFFT	Together forever, forever together	Together Forever
Trece	13 (or thirteenth letter of the alphabet, M)	Mexican gangs
Triple O	Gangster	Bloods
UBN	United Blood Nation	Bloods
YG	Young gangster, new member	All

Street Gang Identification Chart

Gang	Colors	Symbol(s)	Numbers	Affiliation	Clothing
Bloods	Red, black, green	Dog, heart with wings; Piru or P; paw print; Mack truck bulldog insignia; BK; Dawg print (three burn marks)	031; 000	People Nation (not in NYC)	Chicago Bulls; FuBu; Calvin Klein
Crips	Blue, black	Six-point star; C; CK; pitchfork; U on top of I (forms a pitchfork); skull/skull and crossbones	3 (represents C); 6 (represents F for Folk)	Folk Nation	British Knights; Colorado Rockies; University of Illinois
Disciples (Gangster Disciples; Black Gangster Disciples)	Black, blue (or gray)	Three-point star; pitchfork; devil's tail; U on top of I; most Folk Nation symbols	6; 360; 78	Folk Nation	Duke University; University of Illinois; Georgetown University
Dominicans Don't Play (DDP)	Red, white, blue	Dominican flag; three-point crown	4-4-16 (D-D-P)	Dominican mafia; Dominican drug lords	Dominican Republic
Dominican Power	Blue, clear (beads)	4–16 (signifies D and P); three-point crown	416	S/A	Dominican Republic
Five Percenters		Pyramid; crescent moon	5%	Zulu Nation	Fubu

(continued)

Street Gang Identification Chart (continued)

Gang	Colors	Symbol(s)	Numbers	Affiliation	Clothing
Folk Nation	Black, blue	Six-point star; devil's tail; pitch fork, heart with devil's horns or wings; Playboy bunny head with cocked ear, facing right	78; 6; 360	Disciples; Crips; LaRaza; Latin Souls; Two-Sixers; Hoover Criminals	Kansas City Royals; Detroit Tigers; University of Illinois; Nike
La Familia	Red, white (blue)	LF; LFN; L4F; five-point star; Puerto Rican flag	5		Puerto Rico
Latin Kings (Almighty Latin King Nation)	Gold, black, red	Five-point crown; ALKQN	5; 360	People Nation	Los Angeles Kings
Los Papichulos	Green, white	LPC; Dominican flag		DDP	New York Jets
Los Solidos	Red, blue	Joker card; Comedy/tragedy masks	100%	Savage Nomads; Ghetto Brothers	New York Giants
MS-13 (Mara Salvatrucha)	Blue, white	X3; 13; XIII; MS (Old English style); El Salvador flag	13	Mexican gangs	Heavy-metal T-shirts
Mexican	Red, white, green	Cholo symbol; hands praying; Mexican flag; Our Lady of Guadalupe; three-point crown; *Mi vida loca*	100%	Mexican mafia	Pachuco style (baggy)
Netas (Neta Association)	White, black, red	Heart; pitchfork; at symbol; picture of dove	50%	People Nation; FALN; Maceteros	White clothing

Gang	Colors	Symbol(s)	Numbers	Affiliation	Clothing
People Nation	Black, gold (black, red)	Five-point star; five-point crown; dice with 5's showing; Playboy bunny symbol with straight ears, facing left; top hat and cane; Champagne glass; pyramid	5; 360	Latin Kings; Vice Lords; Latin Counts; El Rukns; Black P Stones	Chicago Blackhawks; Los Angeles Kings
Skinheads (racist)	Red, white	Lightning bolt; Celtic cross; swastikas; iron cross; SS	88 (signifies HH); 100%	KKK; American Nazi Party; Aryan Nation	Doc Marten boots; aviator jackets
Together Forever		TF	206 (TF)	Russian organized crime; Italian organized crime	Tommy Hilfiger
Zulu Nation	Red, black, green	Outline of Africa; African mask; peace symbol	5; 15	5% ers	Hip-hop style

CHAPTER 7

JAMAICAN AND NIGERIAN GANGS

The Jamaicans and Nigerian organizations are the two major black organized crime groups. Jamaican gangs have been active in organized crime activities since the mid-1960s, while Nigerian activity began in the early 1970s. Most Jamaican gangs have been mentioned as growers and distributors of marijuana worldwide; in reality, it goes beyond marijuana and drugs because this group has become involved in as many unlawful activities as any other group.

JAMAICAN GANGS

The island of Jamaica was at one time a British Colony in the West Indies. A majority of the island inhabitants are descendants of Africans who were brought to the islands as slaves several hundred years ago. Jamaica has a heterogeneous society that includes Asian as well as European citizens. The literacy rate in Jamaica is 90 percent, and this has created a very proud group of Jamaican citizens who have a productive as well as diversified culture. A large number of the citizenry are either of Protestant or the Roman Catholic religion, but there has been a considerable increase in the total number of people participating in the Rastafarian religious movement.

The immigration of Jamaican citizens to the United States began in the early 1900s. During World War II, there was a noteworthy increase of Jamaican immigrants to the United States because of the decrease in the number of workers available in the United States due to the war, and a majority of these immigrants settled in New York City. The number of Jamaican newcomers to the United States decreased after 1952 due to passage of the McCarron-Walter Act, which reduced the number of Jamaicans entering the United States to 100 per year. This changed in 1965 with the passage of the Hart-Cellar Act, which increased the quotas on Caribbean people entering the United States.

One of the first groups of Jamaican immigrants to arrive in the United States after the passage of the Hart-Cellar Act was the Rastafarians. At first, they were considered by many to be members of some type of gang because of their outward appearance and religious beliefs. The Rastafarians are labeled by many law enforcement officials as the precursors of today's Jamaican posses. This was basically due to the Rastafarians' participation in the growth, sale, and use of marijuana in Jamaica and the United States. The Rastafarians, however, turned out to be more of a religious group than a gang, though some people are still of the opinion that the Jamaican gangs are made up of Rastafarians. Although the Rastafarian sect does not have an inflexible set of principles that guides its members, most sect members conform to a 10-point code. These membership standards include the following (Jamaican Information Service, 1988):

1. They object to the use of sharpened instruments to shave hair off the body or to put tattoos on the body.
2. They scorn the eating of pork, shellfish, scaleless fish, and snails; many sect members are vegetarians.
3. They pay homage to Ras Tafari, or the living God. (Ras Tafari was inaugurated as the king of Ethiopia on November 2, 1930, and immediately named the Imperial Majesty Haile Selassie, which means "the might of the Trinity." This is comparable to Jesus in the Christian religion and Muhammad in the Muslim religion.)
4. They love the brotherhood of man.
5. They detest hatred, jealousy, envy, deceit, and other similar vices.
6. They disagree with modern-day society and all of its evils.
7. They seek a society that consists of one brotherhood.
8. They want to supply benevolence to any brother in anguish.
9. They must comply with the ancient Ethiopian principles.
10. They must shun assistance and accolades extended by a nonmember.

There are several other features that make it fairly easy to distinguish a member of the Rastafarian religious group from Jamaican gang members. The first is the unusual way that the Rastafarians style their hair. This type of hair styling has been called dreadlocks and is worn as a symbol of defiance; they also believe that a person's strength has something to do with the length of his hair. Another feature of the Rastafarian cult is reggae music. This attachment to reggae comes from their use of this type of music to express their protest against the way they were treated by the police and the local government in Jamaica. The third characteristic of a person practicing the Rastafarian religion is the use of ganja, or marijuana. The practice of smoking ganja goes back to the inception of this group and is considered part of the Rastafarian religious ritual (Jamaican Information Service, 1988).

An understanding of the Rastafarian sect indicates that it would be very doubtful that a member of this religion would be a participant in gang activity. Rastafarians may have been involved in the sale of marijuana, but this was done (in many cases) on an individual basis so that a particular person could support himself. In fact, the only probable interaction that would take place between a Rastafarian and a Jamaican gang member is when a Rastafarian purchases marijuana from a gang drug operative.

Jamaican street gangs that are present in our society today evolved over the past 35 years from the same types of gangs that developed in the Jamaican ghettos during the early 1970s. Like their eventual counterparts in the United States, these enterprising young tough Jamaican street kids discovered they could recruit a number of other adolescents from their neighborhoods; in turn, they could form their own criminal organization, which could be used to control a specific territory. The gangs took the name posses, from old western movies in the United States. These posses were based on similarities in neighborhoods, political alliances, and/or notoriety. In most cases, each gang took a name that was associated with its local district; for example, the Waterhouse Posse is from the Waterhouse area of Kingston, Jamaica. There is usually a further affiliation with one of the political groups, the Jamaican Labor Party (JLP) or the Peoples National Party (PNP). A connection to a political party and its elected officials affords the gang favoritism when that specific party is in power. The types of unfair preferences that can be bestowed on a gang include public works projects that allow the gang the right to provide jobs for gang and nongang members in the community. Preferential treatment may also be granted to gang members who are seeking asylum from other authorities or just avoiding some type of required governmental procedure. The gang provides monetary support, which in most cases is accumulated from its participation in drug-trafficking activities, as well as other types of secondary support to the political party (Interpol, 1993).

The influx of Jamaican street gangs into the United States started in the late 1970s. A majority of the first arrivals had prior criminal records in Jamaica and were escaping the Jamaican justice system; they arrived in the United States as illegal aliens. These fugitives from Jamaican justice formed their own posses or assisted others in the expansion of the Jamaican street gangs. The results of this have placed most of these people in either mid-level or high-ranking positions within posses. The more advanced posse members saw immigration to the United States as an opportunity to improve their ranking in Jamaican society by creating and operating some type of criminal enterprise, and they gained an expertise in the way they ran their criminal operations. Recruiting new members into the posses can be fairly easy because Jamaica is an extremely poor country; when a gang member returns to Jamaica with cash assets obtained in the United States, impressionable Jamaican youths see gang membership as a way to obtain a better life. Law enforcement sources in the United States indicate that most of the street-level drug and gun dealers are recruited from within the local Jamaican community (ATF, 1993).

During the 1980s, law enforcement agencies throughout the United States were able to recognize, take advantage of, and start major criminal prosecutions that capitalized on the deficiencies within these Jamaican criminal organizations. Some of the major defects discovered by law enforcement agencies were found in the composition of the Jamaican criminal group. Most of these gangs had a very large and identifiable membership who made little or no effort to hide their gang affiliation. This ultimately led to many gang members being imprisoned, deported, or murdered by members of the same gang or rival gangs (ATF, 1993).

The Jamaican groups were industrious enough to realize their weaknesses and adjusted their structure and operations in order to become a more impressive opponent for the U.S. law enforcement system. These gangs quickly decreased their size and became more secretive organizations. The leaders of the Jamaican posses, through the use of a tier-structured organization, have managed to isolate themselves from the street-level drug dealings. This pyramid type of organization places the leaders or bosses at the top without any direct connection to the street narcotics' dealings but with a majority of the unlawful profits being delivered to them. A leader then hand-picks underbosses or lieutenants to supervise the day-to-day operations of gang activities. The average street gang worker is usually an illegal alien brought to the United States to fill jobs within the gang (U.S. Customs, 1993).

Drug Trafficking

A short time after their arrival in the United States, the Jamaican posses managed to take over a large portion of the street marijuana operations and then set up their own system for trafficking the marijuana. During the 1980s, the Jamaican posses took over a large number of other types of drug markets that were previously controlled by American blacks and other ethnic groups. In just about all these cases, this was done through the use of violence. As the Jamaican posses' participation in drug-trafficking activities increased in the United States, so did the gangs' membership and wealth (see Figure 7–1).

The centralized location of Jamaica has made it an important transshipment site for the large amounts of Colombian-grown cocaine and marijuana that are routed for the United States. Estimates established by federal law enforcement sources indicate that approximately 25 percent of the marijuana shipped from Jamaica to the United States is also grown in Jamaica (U.S. Customs, 1993). Over the past 10 years, law enforcement intelligence information indicates that the Jamaican posses are the major marijuana street dealers in the United States; however, the gangs' recent involvement in the crack cocaine market indicates their desire to increase their wealth and power in the U.S. drug market.

Since the early 1990s, the Jamaican posses have become heavily involved in the crack cocaine–trafficking business. The gangs' in-depth participation in this drug enterprise has expanded to include the operation of street-level crack houses, setting up and managing drug distribution centers (or stash houses) and safe houses throughout the United States. The street-level crack facilities set up by the Jamaican gangs are usually rented by females and managed by armed members of the Jamaican posses and are often referred to as gate-houses by gang members. A majority of the Jamaican drug business takes place within these well-fortified facilities. Included within the definition of a gatehouse facility are houses, apartments, convenience stores, record shops, restaurants, and commercial buildings. Once a location is selected by a gang, construction workers are employed to buttress this

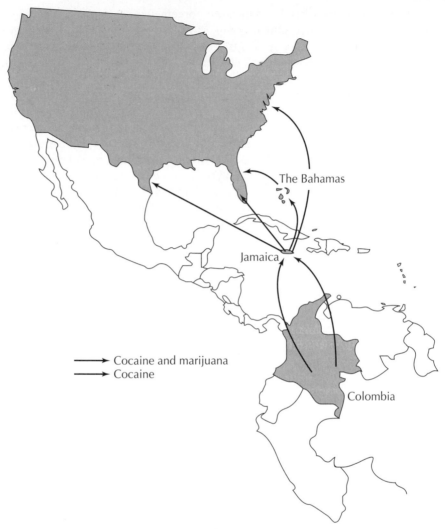

Figure 7–1   Cocaine and Marijuana Routes

Source: U.S. Drug Enforcement Agency, 2004.

stronghold by barricading doors and windows and installing escape doors, hatches, and other devices that could seriously injure or kill anyone who breaches the security of the gatehouse. The types of traps put down in the gatehouses include the following:

- Holes in floor covered by rugs, with beds of nails on the floor below
- Live electrical wires placed in windows and doorways
- Gates and bars on entrances

- Exits and windows electrically wired
- Floor surfaces underneath windows cut away and razor wire laid across the open area
- Bucket-type devices filled with nails or other metal objects and attached to trip wires
- Hanging objects (containing phosphorus, alcohol, and potassium chloride and placed in aluminum foil) that will explode on any type of contact

The exchange of money and drugs is done through Plexiglass shields; in most cases, the buyer must be known by the dealer.

Abundant quantities of various types of narcotics and guns are stored in the distribution or stash houses by gang members. On a daily basis, gang members remove small amounts of narcotics from these locations to be delivered to crack houses for distribution to local street dealers; in turn, all of the profits that have been made by the gang members from the prior drug sales are returned to the stash houses. The gang's bookkeeper maintains records of all monetary and narcotics transactions made between the gatehouses and the stash houses. Security devices are set up to prevent law enforcement agencies from preparing a successful action that could be used to shut down the Jamaican gangs' drug operations. Higher-ranking members of the Jamaican posses may actually live in these stash houses. The safe house or control point is where the gangs store their weapons and keep a hidden reserve of narcotics that is used to restock the stash houses (FBI, 1992).

The amount of drugs found on Jamaican gang members at any given time is usually small, due to the gang's awareness of the penalties associated with federal and state drug laws. Gang members are of the opinion that if they are arrested with a smaller amount of drugs, there is a lesser chance that they will be fined or sentenced to a term in jail. It is also easier for the gangs to continually distribute the drugs in smaller amounts without attracting any scrutiny from local law enforcement agencies. The success of Jamaican posses in the narcotics business has been due to their ability to operate not only as small-time importers but also as industrious drug retailers. For example, the profit gained by Jamaican posse drug merchants starts when a Jamaican posse purchases a kilo of cocaine from a Colombian drug trafficker for $15,000. A posse member will then move the cocaine up the East Coast to New York City or Washington, D.C., and transform the cocaine into 15,000 to 20,000 rocks of cocaine. This rock cocaine's street value will then exceed $125,000, which brings the Jamaican gang a profit of at least $110,000. This makes the Jamaican posse's drug business far more profitable than the Colombian trafficker who originally purchased the cocaine for $5,000 and then sold it to the Jamaican gang members for $15,000 (U.S. Customs, 1993).

Street-level drug dealing for the Jamaican posses is usually conducted by American blacks who are recruited by gang members. The American black is enlisted into the posse but is never truly accepted or depended on by the Jamaican members of the gang. People who conduct street sales are entrusted with only a small quantity of the drugs they are assigned to sell. They are required to then report back to the gatehouse or stash house as soon as possible to turn in their profits to a Jamaican gang lieutenant and to replenish their drug supply. There have been cases in which Jamaican gang members became involved in street drug sales, but in the great majority of these cases, the Jamaican street dealer was far more cautious and secretive than a street drug dealer from any other ethnic group.

Since the late 1980s, the Jamaican gangs have expanded their activities throughout the United States. These posses have moved their operations into cities such as Boston, Dallas, Houston, Kansas City, Philadelphia, Richmond, St. Louis, and Washington, D.C., as well as rural West Virginia. In some of these cities, the Jamaican posses have joined forces with other gangs (such as the Bloods and Crips in Kansas City; the Dominicans in Boston and Philadelphia; and the Nigerians in Washington, D.C.) to enhance their drug-trafficking capabilities.

The Jamaican gangs further strengthen their control over their drug empire through the use of violence. One instance of a gang's ability to recruit new members and then increase their members' affinity for violence is shown in the case of John C. Smith. Smith first became involved in drug dealing when he was 13 years old; 3 years later, Smith was recruited by Jamaican posse members to deal drugs in Dallas. He was given a plane ticket to Dallas and $100 in spending money. A short time after his arrival, he was selling crack out of a Dallas apartment, making an estimated $5,000 a day for the gang. Smith always carried a 9 mm semiautomatic pistol with him; he was arrested and charged by the Dallas police with three murders 2 months after his arrival in Dallas. According to the Dallas police, Smith went on a 36-hour rampage while under the influence of drugs and killed three people. Smith shot one of the victims 11 times (including on the soles of the feet). He is presently serving an 18-year sentence in a Texas correctional institution for the three murders that he admitted to committing just 8 weeks after his arrival in Dallas (Meier, 1989).

In an attempt to destroy the New York–Dallas drug and gun rings, a combined New York Police Department (NYPD) and Federal Bureau of Investigation (FBI) task force raided premises in Brooklyn, Albany, Uniondale, and Long Island, New York, as well as Dallas. The gang's headquarters at 1367 Sterling Place in the Crown Heights section of Brooklyn (which was known as the "White House" or the "killing house") was seized by the police. This location was often used by drug leaders as a place to assassinate rival drug leaders and gang members who stole drugs or money from the gang; it was also a location from which the gang sold drugs in the hallways 24 hours a day, 365 days a year (McKinley, 1990).

This gang, known as the Gulleymen (which takes its name from a neighborhood in Kingston, Jamaica, known as McGregor's Gulley), rented cars in New York to ferry drugs to Dallas. Upon arrival in Dallas, the autos were filled with dozens of illegal firearms for their return to New York. The members of the Gulleymen arrested by the federal task force were charged with 10 homicides; also, a total of 15 guns and $150,000 were seized during these raids. Evidence gathered by federal authorities indicates that this group invested much of their unlawfully obtained profits into real estate in Brooklyn and Long Island, while some portion of the money was shipped back to Jamaica. Federal authorities have indicated that some of this gang's drug money has been used to support political candidates in Jamaica (McKinley, 1990).

Firearms Trafficking

The Jamaican posses have managed to excel in their ability to deal in illegal guns. There are several ways for Jamaican gangs to obtain the weapons for their firearms-trafficking business:

1. *Purchases.* A gang member sets up a residence and obtains all the necessary documentation in a state where a specific amount of time in residence (usually 30 to 90 days) is the major requirement to purchase guns. Once all the residency requirements are met, the gang member can, in a short period of time, buy all the guns desired. These are then transported to New York City or some other large urban center where the guns are sold, usually on the street, for two to three times their original price.

2. *Straw purchases.* This type is very similar to purchases (above) except that a person with a gang affiliation, who already has the necessary residence and documentation, buys the firearms for another gang member and usually receives a percentage of the guns'e purchase price (10 to 15 percent is common). The guns are then transported to major urban centers and sold at high profit levels.

3. *Firearms thefts.* In these cases, gang members either break into gun dealerships or commit gun dealership robberies. Weapons are taken instead of money, and these guns are once again transported to a major urban location where they are sold for a profit.

4. *Home invasion robberies.* The gang members forcibly enter a private residence where they know there are several guns and forcibly take the weapons from the owner. These guns are also transported to a large city where they are sold for a profit.

5. *Hijackings.* When possible, the gang steals a vehicle (using whatever force is necessary) that is carrying weapons; the weapons are ultimately sold at the street level.

6. *Thefts from military bases.* Posse members break into a military installation and remove all the weapons that are accessible to them; then posse members sell the weapons.

7. *Mail thefts.* A gang member or gang associate who works for the U.S. Postal Authority steals packages containing weapons and gives said firearms to the gang for use or for profit.

Just about all the firearms purchases by gang members take place in Florida; Georgia, Texas, and Virginia, then almost all the guns are transported back to New York

City for distribution throughout the United States. Some of these firearms are transported back to Jamaica where the profit margin is far higher than that of the U.S. market—but it is also far more dangerous because of the strict Jamaican gun laws. A gang can use several methods to smuggle firearms into Jamaica:

1. Transporting the weapons in commercial containers that also hold other items such as food or machinery
2. Using female merchants as weapon carriers (These females are chosen because they are Jamaican and regularly travel between Miami and Jamaica.)
3. Using small planes to transport the guns
4. Concealing the firearms somewhere in a vehicle that is shipped to Jamaica from the United States

The Jamaican gangs do their best to remove all identifiable markings on these weapons before selling them.

Economic Crimes

Money Laundering.   The Jamaican gangs have become very much aware of the laws in the United States related to the laundering of currency under the U.S. Bank Secrecy Act (BSA). A majority of the Jamaican gangs, as well as most of the other active criminal organizations in the United States, avoid currency transactions through conventional financial establishments. Yet the vast amount of money that is earned by the gangs from drug operations needs to be moved out of the United States as quickly and safely as possible. There is no doubt that the leaders of the Jamaican posses have managed to successfully transport large amounts of currency to Jamaica without any major interference from U.S. law enforcement agencies. Upon the arrival of the money in Jamaica, must of it is quickly invested in legitimate businesses such as resorts, apartment buildings, restaurants, and other types of investment holdings.

In most cases, an individual member of the Jamaican gang will transport the currency somewhere on his body or in very close physical proximity. Another alternative used by the gangs involves the transfer of U.S. currency into some type of commodity, which is then transported to Jamaica. Usually the merchandise, such as electronic equipment, automobile components, or retail garments, is then shipped to Jamaica by the gangs.

The Jamaican posses have come up with some far-reaching and complicated currency-laundering and money-smuggling conspiracies.

Use of Street Higglers.   Street traders (or dealers) are perceived as higglers within Jamaican society. Street higglers regularly visit the United States to buy articles that they will ultimately sell in Jamaica. In some cases, the higgler is financed by a Jamaican posse; in other instances, a Jamaican gang will pay the higgler's round-trip transportation costs, and on the higgler's arrival in the United States, he is

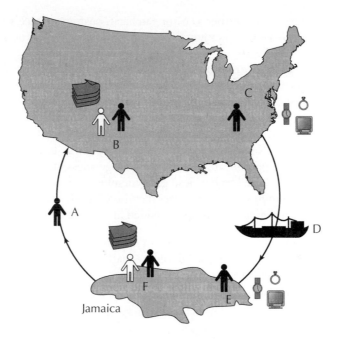

A. Higgler travels to the United States.
B. Gang in the United States provides
   money to higgler.
C. Higgler buys goods in United States.
D. Goods shipped to Jamaica.
E. Goods sold in Jamaica.
F. Money returned to gang in Jamaica.

Figure 7–2   Higgler Money Laundering

Source: U.S. Department of Justice, 2004.

given money to procure retail merchandise. This merchandise is then transported to Jamaica, where the items are sold and the money earned from the sales returned to the posse. Therefore, the money has been laundered by the gang (see Figure 7–2).

Use of 55-Gallon Drums.   A Jamaican gang member will fill 55-gallon drums with currency and then transport the drums to Jamaica. A corrupt airline employee (or a gang member who is employed by an airline at a local U.S. airport) receives the drum, and the employee guarantees that the drum will be put on a plane to Jamaica. Upon its arrival in Jamaica, the drum is moved off the plane and through Jamaican customs without being opened.

Use of Airline Employees.   An employee of an airline that constantly flies into Jamaica is paid a fee to carry money from the United States to Jamaica without claiming the funds at either U.S. or Jamaican customs. Once the employee arrives in Jamaica and passes through Jamaican customs, the money is returned to the gang.

Use of Currency Couriers. The Jamaican gangs (like most other criminal organizations) are very much aware of the possible problems they face when transporting currency. Jamaican posse leaders, after a great deal of discussion, came up with the idea that using many couriers who are carrying lesser amounts of cash would make identification and apprehension a lot less possible. A great deal of the money that travels between Miami, New York, and Washington, D.C., is transported by an emissary in a rental auto. Information gathered from police agencies conducting law enforcement duties on routes of travel used by Jamaican gang members to move money between Miami, New York, and Washington, D.C., indicates that there have been seizures by local police authorities. Those couriers who were apprehended fit into the following categories (DEA, 1993):

1. The amount of money in their possession is usually between $10,000 and $15,000. This is considered a small amount that would not hurt a million-dollar drug business.

2. The sum is considered small by the gang leaders, so the couriers have been told they should not claim ownership of the money.

3. The persons chosen as courier have a low profile and the same basic characteristics as anyone else traveling the highways of the United States. In some cases, three or four people who have never met before are placed in a vehicle and travel as a "family." The only problem with this type of operation is that if the gang's "family" gets stopped by the police and the police question the alleged family members, none of the group can answer questions about other family members. This will immediately make the police highly suspicious of this group.

The gang's purpose, in most cases, is to move the currency from its many nationwide locations to one central site. If U.S. law enforcement organizations manage to stop and seize money from 1 out of every 20 couriers, the whole operation set up by the gang is a complete success.

Use of Automobiles. A member of the posse will purchase a new vehicle at a car dealership. This automobile will be purchased with cash (up to $10,000), checks, and financial assistance. This type of buying is done so that the gang can avoid filling out an Internal Revenue Service 8300 Form, which must be used when a purchase is paid for in U.S. currency and that payment exceeds $10,000. The car is then shipped to Jamaica where it is sold on the open market, and the money originally paid out by the gang member is refunded to him.

Use of Barrels. In this case, the gang contacts an express shipping company, which supplies the gang with one of a variety of barrels. The barrel is filled with money by the gang and returned to the shipper, which transports the barrel to any location in Jamaica. These companies are present in most Jamaican neighborhoods throughout the United States and are frequently used by Jamaicans living in the United States to ship items back to their families in Jamaica.

Use of Express Mail.   The illegally obtained drug money can be moved back to Jamaica by the gangs through the use of overnight express mail. The gangs have found this to be a safe as well as cheap way to move currency.

Use of Western Union.   Jamaican gangs have discovered that they can easily transfer their money to Jamaica through the use of wire transfer companies (see Figure 7–3). The gangs move their money from one location to another in the United States before finally transferring it to a Jamaican Western Union office. In order to avoid the ever-present U.S. government–required Currency Transfer Report (CTR), the gangs will transfer amounts that are smaller than $10,000. One gang member may transfer a total of $20,000 in U.S. currency, but in order to do so, it will involve at least three transactions. In cases such as these, the Western Union office is not required to have the person transferring the money make out a CTR. The only problem is that Western Union records provide police agencies with a paper trail that

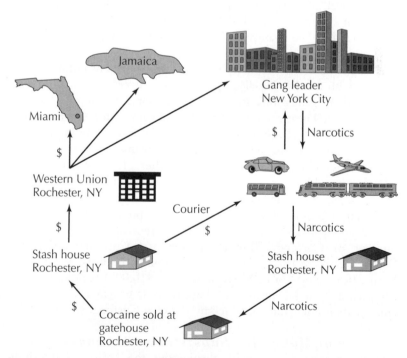

Figure 7–3   Drugs into Currency

Source: U.S. Customs Service, 2004.

may ultimately lead to the indictment of gang officials who are involved in laundering illegally obtained drug money.

Use of Legitimate Companies.   The Jamaican gangs, after having observed other organized criminal groups being successful, are investing their unlawfully obtained funds in legitimate companies. Some of these businesses may be used by the gangs to assist them in their illegal narcotics-trafficking operations. A major portion of these enterprises are kept free of narcotics trafficking and are used to furnish a way for the gangs to turn illegally obtained funds into legitimate currency.

Use of Racetrack Deceit.   Jamaican gang members have discovered a legitimate way to change a large amount of smaller U.S. currency bills into larger denominations. The majority of U.S. racetracks have machines at which chits for wagering can be purchased. U.S. bills in smaller denominations ($1, $5, $10, and $20) are placed in the machine, and a chit for that amount is returned to the person who puts money into the machine. A chit can be used to place a bet or can be cashed in with other chits for larger-denomination bills at a wagering window at the racetrack. In many cases, the posse member purchases chits of all different U.S. currency denominations until all of the drug money in his possession has been changed into chits. These chits are then cashed in for U.S. currency in larger amounts ($50 and $100) in order to reduce the quantity of bills for shipment to Jamaica.

Use of Banks.   Up until recently, most law enforcement agencies considered it doubtful that Jamaican posses would ever use banks to launder their money because these gangs were so aware of the money-tracing devices used by federal law enforcement. These predictions put forth by law enforcement organizations throughout the United States have been found to be false. The Jamaican gangs, like all the other organized crime syndicates, are also using banks as a means to launder their money. They move the money through either a few or many bank accounts, with the currency concluding its journey when it arrives at a Jamaican bank. Late in 1991, a Jamaican marijuana trafficker placed more than $70,000 in a U.S. bank. Currency Transaction Reports indicate that Jamaican posses are depositing money into U.S. savings and loan associations as well as commercial banks. It seems apparent from the number of Currency Transaction Reports, Currency or Monetary Instrument Reports, Foreign Bank and Financial Accounts Reports, and Internal Revenue 8300 Forms (for reports of cash payments over $10,000) handled by federal investigative agencies that the Jamaican gangs have become heavily involved in the use of banks to launder their unlawfully obtained funds (U.S. Customs Service, 1994).

Use of Money for Subsistence Expenses.   Information gathered by law enforcement agencies throughout the United States indicates that some Jamaican gang leaders keep large amounts of U.S. currency in their stash houses. It has also been confirmed that both gang leaders and their lieutenants spend large sums of money to ensure that they enjoy the same lifestyle from day to day. The daily routine of some Jamaican gang members includes a stop at the local racetrack and the betting of large sums of money without any remunerative return. This seems to indicate that a small number of Jamaican posse leaders are wagering with what one could consider disposable earnings.

Use of Counterfeiting.   Like many other ethnic groups, Jamaicans have also been involved in the production and use of counterfeit U.S. bills. The Jamaican posses use this forged currency along with legal currency to purchase drugs in what is usually a planned drug scam. Also, these currency reproductions are sold at about 40–50 percent of their real market value. Just about all the forged money is produced in Jamaica; forged bills are then transported to the United States by either courier or some other safe and easy transfer method. Most of the participants in these counterfeiting conspiracies are also heavily involved in drug trafficking.

Other Criminal Activities

Immigration Fraud.   During the past decade, there has been a sharp increase in the number of illegal Jamaican aliens entering the United States. Approximately 25 percent of the membership of the Jamaican posses is made up of Jamaican aliens. It is very difficult for American authorities to ascertain the identity of many of these illegal Jamaican immigrants because of their ability to skillfully use counterfeit instruments for identification. Jamaican gangs have managed to successfully set up several different types of operations to service illegal Jamaican aliens entering or already present in the United States.

Marriage Fraud.   A classic example of a Jamaican marital scam includes an illegal Jamaican immigrant and a U.S. citizen, usually a facilitator/lawyer with expertise in immigration law and a gang affiliation. The facilitator/lawyer sets up the marriage contract, trains the pair for their meeting with a U.S. immigration official, prepares all the necessary government forms, and arranges for another U.S. citizen who will act as the marriage partner. In most situations, the female partner is supplied by the facilitator/lawyer; she is paid a fee that is anywhere between $1,000 and $10,000. The women who become short-term partners in these marriage schemes are either junkies or prostitutes. The facilitator/lawyer who assists the illegal Jamaican immigrants in completing these spurious plots can make a great deal of money in a short period of time. If the facilitator/lawyer is a gang member, proceeds of this scam return to the gang's liquid assets' coffer; if the facilitator/lawyer has an affiliation to the gang, a specific fee is paid to this person.

Document Counterfeiting.   Investigators from the U.S. Immigration and Naturalization Service (INS) have identified eight different Jamaican posse groups as the generators of a number of counterfeit documents. The major benefit that the gangs reap from these schemes is that all these scams are conducted in Jamaica, which is away from the threat of arrest and prosecution that U.S. government investigative agencies may pose if these activities took place on U.S. soil. One gang will specialize by producing only one or two types of forged documents (e.g., U.S. Virgin Islands or Canadian birth certificates); another gang may generalize and produce many types of forged instruments. The Mavis Anglin Posse produces Jamaican, Canadian, and U.S. passports; Jamaican and U.S. Virgin Islands birth certificates; U.S. voter registration cards; U.S. and Canadian military identification cards; U.S. birth certificates; and many other types of false documents. This gang was able to gather community support for its unlawful activities by putting some of the profits from its illegal operations back into the community (FinCEN, 1992).

Green Card Fraud. Another scam conceived by the Jamaican posses involves fraudulently acquiring green cards. (These cards are to be carried by immigrants who are legally in the United States awaiting an opportunity to become legal residents of this country.) This scheme requires a gang member who has a legally obtained green card or who is an illegal alien to pose as the owner of the green card and falsely report to federal authorities that the green card was lost or stolen. Once this report is made to the U.S. Immigration and Naturalization Service, the deceitful gang member obtains a fingerprint card from the legal green card owner and submits an application for a substitute green card. Once the green card is obtained, the gang member will acquire all the other legal forms necessary to properly identify him as being a legal immigrant in the United States (e.g., state driver's license, Social Security number). It is also possible to revise the identity on the replacement green card once it is secured from the government (FinCEN, 1992).

Other Illegal Ways of Entry into the United States. The Jamaican gangs have designed other ways of smuggling illegal aliens into the United States. One way the gangs have been very successful involves the use of gang members or gang associates who are American citizens. For example, a citizen takes a cruise ship to Jamaica and disembarks upon arrival in Jamaica. The boarding pass is sold to a designated Jamaican citizen, who then uses it to take the ship back to Miami; once the boarding pass is sold, the American citizen will fly back to the United States. An alternative to this scheme involves a gang member passenger who, upon boarding the ship, takes an extra boarding pass and fills it out with all the required information. Upon arrival in Jamaica, the gang member immediately sells the extra boarding pass to an appointed Jamaican citizen. In many cases, the Jamaican purchaser of the boarding pass will travel back to the United States with the gang member, and they will disembark separately upon the ship's arrival in Miami. It is very difficult for U.S. immigration authorities to identify the duplicate boarding passes unless they are found and a comparison is done. In fact, the possibility of either one of these schemes being discovered during the trip back or immediately after docking is slim to none. It was only after an investigation by the U.S. Immigration Service that this latter scam was uncovered. The gangs will charge anywhere from $1,000 to $5,000 to any person seeking this type of illegal entry into the United States (DEA, 1993).

Legitimate Businesses

The Jamaican posses, like all their organized crime counterparts, are putting their illegally obtained funds into legitimate businesses. Through the use of legitimate businesses, the Jamaican gangs make it more difficult for law enforcement agencies to confiscate illegally obtained resources. The Jamaican posses use family members as well as close acquaintances to purchase both commercial and residential properties, which is done to conceal the true property owners. Another method of hiding their involvement in the acquisition of legal ventures used by the Jamaican gangs involves the use of both Jamaican and black American females to purchase land and other types of possessions. Gang members who lease an apartment, house, or car usually put the lease in the name of a female associate. Some of the Jamaican posse leaders have made so much money in the drug market that they have built million-dollar houses in Jamaica.

In the United States, the Jamaican gangs have managed to reinvest some of their money in restaurants, nightclubs, grocery stores, record stores, boutiques, garages, and car services that are located within a local Jamaican community. Originally, these businesses were supposed to remain legitimate after their purchase, but in many cases it is only a short period of time after the purchase that these enterprises become part and parcel of the Jamaican gangs' drug empire, and they are used to launder money as well as dispense drugs. The nightclubs are turned into after-hours' clubs; the restaurants sell food as well as marijuana; the grocery stores sell milk, soda, beer, and crack; and the car services transport drugs and guns that are sold or dropped off throughout the area.

Activities Outside the United States

The Jamaican gangs have managed to increase their drug activities by having working relationships with Nigerian, Dominican, and Asian gangs. These alliances have helped the Jamaican gangs strengthen their operations throughout North America and Europe.

Europe.   The international connections set up by the Jamaican gangs pose a major threat of increased drug activity throughout Great Britain. There have already been several incidents in which Jamaican gangs have used violent tactics during confrontations with the British police; a few of these events involved the shooting of English police officers. Since these incidents took place, British authorities have begun to see an increase in the amount of violence used by Jamaican gangs. The increase in Jamaican gang participation in narcotics trafficking stems from the gangs' ability to move drugs between the United States and England. Jamaican gangs use the same basic drug-smuggling methods in Great Britain as Asian, Nigerian, and Colombian groups use to import illegal drugs into the United States. The drug market in England provides the gangs with a considerably greater profit than does the U.S. drug market-place (FinCEN, 1992).

Since 1987 one Jamaican street gang known as Yardies has made its presence known—first in London, then throughout the United Kingdom. Yardies is the name adopted by any Jamaican who comes from the poorer areas of Kingston, Jamaica, but not all people from Jamaica who call themselves Yardies are members of this violent drug-dealing gang. This Jamaican gangster group dominates and controls Jamaican communities in England. Gang members in England also wear dreadlocks to give people the impression that they are Rastafarians; information shows that is far from the truth.

At first the Yardies were involved in just smuggling and street sales of marijuana, but as the number of gang members in London increased, so did their criminal activities. In 1990 the Yardies started smuggling cocaine into London, and that brought about the processing of cocaine into crack cocaine; within a short period of time, the Yardies controlled the whole crack cocaine market in England. The increased activity in the drug sales market brought a sharp escalation in the number of violent criminal incidents involving gang members. It took over a decade for the London Metropolitan Police to put together a law enforcement task force to attempt to control the Yardies' criminal activities. The Yardies then expanded their criminal activities to all areas of the British Isles, including the English countryside, Wales, Scotland, and Ireland. This move created problems for the Yardies because once the gang members left London, they found that the new locations they moved into had little or no Afro-Caribbean communities. The gang members found it very difficult to operate their drug operation once they moved into these new communities; on the other side, it was fairly easy for the police in these areas to identify gang members.

The Yardies are involved in the same criminal activities in both the British Isles and other communities throughout the world. Gang members participate in drug operations, prostitution, money laundering, robbery, extortion, kidnapping, and smuggling of illegal aliens into England. Presently, the Yardies are the primary gang operating in London.

Canada. The Jamaican posses have managed to set up subsidiary groups throughout Canada that move money and drugs between the United States and Canada. The gangs in Canada are also involved in the Jamaican gangs' illegal alien-smuggling activities. U.S. Immigration Service has gathered information that indicates many of the drug gatehouse workers in the United States are smuggled into the United States from Canada to work in these drug dens (U.S. Immigration Service, 1992). Forged documents are also made readily available to illegal Jamaican aliens by the Jamaican posses. Canadian law enforcement authorities indicate that one of the finest Jamaican document counterfeiters is part of a Jamaican gang in Canada that is producing most of the forged U.S. and Canadian passports (RCMP, 1992).

The subsidiary gangs that have been put in place in Canada are all answerable to the parent groups in the United States. Currency and drugs are conveyed between the United States (New York) and Canada (Toronto), with drugs going north and money coming south. In some cases, Western Union is used to transfer money from the United States to Canada; then the money is sent to its final destination in Jamaica.

JAMAICAN ORGANIZED CRIME GROUPS CURRENTLY OPERATING ON EAST COAST AND IN CANADA

Bantom Posse	Maryland, New York, and Pennsylvania
Barker Organization	Philadelphia, Pennsylvania
Brooks Organization	Philadelphia, Pennsylvania
Bulbeye Posse	Ontario
Bungy Posse	Quebec
Cocaine Cowboys	Philadelphia, Pennsylvania
Cuban Posse	Pennsylvania and Virginia
Delta Force Posse	New Jersey
Douglass Organization	Pennsylvania
Dunkirk Posse	Pennsylvania
Forbes Organization	Philadelphia, Pennsylvania
Glanro Posse	Quebec
Gulleymen Posse	New York City and Philadelphia, Pennsylvania
Hot Steppers Posse	Pennsylvania
Jungle Massive	Ontario
Jungle Posse	Maryland, New York, and Pennsylvania
Lawrence Organization	Philadelphia, Pennsylvania
(The) Mob	Philadelphia, Pennsylvania
Montego Bay Posse	Pennsylvania
Powerhouse Posse	Ontario
Red Shirt Massive	Philadelphia, Pennsylvania
Reema Posse	New Jersey and Pennsylvania
Shower Posse	Maryland, New Jersey, New York, Ohio, and Pennsylvania
Solid Gold Posse	New Jersey
Spangler Posse	Maryland, New Jersey, New York, Ohio, and Pennsylvania
Spanishtown Posse	Pennsylvania
Sterling Organization	Philadelphia, Pennsylvania
Strikers (Strikas) Posse	Ontario and Pennsylvania
(The) Syndicate	Philadelphia, Pennsylvania
Tel Aviv Posse	Pennsylvania
Tower Hill Posse	Pennsylvania
Trinidad Posse	Pennsylvania
Uptown Posse	Quebec
Waterhouse Posse	New Jersey, New York, Ohio, and Pennsylvania
Wet Shirt Massive	Philadelphia, Pennsylvania

(Magloclen, 1993)

Jamaican gangs in Canada sell drugs on two levels. The first involves dealing drugs out of a house, where the buyer uses the drug at this location right after its purchase. This type of place is considered a smokehouse rather than a gatehouse. Presently, there are no U.S.-type gatehouses set up in Canada. A second type of drug dealing involving Jamaican gangs revolves around government housing projects in Canada. Just about all the Jamaican posses' participation in street drug sales in Canada is done in the housing projects environment. As has been seen in the United States, the Jamaican gangs in Canada have also started to move their unlawfully gained profits into legitimate businesses. Some of these ventures remain legitimate; others are used to enhance profits from illegal activities.

Since the early 1990s, there has been a sharp increase in the number of violent incidents involving Jamaican posses in Canada. As the involvement of the Jamaican gangs in drug dealing increased, so did the battles over control of certain areas of government housing projects in Toronto. These Canadian housing projects are the main street locations for the Jamaican gangs' drug sales and the battles for this turf have been ongoing, with constantly increasing amounts of violence by the various gangs. Toronto police have found that victims of this gang violence seldom appear in court to sign complaints against gang members; most of the victims are bought off by gang leaders for a few pieces of crack, some currency, or a free trip to Jamaica (Mascoll and Pron, 1991).

The gang leaders do not live in the projects they control. A number of the gang bosses live with what they call "baby mothers" in houses on the outskirts of the projects. The heads of these posses have anywhere from 6 to 12 of these women who not only serve as mothers for their children but also conceal their drug supplies and money in these houses (Mascoll and Pron, 1992).

NIGERIAN GANGS

Just as the Jamaican posses have spread many of their activities worldwide, Nigerian criminal organizations have been very successful in not only broadening their activities but also expanding the bases for their unlawful deeds. The Nigerian groups are on a level with the Yardies when it comes to broadening their horizons to create unique new swindles to increase gang revenues. These groups' inventiveness also extends to their ability to successfully smuggle and distribute drugs worldwide.

The early 1970s brought a new phenomenon in the New York banking industry: Banks were suddenly receiving fraudulent loan and credit card applications possessing the names and addresses of legitimate university professors. It was later determined that these loans had been submitted by a group of Nigerian students attending universities throughout the New York metropolitan area. A police investigation ascertained that the Nigerian students were obtaining a majority of the information that they used in their criminal enterprises from university yearbooks (IACCI, 1984).

This was the beginning of what has turned out to be a major criminal operation being controlled by several Nigerian organized crime groups. Since the early

TRAITS OF FRAUDULENT APPLICATIONS

The following fraud traits should be considered as alerts and cause for further investigation. Any one trait or combination of traits is an indication of the *possibility* of fraud; however, they should not be considered as absolute without confirmation through additional investigative procedures.

Name

1. There are unusual name configurations such as two first names (e.g., John N. James, Dennis L. George).

2. There are unusual foreign-sounding names that are difficult or nearly impossible to pronounce (e.g., Opriglsn Ameolinadunl).

3. There are foreign-sounding first or last names coupled with common American names (e.g., Richard Ameadonilyme, Oyemeni Miller).

4. There are names of known personalities (e.g., George Burns, Robert Young, George Allen).

Address

1. Addresses are usually "drop" numbers and are not kept for long. Consequently, the address is usually not a pertinent trait. At times, an unusually high number of fraudulent applications may be received from certain cities or locales, but, in general, the organized fraud is widespread throughout the country, and no particular area should be considered as "safe."

2. Always investigate a P.O. box at a large city.

Employment/Salary

1. Job title is misspelled.

2. Job title is unusual or does not appear to fit type of employment.

3. Salary appears out of range for type of employment.

4. Monthly salary includes cents or unusual symbols after base salary.

5. Years employed don't correlate with age.

Credit References

1. They often will look too good. They know what you are looking for and (at times) overdo what would be normal for the references given.

2. Approximately 40 percent of fraudulent applications have bad account numbers. Familiarize yourself with as many configurations as possible (e.g., American Express numbers all begin with 37, Diners with 30 or 38, MasterCard with 5, Visa with 4).

(continued)

(continued)

Nearest Relative

1. The nearest relative is often shown as a doctor in an attempt at credibility.

Signatures

1. Signatures are usually scrawled and undecipherable.
2. They are written over as if someone made a mistake on first try.
3. They are often underscored and angled off signature line.

Miscellaneous

1. The Nigerian group often uses periods incorrectly or in unusual places (e.g., after zip code, last name, account numbers, signatures).
2. The Nigerian group usually makes the "Y" as ppppppppppp.
3. Fraudulent applications in general are usually printed; a few are handwritten, but to date, very few have been typed.
4. Most members of the Nigerian group we have talked with speak very broken English.
5. There are unusual abbreviations (e.g., Street 5 Str., Company 5 Com., Avenue 5 Aven).

(Adapted from New York Police Department, 1994).

1980s, Nigerian groups have expanded their illegitimate activities to include several other types of crimes including the importation of drugs to the United States and Europe.

Since the mid-1980s, drug enforcement officials in the United States have noticed a drastic increase in the amounts of heroin being smuggled into the United States by Nigerian groups. The number of seizures from Nigerian drug smugglers has increased over a hundred-fold since early 1980 (when there was a total of two arrests).

History

Nigeria is located on the west coast of Africa and is approximately twice the size of the state of California. The country consists of 19 states and 1 territory; it encompasses about 554,262 square miles and is bordered by the countries of Benin, Chad, Niger, and Cameroon. Nigeria's coastline extends approximately 511 miles on the Gulf of Guinea. The natural resources of Nigeria include crude oil, tin, columbite, iron ore, coal, limestone, lead, zinc, and natural gas (U.S. Department of State, 1992).

The population of Nigeria was estimated at 115.5 million in 1990; Nigeria is the most populous country in Africa, accounting for nearly one-quarter of the continent's population. The majority of these people are members of 250 tribes that are broken into 4 groups. The major northern tribes are the Housa (21 percent) and Fulani (9 percent), while the Yoruba (20 percent) tribe resides in the southwest and the Ibos (50 percent) reside in the southeast. English is the official language of Nigeria, but there is an extensive spectrum of tribal languages, consisting of 141 dialects, throughout the country. The religious makeup is approximately 50 percent Muslim, 40 percent Catholic, and 10 percent unknown. The literacy rate in Nigeria is somewhere between 25 and 30 percent (U.S. Department of State, 1992).

Native witchcraft also has a strong influence on Nigerian superstitions and beliefs. The majority of the Nigerian population live in what can be considered an impoverished environment, with an average annual income of $700 and a life expectancy of 50 years. In addition, there is also a high rate of HIV in the Nigerian population.

As previously mentioned, the official language of Nigeria is English; this is a result of British influence dating back to the mid-1780s. In 1914, Nigeria was formally united as a British colony and remained that way until October 1, 1960, when it was granted independence. The Nigerian constitution was adopted on October 1, 1979, and it was further amended on February 9, 1984. The present military government banned all political parties in December 1983. This military system of administration had originally promised that a national election for president would take place in the year 1992 (U.S. Department of State, 1992). An election finally took place in 1993, and Moshood K. O. Abiola was elected president of Nigeria. Abiola's election as president was short-term because he was imprisoned soon after the election by the military rulers, the same corrupt military leaders who have run Nigeria since freedom from British rule was gained in 1960 (Magloclen, 1991).

The economy of Nigeria shifted in the early 1970s from one of agriculture to one that now relies on oil for 95 percent of export earnings and for 70 percent of the federal budget resources. This resulted in a massive shift in the population from agricultural to industrial workers. The oil boom of the late 1970s and early 1980s increased the opportunity for people to obtain a better financial position in Nigeria, but it also helped to "erode traditional Nigerian moral values and ethics" (Penn, 1985: 1). According to Larry Diamond, a specialist in Nigerian culture, the oil boom "generated staggering corruption. . . . Public servants became wealthy, basically through white collar crime." He states that these corrupt officials became "role models" for a countless number of Nigerian students (Penn, 1985: 1). The never-ending corruption that has infiltrated Nigeria to date has become a contributing factor in the success of most criminal activities within and outside the country. The desire for bribes (known as "dash" in Nigeria) is open, and bribes are solicited by corrupt officials at all levels of the government. Nigeria, a country with an abundance of oil resources, has gone from what most economic analysts regard as a middle-income nation to one of Africa's poorest countries. This is true even though Nigeria, as a sovereign state, continues to have a productive oil-producing industry.

Organizational Structure

Nigerian organized crime groups are still somewhat loosely knit and (as of yet) not really comparable to the established La Cosa Nostra organized crime families in the United States (Magloclen, 1991). Most traditional Italian organized crime families in the United States control a considerable number of criminal activities in a specific geographic area. In contrast, the makeup of Nigerian organized crime groups is far more connected to their structure and their networks rather than any definitive territorial area of control (see Figure 7–4)

The Nigerian criminal system can be compared to an octopus, with its head (body) being located in the African home base (specifically Nigeria) and its tentacles reaching to other important areas both in Asia and the Far East and in Europe in the north and the United States and Canada in the northwest. New tentacles have recently emerged to the west in South America (specifically Colombia) in a quest for increasing Nigerian control over the cocaine dispersion network throughout Africa and Europe.

The leader of a Nigerian criminal group is known as the baron. He is the person who is more than qualified to make an investment in a criminal operation. These transactions usually involve the purchasing and transporting of drugs such as heroin out of the Far East in bulk into Nigeria for further cutting of the heroin. It is then repackaged for

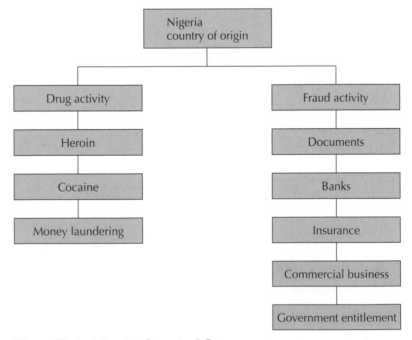

Figure 7–4   Nigerian Organized Crime

Source: Federal Bureau of Investigation

Figure 7–5   Cities with Large Nigerian Populations

distribution to the African, European, and American markets (see Figure 7–5). A baron provides the collateral to a sub-baron (captain) for the initial purchase of heroin in either Southeast or Southwest Asia. Once the procured drug consignment arrives in Nigeria, it is prepared for shipment or sold in bulk to a group of sub-barons. The barons then receive their profits once the drug is distributed to the gangs' major marketplaces.

In this sense, there is a strong disparity between Nigerian and American organized crime. Most of the barons encourage their mid-level employees to go out on their own, which helps to establish a broader base for the leaders' supply of drugs. Any type of individual effort by members of La Cosa Nostra (LCN) would probably result in that individual's death, especially if it occurred in what is considered the traditional U.S. organized crime structure. Since an LCN crime boss or family capo (which is a position that can be considered comparable to the Nigerian gang leader or baron) would more than likely control access to the retail market within his territory, he would (without a doubt) never tolerate any individual enterprising by his subordinates. The Nigerian baron does not have that advantage because the activities of his gang members are worldwide and very difficult to oversee. Consequently, the baron concedes that an underling who decides to go out on his own can broaden his markets as well, so he increases his own profits by encouraging his mid-level subordinates to branch out. Nigerian organized crime families, in some respects, closely resemble both the corporations that distribute their products through their employees' sales and promotion in the United States and the companies that inspire mid-level employees to establish their own supply networks. This expands the base of distribution for the products, with the demand and profits continuing all the way back to the main source of the product, the corporation or company.

Just about every Nigerian organized crime group is divided into cells, and the members of the cells usually participate in several different criminal activities. It is entirely possible that a Nigerian criminal may be involved with more than one gang or in some instances may operate as a singular entity. This is especially true of the individuals who create counterfeit documents for the gangs. There is a great deal of interaction among the different groups and their cells (see Figure 7–6). The gangs exchange knowledge related to their banking and credit schemes, their corrupt contacts in both the public and private sectors, their mail drops, and any other information that may be relevant to their operations (Magloclen, 1991).

A majority of the members of this highly organized crime group have an above-average education. One thing that is highly unusual about the Nigerian gangs is their ability to avoid internal conflict. Thus far, there has been little or no internal resentment, strife, or violent confrontations between members of Nigerian criminal organizations. It is apparent that Nigerian groups go out of their way to work with each other. Law enforcement sources have identified several instances in which Nigerian groups in the United States and Africa have used FedEx to send stolen credit cards to gang associates in Europe so that the cards could be used for several more days (Connolly, 1995). European police recently uncovered a scam involving Nigerian gang members who pilfer credit cards from the Nigerian postal service. Then, over a period of three days to a week, gang members fly all over Africa and Europe purchasing items costing up to $1,500 from airline gift catalogs. Once the members disembark from the

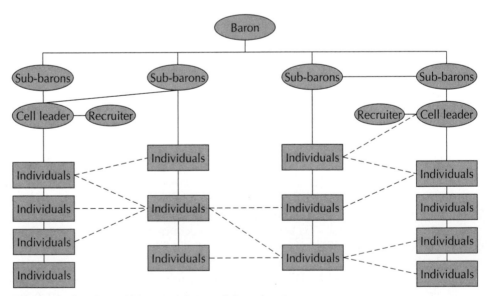

Figure 7–6   Typical Nigerian Criminal Organization

Source: Federal Bureau of Investigation

plane, the cards and the items purchased are handed off to other gang members, who proceed to either reuse the cards on another flight and transport the purchased property to a safe house. This use of stolen credit cards on airlines continues until at least $10,000 is run up on the cards. There is a limit of $1,500 in the amount of purchases that can be made from an airline without verification of the cards (Interpol, 1998).

Since the early 1970s, there has been a sharp increase in the number of criminal activities involving members of the Nigerian community in the United States. Nigerian groups originally participated in several different types of banking and government frauds. The majority of their fraudulent activities involved the swindling of currency from financial institutions. Some of their most popular schemes involve making false insurance claims through the use of crime reports; purchasing autos and other valuable items with a legitimate down payment but using false credit sources; establishing phony credit accounts at large major department stores and purchasing expensive items; opening fraudulent checking and credit card accounts; creating life insurance policies for bogus relatives and then presenting false documents to verify their deaths; and using false identification to participate in schemes that bilk government agencies of large sums of money (Harris County Sheriff's Department, 1986; IACCI, 1984; Penn, 1985).

The ability of the Nigerian criminals to obtain fraudulent documents has increased their capacity to expand their participation in illegal activities. Individuals involved in these schemes have no problem obtaining unlimited counterfeit Nigerian passports. Once they arrive in the United States, they proceed to make the right contacts to obtain the necessary fraudulent U.S. or state government documents. Obtaining forged Social Security cards, driver and nondriver identification cards, and insurance cards poses no major inconvenience to these groups. On several different occasions, investigators have found that these suspects have at least a dozen different driver and nondriver identification cards that contain the same suspect's photo on the front (Duga and Balsamini, 1990).

Involvement in Fraudulent Activities

Early Nigerian Scams.   A raid by federal agents on a Brooklyn, New York, apartment in 1982 turned up four Nigerian students who had fraudulently obtained over $100,000 in federal student loans (Agres and Seper, 1986). In 1985 evidence was presented in the *Wall Street Journal* that 35 percent of all student loan fraud since 1979 was perpetrated by Nigerian students (Penn, 1985). J.C. Penney discovered that in 1983 six Nigerians, all using the same address, submitted over 400 credit card applications using fabricated credentials (Penn, 1985). The ability of the Nigerian gangs to manipulate the credit card companies becomes even more apparent when they are able to use credit cards to fraudulently obtain new high-priced and high-profile vehicles. In fact, a New York City Police Department investigation into a Nigerian gang operating out of Park Hill Avenue in the Staten Island section of New York City turned up 30 vehicles that had been fraudulently obtained by gang members (Duga and Balsamini, 1990).

It was estimated in 1985 that Nigerian crime groups were becoming more and more responsible for the ever-increasing amount (1,200 percent increase in eight years) of credit card ripoffs since 1977 (Agres and Seper, 1986; Duga and Balsamini, 1990; Penn, 1985). A principal U.S. banking agency recently issued an investigative report that places the amount of money swindled from U.S. businessmen by the Nigerian gangs at $1 billion a year. This report also pronounced that 75,000 of the 100,000 Nigerians living on the U.S. East Coast are actively participating in fraudulent gang activities (*South China Morning Post*, 1992).

Many of these criminal groups are made up of illegal aliens from Nigeria, but U.S. immigration investigators have confirmed intelligence reports that verify the fact that a small portion of the members of these groups are from Liberia and Ghana (Duga and Balsamini, 1990; U.S. Customs Service, 1989). Federal law enforcement agencies have also been able to substantiate the fact that the people involved in these frauds have attended and graduated from crime training schools in Nigeria or have been trained in the United States by Nigerians with expertise in fraudulent crimes (Agres and Seper, 1986; Cohon, 1985; Duga and Balsamini, 1990; Harris County Sheriff's Department, 1986; IACCI, 1982; Penn, 1985).

Welfare Fraud. A short time after the arrival of Nigerian gang members in the United States, they are introduced to the U.S. welfare system. The ability of Nigerians to speak English fluently and their knowledge of the American culture make it fairly easy for them to illegally participate in our welfare system. Nigerian gang members usually enter the United States legally by using either a visitor or a student visa. Gang members acquire fraudulent identification documents that identify them as being born in the U.S. Virgin Islands, which entitles them to apply for welfare; within a short period of time, the gang members are on the public assistance rolls. Once this is accomplished, most gang members (using a different set of forged credentials) get jobs driving gypsy cabs. (Gypsy cabs are private vehicles that are owned by a gang and are used as taxi cabs.) The Nigerian gang member usually rents a car (using a fraudulently obtained credit card) and then puts gypsy cab plates from another vehicle on that car. Then the gang member runs his fraudulent activities while maintaining his job driving a taxi cab. Most Nigerians, because of their ability to speak English, are easily assimilated into many black communities in the United States, so it is easy for them to work in these communities as well as live in them.

Student Loans. In the early 1980s, Nigerian gang members arrived on U.S. shores under the guise of being foreign students. Once these alleged students were on U.S. soil, they realized that money could be made by applying for and being awarded guaranteed student loans or Pell Grants. It was not long before these students (in actuality gang members) were creating fraudulent identification documents that were submitted in order to gain entrance into a university. Upon gaining admission to the university, the gang members would go to a loan institution with their letters of acceptance and the forged identification documents and apply for student loans. In a short period of time, the bank would approve the loans and forward the checks to the gang members, who never attempt to attend the university and who do not repay the loan.

Federal investigations into student loan fraud have shown that in some cases Nigerian "students" have submitted several different fraudulent identification documents and letters of acceptance at many different universities in order to obtain multiple student loans from several banks at the same time. One Nigerian "student" in Baltimore had managed to accrue 15 different loan accounts at 3 different universities. At the time of his arrest, he had collected $28,000 of the $42,000 that he had applied for in student loans. In another case, a Nigerian "student," using an assortment of forged credentials, collected a total of $36,000 in student loans while enrolled in 3 different colleges in Alabama and 1 in Maryland (U.S. Customs Service, Subcommittee on Investigations, 1989).

Insurance Fraud.   Nigerian criminals have managed to become experts in the area of insurance fraud. The Nigerian groups have developed skills that assist them in submitting fraudulent personal injury, car theft, death, property damage, and loss claims. Once again, the gangs' ability to produce numerous fraudulent documents makes it easy for one gang member to participate in numerous insurance scams at one time. Some insurance claims are submitted for property theft based on property the gang member recently purchased with a stolen or fraudulently obtained credit card. The allegedly stolen property is identified by a sales draft; once the claim is submitted, the gang member ships the property to Nigeria, where it can be sold for four to five times its purchase price on the black market. This is an interesting scam considering that no one ever actually paid for the property. A fraudulent credit card was used, a false insurance claim was made, and the item was sold for four to five times its actual value in another country.

Another scam involves the use of a fraudulent credit card to buy a vehicle. The auto is purchased within a very short period of time after the gang member receives the credit card. Within a month, the auto is shipped to Nigeria, where it will be sold for several times its value. Shortly after being transported to Nigeria, the vehicle is reported as being stolen to the police and to the U.S. insurance company by the gang member. In May 1991, U.S. Customs Service agents seized 40 recently purchased new vehicles at JFK Airport prior to their being shipped to Nigeria.

The ever-increasing proficiency of Nigerian gang members in insurance scams is evident from the prosperity they have gained from their activity in staged accident schemes. There are several major scams that the gangs participate in that revolve around staged vehicular accidents. One type of scheme requires a Nigerian gang member to have multiple insurance policies on his car. A short time after all the policies become effective, a claim is filed by the insured stating that an unidentified vehicle caused damage to his auto by forcing it off of the road. Appointments for each insurer's appraisal are made, damage to the vehicle is assessed, estimates are made on repair costs, and each insurance company makes what it considers an equitable payment to the insured party. The insurance companies are also unaware that in a majority of these cases, the Nigerian gang member either buys a vehicle that is already damaged or intentionally damages the auto prior to making his insurance claims.

Another type of preplanned accident scam involves the use of two vehicles. Two vehicles owned by the gang, usually containing three to four gang members each, collide at a prearranged location. Police respond to the scene, one of the drivers claims the accident was all his fault, and both the drivers and passengers claim personal injuries. A police report is prepared containing all the facts surrounding the accident. All of the participants in the accident visit doctors, obtain diagnoses of injuries they sustained in the accident, and then proceed to hire attorneys. The doctors submit bills and medical reports to the insurance company confirming that the accident has debilitated the victims and that the victims are unable to work at this time. Once all of this information is evaluated, the insurance company will make an out-of-court settlement that is equitable to all parties.

A deviation from the first two types of staged accidents involves the use of counterfeit documents. Usually two or more Nigerian gang members set up a paper trail that revolves around a bogus vehicular accident. This claim, when filed with an insurance company, contains all of the necessary information concerning vehicles, drivers, passengers, statements of witnesses, and extent of injuries to those in the involved vehicles. This type of conspiracy seldom has any type of police report or documentation of medical assistance being rendered at the scene. Necessary authentication is added to this scam through the use of doctors who verify "injuries" and attorneys who set up civil suits. There is always the possibility that the doctors and lawyers treating and defending the gang members are part and parcel of this criminal operation. Once again, to avoid complications, the impending use of court proceedings can almost assure the claimant that the insurance company will come to a monetary settlement that is equitable to both parties.

A life insurance policy scheme requires that a gang member apply for a life insurance policy using phony identification and naming another gang member as the beneficiary. In many cases, a number of policies are applied for in a short period of time using the same identification and they usually include an accidental death or double-indemnity clause. Several months after the life insurance policies become effective, a death claim is filed by the heir. In this death claim, the beneficiary indicates that the insured died in an accident while on a business trip to or a vacation in Nigeria. The insurance company is supplied with a death certificate, burial certificate, newspaper obituary report, police report of the accident, funeral bills, and (in some cases) a newspaper report of the accident, all from Nigeria. Due to the fact that most insurance companies have neither the capability nor the facilities to properly investigate or refute the evidence from Nigeria produced by members of the Nigerian gangs, either a deal is made on the amount of payment or the claims are paid in full by the company. This scheme has been so successful that members of Nigerian crime groups have put together what they call a death kit. A Nigerian death kit comes equipped with necessary instructions and copies of the fraudulent credentials that will be required in order to consummate the scam.

Bank Fraud.   The average Nigerian gang member is a resourceful con man who has the ability and knowledge to pilfer currency from U.S. banks through the use of what can be considered unsophisticated check scams (see Figure 7–7). There are three main steps involved in these swindles:

1. The gang member opens a bank checking account using counterfeit identification. In almost every case, $100 is deposited in the account.
2. The initial deposit is followed by the deposit of two checks from an out-of-town bank that are made out to the person who opened the checking account. Within a short period of time, these checks will be identified as being from

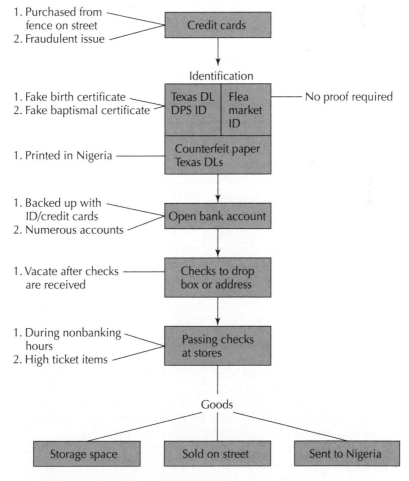

Figure 7–7   Nigerian Check Scheme

Source: Federal Bureau of Investigation

bogus checking accounts, being drawn on closed accounts, or being drawn on accounts with insufficient funds to cover the amount of the checks.

3. The gang member reviews the account to make sure that the deposited checks have cleared the bank. The money placed in this account must be spent as quickly as possible, so the gang member goes out on a Friday and writes as many checks as possible until Monday morning. He knows that the stores where he shops cannot check the balance in his checking account over a weekend. These checks will then come back to the bank, and the bank will be responsible for these checks. It then becomes apparent to the bank that all the identification presented to the bank was counterfeit (Duga and Balsamini, 1990).

Credit Card Fraud.   Nigerian gang members' ability to acquire false identification documents makes bank loan and credit card fraud easy to perpetrate (see Figure 7–8). The Nigerian gang members are also well versed in credit card scams. Nigerian credit card scams are skillfully planned and easily perpetrated by the gangs:

1. The gang member obtains legitimate employment either as a member of a security force or as a health care worker in order to gain personal data on people who work for the company that employs the gang member.

2. The gang member then sets up a credit line using the information that was obtained illegally.

3. Fraudulent identification documents are prepared for a gang member who has a thorough understanding of American culture and banking practices.

4. A change of address is done through the U.S. Postal Service, which is informed that this change of address is only temporary. The new address is usually a mail drop that is run by a private company.

5. A gang member then starts ordering credit cards in the name of one of the company employees whose personnel records have been illegally viewed by a gang member.

6. The mail is inspected by a gang member until the credit cards arrive at the phony address; then the U.S. Postal Service is notified to deliver all the mail to the original address.

7. The gang member then proceeds to go on a buying spree using all the illegally acquired credit cards.

In most cases, this type of scam is not discovered until either the victim receives the bills in the mail or a collection agency employee appears at the victim's door and informs the victim of the unpaid credit card bills. The gang member who perpetuated this crime is long gone, as are the illegally obtained credit cards. In many cases, the property that was secured is on its way to Nigeria.

The majority of Nigerian aliens involved in committing these fraudulent criminal acts attribute most of their success to some or all of these underlying components:

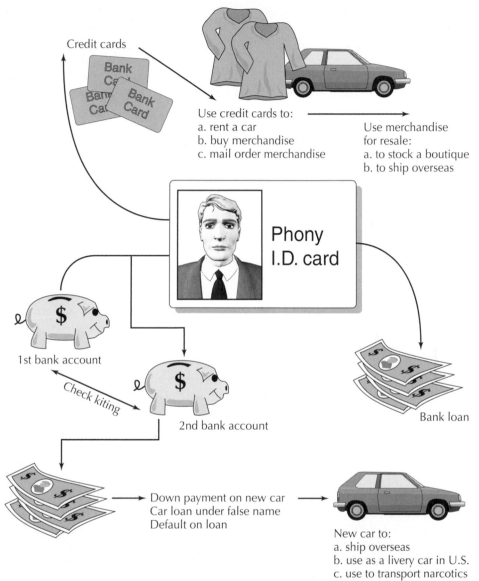

Figure 7–8   Using a Phony ID for Criminal Activities

Source: Staten Island Advance

1. *Creation and availability of counterfeit identification.* This involves the use of many false identities, from which accrue many financial benefits through the use of phony checking accounts, credit cards, and loan applications.

2. *Avoidance of avaricious practices.* These groups believe in advancing their criminal activities through the use of numerous smaller swindles instead of one big ripoff. The use of many minor scams is also very useful because it takes advantage of numerous loopholes within the American economic system and avoids any lengthy punishment by the criminal justice system if a gang member is apprehended.

3. *Family allegiance.* The Nigerian organizations are established based on the abilities of their lower-level workers. The Nigerian criminal groups are both well organized and structured family factions in which everyone is someone else's cousin.

4. *Availability of special training schools in Nigeria.* These schools successfully tutor people in how to adapt to the American culture and how to run schemes that will defraud the American public. These schools teach their pupils the most esteemed identification documents to obtain, ways to acquire these credentials, and ways to best utilize these documents in obtaining money and merchandise after the students' arrival in the United States. Federal agents raided a church in Brooklyn, New York, and arrested 14 gang members for conspiracy to commit bank fraud and to illegally obtain welfare or Social Security benefits. The church was being used as a school to train Nigerian gang members on how to participate in various fraudulent schemes and how to obtain forged documents (Carroll, 1992).

5. *Accessibility of U.S. gang members as contacts for those just arriving from Nigeria.* These contacts will assist the new gang member from Nigeria in obtaining all the necessary documents that are needed for this immigrant to become a participant in the illegal activities of the group in which he is a member (Duga and Balsamini, 1990; U.S. Customs Service, 1989).

Recent Nigerian Scams.   As early as 1990, Nigerian gang members were instituting new con schemes to lure money away from greedy businessmen. One such scam involves the alleged finding of very large sums of money ($10 million to $50 million in U.S. currency) by a government employee, money that the Nigerian government owes to several corporations throughout the world. The Nigerian government worker sends letters out to English as well as American businessmen soliciting their help to obtain these funds by defrauding the Bank of Nigeria. In these letters, the Nigerian employee suggests that he will have no problem modifying both bank and government documents so that the money will be conveyed to this businessperson. The victim is informed that the Nigerian worker needs the victim's foreign bank account to transfer the funds and that the victim will be rewarded when 30–40 percent of the total amount extricated from the Bank of Nigeria is left in his bank account as payment for his cooperation.

Once this businessperson joins this venture, he is informed that blank invoices and business letterhead must be forwarded to the contact in Nigeria. The victim is assured that this is necessary in order to make his corporation appear as the legitimate legatee of these funds. For a period of several months, there is a continual exchange of letters, phone calls, and faxes between the Nigerian worker and the victim. This will continue until the victim finally receives a phony fax or telegram that is allegedly from the Bankers Trust Company. This message informs the victim that the time has come for the Bank of Nigeria to transfer the money to his business account. In many cases, this notification to the businessperson comes on a Friday, so the victim waits patiently until Monday. When the money does not arrive, a phone call is made to the Nigerian worker. At this point, the worker informs the victim that it is necessary for him to pay a standard Nigerian foreign exchange tax of 2.5 percent before the money can be forwarded to him. The businessman, figuring that he is going to receive millions of dollars, forwards by wire transfer the 2.5 percent (or whatever that amount may be) in currency to the worker. Needless to say, that is the last time the victim ever hears from his contact in Nigeria and ever sees his money (FBI, 1993).

An offshoot of this scheme involves contacting American or European businesspersons by sending them what appears to be an authentic business letter requesting their assistance in administering a multimillion-dollar fund. The persons who receive the letter are also informed that they will receive 15 percent of the total sum of the account plus a remuneration for taking care of the fund.

One example of this scheme involved the chief executive officer of a Virginia-based corporation who was contacted by several members of a Nigerian group to participate in this scam. A short time after he received the letter from Nigeria concerning a $28.5 million fund, this person was asked to forward a deceptive statement to the Nigerian government for $18.5 million and also to send a check for $715,000 to take care of expenses until the government finally releases the money in the fund. The victim quickly fulfilled both requests. Solicitations for money to pay advance fees for this fund from the Nigerian gang members continued, as did the money being sent to them by this victim. In 1993, the victim, who paid out $4.4 million to these Nigerian gang members and whose company was $1 million in arrears due to his involvement in this scam, informed the FBI of what had happened to him. Ultimately, the U.S. Department of Justice handed down indictments on the three Nigerians gang members involved in this scam, but there have been no apprehensions made by federal authorities (*Newsweek*, 1994).

In almost every case, the victim of this type of crime will receive a letter, telex, or fax from a person who claims to be a Nigerian "prince," "doctor," "government dignitary," or "notable businessperson" who will pay the victim a large fee if he will help the Nigerian citizen secure a multimillion-dollar fund from the Nigerian government. It is not only businesspeople who are contacted; it is also any organization the Nigerian gangs feel is susceptible to greed. Religious as well as benevolent groups who are approached, in most cases by a person who presents himself as an emissary of an affluent patron.

A sinister spinoff of this scheme concentrates on prior victims of these Nigerian scams. These victims are contacted and informed that they will be compensated for their monetary losses by the Nigerian government's "Presidential Task Force of Debt Repayment." The victim is informed that this can be accomplished by forwarding all of his financial data, including bank account numbers and signatures, to the Nigerian person who forwarded him this information; this must be done within 48 hours, or the offer will be nullified. This information, when made available to a Nigerian gang member, is as good as a certified check made out to this criminal group. Once this information is in the

DR. BLESSING JONAH
NO. 4 HASSAN IDOWU STREET
OFF SANYA ROAD
AGUDA SURULERE
LAGOS – NIGERIA
12th OCTOBER, 2004.

ATTN: THE PRESIDENT
FIRST CARD SERVICES
60 CHARLES LINDBERGH BLVD
UVONDALE, NY 11553 U.S.A.

Dear Sir,

I am the special assistant to the Chief Accountant of Federal Ministry of Aviation and got your particulars through one of your numerous customers. Your customer gave good recommendation of you hence my writing you. I write to intimate you of an opportunity I would like to utilize.

A contract was awarded by my Ministry for the supply of Aviation equipments to our New Federal Capital (Abuja) and Kaduna. This contract was over inflated to the tune of $30.M (Thirty Million US Dollars) to favour the Chairman of the contract Approval Board and other top government functioneries. Now that our government is changing from Military to Civilain rule, I myself and other top officers are interested in politics. With this our mind, we have vital documents that will enable us transfer US $30.M to any incorporation account Overseas. After the transfer for the money, we will resign from our job and go straight into partical politics—The money realised from the transaction will help us in our political campagns.

It is in this regard I am writing you to assist us so that the money will be paid into your account. The mode of sharing is 35% for you as the account owner, 55% for us while 10% is reserved for miscellaneous expenses.

If this proposal satisfies you, please forward to me without delay the following data and documents:-

1. Company's bank account number an Address of the Bank.
2. Three copies of BLANK SIGNED AND STAMPED company's Proforma invoice.
3. Three copies of BLANK signed and stamped company's letter headed papers.
4. Personal telex number, Fax and Telephone numbers.

The blank signed and stamped invoices and letter heading will be used in describing the nature of work done and writingl letter of claims respectively. The documents will then be forwarded to the Ministry where our men who are aware of the transaction will approve the payments. The money, enters the account all the parttis involved will come to your country for our shares after which the documents used in the transaction will be destroyed. Also reply and inform us in time whereby you are not interested.

Please treat as ver y urgent ans confidential. Reply through DHL or call on me through any of the above telecommunication means. The business is 100% risk free.

Thanks for your anticipated co-operation.

Yours faithfully,

BLESSING JONAH (DR.)

hands of the swindler, he can easily forge the victim's signature and move money to gang accounts, and the target of this crime gets victimized a second time.

There are members of these criminal organizations who not only are proficient in speaking and writing the English language but also have available to them many counterfeit government documents. Gang members involved in these schemes even go as far as listing addresses and telephone numbers where the victim can contact them; in some cases, they even invite the target to Nigeria in order to build the victim's confidence and hopefully entice him to participate in this scheme (*Newsweek*, 1994).

Placement of a conspirator inside a stock or trading company has helped the Nigerian gangs create another new scam, which involves the gang member placed inside the company rerouting checks specified for one of the company's vendors to a gang member. A mutual fund money market account is opened using the name of a gang member, and within a short period of time, the gang member has fund checks mailed to checking accounts with disparate identities in a number of banking facilities throughout the area. Once the checks have cleared, they are cashed as quickly as possible but (in most cases) in a way that will avoid arousing as little suspicion as possible. All of the steps involved in creating and working this scheme revolve around the length of time it will take the stock or trading company to realize that the checks have not been sent to the vendor. The conspirator, who was employed by the company, leaves his position a short time after the vendor checks are mailed to gang co-conspirators. Like all the other gang members involved in running scams, this person initially used forged documents to identify himself to this employer, so it is doubtful that his identity will ever be ascertained by investigators.

The establishment by banks and credit card companies of ATM machines, which make it possible for people to get cash allowances at these ATM locations through the use of a credit card, has made the theft of credit far more remunerative to the Nigerian gangs. Members of the Nigerian gangs have found it much easier to go to an ATM machine prior to midnight and withdraw the amount allocated for each cardholder on a daily basis (usually $500) and then right after midnight make another withdrawal for that same amount. Illegally obtaining funds from ATM machines is a whole lot easier for the gangs than obtaining appliances and other goods and then selling these items at a tangible discount or shipping the items to Nigeria and waiting a long period of time prior to finally being reimbursed for their illegal activities.

The participation of Nigerian gang members in what is now known as a visa scam has increased dramatically since early 1990. These unlawful operations involve a written solicitation to the president of a British, American, or European company to personally come or to send a high-ranking official of the firm to Nigeria and participate in what any businessperson would see as a tantalizing business proposal. This business executive is informed that the Nigerian government wants to buy some of his corporation's merchandise. It is further indicated that an agreement with the Nigerian government could be reached almost imminently or as soon as the businessperson

SCAM LETTER 2

FROM THE DESK OF:
DR. BASIL ONUOHA
NIGERIAN NATIONAL PETROLEUM CORPORATION
CHAIRMAN: CONTRACT REVIEW COMMITTEE
FALOMO OFFICE COMPLEX, LAGOS–NIGERIA.

TEL/FAX: 234–1–820123
FAX: 234–90–405621
TEL/FAX: 234–1–5891200
LAGOS–NIGERIA

4th SEPTEMBER, 2004.

STRICTLY CONFIDENTIAL

Dear Sir,

Your esteem particulars was given to me by a valid associate of yours in neighborhood who assured me of your ability and reliability to champion the course of this business transaction requiring maximum confidence.

I am an accountant and a member of "Tender Committee Board" with Nigerian National Petroleum Corporation (NNPC).

We have thirty million U.S. dollars only (US$30,000,000.00) which we got from over inflated contracts from crude oil contract awarded to some foreign contractors in the Nigerian National Petroleum Corporation. We are seeking for your assistance and permission to remit this amount into your account because as civil servants (government workers) the Code of Conduct Bureau made it an offence for us to own or operate a foreign account.

Mode of sharing: It has been agreed upon by all the officials that if you or any company of your choice can take the liberty as the beneficiary, the person or the company will retain 30% of the total amount, 60% for the officials involved, while 10% will be set aside to off-set any bill (expenses) that may come up during the course of the transaction.

Please notify me of your acceptance to do this business urgently through my private phone and fax number. The men involved are men in government, therefore, there is no risk in either side. More details will be sent to you by fax as soon as we hear from you.

For the purpose of communication in this matter, may we have your private phone (home) and fax numbers.

Note: Your entire bank particulars should be included also. Please treat as most confidential. All replies strictly by the above fax and phone number.

The officials involved have agreed to establish viable business venture in your country which you will be a pioneer member on successful transfer of this fund.

Thanks for your co-operation.

Best regards,

DR. BASIL ONUOHA

arrives in Nigeria. The invitation also informs the executive that a visa is not required because the contact can get him through immigration and customs without a visa. All the information the business executive receives is supported by documents containing the letterhead of the Nigerian Defense Ministry or the Nigerian Petroleum Corporation. These letters also suggest that a high-ranking official of the corporation should visit Nigeria as soon as possible to show the Nigerian government that this company is interested in obtaining the contract. The corporation makes a commitment and informs the contact that a company executive will be leaving for Nigeria. Upon the arrival of this high-ranking company official in Nigeria, he is immediately rushed through immigration and customs and then taken to a remote residence outside Lagos (Noble, 1992).

A short time after the business executive's arrival, this person is informed by his original contact that he is no longer free to leave and that the only way out of this predicament is either to pay an ample amount of ransom money or to participate with his kidnappers in a unlawful act (e.g., illegally laundering money for this gang). The gang members emphasize the fact that the executive can be arrested and prosecuted because he does not have a visa stamp on his passport, so the only way out is to pay a ransom or participate in the scheme (Noble, 1992).

The outcome of some of these schemes seems to indicate that some Nigerian gangs may be prone to violence. In July 1991, David Rollings, a British businessman, traveled to Lagos in an attempt to recover $4 million that had been previously taken by fraud from a fellow British business official. A short time after Rollings's arrival, he was found shot to death in his hotel room (*Newsweek*, 1994). Within the same year, Gerald Scruggs, an American businessman who was under the impression that he was a participant in an authorized business venture, was murdered by some of the Nigerian gang members who initiated this scam. Scruggs was first garroted with an auto tire and then burned to death outside the Sheraton Hotel in a suburb of Lagos after he refused to continue participating with Nigerian gang members (*Newsweek*, 1994).

One other type of fraud that has been used by the Nigerian gangs involves contacting a corporate executive who has been doing business in Nigeria. A proposition is made to this person that a tanker full of oil worth $1 million can be purchased at a discount price. He is informed that this oil exceeds the amount of oil that Nigeria, as an OPEC nation, is allowed to produce and that once the amount of oil is deemed in excess of an OPEC-designated amount, it can be sold at a cheaper price on the open market. Once an agreement is made, all the necessary papers are forwarded on bogus Nigerian National Petroleum Corporation (NNPC) letterhead or from communication terminals "on the tanker" confirming the particulars of this transaction. The gang con man then requests the sum of $250,000 to offset the costs of licenses, taxes, and port duties; the victim then forwards this money, in good faith, to his contact. A short time after this transaction is completed, the victim contacts the oil company in an effort to obtain the oil shipment. He is then informed that the deal is phony and that the oil cargo belongs to either the Nigerian government or some major petroleum company. It is also possible that this oil has already been removed from the vessel. It has been established by the Nigerian government that in most of these schemes there are usually several different victims who claim ownership of the same petroleum (Vick, 1992).

Nigerian gang members also run oil tanker scams in which there is no oil, only an empty tanker. Members of the gang will board a tanker and compel the ship's captain to allow them to operate the fax or telex. A prospective buyer is contacted and convinced to participate in this deal. Arrangements are made between the gang members and the client for docking facilities for the tanker. A request is then made by the gang to the purchaser for payment of a fee, usually $250,000, to cover unexpected business expenses (such as bribes or other fees). When the buyer attempts to procure the oil, he finds that there is no oil and that he is out the money invested in the scheme (*South China Morning Post*, February 2, 1992).

Another fraudulent scheme that must be touched on involves the shipment of merchandise to Nigeria. In this scam, European and American corporations are informed that the Nigerian government wants to purchase a considerable amount of products from their companies. The Nigerian gang members further authenticate this scheme by forwarding all the required documents on the letterhead of the Nigerian government's purchasing office. A letter is also sent that guarantees that a check for full payment will be sent once the products arrive in Nigeria and are audited by government employees. Most companies then ship the requested products to Nigeria, only to find out within a short period of time that the check they receive is no good. In a major portion of these cases, the bank this check is drawn on does not exist, or the account this check is written on is closed (*South China Morning Post*, February 2, 1992).

One such scheme took place in 1990 when Nigerian Bisola Chalmers contacted the Belgium-based Quarante Import/Export Company and informed this company that his auto dealership was one of the larger car dealerships in Nigeria. Chalmers proceeded to order 20 1990 Mercedes-Benz, model 260 E, at a cost of 952,500 Belgium francs. A forged irreversible credit letter, which was purportedly validated by London-based Barclay's Bank, was forwarded to the Quarante Import/Export Company by this Ibadan, Nigeria–based corporation. A short time after the arrival of this letter, the Quarante Company realized that the instrument forwarded to it was fraudulent and that the signatures were counterfeit. The Quarante Company has been unable to locate its cars or receive any type of payment for the vehicles (Imasa, 1991).

Drug Trafficking. The deterioration of economic conditions in Nigeria has precipitated a significant increase in the involvement of Nigerian nationals in international drug trafficking. Nigeria is not what would be considered a supply depot for heroin or cocaine because neither opium nor cocoa leaves are grown in Nigeria. Therefore, the participation of Nigerian criminals in a drug-trafficking enterprise revolves around their ability to transport heroin from the Golden Traingle (Burma, Laos, and Thailand) in Southeast Asia and the Golden Crescent (Afghanistan, Iran, and Pakistan) in Southwest Asia to other countries in Europe and to the United States. They also import cocaine from South America for distribution to other African nations and Europe.

Enterprising Nigerian traffickers use both bogus and bona fide passports to travel to heroin-producing Southwest Asian countries such as Afghanistan, India, and Pakistan to purchase heroin. In most cases, they fly into Karachi, Pakistan, allegedly on vacation, and then fly or drive to Islamabad or Peshawar, Pakistan, to purchase heroin at $6,000 to $8,000 per kilogram. Once the heroin is obtained and properly concealed, the smuggler returns to Nigeria. The heroin is then prepared for transportation to the United States or Europe (see Figure 7–9). It is estimated that approximately 5 percent of all Nigerian drug couriers are being apprehended by U.S. Customs Service agents. An indication of the type of Nigerian citizens involved in the drug trade was made apparent in 1987 when Captain Billy Eko, a celebrated Nigeria Airlines pilot, was arrested with 7.5 pounds of brown and white heroin by U.S. customs officers at Kennedy International Airport (*Newsweek*, 1991; *Time*, 1988).

An assessment by U.S. customs officials of Nigerian drug-smuggling rings indicates that it would not be unusual to have 30 to 40 smugglers on any given flight out of various airports in West Africa. These couriers are paid anywhere from $2,000 to $5,000 per trip; the smugglers, in most cases, are accompanied on their flight by a member of the gang who is known as a controller. Nigerian smugglers

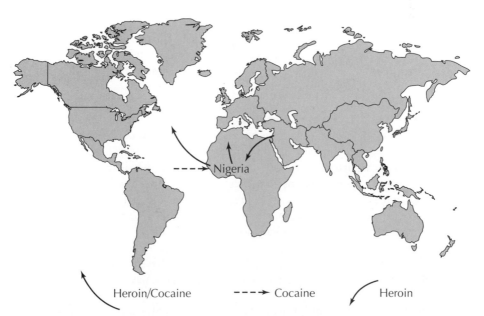

Figure 7–9   Narcotics Movement in and out of Nigeria

Source: U.S. Customs Service

utilize several methods to export their product to the United States. The drug-concealing techniques used are carrying drugs in the body cavity, using the body carry (drug packages taped to body), swallowing drugs, putting drugs in the heels of shoes, and hiding drugs in false bottoms of luggage (Treaster, 1992; U.S. Department of Justice, 1989).

In an effort to avoid customs authorities, the Nigerian gangs have created many new international transportation routes for their couriers to travel and have recruited smugglers from all over Europe and Africa. A smuggler may make anywhere from two to five stops at different transportation terminals throughout the world before arriving at a final destination. The Nigerian drug traffickers, like their Chinese counterparts (discussed in the next chapter), have been using Canada as a stop-off location on route to the United States (*Time*, 1994). The Nigerian gangs participating in drug trafficking have mostly been suppliers, not street dealers. Thus far, the Nigerian gangs have been identified as the entrepreneurs who supply various other gangs with heroin to be sold at street level; the two major purchasers of this illicit Nigerian product are Jamaican and Dominican gangs. The profits that result from the sale of heroin are immense when one considers that a kilogram of heroin sells for about $22,000 in Nigeria and over $200,000 in the United States. This profit margin remains approximately the same with the sale of cocaine because cocaine sells at a much higher price in Britain and Europe than it does in the United States. The Nigerian gangs, which are quite aware of the differences in monetary gain, deal their drugs only in the markets that provide the greatest dividends for them (Magloclen, 1991).

In April 1994, the U.S. State Department disclosed that somewhere between 35 and 40 percent of all the heroin entering the United States is supplied by Nigerian organized criminal gangs. According to the U.S. State Department's report, the international drug activities of these gangs are supported by members of the Nigerian government. Robert Gelbard, the Assistant Secretary of State for International Narcotics Matters, states:

> Nigeria has become a major source of trafficking around the world, as Nigerian trafficking organizations have become one of the most extraordinary, organized phenomena of carrying heroin and cocaine both in the United States and [in] Europe. We calculate that some 35 to 40 percent of all heroin coming into the United States comes from Nigerians who bring it into this country. The smugglers are not random mules, or individuals who are doing this on a free-lancing basis. These people are working for very organized groups, which we have felt is with the protection of Government officials (Sciolino, 1994: A1, A11).

Enterprising Nigerian drug merchants have increased their deployment of non-Nigerian citizens as drug couriers. Within the past 10 years, drug seizures made in numerous countries throughout the world indicate that citizens of West African countries as well as England, Europe, and the United States are employed by Nigerian drug lords as drug runners. The Nigerian couriers are informed that if they are apprehended

NIGERIAN ORGANIZED CRIME

Drug Activity

Methods of Shipment

Standard Scenarios
- Use luggage or carry-on items
- Carry on body
- Hide in laundry powder in luggage
- Hide in clothes, shoes, hair, turbans
  - Use baby bottles (liquid heroin)
- Hide in body cavities
  - Primarily females
  - Rectal or vaginal cavities
- Extreme Cases
  - Dead baby (drugs surgically implanted)

Tools of Drug Traffickers
- Condoms supplied by the United States
- Black electrical tape
- Cream of okra soup
- Heroin for packaging
- Schools for couriers in Africa
- Schools for fraud activities in United States and Africa
- Controllers on flights (not known to couriers)
- Intel analysts
- Dry runs to see what works
- "Witch Doctor"

Source: Duga and Balsamini

Note: As of 1991, other West Africans as well as other nationalities have been recruited as couriers resulting in a drop in purity of heroin, due to the increase in shipment fee.

by law enforcement officials, their families will be provided for until they are released from prison. These drug runners agree to remain secretive and to withhold any information they may have pertaining to the Nigerian gangs. This is done by the couriers because of their fear of retaliation against their families by Nigerian gang members. Just about every Nigerian courier receives training from the drug lords; the training relates to how the drug runner is to avoid apprehension, how to respond if challenged by authorities, and how to answer questions if confronted by law enforcement personnel (Kraft, 1994).

The following two cases indicate the use of foreign nationals by Nigerian drug groups:

1. In October 1984, DEA agents in Seattle seized 334 grams of heroin that had arrived aboard a Japan Airlines flight. It was later learned that the heroin had been originally obtained in Bombay, India, by English females working for Nigerian drug lords. The heroin was transported from Bombay to Tokyo, Japan, where it was repackaged into smaller lots and then dispensed to these same couriers for travel to the United States and England (U.S. Department of Justice, 1985).

2. In September 1988, Japanese police raided the residence of a Nigerian national in Tokyo, Japan, and seized 16 pounds of heroin. At that location, the police arrested one Nigerian national and four U.S. citizens. It was later ascertained that the four U.S. citizens had been recruited by a Nigerian drug dealer to supply heroin to several locations in the United States (U.S. Customs Service, 1989).

Since 1985, one major Nigerian heroin exporter has been using Abidjin, Ivory Coast, as his base of operations. This move was due to an increase in enforcement efforts by the Nigerian government (U.S. Department of Justice, 1985).

One of the major problems facing the Nigerian government's drug enforcement efforts is corruption. A good deal of the progression and prosperity of the heroin trans-porters has been due to the dishonesty of government officials. In many instances, administrative authorities in middle- and lower-level positions have become involved in corrupt activities with drug dealers. Investigative efforts in Nigeria have indicated that corrupt officials assist drug dealers by providing protection and police intelligence data, aiding drug carriers, supplying fraudulent documents, and functioning as "couriers and controllers" (U.S. Department of Justice, 1985: 7).

In 1984, the following government officials in Lagos, Nigeria, were identified as skilled conspirators who were using their positions within the government to assist the Nigerian gangs' drug-smuggling enterprises (U.S. Department of Justice, 1985: 8):

Chief of Immigration, Alagbon Close Street

Chief of Security, Murtala Mohammed Airport

Chief of Criminal Investigation Division, Yaba

In an effort to correct this problem, the Nigerian government cracked down on corruption by either discharging/firing or forcing retirement on many of the police, customs, immigration, and national security personnel. To some extent, this endeavor has been successful: It led to the arrests of a number of drug runners at Lagos Airport and the arrest of a dishonest customs official who was involved in narcotics trafficking; it helped eliminate corrupt officials from the National Security Office; it forced the Nigerian drug gangs to seek new transportation routes for their drugs in an effort to avoid Lagos; and it forced the military government in Nigeria to create a law that makes drug smuggling a capital offense, with a provision related to the forfeiture of the suspect's assets (U.S. Department of Justice, 1985).

In an effort to control drug trafficking by Nigerian nationals, the Nigerian government created the National Drug Law Enforcement Agency in December 1989. This agency increased the government's participation in enforcement of state laws related to narcotics transactions by the Nigerian gangs. This endeavor greatly increased the number of arrests of Nigerian gang members for drug smuggling period.

Money Laundering.   Employees in private industry participating with the gangs in drug conspiracies have also been exposed; included were airline and bank personnel. It has been substantiated by U.S. federal investigators that several privately owned companies established affiliations with the Nigerian drug cartels. These companies were active participants in the drug import and export industry, and they assisted the drug cartels in laundering illicitly obtained money. Some of the Nigerian businesses that were exposed during this investigation are the following (U.S. Department of Justice, 1985):

1. Cool Art Store
2. Ibrahim International
3. Lourdes Disco
4. Mosun Fayemiwo Trading Company
5. O.P.S. International, LTD
6. Vago Associates, Export and Import

The majority of Nigerian gang members smuggle money divested from drug operations back to Nigeria because U.S. currency is much stronger than the Nigerian naira. This is accomplished in several ways, including the use of couriers with a large amount of U.S. currency (usually 50- or 100-dollar bills) in their luggage, bank transfers, goods that can be resold in Nigeria for profit, negotiable instruments, and wire transfers. There has been an attempt by several Nigerian gang leaders to establish offshore banking operations that are similar to those on some of the islands in the West Indies. It must be remembered that drug money is not the only currency that the Nigerian gangs would be trying to launder; they are just as deeply entrenched in other unlawful schemes as they are in drug trafficking, although these gangs are aware that there is a quicker turnover of money in drug dealing than in other scams (U.S. Department of Justice, 1995).

Intelligence gathered by U.S. government investigative sources indicates that some Nigerian drug dealers are becoming active participants in both political and terrorist operations by supplying these groups with monetary support. In one specific inquiry, it was discovered that Nigerian drug groups were using drug money to fund the activities of the Palestine Liberation Organization; in another U.S. government

NIGERIAN ORGANIZED CRIME

Indicators of an organized criminal group:

- Nonideological
- Hierarchical
- Limited or exclusive membership
- Perpetuitous
- Use of violence and bribery
- Specialization and division of labor
- Governed by explicit rules and regulations
- Monopolistic

Criminologists define an organized criminal group as a secret, exclusive society with its own rules and regulations. These groups have been studied by sociologists and psychologists for decades.

Source: Federal Bureau of Investigation

investigation into the activities of the Nigerian gangs, it was ascertained that a terrorist arms supplier was affiliated with these same Nigerian groups (U.S. Department of State, 1992). Therefore, all the money that is obtained from participating in drug trafficking is not being put in the gang leaders' pockets.

CONCLUSIONS

As this chapter indicates, the Jamaican and Nigerian organized crime groups continue to be two of the most futuristic gangs operating worldwide. They have little or no participation by street gangs, except when they occasionally use these gangs to sell their imported drugs on the street. The ability of Jamaican posses to profit from drugs, firearms, and money laundering and the ability of the Nigerian gangs to send unlawfully obtained property (from handheld calculators to luxurious automobiles) back to their headquarters in Nigeria for profitable resale indicate the creativity and resourcefulness of both Jamaican and Nigerian criminal groups.

CHAPTER 8

CHINESE GROUPS

HISTORY

United States and Asian Organized Crime

Prior to 1965, the crime rate in Asian communities in the United States was considerably low in comparison to crime rates in other ethnic neighborhoods. The vast majority of immigrants from China, Japan, and other Asian countries were law-abiding citizens who worked hard and avoided trouble whenever possible (Chin, 1990). Almost all Asian immigrants worked long hours (in a sweatshop type of environment) on a daily basis for minimal pay, which left little or no time to supervise their children. Yet most Asian youths growing up under these conditions spent a major portion of their time concentrating on schoolwork and avoiding trouble. The involvement of Asian youths in street gang crime prior to the 1970s was minimal, but we must also consider that the reason for this scarcity of criminal activity was due to the small number of Asian adolescents in our society prior to 1970.

Asians as a group were always treated as second-class citizens by many members of our society. History shows us examples such as laws that were passed by our legislators to suppress the immigration of Asians (e.g., the Chinese Exclusion Act of 1882 and the Natural Origins Acts of 1924). The incarceration of Japanese citizens and immigrants living in the United States during World War II is another example. We must remember that prior to 1965 Japanese and Chinese ethnic groups were just about the only Asian representatives in this country and that the crimes these groups were involved in (if any) had no impact on our society (Chin, 1990; Kaplan and Debro, 1986; U.S. Department of Justice, 1985). The modification of the immigration quotas in the mid-1960s and the Vietnam War increased the number of Asians immigrating to the United States, which consequently led to a substantial increase in

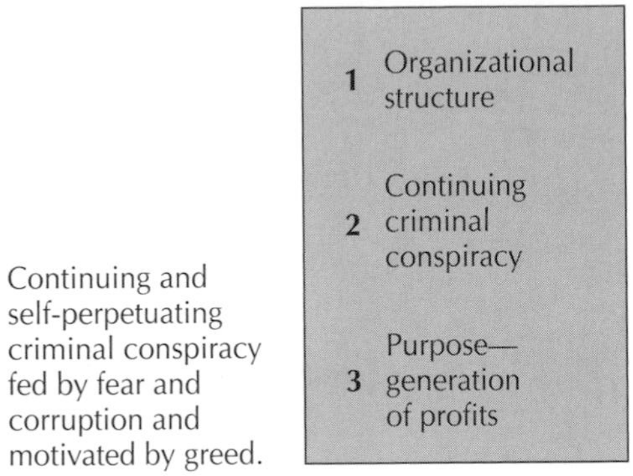

Continuing and
self-perpetuating
criminal conspiracy
fed by fear and
corruption and
motivated by greed.

1	Organizational structure
2	Continuing criminal conspiracy
3	Purpose— generation of profits

Figure 8–1   Organized Crime

Source: Federal Bureau of Investigation

the number of Asian immigrants descending on the Asian communities in the United States. The sudden addition of these immigrants caused a breakdown in stability within these Asian communities because the vast majority of these new immigrants were Chinese and this large influx led to the total fragmentation of social support groups for these new immigrants (Chin, 1990). This opened the door to increased Chinese gang activity (see Figure 8–1).

When we discuss Chinese organized crime groups, we must note some of the major factors that have helped to increase Chinese gang activity in the United States and many other locations throughout the world:

1. There has been an increasing migration of Chinese immigrants (legal and illegal) to the United States since the mid-1960s (see Table 8–1). It is entirely possible that the figures in Table 8–1 could increase anywhere from 25 to 100 percent if we were aware of the number of illegal immigrants entering this country.

2. The increase in Chinese gangs and their membership since the 1970s has also led to the expansion of crimes and criminal activities (kidnapping, robbery, extortion, drug dealing, murder) from small Chinatown-type communities to any locale where affluent Chinese people congregate or live.

TABLE 8–1

Chinese Immigration Figures

Year	Legal Immigrants
1960	237,292
1970	435,063
1980	812,718
1990	1,371,435
2000	1,611,395

Source: U.S. Department of Justice, 2002.

3. During the 1970s and most of the 1980s, Chinese gangs only exploited other ethnic Chinese individuals, but many Chinese gangs (like their Vietnamese counterparts discussed in Chapter 9) then began to expand their criminal horizons to include any other Asian groups that supplied a service or that prevented a Chinese gang from controlling a specific enterprise.

4. Law enforcement officials believe that Chinese organized crime syndicates are going to take over the mafia crime businesses. In reality, this is quite doubtful because the mafia has been entrenched in illegitimate as well as legitimate workplaces for several decades and will not be to easy to supplant.[1] The Chinese have gained a foothold in some criminal activities, but so have Colombian, Nigerian, Japanese, Vietnamese, and Russian gangs. There is just too much competition in the organized crime marketplace for any one group to displace the mafia.

5. The Hong Kong (now part of China) gang connection has been expanding its base from Hong Kong to the United States, Canada, Southeast Asia, and Australia. The Hong Kong consortium controls a majority of the heroin imported from Southeast Asia, which has been force-fed into the world heroin market (Chin, 1990; U.S. Department of Justice, 1993; Dombrink and Song, 1996).

Chinese Roots of Organized Crime

Chinese organized gang activities did not just suddenly appear on the American scene. As students and observers of gang operations, we must review what brought about these criminal gang activities in fairly stable Chinese society, a society that stresses a Confucian code that states that if all persons fulfill their duties toward themselves, their families, their states, and their world, a "Great Harmony" would prevail (Booth, 1991; Freedman, 1966).

When we discuss the evolution of Chinese gangs, we must view the impact that Triads have had on these groups. During an internal revolt against the Ming dynasty, some military leaders from the Ming government requested assistance from the Manchus, a barbarian tribe from Mongolia. The Manchus realized that most of the resistance emanated from a Shaolin Buddhist monastery in southeastern China. A large military force was sent to the monastery in Foochow to kill the rebellious monks; 123 monks were killed by the invaders, and the 5 who escaped eventually went on to form the first Triads (Booth, 1991).

Triad (triangle of heaven, earth, and man) groups first appeared in China in the late seventeenth century (see Figure 8–3). They were formed in an attempt to overthrow the Quig (Ch'ing) government that had been created by Manchu invaders (Morgan, 1964). It wasn't until 1912 that the Quig regime finally collapsed. Some Triad leaders and members attempted to place themselves in the newly created Republic of China's government. A large portion of those not assimilated into the new government reestablished themselves within their Triad associations in order to maintain some type of authority

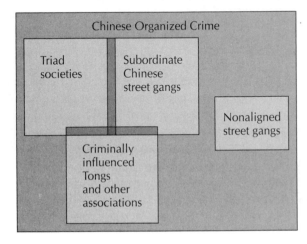

Criminal Activities
• Alien smuggling
• Armed robbery
• Arson
• Blackmail
• Bombings
• Bribery
• Burglary
• Contract murder
• Copyright violations
• Drug trafficking
• Extortion
• Illegal gambling
• Infiltration of legitimate businesses
• Investment fraud
• Loansharking
• Money laundering
• Murder
• Prostitution
• Public corruption
• Tax evasion
• Weapons smuggling

Figure 8–2   Interrelation of Chinese Crime Groups in the United States

Source: McKenna, 1996.

there. The secretive Triad organizations, which were originally civic-minded and devoted to religious camaraderie, slowly but surely deteriorated into what is known as organized crime factions. This took place once the leadership of the Triads was assumed

In 1844 China was conquered by foreign Manchus, who established the Ch'ing Dynasty. The third Ch'ing emperor issued an edict against secret societies, i.e., the Society of Heaven and Earth, whose aims were the moral reform of the people, the maintenance of religious belief and practice, and the encouragement of Chinese nationalism and patriotism. Its famous motto, which remains relevant today in Triads, was "Overthrow the Ch'ing and restore the Ming."

Figure 8–3   Triad Symbolism

Source: New York Police Department.

by self-serving individuals who were able to impose their own standards of conduct on the organization for personal stature and gain (Chin, 1990; Booth, 1991).

Triad societies' involvement in criminal activities increased during the first half of the twentieth century as many Chinese citizens became more uneasy with the various officials struggling to control the government. Several influential organizations recruited Triad members and sanctioned strong-armed methods and violent tactics to ensure that the average person followed organizational rules. The Triads were then authorized by these associations to set up and control prostitution, gambling, and opium houses (McKenna, 1996). As the Triads' enforcer status in these powerful political associations increased, there was a decrease in their patriotic interest and a decline in their leaders' ability to control illegal activities of the membership (McKenna, 1996).

Then, in 1949, the Red Army defeated Chang Kai-shek's Kuomintang Party. This led to a mass migration of Kuomintang Party supporters to Taiwan and Hong Kong. It wasn't long after the defeat of Chang Kai-shek's army that the Chinese Communist Party started harassing and executing Triad members (Chin, 1990). Triad groups were quickly re-formed in Hong Kong.

Hong Kong Connection

Triad societies have been active in China since the end of the seventeenth century, but the groups' participation in Hong Kong's political and patriotic activities started a lot later. Hong Kong was transferred to British control in 1842; three years later, the Triads caused a great deal of social disorder with their unlawful operations. This forced the British government in Hong Kong to enact an Ordinance for the Suppression of Triads (the Societies Ordinances). The statutes banned Hong Kong citizens from becoming members of Triad groups or partaking in any Triad activities (Booth, 1991; Chin, 1990; U.S. Department of Justice, 1993). These laws helped to control the actions of Triad groups by moving most of their operations out of public view until the early twentieth century, when Triad groups started resurfacing in Hong Kong.

In response to Chang Kai-shek's defeat (discussed earlier), many Triad groups moved from China to Hong Kong. It wasn't long before the ranks of the Hong Kong Police Department contained Triad members. This helped to control most criminal activities in Hong Kong and continued the deterioration of a once proud and patriotic group to a sleazy criminal enterprise (Booth, 1991; Chin, 1990). In fact, an investigation into the officers assigned to the Hong Kong Police Department's Triad Society Division disclosed that most of its members also held active Triad membership. This investigation further exposed unbridled corruption within the Triad Society Division. There were 5 police sergeants (Five Dragons)[2] who were the leaders of this corrupt organization; this fact ultimately led to the indictments and exodus of over 40 police officers and the theft of millions of dollars by people who had sworn to uphold the law (U.S. Department of Justice, 1993).

The Triads were reestablished as organizations to provide protection for territories chosen by peddlers. Triads, once again, started to flourish in Hong Kong, but not

FORMATION OF CHINESE SECRET SOCIETIES

Belief	Hung—Heaven, Earth, and Man
Seventeenth century	36 oaths—goodness: patriotism, brotherhood, security, secrecy, "one for all and all for one" 36 strategies—badness
Eighteenth century	Formation of Triads overseas
Nineteenth century	Tongs formed in North America: King Sor, Kung Kuam, Hui; protection for Chinese workers and new immigrants to America; Tong values almost carbon copy of Triad values
Twentieth century	Street gangs formed and used as enforcers by Triads and Tongs; no values, strictly part of criminal enterprise

Source: Royal Hong Kong Police, 1994.

without conflict. A major portion of the problems evolved around the confrontations over the territorial rights of the vendor-Triad members. Triad associations found that members of different Triads had been working the same locations. In an effort to settle these conflicts, the Triad organizations held a joint meeting to start a unification process and to form one association to supervise the activities and settle the disputes. During this conference, all the attendees voted to use the word "Wo" (peace) prior to the symbolic name of each Triad (e.g., Wo Sun Ye On). Ultimately, these Wo groups evolved into some of the most powerful and disreputable chapters of the Hong Kong Triads (Chin, 1990). These are some of the early factors that effected the increased growth and success of the Hong Kong Triad groups:

1. The Triad members had the ability to infiltrate labor unions, recruit new Triad members, and then take control of labor unions.

2. The Triad cooperated with the Japanese military government during World War II. The Triads extended their control over illegal activities by supporting the Japanese officials, who in turn destroyed cooperating Triad members' prior criminal histories and permitted the Triad informers and enforcers to control gambling, prostitution, and opium operations in Hong Kong.

3. Once World War II ended, the Hong Kong Triads continued their rapid growth, but with this increased growth came loss of control over Triad membership, camaraderie, righteousness, and secrecy. A segment of the Hong Kong Triads membership had already sacrificed their nationalism when they joined forces with the Japanese during World War II. After the war, other members also relinquished all the other values of these secret societies by becoming involved in criminal activities.

All these factors, plus doing away with membership registration, led to the further criminalization of what now could be considered fractious criminal organizations (Chin, 1990; U.S. Department of Justice, 1993).

The sudden reemergence of Chinese Triad groups created severe problems for the citizens of Hong Kong. In 1956 and then again in 1967, disturbances between anti-Communist workers and pro-Communist workers created havoc in Hong Kong. Altercations between these same groups also erupted due to the "cultural revolution" that was occurring in China. The results of all the changes in Triad customs and the anti-pro-Communist issue led to a dramatic takeover of almost all the Triads of Hong Kong by mainland Chinese groups (e.g., Big Circle, Ching Societies, 14K, Sun Ye On, and Wo On Lok) (Chin, 1990). All these drastic changes started taking place in the 1970s; since that time, most Hong Kong Triads have become nothing more than groups of street criminals pretending to be nationalistic.

The structure of each Triad society may be slightly different, but most of their organizations are arranged in the same basic manner (see Figure 8–4). Numbers play an important role and are used as signs of identification related to Triad history. When the number four (4) is used as the first number in a specific numberical figure, it signifies the ancient Chinese belief that earth is surrounded by four great seas. The Triads are the dominant Asian group with ties to criminal activity (see Figure 8–5).

As with those of most other secret societies, newly recruited Triad members must participate in a simple initiation ceremony; the Triads call it "hanging the blue lantern." The participants in the ceremony are accepted into the Triad as members once they proclaim the 36 oaths of loyalty, secrecy, and brotherhood (Booth, 1991; U.S. Department of Justice, 1993).

In 1997 Hong Kong became part of the People's Republic of China. Prior to that happening, we observed the tentacles of the major Hong Kong Triads establishing new bases of operation in the United States, Canada, and Australia (Dombrink and Song, 1996). The most powerful and largest Triad group in Hong Kong, Sun Yee On, vastly increased its membership (*South China Morning Post*, October 5, 1992). This group is heavily involved in extortion, money laundering, loan-sharking, drug trafficking, arms sales, prostitution, gambling, credit card fraud, and illegal alien smuggling. The most important gains by Sun Yee On have been in the film industry. This has afforded the Sun Yee On Triad the opportunity to form a potent alliance with members of the Chinese Public Security Bureau. Movies shot on location in China help to provide employment for local citizenry as well as illegal money to local politicians and party leaders. Sun Yee On's control over the film industry in China has afforded it the power base it was seeking with the Chinese government.

Historically, Sun Yee On was formed in 1796 and first appeared in Hong Kong in 1841. The majority of the members were postal workers, and they used the name Sun On Tong Triad (see Figure 8–6). Within a year of Sun Yee On's appearance in Hong Kong, members from Chiu Chow created the Man On Triad. In 1919 the Yee On Triad was forged, with one Henry Chin inducted as Dragon Head. The original income of Yee On came from the import/export business. In 1922 Henry Chin

DESIGNATIONS OF LEADERS AND MEMBERS OF TRIADS

FBI	Chin	San Francisco PD	Job Description
Leader	Shan Chu	Shan Chu	Group Leader
Elder Brother		Leader	Boss of Group
489	489	489	Older Brother
			Slang Tai Lo
Deputy	Yee Lu Yuan	Fu Shan Chu	Second Brother
Incense Burner	Fu Shan Chu	Deputy Leader	Slang Yee Lo
Vanguard Leader		Heung Chu	
		Incense Master	
438	438	438	
		Sin Fung	High Priest
		Vanguard	
		Sheung Fa	Status Rank
		Double Flower	General Affairs
			Recruiter
Red Pole	Hung Kwan	Hung Kwan	Enforcer
Enforcer		Fighter Official	Responsible for gang
426			protection and implementing punishment
White Paper	Park Tse Sin	Park Tse Sin	Planner and advisor
Fan Advisor		White Paper Fan	
415	415	415	
Grass Sandal	Cho Hai	Cho Hai	Messenger
Messenger	Liaison	Grass Sandal	Liaison
432	432	432	Spy
			Infiltrate police and other groups
Members	Sey Kow Jai	Ordinary Member	
	Worker		
49	49	49	
Recruits			
36			

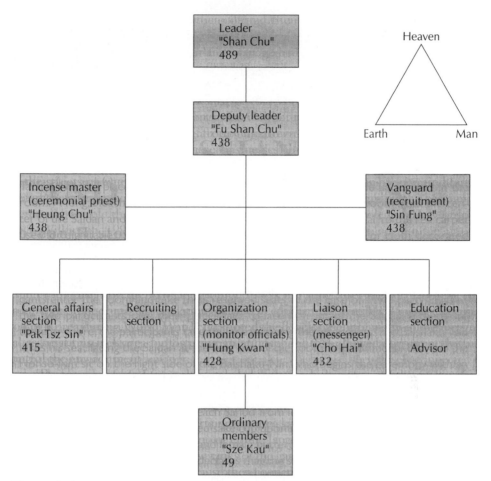

Figure 8–4   Triad Headquarters Structure

Source: U.S. Department of Justice, 2002.

changed the name of the organization to Sun Yee On. These societies continued to grow over the years; in 1987 Hong Kong police estimated the size of this Triad at 35,000 members (Dobson, 1993). Another estimation places membership at approximately 65,000 members (*South China Morning Post*, January 29, 1994).

Until the mid-1980s, the majority of Triads had been anti-Communist and pro-Nationalist, but since the late 1980s, there has been a meaningful shift in loyalty. A major portion of the leaders of Sun Yee On are direct descendants of the people who migrated from Chiu Chow to Hong Kong, and they have become highly supportive of the government in Beijing. According to police intelligence reports, the Sun Yee On Triad has been working with members of the Beijing government since a meeting between the two groups in Kowloon in 1988. This meeting helped form multiple

Subordinate
Gangs

Chinese and Vietnamese street gangs that are affiliated with criminally influenced Tongs. Subordinate gangs are used as enforcers for illegal gambling operations.

Triad
Societies

Ancient secret criminal societies that trace their roots to 17th century China. Today, there are approximately 50 Triads based in Hong Kong and Taiwan. The Royal Hong Kong Police estimate worldwide membership of Triads to be in the tens of thousands.

Nonaligned
Gangs

Chinese gangs that are not affiliated with any Chinatown–based association or Triad society.

Chinese
Tongs

Chinese fraternal and business organizations with chapters in major U.S. cities. The membership of Tongs is composed largely of noncriminals. However, criminal investigations have determined that some have ties to organized crime.

Figure 8–5   Chinese Organized Crime Definitions

Source: U.S. Department of Justice, 2002.

advantageous alliances that have grown powerful as time has gone on. In reality, this association has given Sun Yee On the opportunity to make investments in the People's Republic of China and allowed some members of the Chinese government's Public Security Bureau to enhance their monetary accounts (Dobson, 1993; Torode, 1993).

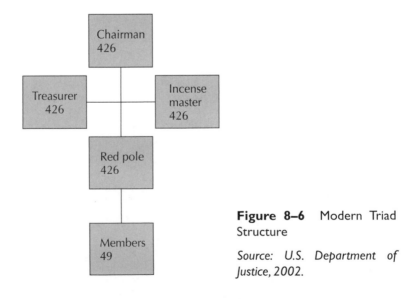

Figure 8–6   Modern Triad Structure

Source: U.S. Department of Justice, 2002.

The Wo Triad group is a combination of societies that, prior to World War II, controlled a major portion of the labor market in Hong Kong. During the Japanese occupation of Hong Kong, most Wo groups aggregated their power base under the aegis of the Japanese military. After the defeat of the Japanese, the British returned to Hong Kong, while the three major Wo organizations—Wo Shing Tong, Wo Yung Yee, and Wo Hop To—not only expanded their business ventures but continued to keep tight control over their labor holdings. An investigation conducted after the war by the Hong Kong police indicated that the same Wo group members managed to accumulate up to 15 million Hong Kong dollars a year by charging local legal and illegal street vendors initiation fees to operate in districts controlled by the Wo groups (Booth, 1991).

During the 1950s, the Wo groups continued their growth by assimilating many other Wo societies into their Triad grouping. The sizes of these associations vary from 20 to 6,000 members. This invariably led to a sharp increase in Wo Triad membership (Booth, 1991). The Wo Triad groups have continued to increase over the past 30 years, with an estimated membership of 29,000 in 1995. The Wo groups have extended their illegal activities by increasing their participation in drug dealing as well as extortion, prostitution, gambling, and the labor market.

The 14K Triad was originally the Hung Fat Shan part of the Chung Yee Wui Society, which was a mixture of different segments of Triad groups brought together to strengthen Triad support of the anti-Communist Nationalist government of Chiang Kai-shek in the mid-1940s. A massive recruitment drive by Chiang Kai-shek and his Kuomintang party attracted close to a million new members. Because of its large size, this group eventually dissipated into smaller and more cohesive groups. The late 1940s brought about the defeat of the Nationalist movement by the Communist insurgents and the integration of members of this Triad from mainland China to Hong Kong and Taiwan because the Communist government did not want organized crime groups operating in China. Originally, the movement of the 14K Triad into Hong Kong was met with animosity by other local Triad groups and caused many conflicts throughout the 1950s (Booth, 1991). During the 1950s, the 14K became the second-largest Triad; its total membership increased to over 80,000. Presently, the 14K has branches in Japan, Taiwan, Macao, Europe, Southeast Asia, Canada, and the United States (Booth, 1991; U.S. Department of Justice, 1988) (see Figure 8–7).

Another Hong Kong group that must be mentioned is the Dai Huew Jai (or Big Circle Gang), which was originally composed of members from mainland China. This group's roots originated in the cultural revolution and reeducation camps in mainland China during the 1960s. Most members of this organization remained in mainland China until the Tiananmen Square massacres. This society has attracted a large number of mainland Chinese refugees and ex–Chinese Red Guard Army personnel who are heavily involved in violent activities. The U.S. Drug Enforcement Agency lists this group as a major heroin importer to the United States (Grennan, 1992). This was quite apparent when one of its members, Johnny Kon, was arrested and convicted of importing over 100 pounds of heroin into the United States between 1984 and 1987 (*South China Morning Post*, October 5, 1992).

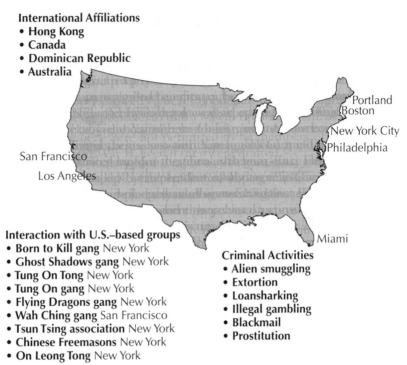

International Affiliations
- Hong Kong
- Canada
- Dominican Republic
- Australia

Portland
Boston
New York City
Philadelphia

San Francisco
Los Angeles

Miami

Interaction with U.S.–based groups
- **Born to Kill gang** New York
- **Ghost Shadows gang** New York
- **Tung On Tong** New York
- **Tung On gang** New York
- **Flying Dragons gang** New York
- **Wah Ching gang** San Francisco
- **Tsun Tsing association** New York
- **Chinese Freemasons** New York
- **On Leong Tong** New York

Criminal Activities
- Alien smuggling
- Extortion
- Loansharking
- Illegal gambling
- Blackmail
- Prostitution

Figure 8–7   Sun Yee On Society Criminal Activities and Affiliations in the United States

Source: U.S. Department of Justice, 2002.

Hong Kong Triads in Canada and Australia.   Hong Kong Triads have managed to enhance their worldwide criminal operations by setting up a base in Canada. The Kung Luk Triad has active illegal programs in place in Toronto, Montreal, Ottawa, Vancouver, Hamilton, and many other urban areas in Canada. This North American Triad is different from the fusion group Triad/Tong operating in the United States. The Canadian Kung Luk Triad is a prototypical Triad that operates in the same fashion as the Hong Kong–based Kung Luk Triad. Members of the Kung Luk Triad are constantly traveling between Canada, the United States, and Santo Domingo; this may be due to the fact that Lau Wing Kui, a reputed leader of the Kung Luk who was deported from Canada, owns an interest in several gambling clubs in Santo Domingo. The President's Commission on Organized Crime indicated that Kung Luk Triad members used the casino in Santo Domingo to launder money prior to depositing the currency in U.S. accounts. We must also remember that a large percent of the heroin brought into the United States by Chinese groups is distributed to Dominican organized crime groups, which then handle street sales (U.S. Drug Enforcement Administration, 1993). The Kung Luk Triad, through its connection in the Dominican Republic, has managed to set up a drug distribution ring that has been very profitable to all of the participating groups (President's Commission on Organized Crime, 1986).

Several members of the Dai Huen Jai (or Big Circle Gang) were recently arrested in Hong Kong for smuggling heroin into Canada. A joint investigation involving Canadian and Hong Kong police led to the arrests of Kong and Chu for importing 6.9 kilos of 97 percent pure heroin into Canada. Police believe that the purity of this heroin led to more than 70 drug overdoses in 1993 (Hughes, 1993).

Australia is another country that apparently has been chosen by Hong Kong Triads as a base for their criminal operations. Since the mid-1980s, several Hong Kong Triads have set up operations in Australia. These groups include the Sun Yee On, 14K, Wo Yee Tong, and Wo Shing Wo Triads. Evidence gathered by the Australian police has thus far led to several large seizures of Southeast Asian heroin and the arrests of Chinese drug importers. In 1988 Australian police, in conjunction with Hong Kong police, seized 43 kilograms of heroin departing Hong Kong for Australia. A 50-kilogram seizure was made at Port Vila, Vanuatu, in 1989; this heroin shipment had departed Hong Kong on route to Sydney, Australia, in 1992. Two additional major seizures were made in Australia: 21.5 kilograms of heroin imported from Taiwan and 12.7 kilograms from three Singapore nationals at Perth's airport (Pierce, 1992).

Taiwan Triads

The operations of Triad associations in Taiwan are basically the same as those of the Hong Kong Triads. The major difference is that the Taiwan Triads (known as "right-handed" groups) support the anti-Communist government in Taiwan, while the Hong Kong Triads (known as "left-handed" groups) started swinging their allegiance toward the government of the People's Republic of China. There are hundreds of gangs in Taiwan that are associated with the six to eight dominant local Triad criminal organizations. United Bamboo is the most powerful Triad in Taiwan, with a membership of approximately 30,000 to 40,000; the Four Seas Triad, the number two gang in Taiwan, maintains control over a major portion of the prostitution, gambling, and protection rackets in Taiwan (U.S. Department of Justice, 1993).

In an attempt to take control of the Triads, the Taiwanese government put an amnesty program in place in early 1997; this program allowed Triad members to turn themselves in to the police and renounce their lives of crime in an effort to avoid prosecution under a new and very strict Organized Crime Prevention Act. Police authorities claim that approximately one-third of Taiwan's 1,200 gangs were disbanded during the Operation Self-Renewal amnesty period. Officials have indicated that the second-largest gang in Taiwan, the Four Seas Triad, was dissolved by its leader Chao Ching-hua (McKenna, 1996).

U.S. Tongs

Chinese immigrants started arriving in the United States shortly after the discovery of gold in California in the late 1840s. Most of the early Chinese settlers were from the southern coastal areas of China. These new arrivals on U.S. soil learned the meaning of discrimination very quickly and found themselves being considered as outcasts because of their ethnic backgrounds. It wasn't long before small Chinatowns started to build up at almost every gold rush location; both family and local associations were set up according to the province in China where the majority of the residents were born. Ultimately, these fraternal organizations were combined and designated as Tongs.

The history of Chinese Tongs goes back to the mid-nineteenth century. Tongs (a term used to describe meeting halls) were originally formed to protect Chinese businesses and new immigrants against the alien and hostile American communities. As time passed, some Tongs were formed to help new members of Chinese communities locate relatives or friends; others assisted immigrants in finding a place to live. The majority of Tongs are national organizations whose members are people involved in assisting legitimate community businesses, ethnic societies, and politics, while a smaller percentage of Tong members use these organizations to benefit themselves and other members of organized crime groups (Chin, 1990; President's Commission on Organized Crime, 1986). Although Tongs were conceived on the North American continent, there is little doubt that the Chinese Triads had a hand in creating these associations. The Federal Bureau of Investigation has gone so far as to state that a major portion of all the crimes in Chinatowns throughout the United States can be traced back to higher-ranking Tong officials. In fact, both the San Francisco and New York FBI offices have linked extortion, gambling, drug trafficking, prostitution, and murder to the local Chinatown Tongs (U.S. Department of Justice, 1993; U.S. Department of Treasury, 1993).

SIMILARITIES BETWEEN MAFIA AND TONG ADMINISTRATION

Mafia	Tongs
Boss	Chairman
Underboss	Vice Chairman
Consigliere	English-Speaking Secretary
Caporegime	Tong Treasurer
Capo	Tong Social Secretary

Source: U.S. Department of Justice, 2002.

Research indicates that Low Yet, a Triad member and a leader of the Taiping rebellion, was the founder of Tongs in San Francisco; Yet formed the Chee Kong Tong, which had over 1,000 members in 1887. This Tong was modeled after the Triad that Yet had been a member of in Hong Kong (Federal Bureau of Investigation, 1996).

The administrative structure of the Tongs is very similar to that of La Cosa Nostra. The Godfather type of rank in the mafia would also be a highly influential position in the Tongs, but one that is shared by a group of members who are perceived as "the elders." The lower ranks of the Tong structure contain the largest proportion of members, and all of these members fall into the rank of soldier/worker (see Figure 8–8).

As far as membership in the Tongs is concerned, there are no restrictions as to the background or the number of newly recruited members, which has led to rapid growth in Tong membership within a short period of time. Tongs have embraced the same basic type of socialization process as the Triads. Initiation rites are mandatory for all new members, as is the recitation of oaths of loyalty, nationalism, and brotherhood. Like the Triads, the Tongs maintain a highly covert operation that restricts the identification of the leadership; this leaves a majority of the membership without any knowledge of the daily activities within the Tong. One problem facing the Tongs is that the politics within the Tong are usually fragmented because of the number of various factions in each association. In many cases, an elected Tong leader can be considered nothing more than a puppet who is controlled by many factions instead of a strong leader who is elected by the majority (Chin, 1990; U.S. Department of Justice, 1993). The Tong associations (presently numbering 100 in New York City) are also part of the Chinese Consolidated Benevolent Association, which is highly influential within the political circles of Chinatowns throughout the United States (U.S. Department of Justice, 1993).

There are several major Tong associations in the United States. According to the Federal Bureau of Investigation (1988), the top three Tongs are On Leong, Hip Sing, and Hop Sing (see Figure 8–9). The first On Leong chapter was established in Boston in 1894. At the start of the twentieth century, On Leong moved its highly profitable coolie trade and headquarters to New York City's Chinatown (Chin, 1990). Shortly afterwards this gang became involved in a Tong war with the Hip Sing Tong over control of prostitution, opium, and gambling in Chinatown. During this eight-year war (1899–1907), both Tongs formed their own "boo how doy," or street gangs, that were used to disrupt each other's legitimate and illegitimate businesses. Research also brought to light that both of these Tongs had managed to form an alliance with corrupt polticians in New York City around the turn of the twentieth century (McIllwein, 1997).

On Leong gained prominence in the mid-1980s when control of the association was taken over by Chan Tse Chin (Eddie Chan). Chan was an ex–Hong Kong police sergeant who immigrated to Mexico during the Five Dragons police scandal in Hong Kong in the 1970s.[2] Within a short period of time, Chan arrived in New York City's Chinatown and set up several successful businesses; this success led to his election as president of the On Leong Tong. Chan proceeded to tighten the connection between the On Leong Tong and the Ghost Shadows street gang, using the gang whenever possible to protect his criminal enterprises and to strong-arm any other groups or persons attempting to move in on his criminal empire.

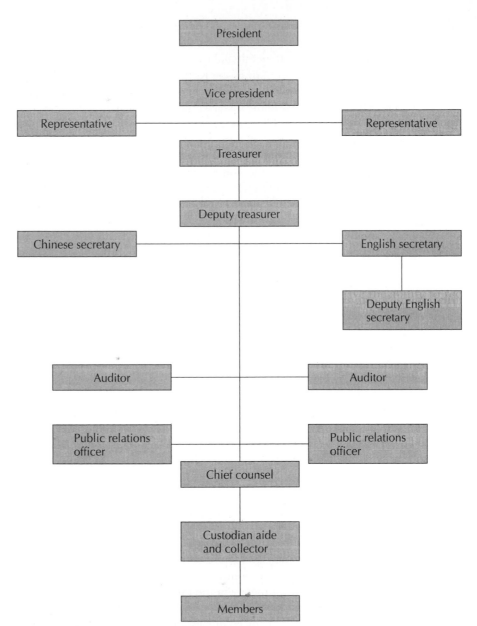

Figure 8–8   Tong Officers Hierarchy

Source: New York Police Department, 1993.

Primary Tongs and Affiliated Gangs

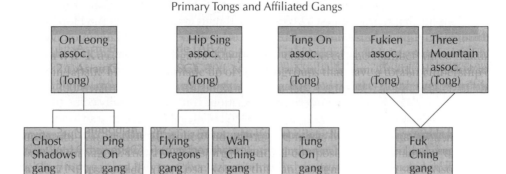

Figure 8–9   Structure of Chinese Organized Crime

Source: Federal Bureau of Investigation

It was not long before a power struggle broke out between Chan and Nicky Louie (head of the Ghost Shadows street gang) over the distribution of money. Louie moved his operation to Chicago and was soon a victim of an attempted murder. It was later alleged that Chan had ordered the shooting of Louie and other discontented members of the Ghost Shadows in Chicago because Chan purported that Louie had extorted money from him. Chan also formed the Continental King Lung Group, a financial investment company, as a front to conduct his fraudulent ventures. Chan was later identified by a Hong Kong Triad member as the Dragon Head (crime boss) of New York's Chinatown (President's Commission on Organized Crime, 1986). Chan helped the On Leong Tong build and control many illegal enterprises prior to fleeing the United States after being subpoenaed to testify in front of the President's Commission on Organized Crime.

The present leader of the On Leong Tong, Chan Wing Yeung, owns 50 percent of Frankwell Management Services, which was seized by federal authorities for participating in illegal trading activities; Frankwell Management Services is a subsidiary of Frankwell Holdings Limited in Hong Kong. Chan Wing Yeung was previously named as a coconspirator with the On Leong Tong in 1990 for participating in gambling and racketeering activities in Chicago, but the trial ended with a hung jury (Chan, 1994).

On Leong's illegal gang activities have continued to flourish. Presently there are chapters in 26 cities in the United States; thus far, in 9 of these cities, the Ghost Shadows street gang is affiliated with the On Leong Tong.

The Hip Sing Tong, like the On Leong Tong, is based in New York City's Chinatown. Its leader, Lei Lo Chat (whose street name was Benny Ong, Uncle Seven, or Uncle Benny), is now deceased. Ong was convicted of murder in 1936 and served 18 years in prison. Besides his criminal record, very little else is known about Ong, except that he was very influential in New York City politics. The Hip Sing Tong has chapters in 16 major cities and has affiliations with the Flying Dragons street gang in 9 of these locations (Chin, 1990; U.S. Department of Justice, 1993).

The Hop Sing Tong operates out of the western section of the United States, with chapters in at least 12 cities; this Tong is associated with the Hop Sing Boys street gang in 9 of these cities. The Hop Sing has been involved in an ongoing turf war with the Bing Hung Tong. Since 1983, these two groups have had more than a dozen different violent confrontations over the control of illegal activities in both Seattle and San Francisco (U.S. Department of Justice, 1988).

The Fukienese American Association/Tong did not really come to light until June 1993 when a ship (the *Golden Venture*) full of illegal immigrants ran ashore off Rockaway Beach, New York. In the 1980s, this organization started to grow, and its street gang, the Fuk Chow/Ching, started getting involved in criminal activities in the Chinatown area of New York City. A 1990 investigation into the smuggling of illegal Chinese immigrants into Canada provided Toronto police with a wiretapped conversation between the alien smugglers and the Fukienese Association's chairperson. The address of this association had also been given as a drop-off point for ransom money for a kidnap victim. Federal authorities have indicated that members of this Fukienese Tong are undoubtedly involved in the criminal activities of the Fuk Ching gang but have thus far avoided any type of prosecution (Kleinknecht, Sennott, and Chong, 1993).

The Tung On Association/Tong is considered one of the largest in New York City. Clifford Wong, the longtime president of Tung On, was charged with operating a criminal enterprise that was involved in the murder of 10 people and with being a participant in numerous other crimes. The investigation of this case disclosed how Tong leaders use members of their affiliated street gangs to safeguard and expand their business empires (Faison, 1994). Federal prosecutors portray Wong as a very successful businessman who has managed to acquire a thoroughbred horse racing stable and a chain of restaurants from New York to Florida. Wong has been the leader of the Tung On since 1984, while his brother Steven controlled the Tung On street gang until his 1988 narcotics conviction. Mr. Wong has managed to build a very profitable criminal federation within the Tung On Tong during his tenure as president (Faison, 1994).

These five—On Leong, Hip Sing, Hop Sing, Fukienese, and Tung On—are the most powerful Tongs operating in the United States today. All these Tongs have many members who are law-abiding individuals, but these Tongs also have members who are constantly participating in illicit activities. Tong members who are involved in criminal actions usually sanction Chinese street gangs, which in turn are affiliated with the Tongs and carry out most of the Tongs' criminal operations.

Most of these gangs can be considered very violent. A great proportion of gang membership is composed of newly immigrated adolescents who are easily recruited into the gangs. These gang members tend to be in their late teens and early twenties, while gang leaders are usually older (some are over 30 years old). A majority of the youths recruited into the Chinese street gangs are school dropouts whose ability to communicate in the English language is very poor; there are very few opportunities for these youths to obtain decent-paying jobs. A major portion of these adolescents join the gangs willingly, but there are some who are compelled to join the gangs. A number of these Chinese gangs have some type of induction ritual that is patterned after the customary Triad ceremony. Although the organizational configuration of most Chinese gangs seems to be diversified, just about every gang seems to have some type of power structure. The upper echelon of the gangs contains leaders who are known as "Dai-los," or big brothers. The Dai-los direct the operations of the gangs and do not normally participate in any of the criminal activities involving gang members. The leaders are also the emissaries who will have contact with other gangs and other Tongs or Triads. The next level contains members who are considered lieutenants, who control street gang members and are known as "Sai Los," or little brothers. The third level of the gang contains ordinary members known as "Ma-Jai" (literally, little horses), or street soldiers, who follow the orders of the bosses.

The members of all these Chinese gangs support themselves in two basic ways:

1. *Freelancing.* The gangs participate in criminal behaviors, such as extortion, robbery, drug trafficking, and kidnapping, that they initiate.

2. *Contracts.* They make contracts with other Tongs or Triads to act as protectors or enforcers of a legal or illegal enterprise.

CHINESE STREET GANGS

West Coast Gangs

San Francisco.   Chinese street gangs started developing in San Francisco during the 1950s. These Chinese gangs were formed and structured in the same manner as other ethnic youth gangs. A street gang known as the Beigs was one of the first street gangs formed by American-born Chinese; this gang's area of criminal expertise was burglary, and gang members could be easily identified by the Beatle-type outfits they wore (Chin, 1990).

The Wah Ching (Youth of China) was the first immigrant gang and was formed to prevent assaults on foreign-born Chinese immigrants by American-born Chinese (Chin, 1990). Within a year of its formation, U.S. immigration laws were modified, which led to an increase in the number of immigrants arriving from mainland China. The Wah Ching took advantage of the changes in U.S. immigration laws to become a more powerful gang by recruiting many of the younger immigrants as new members of their organization (see Figure 8–10). The power of this gang was soon recognized by members of the Chinese community, who hired gang members to run errands and provide strong-arm protection for gambling operations (Chin, 1990).

The Hop Sing Tong, seeing the advantages of being associated with a street gang, brought the Wah Ching under its control by creating a youth branch within its Tong. A short time later, the Suey Sing Tong created a youth gang known as the Young Suey Sing, or the Tom Tom Street gang. Conflict between the Wah Ching and the Young Suey Sing led to many street confrontations (Attorney General of California, 1972). One group, the Yau Lai (Yo Le), or Joe Fong Boys, was formed in 1969 by discontented

International Affiliations
- **Hong Kong**
- **Canada**
- **Taiwan**

Triad Interaction
- **14K group** Hong Kong
- **Sun Yee On** Hong Kong
- **Luen Lok** Hong Kong
- **United Bamboo gang** Taiwan
- **Wo group (confrontational)** Hong Kong

Criminal Activities
- **Murder**
- **Weapons violations**
- **Loansharking**
- **Illegal gambling**
- **Drug trafficking**
- **Extortion**
- **Arson**
- **Bombings**
- **Prostitution**
- **Police corruption**
- **Copyright violations**
- **Tax evasion**
- **Infiltration of legitimate businesses**

Figure 8–10   Wah Ching Gang Criminal Activities and Triad Affiliations in the United States

Source: Federal Bureau of Investigation

members of the Wah Ching gang; many of these dissatisfied Wah Ching members left that gang because of the restrictive controls placed on gang members by the Hop Sing Tong (Chin, 1990).

During the early 1970s, both the Wah Ching and the Joe Fong Boys started to expand their criminal activities by targeting people in the Asian community as victims of their crimes. As the membership of the Wah Ching and Joe Fong Boys multiplied, there was also an increase in the number of violent conflicts between the two groups over territorial rights. This was especially evident between 1973 and 1977 when 27 people were killed in gang-related incidents. On one occasion, 5 people were killed and 11 seriously injured (not one a gang member) during a vicious attack by members of the Joe Fong Boys (Chin, 1990).

The San Francisco area probably has the largest amount of Chinese gang activity on the West Coast. The Hop Sing Boys, the Kit Jars, the Asian Invasion, and the Local

Motion are some of the Chinese gangs that operate criminal enterprises in the Bay area. Wah Ching is considered the largest street gang in California, with about 600 to 700 active members (200 of which can be considered tenacious). The Wah Ching gang formed an alliance with the Sun Yee On Triad in 1987 (*San Francisco Examiner*, May 10, 1987; U.S. Department of Justice, 1993).

Los Angeles.   The Los Angeles branch of the Wah Ching was formed in 1965 by Wah Ching members from San Francisco. Wah Ching was formed in Los Angeles to stop the constant harassment of newly immigrated Chinese youths by Mexican gang members. Despite the formation of the Chinese gangs, conflicts did not cease and have continued up until the present.

One specific area outside of Los Angeles, Monterey Park, saw its Chinese population double between the late 1970s and the early 1980s. The population increase in Monterey Park was caused by two factors:

1. Taiwan police arrested numerous covert individuals in the late 1970s and early 1980s, forcing a multitude of Taiwanese criminals to seek asylum in the United States.

2. The majority of Chinese residents in Monterey Park were from Taiwan, so the Taiwanese criminals settled there.

The transgressors who arrived from Taiwan brought with them enough gang experience to set up two new gangs. The Four Seas gang originally appeared in Taiwan in 1955, only to dissipate within several years. A short time later, the Four Seas gang was resurrected under new leadership, which fortified the gang's economic status by opening and controlling houses of prostitution and gambling casinos. Membership in the Four Seas increased as legal and illegal Taiwanese gang members reached the U.S. shores. The Four Seas gang was soon expanding its criminal enterprises to include legal as well as illegal ventures (Faison, 1993).

Another Taiwanese gang that set up operations in Monterey Park is United Bamboo. This gang was dispersed by the Taiwanese police in 1958 only to reemerge in the 1960s as a dominant street gang. During the 1980s, United Bamboo expanded its operations into the entertainment business and increased its membership with 17 additional new branches, for a combined total of 25 chapters. Although total membership in the United States is unknown, it is estimated that the United Bamboo gang in Taiwan has over 10,000 members (Chin, 1990).

The United Bamboo gang gained nationwide attention in 1984 when some of its leaders were involved in the murder of Henry Lui, a famous Chinese writer. Lui wrote a biography that made derogatory statements about the then Taiwanese president and was preparing a manuscript related to the unethical practices of Taiwanese politicians. Media reports indicate that two United Bamboo leaders, Chen Chi-li and Swei Yi Fund, and the chief of Taiwan's Military Intelligence Bureau, Vice Admiral Wong Shi-Lin, met in 1984 and discussed punishing Lui for what they considered traitorous acts. Originally,

International Affiliations
- Taiwan
- Hong Kong
- Philippines
- Thailand
- Japan
- Saudi Arabia

Chicago

New York City
Atlantic City

San Francisco

Boulder
Denver

Los Angeles

Phoenix

Honolulu

Miami

Houston

Interaction with U.S.–based groups
- **Wah Ching** San Francisco
- **Fuk Ching** New York
- **Flying Dragons gang** New York
- **Ghost Shadows gang** New York

Criminal Activities
- **Contract murder**
- **Illegal gambling**
- **Money laundering**
- **Loansharking**
- **Weapons violations**
- **Public corruption**
- **Drug trafficking**
- **Investment fraud**
- **Extortion**
- **Armed robbery**
- **Prostitution**

Figure 8–11   United Bamboo Gang Criminal Activities and Affiliations in the United States

Source: Federal Bureau of Investigation

the Los Angeles United Bamboo gang was to take some action against Lui but was unable to carry out this mission. Vice Admiral Wong then had Chen and Swei trained to fulfill the contract on Lui. Upon Chen's arrival in the United States, he was joined by United Bamboo's West Coast enforcer Wu Tun. Another gang member from Taipei, Tung Kwei-Sen, soon joined Chen and Wu to partake in this conspiracy. A short time after Tung's arrival, Wu and Tung entered Lui's house and murdered him (Chin, 1990). Besides being involved in the most notorious murder of a Chinese-American writer, the United Bamboo gang is also heavily involved in heroin importing, extortion, and gun running (Grennan, 1992) (see Figure 8–11).

East Coast Gangs

New York City.   Prior to the 1965 immigration law changes, the only active Chinese street gang in New York City was the Continentals. This gang was formed in 1961 to protect Chinese students from attacks by other ethnic groups. The Continentals gang was made up of American-born Chinese youths who did not get involved in street crimes, nor were they associated with any of the Chinatown Tongs (Chin, 1990).

Then, in 1964, the On Leong Tong formed the On Leong Youth Club; it wasn't long before this group became known as the White Eagles gang. This gang was made up of foreign-born Chinese youths, and they were deployed throughout Chinatown to prevent any type of discriminatory activities by outsiders against Chinese businessmen and residents (Chin, 1990). Another gang, known as Chung Yee, appeared on the streets of Chinatown; like its predecessor (On Leong), Chung Yee was made up of new arrivals from mainland China. This gang operated in the same fashion as the On Leong, protecting the rights of Chinatown citizens and businesspeople. Chinese street gangs continued to increase, and gangs such as the Quen Ying, Liang Shan, Flying Dragons, and Black Eagles started appearing on the streets of Chinatown. The early history of these gangs indicates that they were all martial arts clubs used to prevent visitors from harassing local businessmen and residents (Chin, 1990).

The early 1970s saw an increase in the amount of violence being used by Chinese gangs. The three elements that caused an elevation in the amount of violence by Chinese gangs were the increased availability of weapons, the conflicts due to the growing number of street gangs, and the restlessness of new immigrant youths whose violent behavior threatened all the residents of Chinatown (Chin, 1990).

During this period, the youth gangs started extorting money and food from local business establishments through the use of fear and strong-arm tactics and then extended their criminal activities by forcibly robbing local gambling dens. The Tongs, seeing their businesses being extorted and robbed, hired these gang members to perform private security as Tong enforcers and protectors. This led to some of the gang becoming part of the Tong family (the White Eagles joined the On Leong Tong, and the Flying Dragons joined the Hip Sing Tong) (Chin, 1990).

The main problem with the Chinese street gangs was that by 1974 some of these gangs were completely out of control. For example, the White Eagles gang members, hired by the On Leong Tong to protect On Leong members and businesses, were openly robbing, extorting, and humiliating these Tong members on Chinatown streets. The On Leong Tong then started to disassociate itself from the White Eagles by stopping all monetary payments and weapons to the gang and hiring the Ghost Shadows street gang to replace the White Eagles as the On Leong Tongs' street gang (FBI, 1987).

After a short struggle, the Ghost Shadows took charge of just about all of the most profitable locations in Chinatown while the White Eagles removed themselves from On Leong's portion of Chinatown. A realignment of all the territories within Chinatown was completed a short time after the removal of the White Eagles, and all the gangs, seemingly content with territorial adjustments, went back to their separate criminal ventures. But hostilities between the gangs still continued, and street violence increased (FBI, 1987).

The year 1976 turned out to be Chinatown's most violent year, as internal and external gang hostilities increased sharply. Most of the gangs' criminal activities expanded to include the use of coercion, which was so effective that the majority of

Chinatown's businessmen feared for their lives (Chin, 1990). During this time, there were several gunfights between the Flying Dragons and the Ghost Shadows resulting in the killing of one Ghost Shadows member and one innocent restaurant customer and the wounding of one Flying Dragons member and five innocent bystanders (Myers, 1992).

During the gang warfare between the territorial Chinatown gangs, the presence of Wah Ching gang members in the Chinatown vicinity increased drastically. Local gang leaders, worried about Wah Ching's propinquity, set up a meeting of gang leaders to announce that gang warfare would be terminated and that gang members would seek employment. The first indication after this announcement was that the gangs were working together to prevent a turf invasion by outside groups, but purported gang unity and promises of peace were not to last long. Within a month, a dispute over turf rights broke out between the Ghost Shadows and the Black Eagles gangs; this resulted in the wounding of Black Eagles Leader Paul Ma and four other Black Eagles associates. A short time later, a Ghost Shadows member was shot and killed, and this was followed in a week by the killing of a Black Eagles gang member (Moses, July 29, 1990).

Prior to 1976, the majority of confrontations were between opposing gangs over the rights to certain areas in Chinatown. During 1976, problems within different gangs surfaced; internal struggles ensued over control and money, causing increased internal conflict within several major New York City gangs. The intragang hostilities continued, as did the gangs' ability to increase their turf holdings. This became apparent when the owners of a Midtown Manhattan Chinese restaurant were murdered for refusing to pay extortion money to the Black Eagles gang (Moses, July 29, 1990). Another indication of how far out of control gang violence had become was the attempted murder of Man Bun Lee. Lee, the former president of the Chinatown Community Business Association, gained media attention by requesting that additional police units be assigned to remove the gangs from Chinatown. This resulted in Lee being stabbed five times; Lee survived this assault, and his assailant was arrested and convicted of this crime. Both of these incidents sent a definite message to the Chinese community not to cross the gangs because they controlled the streets.

Another factor related to Chinatown street gangs was the fact that it did not matter which gang members or how many of them were arrested and/or convicted by law enforcement authorities. This had been evident since the mid-1970s when the police started taking action against the Chinese gangs; no matter what the police did, the gangs continued to participate in their chosen crime ventures without any serious interruptions. Neither federal nor local law enforcement efforts made any discernible impact.

Since the early 1980s, several new street gangs have appeared in the Chinatown area. Tong On, Fuk Ching, Green Dragons, Born to Kill, White Tigers, and Gum Sing (an offshoot of intragang warfare), are the names of some of these new gangs. The criminal activities of some of these gangs have expanded to all five borougs of New York City. In most cases, these new gangs have attempted to avoid conflict with the original older ones by not impinging on the older groups' territories; instead, the new gangs have taken control of turf outside Chinatown and (in some cases) outside Manhattan. One thing that does seem apparent is that these new gangs are more violent than their predecessors.

International Affiliations
- Hong Kong
- Canada

San Francisco

Los Angeles

Dallas

Houston

Boston

New York City
Philadelphia Newark

Fairfax County,
VA (VFD)

Triad Interaction
- **14K group** Hong Kong
- **Sun Yee On** Hong Kong
- **United Bamboo gang** Taiwan

Criminal Activities
- **Murder**
- **Weapons violations**
- **Loansharking**
- **Illegal gambling**
- **Drug trafficking**
- **Extortion**
- **Armed robbery**

Figure 8–12   Flying Dragons Gang Criminal Activities and Triad Affiliations in the United States

Source: Federal Bureau of Investigation

Flying Dragons.   The Flying Dragons gang has continued to grow; presently, it has five factions. Three of them control gang operations in Chinatown and Manhattan, the fourth group maintains gang business in Queens, and the fifth part is a flying squad that is used as needed throughout the metropolitan area to provide some type of strong-arm assistance to other gang members. This gang is fundamentally the best-run street gang in Chinatown. The Hip Sing Tong keeps tight reins on this gang and, in doing so, has kept its members out of law enforcement's limelight. Benny Ong, the recently deceased head of Hip Sing, set up the original guidelines for the operation of this street gang and never let this organization get out of control. A majority of this gang's members are ethnic Chinese. The Flying Dragons, like other Chinese groups, do use Vietnamese or Korean gang members to handle the extortion, kidnapping, or robbery of Vietnamese or Korean businesses or citizens. The Flying Dragons gang is involved in narcotics trafficking, extortion, prostitution, gambling, and robbery; it also has chapters in San Francisco, Los Angeles, Houston, and Boston (see Figure 8–12).

Ghost Shadows.   Like the Flying Dragons, the Ghost Shadows is an established Chinatown gang that has a long-standing association with the On Leong Tong. There are two Ghost Shadows factions in Chinatown as well as one associate gang. One of the two factions is located on Bayard Street, while the other operates on Mott Street. The associate gang, the White Tigers, operates in Queens under the

International Affiliations
- Hong Kong
- Canada
- Philippines

Boston
New York City
Chicago
Philadelphia
Cleveland
Newark
Baltimore
San Francisco
Los Angeles
Atlanta
New Orleans
Houston
Miami

Triad Interaction
- **14K group** Hong Kong
- **Sun Yee On** Hong Kong
- **United Bamboo gang** Taiwan

Criminal Activities	
• Murder	• Drug trafficking
• Weapons violations	• Extortion
• Loansharking	• Burglary
• Kidnapping	• Alien smuggling
• Bribery	• Gambling
	• Robbery

Figure 8–13   Ghost Shadows Gang Criminal Activities and Triad Affiliations in the United States

Source: Federal Bureau of Investigation

tutelage of the Ghost Shadows. The Ghost Shadows is a notorious gang that is known for its use of violence. In 1990, the Ghost Shadows got involved in a turf war with the Vietnamese gang Born to Kill (BTK). The BTK members were infringing on Ghost Shadows' territory by robbing Tong-controlled gambling establishments. A warning was given to BTK members to cease and desist their criminal activities in Ghost Shadows' territory, but BTK refused to stop. A short time later, Vinh Vu, the second-highest-ranking BTK member, was shot to death. Members of BTK then proceeded to hold an elaborate funeral procession through the streets of Chinatown. During the burial rites in Linden, New Jersey, three of the mourners (actually Ghost Shadows gang members) opened fire with automatic weapons, injuring numerous grieving attendees.

The members of the Ghost Shadows gang are used as mid-level heroin couriers by the On Leong Tong; they are also actively involved in loan-sharking, extortion, robbery, and alien smuggling. The Ghost Shadows gang has vigorously recruited Vietnamese gang members because of their reputation for being violence-prone; this is borne out by the Ghost Shadows membership being 25 percent Vietnamese. The Ghost Shadows gang has chapters throughout the United States and abroad (see Figure 8–13).

Tong On Boys.   The Tong On Boys gang has jurisdiction over portions of East Broadway and Market, Division, and Catherine Streets in Chinatown. The Tong

On Boys are made up of two separate gangs: The first is the Tung On Boys, and the second is known as the Sun Yee On. Most of the leaders of Tung On are also members of Sun Yee On, which is listed by all law enforcement agencies as a Triad gang.

The Tong On Boys are associated with the Tung On, which is run by Clifford Wong, and the Tsung Tsen Tong, which is run by Kwok Too Lai. The main operations of this gang are in the New York and Philadelphia areas, with a smaller branch in Portland, Maine. Like the other gangs, the Tong On Boys are involved in drug trafficking, prostitution, extortion, alien smuggling, and gambling.

Fuk Ching.   A major portion of Fuk Ching gang members are from the Fukien province of China; the gang is associated with the Fukien American Association/Tong. This gang controls parts of East Broadway as well as parts of Christie, Allen, and Eldridge Streets in New York City's Chinatown. The Fuk Ching gang is perceived as one of the most vicious and dauntless Asian gangs. In the past year, the gang gained a great deal of media attention because of gang members' participation in three major events. The first involved the kidnapping and unlawful imprisonment of 61 illegal Chinese immigrants whom gang members locked in a Jersey City, New Jersey, warehouse; these Chinese immigrants were being held until they could reimburse the smugglers who brought them to the United States. The second incident involved a triple murder in Teaneck, New Jersey. Two of the victims of this murder were brothers of Fuk Ching gang leader Ling Kee Kwk (aka Ah Kay). Within a short period of time, law enforcement authorities arrested five Fuk Ching gang members for this crime. The most publicized of the three events was the grounding of the *Golden Venture*, a ship being used to transport illegal aliens to the United States. The ship belonged to gang leader Ah Kay, who made millions of dollars smuggling illegal immigrants into North America.

Green Dragons.   The Green Dragons is a Queens-based gang that evolved from within the Fuk Ching gang. The sections of Queens where members of the Green Dragons can be located are Jackson Heights, Flushing, Elmhurst, Woodhaven, and Long Island City. A major portion of gang members are from the Fukien province of China. The White Tigers gang (discussed later) is the prime adversary of the Green Dragons gang, and there has been a restless respite over the control of specific areas of Queens. The Green Dragons is a gang the Federal Bureau of Investigation claimed it "had by the tail" (Rosario, 1991). This appeared somewhat true when a high-ranking gang member (Stu Man "Sonny" Wong) testified about the participation of other gang members in crimes such as kidnapping, robbery, extortion, and murder. Law enforcement officials dubbed Wong the Chinese Sammy "the Bull" Gravano because of the specificity of his information on the gangs involvement in crimes. All of the gang members in this case were found guilty and given terms of life imprisonment for their participation in these crimes (Dao, 1992).

The pressure from law enforcement failed to permanently dismantle the Green Dragons gang: It is once again resurrected, and gang members are operating in the same Queens neighborhoods from which law enforcement officials allegedly removed them. This gang has continued to thrive by recruiting newly arrived Chinese adolescents and promising them friendship, protection, flashy cars, and plenty of money. Based on the gang's increased activity in extortion, drug dealing, and robberies, there is no doubt that the Green Dragons gang was not mortally wounded by the federal government's indictments and convictions.

Born to Kill (BTK) (or the Canal Street Boys). The Born to Kill (BTK) gang was founded by ex-members of the Flying Dragons gang, and the membership of this gang is ethnically Vietnamese. They are not associated with any Tong or Triad, but they do infringe on the territories of other gangs. The BTK is still being used by Chinese Tongs and other gangs as enforcers and drug couriers. Gang members can be found in Queens and Brookyn and in Jersey City, New Jersey. A more in-depth analysis of this gang is given in the Vietnamese gangs section (Chapter 9).

White Tigers. The White Tigers gang is an affiliate of the Ghost Shadows gang and has branches in Chinatown, Flushing, and Queens. This gang is sanctioned by the Ghost Shadows to operate in Chinatown; it also has an ongoing feud with the Green Dragons over territorial rights in Queens. The leader of this gang, Gary Soo Kee Tam, was indicted by federal authorities for paying gang members $7,000 (per victim) to murder his sister and brother-in-law and their infant son (*New York Times*, August 20, 1994).

Gum Sing. The Gum Sing gang materialized after a major portion of the higher echelon of the Vietnamese BTK gang was arrested, and it is not associated with any Tong or Triad. This gang is based in what is considered Brooklyn's Chinatown (8th Avenue from 40th to 60th Streets). Membership is basically Vietnamese, with a marginal number of members from other Asian ethnic groups. Gang members are very mobile; they move around the five boroughs of New York City, committing various crimes such as drug trafficking, home robberies, and extortion.

CRIMINAL ACTIVITIES

The original purpose of Chinese gangs was to protect Chinatown citizens and businesses from the harassment of other ethnic groups, at no cost to Chinese citizens and owners. It was not long before the profiteers of illegal activities started hiring some gang members to protect their illegitimate businesses. This, in turn, led Chinese street gang members to realize they could make money by shaking down businesses for protection money. Soon after the gangs set up a systematic collection arrangement, the gangs started moving into other types of criminal enterprises, including extortion, alien smuggling, home invasion robberies, business robberies, credit card fraud, commodity scams, prostitution, narcotics trafficking, and money laundering.

Extortion

A short time after their inception, Asian street gangs realized that by extorting money from legitimate as well as illegitimate businesses, they could support themselves. Extortion quickly became the principal moneymaking scheme for the gangs. The gangs discovered various effective methods to extort money or goods:

1. Solicit money from business owners as an investment or contribution for an illegal purpose.
2. Seek a sizable deduction on products made or sold by businesses.
3. Force companies to buy materials that are connected with specific Chinese holidays.
4. Order business owners to pay a specific amount of protection money on a monthly basis.
5. Command owners to pay "Lucky Money" on specific events or the opening of new businesses.
6. Require business owners to put video gambling machines inside their stores.
7. Compel businessmen to purchase either equipment or other merchandise from gang members.

The sum of money the gangs demand is usually based on a classification of the enterprise and the intake of that business. A business owner who either declines to pay or misses a payment finds that gang members retaliate using violence against either him or his business. Any type of operation that does not pay is usually connected to the gangs or to the Tongs. Small-profit businesses are usually charged less ($108 to $208 per month), while high-profit businesses, such as restaurants, are charged more ($300 plus per month). Businesses are also forced to buy specialty items at a higher price; for example, they might be made to buy mooncakes ($7 each in a bakery) from the gangs for anywhere from $50 to $200 each. The money is usually extorted monthly, with additional money being extracted on Chinese holidays and grand openings, as well as on the sale of special objects. In most cases, the gangs extort money from businesses only within gang-controlled territories (U.S. Senate, November 5, 1991).

Recently gangs in New York City's Chinatown started compelling businessmen to put illegal video gambling machines that contain blackjack and joker poker games into their business establishments. The owners of these locations are then obligated to split the profits from the machines with gang members.

Alien Smuggling

The smuggling industry has become extremely profitable for the Chinese gangs. The importation of illegal immigrants was brought to the attention of the U.S. government when a ship called the *Golden Venture* ran aground off Rockaway Beach in New York.

The ship contained approximately 300 illegal Chinese aliens who were paying anywhere from $30,000 to $50,000 each to be taken to the United States. Information gathered by law enforcement sources indicate that the illegal immigrants must pay at least half of the amount prior to departure (Treaster, June 9, 1993).

The two major kingpins of the illegal alien trade are Cheng Chui Ping, known as "Foudu (Stealing Passage) Queen," and Guo Liang Chi, known as "Ah Kay"; the latter is the leader of the Fuk Ching gang. Cheng Chui Ping has been in the smuggling business for the past 10 years and operates out of a variety store called Yung Sim on East Broadway in Chinatown. She purchased the variety store for $3 million and paid in cash. Cheng Chui Ping also runs a money transfer business, which charges a fee of $25 for the first $1,000 and $20 more for every $1,000 after that for money sent to China; she guarantees a prompt three-day delivery period. The other major smuggler is Ah Kay, the notorious leader of the Fuk Ching gang. Ah Kay was indicted for two counts of murder, as he had allegedly ordered the murders of three members of an opposing faction within Fuk Ching. The hit resulted in the killing of two of Kay's adversaries. Kay was seized in a gambling den in Hong Kong, but the most important seizure made by federal agents was two crates that contained the business records of the Fuk Ching gang (Faison, August 30, 1993).

Alien smuggling has become an increasingly lucrative business for the Fuk Ching gang. An estimate by the U.S. Immigration and Naturalization Service indicates that the Fuk Ching gang has smuggled well over 100,000 illegal immigrants from Fukien Province in China over the past two years. At a rate of approximately $30,000 per person, the smugglers would bring in about $3 billion before expenses, which would be minimal. This is why alien smuggling has become such a great short-term investment for Triad, Tong, and other gang leaders (*U.S. News & World Report*, June 21, 1993).

The smugglers, known as "snakeheads," also provide forged documentation to their customers. Once the persons seeking to go to the United States obtain exit visas from the People's Republic of China, they travel to Bangkok, where a gang member supplies them with counterfeit identity documents. The individuals are placed on an airline and taken to another country; from there, they travel to the United States by automobile, airplane, or boat. There are a number of routes that are used by the gangs to transport the aliens to the United States. Almost all these routes run through South and Central America. Countries such as Panama, Bolivia, and Belize are willing to provide the smugglers with necessary visas for the right price (U.S. Senate, November 5, 1991). The smugglers have had no problem finding corrupt officials in most South and Central American countries, so they continually use these routes to bring illegal immigrants to the United States. These same corrupt officials have been helpful to the alien smugglers who are also involved in drug smuggling.

Home Invasion Robberies

Subjects of home invasions are targeted after gang members gather information related to large sums of money or jewelry being kept in a specific house or location. Gang members follow the subject to the residence to verify the site. A short time after the verification of the address, gang members use either subterfuge or force to enter the premises. After entry into the location, the occupants are tied up and the house is thoroughly searched for valuables. If the anticipated amount of money, jewelry, or other valuables is not found, the victims may be menaced, tortured, beaten, or raped or a family member may be taken until a specific amount of money is given to the gang for that person's release. Gang members who participate in this crime are extremely mobile, consistently moving from one site to another.

Business Robberies

Chinese street gangs have also been involved in the robberies of garment factories in Chinatown. The gangs forcibly enter these factories and then rob all the employees. On two occasions, female employees were raped by gang members; in one instance, 3 gun-carrying males entered a factory at 150 Lafayette Street and robbed 50 women employees. All of these robberies took place in the daytime. Thus far 16 businesses have been robbed at gunpoint by gang members (DeStefano, 1991).

Credit Card Fraud

Triads and gangs have gotten involved in credit card fraud. The Big Circle Boys gang uses counterfeit credit cards that are produced through the use of silk screening and encoded with the information of a credit card customer. Cards that have been lost or stolen are modified and imprinted with different names and numbers. Authorities say that these groups can produce a credit card that defies detection. These cards have fairly high limits on them, and the cards are used to charge up to their limits in anywhere from 30 to 60 days.

In March 1992, Hong Kong police raided a factory that was used to produce fraudulent credit cards; 19 employees were arrested, and the police confiscated 50 counterfeit Visa cards and Mastercards and over 200 different credit card numbers as well as counterfeit currency, numerous pawn slips, and some guns. On April 16, 1992, Montreal police expropriated 60 forged credit cards from gang members during a raid on a Chinese gambling den (Cleu Line, 1992).

Commodity Scams

A commodity scam that was set up by Chan Wing Yeung of the On Leong Tong in New York's Chinatown managed to swindle millions of dollars from well over 300 people. The Evergreen International Development Corporation, purported to be trading in gold bullion and foreign currency, while the corporation was really channeling money to Hong Kong. According to Kathy Palmer (a U.S. government prosecutor), "There were no legitimate transactions" (Smith and Chan, August 31, 1994, p. 10). At least half of the Evergreen Corporation was owned by Frankwell Management Services, which is controlled from China by Eddie Chan, a fugitive from charges of murder and racketeering by U.S. authorities. An investigative report by the *New York Daily News* discovered that Chan Wing Yeung and Eddie Chan are very closely connected to the Sun Yee On Triad in Hong Kong. Federal authorities say the scam had well over a 1,000 investors, and most of them worked for the company. Victims indicated that they were guaranteed job training, good jobs, and big profits; ironically, not one of these promises will ever be fulfilled (Smith and Chan, August 31, 1994).

Prostitution

Chinese criminal groups have been involved in controlling houses of prostitution and massage parlors for many years. The participation of these criminal enterprises in prostitution has increased over the past 20 years due to the large increase of Asian male immigrants into the United States. Originally, these houses of prostitution were filled with Korean females and run by Korean entrepreneurs. In most cases, the Chinese groups have (by whatever strategy) now taken over control of these and have filled them with Korean, Taiwanese, and/or Vietnamese prostitutes. A major portion of these women have to be considered indentured hostages; they must work for the group controlling their house of prostitution until all their U.S. immigration costs are paid.

Narcotics Trafficking

According to the U.S. Drug Enforcement Agency, there has been a large increase in the amount of Southeast Asian heroin entering the United States. The Southeast Asian heroin is grown in the poppy fields of the Golden Triangle (Laos, Myanmar [formerly Burma], and Thailand). Once it is processed, the heroin is sent through Hong Kong on its way to some destination in the United States. Of all the heroin seized by federal authorities in New York, 70 percent was identified as being from the Golden Triangle.

Recently confiscated heroin from the Golden Triangle has been found to be 41 percent pure. The purity of this heroin is considerably higher than heroin expropriated by law enforcement authorities several years ago; in fact, the purity of Southeast Asian heroin has consistently increased over the past 10 years. The cost of a kilogram of heroin in the United States will vary from one ethnic group to another. For example, if one Chinese group sold a kilo of heroin to another Chinese group, the cost would be $60,000 to $80,000, while the cost of the kilo of heroin increases an additional $50,000 to $60,000 if a Chinese group sells it to a non-Chinese group.

Evidence gathered by U.S. law enforcement agencies indicates that not all members of Triads, Tongs, and street gangs are involved in narcotics trafficking; however, information does show that Triad-linked groups control more than $200 billion worth of international heroin transactions (U.S. Senate, November 5, 1991). The documented information gathered by the U.S. investigative agencies shows that specific members of the Chinese Triads, Tongs, and street gangs have been regularly involved in the importation of heroin from Southeast Asia. Evidence also indicates that the majority of these

Triad, Tong, and street gang members act on their own or with the help of one or two other members, but without the assistance of a whole organization. In the past, most Chinese groups avoided selling heroin on the street; in most cases, the heroin was wholesaled to other ethnic groups, which then sold the heroin at street level. This has now changed, and New York City's Chinese street gangs are heavily involved in the street sale of heroin on the outskirts of Chinatown (U.S. Senate, November 5, 1991). The monetary gain that heroin trafficking produces is sufficient enough to convince the Triads, Tongs, and street gangs to get more heavily involved in the street distribution of heroin.

Money Laundering

The Chinese gangs, like all other organized crime groups, have had to become involved in money laundering because of their participation in criminal activities. It has been difficult thus far for U.S. law enforcement agencies to make any headway in dissolving these criminal networks. The only dent made by law enforcement was in Boston, where Goon Chun Yee (aka Harry Mook), past president of the Hung Mun Chinese Freemasons Association, pleaded guilty to administering and participating in a worldwide multimillion-dollar money-laundering scheme that was headquartered in Boston's Chinatown. This case also resulted in the arrest of several Boston police officers, who were paid off by Mook to overlook his gambling operations (U.S. Senate, November 5, 1991).

GEOGRAPHIC AREAS

The Chinese groups (the Triads, Tongs, and street gangs) have managed to set up operations throughout the world. In the United States, the Tongs and the street gangs have made a definite impact on all our major urban centers. Listed below are some of those areas not mentioned in this chapter that have seen a large influx of Asian immigrants over the past several years.

As Atlanta's Chinese population increased, so did crimes involving Asians. Thus far, the Hip Sing and On Leong Tong have set up chapters in Atlanta, as has the Ghost Shadows street gang. Chicago—like Los Angeles, New York, and San Francisco—has a long-established Chinatown area, which has been dominated by the On Leong Tong and the Ghost Shadows street gang. Chicago is one of the locations where Chinese organized crime groups and Italian organized crime groups work together. Both of these groups are involved in gambling operations and attempting to locate corrupt public officials to help both groups run their other illegal activities. Law enforcement authorities in Houston have found that Chinese street gangs are present and that they have formed a bond with Vietnamese and Jamaican groups in running drug houses. The Alcohol, Tobacco, and Firearms (ATF) enforcement agency has unearthed evidence that clearly indicates that Chinese groups are investing in properties in Mexico, Belize, and Venezuela. In most cases, the Chinese groups buy legitimate businesses in these countries and use these enterprises to launder their illegally obtained money (ATF, 1993).

Philadelphia has about 17 gangs, half of them Chinese. Representatives from the Flying Dragons, Ghost Shadows, Ping On, Golden Eagles, and Black Eagles are present in Philadelphia, but a major portion of the members are transients fleeing New York or returning to New York after committing crimes elsewhere. Atlantic City has become a center for some of the Chinese groups. Triads such as Sun Yee On, Wo Hop To, 14K, and Kung Luk, as well as the On Leong, Hip Sing, and Tong On Tongs have operations going in Atlantic City. Gambling is very popular with the Chinese, and so is money laundering. During the FBI operation White Mane, one of the Chinese groups was found to be laundering money through the casinos. The Sun Yee On Triad pulled a $3 million baccarat scam at one casino; Herbert Liu, Freemason Tong member, put on shows at the Sands Hotel. Along with Chinese groups has come an increase in extortion (of Asian businesses), drug trafficking, weapons smuggling, and home invasion robberies in all the major metropolitan areas where they have made their bases.

CONCLUSIONS

The information presented in this chapter certainly has to make the reader aware that Chinese groups are definitely making an impact on violence and crime in our society. There is no doubt that gang activity will get worse before it gets better, but there is an explicit need for some organization in our society to stop gang activities. Until that time comes, it is doubtful that there will be any type of decrease in gang activity by the Chinese groups.

ENDNOTES

1. The theory related to the Chinese crime gangs taking over the La Cosa Nostra empire is nothing more than a fantasy created by the FBI to supplement its funding. We must not forget the following three points. First, La Cosa Nostra has become deeply entrenched in illegitimate businesses over a period of several decades, and at this point in time, it will not be easily overthrown. Second, there are presently too many other criminal syndicates operating in the United States, and not one of these has the power or ability to eliminate La Cosa Nostra at this time. These other groups are more like gnats just trying to hang onto the flypaper. Third, the reality is that these other groups are only operating because La Cosa Nostra is letting them operate, and in all likelihood they are paying homage to La Cosa Nostra.

2. The five dragons were identified as Choi Bing Lung, Chen Cheng You, Nam Kong, Hon Kwing Shum, and Laui Lok—all active members of the 14K Triad.

CHAPTER 9

JAPANESE, VIETNAMESE, AND KOREAN GANGS

The remaining three Asian organized crime groups include the Japanese, the Koreans, and the Vietnamese. Japanese organized crime has been effectively operating throughout Japan for over 300 years. Over the past several decades, gang members have broadened their bases of operation as well as their criminal activities to almost everywhere in Asia, Australia, and the United States. A majority of the Vietnamese criminal groups were formed in the United States during and after the Vietnam War. An association was formed with Chinese street gangs; from this alliance came what is now known as Vietnamese organized crime groups. Korean organized crime extended to locations outside of Korea only during the past two decades, with a great deal of those criminal operations being controlled by street gangs in the United States.

JAPANESE ORGANIZED CRIME

The threat of Japanese organized crime to the United States and the world was expressed by U.S. Attorney General William French Smith in December 1982 when he noted that Japanese organized crime members were expanding their bases of operation through Hawaii to the whole North American continent. During the U.S. Congress hearings on organized crime, evidence was produced that showed that members of Yakuza, the Japanese organized crime group, had held meetings with members of La Cosa Nostra (LCN) in both Hawaii and Las Vegas (Cleu, 1993). In fact, law enforcement agencies in Hawaii recorded Michael Zaffarino, a Bonanno family leader, displaying how profitable the pornography business could be for Japanese organized crime families (FBI, 1992). According to FBI intelligence reports, contacts between bosses of La Cosa Nostra and leaders of the Yakuza increased drastically (FBI, 1992).

This threat was enhanced by the fact that the Yakuza is one of the richest organized crime families in the world and that for years gang members have been investing in properties both offshore and on the mainland of North America. Again in December 1987, another warning was sent forth about the threat of Japanese organized crime to the United States. This time the forewarning was given by the FBI through a report published on Asian organized crime in the United States. The FBI informed us that the Boryokudan group was going to create a consequential crime dilemma for most police agencies in the western part of the United States. Apparently these predictions were sufficiently established but totally understated, considering the fact that the Boryokudan has become established in both Guam and the Northern Marianas Islands. The influence of this Yakuza group is continuing to grow in Hawaii and on both the East and West Coasts of the United States. Local U.S. law enforcement agencies that should anticipate the growth of Japanese organized crime groups in their cities are those in Atlanta, Boston, Honolulu, Las Vegas, Los Angeles, Newark, New York City, Portland, San Francisco, Seattle, and Washington, D.C. Four Japanese gangs that have been continually moving parts of their operations into the United States are the Yamaguchi-Gumi, Sumiyoshi-Kai, Inagawa-Kai, and Toa Yuai Jigyo Kumiai (FBI, 1992).

The Boryokudan may become a more dangerous threat to the United States than any other organized crime group because of its ability to launder illegally obtained currency and to penetrate and bankrupt legitimate companies. This is done by using colleagues to combine legally obtained money with unlawfully acquired money to purchase a legitimate company. Once this is accomplished, all of the money then becomes legal currency. The victims of the Japanese gangs are usually members of the Japanese community.

There are approximately 850,000 people of Japanese ancestry living in the United States today. About 88 percent of this population is native-born American, and a major portion of this group lives in either California or Hawaii. This is the major reason why Japanese gang activity is far more common on the West Coast of the United States. Areas of California, Hawaii, Oregon, and Washington, as well as Vancouver, British Columbia, are major vacation spots for Japanese visitors, so these locations provide members of Japanese organized crime with an opportunity to set up fraudulent vacation activities that exploit these foreign travelers. Although these types of activities can be considered trivial, they can also be viewed as a training ground for new members who will ultimately become involved in far more elaborate illegal schemes (FBI, 1992).

Japanese History

Organized crime groups first appeared in Japan over 300 years ago. What can be considered the start of organized crime groups began when the feudal Japanese monarchs did away with Samurai warriors. The new government leaders saw no need for these inordinate soldiers who had served Japan's feudal barons during the sixteenth and seventeenth centuries. The once-proud Samurai warriors found themselves cast adrift by the leaders they would have sacrificed their lives for. These brave soldiers of fortune soon became an undisciplined group of mercenaries who were unable to contend with peaceful times. Many of these warriors found themselves roaming the countryside and committing crimes against local merchants and farmers to support themselves (Kata, 1964). Eventually, the Samurai members were to become a major part of what today is known as the Yakuza (a gambling term for numbers that are considered worthless or useless).

Groups known as the Tekiya or Yashi (street traders) and Bakuto (street gamblers) were formed; a larger group, the Boryokudan (violent ones), has been in existence for over 300 years and at one time was committed to the old customs and cultural traditions of Japan. Many of the early members of Boryokudan regarded themselves as direct descendants of the Samurai warriors. The Boryokudan recruited a vast majority of their members from the Buraku (ghetto); these men constantly complained that they were abused and discriminated against by the rest of Japanese society. Another ghetto group that became part of the Boryokudan was the Eta (meaning much contamination). Eta members worked jobs that the majority of Japanese society considered the most repugnant drudgery (e.g., slaughtering animals, washing and dressing dead bodies). This group was stigmatized with the name "sangoku-jin" (meaning third country people). The ghetto associates comprised different ethnic members, including the Chinese and Koreans, who were seeking ways to rid themselves of poverty. These ghetto-bred individuals quickly became the most violent members of the Boryokudan.

JAPANESE ORGANIZED CRIME DEFINITIONS

Oyabun

Literally, "father role," the overall boss of the Rengo, Gumi, Kai.

Kobun

Literally, "child role," the member of a gang obligated to his Oyabun as a child is to its father.

Yakuza (yahk-za)

Literally, "8-9-3," a term derived from the worst possible score in a card game "Hanafuda." Totaling "20" the player automatically "loses." "Thus, he is a loser, "good for nothing." This term is preferred by Japanese gangsters.

Boryokudan

"Violent ones," the term preferred by the Japanese National Police Agency (NPA) when referring to the Yakuza. The NPA has defined "Boryokudan" an organization that collectively or habitually engages in, or has the possibility of engaging in, violent and unlawful acts.

Source: U.S. Department of Justice, FBI, 2002.

Prior to World War II, members of the Yakuza adopted the American gangster dress style and strut. The majority of gang participants have a plentiful amount of ornate tattoos all over their bodies; a large portion of these tattoos relate to the Samurai warriors, whom most members identify as the original founders of the group. Tattooing was initially used in feudal Japan to classify the criminal elements in Japanese society, and the gangs embraced tattooing as an additional trademark of their mobster image. These modern-day criminals are known as "koika boryokudan," meaning the chic, stylish, and classy violent ones.

When the leader of the Yakuza group decides that one of the members has violated some type of group policy, the member must atone for his mistake by cutting off the joint of his last finger (a ceremonial ritual known as "yubitsume") and presenting it to his boss; it is then up to the boss to decide whether or not all is forgiven. This type of action may be required with other fingers anytime a mistake is made by a koban (solider), and the reparation is accepted by the leader. If the cutting off of a finger is not acceptable as atonement by the boss, then the member might have to commit "seppuku" (suicide) the dignified way by self-disembowelment.

Many of the gangs portray themselves as "mutual aid societies," but most people are aware of this deceptive measure. At the conclusion of World War II, there were many social and economic problems, and the Yakuza quickly gained control of the newly created black market. The gang members then extended their activities to include gambling, extortion, prostitution, labor racketeering, and drug trafficking. A number of new gangs, most of them consisting of delinquents known as "chimpira," started to appear

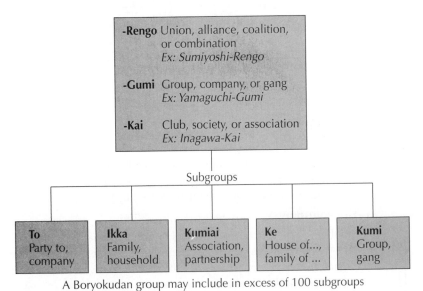

A Boryokudan group may include in excess of 100 subgroups

Figure 9–1   Yakuza Group Structure

Source: U.S. Department of Justice, FBI, 2002.

in Japan; some of these newly organized gangs were also known as "gurentai" or "seishonen-furyo dan." There was a significant amount of turbulent contention among the old and new gangs. Ultimately these new groups were assimilated into either the Tekiya or Bakuto (U.S. Customs Service, June 1993).

The Yakuza's permanence lies in the gang's ability to control power and money; the major purpose of this group is to increase its organization through force. Presently, there are approximately 2,300 Yakuza gangs that contain about 87,000 members (see Figures 9–1 and 9–2). A gang member's rank is decided by that person's productivity as a procurer of assets for his bosses: The higher the person's status is in the organization, the larger the amount of funds that is allocated to him, despite the fact that he is still responsible to the higher-ranking officials in the group. The Yakuza maintains a very competitive association that is designed to provide pressure on each member so that he maintains a high level of productivity. Yakuza members are always seeking ways to create new ventures to gratify their bosses. The two most important functions of Japanese gang members are to remain loyal and productive to their superiors and to be responsible to their specific group.

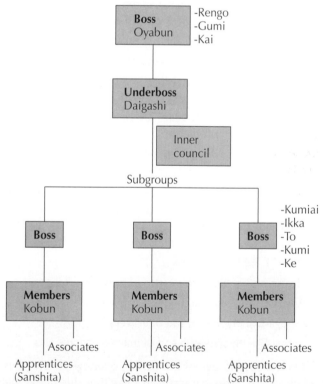

Figure 9–2   Yakuza Subgroup Structure

Source: U.S. Department of Justice, FBI, 2002.

ENGUMI INITIATION CEREMONY

In order for the binding to be fully consummated, the presence of the following people is required:

Toji-Sha—the persons who are to form the relationship by the exchange of cups.

Torimochi-Nin—a mediator, or go-between.

Mitidoke-Nin—a witness to the ceremony.

The foregoing represent the minimum of individuals who must be involved. However, in most cases where there are considerably large families involved or when a family requires strict adherence to formality, other attendants are required as follows:

Koken-Nin—a guardian, or elder. Usually the boss or mentor of the person involved.

Tokubetsu-Koken-Nin—a special guardian, assistant to the mentor.

Maishaku-Nin—a matchmaker who performs the ceremony instead of the Torimochi-Nin.

Kenbun-Nin—an examiner, a special high-ranking witness.

Honso-Nin—an assistant in the mediation process.

Suisen-Nin—a character witness who recommends the suitability of the person concerned.

Sashizoe-Nin—an assistant concerned with the formation of the brother relationships.

Tachiai-Nin—lower-ranking attendants.

Originally, the Torimochi-Nin used to perform the Sakazuki-Goto (Engumi) ceremony, but now the Baishaku-Nin performs the ceremony almost exclusively. Conducted in a specially designated ceremonial room containing a Saidan, or altar, preparations for the ceremony begin with the placing of the likenesses of the Japanese gods upon the top tier, the most honorable place. The gods that are invoked during this ceremony are the following:

Hackiman-Dai-Bosatsu—a god of bravery

Amaterasu-Oomi-Kami—the original god

Kasuga-Dai Myojin—a god of bravery

Katori-Dai Myojin—the god of military/martial arts

On the second tier of the Saidan, offerings to the gods, in the form of food placed on square plates, are arranged. On either side of the Saidan are arranged large nameplates reading:

Toji-Sha

Koken-Nin

Torimochi-Nin

Honso-Nin

Suisen-Nin

Baishaku-Nin

On both sides of the ceremonial room, nameplates for the Mitidoke-Nin and the Tachiai-Nin are placed in order of their ranking, beginning from the upper seat in the room. A long, bleached cotton sheet is spread in the center of the room from the center of the Saidan and extending to the lowest seat in the room, similar to the red carpet used for dignitaries. Sacred sake, called Omiki, is set upon the Sango, or cloth, decorated with origami, folded paper in the form of male and female butterflies. Sacred salt, in the form of a hardened pyramid, is also placed on the Sanpo, along with fresh fish (usually red snapper) and a set of long chopsticks. After everything has been arranged, all attendants enter the room and take their reserved seats. In the case of a two-party Engumi, the two participants take their places face-to-face in front of the Saidan. If there are three or more, the participants take their seats facing the attendants. The Baishaku-Nin takes his seat facing the Saidan at the very end of the room. The Torimochi-Nin and the Honso-Nin sit on the right side of the Baishaku-Nin, who begins the ceremony with an opening speech after which he places the Sanpo with the sacred sake upon the altar and briefly prays. Then, placing three Sanpos in front of the participants, the Baishaku-Nin places the salt, fish, and sake upon each Sanpo from left to right. Taking a Sanpo in front of himself, he then places an unglazed sake cup upon it, bows his head and again prays to the gods. Then, removing the male and female butterflies and the sacred sake bottles, he fills the unglazed cup, drinks it, and declares that the sake is not poisoned. The Baishaku-Nin then fills the remaining two cups on the Sanpo with the sacred sake and again silently prays. After pouring the sake, he touches the sacred salt and the fish with the chopsticks, and moving the chopsticks over the cups, he mingles the salt and the blood of the fish with the sake. Placing the Sanpo with the sake cups on it between the persons concerned, he instructs them to drink half of it. He then mixes the rest of the sake, adding some to the already mingled sake, and presents them to the Torimochi-Nin, confirming that they are well blended, thus concluding the first drinking ceremony.

The second drinking ceremony begins with the Baishaku-Nin approaching the participants again and instructing them to finish the sake in one gulp. The Baishaku-Nin then declares the completion of the Engumi. After finishing the sake, the participants place the sake cups upside down on the Sanpo and wrap them with paper, whereupon each participant places the cup into the breast folds of his kimono. In another version, the Baishaku-Nin takes the handle of a dagger and smashes the sake cups to pieces

(continued)

(continued)

upon the Sanpo, thus symbolizing that as the cups can never resurrect, never can the newly formed relationship be canceled. The Baishaku-Nin then steps to the Torimochi-Nin and reports the final consummation of the Engumi. Occupying the upper seat, the Torimochi-Nin faces the two participants and instructs them to join hands with each other, at the same time joining his hands with theirs. He then advises them to make their best efforts to help each other, while the participants pledge themselves to each other forever. The Mitidoke-Nin and the Tachiai-Nin clap their hands to celebrate the finality of the Engumi and to confirm it. The Baishaku-Nin declares the conclusion of the Engumi to all of the attendees, whereupon the participants express their gratitude to all in attendance. Finally, a sumptuous banquet is held in celebration.

Source: U.S. Department of Justice, 2002.

The ability of the Japanese people to adapt is indicated in the way their industries rebounded after World War II. This was accomplished through the use of Western societies' management and business techniques and was achieved without the Japanese losing sight of their own traditions. Japanese gangs, like the society surrounding them, are just as capable of modifying their workstyles in order to adjust to the organizational systems of criminal gangs in the United States. As already stated, the Yakuza has formed a relationship with La Cosa Nostra, so with the assistance of the LCN, the Yakuza would easily adapt to U.S. activities.

The Yakuza, like many other gangs, has a membership initiation ritual that facilitates the growth of kinship and cohesiveness between the leaders and their workers. This rite is similar to the ceremonial installation conducted by the LCN, but the Japanese investiture involves a deeper commitment to the organization and its objectives. Another component of Yakuza membership requires the newly installed person to become a sworn brother to all other members. The ritual is called "Engumi" and is the first part of a three-part initiation rite of passage that is referred to as the "Sakazuki-goto" (the union of a blood kinship). A second type of rite, a "Shumei," involves the selection of a new leader after either the death or retirement of the present boss. The last ritual, "Teuchi," relates to the issue of two groups that have been involved in a number of violent encounters meeting to agree to a peaceful truce. These rites are ties that remain between the present-day Yakuza and its predecessor, the Samurai (FBI, 1992).

Japanese Gangs

Yamaguchi-Gumi.   The largest Yakuza group is known as the Yamaguchi-Gumi; this gang contains 750 branches that have approximately 20,000 members who control about 80 percent of Japan's prefectures (see Figure 9–3). This group has been beleaguered by hostilities within the ranks and with opposing gangs. A major portion of Yamaguchi-Gumi's problems started after the death of its oyabun, Kazuo "the Bear" Taoka, in 1981; then in 1982, the obvious successor to Taoka, Ken Yamamoto, died in

Figure 9–3   Yamaguchi-Gumi Sphere of Influence

Source: U.S. Department of Justice, FBI, 2002.

Prefectures and Cities					
2. **Akita**	Akita	18. **Kagoshima**	Kagoshima		
3. **Aomori**	Aomori	19. **Kanagawa**	Yokohama	35. **Saitama**	Urawa
4. **Chiba**	Chiba				
		21. **Kumamoto**	Kumamoto		
				39. **Tochigi**	Utsunomiya
10. **Gumma**	Maebashi			41. **Tokyo**	
11. **Hiroshima**	Hiroshima				
		29. **Niigata**	Niigata		
14. **Ibaraki**	Mito			45. **Yamagata**	Yamagata
				46. **Yamaguchi**	Yamaguchi
16. **Iwate**	Morioka			47. **Yamanashi**	Kofu

prison. These deaths left two other Yamaguchi-Gumi leaders, Hiroshi Yamamoto and Masahisa Takenaka, vying for the top position. Ultimately, Takenaka was chosen as the new boss of the Yamaguchi-Gumi. In June 1984, an angry Yamamoto proceeded to withdraw from the Yamaguchi-Gumi, along with 18 top lieutenants and 13,000 members, to form a new group known as the Ichiwa-Kai. Takenaka remained calm and offered the dissidents an expanded benefits package that included amnesty and a retirement income plan. This offer by Takenaka was accepted by 10,000 of the defectors, who were welcomed back by the Yamaguchi-Gumi gang. A short time after these gang members had reaffiliated themselves with Yamaguchi-Gumi, Takenaka and two of his top aides were assassinated by four members of Ichiwa-Kai. This resulted in an emergency meeting being called by the leaders of Yamaguchi-Gumi, who named Kazuo Nakanishi the new boss and pledged an all-out war against Ichiwa-Kai. Over the next six months, Japanese riot police found themselves on constant alert, seizing weapons and arresting gang members. During this time period, about 200 shootings took place, and 26 of these shootings resulted in the death of a Yakuza member.

As the number of confrontations increased, Yamaguchi-Gumi's need of weapons became more apparent to gang leaders. One such member, Masashi Takenaka, set out to obtain new weapons for the gang, but in doing so he made a major mistake. Takenaka approached two undercover U.S. federal agents in Toyko, Japan, and offered to trade 8.5 kilos of heroin and another 8.5 kilos of methamphetamine for 3 rocket launchers, 5 machine guns, 100 handguns, and an executioner (hit man) to murder the entire upper echelon of Ichiwa-Kai by firing a rocket into the headquarters of Ichiwa-Kai. This conspiracy resulted in the arrest of 10 members of Yamaguchi-Gumi, with the ultimate conviction of only 1 (Koyoshi Kajita) and the acquittal of the other 9 members. Even without what one would consider a sufficient amount of guns, the unwavering attacks on Ichiwa-Kai by Yamaguchi-Gumi resulted in the disintegration of Ichiwa-Kai; Yamaguchi-Gumi then assimilated a major portion of the membership of the dismantled Ichiwa-Kai gang (Drug Enforcement Report, October 8, 1991).

There is a total of 92 leaders within the Yamaguchi-Gumi gang. The head of this group is known as the fifth boss, and each one of the other 91 leaders has his own subdivision of the gang. If a member of one of these subbranches manages a prosperous business, he can then establish his own subgroup of the gang. The power of Yamaguchi-Gumi as a group comes from the gang's ability to recruit new members and maintain the largest membership of all the Japanese groups (see Figure 9–4). It is estimated that Yamaguchi-Gumi has approximately 25,000 members. Some of the gang's subgroups have been using corporate classifications to disguise their true identities and their unlawful activities from law enforcement agencies (FBI, 1992).

Prior to Yamaguchi-Gumi's selection of a new leader, the organization embraced a cooperative leadership style of management. Under this type of supervision, the gang avoided controversy by staying out of the media's limelight. This did not last long because the appointment of the new leadership brought with it a desire to aggrandize the treasury and territories of Yamaguchi-Gumi by moving into regions under the control of other gangs. Encroaching on areas under the control of other gangs precipitated skirmishes

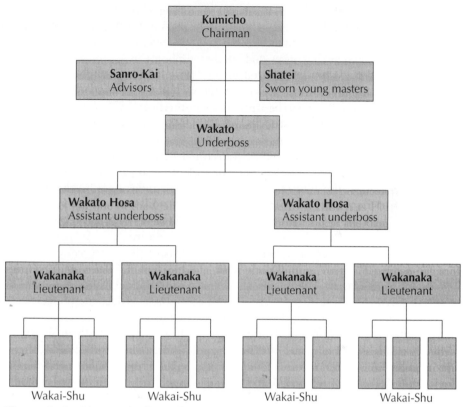

Figure 9–4   Yamaguchi-Gumi Organization Structure

Source: U.S. Department of Justice, FBI, 2002.

between Yamaguchi-Gumi and other Yakuza groups. On December 4, 1990, a meeting in Isogo-ku, Yokohama, was attended by members of the Yamaguchi-Gumi gang to formulate tactics to move in on the Tokyo territories of Sumiyoshi-Kai. The decision made by the Yamaguchi-Gumi gang was to set up business offices as "operational bases" in Tokyo that would also be used to recruit new members. The Sumiyoshi-Kai gang members, in turn, responded by forewarning the Yamaguchi-Gumi members that they would never allow the Yamaguchi-Gumi gang to interfere in the criminal enterprises they controlled in Tokyo.

Yamaguchi-Gumi, in an effort to increase membership, defied an age-old Yakuza rule that forbids enlisting membership from rogue groups and continued to seek out and enroll these outlaw groups in their gang. Strife within the ranks of Yamaguchi-Gumi is another problem that plagued the gang. This discord in the ranks was caused by what some members of the gang considered disparity in the reparations for distinguished deeds performed during the skirmishes with Ichiwa-Kai and the treatment of members recently added from other gangs.

One member of the Yamaguchi-Gumi gang who was highly visible in the media was Masaru Takumi, the wakagashira (or underboss) of the Yamaguchi-Gumi gang. Takumi was refused admittance to Paris in 1992, was linked to tour companies in Vancouver, purchased a house in Vancouver, and purchased a home in Australia (*Vancouver Sun*, October 1993). Takumi was also arrested in July 1992 for violations of the Foreign Exchange Control Law after he purchased a home in Vancouver, Canada; he was one of the first members of the Yakuza to be arrested under this new law that is part of a set of laws being used by the police to arrest and prosecute members of Japanese organized crime.

Under this new antigang legislation (known as the Boryokudan Countermeasures Laws) which took effect on March 1, 1992, crime groups in Japan can be certified by the police as being boryokudan, or violent organized criminal gangs. This new law makes the certification of these gangs easy and quick because the police need only to prove that approximately 4 percent of the gang members have criminal histories. As far as the number of members of the Yakuza gang that have criminal records, a study conducted by the Hyogo Prefecture Police indicated that 50 percent of Yamaguchi-Gumi's senior members had criminal records, while 34 percent of the Inagawa-Kai (discussed later) and 27 percent of the Sumiyoshi-Kai (discussed next) had previous criminal histories (*Japan Times*, weekly International Edition, April 20–26, 1992). Once one of these gangs is recognized as a violent group, the police can raid its business offices, confiscate its weapons, and arrest its members without a warrant. Another part of this legislation deals specifically with prosecuting individuals who are involved in money laundering, and that became effective at the end of 1992.

Sumiyoshi-Kai.   This group is considered a "bakuto" (gambling-oriented) organization. A major part of this gang's revenue has been obtained from illegal gambling operations in Japan. Sumiyoshi-Kai is based in Tokyo; its top leader, Masao Hori, prefers that this group stay out of the limelight. Masao Hori combined all the Sumiyoshi-Kai groups, along with other gambling associations, under the Sumiyoshi-Rengo organization in 1969. The Sumiyoshi-Rengo-Kai gang consists of 177 different subsections and is considered the most powerful Yakuza group in Eastern Japan (see Figure 9–5). In 1969, Hori completely changed the hierarchy of the gang and the areas the gang controlled in Eastern Japan. In 1988, Hori took total control of the gang by making himself the "sosai" (president) of this group (FBI, 1992). Within his newly structured group, Hori created new positions to enable change in the organization that would help this gang sustain its power and not be overtaken by Yamaguchi-Gumi or Inagawa-Kai. The Sumiyoshi-Kai gang uses what can be considered a management team to make decisions (see Figure 9–6). This group of representatives is chosen from the leadership of the Sumiyoshi-Kai subgroups and is responsible to provide the organization with deliberate and concise group decisions. One major advantage to this process is that once a decision is made by this board, this determination can be easily administered without any major opposition within the group.

Gambling is becoming more and more acceptable throughout the United States and Canada. Sumiyoshi-Kai's use of this type of management resolution may ultimately assist this gang in becoming quite successful in their criminal ventures in North America

Prefectures and Cities		
1. **Aichi**	Nagoya	

4. **Chiba**	Chiba	18. **Kagoshima**	Kagoshima
5. **Ehime**	Matsuyama	20. **Kochi**	Kochi
6. **Fukui**	Fukui	21. **Kumamoto**	Kumamoto
7. **Fukuoka**	Fukuoka	22. **Kyoto**	Kyoto
		23. **Mie**	Tsu
		24. **Miyagi**	Sendai
		25. **Miyazaki**	Miyazaki
11. **Hiroshima**	Hiroshima		
		27. **Nagasaki**	Nagasaki
13. **Hyogo**	Kobe	28. **Nara**	Nara
14. **Ibaraki**	Mito	29. **Niigata**	Niigata
15. **Ishikawa**	Kanazawa	30. **Oita**	Oita
16. **Iwate**	Morioka	31. **Okayama**	Okayama
		32. **Okinawa**	Naha

34. **Saga**	Saga
35. **Saitama**	Urawa
36. **Shiga**	Otsu
37. **Shimane**	Matsue
38. **Shizouka**	Shizouka
40. **Tokushima**	Tokushima
42. **Tottori**	Tottori
43. **Toyama**	Toyama
44. **Wakayama**	Wakayama
46. **Yamaguchi**	Yamaguchi
47. **Yamanashi**	Kofu

Figure 9–5 Sumiyoshi-Kai Sphere of Influence

Source: U.S. Department of Justice, FBI, 2002.

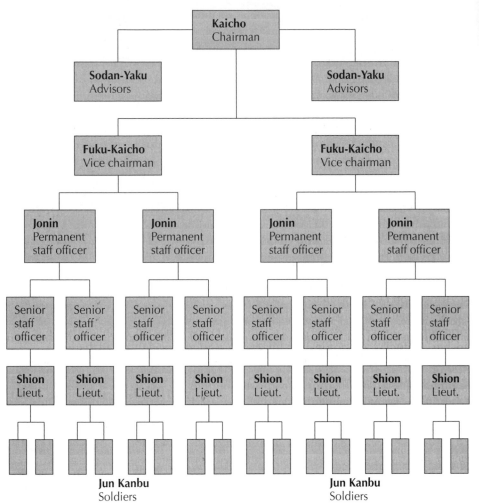

Figure 9–6   Sumiyoshi-Kai Management

Source: U.S. Department of Justice, FBI, 2002.

(FBI, 1992). Legalized gambling has been operating for years in Atlantic City and Las Vegas; several more states have passed laws to legalize gambling, and it is legal for casino gambling to be operated on Indian reservations in some other states. In Japan, betting on *pachinko* (a pinball-type game), bicycle racing, horse racing, and speedboat racing is legal and is run by local organizations. Presently, there are over 10,000 *pachinko* parlors throughout Japan, and Sumiyoshi-Kai direct a major portion of these operations. The Sumiyoshi-Kai gang also controls illegal casinos, off-track bookmaking, a portion of the entertainment industry, pornography, prostitution, stimulants trafficking, and gun running. A majority of these illegal practices would also prosper in either an Atlantic City or Las Vegas type of environment.

Inagawa-Kai.   The Inagawa-Kai gang is considered the number three Yakuza group in Japan. This gang is made up of 313 subgroups that have a total membership of over 6,700 in 20 prefectures throughout Japan (see Figure 9–7). The leader of this group is Kakuji Inagawa; the hierarchy of this gang consists of 18 fixed administrative positions, with Inagawa at the top. Inagawa-Kai is run quite differently from Sumiyoshi-Kai in that all policy judgments are made by Kakuji Inagawa, not by a board of managers. Inagawa-Kai's organizational composition is very similar to that of La Cosa Nostra, and like La Cosa Nostra, this gang assigns to chosen supervisors some communication and coordination activities. The members of Inagawa-Kai, like those in Yamaguchi-Gumi and Sumiyoshi-Kai, partake in a tariff procedure, but the leader of Inagawa-Kai, Kakuji Inagawa, demands that his members pay a much higher levy than those of most other groups (FBI, 1992).

Inagawa-Kai has sustained an ongoing friendly relationship with Yamaguchi-Gumi; it has also managed to improve its long-term alliances with the Aizu-Kotetsu-Kai gang based in Kyoto and the Doya-Kai gang of Nagoya. As this group continues to move its activities into other districts of Japan, it also continues to assimilate other smaller gangs into its membership. In an effort to remain out of the limelight, which attracts both police and media attention, Inagawa-Kai went so far as to remove its gang symbol from the front of its headquarters to avoid observance. The Inagawa-Kai, like the Sumiyoshi-Kai, set its goals on higher stakes by advancing into more complex scams within the financial affairs area.

In the past several years, there has been an increase in the amount of dissension among members of this gang over the ever-escalating amounts of tariffs they are forced to pay. Another factor that has been causing conflict within this group is the fact that their leader, Kakuji Inagawa, maintained an unreasonable number of older members in higher-ranking positions within Inagawa-Kai; this, in turn, denied upper mobility to younger members of this gang. Kakuji Inagawa also caused a sufficient amount of dissatisfaction by attempting to place his son Chihiro Inagawa, who is 50 years old, in the number two position in the group without any consideration for some far more productive and deserving high-ranking gang officials. There is a strong possibility that some of the moves contemplated or made by Kakuji Inagawa have been more harmful than helpful to the gang.

An investigation by the U.S. Department of Justice concluded that the Inagawa Kai gang invested a great deal of its capital in California, Hawaii, and Nevada. Early in this investigation, the FBI discovered direct links among Yamaguchi-Gumi, Inagawa-Kai, and Toa Yuai Jigyo Kumiai (discussed next). The information gathered by the FBI indicated that these groups formed partnerships in order to make investments in various business enterprises in the United States and Canada (FBI, 1992).

Toa Yuai Jigyo Kumiai.   The Toa Yuai Jigyo Kumiai (TYJK) gang—which is also known as the East Asia Friendship and the Enterprise Union and which was

Prefectures and Cities					
1. **Aichi**	Nagoya	17. **Kagawa**	Takamatsu	33. **Osaka**	Osaka
2. **Akita**	Akita	18. **Kagoshima**	Kagoshima	34. **Saga**	Saga
3. **Aomori**	Aomori			35. **Saitama**	Urawa
		20. **Kochi**	Kochi	36. **Shiga**	Otsu
5. **Ehime**	Matsuyama	21. **Kumamoto**	Kumamoto	37. **Shimane**	Matsue
6. **Fukui**	Fukui	22. **Kyoto**	Kyoto	38. **Shizouka**	Shizouka
		23. **Mie**	Tsu		
8. **Fukushima**	Fukushima			40. **Tokushima**	Tokushima
		25. **Miyazaki**	Miyazaki		
11. **Hiroshima**	Hiroshima	27. **Nagasaki**	Nagasaki	42. **Tottori**	Tottori
				43. **Toyama**	Toyama
				44. **Wakayama**	Wakayama
13. **Hyogo**	Kobe	30. **Oita**	Oita		
14. **Ibaraki**	Mito	31. **Okayama**	Okayama	46. **Yamaguchi**	Yamaguchi
15. **Ishikawa**	Kanazawa	32. **Okinawa**	Naha		
16. **Iwate**	Morioka				

Figure 9–7   Inagawa-Kai Sphere of Influence

Source: U.S. Department of Justice, FBI, 2002.

previously (prior to 1979) known as the Tosei-Kai—consists of 6 subgroups with a total of 850 members. Although the membership of this group seems small, the members' active participation in criminal activities in Canada, Japan, and the United States is entirely out of proportion to this gang's size. TYJK controls more than 20 prefectures throughout Japan. This is remarkable considering that Inagawa-Kai, which has 313 subgroups and over 6,700 members, controls about the same total number of prefectures. The theory about strength in numbers is not always true. TYJK is one of the few Yakuza groups that has a number of other ethnic Asians within its membership: Approximately 15 percent of TYJK is made up of ethnic Koreans, and a major portion of TYJK's power structure has a family lineage with Korean members (FBI, 1992).

Information gathered by the FBI showed that one of the top leaders of the TYJK gang is a very formidable Japanese billionaire entrepreneur. According to the intelligence information collected by both the Japanese police and the FBI, this businessman controlled a Tokyo-based corporation with a large number of companies and land resources all over Canada and the United States (FBI, 1992).

TYJK has been identified by both the FBI and the U.S. Drug Enforcement Agency (DEA) as being heavily involved in drug trafficking in Hawaii. This type of activity presented a major problem to the U.S. government for two reasons: the ability of Japanese gangs to set up sophisticated networks of drug importation, and the Yakuza's ever-increasing competency in the money-laundering business.

Japanese Criminal Activities

Money Laundering and Other Illegal Activities.   The Yakuza groups have a profound ability to launder the proceeds of their criminal activities without attracting a great amount of attention from law enforcement agencies throughout the world (see Figure 9–8). Canada and the United States have become primary locations for Yakuza groups to launder their money. Federal authorities have pinpointed Yakuza money-laundering operations in Hawaii, Las Vegas, Los Angeles, and San Francisco as well as Colorado, New Jersey, and Washington. In most areas, the Yakuza has penetrated lawful Japanese and American (usually Japanese-American) companies to launder their money, which in most cases was illegally obtained in Japan (see Figure 9–9).

One thing about the Yakuza that must always be remembered is its ability (as a group of gangs) to make legal profits through the use of illegal funds. The Yakuza used fees assessed on its gangs' members, along with money expropriated from gang-owned businesses, to finance its ventures in Kabutocho, Tokyo's stock market. These earnings were then distributed to the individual participating gangs.

Inagawa-Kai (a Yakuza gang) managed to accumulate a profit of well over 100 million yen through its dealings in the Tokyo stock exchange; in fact, Inagawa-Kai created its own stock transaction company, Hokusho Sangyo, located in Chiyoda-Ku, Tokyo. The president of this stock exchange firm was Susumu Ishii, who was the number two man in the Inagawa-Kai gang (FBI, 1992). Under the leadership of Susumu Ishii, the

Typical Crimes
Likely to be found on Japanese "rap sheets"

Baishun Boshiho Ihan – Violation of
   antiprostitution law
Boko – Simple assault
Chakufuku – Embezzlement
Fuhu Kyoki Shoyo – Illegal possession
   of deadly weapon
Gizo – Forgery
Kakuseizai – Stimulant drugs
   (slang - Shabu or Piropon)
Kenka – Fighting
Kinshi Yakuhin – Prohibited drugs
Kyogino Chinjutsusho – False written
   statement
Kyogino Moshitate – False oral statement
Kyohaku – Extortion
Mayaku – Narcotics
Sagi – Fraud
Satsujin – Homicide
Shogai – Assault and battery
Shogai Chishi – Assault and battery
   resulting in death
Tabaku – Gambling
Wairo – Bribery
Yukai – Kidnapping
Zenka – Criminal record

Typical Occupations
Likely to be found on visa applications

Doboku – Civil engineering (usually work
   obtained by graft)
Fundosan – Real estate
Kanekashi – Money lending (loan shark)
Kensetsu – Construction
Kinyugaisha – Loan company
Kogyo Nushi – Promoter
   (entertainment, theater)
Unso of Unyo – Transportation

Organization and Relationship

Anikibun – Superior (in rank or position)
Bakuto – Gambler
Boryokudan – Violence groups
   (also Soshiki Hanzai)
Gumi – Association, company, gang
Gruentai – Hoodlum
Jiageya – Thugs who remove tenants by
   threats and force
Kai – Association, society
Kobun – Common Boryokudan,
   "child role"
Kuromaku – Behind-the-scenes power
   broker link to legitimate world
Ototobun – Inferior (in rank or position)
Oyabun – Boss, godfather, "parent role"
Rengo – Federation
Riji – Important advisor and link to
   legitimate world
Sarakin – Loan sharks, salary man
   financiers
Sokaiya – Corporate extortionists,
   financial racketeers
Tekiya – Street stall operator, con-man
   (slang - Yashi)
Tokushu Kabunushi – Corporate
   extortionists
Yubitsume – Slicing part of the finger off
   in apology

Figure 9–8   Yakuza-Related Terminology

Source: U.S. Department of Justice, FBI, 2002.

Hokusho Sangyo company expanded its investments to include real estate. The success of this company can be measured by the 12.2 million yen it earned in 1987. Hokusho Sangyo's company then proceeded to build its home office in Kojimachi, where the average 3.3-square-yard plot cost approximately 50 million yen in 1988. There were three

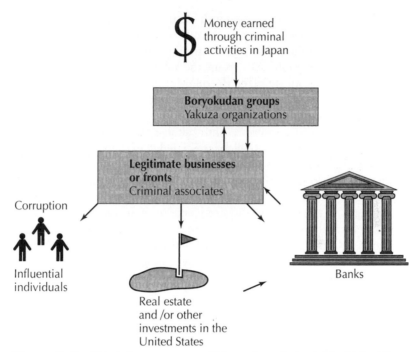

Figure 9–9   Yakuja Investments and Money Laundering in the United States

Source: U.S. Department of Justice, FBI, 2002.

specific circumstances that helped the Inagawa-Kai gang become highly successful in its stock market and real estate ventures (FBI, 1992):

1. The group's ability to legally dispose of illegal funds
2. The procurement of funds from Showa Lease, a finance company associated with the Kyowa Bank of Japan
3. The affirmed support of a major conveyance company

Susumu Ishii, president of Hokusho Sangyo, died in September 1991 (FBI, 1992).

A subgroup of the Yamaguchi-Gumi gang, the Kyushu, managed to make an advance of a substantial amount of currency to a local monetary affairs corporation by channeling this money via a financial consultation firm directed by a "sokaiya" (corporate mobster). This company was so successful that in 1989 it disbursed millions of yen in profits from its stock ventures to Kyushu's upper echelon (FBI, 1992). Historically, stock market investments made by the Yakuza gangs remained hidden from public view; most of this money made by these gangs involved tentative stock or bond ventures. In the past 10 years, Yakuza groups freely and assertively participated in stock market trading.

The Yakuza group is constantly demonstrating its ability to adapt to the world around it in its moneymaking endeavors. The capability to adjust makes the Yakuza a conglomerate of criminal groups controlling an assorted collection of legal and illegal moneymaking operations. As a group, the Yakuza has its own stock market and real estate ventures, and it recently entered the oil painting market by offering to lengthen elevated percentage loans with prestigious works of art as insurance against default on the loans. When the Gekkoso, a distinguished art gallery in the highly trendy Ginza district of Tokyo, went into foreclosure recently, almost all of the gallery's 100 world-renowned paintings were acquired by a gallery associated with the Sumiyoshi Rengo-Kai gang.

The Yakuza gangs' capabilities are expanding as groups and/or agencies seek to attract them to locations outside Japan. Gambling casinos in Las Vegas hired Japanese personnel in an effort to entice affluent Japanese businessmen, whether legitimate or illegitimate, to Las Vegas to disburse some of their money. This, of course, is enticing to Yakuza members, who are looking to transfer or get rid of some of their unlawfully obtained funds. There is no doubt that these trips to Las Vegas by members of the Yakuza led to the formation of friendly relationships between Yakuza and La Cosa Nostra members in the early 1970s.

Corporate Extortion.   The ability of the Yakuza group to diversify its legal and illegal operations caused great concern among members of Japanese society. Japanese citizens requested an expansion of police participation to impede the growth of these gangs, so the police became involved in attempting to control the activities of the gangs participating in corporate extortion.

The Sokaiya gang was originally a separate entity from the Yakuza, but then it joined forces with the Yakuza. Yakuza members are the "muscles" of the operation, and Sokaiya members are the "central processing unit" of the operation. "Sokaiya" was initially a word used to refer to a competent individual who managed to procure an adequate amount of stock in a company so that he could attend the stockholders' meetings and attempt to disrupt the proceedings. The maneuvers used by the Sokaiya member might be as slight as injecting a suitable phrase or as impertinent as disruption of the meetings. In doing this, stockholders would become aware of unethical or immoral activities of either the corporation or some members of the company's executive board. In most cases, the Sokaiya member received a dividend from his stockholdings, which was actually a type of fee paid by the person who hired him to take this action. Some of these Sokaiya claimed to be "grassroots shareholders' campaigners," but in reality they were nothing more than con artists who used these methods to extort money from corporate executives (Jones, 1993).

These types of acts have been replaced by modern-day Sokaiya members who exhibit whatever type of conduct is necessary in order to extort money from a corporation: This conduct could include the threat of having outrageous facts about corporate officials publicized by unethical newspapers, which would not only damage the reputations of company executives but also tarnish the image of the organization.

Shortly after the end of World War II, the number of cases involving the Sokaiya increased at about the same rate as the Japanese economy. The 1980s saw Yakuza members as more active participants in these types of crimes. Up until 1993, over 90 percent of all Sokaiya gangs throughout Japan were controlled by members of the Yakuza. Early in 1980, there were approximately 1,800 active corporations in Japan that reported that they had been targets of extortion by the Sokaiya; however, if one considers the total number of corporations in Japan, the total of 1,800 companies reporting these incidents is very small. In 1992, three senior executives of the Ito-Yokado Company, a 7 Eleven convenience store chain, met with Sokaiya members on three occasions and delivered over 27 million yen to these gangsters. A short time later, both the company executives and the Sokaiya members were arrested for their participation in this criminal activity. The payoffs had been given to the Sokaiya members because they guaranteed the Ito-Yokado Company that they would refrain from making any humiliating revelations at the corporation's annual meetings in June (*New York Times*, 1992).

Another incident in Japan involved the murder of Juntaro Suzuki, a senior executive of Fuji Film Company, who was hacked to death with a Samurai sword near his residence in Tokyo on February 28, 1994. This horrible murder was preceded by numerous attempts by Sokaiya members to extort money from the Fuji Film Company. During a Fuji Film Company meeting in January 1994, about 20 Sokaiya members created a disturbance by badgering Minoru Ohnishi, president of Fuji Film, about company policy related to dividends and other transactions. While the proceedings were continuing, one of the Sokaiya, who was directly connected to the Yamaguchi-Gumi gang, was arrested for tossing three different liquor bottles at Ohnishi (*Toronto Star*, 1994).

During 1981, three Sokaiya who were members of Yamaguchi-Gumi—Koulchi Masada, Chiyousei T. Wada, and Yoshiki Asada—were in attendance at the stockholder meetings of International Telephone and Telegraph, Bank of America Corporation, and Pacific Gas and Electric Corporation (all in San Francisco); after that, they attended the meeting of the Chase Manhattan Bank in New York City. Information gathered by federal investigative sources on these three Yakuza members who attended these meetings indicated that the Yakuza gangs were "testing the waters" in an effort to ascertain whether or not to start using Sokaiya methods to extort money from American corporations (FBI, 1992).

Information gathered by the Japan National Police Agency indicated that Yakuza members with a college education were being recruited to attend American universities in an effort to obtain advanced degrees in business in an attempt to eventually infiltrate and ultimately extort money from American industries. Subsequent data denoted that a Los Angeles Sokaiya group was formed by both Japanese and Caucasian individuals who used the misleading identity Japanese Defense Society (Interpol, 1993).

The Yakuza can apply Sokaiya methods to American corporations in an effort to build a foundation in the United States for the anticipated Japanese gang movement into legitimate businesses. Once the Sokaiya establishes a base within U.S. businesses, the Yakuza can then either extort money from these enterprises or use them to launder money. The Yakuza's average yearly profits are $10 billion, and a major portion of these earnings have to be laundered through a number of different phony companies and financial enterprises and ultimately combined with other Yakuza assets.

Investments. The Yakuza, like law-abiding members of Japanese society, have become involved in real estate ventures, which led to the Yakuza investing in U.S. properties. In Hawaii alone, prior to 1990, Japanese real estate speculators invested over $6 billion, with an expected $1.3 billion in other land deals waiting to be consummated. For example, a company owned and operated by a "former" member and present associate of the Yamaguchi-Gumi gang acquired several parcels of land in Oahu valued at over $164 million; one piece of property included in this real estate is the Turtle Bay Hilton Resort (U.S. Senate, 1993).

One real estate deal that went bad involved Ken Mizuno, owner of Ken International Company of Tokyo and an associate of the Toa Yuai Jigyo Kumiai criminal organization (U.S. Senate, 1992). Mizuno used his corporation to transfer over $265 million in what both the U.S. and Japanese governments considered "illegally obtained proceeds" from Japan to the United States and used $100 million of the laundered money to purchase the Indian Wells Country Club and Hotel near Palm Springs, California, and the Royal Kenfield Country Club in Henderson, Nevada. Mizuna also bought a DC-9 jet, a $2.8 million home, and a $2.3 million condominium in Beverly Hills and acquired three houses and a vacant lot in Hawaii. Between 1989 and 1991, Mizuno managed to lose over $60 million playing the baccarat tables in Las Vegas. According to the *Los Angeles Times*, Mizuno reputedly had strong ties to the Yakuza (*Los Angeles Times*, 1992).

In another real estate deal, a Tokyo developer, Minora Isutani, bought the Pebble Beach Country Club on the plush golf course on the Monterey Peninsula in 1990. Testifying before a U.S. Senate Committee on Governmental Affairs, a Yakuza associate (using the name "Bully") described how Isutani and Japanese gangsters collaborated with the Itoman Corporation of Osaka, Japan, to purchase Pebble Beach and then offer for sale $1 billion worth of $100,000 memberships in a special club at the golf course (*San Francisco Examiner*, 1993).

The Riviera Country Club, on the bluffs overlooking the Pacific Palisades, was purchased by a Japanese investment firm in 1989. The group that acquired the Riviera, members of the Watanabe family, then was investigated by the U.S. government for possibly being involved in a money-laundering scheme. Hiroyasu Watanabe, along with two others, was indicted by the Japanese government for providing $15.7 billion to corporations affiliated with Yakuza organized crime syndicates; for example, Japan's second-largest organized crime group, the Inagawa-Kai, received a total of 95.2 billion yen (*South China Morning Post*, August 15, 1992). In addition, investigators analyzed connections between the Watanabes and Shin Kanemaru, the notorious Japanese political power broker in whose house the Japanese police found over $50 million in cash and securities.

Kanemaru was also implicated both in a tax evasion case and for financial connections to members of the Yakuza. Although there was no definitive evidence related to money laundering, U.S. government officials pointed to the fact that the Watanabes concealed the identities of their investors even after an agreement had been reached and that a total of $53 million for the purchase was paid in cash (*New York Times*, 1994).

Watanabe was accused by the Japan National Police Agency of having Susumu Ishii, head of the Inagawa-Kai Yakuza group, remove a group that was denouncing Prime Minister Noboru Takeshita, who was at that time involved in a campaign to be elected prime minister of Japan; the group known as Nippon Kominto was ultimately removed from the area. Watanabe was also charged with unlawfully utilizing family business funds to make loans and credit warranties of approximately $765 million to corporations that were used as fronts by Inagawa-Kai and other Yakuza groups. This money allegedly produced kickbacks to Japanese politicians (*New York Times*, 1992).

Atlantic City and Las Vegas gambling casinos are other locations where the Yakuza attempted to gain a foothold. During 1978, Takashi Sasakawa, whose father, Ryoichi Sasakawa, is closely associated with the Yakuza, tried to purchase the Shelburne Hotel in Atlantic City with Benihana restaurant chain owner Hiroaki "Rocky" Aoki in order to convert the old hotel into a casino. This effort ultimately failed because of the lack of financial assistance and increasing inquiries by both state and federal law enforcement agencies.

In 1982, Ken Mizuno first appeared on the Las Vegas scene and proceeded to open a restaurant in the Tropicana Hotel. The Aladdin Hotel and Casino in Las Vegas was purchased in 1986 by Ginji Yasuda; Yasuda's funding came from a finance company operated by Yasumichi Morishita, who had direct links to the Yakuza. Morishita apparently used members of the Sumiyushi-Kai Yakuza group as enforcers to collect money owed to him (U.S. Senate, 1992). Yasuda soon became the first Japanese citizen to be issued a Las Vegas casino license. Minori Isutani, another Yakuza associate, purchased the Barcelona Hotel in Las Vegas in 1988 and attempted to obtain a casino license but retracted his application before the Nevada Gaming Board's intensive investigation was finished.

Drugs.   Approximately 33 percent of the Yakuza's earnings are obtained from drug trafficking. The principal drug dealt by Yakuza groups is crystal methamphetamine, which is the primary drug used by most members of Japan's drug culture (where this drug is known as "shabu"); in the United States, this drug goes by the name "ice."

Close to 100 percent of the methamphetamine market in Japan is controlled by the Yakuza. In an effort to create an American market for this drug, the Yakuza started smuggling crystal methamphetamine into Hawaii in the early 1980s. The first indication of the trafficking of crystal methamphetamine into the United States was in 1984 when U.S. undercover federal agents were approached in Hawaii by members of Yamaguchi-Gumi, who attempted to sell the agents 40 kilograms of ice and 8 kilograms of heroin (DEA, 1984). The crystal methamphetamine problem has increased consistently since the mid-1980s. For example, there were 32 deaths attributed to overdoses of crystal methamphetamine between 1985 and 1988 in Honolulu; during the first half of 1989, an additional 12 people died from overdoses. This problem is now on the mainland of the United States, where "ice" is being produced, as evidenced by the seizure of "ice" laboratories in Portland, Oregon, and Sacramento, California. Korea, the Philippines, and Taiwan are the principal suppliers of "ice." An affluent Korean member of the Yakuza group TYJK and a major property owner in Hawaii has been identified by federal sources as a significant "ice" vendor who distributes over 30 kilos of crystal methamphetamine a month (FBI, 1992).

Another drug that has attracted attention from members of the Yakuza is cocaine, with the number of arrests and the total amounts of cocaine seized increasing 50-fold. Japanese police intelligence reports also indicated that large amounts of cocaine were stored in Tokyo. The only reason this cocaine supply did not immediately hit the street was because of the ongoing conflict between Yamaguchi-Gumi and Nibiki-Kai over control of certain areas of Tokyo. There is the distinct possibility that some of the cocaine is exchanged for guns, which are of great value and are difficult to obtain in Japan because of very strict laws regarding the sale or possession of firearms.

Other Illegal Businesses.   The Yakuza has expanded its boundaries throughout the nations and territories of the Pacific Basin. Yakuza members have found that the Commonwealth of the Northern Marianas Islands (CNMI), Guam, and the Philippines, are very well suited for both their legal and illegal business ventures. A major portion of all "Hajika," or heaters (guns) as Yakuza members call them, are made in CNMI, Guam, or the Philippines, although some of the weapons purchased by Yakuza groups initially came from Los Angeles, California.

Both CNMI and Guam have been thoroughly swamped by members of Inagawa-Kai, Sumiyoshi-Kai, and Yamaguchi-Gumi; to make matters worse, there has also been a heavy infiltration of a number of smaller Yakuza groups into these countries. These Yakuza groups have managed to take control of the tourist trade throughout these islands and are currently exploiting the real estate business by creating and operating building contracting firms and phony investment corporations.

The expansion of Yakuza operations on the islands continued during the 1980s. Along with this growth, there has been an increase in the amount of miscellaneous types of drugs being transported through or being used on these islands; law enforcement investigations indicated that the Yakuza also had a reapportioning point somewhere in Japan. The Yakuza's participation in heroin smuggling is purely for profit: A pound of heroin costs about $100,000 on Palau and can be retailed for approximately $1 million in Los Angeles (DEA, 1993; U.S. Department of Treasury, 1993).

Between the 1980s and 1990s, the amount of Japanese organized crime activity in Canada multiplied 10-fold. Canadian police found that the Japanese pavilion at Expo 86 in Vancouver was funded by Ryoichi Sasakawa, one of Japan's leading organized crime figures. Sasakawa, a billionaire, also contributed $1 million to York University in Ontario (Royal Canadian Mounted Police, 1992).

A 1989 heroin conspiracy investigation in Vancouver turned up Atsuki Nagamine of the Matsuba-Kai Yakuza gang as one of the participants arrested. In 1991 Masaru Takumi, of the Yamaguchi-Gumi gang, purchased a home in Vancouver through the TM Canada Investment Corporation, of which he was one of the directors. Investigative information gathered by the Royal Canadian Mounted Police (RCMP) in 1993 indicated that an Osaka-based Yakuza group was actively involved in transporting drugs from South America to Vancouver and Japan for dispersal. Police sources also verified that there was a significant number of meetings in British Columbia involving leaders of several Yakuza groups (RCMP, 1992).

In addition to its presence in Canada and the United States, the Yakuza gained a foothold in Australia. A cooperative investigation involving the Australian and Japanese police led to the arrest of two Japanese gang members. The first arrest was made in Melbourne by the Australian police; Kazuto Furuichi was caught smuggling heroin into Australia. Australian police continued their investigation and passed information on to the Japanese police, which led to the arrest of a coconspirator, Hideo Nistumoto, in Japan. There was an ongoing investigation by the Australian Federal Police into the Yakuza's participation in buying a Queensland casino, and during Australian senate hearings, it was determined that Japanese organized crime was involved in over 25 percent of all the real estate deals in Queensland (Roberts, 1992). In an effort to dissuade Yakuza groups from conducting business in Australia, the Australian government refused to sell a piece of property in Kobe to members of Yamaguchi-Gumi (*Japan Times*, August 10–16, 1992).

The Yakuza crime syndicate moved some of its operations into the lower part of the Yangtze River Basin in southern China. Yakuza syndicates, working together with Triad members from Taiwan, used lawful establishments such as karaoke bars and hotels in an effort to open up and operate their unlawful businesses. A study conducted by a Shanghai professor discovered that Yakuza gangs were located in both the lower Yangtze and the Guangzhoa areas of China and that there were more than 400 Japanese companies operating in the lower Yangtze sector alone. The presence of the Yakuza indicated there was a very strong possibility that the gangs were checking out profitable companies so that their crime syndicates could extort money from them in Japan (*Japan Times*, 1994).

The Japanese gangs, like the Chinese gangs, got involved in illegal alien smuggling. In 1993, three members of the Yamaguchi-Gumi gang were arrested by Japanese police for attempting to smuggle 145 Chinese aliens into Japan. In fact, the total number of illegal Chinese aliens arrested in Japan jumped from 18 in 1990 to 335 in 1993 (*Japan Times*, 1994).

VIETNAMESE ORGANIZED CRIME

Vietnamese History

The Vietnamese people have dealt with over 2,000 years of conflict that goes back to the Chinese invasion of Vietnam around the time of Christ. It was approximately 800 years later that the Chinese were finally removed from power in Vietnam, but the Vietnamese culture was certainly affected by the 800 years of Chinese rule. Vietnam as a country remained fairly stable until the arrival of the French in the mid-1800s. The French invaded Vietnam and within a short period of time took over control of this

Southest Asian country, so the French played a very important role in influencing the present-day culture of Vietnam.

The French controlled Vietnam from the mid-1800s until their defeat by the Vietnamese army at Dien Bien Phu in 1954. During their rule in Vietnam, the French changed not only the way the government controlled the Vietnamese people but also the whole lifestyle of Vietnamese society. The French changed the educational system in Vietnam and modeled it after the French system, without giving any consideration to the long-established Vietnamese educational system. The French administration in Vietnam even went so far as to remove village leaders and replace them with people who had an allegiance to the French administration in either Saigon or Hanoi. The French then took it a step further by changing the various written dialects of the Vietnamese language and consolidating them with the French language.

The changes made by the French represented their perspective of the people in this Third World nation. The notion that all people who were racially or ethnically different than Europeans were on this planet to be exploited by people from European nations was not only a French perception but also a belief that extended throughout Europe and Great Britain. The European opinion that the destruction of a nation's culture would also bring that society to its knees did not hold true in Vietnam's case; in 1954 the Vietnamese defeated the French at Dien Bien Phu and chased them out of Southeast Asia.

It was not long after the demise of the French that U.S. military advisors started appearing in Vietnam to support the democratic government in Saigon against the Communist regime in Hanoi. History tells us what the ultimate result of this U.S. intervention was, but along the way, American interference caused the uprooting of over 25 percent of the villagers in Vietnam. The village and the family are very important to the Vietnamese people; family loyalty is a key factor for members of this society, and this family allegiance is based on the family's village and its philosophy. The Vietnamese family ideals have been conveyed to present-day Vietnamese street gangs, whose members work closely together like a family.

The demise of the democratic government in Saigon and the retreat of the U.S. military from Vietnam occurred in 1975. Once the U.S. troops withdrew from Vietnam, there was a large influx into the United States of Southeast Asian immigrants who were perceived as being Vietnamese, but some of these refugees were actually Cambodian and Laotian; as well as ethnic Chinese from Vietnam. In the first group of Vietnamese immigrants were some important Vietnamese citizens; they had left their country because of their relationship with the U:S. military and their fear of retaliation by the Vietcong regime. A major portion of these people had a good educational background and easily adapted to life in the United States because of their relationships with American military personnel in Vietnam. Many of these new arrivals considered themselves well-qualified personnel who were no threat to U.S. citizens. Because of their credentials, they felt they would be easily incorporated into the American community and would become fruitful members of our society.

Some members of this group who were participants in criminal activities fit right into the Vietnamese communities in the United States. They became active within their local communities and quickly got involved in fraudulent activities and scams, including money transfer schemes and welfare swindles. For example, in 1984 60 Vietnamese pharmacists and physicians deceitfully billed the California Bureau of Medi-Cal for $25 million (FBI, 1993); in most cases, these purported professional people used Vietnamese gang members as their couriers.

The first group that arrived from Vietnam managed to quickly create a number of communities throughout the United States, and a major portion of these neighborhoods were located on the West Coast. These communities would soon become home bases for the second group of arrivals from Vietnam that contained more of a criminal element than the first group (FBI, 1993). The second group of individuals arriving from Vietnam contained true refugees, not immigrants; these expatriates were, in most cases, both socially and educationally different than the people who arrived in the first group. Most of them were from rural regions or coastal communities and had fled Vietnam in boats that were packed with other fleeing immigrants who suffered through the abuses forced on them by pirates from Thailand, who constantly tormented these fleeing "boat people." Within this group of new arrivals were some people who arrived with their families and friends and others who disembarked alone. There were a large number of unescorted children as well as numerous older sons who arrived alone with a strategy that included finding a job and working as hard as possible in order to gather sufficient funds to bring the remaining members of their families to the United States.

There are several reasons for classifying the newly arrived Vietnamese as refugees rather than immigrants. First, a refugee is someone compelled to leave his or her homeland. Second, the circumstances surrounding this person's escape are life-threatening, and third, a refugee is without any specific direction or destination. This experience totally traumatizes most refugees. Another problem facing new refugees can be described as culture shock. When a Vietnamese refugee encounters culture shock, it is experienced by all the family members, not just one specific person. This creates a stress that affects the extended Vietnamese family unit; this stress is further complicated by the pressure placed on Vietnamese refugees to learn a new language in a different culture.

Stress seems to especially affect the adolescent members of Vietnamese society. It is not unusual for a youthful member of a family to set up family members to become victims of home robberies. The situation for some Vietnamese adolescents is even worse when there is no family unit; the youths often become gang members. Once part of a gang, these teenagers adopt the gang as their family and respond to any stress the same way, using desperation and violence (FBI, 1993).

Over the years, many of these Vietnamese progressed from undisciplined and out-of-control groups to street gangs, a major portion of which joined together to form tight-knit organizations linked to other Vietnamese groups throughout the United States. This type of link provided basic needs to members of Vietnamese gangs, as well as self-preservation and profits from gang ventures. The protection of its members is of utmost importance to a gang because of the tight-knit family relationships within Vietnamese society. Gang members in different areas of the United States often provided refuge to members of traveling gangs on route to a location to commit a crime or members retreating from a location where they had just committed a crime.

Vietnamese Gangs

The description of a Vietnamese traveling gang must be preceded by an explanation of what can actually be considered a street gang in general. As street gang members, they do the following (FBI, 1993):

1. Collaborate to perpetrate a transgression against a specific person or group for profit.
2. Identify themselves through the use of a name, sign, or symbol, and have a distinguishable leader.
3. Are involved in criminal activities, which is unusual compared to other identifiable groups.
4. Proclaim that group members are operating in a specific area.
5. Are identifiable by their garments, tattoos, actions, appearance, or communication with other members and seek out the affinity supplied by gang members.

Members of almost every street gang referred to in this book have these five characteristics. It has taken longer for Vietnamese gangs to adapt to these characteristics of gang ideology for two reasons:

1. Vietnamese male adolescents usually come to the United States without any other family members either traveling with them or already having a residence in the United States. These youths are alone and adopt the gang as their one and only family.
2. Vietnamese male adolescents come from a paternal type of society in which everything revolves around a very tight-knit family. The Vietnamese family is totally controlled by the father, whose authority is never challenged. When a male adolescent enters U.S. society (whose members have always questioned authority), it is not long before conflict between father and son develops, which can cause the son to become ostracized from the rest of his family.

It must be understood that in most cases members of other gangs did not come from a war-ravaged and chaotic homeland situation, but many Vietnamese youths entered the United States bewildered and unstable. These adolescents came from an agrarian society, which in most cases lacked any gang-like organizations or groups.

The Vietnamese gangs in the United States have done their apprenticeship under the Chinese street gangs. This experience helped the Vietnamese gangs grow into what now can be considered organized criminal gangs that were well trained during their involvement with the earlier-established Chinese street gangs. The Vietnamese gangs that have come to the forefront after training under the Chinese gangs are the Born to Kill gang, which learned under the guidance of the Flying Dragons gang, and the Hung Pho gang, which was taught by the Wo Hop To gang. Most members of the Vietnamese gangs associated with the Chinese gangs are ethnically Viet-Ching gangs that could be easily assimilated into either group because of their ability to speak both languages and understand both cultures.

The Vietnamese traveling ("hasty" or "phantom") gangs were originally created to perform special tasks. The traveling gang members are usually between the ages of 12 and 25 years old. Like members of all other Vietnamese gangs, the traveling gang members also receive their fair share of the profits, and they are more apt to seek some type of shelter or asylum after leaving the scene of a crime in which they were unlawful participants. The criminal activities these traveling gangs are involved in are not reckless or random; the criminal acts they participate in are thoroughly planned and carried out by skilled gang members. In fact, gang members of traveling gangs routinely recruit members of other gangs who are experienced in perpetrating the same types of crimes that these traveling gang members will be committing.

Almost all these traveling gang members surface prior to a crime and then vanish within a very short period of time after the successful completion of the crime. Activities involving these gangs are preplanned, and the target of the crime was selected long before the traveling gang members chose to participate in the criminal act. The members of these gangs are usually selected from locations throughout the United States so that identification of the perpetrators of these crimes is as difficult as possible for the victims and the police. That is why these gangs are considered "phantom" gangs: Very few of the participants in these crimes have the same home base. The only common identifying factor may be that the participants in these crimes are members of the same gang (but they are all from different locations in the United States).

Considering that the Asian population in California is the largest in the United States, it is not difficult to accept the fact that the first Vietnamese gang appeared in Los Angeles (in 1978). In 1980, Southern California's Vietnamese population was approximately 110, 000; the Vietnamese population in Northern California was about 45,000. Within a short period of time, Vietnamese gangs showed up in Anaheim, Garden Grove, Santa Ana, and Westminister, California. In 1982 there were five organized Vietnamese gangs operating in Southern California, and they concentrated all their criminal activities within the Vietnamese community. These gangs relied on extortion, vehicle theft, business takeovers, and protection rackets to make their gangs profitable.

A major portion of early gang members were ex–South Vietnamese military personnel who had been trained by the U.S. military in the use of military tactics and equipment, a fact which received a great deal of attention in the media. These gangs were originally described as elite military personnel who had received many hours of high-tech military training, including in-depth instruction in the use of explosives and underwater demolition. Much of this media hype proved to be untrue; instead, these gang leaders were usually experts only in the use of violence and in cold-blooded murder.

One of the first Vietnamese gangs to appear in Southern California was the Frogmen (Nguoi Nhu), whose name came from an elite Vietnamese military underwater demolition team. The major criminal activities of this gang, based out of Garden Grove, California, were gambling, murder, prostitution, drugs, extortion, and robbery.

During the early 1980s, a struggle took place within the Frogmen gang, which resulted in the gang splitting into three different factions: Tai gang, Cac gang, and Phong gang.

The second gang was known as the Thunder Tigers (Loi Ho). This gang, based out of Houston, Texas, established a gang in Orange County, California, in 1981. The membership of this gang was also made up of ex-military personnel. The third group was the Catalina Boys, located in both Los Angeles and Orange County, California; this gang was involved in several criminal incidents with the Thunder Tigers. The fourth gang was the Pink Knights, named for a bar in Saigon. This gang operated in the Anaheim area, and their major criminal activity was extortion. The last gang was the Luns, or Little People. Most members of this gang were between 13 and 20 years old and attended Costa Mesa High School. They were involved in extortion and robbery and were associated with the Frogmen gang.

These early Vietnamese gangs had their problems; in 1981 there were three violent incidents involving Vietnamese gang members. The first incident took place on February 5, 1981, when a gun battle occurred between members of the Frogmen and a combined group of Catalina Boys and Thunder Tigers. Then on February 12, 1981, Nguyen Dang, a Los Angeles Restaurant owner, was shot and killed in front of his market by Vietnamese gang members because of his refusal to pay extortion. Another incident took place on October 11, 1981, when two masked gunmen entered the restaurant hangout of the Tai gang brandishing shotguns, which they used during an exchange of fire with members of the Tai gang. This gun battle resulted in the death of one woman and the wounding of eight others (LAPD, 1982).

These early street gangs were the forerunners of the present-day Vietnamese street gangs, and some of these still coexist with the newer and more violent Vietnamese street gangs of today. The number of Vietnamese refugees coming into the United States has tripled since the 1980s, which has caused a widespread increase in the number of Vietnamese gangs, especially on the West Coast. The home base for almost every Vietnamese gang in the United States is California. A majority of these new street gangs are easily identifiable by their names: Viet Ching, King Cobra Boyz, Natoma Boyz, and Orietal Boyz. The makeup of most of these gangs is ethnically diverse. There are also a number of female street gangs of Vietnamese origin that have become visable in Southern California; among them are the South Side Scissors, Asian Girlz Hood, Oriental Raider Girls, and Innocent Bitch Killers (IBK). The female gangs at times work hand-in-hand with the male gangs, but on several occasions some of these female gangs are in direct conflict with their male counterparts. Most of these Vietnamese gangs wear specific gang colors and are all very aware of the territory they control. Like most other California gangs, the Vietnamese gangs adopted hand symbols to show loyalty to their gangs and to notify their own gang members to transmit messages through the use of signals and avoid verbal communications. Some of these gangs use graffiti to mark the boundry lines of their territories, to deliver a challenge to rival groups, and to declare their opinion of other members of society (in many cases, the local police establishment). Gang affiliation can sometimes be ascertained by tattoos and other imprints gang members have on their bodies.

When discussing California Asian gangs, one must consider the Viet-Ching element of Vietnamese gangs. Prior to the fall of Saigon one major portion of this group comprised professional people who owned and operated businesses in Saigon; another portion of the Viet-Ching were involved in medical occupations. The Viet-Ching had acquired the reputation of being an elitist group in Saigon. Because a great deal of the financing, money lending, and banking throughout Asia was controlled by the Chinese, it was logical that the Viet-Ching (or Cholon Chinese) dominated the financial environment of South Vietnam. Most of the ethnic Chinese were from the Cholon district of Saigon, from which they got their nickname the Cholon Chinese, and they formed their own triad groups. These triads may be present in the Little Saigons that have appeared throughout Vietnamese communities in California. Law enforcement sources across the United States believe that these Viet-Ching triads control the activities of the Viet-Ching gangs operating in and around local Vietnamese districts (FBI, 1993).

The Viet-Ching businesspeople have managed to set up their own criminal networks all over the United States. This system allows Viet-Ching entrepreneurs to become leaders as well as operatives who advise the Vietnamese street gangs, and this advice usually involves persons the gangs can victimize during home invasion robberies. The other advantage these networking Viet-Ching groups have is that the secluded Vietnamese community rarely communicates the secrets of its community to any members of outside communities, including the police (whom the Vietnamese hold in very low esteem). The Viet-Ching gangs have to be considered the best-structured Vietnamese criminal organization operating in the United States (FBI, 1993). Most of the Viet-Ching gangs are based in Orange and Los Angeles Counties in Southern California, but they also have large groups operating in San Francisco and San Jose in Northern California and in Houston, Texas.

Many of the Vietnamese street gangs are under the tutelage of a Dai Ka (or big brother) who was at one time a South Vietnamese military officer. These big brothers fashion their advisor position within the street gangs based on their prior military prowess. Often a gang is modeled after the military unit that its advisor served in during the Vietnam War—although in some cases police intelligence units have indicated that some alleged ex-military personnel from South Vietnam now working with gangs as advisors were not old enough to participate in the Vietnam War.

The Vietnamese gangs consist of three different types of members (see Figure 9–10). The first type has to be considered hard-core. A majority of these members are gang leaders, and they control all the criminal activities that involve gang members; they are also the most violent members of the gang. These leaders have the power to select the gang members who participate in various criminal activities, and almost all the hard-core leaders are well liked by gang members. The second type is the associate who participates in activities with the gang to gain some type of status and/or notoriety from other members of his peer group outside the gang. These members need to belong, and other gang members supply them with that sense of belonging. The third Vietnamese type of gang member is a peripheral

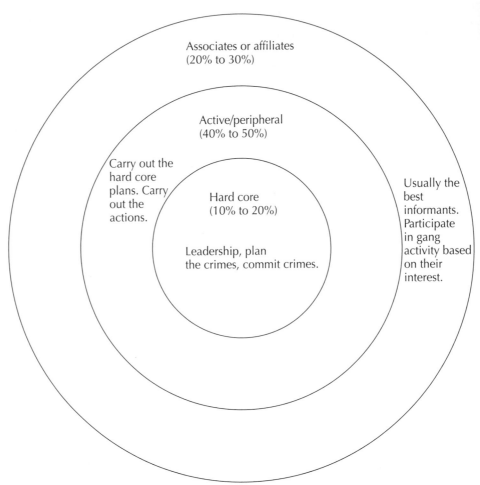

Figure 9–10   Gang Makeup

Source: California Department of Justice, 1993.

member. This type participates in gang activities as long as these criminal operations interest him; in many cases, it would be easy for this type of member to become either a hard-core or an associate member.

One of the major weapons used by Vietnamese street gangs to control a crime victim before, during, and after a crime is intimidation, both verbal and nonverbal. Verbal intimidation is done through issuing various threats that make the victim fearful of gang members from the start to the finish of the crime; for example, a verbal warning may contain the threat to rape, kidnap, or kill another family member or a friend. Nonverbal intimidation (used along with the verbal) usually includes the use of force or violence;

for example, it might include sticking a gun down a victim's throat, burning someone with cigarettes or scalding water, and physically striking someone.

Another type of nonverbal intimidation used by Vietnamese gangs involves leaving a knife or a bullet in plain view so that it is found by the victim. This gives the victim the message that he is not safe and that the gang members can return at any time to inflict harm on the victim or his family (LASD, 1993). This type of intimidation was evident on April 5, 1991, when four members of the Vietnamese street gang Oriental Boys entered a store in Sacramento, California, and held 41 people hostage for more than 8 hours. In an effort to intimidate the police, the gang members shot a hostage in the leg and sent him out of the store. During the ensuing seige with the police, one of the gang members ran down the line of hostages, shooting at the hostages one at a time. When the seige was finally over, 3 gang members and 3 hostages were dead and 15 other people were wounded (Gross, 1991).

There are many more Vietnamese gangs on the West Coast than on the East Coast. In fact, information gathered by U.S. law enforcement agencies indicated that the Vietnamese gang population in California was at least 10 times larger than in any other location in the United States (FBI, 1993). These gang members commit crimes throughout the United States, however, and have gang-related or other types of Vietnamese connections in most areas of the United States, as seen in the ability of Vietnamese traveling gangs to hastily move around. For example, on October 15, 1990, police in Westbrook, Maine, broke up a residential robbery and found Vietnamese gang members from Tai Ho and Tho Quang Ton in what they considered to be the getaway vehicle. A week later, both Tai Ho and Tho Quang Ton members were arrested in San Francisco for robbing a local Vietnamese mechanic inside his garage (*San Francisco Examiner*, 1991). According to San Francisco Police Sergeant Dan Foley, the Vietnamese travel all over the United States committing robberies. Foley states, "They might drive from Texas to Los Angeles, for example, and stop off in Phoenix and do a couple of robberies on the way. Then they will go to Los Angeles, visit some people, do a robbery, and then come up to San Francisco and meet a big brother, who might have a couple more robberies for them to perpetrate" (*San Francisco Examiner*, 1993).

One phenomenon of West Coast Asian gangs is female gangs. There are at least 25 female Asian gangs presently operating in Southern California; a majority of these are ethnically Vietnamese, but there are also Cambodian, Filipino, Korean, and Laotian female gangs. Each one of these female adolescent gangs is affiliated with one or more male gangs. Female gang members have been arrested for their involvement in home invasion robberies both with male gang members and by themselves. The female gangs usually average anywhere from 10 to 20 members, who are somewhere between 14 and 28 years old. Most of the members are fearless and tough; they challenge female as well as male members from opposing gangs to fight; they are known to pull a knife on another female and use it, if necessary, during a brawl. At first, it was believed that female gang members were just used to carry weapons for the male gangs but that was found to be a wrong presumption: Female gang members are involved in almost as much crime as their male counterparts (LASD, 1992).

The Born to Kill (BTK) Vietnamese street gang is an East Coast connection to the West Coast gangs. This gang operates throughout the United States but has established a large operation in the New York City metropolitan area. Members of BTK (originally known as the Canal Street Boys) are noted for their cruel and vicious behavior. Most members of this gang were originally associated with the Flying Dragons Chinese street gang; in 1986, they broke away from the Flying Dragons and formed their own gang under the leadership of David Thai. BTK is one of the very few street gangs that does not have any connections to either a Chinese tong or triad. Its territory includes parts of Canal Street, but this gang infringes on the territories of all the Chinese gangs to extort money from Chinese businesses. The BTK gang is presently operating in Chinatown, Coney Island in Brooklyn, Flushing in Queens, and Jackson Heights. Members sport tattoos of a coffin with three candles on it, which means that members are not afraid to die.

The number one criminal activity of BTK gang members is home invasion robberies, but they also are involved in extortion, gambling, and prostitution, as well as the production and sale of counterfeit watches. The counterfeit watch business was discovered when law enforcement personnel went to the apartment of the head of the BTK gang, David Thai, to question him about a murder investigation. Thai was ultimately arrested and convicted of conspiring to commit and committing the murder of Sen Von Ta, a Chinatown jewelry store owner; Thai was also convicted of attempted murder, a number of robberies, and extortion. Federal prosecutors and law enforcement agencies were under the impression that the convictions of Thai and six other BTK members would destroy BTK, but this was another government pipedream because these convictions only temporarily weakened this gang's New York City operations. The BTK gang has become a formidable force (like other Asian gangs) and is capable of quickly replacing imprisoned leaders without any loss of authority, territory, or profits.

Local BTK Vietnamese gangs have terrorized Chinatown business people and residents by getting involved in daytime shootouts on the bustling streets of Chinatown. These activities are being used in an attempt to gain control of the booming Chinatown extortion business. In one instance, members of BTK entered a garment factory, locked all the doors, and then proceeded to rob the owners and all the employees (*Law Enforcement News*, 1991).

Another New York City Vietnamese street gang is the Gum Sing, which is an offshoot of the BTK gang. The headquarters of this gang is in Brooklyn's Chinatown between 40th Street and 60th Street on Eighth Avenue. Like BTK, Gum Sing has no connection to either a tong or triad. Gum Sing is a highly mobile gang that is made up of Vietnamese adolescents and a few other ethnic Asian youths. Gum Sing members move freely throughout the New York City metropolitan area to participate in their criminal activities; they are involved in drug dealing, home invasions, extortion, and kidnapping (NYPD, 1994).

Vietnamese Criminal Activities

Home Invasion Robberies.   One of the most vicious crimes adopted as a common gang activity by all types of Vietnamese street gangs is home invasion robberies. The Vietnamese gangs perfected their approach to these robberies:

1. They gather all known facts on each and every target prior to making a decision on whether or not a specific location is worth robbing. The gangs also want to be sure that a specific amount of valuables will be at the location when they commit the crime. In most cases, the ideal target for the gangs is either a wealthy business owner or a large group of new refugees living in the same location who do not have any faith in the U.S. banking system or who are trying to avoid the U.S. Internal Revenue System to rip it off.

2. They properly arm all gang members who are going to participate in this crime and supply them with stolen autos.

3. They keep the number of active gang participants in this crime between five and eight (whenever possible).

4. They require that gang members involved in these crimes rehearse the tasks they are required to perform during the crime.

5. They bind and gag all the victims in one specific location in the structure (which is usually the victim's home and all members of the family are at home).

6. They initiate an act of violence (assault, rape, or another type of sexual assault) against one of the victims for no apparent reason. This random violence may be used to obtain more valuables, ascertain whether or not victims will notify police, or to just further terrify the victims.

7. They demand all the valuables in the house that the family owns. Gangs will sometimes threaten to kidnap and/or rape a family member to obtain more valuables; sometimes gang members sexually abuse and rape victims just for fun (*Law Enforcement News*, 1991).

8. They leave the crime scene in various types of transportation that will take them to Vietnamese safe houses in locations throughout the United States (LASD, 1992).

Computer Chip Theft.   The theft of computer chips has become a very profitable business for Vietnamese gangs. This type of crime is prevalent on the West Coast (especially California), but thefts have also taken place in Florida and Texas. In 1991, approximately $1 million worth of computer chips were stolen from a St. Petersburg, Florida, company. During this robbery, the 10 employees of the company were tied up, gagged, and blindfolded by 5 Vietnamese robbers. Stolen chips can be used in almost any computer; the average cost is anywhere between $300 and $700 apiece.

Vietnamese gangs were the first group to realize that the theft of computer chips is a very attractive business because computer chips are valuable and resell at about 80 percent of their value. Computer chips are also very difficult for the police to trace because they do not have any serial numbers on the chips. Computer chips are illegally obtained by Vietnamese crime groups in at least two ways:

1. Use of street gangs to commit robberies of computer chip companies (The method used in these robberies is very similar to that used during the commission of home invasion robberies.)

2. Use of Asian individuals who have become indebted to Vietnamese gangs because of gambling debts to steal chips for the gangs

Law enforcement authorities have identified five major computer chip fencing rings in Southern California alone. The chips taken by these groups are repackaged and then auctioned off to the highest bidder. Many of the pilfered chips either are sold at computer swap shows or are transported to Hong Kong, Taiwan, or Thailand for resale.

Another type of scam involving Vietnamese gangs is the theft of what are known as "valueless chips." The price of these valueless chips may be next to nothing in our ever-evolving high-tech market, but in Third World countries that are a lot less scientifically advanced, these chips have some value because they are made with some type of precious metal. Vietnamese criminals are known participants in the theft of valuable metals and gems, and the jewelry markets of Asia do not ask any questions about the legitimacy of the metals or gems.

Extortion. Three types of extortion involving Vietnamese groups have been identified by law enforcement officials. In the first, a gang member who is affiliated with a newspaper or periodical (whose distribution is limited) contacts businesspersons within the Vietnamese community and informs them that if they do not financially support the periodical, they will either be named as members of the Communist Party or be subject to some other type of harassment. The second type of Vietnamese extortion involves a member of an alleged Vietnamese resistance organization who approaches a businessperson and informs him that if he does not make a contribution to the resistance organization, he will meet with some type of violence. In the third type of extortion, Vietnamese gangs sell protection to community business owners; this is the typical street gang extortion ring (LASD, 1992).

Prostitution. Most prostitution activity within the Vietnamese community involves massage parlors and escort services. Many of the female participants in these prostitution rings were forced into this activity by the Vietnamese street gangs that run the massage parlors and escort services. Gang members who run the prostitution rings keep them well organized and under very tight control. These illegal operations help Vietnamese street gangs operate their other unlawful activities, including currency transfers, narcotic sales, gambling, and acts of violence.

Gambling.   Gambling operations are sometimes set up in residences, and Vietnamese street gangs are used to protect and act as lookouts for these illegal businesses. The street gangs also check out the big winners and may ultimately be involved in home invasion robberies of these patrons. The Vietnamese gangs favor gambling games involving the use of cards; the card games they enjoy betting on are Xap Zam (or thirteen card), and Tu Sac (a game with 112 small multicolored cards with Chinese imprints).

Drug Trafficking.   Vietnamese gang members observed the profits being made by other gangs in drug dealing, so they got involved in the drug trade. Vietnamese gangs are active participants in the crack cocaine business. In both New Orleans and New York City, Vietnamese gangs have been mixed up in the drug business. In New York City, the Vietnamese gangs first moved heroin for the Chinese gangs, but once the Vietnamese gangs realized the profitability in drugs, they quickly became active in the drug market (U.S. Department of Treasury, ATF, 1993).

Auto Thefts.   Since the mid-1980s, Vietnamese gangs have been involved in auto thefts. The gangs made up their own modified keys to gain entrance into automobiles. In many cases, the stolen cars were either Toyotas or Datsuns; the modified keys can be used on any Toyota or Datsun manufactured since 1967. With these keys, gang members can gain entrance into these vehicles in a very short period of time (five seconds). Other people also purchased these keys from Vietnamese gang members for $20 each. It is estimated that members of all the Vietnamese traveling gangs have access to these modified keys (New Jersey State Police, 1990).

Vietnamese gangs are active in almost every major metropolitan area in the United States; Vietnamese gang members are also in countries outside the United States. For instance, Toronto has had an increase in the number of home invasion robberies and shootings by Vietnamese street gangs, the Canadian police have identified BTK gang members from the New York City area as the main culprits in most of these incidents. According to Canadian law enforcement, the BTK gang has a number of criminal associates in Calgary, Montreal, Toronto, and Vancouver (Project North Star, 1993).

Australia has also had an increase in criminal activity involving Vietnamese gangs. Australian police have found that Vietnamese gangs have made a science out of extortion. According to Australian police, Vietnamese gangs practice extortion in four different types of places (Victoria Police, 1992):

1. *Restaurants.* Five or more Vietnamese gang members enter a specific restaurant; each gang member sits at a separate table and stays there for two or more hours. This method decreases the number of patrons who can eat at that location. The gang leader then refuses to pay any of the dinner bills. Gang members return to the restaurant until the owner pays a specific amount of extortion money to the gang.

2. *Businesses.* Vietnamese gang members block the business entranceway, forcing anyone who wants to enter the location to squeeze past or push the gang

member out of the way. The person who is attempting to enter the store then becomes the subject of ridicule from gang members. Gang members continue this practice until the business owner pays them the required protection money.

3. *Nightclubs.* One of the Vietnamese gang's leaders offers to supply protection to the nightclub owner for a specific fee. If the club owner refuses to pay extortion to the gang, gang members enter the club and cause problems by starting fights and damaging property. These gang activities continue until the owner succumbs to the extortion demands of the gang.

4. *General stores.* Vietnamese gang members enter a store and demand that the store owner loan them some money. Most of the store owners ultimately submit to these extortion requests.

Like their American counterparts, Asian members of the Australian community very seldom report any of these types of incidents to the police.

Australian police have found these Vietnamese gangs to be very similar to the Vietnamese gangs in California. The leader is usually older than the other gang members, and all gang members have tattoos that identify them as members of a specific gang. The Vietnamese gangs in Australia are involved in armed robberies of gas stations and convenience stores, thefts of motor vehicles, home invasion robberies, burglaries, and drug trafficking. Australian police have found that most gang members have guns readily available to them (Victoria Police, 1992).

All these Asian organized crime groups have prospered from most of their unlawful ventures, whether they be corporate extortion, computer chip, theft, or smuggling of prostitutes into other countries. Each group has created its own specialties; if it is a profitable scam, other groups use it, too. Yet of the home countries of these Asian criminal groups has taken any major steps to obliterate these groups. Sometimes we have to wonder whether political corruption is the reason these groups seem to be operating without any major roadblocks being put in their way.

KOREAN ORGANIZED CRIME

Federal law enforcement has indicated that Asian organized crime activities in the United States continue to increase sharply. The New York City metropolitan area has the second-largest Asian population in the United States. During 1992, approximately one-third of all the legal immigrants arriving in New York were from Asian countries; that large influx from Asia gave New York City some of the largest Asian ethnic communities in the United States.

One of the largest of these Asian ethnic groups settling in the New York City area was of Korean descent. Most Korean immigrants did not immediately assimilate the ways of American society; instead, they maintained the same moral standards and work ethic that were instilled in them during their upbringing in Korea. Instead of becoming a splinter group in their new environment, the Koreans formed their own communities in the United States and managed to set up their own businesses and housing within those same communities. For example, this type of Korean neighborhood exists in both Flushing, New York, and Koreatown, Los Angeles. The problem with this kind of community in New York City is that, sooner or later, it attracts the attention of the Asian criminal element from either that neighborhood or an adjoining area. At first, it was Chinese gangs from Chinatown in Manhattan who were attracted to Flushing because of the Chinese businesses in the area, but a short time later Korean gangs who were originally affiliated with the Chinese gangs started to appear on the streets of Queens. There are at least six Korean street gangs operating in this area of the city.

Korean History

Korean involvement in organized crime dates back to the early 1800s when an organized group of Korean businessmen was formed to smuggle jewels and drugs out of China to be used by the Korean nobility. It was not long after the formation of this group that other criminal associations started to appear in Korea. The Japanese occupation of Korea during World War II promoted the development of many of these criminal associations in Korea by fostering an atmosphere that allowed corrupt activity to control the environment.

These types of conditions ultimately led to the evolution of one of the most powerful Korean organized crime groups in the mid-1940s (U.S. Customs, 1994). This group, the Samurai Pa gang, became the most powerful force in Seoul by taking control of the central business district and the entertainment area known as Chong No. A major portion of the gang membership was made up of ethnic Japanese, with the minority group comprising Koreans (who were in the low ranks of the gang). Samurai Pa gang members were protected by the Japanese army because they cooperated with the military and provided the army with certain services (such as call girls); gang members also gathered information related to the activities of the Korean freedom fighters for dissemination by the Japanese military rulers.

Another Korean gang was formed when Tu Hwan Kim, a radical Korean independent freedom fighter, reappeared with his associates in Korea and quickly formed the Chong No Pa gang. There was immediate conflict between the Samurai Pa and the Chong No Pa gangs, and most of these hostilities revolved around control of the Chong No district in Seoul. The strife continued until Chong No Pa defeated Samurai Pa and took over control of the Chong No district.

At the end of World War II, Korea was hit with an unusual amount of societal chaos; the outcome of all this turmoil was an increase in the number of unemployed workers, which produced an expanded number of vagrants, beggars, and criminals within Korean society. During these cataclysmic times, the criminal element within this society, especially Chong No Pa, continued to prosper. This led to an increase in the number of gangs in Korea; a number of these new gangs started to appear throughout Seoul, with a major portion of the membership being recruited from unemployed workers. Most of these gangs concentrated on recruiting members from a specific region, town, village, or clan in an effort to create an area they could firmly control. Gang activity and recruitment were extremely intense in the Cholla Do section of the Korean peninsula. These new gangs had problems with previously entrenched rival gangs, such as the Chong No Pa. This led to most of these gangs operating on a hit-or-miss basis on local businesses and stores. This type of activity lasted until the gangs were finally able to take over some of the territories previously controlled by the Chong No Pa (FBI, 1993).

Some of the gangs that survived these trying times and ultimately triumphed over instability were Myong Dong, Tong Dae Moon Pa, Sodae Moon, and Mookyo Done Pa. All these gangs regulated different areas of Seoul, including sections from which these groups took their original names. Each of these gangs was a separate entity that functioned as a broad and adaptable organized crime system; they worked either together or separately. During the 1950s, Korean organized crime syndicates began to be classified into two different categories; political gangs and street gangs.

The most dominant gangs in Korea were the political gangs because of their attachment to corrupt politicians. These gangs were categorized as political groups because they were employed by corrupt politicians to use whatever method necessary to make opposing bureaucrats withdraw from an election race, relinquish their elected position, or throw their support to the criminal syndicates.

Most political gangs, besides being dominant, were well-established organizations that were substantially well connected with government officials. This put the political gangs in a favorable position and the Korean National Police (KNP) in an ineffective and powerless position regarding those gangs. In fact, the KNP very seldom interceded in any activities involving the gangs.

Once police interference was eliminated, the Chong No Pa, Mookyo Dong Pa, and Tong Dae Moon Pa gangs could do whatever they pleased without any interruptions. These criminal syndicates were able to operate all their illegal activities (loan-sharking, prostitution, gambling, smuggling). During this time, investigations by the KNP and the Korean Central Intelligence Agency indicate that the Korean gangs, specifically the Chong No Pa, renewed their relationships with the Japanese gangs. Although contact with the Yakuza was made, the negative effects of 35 years of both occupation and poor treatment at the hands of the Japanese during their reign in Korea made the impact initially insignificant. A working relationship between the Japanese and the Koreans was finally reestablished in the 1960s and firmed up in the 1970s (U.S. Customs, 1994).

Early in 1961, a military coup in South Korea resulted in General Park Chong Hee as the new Korean leader. Park immediately commanded his underlings to arrest all known gang members and place them in military camps to be reeducated on how to change their criminal lifestyle. The military rounded up hundreds of gang members and petty criminals and sent them to a desolate island off the coast of Inchon. A large portion of the gang leaders and their membership either were put to death by members of the military opposed to gang leaders or died because of poor prison conditions. The reeducation programs created by General Park Chong Hee were basically unsuccessful; the only thing these camps accomplished was the killing of numerous gang leaders and members. Ultimately, those who did not die in these camps were released by the government in early 1964 (U.S. Customs, 1994).

The Korean government's attempts to quell gang activities was short term because once the government started releasing gang members from the prison camps, gangs once again started to sprout up all over Korea. San-chong Sin, a camp releasee and a prior member of Chong No Pa, quickly established a new gang, the Cholla Do Pa, whose membership included hundreds of onetime Chong No Pa members. Within a short period of time, this gang took control of almost all the Cholla Do business and entertainment area in Seoul.

Another gang, the Bon Gae Pa (the lighting faction), was soon formed by Chong-sok Pak, a former captain in the Chong No Pa. The Bon Gae Pa gang became the major rival of Cholla Do Pa. These two groups continually battled over control of the main business and entertainment areas in Yongdongp'o, Cholla do, and other similar areas in the major cities of South Korea. After several years of hostilities, Bon Gae Pa took a major step by attacking the headquarters of the Cholla No Pa gang and killing Cholla leader San-chong Sin and many of his underbosses. This action helped Bon Gae Pa become the strongest and most feared gang in Seoul. During the mid-1970s, Bon Gae Pa membership increased so much that the gang was divided into three different groups—the Sobang Pa, the Yang Un Pa, and the Ob Pa—and Chong-sok Pak was in charge of all these gangs (KNP, 1994).

Pak delegated power to run these new gangs to several of his underbosses. Tae chon Kim and Chong chol Oh were appointed leaders of the Sobang Pa; Yang Un Pa was named after and controlled by Yang un Cho, who had participated with Pak in a political gang prior to being imprisoned by the military. The leader of the Ob Pa gang was Tong chae Yi, who also ran the Ho Rang Yi Pa (the tiger faction) gang. Yi took over the leadership of the Ob Pa gang by murdering Pak while Pak was visiting one of his criminal operations in Kwangju, Cholla-do. A short time later, Tong chae Yi moved his headquarters, along with most of his Ob Pa gang members to Seoul. Yi made sure he would remain in control over his unlawful activities in Kwangju by leaving a sufficient number of Ob Pa gang members in Kwangju to supervise operations there (KNP, 1994).

The second form of Korean gang was the street gangs. These groups of paltry lawbreakers roamed the streets of Korea victimizing local businesses and amusement areas. The street gangs' major methods of financing their operations were extorting funds from businesses within the area of their operation and having the rights to black market goods. The street gang members were characterized as street urchins by both the citizens and the Korean police. In most cases, the Korean street gangs did not create the same major type of violent threat to society as present-day street gangs do.

Gang Activity in Korea. During the 1970s, the Korean gangs started expanding their criminal operations by taking complete control of a major portion of the convert economic activities throughout Korea. The profits gained by the gangs from these illegal operations were then reinvested in legal businesses. For years most major media organizations in Korea have alleged that members of Korean organized crime gangs financed some of Korea's major corporations during the early stages of their development (U.S. Treasury Department, 1995).

One Korean organized crime syndicate, the KTA (Korean Tourist Association)—or the KK (Korean Killers) as this chapter calls this gang—instituted a scam in the late 1970s that provided its members with increasing profits. This conspiracy involved the use of Korean females to work as prostitutes in both Korea and the United States. The KK gang created a perfect way for the females to gain entry into the United States as U.S. citizens. The KK used Korean prostitutes, who were in many cases purchased from their families when they were in early adolescence, and sent them to "farms" (locations owned and controlled by the KK) where they served as prostitutes for members of the Korean military.

These females also worked in local bars, massage parlors, and hotels (owned by members of the KK) that provided sexual services to members of the U.S. military. Gang members who owned massage parlors or houses of prostitution in the United States contacted KK members in Korea and made arrangements for sham marriages to be arranged between U.S. servicemen and these Korean prostitutes. KK members expedited all the required paperwork, including visa documents and marital paperwork, and arranged travel to the locations where the females were to work upon their arrival in the United States (KNP, 1994).

Upon arrival in the United States, these women were monetarily obligated to the Korean gang and had to work a number of years to pay back their debt to the gang. In most cases, the women barely survived during the years they worked for the gang because they were paid less than minimum wage for long and arduous hours (FBI, 1993).

As the KK was building its empire, other Korean gangs were also increasing their membership and business opportunities. For example, the Cholla Do gang continued to grow by recruiting new members and by absorbing smaller gangs into Cholla Do membership. The constant expansion of the gang members into legitimate businesses led to the necessity for them to become more complex associations, which resulted in the growth of other organized criminal syndicates in Korea. One of the first and largest criminal syndicates is the Hoguk Ch' Ongyon Yonhap Hae (Korean National Defense Youth Federation), formed and controlled by Sung wan Yi. Later, Tae chon Kim organized the Sin U Hae (Trusted Friendship Association) after his liberation from prison, where he had served time for gang-connected crimes. During his tenure in prison, Kim had become affiliated with the Full Gospel Christian Church; after his release from prison, he induced members of the Full Gospel Christian Church to join his group under the pretense that his association was involved in benevolent work. The Korean government views the Full Gospel Christian Church as a religious organization whose membership is made up of Korean dissidents. This group has expanded to the United States, where it presently has numerous members and several houses of worship. One other group that should be included here is the

Songhap Hae (Pine Tree Association), which is controlled by Hang Hak Kim (U.S. Treasury Department, 1995).

Besides these larger criminal organizations, ATF there are a number of smaller Korean syndicates that are influential and should be part of our dicussion. Included in this group are the Yang Un, Suwon Pa, Ho Rang Yi Pa, Mokpo Pa, Taejon Pa, Tong Song Pa, Hyan Chon Pa, Chil Song Pa, E Sheep Sa Gae Pa, Tae Ho Pa, Tong A Pa, Kukchae Pa, Pusan Yongdo Pa, Piba Ram Pa, and Yong O Pa Uichong Hae Pa. All Korean gangs, large and small, are heavily involved in drug trafficking, control of liquor and food in entertainment areas, gambling casinos, loan-sharking, money laundering, political corruption, credit card fraud, and tax fraud in Korea. Most of these organized crime syndicates have managed to create and maintain exhaustive lists of local and worldwide contacts that are in both legitimate and illegitimate businesses.

Korean Gangs

Prior to the mid-1980s, most Korean organized crime groups were considered nothing more than small subdivisions of either the Chinese or the Japanese organized crime groups in the United States. Since that time, federal law enforcement sources have come to the conclusion that Korean crime syndicates are a considerable threat to American society. These Korean criminal groups are involved in diverse illegal operations in the United States including drug trafficking, money laundering, and production and dispersal of bogus brand-name goods. One example of Korean gang activity is gang participation in the trafficking of crystal methamphetamine ("ice").

Korean syndicates continue to grow and change within our society. Investigative data gathered by several federal law enforcement agencies in the early 1990s indicated there were approximately 150 different Korean criminal syndicates in the United States, with about 35 percent of them actively participating in criminal activities. It was estimated that these active Korean gangs in the United States had somewhere between 2,000 and 3,000 members (U.S. Customs, 1994).

There are three major issues to be examined when considering Korean gangs in the United States. The first is the increasing influence of Korean gangs within Korean communities in the United States. Second is the long-standing relationship between the Japanese gangs (which are becoming increasingly active in the United States) and the Korean gangs. Most gang transactions between the Japanese and Koreans involve the distribution of methamphetamine; both these groups have recognized the potential profits if they work together. The third issue is the unlawful operations in the United States involving already-entrenched Korean groups that are firmly linked to long-established gangs in both Korea and the rest of Southeast Asia, which was evident during a seizure of over 400 pounds of Southeast Asian heroin from Korean gang members (U.S. Customs Service, 1994).

Korean Power Gangs.   In the early 1980s, Korean Power gangs started to surface in several major cities throughout the United States. Newly immigrated Koreans were quick to form Korean Power gangs in Chicago, Denver, Los Angeles, New York, and Washington, D.C. It was not long before the Washington, D.C., group expanded into areas in both Maryland and Virginia. At first, the Korean Power groups were just interested in extorting money from local Korean businessmen, but it did not take these groups long to extend their operations into other criminal activities.

Membership in the Korean Power gang in the New York metropolitan area continued to grow, which generated a great amount of distress within the Korean community there. Gang members intimidated local businessmen in order to extort money; they also committed home invasion robberies. For example, five members of a Korean Power gang were arrested in May 1993 for terrorizing and extorting money from owners of Korean businesses in Midtown Manhattan (between 28th and 48th Streets from Madison to 7th Avenue). These merchants were forced to pay anywhere from $50 to $200 a week protection money plus feed gang members for free (O'Shaughnessy, 1993). According to the New York City Police Department, the Korean Power gang is aligned with the Korean Merchant Association (124 West 24th Street, New York City); in fact, the Korean Merchant Association controls the activities of the Korean Power gang (1993).

A direct spinoff of the Korean Power gang is the Junior Korean Power (JKP) gang, which spread its tentacles throughout New York City. This gang is made up of youths between the ages of 14 and 30 and has an estimated membership of 75 to 100. The JKP gang's criminal activities include extortion, home invasion robberies, protection money from bars and houses of prostitution, kidnapping, and weapons possession. Federal law enforcement investigative reports indicate that the JKP gang is heavily involved in the production and distribution of methamphetamine in New York. This gang is well organized; in many cases, its members are heavily armed. Members of this gang have been arrested for rapes, robberies, and murders in recent years.

The Korean Fuk Ching gang comprises both an older and a younger faction. The older members are involved in traditional organized criminal activities and direct the activities of the younger members (usually 14 to 30 years old), who participate in

---

ACTIVE QUEENS GANGS

White Tigers

Korean Power

Green Dragons

Korean Fuk Chings

Flying Dragons

Ghost Shadows

Taiwan Boys (Mandarin speaking)

Source: NYPD, 1994.

GANG ACTIVITIES

Extortion

Massage parlors

Gambling

Narcotics trafficking

Firearms

Auto theft

Assault

Kidnapping

Burglary

Robbery

Credit card fraud

Protection

Source: NYPD, 1994.

---

extortion, kidnapping, robbery, and drug dealing. Adolescent members are usually recruited from local high schools. The Fuk Ching gang presently operates throughout Brooklyn and Queens.

The Korean Flying Dragons gang is affiliated with the Chinatown Hip Sing Tong gang and its associate, the Chinese Flying Dragons gang. The Flying Dragons gang operates throughout Queens and is involved in robbery, kidnapping, and extortion; members of this street gang are between 14 and 30 years old. In December 1992, seven members of the Korean Flying Dragons were arrested for the robbery of the World Taberah World Mission in Flushing, Queens. The suspects entered the church armed with a machine gun and several pistols; they beat the pastor and forced the parishioners to lie down on the floor while gang members mocked and humiliated them. The robbers then compelled the congregation's members to surrender their money, jewelry, and house keys (Sullivan, 1992).

California Korean Street Gangs.   The first Korean street gang to make an appearance in California was AB (American Burger), which was formed to protect Korean high school students from being assaulted by other high school ethnic gang members. This led to the formation of other Korean street gangs. One of the most vicious gangs was the Korean Killers (KK) street gang; it was also known as the K75K, which stands for Korean [number representing year] Killers. The latter name (using the year) was a way for this gang to identify different sections of its gang.

Another Korean gang that appeared in the same time period as the Korean Killers was the BK (Burger King) gang. The Burger King gang was very active in the Koreatown area of Los Angeles. The leader of this gang was BK Sam (or Mustang Sam), who went on to become one of the most notorious Korean gang members in Los Angeles (U.S. Customs, 1994).

Three other gangs were based out of Garden Grove, California. One was known as the Garden Grove Boys or the Garden Grove Koreans; its total membership was somewhere around 50. Almost all the activities of this group took place in Los Angeles. This gang had an ongoing conflict with both the South Bay Killers and the Wah Ching. Two other gangs that appeared later in Garden Grove were the Korean Town Mob and the Asian Town Koreans. These gangs created problems for the Garden Grove Boys, and there are conflicts between these gangs (U.S. Customs, 1994).

The Los Angeles Korean gangs are similar to the local Vietnamese gangs in that a major portion of the members in both gangs are between 16 and 25 years old. Both gangs have token white members and are very mobile. The Koreans concentrate their criminal efforts within the Korean community, just as the Vietnamese gangs target Vietnamese communities. The Korean gangs and their criminal activities are known to all the Korean communities throughout the United States.

At one time, respect was a very important factor for all members of Korean gangs. More mature gang members came to be known as older brothers, while youthful or newer members were referred to as younger brothers. This respect helped the gangs maintain good relationships in their own gangs and prevented gang members from becoming overzealous. Since the late 1980s, decreasing respect of younger gang members for older ones has created a number of problems within Korean gangs and may ultimately produce gang warfare. Younger gang members are now far more aggressive and violent than their predecessors, who were guided by the respect with which all members treated each other.

The West Coast Korean gangs benefit greatly from street robberies as well as home and business robberies. Gang members carefully preplan all their criminal activities prior to executing them. Victims of these crimes are usually known to gang members and are put under surveillance in order for the gang to gather information prior to committing the criminal acts. Once all the information is gathered, a plan is put in place, which includes another way of carrying out the crime in case something goes wrong with the first plan and a strategy for escape after the crime is committed.

The Korean gangs are involved in burglaries, extortion, kidnappings, and auto thefts. California law enforcement authorities indicate that Korean gangs are involved in street sales of rock cocaine and other illegal narcotics (including marijuana and heroin), but the gangs' major area of narcotic trafficking is in the distribution of methamphetamines. For example, the Honolulu Organized Crime Drug Enforcement Task Force (OCDETF) started an investigation that led to Paciano Sonny Guerrero, who was a major producer and dispenser of methamphetamines throughout Hawaii. The results of this inquiry led the investigators to two Korean nationals: Dae Sung Lee, who headed up methamphetamine trafficking in Hawaii in the mid-1980s and into the 1990s, and

ASIAN GANGS IN LOS ANGELES

1. Asian Boyz, Westside (ABZ)
2. Asian Criminals (ASC)
3. Atwater Villa Pinoy Real (PR)
4. Avenue Oxford Boys (AOB)
5. Cambodian Boyz
6. Crazyies (CYS) (may be inactive)
7. Flipside Trece (FS13)
8. Fliptown Mob (FTM)
9. Ken Side Wah Ching (KWC)
10. Korean Play Boys (KPB)
11. Korean Pride (KP)
12. Korea Town Gangsters (KTG)
13. Korea Town Mobsters (KTM)
14. LA Oriental Boys (LAOB)
15. LA Satanas (STS)
16. Last Generation Korean Killers (LGKK)
17. Lost Boys (LB)
18. Maplewood Jefrox (JFX)
19. Mental BoyZ (MBZ)
20. Oriental Lazy Boys (OLB)
21. Rebel Boys (RBS)
22. Silly Boys (SYB)
23. Sunny Side Wah Ching (KWC)
24. Tau Gamma Pinoy (TGP)
25. Temple Street (TST)
26. Tres Cantos (TCS)
27. Vietnamese Boys (V BOYS)

Ki Woon Kim, who forced Lee to flee to Korea and took over command of the methamphetamine importation business. The final results of this investigation pointed to Los Angeles (as well as Seattle and Tacoma), where half the supply of methamphetamines was produced; the other half came from suppliers in Japan, South Korea, and Taiwan (U.S. Department of Treasury, ATF, 1993).

Korean Criminal Activities

Connections between the Korean gangs and the Yakuza have already been mentioned in this chapter, but some aspects of the relationship between these two groups must be further discussed. Intelligence gathered by Japanese, Korean, and U.S. law enforcement agencies show that the Yamaguchi Gumi and three large Japanese gangs—the Pusan Yongdo Pa, the Chil Song Pa (seven stars), and the E Sheep Sae Gae Pa (twenty centuries)—have been involved in smuggling methamphetamines ("ice"), guns, and other restricted materials between Japan and Korea.

Another major Japanesee group, the Toa Yuai Jigyo Kumiai (TYJK), has taken control of a large portion of methamphetamine distribution in Hawaii and on the West Coast of the United States. As previously mentioned (under the Japanese Organized Crime section of this chapter), about 15 percent of the TYJK gang and most of its hierarchy are of Korean descent (FBI, 1992). The drug-trafficking activities of the TYJK gang were connected to five Korean gangs: Ho Sei Kai, New Obi Group, Yung Gun Pae, Korean White Tigers, and So Bon Pae. Further evidence turned up by federal law enforcement agencies showed that members of Yakuza gang met for several days with the Pusan Yongdo Pa gang in Pusan, South Korea. Another factor that pointed to an affiliation being formed between the Japanese and Korean groups was brought to light by Korean police. Korean police information showed that almost all Korean gangs started adopting Yakuza guidelines related to loyalty, responsibility, and morality of group members. The transferring of mandatory group membership rules from Japanese to Korean gangs members definitely strengthened the development of the Korean gangs and their affiliation with the Yakuza (U.S. Customs, 1994).

U.S. and foreign law enforcement agencies are aware of the ever-increasing criminal activity involving members of Korean organized crime. The emergence of Korean crime syndicates in the United States poses three major problems for law enforcement organizations throughout the world. The first critical issue facing authorities is the proven ability of Korean gangs to easily establish bases for their unlawful activities in major urban centers in the United States. Besides setting up these bases for their gang operations, Korean groups have also been able to establish and run their illegal criminal operations—specifically, drug smuggling, money laundering, prostitution, and production and marketing of fraudulent brand-name goods—with very little or no interference from law enforcement agencies. Added to this is the fact that Korean gangs have already established a working relationship with Yakuza groups and have adopted Yakuza operational policies.

The second major concern of law enforcement relates to the management and operation of Korean organized crime syndicates. Most Korean groups were thought to be loosely knit organizations strewn throughout the United States. These Korean gangs were heavily involved in a number of serious criminal incidents, including the smuggling of 440 pounds of heroin into the United States during the summer of 1993. The only information relating these Korean gangs to any larger organizations was detected by the New York City Police Department (NYPD), whose investigators were able to find a connection between the Korean Merchant Association in New York City and the Korean Power gangs. Data gathered by the NYPD indicated that this relationship was far more involved than first anticipated. In fact, the connection between these two groups is very similar to the relationship between the Hip Sing Tong and the Flying Dragons street gangs. Gang members protect merchants' business enterprises; collect overdue payments from people who fail to repay debts, loans, or bills; and force competitors out of business (1994).

The third issue facing law enforcement relates to the sudden influx of Korean criminals into the United States, which became evident when the Korean media informed U.S. law enforcement agencies that a large number of Korean criminals were immigrating to the United States; this notification was done through the use of Korean TV stations in both Los Angeles and New York. This information was verified when Korean law enforcement sources indicated that they had data showing well over 100 Korean criminals presently involved in developing and operating criminal enterprises in the United States (Interpol, 1993). Intelligence further indicated that many of these Korean criminals set up their operations away from the previously established Korean communities in Los Angeles and New York and set up their bases in areas of the Carolinas, Florida, and Georgia. There is no doubt among law enforcement authorities that these criminals will ultimately form Korean organized crime syndicates throughout the United States. The success of other Asian criminal syndicates in the United States also played an important role in the recent immigration of Korean criminals into the United States.

CONCLUSIONS

It has become quite evident that Korean organized crime groups have already established bases in at least two major urban areas of the United States. As the immigration of Korean citizens to the United States continues to increase, so will the criminal activities of the Korean gangs. The new arrivals from Korea, like their Asian predecessors from China and Japan, will open businesses; once this happens, the Korean gangs will move in and start extorting money from these businesses.

There is no doubt that Korean criminal groups are now operating at the international level, thanks to the formidable relationship the Koreans forged with Japanese gangs. Some criminal activities that the Korean gangs in the United States are already involved in are gambling, extortion, prostitution, alien smuggling, loan-sharking, drug trafficking, and marketing of counterfeited products. Among the gangs that have surfaced in the United States are the Korean Power gangs, Korean Killers, Korean Flying Dragons, White Tigers, Green Dragons, Korean Town Mob, Korean Honam Power, Jul Ra Do, and Korean Fuk Ching. The majority of these gangs model themselves after Chinese street gangs. In some cases, the Korean gangs are outgrowths of Chinese gangs, having originally being formed under Chinese tutelage. Presently, Korean gangs are operating in Atlanta, Baltimore, Boston, Chicago, Detroit, Honolulu, Los Angeles,

New Orleans, New York, Philadelphia, San Francisco, Seattle, and Washington, D.C. The Koreans' ability to set up their gangs and criminal operations in major U.S. cities seems to indicate that there is a bright future for Korean organized crime syndicates throughout this country.

The growth of the newer Korean as well as Vietnamese organized crime groups has also been the result of the increased number of legal and illegal youthful immigrants entering the United States from both these countries (this was especially true during the early 1970s when a large number of youthful Vietnamese immigrants entered the United States). With little or no parental guidance available to them, some of these young men succumbed to peer pressure placed on them by gang members and became active in gang activity.

All these Asian organized crime groups have prospered from most of their unlawful ventures, whether they be corporate extortion, computer chip theft, or smuggling of prostitutes into other countries. Each group has created its own specialties; if it is a profitable scam, other groups use it, too. Yet not one of the home countries of these Asian criminal groups has taken any major steps to obliterate these groups. Sometimes we have to wonder whether political corruption is the reason these groups seem to be operating without any major roadblocks being put in their way.

CHAPTER **10**

HISPANIC GANGS

When Hispanic organized crime is discussed, the first ethic group to come to mind would be either the Colombians or the Mexicans because of their notoriety in the media, but historically the original Hispanic organized crime group was Cuban. This ethnic group was at one time very closely associated with La Cosa Nostra through its gambling activities. The Colombian crime families appeared only after Colombians realized the amount of profits Cuban gangs were accumulating through the sale of cocaine. As the Colombian groups increased their fortunes through the distribution and sale of drugs, Mexican groups started making their mark by forming jail gangs. As these gangs grew, some expanded operations throughout the United States while other Mexican groups enlarged their drug operations in Mexico. Dominican organized crime groups, on the other hand, only appeared on the scene in the last two decades, yet they have received a good deal of attention because of the violent actions they use to control the street drug market. Through the use of violent activities, the Dominicans gained the respect of all the major drug importers. With this information in mind, we now introduce you to the first of our Hispanic crime families.

CUBAN ORGANIZED CRIME

Cuban History

The role of some Cuban crime groups in our society is somewhat similar to that of the Italian mafia, from which the Cuban organizational crime structure emanated several decades ago. Research indicates that there are three basic types of Cuban groups: The first is the older structured gangs that run a majority of numbers, policy, and *bolita* rackets from New York to Florida, with the blessings of La Cosa Nostra; the second type of criminal group evolved out of the Mariel boat lifts of the early 1980s and is noted for its violence; the third group consists of members of Fidel Castro's Communist regime in Cuba.

Historically, the first Cuban organized criminal groups were strongly influenced by members of La Cosa Nostra. The relationship between Cuban organized crime and La Cosa Nostra was formed in Cuba during the Batista regime when gambling and corruption were in vogue in Havana. Just about all the gaming casinos in Havana were controlled by La Cosa Nostra under the guidance of Meyer Lansky. The first two Cuban organized crime groups in the United States were the Corporation and La Compania and were formed by some of the early arrivals from Cuba. They had the following characteristics:

1. They were more far-reaching and much more organized than later groups.
2. They were far more capable than other gangs of forming lasting relationships with other crime groups.
3. They were far less violent than future Cuban gangs.
4. They were heavily involved in gambling and narcotics trafficking but had very little participation in other types of gang crimes.
5. They were more than qualified to create a structured criminal empire.

Cuban Gangs

The Corporation.   A short time after its formation, the Corporation became very active in illegal gambling activities. Some of their original *bolita* and policy operations were set up and run in Dade County, Florida, during the early 1960s. Cuban gambling cartels established their illegal betting businesses so that each part of the enterprise would be capable of booking bets with another faction within the scheme rather than placing bets with Italian gangs. Jose Miguel Battle (also known as El Gordo or Don Miguel) has been the "godfather" or boss since the inception of the Corporation. Battle was originally a soldier in the Cuban army and later became a police officer during Batista's control over Cuba. A short time after he fled Cuba, Battle joined Brigade 2506; he participated in the Bay of Pigs invasion, which failed to get any of the promised support from then U.S. President John F. Kennedy.

Upon his return to Miami, Battle laid out plans to operate and control a Cuban gambling operation in Florida using the help of other veterans of the Bay of Pigs invasion. Once this first business was solvent, Battle set up a meeting with La Cosa Nostra bosses Joe Zicarelli and Santo Trafficante to get an okay to move his gambling operations north. The Italian gangs were slow in showing their support of Battle, so he started using force (whenever necessary) to take control of some northern policy operations. Another meeting was quickly arranged between Battle, Zicarelli, and James Napoli; a settlement was negotiated that permitted Battle to operate his policy and *bolita*, providing he pay a specific percentage of earnings to La Cosa Nostra. Since the inception of this Italian-Cuban criminal conspiratorship, the average gross weekly income averaged approximately $2.5 million to $3 million, with an annual net profit of somewhere between $120 million and $135 million (FBI, 1993).

Under the leadership of Jose Battle, the Corporation garnered hundreds of millions of dollars in profits from gambling ventures. A great deal of this money has been reinvested in both domestic and foreign monetary establishments as well as in the purchase of other types of financial instruments. These investment ventures were coupled with the purchase of a vast amount of property throughout the state of Florida. Some of the following legitimate companies are associated with the Corporation (President's Commission on Organized Crime, 1986):

El Zapotal Realty

Union Finance Company

Union Financial Research Company

Union Management and Mortgage Company

Union Travel and Tours

Jose Battle has had his problems with law enforcement representatives over the years. He was convicted of running a racketeer-influenced corrupt organization, for which he served 13 months, and was charged with both weapons possession and the murder of Ernest Torres (an ex-member of the Corporation). The latter ultimately led to an 18-month sentence for Battle. Considering the time and effort spent by federal, state, and local law enforcement agencies to arrest and convict Battle for these charges, it seems apparent that although law enforcement agencies won some skirmishes and convicted him, Jose Battle easily won the war by doing only a total of 31 months in jail.

In 1982, Battle moved his base of operations from New York to Florida and quickly purchased over a million dollars worth of real estate, paying $800,000 in cash. The purchase of real estate by criminal organizations is probably the easiest way to launder money, even though in most cases it is a long-term investment. In 1983 at two different locations, both Battle's son, Jose Jr., and a very close associate, Humberto Davila Torres, were seized with large amounts of U.S. currency.

The Corporation is consistently seeking ways to launder money so that the money can be utilized for legal ventures. Thus far, the Corporation has managed to build an elaborate network of influence within both the banking and real estate markets. The Corporation invested large amounts of its gambling profits in the Capital National Bank of New York. It turns out that this bank redeems the largest amount of food stamps in the United States; the largest number of food stamp coupons received by this bank came from local bars and restaurants located in established Cuban neighborhoods in Northern New Jersey. According to federal officials, members of the Corporation purchase the coupons from food stamp recipients at rates that are anywhere from 10 to 25 percent higher than the actual value of the stamps; they then allow customers who receive the food stamps to wager using the coupons in place of U.S. currency. In this way, the food stamps are used as a device to launder illegally obtained gambling money (President's Commission on Organized Crime, 1986).

The Corporation's involvement in money-laundering scams does not stop with the purchase of food stamps. During a 1985 federal investigation, it was discovered that members of the Corporation had become mixed up in a deceitful scheme that involved the purchase of winning tickets in the legitimate Puerto Rican lottery. Members of the Corporation had taken control of all the U.S. distributors and salespersons of Puerto Rican lottery tickets. Lottery ticket agents, who worked for the Corporation, were notified to contact the Corporation with the names and addresses of any person holding winning tickets that will pay large sums of money to the holder. Corporation members would then contact the winning person and offer to purchase the ticket from them at a higher price; the usual amount paid for the ticket was anywhere from 20 to 25 percent higher than the actual amount won, so if the ticket paid $125,000, the Corporation would give the ticket owner anywhere from $150,000 to $160,000 for the ticket. A Corporation member would then cash the ticket in Puerto Rico, and the proceeds, after taxes, would be approximately $80,000 in U.S. currency. This scheme enabled the Corporation to launder money it had illegally obtained from gambling or narcotics operations. The U.S. currency would then be legally deposited in a financial institution or invested in stocks, bonds, or realty without any possible indication of the money's true origin. Federal law enforcement officials claim that a total of more than $43 million in currency has been confiscated from the Corporation since the early 1960s. These same officials also assert that Corporation leaders have accumulated so much profit from gambling operations that they are more than willing to pay $2 for $1 in order to launder their money (President's Commission on Organized Crime, 1986b).

The Corporation has maintained a very low profile in communities where it operates gambling enterprises. In fact, in the neighborhoods where the Cubans run gambling operations, most residents have no idea that the men running the operations are of Cuban descent. Strict enforcement of the gambling activities of organized criminal groups is considered a low priority by most law enforcement agencies. The Corporation membership is aware of this fact and operate in the open marketplace using store-fronts and bodegas as their bases of operation in most neighborhoods. In some cases, the Corporation has gone so far as to put slot machines in some of their gambling locations. During the fall of 1994, the New York City Police Department attempted to put a dent in the Corporation's illegal gambling operations by raiding the gang's New York headquarters at 750 Kappock Avenue in the Bronx and a number of other gambling locations throughout New York City. The raid of the Corporation's headquarters resulted in the seizure of $280,000 in currency and approximately $270,000 in jewelry, but no significant information was obtained against Battle or any of his main operatives (Perez-Pena, 1994). Police have found that members of this organization refuse to cooperate with the police or to inform on other gang members or their activities. This is probably one of the major reasons, along with the gang's reluctance to get heavily involved in drug trafficking, why law enforcement efforts against this group have been minimal.

La Compania.   The other long-standing Cuban organized crime group, La Compania, was also formed in the 1960s, but its main activity involved the importation of cocaine, heroin, and marijuana. Prior to the takeover of the cocaine business by Colombian groups, the Cubans were the major suppliers of cocaine on the East Coast, and this operation was run by members of La Compania; presently, this group is still involved in the importation of both cocaine and heroin. It is estimated that total membership of this gang is about 200, with its base of operations in Miami and other chapters in New York City, Las Vegas, Los Angeles, as well as parts of Mexico, New Jersey, and Texas. Information related to La Compania is somewhat limited because this is a very close-knit group that runs a covert drug-smuggling operation. Members are scattered throughout the United States, and all of their narcotics transactions are wholesaled to a select group of buyers and transpire at concealed locations. This group has been fairly successful in avoiding the attention of law enforcement and has managed to stay out of the limelight; in doing so, it has managed to avoid both police and media attention.

Marielitos Banditos.   Just prior to Easter 1980, 25 Cubans gained asylum at the Peruvian embassy in Havana. Castro had originally placed Cuban police around the embassy but then decided that these people were now in the hands of the Peruvian government and to let Peruvian diplomats worry about them. This decision turned out to be a major blunder on Castro's part because on Easter Sunday morning the crowd outside the embassy had swelled to over 10,000 people. Castro apparently had no idea how many disillusioned Cubans would seek asylum at the Peruvian embassy once Cuban security forces left the embassy. Most members of this group at the embassy came from what can be considered the working class of Cuba; several nations, including the United States, volunteered to accept some of these refugees, which would result in a departure of Cuban citizens from Mariel Harbor, about 30 miles outside of Havana, for the United States. Castro finally acceded to the departure of the refugees and charged each citizen $750 to leave Cuba, but in an effort to cause embarrassment to the U.S. government, Castro also ordered all of his military, police, and correctional personnel to locate (if they were not already incarcerated) deviants, including ex-convicts, drug addicts, vagrants, delinquents, and the mentally ill. Once these people were rounded up, they were confined to a high-security makeshift prison camp near the El Mosquito plantation outside of Mariel and became part of the refugee group.

Through the use of the Mariel boat lift, Castro was able to send 25,000 people with criminal records to U.S. shores. This turned out to be about 10 percent of the total number of refugees who arrived in the United States from Cuba during this boat lift. A large portion of the Marielitos (as this criminal element/gang would be known) were criminals who had spent a number of years confined to a torturous Cuban prison environment where cruelty and viciousness were common practice; this atmosphere, with its cruel and inhumane conditions, transformed many of these weak, poor, uneducated Afro-Cuban criminals into psychopaths.

A short time after this group's arrival on U.S. shores, a gang network was set up. Some of the Marielitos were interviewed, issued residency cards, and quickly released into our society. Others were incarcerated so that an in-depth check could be done on their criminal and psychological histories. Once the Marielitos with criminal backgrounds were released into local communities, they quickly established houses that were used for meeting gang members and organizing criminal activities; through the use of these so-called safe houses, the leaders of this criminal organization were able to recruit and consolidate members at several different locations. These locations gave members of the Marielitos gang the opportunity to meet and socialize with other participants in gang operations—both old friends and newly recruited members—in a friendly setting. These houses also presented the gang leaders with a chance to locate and sponsor the release of gang associates who had been held in detention centers since their arrival in the United States. This sponsorship was originally created to get gang members with special criminal skills out of detention camps, but with the gang's increasing involvement in criminal and drug activities, anyone with a criminal background was a possible new recruit for gang membership.

Gang members were recruited by members of both the Corporation and La Compania as collectors for overdue gambling or narcotics debts. They were instructed to injure or maim anyone who refused to pay past liabilities or to kill anyone who declined to pay off large debts or, for that matter, anyone who was considered competition for these groups. The Colombian gangs found work for some of the Marielitos as drug couriers and hit men. Several gang members became involved with local vehicle theft groups. The majority of gang members set up their own criminal operations, using money gained from their crimes to purchase high-powered handguns, shotguns, and rifles.

Along with the formation of the Marielitos gang, there came a drastic increase in the amount of crime within as well as outside the Cuban community. Increases in criminality is somewhat accepted in most U.S. communities, but the violence associated with the unlawful activities of the Marielitos brought an uproar in almost every community where the gang's criminal acts took place. This gang brought a new meaning to the words "violent crime." It seems that members of the Marielitos gang terminated almost every criminal incident they were involved in with some type of brutal and vicious act: Body parts were cut off, words were carved on the bodies of victims, or victims were set on fire, viciously raped, sodomized, and/or murdered in a ritualistic manner.

Marielitos is a gang that has a cult-like image surrounding its membership. A good deal of the gang members have very little education in their backgrounds, but most have served in the Cuban military; under Cuban law, it is mandatory that everyone over a certain age serve time in the military, and a portion of their military service was done in either the Congo or Central America. Most Marielito members have scars on their bodies that either were self-inflicted or resulted from some type of religious ritual. Approximately 90 percent of gang members have tattoos on their bodies, and this tattooing of their bodies by the Marielitos indicates that they realize they are pariahs according to other members of Cuban society. Tattooing is looked upon as a sign of disgrace by legitimate Cuban citizens, who have labeled these criminals "guzanos" (worms) or "escoria" (scum). Gang members have a number of different types of tattoos on their bodies:

1. Saints or other Christian religious symbols
2. Writings or drawings associated with a special saint (e.g., Santa Barbara or Saint Barbara, goddess of vengeance)
3. Names, writings, or drawings in an African dialect (e.g., *Firmas*, which means signatures)

4. Tattoos of their secret society's emblem, with words attached (e.g., Abakwa Secret Society or a Strawman)

5. Tombstones with names of deceased relatives on them

6. Drawings of American Indians (usually with some type of religious meaning attached, such as a drawing of a female Indian, which symbolizes protection from danger)

7. Animals (usually predators such as sharks, snakes, or leopards)

8. Women (usually naked, pictured with weapons and with animals that are predators)

9. Locations (usually associated with their past, such as a prison)

10. Names of wives or girlfriends

Most of these tattoos are coarsely drawn or written during the gang member's time in prison. Dots are also drawn on the hands and indicate that this person has done some time in prison; a tattoo inside the lower lip usually denotes this person's prisoner identification number. In some cases, five dots on a person's hand denotes that this person is a pickpocket, and an arrow-shaped tattoo in the web of the hand will indicate that this person is a member of the Abaqua religious sect. The tattooing tells outsiders that members of the Marielitos gang do not trust anyone.

Tattooing is in many cases associated with the superstition and religious beliefs of the Marielitos gang. Almost all Marielitos are members of what is basically an Afro-Cuban religious group known as Santeria, which combines African religion, Christianity, and superstition into one religious sect. These are some rudimentary Santeria doctrines (DEA, 1990):

1. Every human being has an Orisha, which is a patron saint or guardian angel who should be honored throughout a person's life.

2. As practicing members of this religious cult, they obtain an ability to interpret omens.

3. They hold to the concept of ache, which pertains to the achievement of power.

4. Priests are called Santeros, Santeras, Babalawos, and Espirititas.

5. Believers usually get initiated through a number of other types of rituals.

6. Believers can be tormented for several different reasons: a disregard for the Orishas or other departed souls; curses placed on believers by another person (Brujeria, Bilongo); acts of stealing the head (Eleda) or being given the evil eye (Mal de Ojo); and failure to keep pledges or other acts outlawed by the religion.

What this religion does is give these criminals a sense of power and confidence. Some of the saints gang members pay homage to are Chango who is Saint Barbara, warrior and protector of criminals; Eleggua, who is the Christ child who helps them avoid trouble; Oshun, who is the saint of charity, love, and marriage; Babalu-aye, who is Saint Lazarus, a leper who walks with two dogs; and Oggun, who is Saint Peter, who watches over their weapons and metal objects.

This religion does not use the Bible or any other scriptures. Believers go to graves in cemeteries to steal skulls and bones, which they use in their ritualistic ceremonies, and they get together in family-like groups that have a godfather. The rituals or ceremonies are conducted in a room containing many lit candles; in most cases, animals are sacrificed during these sessions. Rites and ceremonies used in Santeria practices include Trabajos (Works), Limpiezas (Cleansing), Rogaciones de Cabeza (Prayers of the Head), Hacer Santo (Making Saint), Cumpleanos (Birthdays), Feasts of Catholic Saints, Matanzas (Killings), Tanbores, Violines (Drums, Violins), and Ofrendas al Santo (Offerings to the Saint) (Dade County Sheriff's Department, 1991).

Many of the Marielitos also practice Palo Mayombe, which is basically the committing of serious crimes during their mystical-type rituals. These ceremonies involve the use of altars, religious artifacts, human remains, burning candles, and stabbing dolls. These criminals honor the god of hunting, Ochosi, whom they believe will grant them ways to avoid apprehension after committing a crime and help them avoid being sent to prison. If they continually practice these religious rituals, members of the Marielitos gang, gain a sense of invincibility, which has led to their taking great risks during criminal ventures. This type of perception poses a very dangerous threat both to potential victims of their crimes and to the police.

The rituals of the Palo Mayombe sect are centered around the Nganga:

> The body parts of deceased human beings (skulls and bones) used as religious arti-
> facts; dirt collected from a cemetery; twenty-one (21) sticks that were gathered from
> a forest or woodlands (Palos de Monte); bird feathers and railroad spikes; an assort-
> ment of different types of animal bones; rakes, hoes, picks, and other types of small
> farming equipment; firearms, ammunition, and handcuffs; articles that have some type
> of unique meaning to the Palero members (known as sacred stones); pieces of paper
> containing people's names attached to small sticks (Amarres); cowrie shells; pho-
> tographs; and various other items related to the ritual (DEA, 1990).

This group believes that some type of injury or sickness can be imposed on others, whether they be friends or enemies, by the gods. Malevolent witchcraft is a major part of the Palo Mayombe religious sect.

An offshoot of the Palo Mayombe group is the Abacua, which is considered by many Marielitos to be an even more brutal group that attracted a number of former Cuban criminals. One major difference between this group and the Palo Mayambe is that the Abacua is far more selective in choosing new members. The Abacua also requires that all new members take an oath of silence and participate in a secret initiation ritual. During this ceremony, members of this gang specifically are led to believe that they are instilled with some type of special powers that will enable them to feel they are invincible.

A short time after the arrival of Cuban refugees on the Mariel boat lift, the U.S. government realized that Fidel Castro had managed to unload approximately 25,000 criminals on our shores. U.S. Immigration and Naturalization Service attempted to rectify this problem by confining all those who were arrested for partaking in violent crimes in federal correctional facilities until Castro agrees to take them back. Under federal law, the U.S. Immigration and Naturalization Service is required to seize and incarcerate immigrant offenders after their release from state prison. Once imprisoned, these criminals are held until they can be deported back to their country of origin. The Castro government has thus far refused to allow these lawbreakers to return to Cuba, so the U.S. government continues to confine and care for more than 3,000 Cuba criminals whom the Castro government successfully unloaded on us (*Organized Crime Digest*, 1985).

Cuban Criminal Activities

Cuban leaders (sometimes called the Cuban Communist mafia) have been, according to federal sources, actively involved in drug trafficking with the Colombian drug cartels since 1963. Information on the Cuban government's involvement with narcotic trafficking was originally collected by members of the U.S. Bureau of Narcotics and Dangerous Drugs. They place the start of the Cuban government's active interest in the drug business to a short time after Castro took power in 1961 (Arostegui, 1992; U.S. Senate Hearings, 1989). During the late 1960s and early 1970s, Cuban drug dealers controlled a vast majority of the cocaine trafficking in the United States. Any time a police informer was approached as to the identity of the cocaine connection, the officer was informed that Cuban groups controlled the cocaine market. Supplies of cocaine were limited at this time, and cocaine dealing turned out to be a very profitable business for the early Cuban gangs. In the early 1970s, criminal organizations in Colombia realized the profitability involved in controlling cocaine distribution; with this in mind, the Colombian groups took over total control of this market, according to interviews with confidential informants in 1968–1972. In July 1971, information received by the U.S. government indicated that a narcotics operation working out of Havana was importing heroin to the United States in exchange for auto parts, various types of farm equipment, and medical provisions. Reports of the Cuban government's participation in drug-trafficking activities with the Colombian cartels continued to surface during the 1970s, but no truly substantial evidence was provided by U.S. government enforcement sources. During late 1979, Jaime Guillot-Lara, identified as a major drug trafficker by the U.S. Drug Enforcement Agency in 1976, formed what turned out to be a very profitable relationship with several Cuban officials (including Fernando Ravelo Renedo and Gonzolo Bassols Suarez) in Bogota, Colombia. This affiliation put the Guillot-Lara drug-carrying planes and ships under the protective umbrella of the Cuban government while they were transporting narcotics in both Cuban airspace and over Cuban waters. According to U.S. Drug Enforcement Agency sources, Guillot-Lara paid the Cuban government $10 per pound for every pound of marijuana that was transported through Cuba (U.S. Department of State, 1983).

In November 1982, the U.S. District Court in Miami, Florida, handed down indictments for conspiracy to smuggle drugs against 14 people, including 4 Cuban government officials: Cuba's former ambassador to Colombia (Fernando Ravelo Renedo), a vice admiral in the Cuban Navy (Aldo Santamaria Cuadrado), and two high-ranking figures in the Cuban Communist Party and the Cuban government (Rene Rodriguez Cruz and Gonzolo Bassols Suarez). All these officials were named as active participants who assisted Jaime Guillot-Lara, a well-known Colombian drug trafficker, in expediting his drug activities. According to the U.S. indictment, the Cuban officials participated in this venture in a number of different ways (President's Commission on Organized Crime, 1986; U.S. Department of State, 1983):

1. They agreed to let Cuba become a transshipment center for drugs being shipped from Colombia to the United States.

2. They gave him the right to use specially designated Cuban airspace for the drug-carrying planes.

3. They permitted him to operate his drug courier ships in Cuban waters in order to avoid detection by U.S. drug interdiction units.

4. They gave him the okay to offload drugs from larger to smaller conveyors for shipment to the United States.

5. They, in turn, received the right to purchase drugs at a cheaper price or received a specific percentage of the money earned from drug sales.

6. They had an agreement with him to transport weapons to the M-19 terrorist group in Colombia.

In February 1983, David Lorenzo Perez, Jr., testified before a federal grand jury that he and Jaime Guillot-Lara plotted with Cuban officials to ship drugs from Colombia through Cuba to the United States. Perez informed the government jury that he had met with the vice admiral (Aldo Santamaria Cuadrado) and a high-ranking member of the Cuban Communist Party (Rene Rodriguez Cruz) in Paredon Grande, Cuba, in both October and November 1980 to forge a plan to smuggle 8.5 million tablets of quaaludes into Florida. In the middle of this meeting, Cruz commanded Vice Admiral Cuadrado to provide Cuban gunboats as protection for Guillot-Lara's drug operations in Cuban waters. During his testimony, Perez also informed the grand jury that Cruz told him that the Cuban government put up a portion of the money to buy 10 million quaaludes and 23,000 pounds of marijuana and ultimately received $800,000 from the sale of these drugs (U.S. Senate, 1989).

A short time later, Mario Estevez Gonzalez, who had been a member of the Cuban Intelligence Service, informed federal and state law enforcement agencies that he had been selected, along with a number of other members of the Cuban Intelligence Service, to distribute cocaine, marijuana, and quaaludes throughout Florida, New Jersey, and New York. These agents had arrived in the United States during the Mariel boat lift in 1980. Gonzalez disclosed that during a 15-month period, he had given Cuban officials in the United States between $2 and $3 million and that these profits from drug sales were used to promote terrorist activities in Latin America (Westrate, 1985; U.S. Senate, 1989). Information in hearings before the U.S. Senate Drug Enforcement Caucus in 1983 implied that Castro was just as much involved with drug traffickers and drug activities as other Cuban government officials (U.S. Senate, 1989).

Since early 1980, a substantial amount of valid information related to the active participation of Cuban officials with members of Colombian drug cartels has surfaced. One report in 1987 indicated that Carlos Lehder Rivas, the renowned Colombian narcotics trafficker, convinced Cuban government officials to set up a cocaine-processing plant in Cuba. According to this report, the Cuban government built this cocaine-processing plant on a military base in order to ensure greater security. The Cuban government also assured Rivas of safe passage for his drug boats that were traveling in Cuban waters on the trip from Colombia to the United States (*U.S. News & World Report*, 1987). A short time after a $15 million cocaine seizure in New York City, Sterling Johnson, the special narcotics prosecutor for New York State, disclosed that the seized drugs had been transshipped through Cuba (U.S. Senate, 1989).

During Senate subcommittee hearings, Jose I. Blandon, a member of General Manuel Noriega's staff in Panama, testified that Castro and Noriega worked in concert, using drug money to advance terrorist activities in Latin America. Blandon further stated that both Castro and Noriega instituted a strong relationship with the Colombian drug cartels, which proved to be very profitable for both Castro and Noriega. A portion of the money made by these dictators was eventually used to fund terrorist guerilla movements in South America (U.S. Senate, 1989). In February 1988, the *Washington Times* reported that a Colombian drug cartel that had transported about a ton of cocaine through Cuba had been broken up by agents of the U.S. Drug Enforcement Agency. The *Washington Times* revealed that Cuban-flown Russian-made MIG jet fighters were observed escorting Colombian drug planes and that Cuban military personnel were discovered participating in the offloading and securing of the drugs. The *Times* also disclosed that during May 1987 members of the Cuban Air Force and Coast Guard and the Cuban General Intelligence Directorate (DGI) participated in a cocaine-smuggling ring (U.S. Senate, 1989).

A great deal of evidence came to light in March 1989. Videotaped confessions by gang leaders Reinaldo Ruiz and Ruben Ruiz confirmed that Cuba was used as a refuge for the storage and transfer of drugs as well as a refueling point for planes and boats. Ruben Ruiz explained that he had piloted planes containing at least a 1,000 pounds of cocaine from Colombia to Cuba and that he had landed at a military air base in Varadero, Cuba on several occasions during 1987. The Cuban military, after offloading the drugs, proceeded to transport the drugs to a coastal location where the drugs were transferred to a boat named *The Florida* for shipment to the United States. The Ruizs also identified their contacts as Tony de la Guardia, Amado Padron, and Miguel Ruiz Pau (U.S. Senate, 1989).

The information gathered during research into the Cuban government's participation in drug trafficking indicates the following:

1. An organized criminal group does exist within the Cuban government.

2. The Cuban government's involvement in drug trafficking is real. Although
    Fidel Castro vehemently denies these charges, all the evidence gathered
    during this investigation indicated that both Fidel and his brother Raul are
    far more than observers in this drug conspiracy. Evidence gathered from
    hearings in front of the U.S. House of Representatives and the U.S. Senate
    indicated that both brothers collaborated with other members of the Cuban
    government and with the Colombian drug cartels to move drugs through
    Cuba to the United States. A number of former Cuban government officials
    as well as military officials testified that nothing happens in or around Cuba
    without the okay of the Castro brothers. But according to Susan Kaufman
    Purcell of the Americas Society, Latin American Affairs, Castro, as "the
    leader of a highly centralized, personalistic autocracy, characterized by an
    intelligence and security apparatus that permeates all aspects of life on a small
    island of ten million people, remained in the dark about elaborate drug
    trafficking maneuvers that involved the use of Cuban waters, airspace and
    territory" (U.S. Senate, 1989, p. 167). Another piece of evidence came from
    a former high-ranking U.S. State Department official, Elliott Abrams, who
    stated on the "MacNeil Lehrer Newshour" on July 6, 1989, "We know that
    when a yachtsman by accident edges into Cuban waters, he is immediately
    found and picked up by Cuban radar. We know that regularly boats from
    Colombia use Cuban waters; planes from Colombia fly over Cuba. This can-
    not happen without Cuban government knowledge." Abrams continues by
    stating, "The idea that this has been going on for 10 years and Fidel just
    learned about it just defies logic. Nobody in Cuba except Fidel Castro has the
    power to say 'Yes' for 10 years. . . . No general, no admiral is going to risk
    doing that without Fidel's knowledge" (Arostegui, 1992). The former U.S.
    ambassador to Colombia, Thomas Boyett, testified during U.S. Senate
    hearings that "the Cuban government, as a matter of policy, for a long
    period of time—until exposed—was involved in drug smuggling. It was a
    [Cuban Intelligence] operation with the blessing of Fidel" (U.S. Senate,
    1989, pp. 104–105).

3. The Cuban government has involvement with Robert Vesco, who is wanted
    in the United States for stealing more than $200 million and who was granted
    asylum in Cuba by Fidel Castro in 1983. In 1984, Vesco set up a deal between
    the Colombian drug cartels and the Cuban government to transship Colombian
    drugs through Cuban territory for a fee. Law enforcement sources also believe
    that it was Vesco who initiated the Cuban government's involvement in shaking
    down drug boats passing through Cuban waters. Vesco, one must remember,

created an almost flawless system of laundering money by moving currency in small bills from bank to bank and nation to nation. Vesco is presently under indictment both in New York (for embezzling over $200 million from a mutual fund) and in Florida (for involvement in Cuban drug conspiracies) (Arostegui, 1992).

4. The easy money gathered from drug trafficking was used to purchase guns, ammunition, and explosives for terrorists' groups in both Central and South America. Drug money was easily available to Castro; by using these funds, Castro avoided using money from the depleted Cuban economy. In the late 1970s, Castro understood the relationship between drug money and the funding of revolutionary groups in Central and South American countries. The development of this relationship was fortified in the late 1970s and early 1980s when Jaime Guillot-Lara, a major Colombian drug trafficker, was given permission by the Cuban government to move his drugs through Cuba to the United States. Permission also included protection for Guillot-Lara's boats and planes, which was provided by the Cuban military. Guillot-Lara paid a specific fee for each pound of drugs transported through Cuba; the fee was usually $10 per pound. This money, in turn, was used to pay Guillot-Lara to purchase and ship guns to the Colombian terrorist group M-19 (U.S. Department of State, 1983). An article in *U.S. News & World Report* indicated that members of the Colombian cartels approached the Cuban ambassador to Colombia in late 1975 in an effort to gain passage for their drugs through Cuba. The cartel members were informed that the fee would be $800,000 per boatload of drugs. Drug traffickers were told that they could fly the Cuban flag and that their boats would be escorted through Cuban waters by Cuban Coast Guard gunboats. Monetary fees gained from the tolls paid by the drug cartels were then used to buy guns and explosives in the United States that were transported back to Cuba for shipment to terrorists' groups in both Central and South America. According to the U.S. Drug Enforcement Agency, the Guillot-Lara case was only the "tip of the iceberg of Cuba's ultra-secret involvement in the drug trade" (DEA, May 4, 1987, pp. 34–35). U.S. drug enforcement officials documented over 50 cases related to Cuban involvement in drug trafficking with the Colombian cartels between 1982 and 1987. A participant in one of these cases, Carlos Lehder Rivas, was forced by Cuban authorities to transfer his cocaine-processing operations to Cuba. Intelligence gathered by the Drug Enforcement Agency indicates that the Cuban government took over the operation of this extremely lucrative cocaine-processing plant (*U.S. News & World Report*, May 4, 1987).

5. In 1989, an intriguing undercover drug operation was set in motion by the U.S. Drug Enforcement Agency. It was intended to be used as a trap to entice and then arrest Cuban Interior Minister Jose Abrahantes. Undercover U.S. Drug Enforcement Agency agents set up a meeting with Abrahantes on a yacht at a location outside Cuban waters. At the last minute, one of the Cuban

informers, out of fear for his life, told Cuban Ministries Intelligence that the people setting up the operation were U.S. drug agents. Abrahantes controlled drug operations (including storage of cocaine) for the Cuban government; he was also the person Antonio de la Guardia Font turned his $3 million drug profits over to just prior to his arrest (Arostegui, 1992).

In response to pressure being placed on him and his government, Castro instituted charges of corruption and larceny of government resources against 14 members of the Cuban military in June 1989; 4 of the 14 defendants were very close associates of both Fidel and Raul Castro. One, General Arnaldo Ochoa Sanchez, had been selected by the Castro brothers to become the commander of the Western Army Forces, which is the most distinguished and highest-ranking position in the Cuban military forces known as the Fuerzas Armadas Revolucionarias (FAR). The charges against Sanchez and other members of the Cuban military included allegations that members of the Cuban military were involved in a joint conspiracy with Colombian drug dealers. According to the allegations brought by the Cuban government, the collaboration between the Cuban military and the Colombian drug cartels included a combined narcotics smuggling operation in which airdrops, refueling stopovers for drug aircraft, and transferring of drugs from planes to boats were completed prior to drug shipment to the United States. All this was done under the guidance of the (arrested) members of the Cuban military without the knowledge of the Castro brothers and the Cuban government (*Financial Times*, 1989; Lupsha, 1991; Uhlig, 1989; U.S. Senate, 1989).

The trials ended on July 7, 1989, with General Sanchez, one of his aides (Captain Jorge Martinez Valdes), Colonel Antonio de la Guardia Font of the Cuban Ministry of the Interior, and de la Guardia Font's aide (Major Amado Padron Trujillo) being sentenced to death. All 4 of these convicts were executed on July 13, 1989, while the other 10 convicted military officers were sentenced to anywhere from 10 to 30 years' imprisonment.

After the completion of these trials, it became evident to members of the media and the Cuban community in exile that Sanchez was aware of drug trafficking but was not an active participant in any of the drug conspiracies. According to Lupsha (1991), neither Sanchez nor his aide (Martinez Valdes) was involved in any of the drug schemes. Colonel de la Guardia Font and his aides had been designated to run the Cuban drug cartels' operations; if anything, de la Guardia Font and Sanchez were in competition with each other politically, and de la Guardia Font had successfully put Sanchez in a position that eliminated him from any type of participation in the drug business (Lupsha, 1991). There is no doubt, however, that de la Guardia Font and other members of the Cuban Ministry of the Interior (MININT) were active participants in drug conspiracies. It also seems quite apparent from the evidence that it is far more than a possibility that the real coconspirators in the drug plot were the leaders of the Cuban Communist government, not Sanchez and his aide. Arostegui (1992) stated that a letter smuggled out of Cuba by Hector de la Guardia Font, son of Antonio de la Guardia Font, proved that Castro used his so-called war on drugs to eliminate two of his major opponents in the military: de la Guardia Font and Sanchez.

The article by Arostegui indicated that the Cuban government is as deeply involved in drugs as it was prior to the arrest and conviction of the 14 military leaders (Arostegui, 1992). In turn, this leads us to the same conclusion as Arostegui: There is a Cuban Communist mafia that is involved in drug trafficking as well as money laundering, a gang that, through the use of the Communist Manifesto, created its own organized crime kingdom with tentacles that are always seeking new domains to control. Terrorist tactics, which are supported by drug money, are used to take control of areas in other countries that will then be used as bases for Cuban gangs' illegal drug activities.

The Cuban gangs vary from organized crime families to what might be considered somewhat fanatical street gangs to government-organized political groups. As we move on to the Colombian groups, we will see more groups that are fashioned after La Cosa Nostra.

COLOMBIAN ORGANIZED CRIME

All phases of cocaine trafficking, including cultivation, processing, and distribution, have expanded since the early 1980s. The world's cocaine supply is based out of South America, with the coca being cultivated in Bolivia, Colombia, Ecuador, and Peru. The majority of cocaine conversion laboratories are located in Brazil, Colombia, and Venezuela. The cocaine industry, as well as the long-established marijuana-trafficking enterprises, flourished and benefited the Colombian drug cartels for the past 40 years. Not to be outdone by the Asian drug rings, the Colombian cartels also created their own heroin business, going so far as to market their heroin at half the price of heroin from both Southeast and Southwest Asia. One problem with Colombian heroin is that, thus far, it does not have the same potency and doesn't give the addict the same high as the Asian heroin does. The Colombian cartels entered into the heroin industry later, but their heroin will probably continue to improve until it reaches the same quality as the Asian product. With their ever-increasing participation in the drug trade, Colombian drug cartels created an economy in Colombia that could not survive without the contributions of the drug traffickers.

Colombian History

The country of Colombia is located in the northwest part of South America and borders Ecuador, Panama, Peru, and Venezuela; it is also bordered by both the Pacific Ocean and the Caribbean Sea. Colombia, the fourth-largest country in South America, has a total landmass of approximately 440,000 square miles. As a nation, Colombia has a very diverse population, the result of the blending of the native Indians, Spanish colonists, and African slaves. There are approximately 31 million people presently living in Colombia.

As a country, Colombia survived 50 civil wars between 1850 and 1900, losing over 100,000 people out of a population of 4 million during the last years of these revolutionary conflicts. These constant hostilities erupted into what is known as La Violencia. La Violencia started in 1946 and ended in the mid-1960s; an estimated

250,000 people lost their lives during these violent encounters. Ever since the early 1970s, Colombia has been a nation overrun with violence and crime. The level of violent crime in Colombia is seen in the number of homicides per year: Since 1972, there has been an average of 15,000 homicides annually, which breaks down to approximately 68 murders per 100,000 people; in comparison, the U.S. average is about 18 killings per 100,000 people. Its commonplace to read about the murder of a Colombian political leader or judge. For example, between 1979 and 1982, a total of 30 judges were viciously assassinated in Colombia. There has also been a great deal of regional strife and terrorist attacks from either the 19th of April Movement (also known as M-19) or the Revolutionary Armed Forces of Colombia (FARC). A constantly elevated inflation rate, violence, and poor economic conditions have created a Colombian nation that depends on the drug cartels to support its ever-increasing monetary deficit (McGee, March 26, 1995).

Problems created by inflation as well as the ever-increasing crime problems led to the immigration of a large number of Colombian citizens to the United States. This increased immigration in the mid-1960s resulted to the eventual takeover of the cocaine importation business by the Colombians. All the cocaine coming into the United States had been controlled by the Cubans in the 1960s. The immigration of a large number of Colombian citizens to the United States opened the door for smaller Colombia drug dealers to set up their own drug operations in the United States. At first, these smaller operational bases were located in cities that had what leaders of these drug groups considered a visible and viable Hispanic community. Colombian drug cartel bosses realized that couriers and dealers would be a lot less conspicuous to law enforcement officials when they were operating out of a Latin community. As Colombian immigration rates increased, so did the amount of cocaine being smuggled into this country. As a country involved in drug trafficking, Colombia has the following characteristics:

1. It is geographically well positioned in order to receive coca from other countries in South America.
2. It has coastline on both the Pacific Ocean (900 miles) and the Caribbean Sea (1,100 miles) for drug shipment to the United States.
3. Its sparsely populated eastern section, with vast central forests, effectively conceals clandestine drug-processing labs and airstrips.

Colombian Gangs

As the Colombian cartels continue to grow, so does their political power within that country. The Colombian organized crime groups effectively transformed themselves from small unattached gangs into distinct organizations. Colombians who have immigrated to the United States and other countries throughout the world supply the cartels with access to those countries; in turn, they continue to work within the Colombian drug systems. Two major Colombian drug-trafficking groups have structured their organizations so that they maintain complete control over all the steps involved in drug trafficking, everything from growing the drugs to selling the drugs on the streets. Modeled after La Cosa Nostra, the Colombian factions are built of interconnected and component groups; these groups require each specific sector to maintain its own responsibility for its area of productivity. Participation in these gangs requires members to be involved as laborers, processors, transporters, financiers, and enforcers. Regular membership in most cases is supplemented with outside criminal affiliates, who perform certain tasks for a fee. Colombian gangs, in most cases, use other Colombians to carry out actions against group members who steal or cheat, but gang leaders also seek out members of other ethnic organized crime groups for specific purposes.

In recent years, the Medellin and Cali groups worked together to resist extradition proceedings against their leadership by the government of the United States. We also observed a close relationship forming between the Cali cartel and members of La Cosa Nostra over the past several years. The Colombian and Italian factions found that there is more to be gained financially by working together than by feuding with each other. The Sicilian mafia formed a relationship with the Colombians that permits them to control a large portion of the fertile cocaine market in Europe; this turned out to be a very productive venture for both groups, especially when one considers that the Colombians wholesale the cocaine to Sicilians and then let the Sicilians run their own drug operation. This frees up the Colombians from having to set up and run cocaine sales in Europe on a day-to-day basis. Colombian groups make their money up front and distance themselves from the drug operation.

The Colombian cocaine gangs' methods of survival are listed in a manual written to protect Colombian drug traffickers. These guidelines were put together by Lizardo Marquez-Perez, who is presently serving a 45-year sentence for drug importation to the United States. The guidelines specifically set standards to be followed by cartel members while participating in drug-trafficking ventures (DEA, 1987):

1. Conduct all drug transactions in code.

2. Have security devices such as pocket alarms, beepers, electronic briefcases, mace, pepper spray, stun guns, security flares, tear gas, bulletproof vests, safety shields, and portable phones in your possession.

3. Distribute drugs prior to six in the morning and after six in the evening.

4. Always identify yourself as either the butler or the handyman and say that the people who own the house are away on vacation when conducting drug business out of a house.

5. Use residential areas where there is very little street traffic, and find a house with a big lawn and a two-car garage that is out of any neighbor's sight.

6. Try to imitate an American home owner. Wash your car, mow your lawn, and have barbecues. Stay away from extravagant social events, and have some type of watchdog.

7. Avoid having furniture you do not need.

8. Avoid using work vehicles for personal activities.

9. Never leave the house unguarded.

10. Always have available airline tickets, money, a safe house, a trusted lawyer, and a nondescript vehicle.

During the early 1970s, a number of turf wars were fought over the control of the cocaine business in the United States. As previously stated, the Cubans controlled almost all the cocaine imported into the United States prior to the early 1970s. Once the Colombians took control of the drug industry, they successfully regulated this drug trade through the use of high-profile intimidation and violence. This persisted through the late 1970s and the early 1980s. For example, in 1979 in East Elmhurst, New York, Susana Toro, a Hispanic female, was found strangled and hung from a basement pillar in her residence; she had a Christmas wreath around her. Nine days later, her brother, Oscar Toro, and a babysitter, Liliana Bustamante, were found strangled and stabbed, hanging frozen on mail bag hooks in a deserted post office in Long Island, New York. Oscar Toro, Sr., the father of the murdered children, was a lieutenant in a Colombian drug group that had cheated the organization out of money. In January 1982, Orlando Galvez, his wife, and their two children were found shot to death in his Mercedes-Benz along the Grand Central Parkway in Queens, New York. A search of the Galvez apartment turned up $980,000 in U.S. currency and $15 million worth of cocaine. Galvez had also been a dishonest employee of the Colombian drug cartels.

Groups such as Los Pistoleros, led by Michael Sepulveda, were responsible for 50 to 60 murders in both Florida and New York. Most of the members of this group were recruited hit men who came from Medellin, Colombia. Two members of this group, Hugo Echevirri and Carlos Arrango, took their victims to an apartment in Queens and drained all the blood out of them in a bathtub and then proceeded to put the bodies in discarded cardboard television boxes or stereo boxes. These cardboard containers were then placed with other garbage on the street for pickup by sanitation workers. All these actions taken by the Colombian gangs certainly reveal their dedication to the use of intimidation and violence to control members of their organization.

Medellin Cartels.   Colombian cartels are basically nontraditional in character. They believe in conducting "in-house" justice carried out through the use of vendettas, which are considered a legal principle of these organizations. Family members are active participants within their own drug group, and it would not be unusual to find a female in a high-ranking position in any of the Colombian drug groups. Many leaders of the Colombian groups have become active participants in legitimate businesses including import/export companies, travel agencies, investment corporations, ranches, and the entertainment industry. Over the past 35 years, Colombian groups managed to take a large percentage of control of the marijuana (70 percent) and cocaine (90 percent) industries while still being fairly active in methaqualone trafficking (40 percent).

The Medellin cartels formed in the early 1980s were at one time considered the most powerful Colombian drug group. Originally, they were set up and run by Pablo Escobar-Gavaria, a former Colombian politician. Escobar-Gavaria started as an enforcer for a small drug-smuggling group in Colombia, but within a short period of time, he was able to save enough money to set up his own drug organization in Medellin. Escobar-Gavaria's drug ventures quickly made him a billionaire; he spent large amounts of money importing African wildlife into Colombia to stock his own personal zoo. Escobar-Gavaria was considered a Robin Hood type of character by some citizens of Colombia because he built low-cost housing and soccer fields for the people. The other side of Escobar-Gavaria was illustrated in an article written by Jose De Cordoba a short time after Escobar-Gavaria's death. De Cordoba claimed that Escobar-Gavaria was responsible for the bomb that exploded on an Avianca flight in 1989 that killed 107 persons onboard the airline. He said that Escobar-Gavaria was also the Colombian drug trafficker who instituted a great deal of the violent activities associated with the Colombian cartels and estimated that Escobar-Gavaria was responsible for 25,000 killings in Colombia in 1992 alone (De Cordoba, 1993).

As the drug ventures expanded, so did the number of well-known participants, such as Jorge Ochoa-Restrepo and his sons Fabio, Jorge, and Juan as well as Carlos Lehder-Rivas (who was a noted car thief in the early days of his criminal career). Ochoa-Restrepo, also known as Don Fabio or El Gordo (the fat one), assumed national prominence as a drug cartel leader in 1977, the year he took over the leadership of a drug cartel by ordering the assassination of his boss. The assassination plus many other acts of violence helped Ochoa-Restrepo become the godfather of the Medellin cartels. Ochoa-Restrepo formed a very profitable drug-smuggling alliance with Escobar-Gavaria. As a result of this affiliation, Ochoa-Restrepo was able to participate in a large number of drug-smuggling endeavors that increased his wealth. Ochoa-Restrepo was also able to build a fleet of airplanes that included props as well as jets; in addition, he had private and commercial seagoing vessels to ship his cocaine from Colombia to the United States. His son Fabio Ochoa-Vasquez became known as the father of international cocaine trafficking and a "notable" millionaire businessman with a number of legal investments in both agriculture and horse breeding. (It is a Spanish custom for the children of a marriage to use their mother's maiden name as the last name while the family name is usually placed in front of the mother's maiden name. This is why the father is Ochoa-Restrepo and the sons are Ochoa-Vasquez.)

In 1991, when they took advantage of a Colombian government plea bargain agreement for their participation in drug trafficking, Jorge Ochoa-Vasquez and his brothers, Fabio and Juan, were confined to a medium-security prison about 10 miles from Medellin. During their stay in prison, all their food preparation was taken care of by their mother, Margarita de Ochoa. The brothers completed their sentences and were released from jail sometime toward the end of 1995. The brothers claimed that all the money they made from their drug-trafficking business was spent on lawyers and family security (Brooke, February 28, 1995).

Carlos Lehder-Rivas was originally arrested in Miami in 1973 for possessing 230 pounds of marijuana and was indicated again in 1981 for shipping cocaine through

Florida and the Bahamas. In the early 1980s, Lehder-Rivas smuggled an average of 500 to 1,000 kilograms of cocaine a month into the United States. Lehder-Rivas has been given credit for setting up transshipment routes from Colombia through several Caribbean islands to the United States (*Organized Crime Digest*, 1984). In 1988, Lehder-Rivas was convicted and is currently serving a life sentence in a U.S. correctional facility.

Another group within the Medellin cartel that deserves mention is one that was formed by the now-deceased Jose Gonzalo Rodriguez-Gacha (also known as the Mexican). Rodriguez-Gacha and his group emerged as a very powerful force after the conviction of Lehder-Rivas in Florida in 1988. Rodriguez-Gacha's drug operation was run somewhat differently from some of the other Medellin cartels. Rodriguez-Gacha personally maintained very tight control over both the transportation and dispersion networks of his drug operation. All the people who represented Rodriguez-Gacha's organization throughout the United States were employees of his group; these workers put in regular business hours; wore shirts, ties, and suits; and did their best to maintain a very low profile. Rodriguez-Gacha's employees were paid a weekly salary, unlike most other cartel employees who worked on a commission basis (U.S. Department of Justice, 1989).

In 1989 Rodriguez-Gacha offered to wipe out Communism in Colombia if the Colombian government would give him amnesty for his past narcotics trafficking. In an effort to show he would fulfill this promise, Rodriguez-Gacha went so far as to hire American, British, and Israeli mercenaries to train his own personal army to carry out the task of destroying Communism in Colombia, but he actually created a reign of terror with his paramilitary group. According of Colombian sources, his mercenary military units were responsible for over 200 killings, including those of Justice Minister Lara Bonilla, newspaper owner Guillermo Cano, radical leader Jaime Pardo Leal, and presidential candidate Senator Luis Carlos Galan. Rodriguez-Gacha's army was also responsible for the wanton killings of numerous other leftist leaders and political figures, including judges and police officials who allegedly stood in the way of his effort to "defeat Communism" in Colombia. In reality, Rodriguez-Gacha was nothing more than a petty thief and hustler until he became associated with Escobar-Gavaria, who considered Rodriguez-Gacha, prior to his demise, as being totally out of control. During the search of his ranch a short time after his death, the police found a large cache of Israeli-manufactured weapons and ammunition. An investigation revealed that these weapons had originally been sold to the Antiguan government. Eventually the Antiguan government found that the shipment was made by two former Israeli army officers who through the use of a scam, managed to have the weapons shipped through Antigua to Colombia. One of the ex-Israeli military officers was wanted in Colombia for both illegally transporting weapons into Colombia and teaching members of drug-trafficking groups how to properly use subversive military procedures. U.S. federal law enforcement officials have labeled Rodriguez-Gacha as nothing more than a deceitful common crook who would steal or kill anyone (Eisner, September 10, 1989). Rodriguez-Gacha's drug group continues to operate but on a smaller scale since his assassination in December 1989.

Although Escobar-Gavaria was confined to a Colombian correctional facility in 1991, he still had enough free time to run his drug operations without any interference from government officials. Escobar-Gavaria escaped from prison in 1991 and was later killed during a police raid on one of his hideouts in December 1993. Information has surfaced since his death that members of the Cali cartel, using a group known as Pepes (People Persecuted by Pablo Escobar), played a major part in locating and eliminating Escobar-Gavaria. As the control of the Colombian drug-trafficking business was increasingly taken over by the Cali cartels, there came growing concern over the extensive use of violence by the Medellin cartels. Bombing, murders, and other violent acts brought too much attention to the Colombian cartels, so cartel leaders such as Escobar-Gavaria were considered liabilities who could no longer be tolerated by the leaders of the new Cali drug cartels. These newer cartels were run on the basic management principle that advocated the use of bribery instead of violence (De Cordoba, 1993; Wilkinson, 1994).

The Medellin cartels set up organizations that were family-oriented and whose associates were carefully selected by family members. The Medellin groups' ability to stay within their own confines was illustrated by the drug alliance set up between Escobar-Gavaria and Ochoa-Vasquez. The Medellin cartels set up organizations that had a very tight span of control over all aspects of their drug ventures from cultivation through distribution. This span of control also encompassed the close monitoring of processing, transporting, and dispersing the drugs. The Medellin cartels were the first drug groups to do the following:

1. Purchase fields producing coca in Bolivia, Colombia, and Peru.
2. Compensate the farmers through an agent.
3. Employ chemists as associates in the group.
4. Use many small processing laboratories set up and run by family associates, instead of one or two major labs.
5. Use coca paste, which was, in most cases, provided by growers.
6. Use brokers to devise and carry out transportation and to supply aircraft, airstrips, pilots, and vessels.
7. Use close associates in the United States and Europe for high-level distribution. Lower-level distribution was usually done by members of other ethnic gangs.
8. Have sufficient funds available to spread plenty of money around to both bribe and intimidate politicians and other law enforcement officials.
9. Maintain a strong home base operation that kept a tight rein on all overseas operations.
10. Maintain links between the base of operations in Colombia and other locations throughout the world through the use of fax machines. (All supervisors were rotated from one location to another to avoid the temptation of cheating the cartels out of some of the large amounts of money they controlled daily.)

11. Have the capability to form business alliances with members of other criminal organizations in order to reach a specific goal.

12. Launder money through diversified schemes:
    a. Front businesses
    b. Small deposits (less than $10,000)
    c. Computer transfers
    d. Money orders
    e. Money transfers through banks in Colombia, Panama, and Switzerland as well as other foreign banks
    f. Wire transfers (This was known as smurfing, breaking each transaction down to less than $10,000 so that it does not have to be reported to the U.S. Internal Revenue Service. Storefront money transfer agencies usually get 8 percent for breaking down and wiring money in this manner.)
    g. Casinos

Federal law enforcement agencies instituted a strict enforcement policy for the Currency and Foreign Transactions Reporting Act of 1970 (or as it will be referred to here, the Bank Secrecy Act) in early 1980. This act required financial institutions, including banks, savings and loans, currency exchanges, currency brokers, and credit unions, to file Currency Transaction Reports with the U.S. Treasury Department on all cash transactions that exceeded $10,000. Strict enforcement of the Bank Secrecy Act hindered money laundering by the Colombian cartels as well as other organized criminal groups. It did not take long for the members of these criminal organizations to realize that there was a "legitimate" way to launder their profits without government authorization: Gambling casinos could be used to launder their unlawful profits. Casinos do not have to file any Currency Transaction Reports, so they presented gang members with a perfect remedy for their money-laundering dilemma. Money laundering through casinos is done in several ways (DEA, 1984):

1. Bills in smaller amounts are exchanged for bills of larger denominations. This makes it easier for drug groups to transport the money.

2. Casino personnel in on a money-laundering scheme wire clients' money to an offshore account. Casino employees also make loans available to gang member patrons, knowing payback will be almost immediate and will include a cash bonus.

3. Money deposited in one casino can be transferred to a specified account in another associated casino, usually one outside the United States. After this transfer is completed, credit can be issued to the person whose name is on the account; this person is, in most cases, a high-ranking member of the drug cartel.

4. A casino can claim that money in a person's account is the result of successful gambling. This method gives the money (minus taxes) back to the depositor

which is still an advantage for the drug trafficker. Under what is designated as "high roller status," people can open accounts with the casinos. Under the guidelines set forth by the casinos, airline fare, room, and board are paid for by the casino, but the gamblers must put a specific amount of money in this "high roller" account; the gamblers must also bet or spend a specific amount of money during this gambling venture. They can win as well as lose money and large sums of money can be placed in the account, and any money in the account can then be designated as winnings by the casino.

5. A member of a drug cartel can gamble away a sum of money originally deposited in an account (usually $10,000), then enter a much larger sum of money into the gambling account (usually $100,000 or more), and then quickly withdraw this amount in a check or very large bills.

Cali Cartels.   Cali drug cartels started to take over control of the Colombian drug industry during the late 1980s. The continuing violent and destructive acts by the Medellin cartels during the mid-1980s and late 1980s quickly worsened the working relationship that had been agreed on in the early 1980s by both the Medellin and Cali drug cartels. Suddenly in the late 1980s, the Medellin cartels found that their unchallenged power was starting to deteriorate. The arrest and conviction of Carlos Lehder-Rivas in the United States was followed by the assassination of Jose Rodriguez-Gacha in 1989, the conviction and jailing of the Ochoa-Vasquez brothers, and the killing of Pablo Escobar-Gavaria by the Colombian police in December 1993. All these events helped to decrease a major portion of the Medellin cartels' narcotic-trafficking activities.

Leaders of the Cali groups participated in some of the events that helped to reduce the power of the Medellin cartels. Cali leaders quickly seized this opportunity to take control of the Colombian drug business. Unlike the leaders of the Medellin cartels, the Cali groups cautiously set up their drug operations in an attempt to avoid the mistakes made by leaders of the Medellin cartels. Cali groups devised plans for corporate-type narcotic-trafficking organizations; in some cases, these were run in the same clandestine manner as the U.S. Central Intelligence Agency. In order to avoid interception of either communications or drug shipments, the Cali groups went so far as attempting to purchase their own communications satellite. When they shipped drugs, they usually secreted the drugs in another item, such as Brazilian cedar boards. Using Brazilian boards was very successful for the Cali groups because it took U.S. customs and U.S. drug enforcement officials nine years to finally catch on to this diversionary method of smuggling drugs. The Cali groups made sure these shipments contained a very large number of boards and then proceeded to drill out the centers of only a very small portion of the boards to avoid detection of the hidden drugs. This method of smuggling was devised by members of the Santacruz-Londono Cali group in 1988, and it was discovered only by a stroke of luck. The drilling of a hole in a board was done by a U.S. customs official after he observed some suspicious actions by a crew member; that U.S. customs official found drugs. In reality, only a very small number (700) of the 9,000, planks had been drilled out and filled with cocaine (Shannon, 1991).

The Cali drug organizations are structured in a patriarchal manner while maintaining an autocratic system that requires the necessary amount of discipline to maintain total allegiance to the leadership. Although these organizations have a great deal of discipline and control, they also need creativity in the drug-trafficking business. An example of the inventiveness of this drug cartel surfaced when a drug sub washed ashore in Santo Domingo. These miniature submarines are anywhere from 17 to 30 feet long and are made of fiberglass and wood. They have no sharp edges, which helps them avoid radar detection. There are two crew members, and the range of these boats is about 600 miles. It is estimated that these boats can carry up to several hundred kilos of marijuana, cocaine, or heroin. Intelligence information indicates that these miniature submarines are being built at the seaports of Santa Marta and Barranquilla and that these boats are leased to the Cali cartels at somewhere between $100,000 and $200,000 per drug load (Copeland, 1994).

Jose Santacruz-Londono (also known as Don Chepe or El Gordo) is the leader of one of the Cali cartels. He, along with Gilberto Rodriguez-Orejuela, put the Cali drug operation together during the mid-1970s. This group set up its base of operations in the Cauca Valley city of Cali. Thus far, these groups have managed to successfully work hand in hand in taking over control of the importation of Colombian drugs worldwide. Santacruz-Londono and the other members of the Cali drug consortium groups set up cell-type operations that are totally controlled by the group leaders residing in Cali. Cartel bosses in Cali go so far as to vigilantly check the expenditures and liabilities of each cell, oversee and make decisions on what tasks should be performed by hit men, keep a watchful eye on the activities of their money couriers and lab employees, and oversee the transporting or smuggling of persons. Cali leaders feel that the control by the employer over the employees is made easier through the use of placing skilled and trusted workers from Colombia in charge of these cells. Cartel bosses also use the threat of violence against family members in Colombia to keep workers in line. The Cali leaders find that is very important to keep each cell and its cell leaders and workers isolated from all other cell locations and their leaders and employees. In fact, few high-ranking officials in each cartel are aware of the identity of the people who work in these cells.

Cells are set up in centralized locations throughout the United States. U.S. drug enforcement estimates that each Cali group has anywhere from 6 to 10 of these cells presently operating throughout the United States. These cells are made up of trusted employees from Colombia who worked their way up the organizational ladder in either Colombia or the United States. All of the cells are supervised by a person who is known as a Caleno. Some of the cartels staff their cells with relatives or close and trusted friends. Salaries for cell leaders and employees are deposited in banks in Cali; if there is a monetary error made by a cell member, the amount of the error is withdrawn from the employee's bank account in Cali (Shannon, 1991).

Each one of these cells operates independently from all the others. They are stocked with arsenals for the protection of the cell as well as its product, and they are set up to be impenetrable by outsiders, especially informers and law enforcement agents. The major task of each cell is to properly apportion either cocaine or heroin to distributors within its operational area; the distributors retail the drugs to street vendors. A Celeno (or cell leader) sells drugs only to people he has been acquainted with over a period of time; this usually means other Colombians. Prospective drug purchasers must have been checked out and given an endorsement by cartel leaders in Cali prior to being sold drugs by any cell. Cali leaders may go so far as having a background and credit check done on prospective customers. Prior to being given approval, these people are made aware of the fact that they must have some type of security to put up in case they are apprehended by law enforcement officials; some of this collateral may include family members in Colombia. At the present time, the U.S. Drug Enforcement Agency estimates that the Cali cartels control 80 percent of the worldwide cocaine-trafficking business (McGee, March 26, 1995; *Newsweek*, 1989; Shannon, 1991).

Gilberto Rodriguez-Orejuela and his brother, Miguel Angel Rodriguez-Orejuela, are the leaders of one of the Cali drug cartels. Gilberto is known as El Ajedrecista (the chess player) because of the way he methodically maneuvers his drug operations to avoid detection by both U.S. and Colombian law enforcement agencies. Gilberto was arrested on June 9, 1995, by Colombian authorities; on two prior occasions, he had been arrested but was released within a short period of time without any type of prosecution being initiated by the Colombian government. There is a distinct possibility that Gilberto was arrested this time because of a taped telephone conversation that involved the Cali cartels agreeing to make a contribution of more than $3.7 million to the 1994 presidential election campaign of Ernesto Samper-Pizano. Samper-Pizano, after being elected Colombian president, denied any knowledge of campaign contributions by the Cali cartels and encouraged a full assault on the Cali cartels. This would indicate there was some truth to the campaign contributions allegations and taped telephone conversations and that this enforcement effort was being used to cover up any improper practices involving the president (McGee, March 28, 1995).

Gilberto and Miguel, like other members of the Cali cartels, find it much easier in many cases, to bribe people than to kill them; it is also more useful to work a member of the organization into an official position within the Colombian government. In spite of this, someone being killed by the Cali cartel is just as likely as someone being murdered by the Medellin cartel. A New York journalist, Manuel de Dios Unanue, did a continuing exposé on Cali cartel leader Jose Santacruz-Londono in the Spanish language newspaper *El Diario-La Prensa* until he was assassinated while having a drink in a Queens bar in 1992. According to U.S. Drug Enforcement Agency informer John Harold Mena, Santacruz-Londono ordered the hit on de Dios Unanue (McGee, March 27, 1995).

In many cases when the Cali cartels use violence, they attempt to keep that violence fairly low key. Although intelligence information gathered from Colombian law enforcement officials seems to indicate that Santacruz-Londono and his Cali group would sanction a terrorist-type action against the Colombian government, this type of terrorist action would probably be similar to the seditious type of campaign Pablo Escobar-Gavaria carried out against the Colombian government (*New York Times*, 1995). Up to now, the Cali cartels have stayed away from participating in mass killings and bombings to gain notoriety, although there are one or two exceptions to this rule.

Another major achievement accomplished by the Cali cartels involves their inventiveness in seeking working agreements with other ethnic gangs. This is especially true when we consider the Cali cartels' dealings with La Cosa Nostra in Italy:

1. The Cali cartels' connections to the Sicilian mafia are well documented and include money laundering and a drug connection to Pasquale Locatelli, a Sicilian crime boss. He and 60 other people were arrested for their involvement in laundering Colombian drug money through a bank set up by U.S. federal authorities to trap drug money launderers. This operation, called Operation Dinero, also led to the arrest of Roberto Severa, a member of the Banda Della Malgliana, a criminal group based in Rome. Operation Dinero successfully helped law enforcement agencies to seize $40 million and very expensive paintings by Picasso and Rubens (Janofsky, 1994).

2. Another U.S. law enforcement money-laundering operation set up in 1989 to catch drug cartel members resulted in the arrest of members of the Sicilian mafia, the Neapolitan camorra, and the Calabian ndrangheta. A person identified as Jose Duran (also known as Raul Grajales), who according to Italian law enforcement authorities is "the most important distributor in the world for the Colombian drug cartels," was also arrested in Italy. Apprehended with Duran was Betten Martens, a significant money launderer from the Netherlands, and Pedro Felipe Villaquiran, a Colombian national who was being introduced to organized crime connections in Europe by Duran (Ostrow and Montalbano, 1992, pp. A1, A6).

3. FBI agents in Florida arrested several members of the Calabian drangheta in Sarasota, which had been combined with a group of Colombian traffickers to set up and run a heroin- and drug-trafficking conspiracy in the United States and Canada (*Narcotic Control Digest*, April 1993).

4. According to law enforcement sources, an alliance was set up in New York City between members of both the Gambino crime group and Colombian organized crime cartels to deal both drugs and guns (Parascandola, 1995).

5. Russian drug enforcement chief Aleksandr Sergeyev documented information that indicates there is a direct working relationship between the Cali drug groups and the Russian and Israeli organized crime gangs in Europe. The Cali connection to the Israeli and Russian groups was evident during a seizure of over 2,400 pounds of cocaine packed in food containers that were marked "meat and potatoes" on a truck in St. Petersburg, Russia. An Israeli, who had been a resident of St. Petersburg, was the only person arrested by Russian police (*Narcotics Control Digest*, May 1993; *Newsweek*, December 1993).

One must remember that seizures and arrests only indicate approximately 10 percent (if not less) of the total activities of organized crime groups in drug trafficking and money laundering. So the examples used above only give us a modest insight into the connections among organized crime groups. There is no doubt that the total number of conspiracies involving these criminal groups is a lot larger than depicted in the above-described situations.

An associated group of the Rodriguez-Orejuela family is the Orjuela-Caballero family, led by Jaime Orjuela-Caballero, who is a cousin of Rodriguez-Orejuela. There are two other major Cali groups that require mentioning. The first is the Pacho Herrera group, whose leader is said to be the son of Afro-Colombian drug smuggler Benjamin Herrera-Zuleta (also known as the Black Pope). The other group, the Urdinola-Grajales family, is known as the Northern Cauca Valley Cartel and operates out of the fairly wealthy sugarcane growing area north of Cali. The leader of this group, Ivan Urdinola-Grajales, was arrested by Colombian police in April 1993 and quickly pleaded guilty to drug charges, for which he received five years and six months in prison. Prior to his arrest and conviction, Urdinola-Grajales was somewhat of an idol to some local gang members. Urdinola-Grajales had built a reputation for killing people with a chain saw and then depositing their bodies in the Cauca River; these bodies, some of them with their hands tied behind their backs, would eventually turn up in villages and towns along the river. Colombian officials estimate that Urdinola-Grajales was responsible for well over 100 mutilation-type murders. Since his arrest and conviction on drug charges, not one new body has turned up in the Cauca River (De Cordoba, 1993; Wilkinson, 1994).

Henry Loaiza-Ceballos (nicknamed the Scorpion and labeled the Cali cartel's minister of war by local Colombian newspapers) was a notorious drug trafficker who surrendered to Colombian police authorities on June 20, 1995, in Bogota. According to Colombian police officials, Loaiza-Ceballos (whom villagers in his home base of Venadillo, Colombia, consider a Robin Hood type of character because of the good-will he spreads in that community) was involved in the killings of over 100 of his workers who attempted to form a labor union on his ranch in Trujillo, Colombia, in 1990. Loaiza-Ceballos, along with a group of Colombian army deserters, allegedly tortured the victims with water hoses, blow torches, and chain saws. Most of the casualties were then cut up with chain saws and, like Urdinola-Grajales's victims, dumped into the Cauca River (Brooke, March 27, 1995).

Just as the Cali cartels have grown and increased their profits from drug trafficking, so have a number of small-time drug dealers, with their violence-prone activities. Men known as *traquetos* (Spanish for machine gun fire) have popped up throughout Cali carrying walkie-talkies in their hands and semiautomatic pistols in their waistbands. A majority of the *traquetos* are in their early 20s and have made their money by smuggling drugs into the United States for members of the Cali cartels. Presently, the *traquetos* are licensed to operate by the godfathers of the various Cali groups and will probably become more heavily involved in the drug-trafficking business as the Cali bosses continue to franchise out their drug operations and move into legitimate business ventures. The problem with continuing to license the *traqueto* groups to operate under the umbrella of the Cali cartels is that in the future these *traquetos* could become clones of the Medellin cartels, Rodriguez-Gacha's and Escobar-Gavaria's vicious murderous groups (Wilkinson, 1994).

The ingenuity of the Cali cartels is also indicated by the way they suddenly moved into the heroin market in early 1990 in an effort to increase their earnings. This was done by having farmers in Colombia convert their crops from coca plants to poppy plants. Cali cartel leaders paid the farmers $3,000 for each pound of opium grown. Presently, the Colombian cartels have more acreage in Bolivia, Colombia, and Peru dedicated to poppy growing than every other country in the world except Myanmar, the worldwide leader in poppy production. In an effort to properly cultivate their heroin product, the Cali cartels imported Chinese chemists. Results seem to indicate that the procedures used by the Cali groups produced a poppy that produces more opium-containing bulbs than the opium grown anywhere else in the world. The highly fertile fields in Colombia make it possible to produce a new crop of poppy plants every five months (Ebron and Mustain, 1993).

The Cali cartels then proceeded to compel cocaine merchants to purchase heroin as well as cocaine from them. Since it first appeared on the drug scene, Colombian heroin is probably the purest heroin produced in the world. The purity of the heroin makes it possible for it to be smoked or inhaled as well as injected into the body. Another factor that makes the Colombian heroin so inviting is that it is much cheaper on the street than heroin from either Southeast Asia or Southwest Asia, which lacks the purity of the Colombian heroin. Colombian heroin traffickers are presently selling a kilo of heroin for $65,000 to $70,000, while the Southeast Asian and Southwest Asian heroin usually costs about $130,000 per kilo.

Other Colombian Cartels.   There are two other major drug groups that operate in Colombia that deserve some type of mention, although both these groups have managed to keep a low profile and avoid media attention. The first cartel, the Bogota cartel, has over the past several decades maintained connections to both La Cosa Nostra and two Cuban groups, the Corporation and La Compania. Historically, the Bogota group formed a relationship with both La Cosa Nostra and the Cuban groups through Meyer Lansky in the late 1950s when they were running contraband items into Colombia. This group is probably the oldest organized crime group in Colombia. The Bogota group's first connection to drug trafficking involved the earliest cocaine dealers in the United States, who were Cubans; the Bogota cartel supplied the Cubans with cocaine during the 1960s and early 1970s. In most cases, the Bogota cartel is still supplying many Cuban and La Cosa Nostra organized crime groups with cocaine. A major portion of the Bogota cartel's cocaine is processed through plants cartel members have built adjoining coca plant farms in Colombia. As a group, the Bogota cartel has managed to maintain its political contacts in Colombia over the years by staying out of the limelight and avoiding direct contact (whenever possible) with both Colombian and U.S. law enforcement agencies. Most of their profits from drug trafficking have been reinvested in properties outside Bogota.

The second Colombian cartel is known as the North Atlantic Coast group. This group is small and lacks the cohesiveness that most other Colombian groups exhibit. As a group, the members are spread throughout the Colombian port cities of Barranquilla, Cartagena, Rio Hacha, and Santa Marta. Similar to the Bogota cartel, the North Atlantic Coast cartel was originally involved in supplying contraband products to

Colombia. These group members were some of the earliest participants in smuggling marijuana into the United States. Once they observed the profits being gleaned by other Colombian cartels, they also got involved in cocaine smuggling. Through the years, the North Atlantic Coast cartel managed to set up solid drug bases in California, Florida, Georgia, Massachusetts, and New York. Since the late 1980s, this cartel has managed to expand its activities to include smuggling and money-laundering assistance to both the Cali and Medellin cartels (U.S. Department of Justice, 1989).

As with all the other organized criminal groups, the Colombian cartels continue to survive and increase their profits from unlawful activities. The Medellin cartels have lost a number of their leaders over the past several years but will more than likely regroup in the near future in an effort to once again increase their participation in and profits from drug-trafficking ventures. As far as organized criminal groups are concerned, the Cali cartels have to be considered one of the best-managed and best-organized groups in the world, but (like the Medellin cartels) they will ultimately get caught up in the violent activities that will destroy their continued joint alliances with other groups. One must also not forget the continued attention paid to the Cali drug barons by tenacious U.S. law enforcement agencies. As indictments and money seizures continue, so will the pressure on the Colombian government to arrest and extradite members of the Cali drug cartels to the United States for prosecution.

As we have seen in this section of the book, the Colombian cartels' names may change, but they remain financially sound and politically strong in their homeland. For all the aforementioned reasons, we must consider the Colombian cartels similar to large corporations that profit from illegal activities.

Next, we discuss how Dominican crime groups, some of whom were modeled after the Colombian cartels, that have become organized crime families.

DOMINICAN ORGANIZED CRIME

Dominican History

The island of Hispaniola was originally discovered in 1492 by Christopher Columbus. Santo Domingo, which is the oldest European settlement in the Americas, was designated as the capital of La Hispaniola in 1496. There has been a considerable amount of turmoil in the Dominican Republic since the late 1700s. France took over control of this colony in 1795; in 1801, Haitian soldiers, under the command of Toussaint L'Ouverture, overthrew the French government. A citizen revolt in 1808 resulted in Santo Domingo being seized by what were considered the local rebels, who immediately set up a republic. During the early 1800s, Spain reacquired and lost power on several occasions, as did a number of local representative governments that disappeared as quickly as they surfaced. Haitians controlled the Dominican Republic again between 1822 and 1844; then Spain once again seized control of this country from 1861 to 1863. In 1916, an occupation force of U.S. Marines took over control of this country until a democratic type of government was installed in 1924.

The worst possible thing that could happen to this nation took place in 1930 when General Rafael Trujillo-Molina was elected president of the Dominican Republic. Within a short period of time, Trujillo quickly set a military dictatorship that ruled through the use of murder, torture, and brutality. After 31 years of civilian torment by this military regime, an assassin finally stepped forward and killed Trujillo in 1961. His successor, Joaquin Balaguer, was forced to step down in 1962; Juan Bosch, who was elected in 1962, was overthrown in 1963. Then in 1965, Bosch and a group of his followers created their own rebellion in an attempt to take over the government. Within four days of these disruptions, U.S. Marines were dispatched to the Dominican Republic, along with troops from several other South American countries, and they quickly quelled the activities of Bosch and his associates. In 1966 a presidential election was held in the Dominican Republic, and Joaquin Balaguer defeated Bosch and took control of this new democratic government. A short time after the election, the outside military forces left the Dominican Republic. In 1978, in an attempt to gain a fourth term as president, Joaquin Balaguer had the military delay the processing of election ballots. President Jimmy Carter intervened and warned Balaguer to have all the ballots counted as quickly as possible. A short time later, a member of the Dominican Revolution Party, Antonio Guzman, was named the winner of the presidential election. In 1986, Balaguer was once again elected as president of the Dominican Republic on a platform that promised not only an improvement in issues related to the economy but also the creation of a diversified policy in an attempt to control the Dominican economy. Balaguer won his reelection campaign in 1990 and continues to run the Dominican government.

The Dominican government is a democracy that consists of 30 delegates who are elected from the 29 provinces and 1 national district. The president, who must run for election every four years, has executive power bestowed on him by a constitution that was created in 1966.

Located on the island of Hispaniola (which it shares with the country of Haiti), the Dominican Republic is a nation that has suffered through many years of distressing poverty and depression. Haiti is probably the only country in the Caribbean that is poorer than the Dominican Republic. The national average per-capita income for a citizen of this country is $697 per person; the Dominican Republic is one of the four most poverty-stricken countries in the Northern Hemisphere.

This level of indigence within the Dominican Republic has created an increase in immigration to other nations within the Northern Hemisphere, including the United States. An ample number of Dominicans escape the poverty of this country by immigrating to the United States. Many of these immigrants end up in New York because family sponsorship comes from the large Dominican community in New York City. Some Dominicans who do not have a legal way to gain entry into the United States usually reach their objective by obtaining illegal identification and then entering the United States from either Puerto Rico or Mexico. Information gathered by both the U.S. Customs Service and the U.S. Immigration and Naturalization Service indicates that illegal Dominican immigrants often set sail from the Dominican Republic on a raft (*yola*) constructed of wood and cross the Mona Passage on their voyage to the western shores of Puerto Rico. The cost of this trip would be $400 to $700. Another means of transportation would be to set sail in a legitimate vessel that sails north and then drops the illegal aliens off on the eastern shores of Puerto Rico for a mere $1,500 (DEA, February 1993). The U.S. Immigration and Naturalization Service indicates that there has been a significant decrease in the number of visa applications being received from the Dominican Republic since 1989 (over 209,412 in 1989 to 60,000 in 1992). According to the U.S. Immigration and Naturalization Service, this decrease in visa applications is an indicator of the increase in the number of Dominicans entering the United States as illegal aliens (DEA, February 1993).

The lifestyle in the Dominican Republic in most cases has to be considered very difficult for most of the inhabitants of this country. The unemployment rate in the Dominican Republic is a constant 25 to 30 percent. It was ascertained in the early 1990s that the Dominican Republic has the second-highest total number of AIDS infection cases in the Caribbean. This country has still managed to maintain a literacy rate of 83 percent, which is fairly good considering it has an ever-increasing population that is presently somewhere around 7.5 million people. The government of the Dominican Republic has also had continuing problems attempting to decrease the foreign debt from an economy that finds it impossible to survive without an agricultural base that supplies the raw materials for the survival of that nation's processing plants.

Dominican Criminal Activities

Dominican groups first started appearing in the mid-1960s on Manhattan's West Side between 105th and 109th Streets. Over the following 30 years, the Dominican gangs expanded their activities throughout Upper Manhattan; in fact, the criminal activities of these gangs are visible in four of the five boroughs of New York City. The Dominican gangs have taken over a major portion of the drug trafficking from 110th Street to the northern tip of Manhattan, the West Side of the Bronx, and the Bushwick and East New York sections of Brooklyn. They are also found in Elmhurst and Corona and in parts of the Jackson Heights sections of Queens.

Realizing the possibility of easily netting anywhere from $20,000 to $30,000 a day from street drug operations, the Dominicans continued to expand their street drug activities. The Dominican gangs employ addicts to deal their drugs at street level and use armed supervisors to scrutinize the movements of the addict-dealers. Observers are usually put in place by the boss of this drug operation to ensure that the seller does not leave with either the drugs or the money. In most cases, the addict-dealers are given small amounts of heroin/crack so that they must continually return to the stash or to the holder to replenish their supply. This type of operation almost guarantees that revenue from drug sales will be turned over to the main operator within a short period of time. Most supervisors are put in charge of several addict-dealers within a small area. Gang bosses employ other Dominican gang members in the mid-low to mid-high positions that involve the members in the apportioning of the heroin and/or cocaine; these are positions of trust within the organization because they require the gang members to be accountable for both the drugs they distribute and the amounts of money they collect from street dealers.

The Dominican gangs set up an area of Manhattan known as Washington Heights as the base of their criminal activities. It is estimated that there are approximately 650,000 Dominicans living in the Washington Heights section of Manhattan. Dominicans have adapted to the New York City environment by creating a Dominican type of habitat within their Washington Heights surroundings. The focal point for each group's activities in all of these smaller neighborhoods revolves around the local food store, or bodega. These stores function as both a market and a cultural center for legal and illegal aliens entering the New York City setting from the Dominican Republic.

Members of most major Dominican organized crime gangs are originally from the villages of San Francisco de Macoris and Santiago de los Caballeros. Most Dominican gang members arrested for drug violations identify themselves as being from the village of San Francisco de Macoris. It is a village that has received a great deal of notoriety over the past several years and is located 100 kilometers northeast of Santo Domingo. This village has seen an influx of drug dealers known as Dominican Yorks, who are considered the nouveau riche because they gained their assets by working as drug runners and dealers on the streets of New York City. A major portion of the economy in this village is controlled by these rich opportunists who, after making their money on the streets of New York, come home to San Francisco de Macoris to create work for citizens of this city. The drug lords have built modern houses that contain turrets, balconies, skylights, statues, and many other types of geometric shapes that in some cases liken them to spaceships. Gang members paint both the interior and the exterior of their homes in resplendent tropical colors such as orange, raspberry, lime, peach, and mango; in many cases, these colors are painted as stripes going up, down, or around the house. They use businesses, usually supermarkets or casinos, that they have purchased in both San Francisco de Macoris and Santo Domingo to launder their drug money. The lack of respect that some of these drug cartel members have received in their hometowns in the Dominican Republic have forced them to move to other locations. Most of these areas are in the United States, specifically the west coast of Florida and Long Island in New York (O'Connor, 1992).

Once drug gang members, resettle in the Dominican Republic, they immediately start recruiting others to become part of their cartels. It is apparently quite easy to recruit new members because most of these young and poor local residents have observed the families of drug gang members freely spending money sent to them from the United States. These youths also take note of the drug dealers returning to town driving fancy autos, wearing expensive jewelry, and building costly mansions. The gang newcomers are given a loan that will pay for their passage and whatever type of identification that is required to gain entry into the United States. A short time after these new gang members arrive in New York, they are set up to become involved in the gang's drug enterprise. As more and more illegal young Dominican aliens arrive in New York, the unemployment rate among these Dominican youths continues to rise to anywhere between 300 to 500 percent higher than the national U.S. average. It is easy to see why these adolescents would find that participation in the drug business would be a feasible moneymaking option. When we consider the fact that 60 percent of the Dominican males living in New York are under 24 years old and 41 percent of them are unemployed, it is even more conceivable that they become actively involved in the drug trade.

One problem with involvement in the drug business has been the number of young Dominicans being sent back to the Dominican Republic in caskets after being murdered in New York because of their participation in drug trafficking. In 1991, there was a total of 122 drug-related homicides in the Washington Heights section of New York City. A number of these murders were related to Dominican drug activities, with Dominican gang members killing other Dominicans over drug-related issues (also known as "business competitiveness") (NYDETF, 1992).

Washington Heights is the home base for Dominican drug dealing in the United States. According to local law enforcement, the Washington Heights area is separated into two sections, with the purchasing and peddling activities taking place in the southern part and the storage or stash houses being located in the northern part. Just about all these stash houses are equipped with various types of devices that are set up to hinder anyone seeking either to gain unauthorized admittance or to conduct an in-depth probe to locate drugs.

It has been discovered by the law enforcement community that the Dominican drug gangs set up complex systems to prevent easy detection and arrest. Specific code words and phrases have been created by the gangs in order to caution each other about some possible liability. The gangs use gestures or special buzz words such as *suviendo* (coming up), *agua* (water), or *bajando* (coming down) to notify other gang members that the police are somewhere in the immediate area. A newer way to transmit an alarm to gang members is through the use of cellular phones, which are reasonably priced. Each gang member who is watching a location can be easily notified by cell phone of any nearby police activity.

Some of the gangs use surveillance equipment and special remote alarm mechanisms outside a location to warn them of police movement in the area. These same methods of protection are usually set up in a drug dealer's apartment door or in the hallway approaching the entranceway to observe all the movements in the hallway. Drug gangs also use lookouts equipped with cellular phones or other alarm devices and positioned on rooftops, in doorways, on bicycles, and on street corners to notify them of pending police activity. These devices and lookouts are also used by the drug gangs to avoid the spot robbers, those who pose as narcotics officers to rob the drug locations (NYPD, 1991).

The Dominican gangs have adapted the use of booby traps in their drug locations in a manner similar to that used by Jamaican gangs. These booby traps are put in place to discourage police efforts to raid their locations, seize their drugs, and arrest their employees; booby traps are also a viable means of stopping other drug gangs from entering the premises and stealing money and drugs. Some types of devices used by the gangs include electrified wires on wet floors, electrified doors and windows, and hanging wires. Trip wires are set up at entranceways to darkened rooms, and on the floors of these rooms are what the gangs call "pungi boards." Pungi boards are plywood boards full of three- to four-inch nails. These boards are set up on floors so that when a person trips on the wire, he will fall face forward into the nail-filled pungi boards. Another deterrent used by the Dominican gangs is vicious pit bulls that have had their vocal cords extracted (NYPD, 1991).

Throughout the New York metropolitan area and most of the East Coast, the Dominicans have formed a beneficial alliance with the Colombian drug cartels. This relationship has progressed since the 1980s when the Colombian drug traffickers designated the Dominican Republic as a refueling stop and a location to ship drugs to other points in the world. Since the late 1980s, it has become quite apparent to federal law enforcement agencies that Dominican organized crime gangs have moved up the drug distribution ladder to the point of importing and allocating both cocaine and heroin for the Colombian drug cartels. Colombian drug cartels believe that the Dominican gangs can be trusted to handle the distribution of both cocaine and heroin because of the Dominican gangs' ability to regulate, supply, and dominate street-level drug operations of Dominican as well as other drug-trafficking groups (NYDETF, 1992).

The Dominican gangs have managed to stretch their tentacles throughout the New York State area; for example, Dominican drug gangs set up drug operations in the western portion of Buffalo. A large amount of the drugs they sell are imported from New York City and transported to Buffalo on the New York State Thruway. In Syracuse, the Dominican gangs supply crack and cocaine to both black and white street drug dealers; once again, the Dominicans bring the drugs to Syracuse from New York City. Members of some Colombian gangs have attempted to remove the Dominicans from the drug business in Syracuse. In Rochester, the Dominican gangs have taken over complete control of the cocaine market from Jamaican gangs. The Dominicans set up their base for drug dealing in the northeastern section of Rochester, and they strengthened this foundation by importing and selling heroin in the Rochester area (NYDETF, 1992).

The Dominican gangs have formed relationships with several other organized crime gangs besides the Colombians. During incarceration in various prison facilities throughout New York State, Dominicans formed working relationships with members of Chinese criminal gangs. A drug raid conducted by both federal and local law enforcement officers uncovered a large amount of heroin wrapped in Chinese newspapers in a Dominican drug house in Queens, New York. In 1989, a New York City Police Department Narcotics Unit uncovered a Dominican heroin operation that was run by two former police officers from the Dominican Republic. This was followed up by an investigation conducted by members of the New York City Drug Enforcement Agency, who discovered a Dominican-run heroin ring that supplied heroin to Connecticut, Massachusetts, New Jersey, New York, and Rhode Island. Evidence showed that this Dominican group was purchasing large amounts of Southeast Asian heroin from Chinese gang members (DEA, 1993). Dominican gangs also managed to form a drug-related relationship with

Nigerian organized crime groups, which supply the Dominicans with heroin for street sales (NYDETF, 1992).

A 1993 article in the *New York Daily News* described the rise and fall of a Dominican drug gang leader in Washington Heights. The leader of this gang was Euclides Rosario Lantigua, a 30-year-old Dominican known on the street as Un Rey (the king) who drove a flashy Toyota Pathfinder throughout Washington Heights and who was assisted by his wife, Vanais, and his brother, Franklin, in running the gang. Lantigua wore fancy jewelry, silk shirts, and linen pants and flaunted his money. This gang, set up by Lantigua, had 50 different groups in Washington Heights alone. A great deal of the money from drug trafficking by this gang was set back to the Dominican Republic for investment. Law enforcement official records show that the Lantigua organization set up an apartment building in Washington Heights that included both of the following (Sennott, 1993):

1. On the second floor, long wooden tables were used by employees to cut the drugs, check their weight, bundle the drugs in plastic bags or containers, and record all necessary information in a book.
2. On the eighth floor, a special armed security force was constantly patrolling. Chinese, Colombian, and Nigerian drug importers were brought to this floor to set up large drug deals and then finalize these drug transactions.

The Lantigua drug operation was successful enough to eventually wholesale approximately 15 kilos each day at $20,000 per kilo; it is estimated that the Lantiguas made $3,000 per kilo. Some of the money from these sales was used to purchase the D'Cachet Restaurant on Nagle Avenue and the Vanassiel Travel Agency on Amsterdam Avenue. A majority of the proceeds were sent back to the Dominican Republic through the use of either wire transfers sent from the Lantigua's travel agency or smurfing (money is bundled in amounts of less than $10,000 each and then forwarded to the Dominican Republic). Anyone shipping U.S. currency in amounts of $10,000 or more is required to file paperwork with the U.S. government prior to shipment (Sennott, 1993).

This drug operation was highly successful until the police overheard a telephone conversation on August 4, 1993, between Lantigua and a Colombian courier that involved the purchase of 30 kilos of cocaine. Police moved in once the delivery was made and arrested two of Lantigua's lieutenants and the Colombian courier. Lantigua quickly paid the $50,000 bail on each of his lieutenants and shipped them both back to the Dominican Republic. Then on September 15, 1993, another telephone conversation between Lantigua and a Colombian courier about the purchase of 10 kilos of cocaine gave the police the information they needed to arrest Lantigua. Lantigua and his wife, Vanais, were both arrested in their Wadsworth Avenue apartment, where the police recovered $120,000 in U.S. currency. A search of the Lantigua's travel agency turned up drug records and $20,000 more in U.S. currency. Lantigua's drug headquarters, nicknamed Heartbreak Hotel, was seized after the raid and was shut down and locked up (Sennott, 1993).

Money Laundering. Federal law enforcement agencies have concluded that approximately $800 million in U.S. currency is legally shipped to the Dominican Republic each year from the United States. A great deal of this money is sent home by legitimate hardworking native-born Dominicans. On the other hand, there is no way of truly knowing the amount of money shipped to the Dominican Republic by the drug gangs. There are several methods used by members of Dominican drug gangs to ship money back to the Dominican Republic:

1. Money is placed in a legal enterprise, and currency can then be legitimately transferred anywhere in the world's economics system without attracting any major attention. Once a business is set up by the drug lords, the illegally obtained drug money is used to purchase commodities at a higher price in another country, shifting money from one country to another under the guise of a legal business transaction. The gangs have found it easy to move the money out of the United States either as U.S. currency or as legitimate money orders. The currency or the money orders are secreted in cargo being exported to the Dominican Republic.

2. The Dominican drug cartels launder money through the use of electronic transfers. Money is moved from the United States to the Dominican Republic by wire services, usually Western Union. This type of transfer was exposed when a New York County grand jury handed down indictments against three Dominicans who owned and operated the Dominican $ Express Inc. The three were charged with unlawfully using 500,000 different transactions to transfer over $70 million to the Dominican Republic (DEA, 1993). In many cases, the drug gangs purchase a large number of money orders in denominations less than $10,000 and usually in amounts much lower than those that require a U.S. government report. In one case, Dominican drug dealers left U.S. currency with an electronic transfer company, which would then change the U.S. currency into money orders. The drug traffickers would pick up the money orders several days later and then ship the money orders to relatives in the Dominican Republic. Money laundering through the use of wire services, is far from complicated when the methods used by the Dominican drug gangs are reviewed (Guart, 1995):

    a. U.S. currency is delivered to a messenger.

    b. The messenger then delivers the cash (usually in tens, twenties, and fifties) to a corrupt wire services agency.

    c. The currency is then broken down into separate money orders or invoices of less than $10,000 each. Fraudulent identifications, including residences and phone numbers, are then placed on the money orders or invoices.

    d. The money is deposited by the New York State–licensed wire services agency into a bank account.

    e. An authorization is given by the licensed wire services agency for the bank to shift the funds via wire to the foreign accounts.

f. This transfer is set up so that once the money reaches its foreign destination, a representative (usually a lawyer) shows up at this transfer office with a document that enables him to take possession of the money. The person with the state-authorized license to transfer the money receives about 7 percent of each transaction while the agent gets about 3 percent of the transferred amount.

3. The profits from drug enterprises that are not sent back to the Dominican Republic are usually invested in bodegas, laundromats, money transfer businesses, travel enterprises, beauty shops, and large food markets. Most of these businesses are operated somewhat legally but are used to launder drug money for the gang leaders.

4. The Dominican gangs, following the example of both the Colombian and Nigerian drug swallowers, fill the fingers of latex gloves with ten $100 bills. The gang leaders would then have one of their couriers swallow the fingers from the gloves and return to the Dominican Republic with the money. In one specific case, two of the gang's representative swallowers ingested 125 fingers that contained a total of $125,000. In turn, many of these couriers would swallow heroin for their return trip to the United States (DEA, 1993).

5. The drug gangs have also been known to secret the money on the bodies of relatives or close friends and have them carry it back to the Dominican Republic.

Robberies.   Robberies committed in the Dominican community are called *tumbes*, which actually means takedowns. Tumbes is also the name given to Dominican gangs that participate in "push-in" robberies. Push-in robberies are a trademark of Dominican gangs throughout the United States. This type of robbery involves the choosing of a target, usually a person who has large amounts of money or jewelry at his or her home or business. Many of the targets first picked by the gangs were Dominican drug dealers, who were known to hide money at their residences or stashes. Then the types of targets changed to houses legitimate Dominican businessmen who owned grocery stores (bodegas), restaurants, bars, jewelry stores, or supermarkets. The gangs found that most legitimate businesspeople were not armed, nor did they have body guards around them at all times. Once a target was chosen, observations of the target were conducted by gang members in an attempt to find out when the greatest amount of money would be present at the location where the robbery would take place.

An area that has any type of Dominican population soon finds that push-in robberies also become part of this Dominican community. During 1993, a total of over 500 push-in robberies were reported in the Washington Heights area of Manhattan and the southeastern section of the Bronx; both of these areas are densely populated Dominican communities (NYPD, 1993). Inquiries to the New York City Police Department in relation to these types of push-in robberies have come from other police agencies in Bangor, Maine; Lawrence, Massachusetts; Providence, Rhode

Island; Reading, Pennsylvania; Washington, D.C.; and Westchester, Suffolk, and Nassau Counties in the New York metropolitan area (NYPD, 1993).

A number of these robbers were originally part of the drug gangs, but fearful of the harsh sentences that a second drug sale conviction presented to them, they became part of the Tumbes gangs. These Dominican Tumbes groups usually have three to six members, and the victims are almost always Dominican. The gang members are aware that most Dominicans distrust the police, so they realize that most of these crimes would not be reported to the authorities (Moses and Furse, 1991).

There are two basic methods used by the gangs to gain entrance to a location without alerting the police. The first method requires gang members to conceal themselves somewhere in very close proximity of the victims' front door. They wait in seclusion until the target unlocks the door; the gang members, who are all armed, then rush up behind the victims, forcing all parties inside. Once inside the premises, gang members immediately disconnect all telephone wires and then proceed to tie up any family members. Questions concerning the whereabouts of money and other valuables commence once all the family members present at the location are bound with cords or wires. Some Dominicans like to keep large sums of money in their homes because the money might have been earned unscrupulously, hidden to avoid taxes, or kept at home because of mistrust of financial institutions. Valuables are usually secreted in homemade vaults. A victim who fails to cooperate with the gang (that is, tell gang members where the money is hidden) finds that the gang quickly terrorizes other family members, especially female ones. These gang members have no compassion toward wives, daughters, or other female relatives; they will assault, sexually abuse, rape, or torture them or do whatever else is necessary until the location of the valuables is disclosed to them. In some cases, gang members have cut body parts off or have branded family members with hot irons or spoons (NYPD, 1991).

The second technique used by gang members involves the use of a ruse to gain entry into the victim's residence. In many cases, the robbers identify themselves either as police officers (and actually display police shields and identification cards) or as electric company employees, building inspectors, mailmen, UPS workers, or telephone company employees to obtain entrance to the location. Once the gang members enter the victim's residence, they use the same procedures as described above (Moses and Furse, 1991).

Extortion.   One specific Dominican gang found a better way to extort money. The C & C gang, in the Mott Haven section of the Bronx, set up an extortion racket that involved forcing drug dealers on the streets of the South Bronx to pay rent in order to operate on these streets. Originally, the C & C gang was involved in street drug dealing using the name D.O.A. on its heroin, but the leaders of this gang saw extortion as a lot safer and almost as profitable as drug dealing. This gang was named for its two leaders, George Calderon and Angel (Cuson) Padilla, who together managed to collect anywhere from $100,000 to $500,000 weekly. Calderon and Padilla set up a complex blackmail system that made money using duress. This enabled them to totally control a seven-block area in the South Bronx.

The first thing that Calderon did was set up a treaty within the community forbidding drug dealers to sell drugs either during the times children were going back and forth to school or in areas where the dealers could be seen from the school. A limit was also placed on the number of drug addicts who could assemble at one specific location at any time. Anyone setting up business in the area controlled by the C & C without the permission of C & C would be kidnapped, assaulted, robbed, or murdered. Anyone dealing drugs in this area had to abide by the rules set forth by C & C and pay rent on their designated spot. In some cases, the gang would actually specify a site for the drug dealer to work. In most cases, the rent on each location was determined by the amount of money a dealer could make at a specific locale, but in some cases, a flat rate was paid each week (Faison, May 27, 1994). Gang rule changed in 1992 when Calderon was shot and killed after leaving his parole officer in the Bronx. Two months later, Calderon's sister, Lourdes Cintron, was shot and killed sitting inside a car in the Bronx. According to federal investigators, both these hits were ordered by Padilla (Purdy, October 19, 1994).

Homicides.   A review of homicides in the Washington Heights section of New York City showed there was a total of 122 murders in that area in 1991. A total of 97 of the victims were Dominican; of that total, 80 were killed with a gun, and 54 of those shot were confirmed drug gang members. Most of these homicides were carried out by hit men brought in from the Dominican Republic by the gangs.

Information received from the Dominican National Directorate of Drug Control (DNCD) indicated that between January and August 1992 a total of 144 bodies were returned to the Dominican Republic from the United States; the DNCD reports also indicated all these citizens of the Dominican Republic suffered violent deaths in the United States. Information on the ages of these victims revealed 15 percent of them were 18 to 20 years old, 70 percent of them were 21 to 35 years old, and 15 percent of them were 36 years old and older (DEA, 1993). The location of the deceased person's birthplace or residence was judged by location of burial. The reports revealed that 57 percent were from Santo Domingo, 29 percent were from San Francisco De Macoris, and 14 percent were from various other locations in the Dominican Republic (DEA, 1993).

Investigators say that one Dominican gang, the Wild Cowboys, was responsible for a number of murders of other Dominicans over the past several years and that just about all these murders were connected to the control of drug trafficking in Washington Heights and the Bronx. In fact, the two gang leaders, Nelson and Lenin Sepulveda, and their number one enforcer, Jose Llaca, are in the New York City prison system awaiting trial on numerous charges. NYPD investigators pinpointed the leaders of the Wild Cowboys as having participated in over 30 homicides in New York City (Faison, May 27, 1994). A Supreme Court indictment charged the Sepulveda brothers and seven of their appointed gang lieutenants with 105 counts of murder and numerous counts of attempted murder, felonious assault, and drug trafficking (Faison, April 4, 1994).

Both the Sepulveda brothers claimed they were destitute and couldn't afford to pay for an attorney. They were assigned court-appointed lawyers, leaving the tax-paying citizens of New York City responsible for their legal bills. Obviously crime does pay for the Sepulveda brothers, who shipped millions of dollars in illegal drug money back to the Dominican Republic and then turned around and forced the New York City court system to pay for their attorneys (Faison, April 4, 1994).

In the Bronx, another Dominican drug gang, led by Jose Reyes and known as the Reyes Crew, savagely controlled the University Heights community for over five years. Reyes, paralyzed due to prior gunshot wounds, was nicknamed El Feo (the ugly one). This group was aware of police operations and was constantly moving its stash houses and distribution centers to avoid police surveillance. Reyes Crew still managed to earn over $500,000 a year from its drug businesses. Members communicated with each other through the use of beepers and cellular phones; all the gang's records were kept on a computer by Reyes. The gang's drug operations were modeled somewhat like a big corporation, with a different set of managers, steerers, and sellers for the heroin, crack cocaine, and cocaine divisions of its drug business. When Reyes was arrested in Miami, he had in his possession records that showed all his gang's drug transactions. Bronx Supreme Court indictments charged Reyes and his two lieutenants, Thomas "Cruel" Rodriguez and Francisco "Freddy Kruger" Medina, with murder, narcotics trafficking, and weapons possession (Parascandola, 1994; Perez-Pena, 1994).

The New York City Police Department discovered a recent phenomenon in the Washington Heights community. These abrupt and strange happenings indicated that there had been a sudden surge in the number of Colombians being murdered in Washington Heights. Police intelligence indicated that this was due to the fact that the Dominicans tenaciously observed the movements of the Colombian drug dealers. After the completion of a couple of drug deals, the Colombian couriers were murdered, and the drugs and currency were kept by the leaders of the Dominican drug gangs (NYPD, 1993).

Auto Thefts.   The Dominican gangs have become increasingly involved in auto thefts since the early 1990s. One gang designates Nissan Pathfinders and Toyota Forerunners as their choice of vehicles to rob, mainly because the gang found these vehicles somewhat easy to steal. In cases involving these vehicles, gang members need only to get the car door open to procure the code number of the ignition key. Once the code number is obtained, the thieves need only a portable key maker to reproduce the key; then they can quickly drive off in the auto.

The gangs used two other methods to steal vehicles, both of which were more drastic. One method that was used was bumping a vehicle at a red light and then forcibly taking the car at gunpoint. The other technique involved stealing an auto from a parking garage. This was accomplished in two easy ways:

1. Stealing the keys
2. Paying the attendant for the keys

A number of these vehicles were transported out of the United States. Getting a stolen auto out of this country can be a very difficult task. In most cases, it is necessary

to get the assistance of a person with some substantial knowledge of the shipping business; more than likely gang members used freight forwarders. A freight forwarder
receives fees to organize and then provide the necessary shipping papers. This person
seldom has an opportunity to see the type of property being shipped, so it is fairly easy
to ship cargo without the freight forwarder having any knowledge of whether or not
the property being shipped is stolen.

This resulted in many shipping documents being poorly prepared and containing
erroneous information. First, the car thieves placed inaccurate vehicle identification
numbers on the information supplied to the freight forwarders for listing on the shipping papers. A number of the stolen cars were taken to the Bronx Terminal Market,
where they were containerized; the cars were then shipped to Elizabeth, New Jersey,
and finally transported to the Dominican Republic for resale.

It was not long before local law enforcement officials realized what the car thieves
were doing and shut down this operation. There is a great deal of profit for the gangs in
stolen vehicles. A stolen car that would cost $25,000 new in the United States can be
sold for $50,000 outside the United States. Therefore, stolen autos are pure profit for
the gangs, especially with the escalating prices of the new and fancier vehicles.

A Dominican auto theft ring that was shut down by federal law enforcement
authorities had stolen over $8 million worth of luxury cars beginning in 1993. This gang,
which worked out of an auto body shop in the Bronx, bribed officials in the Dominican
Republic and stole hundreds of auto manufacturer certificates (also known as certificates
of origin) that authenticate the age of new vehicles sold in the Dominican Republic. The
cars that were stolen were a close match to the vehicle described on the certificates of
origin. Vehicles were then taken to the auto body shop where workers removed the
actual vehicle identification number plates and replaced them with plates that matched
the vehicle identification numbers on the certificates. These stolen cars were then sold to
unaware buyers by dealers in both the United States and the Dominican Republic. Types
of autos stolen included the Lexus, Infiniti, Jeep Grand Cherokee, Mercedes-Benz, and
BMW. This investigation led to the arrests of 17 people, including the gang leader,
Fernando Pena, of the Bronx; two car dealership owners in New Jersey; a State Department of Motor Vehicles employee; the owner of two auto body shops in the Bronx; and
the owners of four auto dealerships in the Dominican Republic (McKinley, 1995).

Geographic Areas

Dominican gangs have become the most active participants in cocaine trafficking
throughout Montgomery and Prince George's County as well as the city of Baltimore
in Maryland. In New Jersey, the Dominican gangs teamed up with Colombian gangs
in the cocaine-trafficking business. Law enforcement officials in New Jersey have
come to the conclusion that the Dominican gangs are organized and pinpointed the
Dominicans as the major suppliers of cocaine in the city of Trenton and the counties of
Camden, Passaic, and Middlesex. Police agencies in both Camden and Middlesex
Counties gathered information that verified that the Dominican gangs were active

participants in not only narcotics operations but also unlawful gambling businesses, illegal importation of Dominicans into the United States, and counterfeiting of documents and U.S. currency (Magloclen, 1993).

Dominican gangs in Ohio have been active participants with Colombian groups in the dispersal of cocaine in the major urban centers of Ohio. The Dominican groups worked out cooperative agreements with Hispanic as well as other street gangs in Philadelphia in order to conduct their drug-trafficking business. These Dominican gangs have spread their tentacles throughout the state of Pennsylvania, with operations in the Allentown/Bethlehem areas, Douphin County, and areas around Lancaster/York and Reading. Almost all these operations were related to heroin/cocaine trafficking. Some of their other activities included counterfeiting of all types of federal, state, and other documents; illegally bringing immigrants into the United States; money laundering; drive-by shootings; and committing robberies, assaults, and arson (Magloclen, 1993).

The Dominican gangs have continued to operate as autonomous groups with a very loose-knit structure. Dominican gang members are citizens of the Dominican Republic and from the same basic environment. These gangs have remained unable to combine into one large organization with all members working together. Smaller Dominican gangs fostered characteristics of greed and rivalry, and these traits prevented these groups from being able to band together as one major organized ethnic gang. It is possible that sometime in the future all these smaller Dominican gangs will unite to form one large and well-organized criminal enterprise, one similar to the Colombian cartels.

MEXICAN ORGANIZED CRIME

Mexican History

The history of Mexican organized crime groups starts with the Mexican Mafia, or La Eme (which is Spanish for the letter *M*). The Mexican Mafia formed its roots in East Los Angeles in the early 1950s. Prior to the formation of the Mexican Mafia, there were approximately 20 loosely knit gangs, most of which were created in the early 1940s. Some of these organizations were actually remnants of gangs that had been formed in the barrios of East Los Angeles during the mid-1920s. According to early gang observers, some of these Mexican street organizations emerged from groups formed during the Mexican revolution.

During the 1930s and 1940s, gangs that came to be known as Pachucos started sprouting up in Arizona, New Mexico, Southern California, and Texas. These gangs became modish because of their unique way of dressing: On most occasions, gang members wore baggy, pegged pants worn high above the waist, patent leather shoes, knee-length suit coats, and broad-brimmed hats. Many of these gangs, because of their style of dress, quickly attracted the attention of local police departments. In a majority of cases, these gangs were more of what today would be considered trendsetters rather than criminal organizations. A murder in East Los Angeles during World War II resulted in off-duty police officers and military personnel roving through the streets of East Los Angeles preying on these gangs that were known as zoot-suiters. A segment of the present-day Mexican gangs can be traced back in some ways to the earlier zoot-suiter gangs (Governor's Organized Crime Prevention Commission, 1991).

Mexican street gangs continued to appear on the streets of East Los Angeles, but the composition of these groups changed somewhat beginning in the mid-1940s. During the early 1950s, the makeup of these groups began to include a large number of hard-ened criminals who had participated in numerous types of criminal operations in East Los Angeles. Many of these smaller gangs were ultimately linked together into one large gang, the Mexican Mafia, which occurred during the imprisonment of gang members in the Deuel Vocational Institute in Tracy, California, in the mid-1950s. Within a short period of time, the majority of members of these smaller gangs were assimilated into one big gang, the Mexican Mafia, that would ultimately create a prison empire victimizing white, black, and Hispanic inmates. It was not long after the incorporation of these smaller gangs into one high-profile gang that this criminal organization started moving into more profitable unlawful activities.

Mexican Gangs

Mexican Mafia and La Nuestra Familia.   At first, members of the Mexican Mafia set themselves up as a protection service for other members of the prison community. In an effort to follow up on this successful endeavor, the gang members quickly became active participants in gambling, drug dealing, and male pros-titution rings within the California prison system. During the mid-1960s, the Mexican Mafia took complete control of the prison drug trade as well as a large portion of the other unlawful activities found within penal institutions. A majority of the members of the prison population whom the gang provided services for were either black or white. As the membership of the Mexican Mafia continued to increase, so did their use of brutality against all nongang members—whether black, white, or Hispanic—within the California prison system. This type of treatment led to the formation of another Mexican prison gang, La Nuestra Familia (Our Family), which objected to the brutal actions of the Mexican Mafia used against other prison groups.

La Nuestra Familia originally comprised U.S.-born Mexicans who lived outside the major urban areas of California. This gang was (and still is) involved in a fierce con-flict with members of the Mexican Mafia, a conflict that began with La Nuestra Familia's inception in 1958. When La Nuestra Familia was originally formed as a prison gang, just about all the members were from an area outside Los Angeles known as Central Valley. As time progressed, membership in this gang changed to include urban as well as rural members. This organized crime group managed to form a business rela-tionship with several Chinese gangs, including the Wah Ching and Chung Ching Yee; these alliances helped La Nuestra Familia increase its involvement in the street sales of heroin (DEA, 1993).

In the mid-1980s, La Nuestra Familia started to encounter some serious prob-lems within its ranks, a major portion of which were related to members deserting the gang. The gang leaders made several attempts to negate this problem by trying to influence the defectors to return to the gang by promising them that changes would be made to improve conditions within the gang. This attempt proved to be an unproductive measure that enticed very few members back to the gang. Two other issues had an effect on the stability of La Nuestra Familia. First is the continuous growth of its number one adversary, the Mexican Mafia, which has been moving into territory once controlled by La Nuestra Familia. Second is the arrests and prosecutions of street leaders and gang members by the federal government under the Racketeer Influenced and Corrupt Organizations (RICO) laws.

Mindful of all these difficulties, La Nuestra Familia's leadership created a far more controlled type of family environment within its organization. The gang leaders stressed the importance of having a disciplined and profit-making group. Within the prison environment, La Nuestra Familia formed a working relationship with the Black Guerrilla Family, which is a militant prison gang. This was done by La Nuestra Familia to gain an ally in its war against the Mexican Mafia, not to advocate prison militancy. One of the main results of this organizational change by La Nuestra Familia was a militaristic attitude within the rank and file of the gang. With this in mind, the leaders of La Nuestra Familia created a constitution known as the Supreme Power Structure of La Nuestra Familia. The first, third, fourth, and fifth of the six articles of this constitution describe the authority, competency, and obligations of all members of La Nuestra Familia. Rank structure in La Nuestra Familia is similar to that of the military, with one leader who is designated as a general in command of all the prison groups and another general who commands all the gang's street activities. Each general has up to 10 captains; the captains control a large number of lieutenants, who in turn supervise La Nuestra Familia soldiers or members.

Any member can become a gang leader after he participates in or performs a number of killings. Once a soldier (*soldados*) carries out a hit (usually wounding a specific person in the leg or arm with a gun, not killing someone), this gang member is given the title of warrior. There are two ways to attain the rank of captain: The first is by performing three killings; the second is according to the executive abilities of the member. It is not mandatory that a gang member be promoted under either one of these standards. A gang member can quickly achieve the rank of lieutenant by killing any person listed by La Nuestra Familia as one of its top 10 enemies (LASD, 1992).

The other two articles (the second and the sixth) in La Nuestra Familia's constitution relate to the membership. The second article discusses the main objectives of the organization. According to this constitution, the gang's purpose is to serve the membership, improve the conditions within the gang, and work toward solidifying an effective association. In article six, guidelines related to the proper behavior of all gang members and the associated punishments for improper actions are described; this is in addition to the guidelines related to the denial of the existence of the gang when members are questioned by law enforcement officials (LASD, 1992).

La Nuestra Familia's constitution also outlines a three-part agenda to create financial security:

> [La Nuestra Familia will keep funds] containing not less than $1,000 for each La Nuestra Familia "regiment" and a main bank. The regimental bank, designed for each regiment's own use, will provide the payroll, pay attorney's and doctor's fees, pay bail money, and also buy into legitimate businesses. A main bank will exist as a financial resource for purchasing legitimate businesses. However, the businesses purchased through their main bank, unlike the regiment bank, is to be kept strictly legal (U.S Department of Justice, 1989; LASD, 1992).

It would be possible for the leaders of La Nuestra Familia to fulfill the first six articles of this constitution, but until the gang built up a large fund, there would be a great deal of difficulty in implementing the three-part agenda. The present strength of this gang is somewhere around 400 members; its area of operation includes Bakersfield, East Los Angeles, Fresno, Gilroy, San Diego, San Francisco, San Jose, Santa Barbara, Stockton, and Visalia. As for the Mexican Mafia, the major moneymaking activity for La Nuestra Familia is narcotic trafficking, both in the prisons and on the streets. Many gang members still participate in crimes such as burglary, robbery, and larceny.

As far as size is concerned, the Mexican Mafia has to be considered a much larger and more powerful gang than La Nuestra Familia. This strength was built on the ability of the Mexican Mafia to use violence to protect themselves and other members of the prison community. In addition, the Mexican Mafia prevented other groups from attempting to take over control of its unlawful prison and street operations. This reputation for violence also helped the Mexican Mafia to attract new members at twice the rate of La Nuestra Familia. Since the early 1970s, both Mexicans and Mexican-Americans entering the California prison system have been compelled to become members of the Mexican Mafia, La Nuestra Familia, the Texas Syndicate, the Border Brothers, or the Fresno Bull Dogs. Mexican Mafia gang members have thus far avoided being involved in any type of radical activities; instead, they work to make money and, whenever possible, continue to exploit the system, whether it be inside or outside prison. Recent intelligence information indicated that the Mexican Mafia formed a business relationship with La Cosa Nostra. These combined business operations include performing strong-arm activities, collecting debts, protecting gambling and prostitution establishments, and supplying heroin or cocaine to the Italian gangs. Members of the Mexican Mafia have always had a propensity to be more violent than their counterparts in other Mexican gangs. One must remember that this gang found it easy to kill rival gang members as well as Mexican Mafia members who failed to follow gang policy and any other people who got in their way, including members or workers of other ethnic gangs. Mexican Mafia members killed without hesitation, whether they were hired to do so or simply wanted the thrill of killing a rival gang member.

Members of the Mexican Mafia have a tendency to be arrested and charged at a far more frequent rate than members of other Mexican gangs; there are several possible reasons for this. One is the inability of some gang members to cope with the world outside of prison. Another possible reason is that when gang members are arrested and go back into the prison system, they are going back to the only family relationships they know and to the only place where they feel safe. In turn, these feelings create a very strong and structured family-type group and produce an environment for expanding unlawful operations and attracting new members to the gang (U.S. Department of Justice, 1989).

One early problem Mexican gangs faced revolved around members who deserted the gangs after their release from prison. When the gangs were originally formed, a person who was a member while serving time in prison could, upon release from prison, return to his home and have no further relationship with the gang; however, this is no longer tolerated by the gangs. Once a person becomes a gang member, that person must remain a member until death. After release from a correctional institute, a gang member must join other gang members and must partake in criminal activities. Members are not permitted to resign; people who desert the gang are usually found dead because all gang members have a responsibility to kill anyone who defects from the organization.

A large percentage of drug dealing in East Los Angeles is controlled by members of the Mexican Mafia. In most cases, the Mexican Mafia supplies the drugs to local Hispanic street gangs, which then distribute the drugs to their members who sell the illegal substances at street level. East Los Angeles is the number one location outside prison that the Mexican gangs control. The distribution of heroin, cocaine, and other drugs to street gangs resulted in these organized Mexican gangs accumulating large revenues for their leaders. Any intruders who think they can move into a gang's territory to deal drugs are quickly eliminated by gang members. Another high income producer for the gangs has been the armed robbery of businesses or banks within the gang's area of control. The gangs have found that robbery is an easy way to increase their income and finance other types of criminal activity.

The Mexican Mafia was controlled and run by Joe (Pegleg) Morgan for the greater part of 25 years. Morgan was a Slavic-American who spent 40 years of his life in prison and managed to climb the ladder to become the Mexican Mafia's godfather. Morgan's criminal career began in 1946 at the age of 16 when he was convicted of murdering his 32-year-old girlfriend's husband with a tire iron. Morgan was released from prison after serving 9 years, but within a year he was back in prison for committing a bank robbery in West Covino, California. Morgan escaped from several correctional facilities in California; one escape was facilitated by tools hidden in his prosthetic leg. In early 1993, Morgan threatened to use members of the Mexican Mafia as violent enforcers to stop drive-by shootings by members of the Latino street gangs in Southern California. There was a decline in the number of drive-by shootings after Morgan's announcement, but a short time after this proclamation, Morgan was diagnosed with cancer and died in early November 1993 (Katz, 1993).

Law enforcement officials in California consider the Mexican Mafia a well-established, highly meticulous, and very complex organized crime family. Each prison has one specific leader who is answerable only to the principal leader of the Mexican

Mafia. There are many notable similarities between the Mexican Mafia's prison and street gang leadership and tactics and those of the different family groups within La Cosa Nostra. The basic structure includes two systemwide leaders, a godfather/president at the top and an underboss/vice president underneath him. Regional-level generals are in charge of each institution; lieutenants and sergeants are at unit level, with soldiers or workers at the bottom with associates or sympathizers. The prison leaders and street leaders will change, according to whether a leader is in or out of prison (DEA, 1987).

Membership in the Mexican Mafia has continued to grow over the past several decades, and there are presently about 700 hard-core gang members. In an effort to strengthen its control in the California prisons, the Mexican Mafia formed an alliance with the Aryan Brotherhood, a white supremacist gang. The Aryan Brotherhood assists the Mexican Mafia in some criminal activities but on occasion also takes a contract to kill someone from the Mexican Mafia. The Aryan Brotherhood has no real written code but usually adheres to the following doctrine:

> A member is to share all and everything. I have one leader to boss all members and to swear their lives to the group with the understanding that death is the failure to comply with the codes of the group. Once an inmate is accepted into the group, he can no longer drop out (Commitee on Governmental Affairs, December 1992: 32).

The Mexican Mafia, like other gangs, managed to become actively involved in acquiring government-subsidized grants. Once gang members become active participants in a project, they immediately take control of the grant. An example of the gang's activity in a project can be seen in the following information gathered by California correctional authorities:

> In 1976, a project was established in East Los Angeles with $228,000 of government funds to help ex-convicts readjust to living in society. Vehicles bought by the project's funds for field counseling were used by Mexican Mafia members in at least seven murders. Funds were also used to purchase heroin in Mexico which was then flown to California by couriers using the project's credit cards. Prison inmates released into the care of the project were provided with heroin by the Mexican Mafia and encouraged to establish dealerships in East Los Angeles. A percentage of the profits was then kicked back to the Mexican Mafia. When the wife of a Mexican Mafia member threatened to tell the authorities about the misuse of the project's money, she was killed on the orders of her husband (DEA, 1987: 97).

SNM Gang.   Another prison gang, the Sindicato Nuevo Mexico (SNM), or the New Mexico Syndicate, is an expansion of the Mexican Mafia. The SNM is the largest gang operating in the New Mexico prison system. This gang follows the same philosophy as the Mexican Mafia and exerts influence throughout the New Mexico prison system by controlling drug operations, extortion, and prison violence. The objectives set forth by this group are explicit (Governor's Organized Crime Prevention Commission, 1990):

1. Regulate all narcotic trafficking throughout the New Mexico prison system.
2. Direct all extortion and protection activities.
3. Achieve and maintain authority over the entire correctional facility, all of the inmates and prison staff, through the use of violence.

The SNM gang requires the following of all new gang members (Governor's Organized Crime Prevention Commission, 1990):

1. Sponsorship into the gang is mandatory, and the sponsor should be of good character and willing to be accountable for the conduct of this newly sponsored member.
2. The new gang participant must be ready to devote his life to the gang.
3. A plurality of the membership's vote must be obtained to become a member.
4. Betrayal of the gang or disobedience to an order by a gang member means death.
5. All new gang members have anywhere from six months to a year for a probationary period. During this time period, the new member must perform different tasks to prove his worth to the gang.
6. It is mandatory that all gang members have a high regard for each other.

The SNM maintains a very good relationship with the Mexican Mafia, and this alliance helped the SNM strengthen its ability to recruit new members into the gang. The structural makeup of the gang includes a systemwide don and godfather. At the regional level, there are generals who control prison and street activities, while unit-level supervisors are known as lieutenants. The soldiers, associates, and sympathizers are at the bottom of the gang hierarchy.

Mexikanemi Gang.   In 1984, the Texas version of the Mexican Mafia was formed in the Texas prison system. This gang was not only patterned after the California version of the Mexican Mafia but also used the name Mexikanemi (Soldiers of Atzlan). The Mexikanemi gang has been involved in continuous hostilities with the Texas Syndicate since the Syndicate declared war on the Mexikanemi in 1985 (Governor's Organized Crime Prevention Commission, 1991). The administrative structure of the Mexikanemi gang is the same as its California forerunner, but there are some differences in the guidelines set forth by this criminal organization (LASD, 1992: 91–94):

1. Once a member, always a member—"blood in, blood out."
2. All members must be ready to forfeit their existence or to kill another if it is required of them.
3. Members shall struggle to conquer their faults in an effort to obtain and maintain control of the gang's membership.

4. No matter what happens, members must never disappoint or fail the gang.

5. A mentor to a new member is fully responsible for that member's actions, and it is the mentor's duty to dispose of any person he sponsors who turns out to be a defector or dropout.

6. The membership of Mexikanemi will strive to eliminate any person or group of people who takes contemptuous actions against the gang or the gang's membership.

7. The maintenance of honor and principles is a very important factor to all gang members.

8. A member must never discuss the gang's activities with outside people or agencies.

9. All of the members have the right to participate in and agree or disagree with the gang's philosophy or regulations.

10. A member of Mexikanemi has the right to guide and protect the gang.

11. Once a person has attained membership in the Mexikanemi, he can sport the gang's tattoo.

12. The Mexikanemi is an organized criminal group that will continue to partake in any criminal activity that will produce dividends for the gang.

Mexican Street Gangs.   It is important to remember that when there is any discussion involving Mexican organized crime groups, some time must be spent reviewing Mexican street gangs because a major portion of the members of Mexican organized crime evolved from these street gangs. A majority of the East Los Angeles street gangs of today emerged from the original street gangs of the 1940s and 1950s; these gangs were formed within local Mexican communities as the defenders of local ethnic domains against any attacks from outside ethnic groups. Participation in these Mexican groups became a handed-down practice; in fact, the Los Angeles County Sheriff's Department found that grandfathers, fathers, and sons have held membership in the same street gangs. In some cases, it is possible to have members who are third- or fourth-generation gang members. It has also been discovered that machismo is a key factor in actions taken by most members of these street gangs (LASD, 1992).

The enticements each gang presents for becoming a member include the following (LASD, 1992):

1. The member becomes part of a group or family and joins the gang in an attempt to gain that identity.

2. Once attaining membership in a gang, this person becomes an acknowledged member of gang society—a "home boy"—who has a unique identity and usually a nickname that fits him or her.

3. Belonging to the gang leads to an existence that converts the new member to a home boy. Being a home boy is very significant to the new member.

A large proportion of gang members use some type of drugs, whether it is PCP, crack cocaine, speed, LSD, or heroin. Street gang members wear clothing that sets them apart from members of other gangs. Most Mexican street gangs prefer khaki pants that are very baggy and pulled above the waist. At one time, Pendleton shirts were a common part of their dress style, but this has changed in recent years. Nicknames are a major part of each gang member's identity; names such as Maton (Killer), Gordo (Fat), Toro (Bull), Flaco (Skinny), and Oso (Bear) are some of those given to gang members by other gang members (LASD, 1992).

The role of the leadership in most of these gangs is loosely structured and is based on the needs of the gang. A gang member who becomes a boss is usually only placed there on a temporary basis because of some unique talent this gang member may possess. It is very seldom that any of the street gangs select a permanent leader, so there is no firm foundation to the supervisory structure in most of these Mexican street gangs. In many cases, street gangs are somewhat under the guidance of older gangs such as the Mexican Mafia. These are some of the major differences between Mexican street gangs and other street gangs (LASD, 1992):

1. Mexican street gangs are very protective of what they consider their turf and protect this territory by whatever means necessary.
2. In most cases, Mexican street gangs do not leave their turf, so mobility is not one of the gangs' assets.
3. Mexican street gangs are considerate to people and protective of places in their own territory.
4. Mexican street gangs are loyal—gang members come first and everyone and everything else comes second.

Graffiti, in most cases, is used to designate an area that a Mexican street gang controls. This wall writing also leaves an explicit message to other gangs about who controls this territory and what will happen if any other gang attempts to infringe on this area. Graffiti is also used to heap praise on the gang and its members. Mexican street gangs are prevalent throughout California, the West Coast, the Southwest, and some cities in the Midwest, especially Chicago. Presently, there are 15 active Mexican street gangs in Chicago; most of these gangs are composed of Mexicans, whites, and blacks. Mexican street gangs on the West Coast and in the Southwest are ethnically Mexican and Mexican-American (Chicago PD, 1993; LASD, 1992).

Mexican Criminal Activities

Organized crime groups in certain areas of Mexico are highly influential and very heavily involved in drug trafficking; this was especially true in the city of Culiacan in the northwestern Mexican state of Sinaloa. Through the mid-1980s and into the 1990s the U.S. Drug Enforcement Agency estimated that approximately two tons of cocaine were transported from Culiacan to the United States each month. In 1989, the Mexican army arrested Felix Gallardo, the leader of the Culiacan gang and a major cocaine smuggler; the chief of police in Culiacan, Robespierre Lizarraga Coronel; the director of the Sinaloa State Judicial Police, Arturo Moreno; the leaders of the Mexican state of Tamaulipus that is on the border of Texas; a federal highway police unit; and 300 members of the Culiacan Police Department (Rohter, April 11, 1989).

The drug gangs in the Mexican state of Sinaloa have been involved in the trans-shipment of narcotics from Colombia to the United States since the 1980s and have grown Mexican brown heroin and marijuana since the late 1940s. The Gallardo drug gang has become completely in control in the state of Sinaloa. Members of this gang were not only growing, importing, shipping, distributing, and selling drugs but were allowed to openly kill people who opposed them right on the streets of Culiacan. Gang members also kidnapped and raped young women of Sinaloa without any opposition from any police agency (Rohter, April 16, 1989).

Drug trafficking in and around the city of Culiacan in Sinaloa has not decreased since 1989; in fact, Culiacan has been nicknamed "Little Medellin" because of the amount of drug activity in and around the confines of this city. Felix Gallardo controlled his high-profile drug organization from his prison cell in Mexico City's Southern Prison. Gallardo's prison cell was equipped with a cellular telephone, fax machines, and body guards who performed clerical work. In 1993 in an attempt to control Gallardo's drug activities, the Mexican government transferred Gallardo to a high-security prison in the state of Mexico. Gallardo, who was a state police officer in Sinaloa prior to his involvement in drug trafficking, still managed to communicate with his gang by sending coded messages through his lawyers. In 1993, the U.S. Drug Enforcement Agency estimated that about 70 percent of all the cocaine that entered the United States was transported through Mexico (Golden, January 10, 1993).

Conditions in the state of Sinaloa continued to deteriorate; the total number of people killed in Sinaloa between 1981 and 1993 was over 7,000 (Golden, March 8, 1993). These murders, plus Gallardo's ability to operate openly while in prison, indicated that the drug gangs adjusted very well to the measures taken by the Mexican government to control drug trafficking in the state of Sinaloa (Golden, August 7, 1993). Violence of the Mexican drug gangs, erupted in May 1993 when Juan Jesus Cardinal Posadas Ocampo, was shot and killed (along with five other people) as he inadvertently walked into a drug shootout as he was leaving the airport in Guadalajara, Mexico. The person arrested for this crime was Joaquin Guzman Loera (also known as El Chapo or Shortie), who was the head of a Sinaloa-based drug cartel. Loera was apprehended in Guatemala along with five other gang leaders (Golden, June 11, 1993).

A short time after the murder of Cardinal Ocampo, the Mexican government pledged to dismantle the organized crime groups and the drug trade they controlled. This vow apparently went unfulfilled because the Mexican gangs continued to openly operate in the state of Sinaloa. In August 1994, Mexican police made a large seizure of marijuana on a 220-acre marijuana plantation in the Chihuahua desert through a tip given to the Mexican police by the U.S. Drug Enforcement Agency (Golden, 1994).

This seizure was followed in September by the arrest of Antonio Abrego, the nephew of the boss of the Abrego organized crime family, and his associate, Alejandro Diaz. A former Mexican government official has accused the Abrego cartel of being involved in the assassination of presidential candidate Donaldo Colosio (*New York Times*, 1994).

Members of Mexican drug cartels also used old Boeing 727s and French-produced Caravelle jets. In Colombia, these planes would be loaded with six tons or more of cocaine for a flight to Mexico. In Mexico, an airport would usually be built on short notice on a large farm area or in a Mexican desert by just flattening out and hardening the dirt surface with a steamroller. After the planes landed and were unloaded, the Mexican gangs would transport the drugs by land or sea to the United States (Golden, 1995).

The organizational structure of Mexican organized crime groups is a combination of La Cosa Nostra and the military. A leader is both a boss and a godfather. As a boss, he runs the whole operation, with the assistance of several underbosses and advisors, but as a godfather, he has total control over this organization. Under his command are captains who control specific operations and who are answerable to the godfather. Next in command are lieutenants who control the daily movements of the gang members; under the lieutenants are soldiers or workers who perform the activities assigned to them by the lieutenants (DEA, 1993).

The Mexican drug cartels in Sinaloa capitalized on their relationship with Colombian drug lords. U.S. law enforcement officials estimated that anywhere from 60 to 75 percent of the cocaine being imported into the United States was transshipped through Mexico. As a result of this increased cocaine distribution, many members of Mexican drug cartels became millionaires. Along with this newfound wealth came the power and the ability to corrupt both political and police authorities throughout Mexico, resulting in increases in both crime rates and drug use. There is no doubt, that these organized crime gangs will continue to flourish in Mexico until a method is found that prevents these gangs from having access to their drug suppliers. As the different types of Mexican organized crime groups continue to grow and flourish, it seems doubtful that either the Mexican or the U.S. government is taking the proper steps to deter the gangs' criminal activities.

CONCLUSIONS

There is little doubt that all the Hispanic organized crime groups continue to prosper due to the vast drug market available to them, whether they grow, process, smuggle, distribute, or sell drugs at street level. A major portion of the Hispanic groups come from countries run by governments whose integrity is questioned by their citizens as well as by the media, so until some drastic changes are made or laws are introduced and strictly enforced—without corruption playing a major role—nothing will hinder these gangs and their criminal activities.

CHAPTER **11**

RUSSIAN AND ISRAELI GANGS

Russian and Israeli organized crime groups have both similarities and differences. Although based out of two different countries, both groups have worked successfully in drug-trafficking and money-laundering businesses. The groups also profited very handsomely from scams they perfected and worked on together. However, each of these groups is controlled by a separate faction whose leadership is chosen by its membership. The first criminal organization we shall view is the Russian groups.

RUSSIAN GANGS

Russian History

Historical records indicate that the criminal operations of organized gangs in Russia have existed for several centuries. It seems that the earliest criminal groups that formed in Russia based many of their guidelines on procedures followed by the Russian Cossacks. Varery Chalidze, in his book *Criminal Russia: Essays on Crime in the Soviet Union*, compares what he considers to be the significant relationships between the members of the seventeenth-century Cossacks and the first underworld gangs in Russia that later became known as Russian organized crime groups. Chalidze found the following (Chalidze, 1977):

1. Both groups conformed to policy set by the government, but each association had some kind of self-government that ruled from inside the organization.
2. Within the group, the members were treated the same. There was little or no preferential treatment for anyone, although with leadership received some special recognition from the members of the organization.

3. All the leaders were selected and elected by the members and sat on councils at which every member had to express an opinion either for or against a policy set by the council. Members' opinions were given without any fear of retaliation.

4. There were no written procedures or policies relating to the group's legal or illegal activities, but each member understood the necessity of unity and of punishment for members who committed some type of serious error (e.g., treason, cowardice, or murder) against the association. Serious infractions against the organization usually resulted in death of the offender.

5. As in other secretive associations, a code of silence concerning the organization and its activities was maintained by all.

Early studies on crime in Russia indicated that almost all previous criminal groups were considered to be Robin Hood types of gangs that robbed the rich and seldom bothered the poor. As years passed, members of these groups also became involved in extortion of business enterprises within their local villages. As times in Russia changed at the turn of the twentieth century, so did the opinions of leaders among the Bolshevik revolutionaries toward criminal groups. The gangs were used by both the Bolsheviks and the Social Revolutionaries as vehicles to procure collateral through both extortion and robbery. Lenin went so far as to state that "We stole what had been stolen" (Chalidze, 1977, p. 22). Stalin created his own gang, with Semyon Terpetrosyan (an Armenian Bolshevik who was also known as Kamo) as the leader, to carry out robberies to enrich the Bolsheviks' treasury and support their upcoming revolution (Chalidze, 1977). A short time after the revolution, Kamo died under very suspicious circumstances. Stalin denied any type of criminal association with Kamo and denied being involved in any of Kamo's criminal activities prior to, during, or after the revolution. Chalidze claimed that Stalin had very close ties to criminals and their organizations that were built during the early days of the Bolsheviks' rise to power. During the early part of the revolution, Stalin used these connections to carry out numerous robberies and other crimes that would bankroll the party and enhance his position in the revolutionary group (Chalidze, 1977).

As we continue to examine the Russian gangs, we also become aware of the way the Communist government in Moscow totally controlled all the Soviet Socialist Republic for a period of 75 years. Almost every person put in a political position by the Communist Party was placed there to extort money from either businesses or citizens of the Soviet Republic. People placed in these governmental positions were there because they were politically connected to the Soviet regime or because they paid a government official to be appointed to that position; only people the Communist Party trusted were placed in these posts.

Corruption existed in every phase of the Russian government's operations. A Russian citizen in need of housing was given preference according to his or her ability to supply something to the person(s) in charge of assigning residences to citizens. In many cases, a person seeking housing had to participate in an auction-type situation and had to bid on properties. It was usually required that a specific amount of money be paid to a government official in order to obtain accommodations. This system also gave those who could afford to pay bribes (and who in most cases also managed public supplies) the ability to barter their goods by way of either legal or illegal markets. Back-door business deals were common, as was the exchange of items in illegal markets. The Communist Party created a well-organized extortion-oriented system that revolved around bribery. Money obtained from corrupt activities moved up through the Soviet power structure and became tribute to higher-ranking officials in the Communist Party. The money became what was to be considered an unofficial tax that was paid in order to operate a business in the Soviet Socialist Republic (Leitzel, Gaddy, and Alexeev, 1995).

Russian Gangs

Under the Bolshevik's regime and the Communist Party, activities of organized crime groups in Russia gradually increased without any major intrusion into their operations from members of the easily influenced Russian law enforcement establishment. Russian history does not acknowledge the fact that in many cases the clandestine and coercive activities of both the Soviet government and its secret KGB police–type organizations were very similar to those of La Cosa Nostra organized crime families in the United States. As time went on, these types of tactics were found to be effective for the Soviet rulers to use to rid their nation of adversaries. It also assisted them in regulating the economy and assuring them of an ever-increasing corrupt income on top of their governmental salaries (Klebnikov, 1993). There had always been a considerable amount of organized criminal activity within the Soviet Union, but few of these groups' unlawful operations actually became public knowledge until the latter part of 1970, even though most parts of the old Soviet Republic were aware of the actions of these organized gangs for decades (U.S. News & World Report, 1993b). Throughout Russia, criminal operations are carried out on a daily basis by these gangs. In fact, during a 1995 meeting in Moscow, members of a very influential roundtable organization demanded that something be done by the government to reduce the ever- increasing attacks on Russian businesspeople by gang members; since January 1 of that year, there had been a total of 90 assaults on rich business owners, with 46 of those attacks killing the victims (New York Times, 1995).

Most of the gangs were built around a strong leader who in many cases had prior gang experience, had spent some period of his life within the confines of a prison, and had a very strong autocratic disposition. Gang participants selecting a leader felt that these variables gave the newly appointed group boss sufficient criminal experience to run a profitable gang operation. Most of the early gangs had a power structure that included the boss; several lieutenants, workers, and apprentices; and people who were considered the gangs' connections to legitimate society. This last group included receivers of stolen property, dealers in stolen property, informers who set up places for people to rob, and people who would participate in the escape of a thief or gang member after the completion of a crime. Although this latter group of individuals were really criminals, the gangs considered them "legitimate" citizens because they were not true gang members.

The gangs in Russia that formed after the revolution had their own body of laws to guide their operations (Chalidze, 1977):

1. Gang members lived segregated from the legitimate outside world.
2. Gang members rejected all the responsibilities of a normal life.
3. Gang members vowed to never cooperate with state authorities in any way and (whenever possible) to find a way to rip off the state or one of its agencies.
4. Gang members were not permitted to be members of the Russian military during World War II, even if they were drafted.
5. Gang members avoided any connections that interfered with their autonomy in gang activities.
6. Gang members maintained integrity when dealing with other gang members.
7. Gang members made their family members understand that they were to avoid any type of contact with the outside world.

Russian gangs also use special terms to describe their members and some of their activities. Some of these terms are *pakhany* (bosses), *vory v zakone* (regular criminals or thieves professing the code), *vorovskoy mir* (thieves' world), *krestnii otets* (godfather), and *vory v ramke* (thieves in a frame). These terms have different meanings for gang members than for outsiders. For example, according to Russian police officials, a person designated a *vory v zakone* is a member of "thieves in law," which to them means that person is a leader in Russian organized crime (Raab, 1995).

Another characteristic of many members of Russian crime groups is their ability to withstand pain. This attribute manifests itself when gang members are confined to prison. In many cases, actions taken by gang members in prison impair them as well as cause pain, but the actions have a purpose. For example, while confined to a correctional facility, gang members may swallow nails, barbed wire, mercury thermometers, chess pieces, dominoes, needles, ground glass, spoons, knives, or other foreign objects. According to Chalidze, prisoners who are gang members will "sew up their lips or eyelids, nail their scrotums to a bed, cut open the skin on their arms or legs and peel it off their bodies" (Chalidze, 1977). All these activities are done so that gang members are sent to the prison hospital, where they receive special treatment that includes better food, needed drugs, and a work-free environment for a period of time (Chalidze, 1977).

The number of organized crime groups and their illegal activities in Russia increased dramatically between the 1960s and 1990s. A great deal of gang expansion was due to the lackadaisical attitude of the Communist government, which denied all allegations of the existence of organized crime in Russia. Many of the gangs were actually started in locations such as the Central Asian (Uzbekistan and Kazakhstan), Caucasus (Georgia and Azerbaijan), and Ukraine areas of what was then Communist Russia.

One of the most disreputable yet adaptable gangs within Russia has been the Chechen organized crime groups, which originated in the Chechnya area of the Northern Caucasus. Although many of these Chechen gangs were not affiliated with each other, they managed to rely on each other and on a corrupt government to avoid prosecution. It is estimated that the Chechen gangs have a force of 600 in Moscow, where they are feared and despised. Russians consider them a braggadocio bunch of hoodlums who are attempting to bully their way into taking control of the streets in Moscow as well as those of Berlin, Prague, and Warsaw. Chechen gangs have become involved in car thefts throughout Europe and the United States; they also have smuggled drugs all over Western Europe and created scams that were used successfully to bilk money from both the public sector (government) and private enterprises in the United States (Sterling, 1994). Chechen gangs' activities such as robbery, extortion, fraud, prostitution, and murder continued to thrive, and their increased participation in the lucrative Russian black market enhanced the gangs' treasury and slowly but surely helped expand the number of gangs and their total membership.

Russian Gangs Since Glasnost.   The formation of the Commonwealth of Independent States (CIS) that came with the fall of Communist rule in Russia apparently caused a large increase in the number of organized crime groups within the newly created CIS. According to various law enforcement sources, the number of gangs in the CIS ranged from 3,500 to 5,700, with total membership somewhere in the area of 200,000 to 1,000,000 and a total of 500 to 18,000 leaders. One must remember that within this Russian organized crime environment, a majority of the gangs have an average of only 2 to 5 members; there are some very large organized crime groups, but most are small cells that have some type of affiliation to the bigger crime groups. In most cases, an alliance with a larger gang requires some sort of monthly compensation for the protection afforded to the smaller group. Present-day Russian law enforcement discovered that of the large number of criminal groups in operation in the CIS, the vast majority were under the control of anywhere between 150 and 200 confederations. These confederations provide the necessary protection and guidance so that the smaller groups can avoid conflict within the various criminal environments or criminal operations that these gangs are participating in at the same time (Klebnikov, 1993).

The Russian Ministry of Internal Affairs (RMIA) indicated there were approximately 4,350 criminal groups within Russia; there were 275 intraregional gangs, 168 universal gangs, approximately 150 "criminal communities" that consist of two or more gangs working together, and about 150 ethnically based gangs. Intelligence information gathered by RMIA indicated that the 4 groups that have caused the most problems within the CIS were originally from the Azerbaijian, Chechen, Dagestan, and Georgian regions of Russia. A majority of the Russian gangs have done fairly well financially because of their participation in banking fraud, auto thefts, and contract murders.

Many Russian criminals who were deported during the 1980s under the guise of being Jewish immigrants went back to Russia after the collapse of the Communist regime in 1991. These criminals, working hand in hand with a criminal element that never left Russia, managed to infiltrate the Russian banking operations through the use of kidnapping and murder. Once these gangs took control of the banks, they used them to launder money from unlawful gang operations and foreign drug cartels and to embezzle money from local business accounts. Gang members used information obtained from bank records to decide what businesses to exploit and how much money to embezzle from them. The gangs formed by the former deportees also successfully set up a scheme that forced 70 percent of all private-sector enterprises to pay the gangs a monthly fee for protection against anything happening that could hurt or destroy their businesses.

Researchers studying organized crime groups in Russia found three basic types of group structures. The first shows a pyramid type of structure that has elite leaders at the top who control the activities and profits of the organization. These elite leaders live the good life; in many cases, their street operatives are unaware of their identities. The support and security part of this organization manages to shield the identities of the leaders.

Members of the support and security part of the gang may include doctors, corrupt government officials, and persons involved in the distribution of media information. All the workers in both the support and security branches have an agenda to fulfill (Serio, 1992):

1. Ensure that all orders given by the elite group are properly followed and that the planned criminal activity is successfully completed by gang workers.

2. Maintain peaceful coexistence within the gang's lower ranks by resolving any disagreement or disputes.

3. Perpetuate a peaceful coexistence between the gangs and both other criminal groups and other criminals.

4. Distribute promotional information that helps expand the group's illegal beliefs.

5. Ensure that members of the elite group receive the proper accolades they deserve and that the local community is aware of the plaudits being heaped on each group leader. This is carried out in order to increase the productiveness within the criminal society or group.

6. Do whatever is necessary to hinder the effectiveness of any procedures that might be used by outside government agencies against the gang.

7. Have a plan and people available to assist in dealing with agencies that arrest and prosecute members of the gang.

8. Provide all types of fraudulent documents to gang members either to bring a criminal act to a successful conclusion or to avoid arrest and/or prosecution.

The third group of members that works in a pyramid structure of a Russian organized crime gang is the workers or street operatives. These workers, as members of the gang, are required to successfully complete all the criminal schemes formulated by the elite members of this criminal enterprise. In most cases, these members are usually career criminals who have expertise in a specific type of crime (e.g., burglary, robbery, fraud, kidnapping, or murder). It is possible for a member of the lower echelon to climb the ladder and join the elite group, but it requires that person to be very productive and capable of putting a lot of money or other assets into the group's accounts. Another alternative for an ambitious worker to gain group status is to save a sufficient amount of money to start his own gang.

The second type of organizational structure discovered by investigators of Russian organized gangs is a tetrad type of association. This four-tier criminal organization is controlled by a person identified as a boss. According to Russian police sources, in 1993 there were approximately 500 crime bosses throughout the CIS (U.S. Department of Justice, 1995). An organizational boss or leader has employees directly underneath him who are known as spies. Each boss usually controls two spies, whose job it is to make sure that the next-highest-ranking person (called a brigadier) maintains allegiance to the organization and does not become more influential among the workers than the boss. Workers within this structure are put into smaller units; these smaller units (or cells) are labeled according to their specialties (e.g., narcotics unit, prostitution unit, governmental contacts unit, enforcer unit). Naturally, each specialized unit would control a specific area of organized criminal activity for the gang. Russian organized crime bosses seem to feel that an organization that has specialty employees has several advantages:

1. These gang employees know their jobs and how to perform them without being a jack-of-all-trades and attempting to create new opportunities for this organized crime family in other areas.
2. If arrested and turned into informers, these specialty employees can supply particulars on only one area of criminal activity.
3. These gang employees can't blame their inability to perform their jobs properly on being overburdened with a number of tasks required of generalist workers.
4. Specialty employees find it difficult to gain total knowledge of an operation so that they can form their own group using information gathered from this gang and become another competitor in this field.

The third type of Russian organized crime group structure discovered by the researchers is the one used by the Chechen gangs, most of which are very clannish groups. It is estimated that there are 1 million Chechens presently living the northern area of the Caucasus; the majority of all Chechens are members of the Islamic religion. As a group, they work throughout Russia as well as in Germany, Saudi Arabia, and the United States. There are five godfathers: four in Moscow and one in Groznyy. Each godfather controls four different underbosses, who are usually placed in charge of all the groups' operations in each country. The underbosses, in turn, control at least 50 gang leaders, who oversee various gang members throughout the world. Gangs that these leaders manage are usually made up of criminals who are members of these gangs and who perform specialized criminal tasks for each group; most of the specialists are considered workers.

Intelligence gathered by U.S. law enforcement agencies indicated that Russian organized crime membership came from four different types of groups (FBI, 1993):

1. Some criminal enterprises came from the membership of the old Communist Party, which was a circle of dishonest ex-Soviet officials who worked in various government positions under the old Communist regime.

2. Regional ethnic groups had been operating as organized gangs within the Soviet Union for decades, even though the Communist government denied their existence. Some of the groups that fall into the ethnic organized criminal gang category are the Azerbaijians, Chechens, Dagestans, Georgians, Ukrainians, and Uzbeks.

3. Regular criminals or thieves who came to power in their gangs after being elected to the position of *vory v zakone* (thief professing the code) while serving a term in a Russian prison also formed gangs. These gang members are considered the bosses of most Russian organized crime groups and are elected by the membership to this position. They have the capacity to create their own organized crime gangs and, in doing so, have the ability to recruit membership to their gangs from any other Russian groups. The majority of these bosses shun attention whenever possible to avoid identification by the government. A person is selected to be a *vory v zakove* because of his prior criminal history (being both a successful and notorious criminal) and his leadership qualities. Upon being chosen, this person is obliged to take an oath of office; during an initiation ritual, he is awarded the title of master thief and leader.

4. Another type of criminal enterprise is formed as an offshoot of one of the previously mentioned organizations. Many of these gangs have been formed since the downfall of the Communist regime. The leadership of these types of organizations is usually very strong, with many of the gang's members being career criminals who have spent a good portion of their careers in prison.

In an effort to legitimize their gang operations, the godfathers, bosses, and *vory v zakone* held a series of meetings in an attempt to eliminate the hostilities between some of the gangs and create one big happy family. The first truce was made during meetings between gang leaders in Dagomys on the Black Sea in 1988; peaceful coexistence between the gangs lasted almost a year. Then during 1991 and 1992, more conferences were held with gang leaders. Peace was again restored, with the gangs being assigned different territories of authority by the leaders. Gang leaders felt that peace between all gangs was mandatory because there were opportunities for the gangs to purchase newly privatized businesses in Moscow. In doing so, the gangs would create an even larger power base for themselves. In a combined venture, the gangs managed to purchase over 50 percent of the businesses that had been put up for auction after the government privatized them. It was estimated by the government heads in Moscow that the sale of these businesses would bring approximately 1.6 billion rubles into their treasury. Gang leaders, realizing that the government anticipated a large profit on these sales, intimidated bidders on many properties. This resulted in a total amount of 200 million rubles being made by the Moscow government for properties whose estimated value was in the range of 1.6 billion rubles (Sterling, 1994).

A major advantage that organized crime groups had in Russia was the inability of the reorganized government to set up or pass the legislative tools necessary to help police and prosecutors to arrest and convict group members for their gang activities. As of now, there has not even been an attempt by the government to create laws that are comparable to U.S. antigang laws such as the Racketeer Influenced and Corrupt Organizations (RICO) Act, which allows U.S. government attorneys to prosecute bosses as well as workers. Russian leader Boris Yeltsin called for legislation that would help the government prosecute members of the Russian organized crime groups, but little was accomplished because of the lack of support within the Russian parliament. An attempt was made to strike out at the growing crime rate by strengthening prosecutors' offices in areas with high rates of criminal activity, but because of the staggering increase in crime, augmentation of these staff in these offices did not help the system.

Corruption within the Russian criminal justice system flourished even prior to the change in government. Indications of police corruption came to light in 1988 when the old Soviet government eliminated a total of 15 percent (100,000 members) of its police force because of corrupt activities within that agency. During a speech, Yeltsin admonished the politicians and the police in Russia by commenting, "Corruption is devouring the state from top to bottom" (Sterling, 1994, p. 93). Three years later in 1991, over 20,000 more police officials were terminated because they were participating in unlawful activities with members of organized crime. This—plus low (or no) pay and an ever-increasing number of serious assaults on police officers by members of organized crime—had an effect on the actions taken by law enforcement against members of these organized crime gangs. The total number of attacks with guns on police officers increased from 186 in 1989 to 719 in 1991 in just one city, St. Petersburg, Russia. This is meaningful because it indicates a 386.5 percent increase in attacks on police officers within a two-year period, a figure which was far higher than for other areas of the world, such as Sicily or Colombia, that were also dominated by members of organized crime families (Sterling, 1994).

Since the change in Russian government, there has also been a significant increase in the number of crimes committed within the old Soviet Union. The cause of this crime wave can certainly be blamed on both the sudden growth of organized crime groups and the lack of stability within the newly formed government. There were no real indicators as to which of these two factors had the bigger effect on crime in Russia; both factors probably had some impact on the total number of crimes committed, as seen in Table 11–1.

TABLE 11-1

Effect of Organized Crime on Crime Rates

Type of Crimes	Crimes Reported to Police		
	1987	1989	1993
Murders	9,199	13,543	29,200
Firearms possession	5,656	14,551	22,100
Acts by organized gangs	110,921	175,092	355,500
Serious injury to victims	20,100	36,872	66,900
Total crimes	1,185,914	1,619,818	2,799,600

According to a 1995 CNN special and several other reports, the following are true of organized crime groups in Russia:

1. They were a major factor in the ever-increasing crime rate in Moscow, which saw murder up 40 percent, rape and robbery up 42 percent, and fraud up 170 percent in one year.

2. They used crime as a tool to oppress the people just as the old regime used Communism to instill fear in citizens.

3. They fought over control of the wealth of natural resources within Russia.

4. They controlled over 40 percent of all Russian exportation of indispensable metals such as cobalt, copper, nickel, and uranium. Gang members also managed to make an average of 50 train tank cars (each carrying 147 barrels of oil) disappear every day during 1993 for sale on the black market.

5. They were involved in smuggling both historical and religious icons and art treasures out of Russia to be sold to the highest bidders throughout the world. During 1993, Russian customs officials seized over 400,000 antique art objects. According to Russian intelligence sources, the gangs were connected to every security agency in Russia, so smuggling objects out of Russia was not a problem for them.

6. They extorted protection money from about 90 percent of the street vendors in Russia.

7. They controlled over 35,000 Russian businesses, including 400 banks. Gang members used these businesses in every way possible to increase their assets. One specific scam involved obtaining a 25 percent interest rate to be paid on employee wages or overdue accounts in a business. This money was put into a commercial banking establishment that was associated with the business. Then it lent the money out at a 250 percent interest rate, with the excess interest money gained being placed in gang members' bank accounts outside Russia.

8. They established both significant relationships with Israeli organized crime groups and strong ties with many major U.S. gangs.

9. They worked hand and hand with Colombian drug cartels to distribute drugs throughout Europe and to launder their drug money. They also worked with La Cosa Nostra organized crime groups from Italy in drug distribution, money laundering, and auto thefts from both the United States and Europe.

10. They controlled who did or did not get a visa at the U.S. embassy in Moscow.

11. They were involved in the real estate market. With the upsurge of the real estate market covered by Russian tenants being allowed to purchase the apartments and houses they had rented from the old Soviet government, the gangs saw an opportunity. They used violence and kidnapping to force these citizens (the majority of whom were older members of Moscow society) either to hand over ownership papers or to sell their apartments and houses at a rate far below the average market price.

12. They managed to gain control over the illegal movement of military equipment, specifically guns. (This was apparent in the increase in crimes committed with guns from 4,000 to 22,500 in three years.) Ammunition and explosive devices, plus if available, nuclear weapons and their energy supply, they then sell these materials to the highest bidder on the world market. During 1994, German customs officials seized 17.6 ounces of plutonium 239, which is the primary material used in atomic warheads, from three non-Russian citizens traveling from Moscow to Munich. As of 1994, it was the largest seizure of this type of nuclear material (Handelman, 1994; Hersh, 1994; Hockstader, 1995; Klebnikov, 1993).

13. They controlled the organ donor market in Russia. Gang members kidnapped children and adults, removed their organs, and offered the organs for sale in countries outside Russia. Members of Russian organized crime groups were also involved in the removal of organs from unclaimed bodies in city morgues; the gangs then sold the highly profitable organs, which were then used either for organ transplants or for medical experiments (Hersh, 1993).

Several major gangs operated in Moscow. Dolgoprudny (or Dolgoprudnaya) members were involved in criminal activities centralized in the northwest section of Moscow. This was one of the oldest organized crime groups in Moscow, and a major portion of this gang's income came from its long-term protection rackets. The Lyubertsy group was originally made up of weight lifters from the southeastern section of Moscow; it became recognized as a gang in the mid-1980s. Members of this gang were initially considered to be western-type cowboys who beat up on (what they considered) punks or hippies, but they eventually became involved in running prostitution rings, extortion operations, and robbery rings and carrying out contract hits. Subsequently, a large number of the members moved on to form their own gangs throughout Russia.

The Solntsevo gang emerged from the southern part of Moscow where they were heavily involved in illegal gambling and limousine businesses. This gang's *vory v zakone* was murdered during the fall of 1994 when a bomb exploded in his vehicle. The Ingushy gang was involved in the theft and illegal trafficking of leather and animal skins, selling these to various parts of northern Italy. Assyrian, Azeris, and Chechen gangs control a majority of the drug trade in the present-day CIS (Hockstader, February 27, 1995; Sterling, 1994).

The Chechen gangs are the largest group and have been active throughout both the old Soviet Union and the new CIS; they have also increased their worldwide operations. Gang members participate in almost every type of criminal venture available to them and are presently considered the most powerful criminal group in Moscow. They are feared and despised by the citizens of Moscow, who think of them as nothing more than arrogant hoodlums who cannot be eliminated from the streets of Moscow. Chechen gangs also expanded their horizons and have taken over criminal activities on the streets of Berlin, Prague, Stockholm, and Warsaw. Within these cities, Chechen gangs participated in auto theft, drug trafficking, fraud, and counterfeiting. This group even expanded its unlawful activities to the United States in the areas of swindles and drug trafficking.

Russian Gangs in the United States.   During the early 1970s, the U.S. government used detente in an effort to create a better relationship with the Communist government in the Soviet Union. Part of the agreement worked out with the Soviet leadership involved the immigration of a large portion of the Russian Jewish population to Israel or the United States. A short time after an agreement was reached, a large number of these Soviet immigrants left Russia; some settled in Israel, while others ultimately ended up in the United States. In fact, by the mid-1980s over 250,000 Russians who were members of the Jewish religion had immigrated to the United States.

The Russians, like their counterparts in Cuba in 1980, played a dirty trick on the U.S. government in that a large percentage (40 percent) of these alleged Soviet Jews were not of the Jewish religion but were from the criminal ranks of Russian society; many of these new immigrants had been arrested and convicted of serious crimes and had done time in Soviet prisons. The majority of these Russian criminals ended up settling in major U.S. cities such as Chicago, Los Angeles, Miami, New York, and San Francisco. Once these criminals settled in a large urban community, it was not long before they started establishing small criminally oriented gangs and creating moneymaking ventures for gang members. At first, the gangs were involved in robberies, extortion, burglaries, larcenies, and auto thefts. Then they expanded their operations to include various con games, insurance fraud, medical scams, counterfeiting, credit card thefts, forgeries, and murders (Adams, 1993; Blumenthal, 1989; Freedman, 1994; *Organized Crime Digest*, 1982; Sterling, 1994).

There are a great many similarities between these Russian gangs and other ethnic gangs that formed in the United States over the past 100 years:

1. Most ethnic gang members arrived here from another country rather than being born here.

2. Ethnic gangs made their bases of operations in modest areas of large urban centers.

3. As these different ethnic gangs formed, they were based on nationality and language.

4. A vast majority of ethnic gang members left countries that were suffering from both economic problems and depleted national resources.

5. Most of the crimes ethnic gangs committed were against other members of their own ethnic group.

6. In each group of immigrants, outlaws and criminals banded together to form their own gang and initially were not affiliated with any other ethnic groups. Later on, relationships were formed with other ethnic gangs that would be mutually beneficial.

7. Whenever possible, ethnic gangs made connections to organized groups back in the homeland for support services and leadership.

Brighton Beach in Brooklyn, New York, was the home base for most Russian organized crime operations in the United States and had over 200,000 Russian immigrants within this community. According to intelligence gathered by members of local and federal law enforcement, there were three major groups operating out of Brighton Beach. A majority of the membership of the first group was Jewish and came from Odessa in Russia; the second group consisted of immigrants from Tashkent in Uzbekistan, and a majority of these members were alleged to be Muslims. Most of the members in the third group were ex-citizens of the city of Ekaterinburg in Russia (Freedman, 1994). It has been alleged that a number of New York City Police Department (NYPD) officers from the 60th and 61st Precincts in Brooklyn worked as chauffeurs and bodyguards for members of Russian organized crime. It was reported by Roger Berger, an investigator for the New York State Department of Taxation and Finance, that these same NYPD officers worked as bouncers at two local Russian nightclubs, the Rasputin and the Metropole and that these officers were active participants in some of the phony accident scams staged by members of Russian organized crime (Freedman, 1994).

One of the first known members of Russian organized crime to arrive in the United States was Evset Agron. Agron had been in jail in Russia for murder and had left Russia in 1971 to open up both gambling and prostitution operations in West Germany. He was one of 5,250 alleged Russian immigrants of the Jewish faith who came to the United States in 1975 who were really gangsters. A short time after his arrival in Brighton Beach, Agron set up his own organized crime family; his first moneymaking venture was extortion. Agron hired the most violent members of the Russian community in Brooklyn to brutally intimidate Russians immigrants into paying protection money to him and his gang, and anyone who refused to pay tribute was either beaten or tormented with an electric cattle prod until they did pay. This gang was bringing in over $50,000 a week in extortion money by the end of 1980. Agron continued his successful extortion business from his offices in the EI Caribe Country Club in Brooklyn until May 1985, when he was shot and killed in his Park Slope residence (Adams, 1992; Freedman, 1994).

Marat Balagula was quickly ordained Agron's successor. Balagula professionalized a gasoline bootlegging scam by setting up numerous dummy corporations and then moving the gasoline (on paper) from one spurious franchise to another until it reached a bogus company that was set up to pay the taxes; however, all this bogus corporation did was sell the gasoline and stamp "all taxes paid" on the bill. All the money was then taken by gang members, and the company, which had nothing more than a post office box and a nonexistent corporate head, from the face of the earth (Freedman, 1994). Balagula was convicted of credit card fraud in late 1986 and fled to Germany, from which he was returned to the United States two years later to serve a prison term.

Once Balagula was no longer in control of the Russian gangs, Boris "Papa" Nayfeld took over command. According to investigative sources, Nayfeld was responsible for the demise of Agron in 1985 (Freedman, 1994). As leader of the former Agron gang, Nayfeld had an ongoing conflict with Monya Elson, an enforcer for the Zilber brothers gang. There were four unsuccessful attempts on Elson's life that were allegedly engineered by Nayfeld: a hand wound to Elson, a perpetrator's jammed gun, a car bomb that exploded with the bomber still in the auto, and shotgun wounds received by Elson, his wife, and his nephew in a botched attempt by an unknown assassin. Elson fled to Israel in order to escape the never-ending attempts on his life (Freedman, 1994). Elson was charged with the murders of Vyacheslav Lyubarsky and Alexander Lyubarsky in January 1992 and of Alexander Slepinin in June 1992 as well as the attempted murder of Boris Nayfeld in 1991; he was arrested in Italy in March 1995. Then Nayfeld was arrested in January 1994 for being the leader of a conspiracy that smuggled tons of heroin from Southeast Asia through Poland into the United States, where the heroin was ultimately sold to members of La Cosa Nostra.

Vyacheslav Ivankov was known both as Yaponchik (or Little Japanese) and as the father of Soviet extortion. Ivankov, identified as a *vory v zakone* in Russia, had originally formed his own group, the Solontsevskaya gang, in Moscow in 1980; the members of this gang posed as Russian police officers in order to carry out robberies in Moscow. Then in 1982, Ivankov was arrested and convicted on robbery charges in Moscow and sentenced to 14 years in a Siberian prison (Raab, 1995). After serving 9 years of a 14-year prison sentence, two prominent Russian politicians, one a member of the Russian parliament and the other a Russian supreme court judge, had Ivankov's prison sentence shortened by 5 years. Within a short period of time after these two politicians intervened, Ivankov walked away from prison a free man and in early 1992 moved his operations to the United States (Hockstader, February 27, 1995).

A short time after his arrival in the United States in 1992, federal law enforcement authorities described Ivankov as the most influential Russian organized crime leader in the United States. Intelligence information on Ivankov indicated that he was sent here by other Russian organized crime bosses to guide, control, and enhance the relationships between the Russian gangs throughout Europe and Russia and the ever-expanding Russian gangs in the United States.

Ivankov set up his base of operations in Brighton Beach, Brooklyn. Because of his status within the structure of the Russian gangs, he was clever enough to survive quite well on tribute paid to him by the gangs. He was also involved in several swindles, including one for which he was arrested by the FBI. Ivankov and eight other Russian gangsters had participated in an extortion ring. Law enforcement sources stated that Ivankov had been actively engaged in attempting to coerce $8.5 million from the owners of the Summit International Corporation between November 1994 and May 1995. A demand was made for payments of $3.5 million and $5 million; this demand was accompanied by threats of violence. In April 1995, one of the complainants, Vladimer Voloshin's father, was beaten to death on a Moscow subway station. A short time after this incident, four armed males forced the complainants at gunpoint to accompany them to the Troika Restaurant in Fairview, New Jersey. Gang members then forced the complainants to sign a contract ensuring payment of $3.5 million to gang members. A month later, Ivankov and his eight associates were arrested and charged with extortion by federal authorities (Ball, June 11, 1995; Raab, 1995).

Some of the Russian gangs that have become highly visible in the United States include the Odessa Mafia, which originally operated in Brighton Beach in the mid-1970s. This gang then proceeded to set up other gang operations in both Los Angeles and San Francisco, but gang leadership remained based in Brooklyn, New York. The California Department of Justice found this gang to be well controlled and organized. A gang known as the Evangelical Russian Mafia first appeared on the West Coast in early 1993. Law enforcement sources indicated that this gang had no roots in Russia and was formed by young Russian immigrants in Sacramento, California. There are presently about 60 members of this gang; they have not, yet expanded outside California. A Russian-Armenian mafia group formed in New York City in the early 1980s expanded its operations to both Hollywood and the San Fernando Valley in California during the later 1980s. Gasoline bootlegging was a very profitable business for this group, and it also became heavily involved in drug trafficking. Another group, the Molina/ Organizatsiya, combined ethnic Russians, Armenians, and Chechens as well as any others with ethnic roots in the countries of the Commonwealth of Independent States. As a group, they managed to connect with other international organized crime gangs. Molina/Organizatsiya members were very active in credit card scams, drug trafficking, extortion, fuel tax and medical fraud, robberies, and murder (California Department of Justice, 1993; FBI, 1993).

Many Russian organized crime gangs can be differentiated from other gangs by distinct characteristics (Freedman, 1993; Mitchell, 1992; Pennsylvania Crime Commission, 1996):

1. Russian gang members are usually from the same city or country in the CIS.
2. Russian gang membership is small, with most gangs ranging anywhere from 3 to 20 members.

3. Leaders and members of Russian gangs are not confined to certain activities; they participate in anything that brings them some type of profit.

4. Russian gang members avoid any disclosure of assets because that draws attention to the gang.

5. A great number of Russian gangs' members are highly educated and fluent in several languages.

6. Use of violence is somewhat controlled by the Russian gangs, with most violent acts used for expedient reasons. Aggression, when necessary, may be used.

7. All Russian gang business is discussed outside any area where listening devices could be installed or used.

8. Russian gangs believe all law enforcement agents can be bribed.

9. Russian gangs believe neither the government nor elected officials can be trusted.

10. Members of Russian organized crime groups constantly use fraudulent activities as tools to swindle private- as well as public-sector organizations.

Russian Criminal Activities

Scams. One of the earlier and most successful fraudulent operations run by the Russian gangs was a bootleg gasoline scam that bilked federal, state, and local governments out of billions of dollars in excise taxes over 10 years. During the early 1980s, a partnership was formed between the Russian gangs and members of four of the local (Italian) La Cosa Nostra families (Columbo, Gambino, Genovese and Luchese). Members of La Cosa Nostra formed a coalition that often allowed the Russian gangs to keep approximately 25 percent of the profits while the four La Cosa Nostra families received about 75 percent of the profits; in other cases, members of La Cosa Nostra received 2 cents for every gallon of bootleg gasoline sold by the Russian gangs. Members of one La Cosa Nostra family (Gambino) were used primarily as enforcement agents for the Russian gangs, and they collected 2.26 cents for each gallon of gasoline and fuel oil sold through the dummy corporations. A 1993 federal court indictment claimed that Gambino family members were paid a total of $6.7 million for their participation as enforcers for the Russian groups (Strom, 1993).

This unlawful scam was set up to avoid the collection of various excise taxes placed on gasoline by federal, state, and local governments and became known as a "daisy chain." It involved setting up numerous small corporations that were involved in a large number of sales and purchases of gasoline. One of these paper corporations was set up as a burn or pony company, which was used to sell gasoline to a purchaser. This burn or pony company indicated on paper that the taxes on the sale were included in the bill, but this was not true because no taxes were paid on gasoline at any time during any of the transactions. When the time came for a tax collector to try and collect the taxes allegedly paid to the burn or pony company, it would no longer be in existence.

As law enforcement agencies became wise to this type of illegal operation, the Italian and Russian gangs changed their procedural methods. The groups started purchasing the facilities related to the operation of an oil company, including transportation vehicles, gasoline stations, and petroleum terminals. Intelligence gathered by several law enforcement agencies indicated that a coalition of La Cosa Nostra and Russian mobsters was conspiring to obtain several tankers as well as an oil refinery. These groups managed to buy a number of gas stations/truck stops throughout New Jersey and New York. An offshoot of this scam involved the gangs buying large amounts of number 2 home heating oil, which is tax-exempt and is the equivalent of diesel fuel. Through the use of dummy corporations, the home heating oil moved from company to company until it was changed on paper from number 2 home heating oil to diesel oil. This newly designated diesel oil was either sold by gang members at their privately owned gas stations/truck stops or purchased by an unsuspecting retailer; once again, all the tax money was pocketed by gang members.

Another scam contrived by the Russian gangs involved purchasing waste oil from both gasoline stations and oil container cleaning companies throughout the East Coast and Canada. This contaminated oil was then combined with unadulterated oil and sold to unsuspecting customers. Law enforcement sources estimated that well over 8 million gallons of contaminated oil were sold on the open market (Block, 1994; Strom, 1993).

One of the other early scams run by Russian gangs included what was called a potato bag scam. Con men, who were members of a Russian gang from Odessa, posed as merchant seafarers and offered to sell customers antique gold Russian rubles at a bargain price. A genuine antique gold ruble was shown to the person, usually another Russian immigrant whom the gang knew had money, for examination. The customer was permitted to scrutinize several antique gold rubles prior to the completion of the deal. After an agreement was reached, both parties decided on a delivery location where a bag of these antique gold rubles would be handed over to the purchaser. Once the exchange was made, gang members made off with the money while the victim opened the bag of rubles and found a bag of potatoes. The victim believed he was getting a bag of antique gold rubles, but in reality it was a potato bag scam (Blumenthal, 1989).

Another swindle involved Jardinay, a watch and jewelry manufacturer in downtown Manhattan. Approximately 25 Russian immigrants managed to gain employment with the Jardinay Company and stole over $54 million worth of diamonds and gold in a period of 1 year. Investigators theorized that most of the stolen jewelry was diverted to smaller jewelry stores owned by members of the gang who were stealing the jewelry. A similar type of swindle was perpetrated on the SoHo-based NGI Precious Metals company. In 10 years, four members of a Russian organized crime syndicate stole over $35 million worth of jewelry from NGI. Most of the stolen jewelry was smuggled to Europe, where it was easily sold to jewelry dealers. Almost all the money from this swindle was deposited in Swiss banks, with a large portion of this money then used by the same gang in a money-laundering scheme (Blumenthal, 1989; Smith, 1995).

Russian gang members (along with their La Cosa Nostra counterparts) increased their participation in auto insurance scams. Russian gangs had a monopoly on the reports of (falsified) injuries from auto accidents. Federal authorities indicated that this type of scam netted Russian gangs an estimated $500 million to $1 billion a year. The targeted insurance victim drove on a busy roadway or highway. The driver of the scam vehicle was usually a drug addict recruited and trained by the Russian gangs to participate in the scam by either crashing into the victims car or causing the innocent motorist to crash into his vehicle while on the busy roadway. Russian gang members then had the accident victim (drug addict) and any of his passengers visit a clinic that was owned and operated by gang members and that used imported Russian-trained medical doctors. These doctors diagnosed and treated the (mostly false) injuries of the persons hired to be participant in this insurance scam. If there was any reluctance on the part of any paid participant to go to the clinic for diagnosed (but usually unnecessary) treatment—including chiropractic sessions, counseling, physical therapy, and dental work—this person would receive a visit from an enforcer, who was a member of a Russian or Italian organized crime group, to ensure attendance at the clinic. Gang members had their own Russian-owned law firms in the areas where they ran these swindles. One law firm in Brooklyn, New York, on the average defended over 3,000 "victims" of these staged crashes each year, with profits of over $30 million a year (Lehmann, 2003).

The staged accidents involved the use of several different tactics by members of Russian and Italian organized crime. The driver of the staged accident vehicle would attempt to target either senior citizens operating vehicles or drivers preoccupied with operating their cell phones. In most cases, the brake light bulbs were removed from the rear tail lights of the scam vehicle. The scam vehicle would pass the targeted vehicle, proceed to move in front of the chosen victim's car, put the car in neutral while advising any passengers to prepare for a crash, and suddenly put on the brakes of the scam vehicle (Lehmann, 2003). All these tactics ensured the commission of a successful staged accident and the falsified injuries of the driver and passengers in the vehicle struck by the targeted victim. The profits from this conspiracy were paid by the insurance company. Usually one-third of the claim was profit for the gang and two-thirds of the paid claim (as well as increased insurance costs) went to the victim (the licensed and insured driver).

The Russian gangs also became active participants in both counterfeiting and forgery. Members of Russian organized crime groups have been implicated in the production of over $4.5 million worth of forged American Express checks and another $15.5 million in bogus checks from banks such as Citibank and Manufacturer's Hanover. These same Russian gangs also gained expertise in the forgery of artwork. Shops were set up in Queens, New York, to produce forged bejeweled Faberge eggs, which are quite valuable and highly marketable throughout the world.

In Los Angeles, Russian gang members set up a scam that brought Russian immigrants (a good portion of them criminals) to the United States, where they were supplied with false identification and a legitimate checking account. They were then sent out with a gang member to make numerous large purchases of goods at the foremost stores and auctions in Southern California. Russian con artists discovered several weaknesses in banks' checking account systems, including the fact that an amount in a checking account may be verified over a phone but that it takes a day or two for the bank to receive the check. The swindlers also realized there was a distinct possibility that the check could be delayed several days longer if someone in the bank's check-clearing department put the check aside for a few more days.

With all this information in mind, members of a Russian gang proceeded to open checking accounts in several different banks in Los Angeles. People selected to work for the gang were permitted to operate for no longer than two weeks, and the amount in each checking account was never exceeded at any shopping location. Merchandise purchased by the people working for the gang was ultimately sold off, and the gang's members received 80 percent of the profits. Just prior to the checks being presented for payment, the money in the bank checking accounts was removed by gang members. Profits from this swindle netted the gang over $50,000 per month. Eventually the gang leaders involved in this scam were viciously murdered by two of their employees. A search of the murder location turned up numerous items including camcorders, television sets, computer equipment, fax machines, highly valuable Persian rugs, antiques, and works of art (Mitchell, 1992).

One of the most productive fraudulent schemes conducted by members of Russian crime groups involved a $1 billion Medicare/Medicaid billing scam. A total of 350 front companies (phony companies incorporated to advance fraudulent activities) were instituted so that group members could falsify their invoices. Customers were solicited by phone to participate in what they were told was a free medical examination to be conducted at a mobile clinic (actually owned by one of the gangs). Once consumers, either senior citizens or homeless persons recruited off the street, appeared at one of the mobile clinics for the examination, they were given several forms to sign that (they were told) were for clearance to perform the tests, but the papers they signed were actually insurance claim forms that gave the clinic the right to submit bills to the customers' insurance companies for tests conducted on them. The average bill to an insurance company was $8,000.

This group also set up scams throughout Russia. After fraudulent employment agencies were set up in Russia, people would respond to advertisements for employment opportunities in the United States and would pay a fee to members of this group. A short time after the fee was paid, both the employment company and the monetary fee would vanish (*Newsweek*, 1993).

Russian gang members, who came from an environment where it was only natural to steal from the government, set up all types of fraudulent activities targeting the U.S. government. Medicaid and Medicare fraud alone brought millions of dollars into the Russian gangs' bank accounts. Many new immigrants from Russia who arrived in the United States and who were somehow involved with Russian gangs were immediately put on welfare, food stamps, and Medicaid. Another gang method of ripping off Medicaid was by double- and triple-billing the government through the use of a visiting nurse service owned by gang members. This gang-owned nurse service billed the government using legitimate Medicaid numbers either obtained fradulently by people working for the gang or obtained from drug addicts and homeless people whom the gang paid to gain this information.

Another Russian gang scam involved travel by members of the gang throughout the United States. As the members reached specific destinations in the United States, they would lease stores under false identities and immediately submit anywhere from 10 to 15 orders for gold and other jewelry to out-of-state jewelry vendors. In almost every case, the jewelry order was well over $5,000, and the vendor was informed that the bill for the jewelry would be paid upon delivery of the order; however, the cash on delivery was nothing more than a counterfeit cashier's check (Mitchell, 1992).

The fradulent use of credit cards was pulled off by Russian gangs in Brooklyn. Gang members managed to get master keys to mailboxes in multiple-dwelling buildings. They would check the tenants' mailboxes a short time after mail delivery for any credit cards. Upon finding a credit card in an envelope, gang members would remove the envelope containing the credit card, unseal the envelope, and run up at least a $10,000 bill on the account. The credit card would then be resealed in the envelope and the envelope redeposited in the original tenant's mailbox. Needless to say, within a couple of weeks the credit card holder would get a bill for several thousand dollars from the credit card company and then notify the credit card company that he or she had not run up these bills.

Members of the Russian mafia have chosen Russian athletes as targets for extortion. Media and investigative reports indicated that Russian gangs targeted for embezzlement some Russian hockey players in the National Hockey League. Some of the players (e.g., Alexei Zhitnit of the Los Angeles Kings, Pavel Bure of the Vancouver Canucks, Viacheslav Fetisov of the New Jersey Devils, and Alexander Mogilny of the Buffalo Sabres) complained to U.S. authorities about being approached by members of Russian organized crime groups who attempted to extract extortion money from them (Beacon, 1993; MacIntyre, 1993; Middleton, 1993).

Drug Trafficking.   Russian organized crime groups' participation in drug trafficking in both the United States and Russia has constantly increased, as evidenced by the following (Dahlberg, 1993):

1. Members of Russian gangs formed working relationships with members of organized crime groups who were already heavily involved in drug trafficking (e.g., Chinese, Colombians, and La Cosa Nostra members).

2. Lack of any type of major drug enforcement agency within the newly formed CIS gave Russian gangs an opportunity both to set up new routes to transport drugs into the CIS and into Europe and to participate in the distribution and sale of drugs.

3. Russian gangs used areas within the CIS (with the proper soil and climate) to grow and process drugs so that the gangs were no longer middlemen for drug kingpins from outside the CIS. For example, there are areas in Russia where marijuana plants grow undomesticated in open fields in the country; opium poppies are grown freely in the Central Asian republics of Tajikistan and Uzbekistan, and a crop was planted in the Northern Caucasus. In 1992,

approximately 40 percent of all the drugs coming into Russia came from the former Soviet Republic of Azerbaijan, and ethnically Azerbaijanis accounted for 82 percent of the people arrested for drug possession in Russia.

4. Throughout the CIS, there is an ever-present demand for drugs, with an estimated 3.5 to 4 million drug users, and these numbers are increasing. Networks were already in place that smuggled guns, precious gems, metals, art, and other valuable materials from the CIS to the Americas, Asia, and Europe, so it was easy to also smuggle drugs through these networks.

5. Russian gangs have been cautious in their dealings with other organized crime syndicates throughout Asia, Europe, and North and South America. The Russian groups, in most cases, have gone out of their way to have peaceful negotiations with all the other crime groups. In the United States, they have been more than willing to share their wealth with other criminal gangs, as can be seen in their participation with La Cosa Nostra in the gasoline tax fraud scheme throughout the New York metropolitan area. In their dealings with other gangs, the Russian gangs have gone out of their way to share the wealth accumulated during their illegal scams in order to further camaraderie among all the gangs. For example, in the CIS and Europe, the Russian gangs laundered money for both the Colombians and the Italian mafia.

6. Ever-increasing maritime trade between members of the CIS and businesses in every major port city in the United States and Canada added more routes to the expanding criminal networks of Russian organized crime groups. The involvement of Russian sailors in the drug trade surfaced during 1992 when a Russian seaman was arrested in Melbourne, Australia, in possession of 12 pounds of heroin. Two other sailors were arrested in the Belgian port of Seebrugge with 24 pounds of cocaine in their possession. The U.S. Drug Enforcement Agency received documented information that over half the sailors in the Russian merchant marine on ships that run the Colombia to Russia route were smuggling cocaine back with them.

ISRAELI GANGS

Israeli History

Discussions involving Russian crime groups should always include mention of Israeli organized crime groups. In many scams, these two groups worked and profited together, but they are two distinctly different crime families. During the late 1960s, a group of Israelis between the ages of 20 and 35 years started migrating from Israel to California. This (and later migrations) was probably due to a dynamic enforcement effort by the Israeli National Police to rid Tel Aviv of some of these gangs. A major portion of the gang members had formed friendships while on active duty with the

Israeli armed forces or while serving sentences in Israeli correctional facilities. Most members of this group were originally from a poverty-stricken suburb of Tel Aviv known as Bat-Yam, and most of the members were from the Sephardic Jewish sect that has family roots throughout the Middle East, North Africa, and Spain. In most of these cases, the families of gang members or the gang members accompanying their families moved to Israel because of religious persecution they were subjected to while residing in Arab countries.

Israeli Criminal Activities

As members of what is now called the Israeli organized crime group, they did not come to the attention of the Los Angeles Police Department until 1975, when members of this syndicate were found to be actively participating in extortion, arson, bankruptcy scams, and insurance fraud operations. At first, most of this group's activities existed in either Los Angeles or Calexico, but by 1978 this organization had expanded its activities throughout Southern California. Originally, gang members profited by extorting money from elderly Eastern European Jews who owned butcher shops and Judaic retail stores in what was then the predominantly Jewish community of Fairfax within the confines of the city of Los Angeles. These gangs also increased their revenues by running "bust-out" schemes: A business is set up and a credit line is opened by gang members; once everything is in place, the gang members place large orders for jewelry, clothing, appliances, or whatever products they are supposedly selling. Once the "business" receives the commodities, it disappears.

Along with the extension of their criminal activities came an increase in membership and an expansion in the amount of violence used by the members. For example, in 1979 Eli and Esther Ruven were brutally murdered in Los Angeles and their bodies were cut into pieces by three members of an Israeli organized crime group who were later arrested and convicted of this heinous crime. It seems the Ruvens were dealing cocaine for the gang and failed to pay a $70,000 fee on a drug delivery to gang members. After this incident, four other murders were linked to this Los Angeles–based gang (Derfner, 1990; *Organized Crime Digest*, 1982).

Drug Trafficking.   The rapid growth in gang membership continued into the early 1980s, as did Israeli gang participation in drug-trafficking activities. During 1981, various federal, state, and local law enforcement agencies in Southern California arrested 33 gang members for narcotics-related offenses. Evidence of this expansion of Israeli gangs was seen in 1986 when 5 gang members were arrested in Brooklyn, New York, for their involvement in a drug-trafficking ring that supplied the New York metropolitan area with over $1 million worth of heroin on a weekly basis. This gang was connected to the group in Los Angeles, and in 1986 this New York–based group was made up of more than 200 hard-core members. These Brooklyn gangs based most of their activities out of Brighton Beach but maintained headquarters in Bensonhurst. Most Israeli gangs average anywhere from 5 to 25 members but are always increasing. One of the gangs that formed in Brooklyn was under the guidance of Johnny Attias and became known as the Johnny Attias gang; this gang imported cocaine from Colombia and heroin from Southeast Asia. After a number of disputes over drug transactions, Attias killed several members of this gang, and eventually other gang members, who were fed up with the actions of their leader, killed him (Ross and Gonzalez, April 27, 1994a).

The increasing participation of Israeli gangs in drug trafficking led to a more active involvement in each aspect of the drug business by members of the Israeli crime organizations. In order to upgrade their drug operations in the United States, Israeli gangs started to set up bases in South America. Police officials and U.S. drug enforcement agents in Colombia observed a conspicuous increase in the number of Israeli refugees in the Colombian cities of Barranquilla and Cali, in a 10-year period (Moses and Pelleck, 1986; Ross and Gonzalez, April 27, 1994a). Worldwide operations for drug trafficking and money laundering were also put in place by members of Israeli organized crime. Intelligence gathered by members of the U.S. Drug Enforcement Agency on assignment in Europe and Asia indicated that members of Israeli organized crime groups set up operations throughout Europe. Other bases for drug trafficking and money laundering, (in addition to those in Brazil, Canada, Colombia, and the United States) have been set up in Belgium, England, France, Germany, Holland, Poland, and Russia in Europe as well as Hong Kong and Thailand in Asia and Israel, Pakistan, and Turkey in the Middle East (DEA, 1993).

A U.S. narcotics enforcement agency produced some fairly solid evidence that Rehavam Zeevi, a retired general from the Israeli military and an appointee to the Israeli cabinet in 1991, was a participant in drug-trafficking deals with members of Israeli organized crime groups starting in the early 1980s. Information related to Zeevi was uncovered by Michael Levine (a retired undercover agent in the U.S. Drug Enforcement Agency), who stated that during an interview with an arrested member of the Israeli organized crime group called Sam Shapiro, he was told by Shapiro himself that Israeli gangs had set up a working operation with La Cosa Nostra in both the United States and Italy. Shapiro also informed U.S. government agents that Zeevi, who was appointed an advisor to Prime Minister Yitzhak Rubin on terrorism in 1974, traveled to Colombia in 1977 with antiterrorist advisors. Shapiro alleged that Zeevi had 1,000 pounds of hashish with him in order to exchange the hashish for cocaine, which was then shipped to Florida for distribution throughout the United States. This, according to Shapiro, was the beginning of a fruitful drug-trafficking relationship between Colombian drug lords and members of Israeli organized crime groups. On his travel to South America, Zeevi was accompanied by Betsalel Mizrahi, alleged to be the major financier behind organized crime groups in Israel. According to a media report in the *Jerusalem Report*, information from Israeli police wiretaps published in February 1991 indicated that Zeevi was connected to a number of Israeli criminal group members, including Tuvia Oshri, a major narcotics trafficker who was serving a life sentence for two gang-related murders (Marshall, 1991).

Israeli gangs have used varied routes to transfer heroin from either Southeast Asia or Southwest Asia to the United States. One path took heroin from Pakistan to Japan: A member of an Israeli gang would create a deceptive bill of lading that indicated that the product in which the heroin was hidden originally came from Japan; the product was then shipped to Europe, usually the Netherlands, from where it was rerouted to Belgium, France, Germany, or North America for distribution. Another route sent heroin from Turkey to the Netherlands and then on to Canada or the United States. A third path took heroin from Thailand to either France or the Netherlands and then on to Canada or the United States; a fourth route moved heroin from either Pakistan or Thailand into Italy, where it was secreted in a shoe shipment and forwarded to the United States (DEA, 1993).

Cocaine purchased in Colombia by members of Israeli organized crime was transported through Mexico, with the cooperation of members of Mexican organized crime families, to California. Another variation involved the transportation of cocaine to Brazil, where it was secreted in shoes and conveyed to Canada or the United States. A third route took cocaine to Brazil, where it was hidden in shoes and shipped to the Netherlands. There it was distributed for sale in Europe or Israel or exchanged for heroin that was then transported back to the United States for distribution. In most cases, the Israeli gang members were not involved in the street sales of either heroin or cocaine. Almost all drugs brought into the United States by Israeli gang members were sold to other racial and ethnic groups that were involved in street sales (DEA, 1993).

Scams.   The Brooklyn Israeli gangs have been active participants in gasoline tax scams since the early 1980s. In fact, the ability of the Israeli gangs to work these gasoline scams in concert with members of other Israeli groups, as well as with members of Italian and Russian organized crime groups, helped to increase their credibility with organized crime groups in the United States. Israeli gang members quickly moved the profits from their gasoline scams into drug-trafficking and money-laundering schemes.

Israeli organized crime members in Los Angeles found the use of credit card scams a successful way to make money. One of their favorite schemes involved going through trash bins of retail stores to locate carbon paper and tissue from credit card sales. Once the carbon paper and/or tissue was discovered, gang members obtained names and credit card numbers from these items. A small factory would then be set up with the necessary laminating equipment and plastic necessary to produce counterfeit credit cards using the names and credit card numbers of real people. Phony retail jewelry businesses with commercial bank accounts were devised, and credit card vouchers for bogus purchases were submitted to credit card companies. These companies, in turn, would reimburse the phony businesses where the credit cards were allegedly used. A number of Hollywood celebrities' names turned up on these spurious purchases made with counterfeit credit cards.

Money Laundering.   Members of Israeli gangs found an excellent way to profit from drug trafficking. They managed to launder money through the Diamond District businesses in New York. Israeli gangs also recruited leaders of Jewish religious institutions on both the East and West Coasts to work money-laundering scams with them. A Satmar rabbi, Abraham Low, charged a 30 percent fee on all the money he laundered through the Mogen Abraham Synagogue in Los Angeles. He openly bragged to an undercover FBI agent that he could launder approximately $5 million a week through a network of charitable Satmar organizations throughout the United States as well as in Europe. In another case, Joseph Krozer bragged to people that he was involved in a business that processed over $300,000 in drug money on a daily basis. A U.S. Drug Enforcement Agency surveillance team followed Krozer to the offices of Ahron Sharir, a New York City gold manufacturer and an Israeli underworld figure, where Krozer picked up bags of cash and then delivered them to Congregation Chesed and Tsedeka a schteebel (little place of worship) in Brooklyn.

This group turned out to be one of the largest money-laundering operations for the Colombian drug cartels in the United States. Federal prosecutors estimated that this group laundered over $3 billion for the Medellin drug cartels. One of the largest money-laundering scheme involved Israeli organized crime member David Vanounou. He recruited Mendell Goldberger, who set up a money-laundering operation through the Mesivta Tifereth Jerusalem, one of the oldest yeshivas in New York City, for Colombian drug traffickers. A total of $23 million was laundered through this yeshiva. Ultimately, six different business firms and nine people, including Rabbi Yisrael Eidelman (executive vice president of Mesivta), were convicted of various tax evasion infractions (Ross and Gonzalez, April 29, 1994c). All these operations were put in place by Israeli gang members, who shared the profits from the money-laundering ventures equally with the participating religious institutions.

Federal officials were ultimately able to break up all these Israeli organized crime money-laundering rings and arrest all the participants. One very active member of one of these money-laundering rings was Diamond District business owner and mob figure Ahron Sharir. Sharir had set up one of the largest money-laundering businesses in the world for members of Colombian drug cartels by using the following methods (Ross and Gonzalez, April 28, 1994b):

1. Direct deposits of money into various banks were made as if the money was profit from Sharir's jewelry business.

2. Sharir then purchased airplanes as an investment; these planes were then used to ship drugs by the Colombian cartels.

3. Sharir procured gold at inflated prices and sold the same gold to other associates in this conspiracy at a cheaper price.

4. Wire transfers of money were sent throughout the world under the guise of Sharir's business deals.

5. Cash was exchanged by Sharir for legitimate checks that were from the bank accounts of either other businesses or religious institutions.

Israeli gangs broadened their criminal environments by participating in other unlawful activities that also helped to increase their profits:

1. In insurance fraud, gang members operated businesses and reported staged larcenies and burglaries to local law enforcement agencies in order to bilk an insurance company of money. The operator of the business purchased large quantities of items that the retail store was going to sell and then transferred the products to another location and reported the property stolen. Other store owners removed the property from the store and burned down the store to obtain insurance reimbursement.

2. Bogus identification was used to obtain large quantities of retail items such as cameras, televisions, and video recorders. This equipment was picked up and taken to a storehouse owned by gang members. The supplier submitted the bill to the credit card company or the check to the bank only to find out that all the information, the checks, and the credit card slips were phony and that there would be no reimbursement.

3. Both a business and a business credit line would be set up by gang members. Payments were then made on small orders for about a three-month period. Once the business had established a good credit line, the business owners would purchase large quantities of merchandise on the business credit line. After the newly purchased merchandise was moved to a different location, the business would go into bankruptcy.

4. Both U.S.- and Israel-based members of Israeli organized crime were involved in counterfeiting U.S. currency. The arrested Israeli gang members had immigrated from Russia to Israel and had set up three counterfeiting money shops in Israel and one in Clifton, New Jersey.

CONCLUSIONS

It is difficult to estimate which ethnic gangs—Russian or Israeli—made an appearance on the American scene first. Israeli gangs were probably first because they were working their scams in Los Angeles a short time prior to the arrival of Russian gangs on U.S. shores. Some researchers try to confound the situation by announcing that Russian and Israeli gangs are one and the same, but the following factors seem to indicate that is not the case:

1. Members of the Russian mafia started moving large amounts of money into the Israeli economy because of Israel's liberal money-transferring policy; as of June 1995, $4 billion had been transferred. This accompanied the mass immigration to Israel of Russians (after the fall of Communism), of which approximately 35 percent were not of the Jewish faith. Of the money invested in Israel $2.5 billion was placed in Israeli banks, while the other

$1.5 billion was used to purchase land in the Tel Aviv area of Israel (*Agence France Presse*, 1995; Linzer, 1995).

2. Members of Russian organized crime worked scams against the Israeli government. The Russian gang members prepared counterfeit Israeli immigration documents so that Russian immigrant gang members could enter Israel and receive the same benefits as legitimate Jewish immigrants to Israel. Included in the benefits were a six-month grant, money to buy appliances, free medical insurance coverage, partial payment of rental fees, and a *mashkanta* (mortgage loan). Russian gang members set up these newly immigrated families so they could purchase apartments in Israel using the *mashkanta*. The *mashkanta*, along with a bribe or a threat of injury or death, was supplied by a gang member, which certainly helped with the quick acquisition of an apartment for the gang member. Once the apartment was officially owned by the gang member, it was put on the market at double the price and, in most cases, quickly sold for a large profit—usually anywhere from $50,000 to $100,000 dollars (Polyak, 1994).

3. Russian gangs took over control of 80 percent of the sex industry in Israel by using counterfeit documents to import prostitutes from the CIS (Walker, 1995).

4. Many of the original Brighton Beach gang members were ethnically Russian, and their religious background was Jewish.

5. Russian and Israeli gang members set up and ran the original gasoline tax scams during the early 1980s.

The above information seems to indicate that there was some type of relationship between the Russian and Israeli organized crime groups. For example, there were major connections between the similar types of scams that both groups perpetrated against other Russians, other Israelis, and the U.S. government. Israeli gangs have become deeply involved in money laundering and lightly involved in scams and drug trafficking; Russian gangs have remained very actively involved in crimes such as robbery, extortion, fraud, and drug trafficking. Several points should be mentioned regarding both these groups. The Russian gangs probably would not have had the ability to move all that money, had such extensive knowledge of the social services system in Israel and been able to scam the government, and been able to take over control of Israel's sex industry without the assistance of the Israeli criminal groups. A slim possibility does exist that the Russian and Israeli gangs could be one and the same, but at this juncture it is truly doubtful. There is no doubt, however, that these two groups will continue to work together as long as there are scams from which they can both profit.

CHAPTER **12**

OTHER WORLDWIDE ORGANIZED CRIME GANGS

This chapter discusses the organizational characteristics and activities of smaller and somewhat unheralded (outside their own region or place of operations) ethnic organized crime groups throughout the world. It outlines each organization, the home base from which each group operates, the locations of each group's businesses throughout the world, each group's types of activities, and each group's connections (if any) to other organized crime families or groups. Although many of these groups are connected with other criminal organizations, few of them are as well structured or are run like La Cosa Nostra. Yet all these gangs are in the business of making as much money as possible for their leaders as well as their organization. The reader will see that some of these gangs, even though they are of the same ethnic background as other groups in the same area or country, have different agendas. What this means is that one ethnic gang may be involved in murder, robbery, and drug trafficking while another ethnic gang from the same country is involved in scams and terrorism. The use of fraud to support terrorism became quite apparent from a yearlong inquiry conducted by investigative reporters of "West 57th Street," a news television show. The results of this examination enlightened us with information about a loosely knit ethnic organized crime group, which is discussed in the Palestinian section, called the Worldwide Organized Crime Groups chapter (CBS News, 1989).

THIRD WORLD GANGS

Palestinian Gangs

A Palestinian group that has received a good deal of attention throughout the United States is the Deir Dibwan criminal organization. It is composed of a small group of citizens from the village of Deir Dibwan on the West Bank of Israel. Members of this gang first came to the attention of law enforcement officials in the mid-1980s when the investigative television program "West 57th Street" did a segment on their criminal activities. This investigative program indicated that members of the Deir Dibwan group worked in an organized crime network that was involved in numerous types of unlawful business scams. Law enforcement sources felt that a good portion of the money that was illegally obtained by this group was used to fund the terrorist activities of the Palestinian Liberation Organization (PLO). Members of this criminal organization traveled throughout the Arab world and the United States setting up their unlawful operations (CBS News, 1989).

During the 1980s, stores were rented and legitimate businesses (either clothing stores or appliance shops) were opened along the West Coast of the United States. Some of the first "bust-out" operations by this Palestinian group appeared in the eastern section of Washington State. All these businesses were legitimately purchased by gang members, who then proceeded to stock the stores with products that were paid for within a short period of time after their purchase. Once group members were able to stabilize the business operations and show a profit, they immediately ordered extensive amounts of the types of merchandise they were selling at these stores. The goods were purchased on the stores' credit lines, which were built up by paying for acquisitions on time. Upon delivery of the merchandise, it was immediately transported to another location to be either hidden or disposed of as quickly as possible. In most cases, the merchandise was sold off at anywhere from cost to 50 percent less than cost.

After a short time, bills would be received by the purchaser, who claimed that the bills could not be paid because the items were no longer in his possession. Also due to extenuating circumstances, he no longer had any assets to assist him in paying this liability and immediately filed for bankruptcy. The owner of the business then declared that either the money was lost while gambling, the property was taken during the commission of a burglary, or the books and records were either misplaced or taken by a burglar. In every case in which the business owners presented either a gambling or a burglary excuse, there was no actual way for the purported bankrupt victim or a bankruptcy court investigator to actually verify the claimed losses. The same was true for the theft of money or property during the commission of a crime. This is why bankruptcy courts in some cases did not accept bankruptcy claims (CBS News, 1989).

These scams indicated that the Deir Dibwan group found a way to ensure for themselves profits for the PLO through innocent creditors. Although the first three gang members to pull this scam off successfully were allowed to claim bankruptcy, which was accepted by the courts, the last five claims were not accepted. This negative verdict gave the creditors the opportunity to continue their pursuit of the amount of money owed them until some or all of it is paid. The gang member (the scammer) either leaves the United States and returns to Deir Dibwan or adopts a new identity. A majority of the members of Deir Dibwan gangs are highly mobile and capable of traveling to any destination in Canada or the United States in order to set up a new type of business bust-out scam (CBS News, 1989).

Another scheme instituted by members of a Palestinian group involved the use of stolen telephone access codes. Telephone toll codes were accessed by Palestinian organized crime groups in several ways:

1. Searches of dumpsters outside businesses were made in an effort to locate telecommunications printouts.
2. Gang members were involved in shoulder surfing, the theft of a phone code by watching a code subscriber use the credit card calling number at a pay phone.
3. Gang members gained access to phone codes by having office cleaning staff search desk tops, drawers, or trash pails for company or customer codes.
4. Pickpockets employed by the gang obtained codes from stolen identifications.
5. Employees of telecommunication companies shared information with gang members.
6. Computer hackers were paid by gang members to target a company that had an 800 number. The hacker would break the security code; usually this was done through the use of the hacker's computer modem. The computer would automatically dial numbers continuously until the computer located and identified the proper number grouping sequence. This enabled the hacker to break into the private branch exchange (PBX). Once the hacker obtained this 800 number, a second dial tone would allow the hacker, a gang member or a purchaser of the phone line time to make calls anywhere in the world. The hacker would give the access code(s) to gang members, who then would sell the long-distance lines to other illegal immigrants (Holmes, 1994; Mallory, 1994).
7. Using a scanner with special software along streets, parkways, expressways, and roadway overpasses, gang members intercepted identification numbers from cellular phones that were in passing vehicles. Numbers obtained in this manner were then placed into a computer so that these numbers could be transferred to another phone. It takes about five minutes to complete this procedure. The cloned phones can use the identification numbers stolen from the authorized consumer, whose account is ultimately billed for this illegal use (James, 1994).

The utilization of these diverse types of illegal tactics led to losses of over 1.8 billion for corporations throughout the world in 1993.

The scheme was initiated by a scam artist named after a U.S. citizen of Palestinian ancestry, Frank Fahmi Amigo. When this scam was uncovered by investigators from telephone company security and law enforcement, they named it the Amigo scam after Frank Fahmi Amigo. Fahmi Amigo was ultimately arrested, tried, convicted, and sentenced in August 1992 to 52 months in prison for setting up and perpetrating telephone swindles. In fact, in 1992 it was estimated that members of Palestinian and Jordanian organized crime groups yearly swindled worldwide telephone service companies out of approximately $40 million (Holmes, 1994; Lawlor, 1993). Palestinian gangs continue to use their workers to run these various types of telephone scams because they have become big moneymakers for these groups; it is what gang members call easy money, which can be quickly reinvested in drug operations or other money-making schemes.

A second type of Palestinian gang is found on the West Bank in Israel and is very similar to the street gangs operating in major urban areas of the United States. Most of these gang members range in age from 12 to 30 years old, with the older members being the gang leaders. A vast majority of the members are armed and present a considerable threat to honest Palestinian and Israeli citizens on the West Bank.

Two major West Bank gangs are the Red Eagles and the Black Panther Brigades. Both of these gangs base their operations out of the West Bank town of Nablus. The Red Eagles gang was formed and is supported by the Popular Front for the Liberation of Palestine (PFLP), an extremist PLO faction that conducts most of its operations from a Syrian base and is totally opposed to any type of peaceful agreement or negotiations with Israel. The Black Panthers gang is affiliated and supported by Yasser Arafat's Al-Fatah wing of the PLO. Originally, these gangs were used to eliminate Palestinians who collaborated with the Israeli government, but the PFLP and the PLO let the leadership of these groups get completely out of control. They killed anyone they thought was collaborating with the Israeli government as well as members of the Israeli police or military who got in their way. This resulted in an intervention campaign by the Israeli government, which led to the killings of the leaders of both the Red Eagles and the Black Panthers gangs. In the first incident, Ayman Arruzeh, the boss of the Red Eagles gang, was shot and killed by Israeli soldiers after he had killed an alleged Israeli collaborator with an ax. Several weeks later, members of the Israeli military, disguised as Arabs, killed Imad Annaser, the anointed leader of the Black Panthers organized crime gang, during a shootout in a Nablus barber shop (*Los Angeles Times*, 1989).

These killings forced both gangs to slow down their criminal activities during the latter part of 1989. In early March 1990, gang activity picked up with a sharp increase in the number of robberies of jewelry exchanges in Nablus. Assets gained from these types of robberies helped to support unlawful gang activities against the Israeli government. One of the gangs, the Black Panthers, increased the number of its members to well over 300 since early 1990. This loosely organized criminal gang also expanded its illegal activities to include extortion, kidnapping, and drug dealing. In fact, this gang went so far as to kidnap an Israeli solider and kill him five days later during the Israeli/PLO peace talks in October 1994 (*Bergen Record*, 1994).

Although the Israeli government has attempted to crack down on these street gangs through the use of the Israeli military, most of these actions caused only a temporary decrease in gang activity. Within a short time after a more strict enforcement policy is lifted, there is a sharp increase in the number of new members for older gangs and the creation of new gangs. As the number of gangs increases, the Israeli government also found an increase in the number of crimes being committed on the West Bank. The Israeli government seems hopeful that the peace agreement reached with the PLO, which affords the Palestinians the right to police their own territories, will cause a decrease in the number of criminal activities and acts of violence involving these street gangs.

Syrian Gangs

Although a great deal of information related to Syrian gangs is conjecture, there are a number of Syrian organized gangs operating throughout the Middle East, and most of them are involved in drug smuggling. U.S. drug enforcement intelligence reports indicated that anywhere from 25 percent to 35 percent of all heroin imported into the United States is grown in the Syrian-controlled Bekka Valley in Lebanon. In 1989, it was estimated that Lebanon's drug crop produced over $600 million in profits for Syrian drug lords; estimates in 1992 put the Syrian drug profit figure at over $2 billion. Escalating drug profits were realized when members of Syrian drug gangs recruited Turkish and Iranian agricultural experts to help the Syrians convert the hashish drug crop to a heroin drug crop in 1986, and these experts convinced the Syrians to institute a crop rotation that would produce at least two drug harvests per year. The rotation would increase the total heroin crop in the Bekka Valley so that drugs would be grown on 90 percent of the land instead of 10 percent of the land. According to published reports, the recommendations by the Turkish and Iranian drug agriculturists were put into action when Rifaat Assad, brother of the Syrian president, and Mossar al-Kassar, a major Syrian drug trafficker, took over control of drug production in the Bekka Valley in the mid-1980s. During this same time period, the Syrian military were placed in charge of the security of the ever-increasing drug crop in the Bekka Valley of Lebanon (Builta, 1994; Rowan, 1992; Widlanski, 1992).

Syrian gang members also made connections with other members of ethnic Syrian gangs in South America, specifically Colombia. Coca base was shipped from locations in South America to locations in both Syria and Lebanon, where the cocaine was refined, packaged, and shipped to both Europe and the United States. Syrian drug lords had an easy outlet for their heroin and cocaine in the United States through gang members already in place within Syrian and Lebanese communities in and around Detroit, Michigan (Widlanski, 1992).

There has been some evidence uncovered that indicated that the Syrian government used the money derived from drug trafficking to support its participation in terrorist activities. An article by Michael Widlanski claimed that the Syrian government, its leader (Hafez al-Assad), and the military were connected to the drug lords. Information gathered by Widlanski indicated that every member of the Syrian military received some type of salary enhancement from the profits accumulated by the Syrian and Lebanese drug traffickers (Widlanksi, 1992).

An article in *Time* magazine in 1992 went so far as to indicate that there was a connection between the terrorist bombing of Pan Am flight 103 over Lockerbie, Scotland, and a Syrian drug gang boss named Monzer al-Kassar. Kassar was connected to the Syrian government through his brother-in-law Ali Issa Duba, Syrian intelligence chief, and President Assad, a blood relative of Kassar's wife. This article further stated that the U.S. Central Intelligence Agency (CIA) allowed Kassar to legally operate his drug-trafficking business in exchange for his assistance in gaining the liberation of the U.S. hostages being held by terrorists in Lebanon. The U.S. Drug Enforcement Agency (DEA) also used Kassar's drug-trafficking business in a sting operation to arrest persons participating in this drug conspiracy (usually other Lebanese or Syrian nationals) in the United States. According to a report from Mossad (an Israeli organization that gathers intelligence information related to terrorism and terrorist groups), Kassar was connected to Ahmed Jabril, leader of the Popular Front for the Liberation of Palestine–General Command (PFLP-GC). This group allegedly received a majority of its financial support from Syrian drug enterprises. Jabril set up a meeting with Kassar in a Paris restaurant in 1988, and Kassar assured Jabril of his support for the terrorist attack on a U.S. airline. Kassar did notify the CIA of the intent of the PFLP-GC sometime in mid-December 1988, but that did not seem to help because Pan Am flight 103 exploded in the air over Lockerbie, Scotland, on December 21, 1988, killing all the passengers and crew members (Rowan, 1992).

Evidence gathered in the *Time* article indicated that a member of the U.S. military's Defense Intelligence Agency (DIA), Charles McKee, was on board Pan Am flight 103, along with CIA's deputy station chief in Beirut, Matthew Gannon. They were en route to CIA headquarters in Virginia to condemn the CIA's association with Syrian drug trafficker Kassar. An investigation conducted by McKee and Gannon had discovered not only that Kassar was a major Syrian drug dealer but also that he was very closely connected to both Jabril and his PFLP-GC terrorist gang. The threat that Kassar presented to these two government agents was his terrorist connections to Jabril because the two agents were in the process of setting up a plan to free the American hostages held in Lebanon. In turn, Kassar, fearing that without U.S. support his drug operations would be shut down once these agents reached Virginia, continued his support of the terrorist activities related to bombing of Pan Am flight 103 (Rowan, 1992).

No matter how anyone views this information, it was disparaging enough to indicate there was a definite connection between the Syrian drug gangs, the Syrian government, and some terrorist groups based outside Syria. As previously stated in this book, there are numerous types of gangs and gang activities. These Syrian gangs, like some of the other gangs that will be described in this chapter, can be placed in the same category as the Cuban Communist Mafia that is controlled by the Castro government in Cuba. All these organized criminal groups participate in drug trafficking both to embellish their own assets and to support terrorist activities in an attempt to overthrow other governments, to increase the power of their leaders, or to just get even with another nation.

Turkish Gangs

When one discusses Turkish gangs, the one group that comes to mind is the Kurdistan Workers Party (better known as the PKK). This group changed its name in 2002 to the Freedom and Democracy Congress of Kurdistan (KADEK); we will refer to the

PKK-KADEK as the PKK for events until 2002, and for events after that, they will be called the PKK-KADEK. Originally instituted as a radical group for the overthrow of the Turkish government, this group has become known as a highly violent drug gang whose members think nothing of taking control of small villages in Eastern Turkey to extort money from local businesses, and they also torture villagers who do not agree with their radical philosophy. This gang began in 1974 in Ankara, Turkey, when a meager band of fanatics who were associated with a Turkish revolutionary youth group decided to start their own gang. The person who got this group together and who was eventually appointed leader of this gang, Abdullah Ocalan, formed the Kurdistan Workers Party, or the Partiya Karkeren Kurdistan (PKK), in 1978. Ocalan was convicted in 2002 of treason and is presently serving a 36-year term in a Turkish prison (*Financial Times*, 2002). This gang's premise since its inception has been that people who disagree with its fanatical logic are its enemies. In order to understand the radical views of this group, you must understand that its tactics include the wanton murders of all members of society who oppose their ideals. Some of their heinous crimes involve killing schoolteachers in front of classrooms of children and murdering women and children to maintain control over a village. The levels of violence involving the PKK gang members are shown in Table 12–1.

Until the late 1980s, a majority of the funding for this gang was obtained through extortion, arms smuggling, smuggling of workers, or robberies. Gang leaders then discovered the money that could be easily made in drug trafficking. Operations to import drugs into Eastern Turkey were quickly set up by the gang, and PKK members started importing drugs from both Southeast Asia and Southwest Asia; a majority of these drugs that are processed in Turkey come from Southwest Asia (Iran and Pakistan). In most cases, after the arrival of morphine-based drugs in Turkey, gang members processed the morphine into heroin in makeshift labs set up by the gang in Eastern Turkey. Once this process was complete, the heroin was shipped to either Europe or the United States.

TABLE 12–1

Killings by Members or Associates of PKK

Year	Terrorists	Civilians	Soldiers	Police	Villagers
1984	11	20	24	0	0
1986	64	74	40	3	0
1989	165	136	111	8	34
1991	356	170	213	20	41
1993	1,699	1,218	487	28	156
1994	4,114	1,082	794	43	265
1995*	2,292	1,085	450	47	87
Total	8,701	3,785	2,119	149	583

* The 1995 figures are for the first 6 months of that year.

Source: Internet PKK and Terrorism, December 1995.

Since 1990, arrests of PKK members have become more and prevalent throughout Europe. In Germany, members of the PKK used juveniles to transport and sell drugs in most major German urban centers. Hamburg police arrested children between the ages of 10 and 12 for drug sales and arrested an 8-year-old for possession of a loaded firearm and for drug sales. Police in Wandsbeck arrested 14- and 16-year-old youths for participating in drug trafficking. All these children had been transported to Germany from Eastern Turkey by members of the PKK gang. Other members of the PKK took over control of drug-trafficking activities in the German cities of Bremen, Essen, Frankfort, and Hamburg. German narcotics police reported in October 1994 that PKK members transferred 15 million Deutsch marks from Germany to their gang leaders in Eastern Turkey. German police statistics further indicated that in 1991, 400 of the total 735 drug sales arrests involved PKK members, and the numbers for 1992 increased to 735, of which 450 were PKK members; in 1993, the total number of PKK members arrested for drug sales was 300 of 457 arrestees. In November 1993, a drug courier, Sengul Karacan, was apprehended in Caracas, Venezuela, carrying 3.5 kilograms of cocaine, and during interrogation by Venezuelan police, Karacan confessed that she was a courier for the PKK (Internet, PKK and Drug Trafficking, December, 1995).

In 2002, it was estimated that the PKK-KADEK was involved with over 450 organizations throughout Europe and Turkey, with over 6,000 armed militants stationed throughout Europe and the Middle East. These organizations continue to exist thanks to profits produced from their involvement throughout Europe in illegal activities, including arms smuggling, counterfeiting, and drug trafficking. PKK-KADEK took control of the drug markets in Belgium, Bulgaria, Germany, and the Netherlands; in countries such as Austria, Denmark, England, France, Italy, Russia, and Sweden, the PKK-KADEK continued to operate its drug-trafficking and worker brokerage schemes. In all of these countries, the PKK-KADEK operated newspapers as well as radio and television stations to continually spread their terrorist propaganda (Sik, 2002).

In recent years the PKK-KADEK received monetary as well as weapons and equipment support from Iran and Syria. This equipment included light infantry armament, antitank and antipersonnel mines, heavy air defense machine guns, and radio transmission stations plus a large amount of guerilla warfare training and supplies. A major portion of these supplies were used by PKK-KADEK military forces in Northern Iraq, where they have been under constant attack from another Turkish terrorist group known as the Revolutionary People's Liberation Party Front (DHKP-C). The DHKP-C is considered the most dangerous and active Marxist-Leninist organization operating in the Middle East today and has been in constant conflict with PKK-KADEK. DHKP-C considers the PKK-KADEK an enemy and is doing everything possible to undermine PKK-KADEK activities (Tudor, 2002).

Turkish police investigators working with U.S. DEA agents seized the Panamanian registered ship *Lucky S* in January 1993 and found 2.7 tons of morphine base hidden in the anchor chain storage area of this 200-foot boat. That was the fourth morphine base seizure by police in two months, bringing the total of morphine base seized by drug authorities to 7.5 tons. Turkish police suggested that evidence from these seizures indicated there was a much closer connection than originally anticipated between the Turkish drug mafia and the PKK gangs in Eastern Turkey in the drug smuggling market (Cowell, 1993).

The *Lucky S* seizure led to the arrest of Necat Des, leader of the Des drug gang, and Derya Ayanoglu, part owner of the vessel, for drug smuggling; a leader of another major Turkish drug gang, Huseyn Baybasin, has been in hiding in Eastern Turkey since the seizure of the *Lucky S*. Police established direct connections between leaders of the Des and Baybasin drug gangs and leaders of the PKK in the drug-trafficking business (Cowell, 1993).

In an effort to destroy PKK drug operations, the Turkish police and military initiated raids on their bases in Eastern Turkey and Northern Iraq. Knowing that PKK gangs have been conducting drug-trading operations in Zaho, Northern Iraq, the Turkish government decided to conduct some police and military drug seizure maneuvers in that area. In fact, during raids into PKK-controlled villages in Eastern Iraq, the police and military authorities uncovered a cannabis cultivation center and farm. This farm property producing a very large crop of cannabis was located in PKK's Pirvela Camp in the Bahara Valley of Northern Iraq. A total of 4.5 tons of cannabis plants and hashish were seized by the Turkish police and military during this raid.

The expansion of the Turkish mafia's drug-trafficking activities became even more prevalent in 1994 when an undercover member of the U.S. DEA purchased 23 kilograms of pure heroin from Seref Karanisoglu, a notorious Turkish drug trafficker. In an effort to eradicate both the Turkish mafia and the PKK drug rings, the Turkish government signed agreements to set up drug task forces to destroy PKK drug-trafficking activities, activities that have been major monetary resources for this Turkish terrorist and drug gang. The Turkish government already had an agreement with the U.S. DEA and recently set up the same type of arrangement with the Israeli government (Onishi, April 20, 1994; *Reuters World News Service*, 1994).

Lebanese Gangs

In most cases, Arab gangs operate within their own countries; drug gangs are the exception. For example, Lebanese drug gang members were arrested in Israel for smuggling over a quarter ton of heroin (with an estimated value $21 million) into Israel during the early 1990s. Police in Israel conducted a 30-month investigation into these drug gangs. As a result of this inquiry, members of six different Lebanese gangs (including members of two Bedouin gangs from southern Israel) were arrested throughout Israel. This drug operation was set up by two Lebanese brothers, who made sure there were sufficient amounts of heroin available at all times to supply most areas of Israel. Mufid Nahara and Ramsi Nahara had been previously arrested by the Israeli police for their participation in a hashish-smuggling ring. The gang bosses, Shawki Latiff and Itab Tuba, owned a contracting company on the outskirts of the village of Rama in Galilee (Rudge, 1992).

Iraqi Gangs

During the latter part of 1994, Lebanese police seized three members of an Iraqi gang who were involved in counterfeiting currency. When apprehended in the village of Ajaltoun on the outskirts of Beirut, Lebanon, the gang members had counterfeiting equipment and counterfeit money in their possession. Law enforcement sources in Lebanon estimated that gang members had produced well over 162 million (mostly in denominations of 50,000 and 100,000) in Lebanese pound currency. A number of forged samples of other foreign paper money, including Kuwaiti dinars, Turkish liras, and United Arab Emirates dirhams, were also found. This gang of forgers had not stopped with Arab currency; in their possession were also forged German bank notes (marks) and Swiss franks. Lebanese government officials estimated that the forgers had placed roughly 45 million pounds of Lebanese currency in circulation prior to their apprehension (*Reuters World News Service*, October 6, 1994).

United Arab Emirates Gangs

The United Arab Emirates government faced its first major problem with gangs when 10 members of a local motorbike gang killed a night watchman for no apparent reason. Apparently, the 10 gang members (6 of them born and raised in the United Arab Emirates, 3 Iranian nationals, and 1 from Yemeni) were sniffing glue just prior to the savage attack on the security guard. Gang members between 15 and 18 years old first attacked the guard at a municipal car pound in the town of Sharjah. After being struck on the head with an iron bar, the guard ran inside a building and bolted the door, but the gang members proceeded to demolish everything in their way until they managed to gain entrance into the room where the guard was hiding. Once the gang members entered the room, they proceeded to unmercifully beat the security officer to death with sticks, bats, and iron bars. Prior to leaving the crime scene, gang members stole five motorbikes that had been taken from them during a previous confrontation with the police (*Reuters World News Service*, March 29, 1994). Prior to this episode, the only gang activity in the United Arab Emirates involved drug gangs. In each case, these gangs were made up of Pakistani nationals who found it easier and faster to smuggle drugs (heroin or hashish) through the United Arab Emirates on route to Europe.

Iranian Gangs

In 1989, the Iranian government passed some very strict drug laws that stipulated that any drug trafficker apprehended with 30 or more grams (1 ounce) of heroin or 5 kilograms (11 pounds) of opium would be sentenced to death. Once these laws were put in place, it was anticipated that drug trafficking by Iranian gangs would cease, but the government has come to the conclusion that this did not happen. A total of more than 2,500 drug traffickers were hung between 1989 and 1994; drug arrests steadily increased in spite of the new laws, as has the number of pounds of heroin seized by

Iranian police, so over half the Iranian prison population is now serving time for drug infractions. Major General Reza Seifollahi, chief of Iranian law enforcement, indicated that 14,612 narcotics traffickers and 43,464 drug addicts were arrested in Iran between April 1993 and February 1994. Seifollahi further stated that the police had seized over 175,000 pounds of heroin (*Agence France Presse*, 1994).

The drug-smuggling activities of Iranian drug gangs continued even though the Iranian government had instituted a strict enforcement policy, so this policy did not seem to be totally effective. As strict as drug law enforcement was in Iran, the drug gangs' trafficking businesses seemed to be prosperous. For example, on November 13, 1994, Iranian police arrested 89 members of an Iranian drug gang and seized over 191 kilograms of heroin. In another instance, on March 28, 1995, the Iranian police seized 2,058 kilograms of heroin and killed 20 members of an Iranian drug-smuggling gang (*Reuters World News Service*, 1994; Xinhus News Agency, 1995). Between March 1993 and February 1994, a total of 68 tons of drugs were seized by the police. Also between March 1994 and February 1995, the Iran police seized over 135 tons of drugs (*Reuters World News Service*, September 18, 1995). This certainly seemed to indicate that tough drug laws were not a hindrance to most drug gangs.

Iranian drug gangs such as the Kamrani-Bameri were connected to drug growers in Afghanistan and Pakistan, who were supplying them with large quantities of both heroin and opium. These drug gangs usually have anywhere from 20 to 150 members who are well armed and who distribute large amounts of heroin daily; the Kamrani-Bameri gang actually distributed over 100 kilograms of opium a day. In many cases, drug gangs in Iran kidnapped local villagers (male and female) and forced them to become gang slaves (the Kamrani-Bameri gang had 200 male and 300 female slaves when the gang was trapped once by the Iranian military and police). Some gang slaves were sold back to their families, while others were used to transport drugs, carry weapons, clean animals, or have forcible sex. Most of these gangs used camels as their transportation vehicles because it is easier for camels to travel through hot sandy deserts and over other types of rugged terrain (*Reuters World News Service*, September 18, 1995).

A majority of drug trafficking in Iran is confined to the Baluchins. There are a total of 1.5 million members of the Baluchin tribe living in Iran, and a majority of them are Sunni Muslims (unlike the majority of the population in Iran who are Shiite Muslims). Many members of the Baluchin tribe are involved as leaders and members of Iran drug gangs; in fact, Baluchins who participate in the highly profitable drug-trafficking business receive the blessing of the Baluchin clergy. The clergy established that Baluchins have a divine right to form drug gangs and to participate in the drug-trafficking business (Ghazi, 1990).

Pakistani Gangs

The involvement of Pakistani nationals in drug-trafficking gangs has increased 10-fold since the early 1970s. Customs officials in airports in Atlanta, Boston, Chicago, Houston, Los Angeles, Miami, Newark, New York, San Francisco, and Seattle as well as our Canadian neighbor's airports in Montreal, Toronto, and Vancouver have seized Pakistani gang members attempting to smuggle in heroin. In most cases, the heroin was concealed in suitcases or briefcases with false sides or false bottoms, was sewn into suits or jackets, or was secreted in hollowed-out items such as candlesticks and furniture legs. Heroin that gets past customs officials is then given to a member of the Pakistani gang who is either a registered alien or a naturalized U.S. (or Canadian) citizen.

Drug couriers leaving Pakistan for North American cities seldom carry the concealed drugs onto the plane with them; most couriers pass through customs in Pakistan prior to being informed of the location of the heroin. Once the drug trans-porter reaches the departure area of the airport, he is either handed a claim check for luggage that contains the heroin or given a carry-on item that holds the secreted drugs. Pakistani drug gangs usually place a member who is known as a controller on all planes that contain drug couriers to ensure the integrity of the couriers. Once the plane arrives at the designated destination and the drug courier passes through customs, one of two things will happen: Either the courier passes the heroin to the controller, who then arranges to deliver the heroin to its final destination, or the courier follows instructions given to him requiring him to register at a specifically chosen hotel, from which the courier calls Pakistan for instructions on how to make the delivery to the purchaser (DEA, 1987).

An example of a Pakistani drug gang's smuggling operation took place in 1991 when U.S. drug agents seized three kilograms of pure heroin imported from Pakistan and arrested Guiseppe DiFranco of New York City, the buyer and ultimate dispenser of the heroin on the streets of New York. Khalillullah Kakur, a native of Afghanistan and a resident of California, was an associate gang member who received the heroin after its arrival in the United States, and Parvis Khan, a Pakistani sheep herder, was the drug mule. Khan had arrived at JFK International Airport on November 4, 1991, and then proceeded to a Hauppauge hotel. He was joined at the hotel by Kakur on November 5. Kakur then proceeded to the Kew Motor Inn in Kew Gardens, Queens, where he held a meeting with DiFranco. Once the deal was consummated on November 6, federal drug agents moved in and arrested all three participants. Khan and Kakur were arrested in the Hauppauge hotel where the three kilos of heroin were recovered, along with the $25,000 fee that Khan had received for smuggling the heroin into the United States. DiFranco was apprehended in his Brooklyn restaurant (Kessler, 1991).

In an effort to crack down on both the drug and kidnapping activities of orga-nized crime groups in the southern province of Sindh, which is on the outskirts of Karachi, the Pakistani government, on June 19, 1992, staged raids on all locations that were known to be frequented by members of these criminal organizations. With mili-tary assistance, the police conducted house-to-house searches in an effort to confiscate drugs and weapons that were hidden by local gang members. During this same time period in Sindh province, there was an ongoing conflict between past and present members of the Mohajir Qaumi group over control of this gang's criminal activities in the southern region of Pakistan. Police and military personnel in Sindh province suddenly found themselves in the midst of an all-out gang war. Within a short period of time, this conflict spread into Karachi, where the police found themselves dodging a raging fusillade of bullets that were being exchanged between opposing factions of the Mohajir Qaumi group. It took until June 21, 1992, for the police and military to finally squelch the fighting and subdue the rebellious gangs. Once peace was restored to this area, the police announced that 10 people had been killed during the skirmishes and that over 700 gang members had been arrested by the police. Ruling government officials in Sindh were removed by Pakistani president Ghulam Ishaq Khan because of their inability to suppress gang activities in the province (Iqbal, 1992).

Problems with drug gangs in Sindh province is only one example of the Pakistanis' inability to control gang activities. A U.S. CIA report dated February 1993 indicated that Pakistani drug gangs supplied funding to elect many of the government leaders in Pakistan. Drug money was used to buy votes throughout the country, which helped the drug gangs win seats for corrupt politicians in the Pakistani National Assembly. This money even gave drug gang leaders access to both the prime minister and president of Pakistan. One of the leading Pakistani drug gang leaders, Sohail Zia Butt, was the brother-in-law of Nawaz Sharif, the prime minister of Pakistan. One must remember the importance of a marital relationship in Pakistan: According to Pakistani custom, marriages are actually affiliations that in many cases are made in order to combine both prosperity and power. After the Sharif and Butt alliance took place, both families prospered; Sharif became prime minister, and Butt (a notorious heroin trafficker and a very influential multimillionaire) was protected from arrest and imprisonment by his family's political and monetary associations. This prosperity spilled over to other members of the Butt family. Aslam Butt became the emissary to other drug-trafficking groups, and Haji lqbal Butt, also a major part of the Butt narcotic-trafficking gang, became an effective and important advisor to Prime Minister Sharif (Royce, 1993).

The Butt family was not the only one with drug-trafficking connections in the Pakistani government. According to CIA documents, Malik Mohammed Ayub Khan Afridi (also known as Haji Ayub Zakha Khel), the number one drug trafficker in Pakistan, used his drug money to get himself elected to a seat in the National Assembly. Khel (known as the King of Khybur Heroin) gained a great deal of influence in the Pakistani government. Through the use of corrupt methods, Khel created a situation for himself that gave him direct access to the president of Pakistan, Ghulam Ishaq Khan; to leaders of the ruling political party; and to high-ranking members of Pakistani military intelligence. Khel complied most of these benefits by spending large amounts of money to entertain as well as support the reelection campaigns of high-ranking Pakistani politicians. In an effort to take away Khel's power, some previous government officials (including former Prime Minister Benazir Bhutto) had warrants issued for his arrest on drug-trafficking charges, but Khel evaded arrest by remaining out of sight. Once the government of Bhutto had been removed from office, Khel had members of the next government suppress these arrest warrants (Royce, 1993).

A 1993 CIA report indicated that one of the few Pakistani leaders who was not entangled in any of the Pakistani drug conspiracies was former dictator Zia ul-Haq, who was killed when his plane exploded in 1988. Yet some of his associates, including the pilots of the presidential plane, were identified as coconspirators in a drug-smuggling operation. CIA sources also indicated that large amounts of drug money were used by the Inter Services Intelligence Directorate (ISI) to support either Sikh radicals in India or Mashmiri revolutionaries in Kashmir. One drug gang, controlled by Chaudhury Shaukat Ali Bhatti, supplied large amounts of money to the Sikh revolutionaries to buy weapons. In return, the Sikh militants guaranteed that the transportation of all the heroin across the Pakistani border into India was done without any interference from either other rebel groups or other drug gangs (Royce, 1993).

Religious laws related to opium cultivation, heroin production, and drug gangs within the Pakistani Muslim hierarchy were similar to those of Baluchin Muslims in Iran. In the Koran (the Islamic bible), it forbids the use of narcotics, but devout Muslim savants in the heroin-producing locations in Pakistan declared that under Muslim law it was legal to both grow poppies and produce heroin. What these religious leaders did was to create a *fatwah* (legal doctrine) that justified the tillage of the soil to produce opium as long as the by-product, heroin, was sold to or used by Muslim drug addicts. This is almost the same stance taken by Islamic Shiite religious leaders in Iran and leads one to believe that the so-called fanatical Islamic religious leaders feel that violations of Islamic religious laws can only be committed against Muslims and that there is nothing wrong with selling heroin to members of other ethnic and religious groups. This is noteworthy because most Muslim religious sects consider the Islamic religion the only pure and true religion on earth while justifying drug gangs, violence, and drug trafficking.

Pakistani drug gangs have been operating since the late 1970s, but the amount of drugs being smuggled out of both Afghanistan and Pakistan has risen dramatically since the late 1980s. Opium production in Afghanistan, for example, increased extensively once the Soviet military left in 1989. Anywhere from 70 to 80 metric tons of opium are processed through Pakistani heroin-producing labs yearly; this heroin is then shipped to either an American or a European market.

There are three major drug gangs operating out of Pakistan. The first gang is based out of the Lahore area of Pakistan and is known as the Haji Baig group. This gang is a loose coalition of major drug gangs that prospers in spite of the fact that three major leaders were imprisoned in Pakistan on drug charges; the U.S. government then succeeded in extradition proceedings against them. The three leaders of this consortium included Haji Mirza Iqbal Baig, who amassed (both legally and illegally) over $20 million in assets in the past 30 years. Anwar Khan Khattak, the second member of this drug gang, was the mastermind behind the transshipment of heroin from Lahore to Karachi and then by sea or air to either Europe or the United States. The third member of this coalition was Tariq Waheed Butt, who provided the alliances with both American and European markets for Pakistani drugs (Witkin and Griffin, 1994). In an effort to show that the Pakistani government was cooperating with the U.S. effort to prosecute foreign drug gang leaders, both Baig and Khattak were extradited to the United States in April 1995.

Haji Ayub Afridi, a drug gang leader who was at one time a member of Pakistan's National Assembly, has become possibly the most powerful drug lord in Pakistan. Afridi built his own drug barony 35 miles outside of Peshawar. Afridi's compound is surrounded by 20-foot-high walls for protection; he also has his own private drug army with a membership of over 1,000 well-trained soldiers. Also, a number of antiaircraft guns protect Afridi from both aerial and ground attacks. Within the confines of the Afridi estate are both a large ranch and a well-stocked zoo. To some extent, Afridi seems to have modeled his drug operations after his Colombian counterparts (Witkin and Griffin, 1994).

A third drug gang, the Quetta Alliance, is similar to the Haji Baig group mentioned earlier, but one major difference is that the Quetta gang elected one of its members as the head of the gang, This gang's labs produce a morphine base product that is converted to heroin in Turkey. Sakhi Dost Jan Notezai, an elected member of the Pakistani Provincial Asembly, ran the day-to-day operations of the Quetta gang even while confined to a Pakistan prison awaiting trial on drug charges. Of the two other leaders of the Quetta gang, the Rigi family controlled all the transshipment of drugs in and out of Pakistan; Mohammed Issa, an Afghan national, controlled the markets for heroin in both America and Europe. This group's base of operations is located in Pakistan several miles from the opium-rich Afghanistan province of Helmand (Witkin and Griffin, 1994).

As far as these gangs' drug operations are concerned, most of their heroin is transported across Europe; then it is transshipped to either Canada or the United States. Heroin produced by the Pakistani drug gangs is imported into the United States through Los Angeles, Newark, New York, and San Francisco. Chicago, Detroit, and New York contain the largest markets for Pakistani heroin because all these cities have a large population of Pakistani nationals. In almost all cases, the heroin is sold to other ethnic groups, which then sell it at street level.

Even though Islamic religious leaders in Pakistan have justified members of their religion dealing in heroin, they did not anticipate the increased use of heroin in their own country. In 1994, over 1.5 million Pakistani citizens were addicted to heroin and consumed over 40 percent of all the heroin produced in Pakistan that year. In Karachi, for example, the heavily armed drug gangs became so powerful that they took control of a major portion of the city.

Pakistan's problems with corruption from drug gangs has gotten so far out of hand that deposed Prime Minister Nawaz Sharif accused then General Aslam Beg, military chief of staff, and General Assad Durrani, head of the ISI, of approaching him and proposing a plan to raise money for clandestine foreign campaigns by working with local drug gangs (Anderson and Khan, 1994). According to Sharif, money gleaned from narcotics trafficking was used by the ISI to support dissident actions throughout India (1993). Other reports indicated that drug gang leaders managed to use money to reach the highest-ranking political officials in Pakistan to avoid arrest and prosecution for drug trafficking (Royce, 1993).

In early 1995, the Pakistan government, in an effort to take back control of the country from the drug gangs, staged raids throughout the Islamabad area of Pakistan.

These raids resulted in the tearing down of 15 drug labs and the seizure of over 6.3 tons of heroin. A prior raid by the military in January 1995 in Bara, Pakistan, led to the seizure of 480 kilograms of heroin and 165 tons of hashish. The only problem with these raids was the way they were viewed by both Pakistanis and Western drug authorities: Both groups indicated that these raids were conducted against groups that were not involved in the major Pakistani drug market and that most of the people seized were poor Khyber tribesmen. Some observers went so far as to say that in both cases the raids were orchestrated by the Pakistani government just to gain U.S. support (Clerc, 1995). What these observers really wanted to know was why the Pakistani government refused to seize this opportunity to go after members of the three major drug gangs who were still at large. Arresting members of the Khyber tribes, who plant and gather the opium crop for sale to major drug traffickers for very small amounts of money, would not be the answer to Pakistan's drug gang problem. Claims that large quantities of heroin were recovered and drug labs were destroyed had no visible evidence to back up these assertions. One must remember that a majority of the raids conducted by the Pakistan government were in inaccessible areas of the Khyber Pass, so all information related to these raids and the amount of drugs confiscated was released by members of the Pakistani government's public information unit and not by any outside media or government agency.

Criminal activities by Pakistani gangs also began to appear outside Pakistan. For instance, in Japan during 1994, the Japanese police arrested Mohammed Naeem, a Pakistani national and the head of a Pakistani crime group that made counterfeit 1,000 rupee notes. It seems that Naeem had set up a factory in Koshigaya in Saitama Prefecture and had employed several Japanese workers who assisted him and his gang members in producing over 4,000 counterfeit 1,000 rupee notes. Many of these notes were smuggled out of Japan and then converted into either Japanese or U.S. currency in Bangkok. Tokyo police also arrested Jun Furusawa and four other Japanese suspects on extortion charges. It seems that Furusawa and his gang of four were hired by Naeem to pose as immigration officers and to seize four Pakistani nationals who were arriving at the Tokyo airport. After their arrival, the Pakistani nationals were approached by Furusawa and his associates, who placed them in handcuffs for allegedly violating Japanese immigration laws. The four Pakistanis were then taken to Naeem, who informed them that if they paid a specific amount of money to him, he could ensure that they would not be charged with any violations of Japanese immigration laws. During interrogation by Japanese police, Naeem admitted that he had made up counterfeit immigration officer identification cards for members of his gang as well as for Furusawa and his four associates. He further stated that once the counterfeiting money scheme was finished, he and his gang members had a list of Pakistani nationals living in Japan from whom they planned to extort money (Shimbun, 1994).

Besides their drug and extortion businesses, members of Pakistani organized crime groups in the United States initiated scams to bilk the government as well as private citizens of U.S. currency. These gang members instituted swindles that involved fraudulent automobile accidents and phony injury claims; then the claimants used medical clinics that often only existed on paper. In some cases, a clinic was opened by gang members, who then used both corrupt doctors to make false reports and underhanded lawyers to file insurance claims. Gangs employed their members to act as runners, who were issued fraudulent driver's licenses, a legitimate vehicle registration, and a valid insurance card. A vehicular accident would then be staged, and three to four fictitious injured passengers would be created by the runner when he reported this false incident to the police. This scam was successful in most major metropolitan areas because the runner had to go to the local police precinct to report the accident, unless there is a serious injury involved, metropolitan police do not respond to vehicular accidents. Once the accident was reported to the police, the gang member would hand the information over to gang members running the clinic, who in turn would forward medical bills to insurance companies. Insurance companies would be billed for 25 to 50 different types of therapies that the gang's corrupt doctor would state are necessary for the injured parties to successfully recover from the physical and mental impairments they suffered during or after the accident.

Gang members also set up a phony car service that is used by the injured driver and passengers for transportation to and from the clinic; the car service then bills the insurance company for these bogus services. The gangs also paid illegal aliens or newly arrived immigrants to have X-rays taken so that there were bodies available for the insurance company in case of any type of follow-up investigation. Most insurance companies settled claims such as these as quickly as possible to avoid going to court and having to pay a larger settlement (Koleniak, 1995).

Pakistani organized crime groups are similar to other criminal gangs at this stage of their development. The U.S. market was new to Pakistani leaders and gang members, but it did not take any great period of time for the gangs to adapt to the criminal opportunities in our environment. Most Pakistani gangs are presently loosely knit, but there is a kinship based on both their ethnic and religious backgrounds that could help to create one larger tightly bonded organized crime group sometime in the future.

Indian Gangs

Organized crime groups first appeared in India in the early 1800s. Prior to the appearance of these organized crime groups, a majority of the wealthy people in India (known as *zamindars*) hired large groups of men known as *paiks* or *lathials* and kept them under their control, mainly for their own protection. A majority of these *paiks* or *lathials* were well trained and were used by the *zamindars* as enforcers who collected rents, forcefully took land back from renters, supplied their bosses with women, and provided protection for them and their families.

The first organized gang was known as Thuggees, a secretive group of gangsters involved in robbery, extortion, and murder. Members of this gang traveled throughout India in smaller groups and represented themselves as members of a religious sect in order to gain the trust of victims. Through the use of various types of deception, gang members built up the victims' confidence in them; a short time later, gang members would rob and kill the victims. These gangs got so far out of control by the mid-1830s that the British government in India passed special legislation that allowed the military and other law enforcement agencies to arrest these gang members on sight. Some were put to death, while others were banished from India and told that if they ever returned, they would also be put to death (Ghosh, 1991).

Late in the 1850s, the problem of loosely organized crime gangs again appeared in India. These gangs were bandits who roamed the highways and byways of India committing crimes such as robbery, burglary, extortion, kidnapping, and murder. Gang members used trained dogs to protect their camps and hideouts from government attack; gang leaders also managed to get the police to work with them by using female members of the gang to corrupt local members of the constabulary. During this time, these gangs had approximately a quarter of a million members. They, like the Thuggees before them, forced the British government in India to enact what became known as the Criminal Tribes Acts in 1871. This act was strictly enforced by both the military and the state police agencies. Stern enforcement of these acts led to a decrease in the crimes committed by members of these organized crime groups, but it was not long before other types of groups started appearing in India (Ghosh, 1991).

At the beginning of the twentieth century, information on a tightly run organized crime group started to appear in Calcutta. Police intelligence information indicated that this group, known as the Bengal Goonda gangs (thieves or gangsters), had formed a coalition with Indian revolutionaries as well as smugglers and drug traffickers. These gangs created their own criminal organization that supplied guns to revolutionaries and drugs to local drug dealers. Once again, the British government stepped in and passed legislation that allowed the Indian government to proclaim that if a person was a member of a Goonda gang, that person could be banished from the state of Bengal for an indeterminate amount of time. Again, this type of banishment worked for a period of time but was not strong enough to totally remove the Goonda gang members from the Indian state of Bengal (Ghosh, 1991).

A short time after the outbreak of World War II, the Goonda gangs, which had been operating covertly in India since the Goonda Act of 1923, reappeared in Calcutta. These gang members immediately set up their own brothels and drug dens throughout what became red light districts in Calcutta as well as in every other major urban area in India; Goonda gangs also set up protection rackets for other ethnic brothels in India. The gangs became involved in supplying girls to the various ethnic brothels in India, which required gang members to get involved in rape and kidnapping of females of all ages and ethnic backgrounds in order to produce the number of women required to stock these brothels. The abducted women were usually auctioned off to the brothel owner who bid the highest price. In many cases, the gangs' participation in this type of crime provided outright profits, but in some cases, the gangs had a deal with the brothel owner that provided them with a small percentage of the abducted woman's earnings even after she was paid for by the brothel owner (Ghosh, 1991).

During this time, gang activities increased not only because of the number of foreign military personnel who were given leave from the war in Calcutta but also because of the atrocities being committed by members of the Muslim community against members of the Hindu community. Muslims in Calcutta started by recruiting other gang members from throughout India for a reign of terror on the Hindu community in Calcutta. Muslim crimes included raiding Hindu houses and robbing and killing the owners, abducting and raping all the females, and burning houses to the ground. In retaliation for these crimes, members of the Hindu community hired the Goondas to provide protection for them and their families (Ghosh, 1991).

Gang activities in India continued to flourish, and the gangs established themselves during the 1950s, 1960s, and 1970s. Today gang members are as much a part of Indian society as are members of both the Muslim and Hindu religions. People who joined gangs were usually between 16 and 18 years old, were unemployed, and were involved in some type of criminal activity before seeking gang membership. Once they became members of a Goonda gang, they were totally faithful to the gang and its leaders. Some leaders were chosen from within the gang, but a majority of the leadership came from the middle-class level of Indian society. Most leaders reached this level in Indian society because of their past criminal activities in a gang. A leader, called a *dada* or *mastan*, would have extremely good abilities to organize and run a business or a criminal association. Many gang bosses were between 40 and 50 years old and were fairly literate. Bosses got a specific percentage of the money made by their underlings for deciding the criminal strategies of the gang; they directed gang members on how to carry out these crimes without being apprehended by the police and made the proper connections to corrupt government officials in order to prevent the arrest and prosecution of members who participated in the gang's criminal activities.

Once a gang member became somewhat prosperous, he could break away and form his own gang. Organizing a new group was done without any conflict from gang leaders, and it was often done with the leaders' blessing because when a member formed his new group, he remained loyal to his original gang and continued to support all the old gang's criminal endeavors. Gang research done by Ghosh indicated that Indian gangs were divided according to social status or religion (Ghosh, 1991).

Like other wealthy people before them, members of India's political parties used gang members for their benefit. Gang members were used by politicians to persuade citizens to vote or not vote for certain politicians, to discourage political opponents from seeking office, to gather election funding for candidates, and to maintain the ability to manipulate the electorate. One Indian politician, Kapil Deo Singh (a minister in the Karpoori Thaker Cabinet), acknowledged on the floor of the Bihar Assembly that he had his own gang of Goondas and that without its assistance he would never be elected to office. Goonda members' participation in political activities first appeared in 1969 when India's two major political parties were involved in a bitter dispute. During this time, gang leaders decided to start seeking closer associations with politicians; between 1969 and 1980, gang leaders worked toward accomplishing this goal. First, contributions were made by gang leaders to gain the confidence of the politicians. This was followed by having gang members along with their leaders, take an active role in the election of their candidates, which in many cases, involved the use of intimidation by gang members to get people to vote for the office seeker supported by the gang.

In 1980, the association between gangs and politicians became far more obvious when gang leaders decided it was cheaper and easier for them personally to seek election to office. After acquiring the necessary knowledge over the past 11 years by working for the politicians, the gang members set up their own well-oiled political machine. Once this was accomplished, gang leaders used whatever techniques were needed to gain the votes necessary to be elected to government office. Since gang leaders first started running for office in the early 1980s, gang leaders began to control a great deal of the activities of both the politicians and the government. In many of the Indian states, politicians are under the total control of the gangs and cannot vote on any controversial issue or do anything else without consulting gang leaders. The gangs also took the time to set up good relationships with lawyers, court officers, police officials, and members of the media. All this, of course, gave gang members all the power they needed to run their illegal activities without any interference from most government agencies or the media.

Gang activities during an election became more brutal as time passed. In 1989, during general elections in India, over 150 people were killed during three days of voting by gang members because the victims opposed the persons supported by the gang leaders. Gang leaders assured themselves of continued political support by what is known as "booth capturing," a tactic that we would call stuffing the ballot box. Through the use of force, gang members would take over control of an election booth and then stamp all the ballots in that booth for their candidate. This is done without any government interference (Ghosh, 1991).

Organized crime gangs in India participated in numerous legal and illegal activities (Ghosh, 1991; Hazarika, 1993):

1. *Unions.* During the mid-1960s, the gangs were used to eliminate unions striking in Bombay. Since then, gang members have penetrated into the unions as both workers and union representatives. In this capacity, gang members used intimidation, kidnapping, assault, and murder to gain results from the management of any company with which the union had a dispute. Gang members used the same tactics against union members who did not support them.

2. *Private companies.* Private companies hired gang members to eliminate their competition, usually accomplished by murdering the owner of the other business. These private businesses also used gang members to help them bilk insurance companies. A businessperson would order an expensive piece of machinery and make sure that this item had insurance coverage. Once the businessperson knew the location where the machinery was to be dropped off for him to pick up, he would notify gang members, who would steal the machinery. (It would later be delivered to him.) When the businessperson was informed that the property had been successfully stolen (usually from a shipping dock), he immediately would inform the insurance company, which

had to then reimburse him for his loss. A percentage of the insurance claim would be paid to the gang leader.

3. *Contract murders.* Gang members murdered anyone for a price.

4. *Real estate.* Gang members were used by landlords to remove any problem tenants. In other cases, the gang leader would offer to buy the apartment or house for half its market price, would purchase the apartment, and would forcibly remove the tenants. The apartment was then sold for its true price. Builders and contractors used gang members to assist them in removing tenants from slum housing so that the builders or contractors who had purchased the property, could knock down the old tenement and replace it with a larger modernized building. If tenants refused to move, a group of gang members would either beat up the tenants or sexually assault the tenants' wives and daughters until they agreed to leave the apartment.

5. *Hafta collection.* Gang members were involved in extortion of businesses and stores, including jewelry and diamond shops, movie theaters, restaurants, hotels, limousine and taxi businesses, brothels, food stores, gambling dens, and money-lending businesses. There was a set payment based on the profit made by each business. Refusal to pay this protection money led to the owner being assaulted, kidnapped, or murdered.

6. *Movie industry.* Owners of movie distribution centers used gang members to ensure that no one made copies of their movies. Gang members were so involved in extorting money from Indian moviemakers and movie stars, charging them a monthly fee for protection.

7. *Havala business.* A loan-sharking operation was run by Indian gang members for stock market investors. An interest rate of 24 percent was charged on money loaned to these investors. Gang enforcers were used to collect the debt in cases in which investors refused to either pay the interest or repay the loan.

8. *Narcotics and liquor.* Gangs controlled the distribution and sale of all drugs and alcohol throughout India. Indian organized crime gangs were also heavily involved in supplying drug gangs in Afghanistan, Myanmar, and Pakistan with a chemical known as acetic anhydride, which is used in the production of heroin.

9. *Smuggling.* All types of goods—from human beings to textiles and drugs—were smuggled to make money for the gangs.

The power of the gangs was evident in Bombay in early 1993 during riots that started out as a dispute between local Hindu and Muslim groups. Bombay police reported that organized crime gangs had spread the fighting and violence throughout Bombay. During these riots, gang members robbed people on the streets, assaulted or murdered anyone who opposed their actions, and broke into stores to steal anything of value. In March 1993, Bombay was hit with 13 explosions that killed 317 people and wounded 1,500 citizens; these bombs exploded in the Bombay stock exchange, in three hotels, and in several corporate offices, including the central office of Air India. In the aftermath of these bombings, the police investigation traced evidence located at and around these bomb scenes to a gang run by the Memon brothers. Another organized crime leader, Dawood Ibrahim, was mentioned by the police as a coconspirator in this crime. Ibrahim became a power in organized crime in India in the late 1970s when he took control of many smuggling and protection rackets in Bombay. In the mid-1980s, Ibrahim moved his base of operations from Bombay to Dubai but was still able to totally control his gang's activities from there. A short time after the bombing, the police responded to the Memon residence in Bombay to find that the family had packed up and left for Dubai (Gargan, 1993).

In August 1994, Yakub Abdul Razak Memon was apprehended by police at a New Delhi train station. The Indian government claimed that the Memon brothers, along with Ibrahim and other gang members, had planted the bombs throughout Bombay and then had watched as the bombs were set off. Further information obtained from the Indian government indicated that both the Memon and Ibrahim gangs were contracted and paid by Pakistani militants to carry out these bombings; in fact, members of both gangs were trained and paid by Pakistani terrorist groups prior to the bombings (Bidi, 1994; Burns, 1994; Chakravarty, 1994).

The activities of most Indian organized crime groups have not yet impacted the United States too heavily. However, the Patel Indian organized crime group has been visible in this country since the mid-1960s and has been involved in loaning money to newly arrived Indians to open businesses in the United States. A U.S. government investigation in 1985 showed that the Patel group owned 28 percent of small motels and hotels in the United States and owned about 90 percent of all the independently owned motels and hotels in this country. In most of these establishments, gang members also controlled and operated a prostitution business. Members of this organized crime group have managed to keep a very low key profile and to avoid conflict with members of law enforcement. They are fairly well organized and (in most cases) operate as cell groups in major cities throughout the United States. U.S. Drug Enforcement Agency sources indicated that the Patel group also used its hotel/motel businesses as drop-off and pickup points for its hashish/heroin-trafficking businesses (DEA, 1993).

Like many other ethnic groups before them, the Patel crime gangs were involved in the forgery of documents that can be purchased by people with money looking for an easy entry into the United States. Members of this gang were also involved in the forgery of food stamps, U.S. Treasury checks, and traveler's checks and the theft of food stamps and personal checks. One scam by members of Indian organized crime involved the theft of thousands of copies of major magazines such as *Cosmopolitan*, *Time*, and *Good Housekeeping*. Patel gang members set up a major theft conspiracy and stole thousands of copies of major weekly and monthly magazines; then they sold the magazine to other members of the Patel gang who owned and operated newsstands throughout New York City. A total of 13 members of this operation were arrested by investigators from the U.S. Department of Labor for their participation in this theft (McCoy, 1994).

Burmese Gangs

Burmese organized crime groups first appeared in Burma (now known as Myanmar) when Khun Sa organized the Mong Tai Army (MTA) or the Shan United Army to protect his newly established drug empire. Khun Sa's base of operation was in the town of Homong in the southern Shan state of Burma. Over the past several decades, Sa created his own personal military-type gang; he claimed that he does not participate in the drug-trafficking business but only extorts money from the drug growers and dealers to support his group. In reality, Sa formed an alliance with local farmers who grow the opium for him, and he then refines the opium in his refineries on the Burmese-Thailand border. Sa's gang is a military type of organized crime family, which includes himself as the boss and three underbosses or lieutenants assisting him. One lieutenant runs the day-to-day operations of the gang, another lieutenant takes care of security and intelligence gathering, and the third lieutenant is the comptroller and runs the opium refineries (Witkin and Griffin, 1994).

The Sa gang and its 20,000 members are considered one of the most ruthless gangs in Burma. On occasion, the gang entered a village where there was opposition to them and their drug-trafficking activities and killed or mutilated all the people in the village. These brutal activities, plus Sa's eccentricity, brought a great amount of attention from the Burmese government, which sent a number of military detachments to confront and arrest Sa and to destroy his militaristic gang's drug operations (Lintner and Mai, 1994). During 1995, the Burmese government conducted an all-out attack on Sa and his army that resulted in Sa surrendering to government troops in early 1996. An agreement reached by Sa and representatives of the Burmese government gave Sa amnesty from any government charges for his drug-trafficking activities since the 1960s. It was not known what other deals were worked out between Sa and the Burmese government (Shenon, 1996).

Following in the footsteps of the Sa gang were several other major drug-trafficking groups; among them was the United Wa State Army. This group was formed by two former members of the Communist Party. The United Wa State Army had two wings: a political wing and a military wing. The gang had an elected leader, Chao Nyi-lai, and a military leader, Pao Ya-chiang. Total membership in this loosely knit group was estimated somewhere between 15,000 and 35,000. At one time, the United Wa sold drugs to the Sa group, but then this gang set up its own opium-refining locations along the Burmese side of the Chinese border. There have been a number of confrontations between the Shan United Army (another drug gang) and the United Wa State Army caused by both groups' desire to control Doi Lang, a drug-producing area near the town of Fang in Burma (Witkin and Griffin, 1994).

Probably the most dangerous drug gang leader was Lin Mingxian. Like the leaders of United Wa, he was originally a member of the Communist Party of Burma. Lin Mingxian set up his home base in Mong La in Burma, from which he directed his heroin operations that ran from deep inside of China across Laos and into Vietnam and Cambodia. There was no Burmese military presence within miles of Lin's base in

Mong La, which is considered the lawless frontier of Burma. The lack of any type of narcotics control in this area gave Lin total freedom to openly operate his drug business. Lin also owned and operated the two largest opium-processing plants in Burma and a third plant in Laos (Lintner and Mai, 1994).

There were several other organized drug gangs operating in Burma, including the Yang and Pheung gangs in Kokang, the Lo Hsing-han gang in Lasho, and the Wei brothers gang that worked hand in hand with the United Wa State Army. Most notable gang leaders were at one time members of the Communist Party of Burma who saw a greater opportunity for moneymaking in drugs than in terrorism. The movement of these prior leaders into drug trafficking caused opium production to more than double. Unlike the Shan United Army and the United Wa State Army, these gangs did not claim to be using drug money to support some type of ethnic freedom fighting for the people. They were strictly drug gangs that operated to make money and that killed anyone who interfered in their moneymaking business (Lintner, 1994).

The activities of Burmese gangs has remained within Burma borders, and virtually all their heroin was brokered through locations such as Bangkok or Hong Kong. Most of these brokers ran what seemed to be legitimate businesses, but in reality these legitimate operations were a front for brokering drug transactions. One of the most notable drug brokers was Thai gangster Thongchai Sanguandikul, who is presently confined to federal prison in the United States. Sanguandikul shipped thousands of kilograms of Burmese heroin from Hong Kong through his Mexican organized crime connections in Sinaloa, Mexico, to the United States. A great deal of the processed heroin was also sold to ethnic Chinese who were residents of the United States. Once the heroin arrived in the United States, it changed hands once again and was sold on the street by local drug dealers (Woolrich, September 26, 1993).

EASTERN EUROPEAN GANGS

Since the fall of the Soviet Union and its loss of authority over Eastern European countries, there has been a drastic increase in the number of organized crime groups taking control of criminal activities in these countries. Prior to the fall of Communism, most criminal actions were controlled by members of the Communist Party, the secret police, the military, or a combination of all three. After the demise of Communism, these people remained in power in many cases but lost the Communist or secret police designation; they became leaders or founders of ethnic organized crime groups in Eastern Europe. Besides these gangs' involvement in extortion, forgery, fraud, prostitution, and people smuggling, there was a tremendous increase in the gangs' participation in drug trafficking. In fact, the countries in Eastern Europe have become major transshipment points for drug traffickers from both Southeast Asia and Southwest Asia. There was not one country in Eastern Europe that was prepared for the unlawful activities, especially the drug activity, that took place after the fall of Communism. Even today, most military and law enforcement agencies in these countries have little or no training, nor do they have proper laws in place to deal with most of the crimes. There-fore, just about every Eastern European country has gang activity, drug use, and drug trafficking that are totally out of control—and they will remain that way until each government provides the military and the police with the necessary expertise and laws to eliminate a great deal of these illegal activities.

Albanian Gangs

Albanian gangs built their numbers and their bank accounts throughout Europe by operating the majority of prostitution businesses. Gang members recruit females between the ages of 14 and 25; this recruitment involves convincing the females there is a better life for them in other European environemts. Women who are recruited believe that employment in another European country has been set up for them by the recruiter, who (unknown to them) is actually a gang member. A majority of the women are recruited from Eastern European countries (e.g., Albania, Poland, and Yugoslavia), while others are recruited from various parts of Africa (mainly Nigeria). Any women being recruited who decide against participating are kidnapped and taken to another country in Europe as prostitutes, and the women who go willingly are also immedi-ately forced into prostitution upon their arrival in the new country. These illegal oper-ations go on throughout most countries in Europe. In Italy, for example, Albanian gangs are allowed to operate their illegal prostitution activities with the permission of Italian organized crime, and a percentage of the profits from prostitution is paid to Italian organized crime families as a tribute for operating in Italy.

It is estimated that the total number of Albanian nationals living in the United States is about 300,000. Most of these immigrants settled in major U.S. urban centers such as Chicago, Detroit, Los Angeles, and New York. Like most other groups, ethnic Albanians (most of them born in Yugoslavia) formed loosely knit organized crime factions that are interconnected from city to city. A major portion of Albanian gang members are illegal aliens who fly from Europe to Mexico; there they obtain forged documents and illegally enter the United States. Once here, most head toward a major U.S. urban center to join with other family members or to become part of an Albanian community. A num-ber of the illegal Albanian immigrants smuggle in drugs, which are then dropped off with a member of a Mexican drug cartel. The cartel, in turn, supplies the illegal aliens with the necessary forged documents and a contact person to guide them across the border into the United States. Money these Albanian aliens receive for smuggling drugs usually pay all the costs of their travel and fees to get to the United States.

Albanian gangs follow a code very similar to La Cosa Nostra's guidelines related to honor and silence. The code, which is called either "Che Basa" or "Leke Dukagjini," sets forth for gang members and outsiders what honor and personal trust are and what happens if someone violates this code. In some cases, a violation of this code results in some type of revenge, usually the killing of the code violator. This is one of the reasons why few (if any) Albanian gang members ever become police informants. Knowing this code and what will happen to them also impacts legitimate members of the Albanian community who have nothing to do with gang activities. They refuse to cooperate with the police in apprehending these criminals because they are aware of the types of retaliation the gang uses against informers.

One other Albanian practice that may have an effect on the social values of male members of Albanian society is that right after birth a firearm is procured for the newborn infant. As the child grows up, he becomes highly accomplished in both the handling and use of the firearm. In most cases, this is as much a cultural thing as it is a bonding thing among the males in an Albanian family. Estimates indicate that about 90 percent of all Albanian males in the United States own some type of firearm. This custom, along with the code of honor, has led to an abnormal number of serious assaults as well as murders among males in most Albanian communities throughout Europe and the United States (Sherman and Goldfarb, 1996).

With the large influx of Albanian nationals into the United States came a sharp increase in the number of crimes involving Albanian males. New York police found that Albanian gang members who formed what they referred to as crews within the gang became specialists in the crime of burglary. Gang members, acting as visiting tourists from Europe, would go through various food markets, clothes outlets, jewelry stores, department stores, and banks throughout the New York metropolitan area videotaping the insides of these places. A short period of time after the videotaping, gang members would return, breaking into one of these locations from the roof and climbing down ropes into the store. They would use a gang member who is an electronics expert to quickly disarm the alarm and video security systems; then they find the safe or other money container and use equipment to gain access to the money. Gang members often purchase a safe to practice the techniques they need to use to gain entry to a safe. Albanian gangs place well-trained lookouts, equipped with walkie-talkies and police scanners, outside the location they are burglarizing to further thwart police efforts to apprehend them. In some cases, the gang purposely set off an alarm in a business and waited outside to watch as the police responded to the scene. Once the police left the scene, Albanian gang members entered the location and proceeded to commit the burglary, figuring that a second alarm would be viewed as nothing more than a nuisance by the police and that the police would not come to the location again.

Law enforcement agencies from throughout the East Coast and the Midwest indicated that Albanian gangs have committed similar types of burglaries within many of their jurisdictions. Police agencies substantiated their claims of Albanian participation in these crimes due to the use of the same types of equipment, personnel, and methods of operation by Albanian gang members in all their criminal ventures. In many cases, gang burglaries of superstores (very large retail outlets and supermarkets) and cash-rich businesses would give the gang a profit of anywhere from $500,000 to $10 million for each burglary. A more recent gang activity has been breaking into automatic teller machines (ATMs) to gain instant cash. Members of Albanian burglary gangs use what is known as a "slice pack," which consists of an oxygen-fueled device with burn rods that can be used to promptly reach a heat of 10,000 degrees Fahrenheit, that helps the criminals to bore through a safe wall or an ATM in a very short period of time.

Always standing by during these jobs is another gang member known as a "hack and whack" artist, who has a 20-pound sledgehammer in case the gang needs physical force to gain entry into the safe or ATM. Law enforcement figures indicated that Albanian gangs have burglarized over 200 large supermarkets, 50 ATM machines, and 35 to 40 jewelry manufacturers and stores in the New York metropolitan area in two years (Purdy, December 17, 1994; Sherman and Goldfarb, 1996).

Albanian gangs use social clubs that they created as bases for their criminal activities. Gang members inform the Albanian community that these ethnic clubs help them to maintain their own culture in a new and different environment, but in reality this is far from the truth; instead, Albanian gang members use these social clubs as locations where they plan their criminal endeavors, recruit new members, and split the proceeds of their crimes. An outgrowth of these gang-run social clubs has been the formation of street gangs that spew hate for other racial and ethnic groups either inside or outside their neighborhoods. Unlike the Chinese street gangs who work for the Tongs, these Albanian street groups seem more inclined to work for their own benefit, without any type of major connection to the older Albanian gangs. The lack of recognition of these street gangs by the established Albanian gangs is based on the fact that members of the street gangs are predominantly U.S. born and do not have the same maturity, discipline, understanding, or dedication as the foreign-born gang members. One must remember that just about every member of an established Albanian gang comes from an Eastern European environment where the law enforcement establishment could, under the old Communist regime, do whatever it pleased to obtain a confession or to force criminal activity to desist. Gang members who end up dealing with law enforcement in the United States have no fear of the police because they know they can control most situations and that the police cannot threaten or use force to intimidate them (Gonzalez, 1992).

Members of Albanian organized crime also became fairly active participants in the drug-trafficking business. The group made a connection with the Colombian cocaine cartels in Flordia, and this relationship proved very profitable for Albanian gang members because once they obtained the cocaine in Florida, they moved it to Detroit, New York, or Chicago. Upon arrival, the cocaine was cut by members of the Albanian gang, who then retailed it to other ethnic groups that sold it on the street. Law enforcement sources in the Midwest considered the Albanian gangs the major suppliers of cocaine to both the Chicago and Detroit areas (DEA, 1993). Some other activities of the Albanian gangs included alien smuggling (most of which was done through Mexico and Canada into the United States), forgery, and gun running.

Albanian gangs discovered a method of scamming using phony ATM machines. Members of Albanian organized crime installed what was believed to be an ATM machine in a grocery store on the East Side of Manhattan. The store owner, who was under the impression that the ATM machine was legitimate, soon found out that the four Albanian criminals had actually installed a machine that recorded the ATM card information of people attempting to use it. Once the information related to the ATM cards was registered in the machine, gang members returned and removed the information, which was then transferred onto plastic ATM-type cards. These cards were then used to remove over $225,000 in U.S. currency from victims' accounts in both Chase and Citibank accounts on the Upper East Side of Manhattan (Italiano et al., 2003).

Polish Gangs

Like most other groups from Eastern Europe, Polish organized crime groups started to appear a short time after the fall of the Soviet Union. In Poland, almost all the members of these new criminal groups were active participants in the Communist Party, the military, and/or the secret police. Organized criminal groups in Poland became involved in bank frauds that led to the loss of billions of dollars from the Polish banking system.

In August 1994, shop owners in Warsaw closed down their stores in a protest over the actions of members of organized crime and the inability of the police to control the gangs' activities. Gang members had set up an extortion ring that required stores in Warsaw to pay anywhere from $500 to $7,000 monthly to the group. In several cases, gang members went to the homes of the shop owners and in one case actually threatened to chop off the hand of the child of one of their intended victims. Several days prior to the store owners' protest, gang members attacked several restaurant owners and vandalized half a dozen businesses. The protest worked because several days after these demonstrations, the police arrested a gang member known as Pershing when he attempted to force a Warsaw businessman to pay him $40,000 (Turek, 1995).

The inability of the police to control the activities of organized crime gangs may be due to corruption within Poland's police agency. This police corruption became very visible in the summer of 1994 with the arrest of Mieczyslaw Grzybowski, chief of the Polish police agency's economic crime section; he was arrested for accepting bribes from members of organized crime. A short time later, several dozen Polish police officers, four state prosecutors, and a number of criminal court judges were arrested and charged with taking bribes from members of organized crime. This was followed by the arrest of several other high-ranking police officials for participating in the hijacking and selling of thousands of bottles of scotch (*New York Times*, August 7, 1994).

Corrupt police practices forced the prime minister of Poland, Jozef Oleksy, to select Jerzy Stanczyk to become the leader of the Polish National Police. Upon taking office, Stanczyk immediately declared war on all organized criminal groups in Poland. He demanded that sufficient funding be apportioned by the government to support the police and prosecutors in their battle against Polish organized crime. One major problem with the gangs was their use of explosive devices. In 1994–1995, Polish gangs planted 150 bombs throughout Poland in an effort to settle disputes with rival gangs, and these bombings killed 10 people and wounded 36 others. Police intelligence information indicated that the Pruszkow and the Wolomin organized crime groups were the two major factions involved in the bombings; most of the explosions were the result of a battle over which gang would control drug trafficking, prostitution, auto theft, and extortion. There were no arrests of any of the members of these gangs (Barker, 1995; Spolar, 1995).

In the early 1990s, Polish organized crime groups set out to establish alliances with members of international drug groups from Colombia, Nigeria, and both Southeast Asia and Southwest Asia. Drug trafficking in Poland increased sharply once these affiliations were agreed on and set in place. After the gangs planned their strategy to avoid detection and set the different routes to be used for drug transporting, the gangs started moving the drugs throughout Poland. The gangs knew that Poland lacked any strict drug laws or law enforcement methods to cope with the transshipment of drugs throughout the country.

The extent of the participation of Polish organized crime groups in drug trafficking was shown by the increased number of drug seizures involving Polish nationals. During 1993, Polish customs agents seized 220 pounds of cocaine on a Polish ship in the port city of Szczecin; in January 1994, over half a ton of cocaine was seized by customs agents from the Polish freighter *Lublin II* during a stopover in Antwerp and a member of a Polish organized crime group was arrested immediately after the seizure. In February 1994, British customs officials, working hand in hand with Polish law enforcement officials, seized 1,200 kilos of cocaine in Liverpool aboard a ship bound for Poland. Then in May 1994, Polish authorities seized 88 pounds of heroin at the border of Germany and Poland that were being transported in two automobiles by members of Polish organized crime.

Additional seizures from members of Polish organized crime included 1.2 tons of Colombian cocaine aboard the Polish ship *Jurata* and 2.2 tons of hashish found in raisin containers on a train that arrived in Warsaw from Blearus. In Morocco, there was a seizure of 3,135 pounds of hashish secreted in containers of sardines and olives; Moroccan officials arrested Pawel Skowronski in connection with this drug seizure, and he was later identified by Polish authorities as a member of a Polish organized crime group. In February 1994, Polish customs officers apprehended two gang members at the Polish border attempting to smuggle into Poland 200 gallons of the ingredients used to produce amphetamines. Polish organized crime gangs also set up numerous labs that produced synthetic drugs. These illegal labs made Poland the second-largest producer of illegal synthetic drugs in the world behind Holland (Associated Press, 1994; McKinsey, May 27, 1994; *New York Times*, August 7, 1994; United Press International, 1994).

Ever-increasing participation in narcotics trafficking by Polish organized crime members helped to expand the number of drug addicts in Poland. Since the collapse of Communism, the number of drug users in Polish society increased from about 7 percent in the 1980s to approximately 25 percent in the 1990s. This indicated that all the heroin, cocaine, and amphetamines entering Poland from outside were not just passing through on the way to another country; instead, Polish organized crime groups made sure that a certain portion of the drugs they were smuggling were sold for a profit on the streets of Poland (McKinsey, July 19, 1994).

Prior to their involvement in narcotics trafficking, Polish gangs in both Europe and North America operated very successful car theft rings. Polish auto theft gangs in the United States based a major portion of their operations in the state of Illinois. These activities first surfaced in Chicago in the late 1980s when the Chicago Police

Department's Auto Crime Unit discovered how Polish gangs participated in these auto thefts. During an investigation that originated in August 1989, the Chicago police started coming up with specific information related to the vehicle theft by members of Polish organized crime groups. Members of the gang would steal luxury cars from showrooms and display lots in the Chicago metropolitan area and then transport the vehicle to a garage in Chicago, where vehicle identification numbers would be altered and where counterfeit license plates would be placed on the vehicles. The cars would then be transported to the Portsmouth, Virginia, marine terminal where the autos were containerized and shipped through Goteborg, Sweden, to their new owners in Poland. Gang members in Poland would contact other gang members in the United States with a list of vehicles that they had received orders for from clients in Poland. Usually the list consisted of cars such as BMW, Corvette, Jeep Cherokee, Lincoln, Mercedes-Benz, TransAm, and Volvo, as well as Harley-Davidson motorcycles. Chicago police discovered that the Polish gangs were also shipping cars in containers to Toronto and that the vehicles were then shipped to Europe from Canada. While Polish gang members in the United States were shipping autos back to Poland, the gangs in Poland were stealing cars throughout Europe and selling them in Poland and other parts of Europe (Kiefer, 1992; Skonie, 1991).

Hungarian Gangs

There is organized criminal activity throughout the rest of Eastern Europe, but not on the same scale as in Albania and Poland. Some countries, like Hungary, are having problems with street gangs. In Hungary, there has been an enormous increase in the number of crimes involving juveniles since 1991. Many of these gangs have the same ideology as their counterparts, the American skinhead gangs. The Hungarian skinheads commit numerous types of crimes, but most of the crimes are aimed at certain types of ethnic or racial groups. Hungarian gang robberies, assaults, and other violence are directed against Arabs, Turks, and other non-Hungarians. These street gangs have also become heavily involved in street-level drug trafficking. Gang members have entered cemeteries at night, drinking or using drugs and then vandalizing the graves and mausoleums. In many cases, Hungarian gang members wear black clothing, have shaved heads, and have both their lips and cheeks pierced with metal objects (Viviano, 1994).

Hungary has had a drastic increase in the amount of activity involving organized crime groups, specifically activities involving drug trafficking and money laundering. Like their Russian organized crime counterparts in the United States, Hungarian gangs became participants in rings that sell heating oil, which is the same as diesel fuel but one-third cheaper at local petrol stations. To counteract the gangs' actions, the Hungarian government put a harmless but observable red dye in the heating fuel. The placing of the red dye in the heating fuel did not deter gang members, who quickly found several oil refineries that removed the red dye from the fuel so that gang members were back in business.

Bulgarian Gangs

Bulgaria faced the same problems with gangs as the rest of Eastern Europe. Bulgarian gangs have been involved in trafficking Turkish drugs into Western European countries. During the ongoing armed conflict in Yugoslavia, members of Bulgarian organized crime made thousands of dollars transporting gasoline across the border to the warring factions in Yugoslavia. Besides the activities related to black market gasoline, the gangs also became involved in extortion, drug trafficking, smuggling, prostitution, and counterfeiting. Thus far, estimates by Bulgarian law enforcement officials of the organized crime activities in Bulgaria indicated that gangs managed 70 percent of all gambling, 80 percent of all alcohol and tobacco businesses, and 50 percent of cabarets and casinos. A large percentage of Bulgarian gang members were either wrestlers or weight lifters, which is why most Bulgarians called gang members *bortsites* (wrestlers). Many gang leaders were former members of the Bulgarian Communist secret police, and these leaders attempted to pass their gangs off as security companies (without much success). One other problem the Bulgarian government faced in dealing with these organized crime groups was that a good deal of the gang membership had previously been members of the Bulgarian police. What this created was a group of organized crime members who not only could act as Bulgarian police officers but also would have available to them all the police equipment and all the police accoutrements necessary to perpetrate crimes (Perlez, 1995).

The power of Bulgarian organized crime groups came to light after a shootout in a luxurious gambling club in Sofia owned by a former member of the secret police. One day later, members of the Bulgarian police asked the leader of one of the gangs to stop in at the local police station for coffee; a short time after his arrival, he was placed under arrest by the police. A large group of gang members quickly gathered in the courtyard of the police station. In an attempt to calm this situation, the police sent two supervisors out to attempt to settle this dispute. Unbeknown to the police, another squad of officers was sent out from another location to apprehend the same person. Ultimately, these two groups of officers confronted each other, which resulted in a shootout that caused the death of two officers. As an end result, the Bulgarian government had two police officers dead and the suspect in the shootout at the club still a free man (Borger, 1994). This situation was indicative of what happened in Bulgaria after the fall of Communism. Like most of the other Eastern European countries, Bulgaria is a democratic country that does not yet have the tools to deal with the problems presented by members of organized crime. They must make the adjustments to eliminate the criminal activities of Bulgarian organized crime groups.

Czechoslovakian Gangs

Since the fall of the Iron Curtain (Communist control) around Czechoslovakia, there has been an increase in the number of activities involving organized crime groups in the Czech Republic. These organized gangs brought with them criminal activities such as narcotics trafficking, auto theft, prostitution, gambling, extortion, art theft, money laundering, fraud, blackmail, and people smuggling. Some of the favorite targets of these organized gangs were historical locations such as museums and castles, from which gang members stole valuable works of art and ancient artifacts. Prizes such as these were immediately sold on the black market for a large quick profit; many of these items were difficult to trace.

Gypsy Gangs

There is one more fairly well organized crime group that deserves some recognition: the gypsies. Gypsy groups are an international organized crime group that has its tentacles spread throughout the world. Gypsies should be thought of as a nation of people as well as a very large organized crime family; as both a nation and an organized crime family, gypsies have their own banks, bankers, courts, lawyers, and kings. Gypsy groups can be considered a traditional as well as a nontraditional organized crime group.

Their historical roots reach back to both the Punjab province in India over 1,200 years ago and to Israel over 2,000 years ago. History indicated that gypsies were descendants of two northern Indian tribes known as the Dom and the Luri. Somewhere around 1000 A.D., these tribes left India and traveled through most of Southwest Asia, Northern Africa, and Eastern and Western Europe until they reached their final destination in what is now known as Hungary sometime during the fifteenth century. These gypsy groups attempted to settle in many of the countries they traveled through but were not accepted by citizens of these countries. Most people in the countries where they attempted to relocate were apprehensive of the gypsies because they were different due to their customs, their language, and (more than anything else) their purported mystical and esoteric powers. As the gypsy groups traveled through many of the towns and villages of these countries, laws were passed by the rulers of these governments to imprison, banish, or kill the gypsies. During the Hitler years in Europe, the gypsies were singled out as one of the groups to be placed in concentration camps and put to death.

Hate for and distrust of gypsies remain even today, and there is a great deal of apprehension and condemnation throughout the European community when it comes to dealing with gypsies. Some of these feelings are based on the skepticism surrounding gypsies' reputation as thieves who perform mystical feats. According to legend, gypsies became world wanderers and criminals for several reasons:

1. Ethnic gypsies refused to help Mary and Joseph when they were fleeing from Bethlehem with baby Jesus after King Herod's proclamation to kill all newborn male children.

2. Gypsies willingly forged the nails used to crucify Jesus while all the other blacksmiths refused to make them.

3. One gypsy blacksmith made the nails to crucify Jesus, but when he was informed by a Roman soldier that the fourth nail was to be used to pierce the heart of Jesus, this gypsy swallowed that nail. Myth has it that a short time

after the gypsy swallowed the nail, Christ looked down on him from the cross and gave him permission to wander the earth and live off whatever he could obtain illegally or steal.

There is very little recorded gypsy history because most gypsies were illiterate and lived from day to day with absolutely no thought about their past history. The historical reasons why gypsies are wanderers and thieves are unknown.

As far as the lineage of a gypsy family is concerned, usually each member of a family is a direct descendant of the eldest group leader, who in most cases is known as the vista chief or baro (big man) (see Figure 12–1). The family consists of a husband, a wife, and nonadult children and their sons. The father is responsible for the actions of his wife and children; once a woman marries, she is considered part of her husband's family and not part of her birth family. Gypsies usually travel together in groups of anywhere from 8 families to 100 or more families. Besides their participation in criminal activities, these groups also stay together because it is a lot easier for them to survive economically and to locate and maintain living quarters during their short stays in various locations. Groups that travel like this are known as *kumpanias*, and all group members equally participate in the work as well as contribute and share any profits from their illegal activities (see Figure 12–2). Members of the *kumpania* elect a leader who is known as a *rom baro* (a king); this leader is picked because of his leadership capabilities, moneymaking potential, maturity, and knowledge.

The organization of both the gypsy family with a vista chief and the *kumpania* has a fairly strong correlation with the way traditional organized crime groups, such as La Cosa Nostra, are set up (see Figure 12–3).

Wandering from one location to another by an organized crime group is somewhat unusual. In almost every urban or suburban area where a traveling gypsy crime group may choose to stop and operate from for a while, there would usually be a

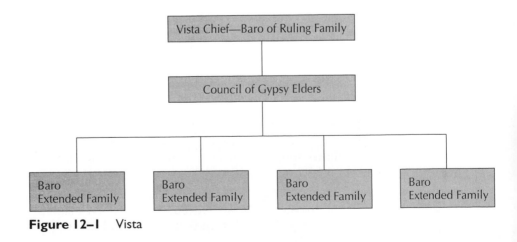

Figure 12–1   Vista

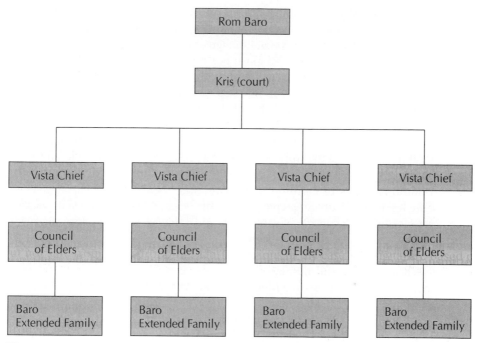

Figure 12-2   *Kumpania*

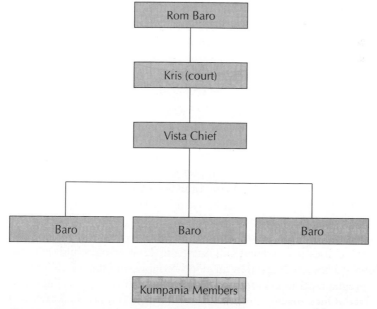

Figure 12-3   Nontraditional Gypsy Organized Crime Family

kumpania already in place. An outside gypsy group entering one of these areas must seek the permission of the local *rom baro*, and before leaving this location, the visiting *kumpania* must pay some type of homage to the local *rom baro*. In many cases, upon the visiting group's arrival, a safe deposit box is rented; one key is held by the local *rom baro* while the other key is given to the visiting *rom baro*. When the travelers are ready to leave, both *rom baros* go to the safe deposit box, any stolen property is removed, and a certain percentage is given to the local *rom baro*.

One interesting part of the gypsy lifestyle is the type of clothing they wear. Most of the older male members of gypsy families are fairly corpulent and wear extra-large clothing, such as suits, shirts, ties, and hats, that went out of style 20 to 30 years ago. Younger gypsy males wear very glittery clothing. During their youth, gypsy girls wear traditional types of clothing; it is only after their first menstrual cycle that gypsy females' mode of dressing changes. At this point, gypsy women start wearing customary clothing that consists of a long skirt and a sleeveless blouse with a very low neckline that practically exposes their breasts. This type of low-cut blouse also gives gypsy women quick access to their undergarments, where they usually store small articles (such as jewelry and money) that they have stolen. Skirt lengths on gypsy women symbolize their age, with a longer skirt indicating an older woman. In relationship to gypsy women and skirts there is an interesting maxim that states that the woman's body from the waist down is unchaste and must at all times be hidden from view. The style of a gypsy woman's hair also can indicate her age: Younger women wear their hair in a bun; older women wear braids. A successful gypsy female is easily identifiable because she wears a great deal of jewelry.

All gypsies have three names. The first name is given to the child right after birth when the mother whispers a secret name into the baby's ear out of earshot of any other person. According to gypsy custom, this is done to fool the evil spirits. The second name given to a gypsy child is his or her given name; this is the name by which gypsies can be identified by each other. Most gypsies adopt a third name, which is usually a nongypsy surname, that can be changed each time they are apprehended for a crime. During their criminal careers, most gypsy offenders amass anywhere from two to three dozen aliases that can be used at any given time.

Ethnically, gypsies are divided into several different groups: American, Hungarian, Irish, Polish, Romanian, and Scottish. Each ethnic gypsy group has one special criminal method of operation. American gypsies are noted for their ability to sell people cheap remodeled used trailers as being brand-new. Police estimate that this scam nets gypsies over $2 million per year. Polish Gypsies are known for their deceptive methods of committing burglaries. Their most famous scam involves the use of a deceitful method to gain entry (usually into the residence of a senior citizen). It involves two to three gypsies, in most cases two women and one 8- to 12-year-old child. The two women go to the door of a house occupied by an elderly couple, and one of the women feigns sickness due to pregnancy and asks for a drink of water. In most cases, entry to the home is easily gained. Once inside, the two females distract the person(s) who let them in while the adolescent, who was hidden under one of the female's skirts, slips out and searches the house for valuables. Once the juvenile has completed the search and gathered some costly items from the house, he or she signals the two females, one of whom once again manage to secret this person under her clothing. They all leave without the residents having any idea what took place. Another scam uses three females, who state that they are good friends of the next-door neighbor and that they need paper and pencil to leave a message. This has also been very successful in helping gypsy women gain access to a residence to commit burglary. Each of these scams can net anywhere from $1,000 to $50,000 worth of money and jewelry.

Yugoslavian gypsies are experts at creating a distraction in order to steal property from stores. One of their diversions involves two to three different teams of two to three gypsies each that enter a store. The first team gets a salesperson to open a display case containing some valuable items. Once this is completed, the second team enters the location; upon their entrance to the store, the second group finds a way to distract the clerk (usually by creating some type of disturbance). In an effort to quell the commotion, the clerk leaves the first two gypsies alone at the open showcase. Members of this team quickly either raid the register or take expensive jewelry from the showcase and replace it with zircons or costume jewelry. These thieves then quickly flee the scene, and the theft is not discovered until the jewelry is examined at a later date. This is a very profitable scam for gypsies and nets them anywhere from $15,000 to $20,000 or $300,000 in jewelry or currency.

Other gypsy crimes include house scams and auto scams. In the house scam, two or three males pull up at a victim's house and offer to fix a roof, chimney, or siding for what seems to be a cheap price. In reality, they only put a little tar on the roof or a small amount of glue on the chimey or some paint on the siding; then they collect the money and leave. In the auto scheme, male gypsies say they will take a dent out of a car, but they just put some plastic filler on the dent and leave with the money. A short time later, the plastic filler falls out, exposing the original dent. Federal officials have also discovered that wandering gypsies collect welfare checks and food stamps in several states using some of their many aliases. During their travels, they stop in one state and apply for welfare and food stamps. Once they are cleared to receive both welfare checks and food stamps, they always make sure that they stop at that designated location whenever necessary to pick up both their welfare checks and their food stamp allotment.

CONCLUSIONS

As this chapter indicates, gang activity worldwide has increased drastically. These types of organized crime groups and their unlawful activities will continue to flourish until all the nations can come together and institute national guidelines, laws, and enforcement policies that are used to force organized criminal gangs to cease their existence.

CHAPTER 13

TERRORISM

It is the intent of this chapter to show the reader that discussing organized crime without including terrorist gangs as an organized crime group is a mistake. There is no doubt that all terroirst gangs are well organized; like organized crime groups, they are involved in various types of criminal activities, especially narcotics, and they create a great deal of profits for their leaders and for terrorist gang members through their legitimate and illegitimate activities. Like other organized crime groups, terrorists kill those inside and outside their organization without any compassion. It is all about power and profits, with most of the revenues coming from illegitimate transactions. Intimidation is a major part of all terrorist gangs, which is the same policy followed by La Casa Nostra members. No matter what type of activity we look at, there is no difference between terrorist gangs and organized crime groups. The rest of this chapter will show the reader that terrorist groups and organized crime groups are one and the same type of gang.

SYRIAN TERRORIST GANGS

Since the inception of terrorist attacks throughout the world, there has been a great deal of research into the funding of these groups. It was assumed that most of the financial support for these groups came from terrorist sympathizers. It wasn't until the late 1990s that the intelligence communities of the world realized that over 90 percent of terrorist gangs' support comes from the growing, transportation, and sale of narcotics and the extortion of drug traffickers. This was extremely evident after Pan Am flight 103 was blown up in 1988 when evidence from this terrorist act proved beyond a reasonable doubt the Syrian drug kingpin al-Kassar had helped to sponsor this terrorist act (Grennan et al., 2000). It was also disclosed that Kassar was at the time a double agent employed by the Central Intelligence Agency (CIA), with a guarantee from the CIA that if Kassar provided the CIA with pertinent intelligence information on terrorism, Bekka Valley heroin could be transported through Europe on its way to the Americas without any U.S. drug enforcement intervention (Grennan et al., 2000).

Syria has always been a major supporter of Muslim terrorism, but since the death of President Hafez al Assad, the assistance to radical terrorist groups has increased drastically. New President Bashar al Assad, son of Hafez, continues to monetarily support these terrorist gangs, allows terrorist training camps to be conducted in Syria, grants terrorist fugitives asylum, and allows terrorist organizations to settle in Syria. Bashar openly supplies gangs such as al-Qaeda, the Democratic Front for the Liberation of Palestine (DFLP), Hamas, Hizballah, Islamic Jihad, and the Popular Front for the Liberation of Palestine (PFLP) with all types of military weapons (including rockets). He calls Israeli retribution against Palestinian terrorist groups "Zionist aggression" and states that Palestinian bombings are "acts of despair that are caused by Israel's barbaric practices against an unarmed people" (Levitt, 2002: 2–3). Statements like this come from one of the biggest drug barons and a supporter of murderers of innocent people around the world. This is the son of the same man who converted the Bekka Valley in Lebanon from hashish to heroin and paid members of the Syrian military a bonus based on the profits the government made on drug sales. A major portion of profits from drug trafficking was then used to support terrorist gangs (Grennan, 2000).

Syria is also a location that terrorists wanted worldwide consider a safe haven. Many members of al-Qaeda, Hamas, and Hizballah are secreted away in different safe houses or remote areas in Syria. Mohammad Heidar Zammar is a senior al-Qaeda commander; the Syrian government has refused to allow U.S. intelligence to interview him. Syria, along with Iran, is the worst offender, with its monetary and weapons assistance to terrorist gangs. We know that Mohammad Atta (the mastermind of the September 11, 2001, terrorist attack on New York) spent a great deal of his life in Syria. But once again, no U.S. agency or any other intelligence agency has been allowed to interview people still in Syria who have knowledge of Atta (Levitt, 2002). In viewing this information, we recognize the fact that the Syrian government actually functions as a narco-terrorist gang that supports all the ongoing terrorist attacks around the world, especially those against Israel and the United States. The other issues that come to mind are the decisions to invade Iraq instead of Syria and to have diplomatic relations with a Syrian terrorist government that is involved in an aggressive effort to destroy the United States and its allies.

This introductory information only scratches the surface of the parts that organized crime groups and drugs play in supporting terrorist activities, especially against Israel and the United States. As this chapter continues, it will show that both organized crime groups and drug cartels play roles as major supporters of terrorism activities throughout the world.

EASTERN EUROPEAN TERRORIST GANGS

We can start with the Eastern European groups that operate in Albania, Poland, Russia, Yugoslavia, and many of the other older ethnic countries that were at one time controlled by the United Soviet Socialist Republic (USSR) and that were reestablished when the Communist government in Russia was replaced by a democratic government in Moscow. It seems apparent that the Communist government controlled organized crime activities in Russia with an iron fist prior to the change in political ideology in the late twentieth century. There seems to be few (if any) people outside the Soviet Union who ever heard of any type of organized crime activities in Russia prior to the change in the government's political philosophy. Suddenly, like the outbreak of a plague, organized crime groups manifested themselves throughout Eastern Europe, especially in Russia. History does indicate that prior to and during the early stages of Communism, organized crime groups did exist in Russia; in fact, in the section of this book on Russian organized crime, there is significant coverage of these early groups and their participation in supporting terrorist activities perpetrated by the Communist regime controlled by Joseph Stalin. Stalin went so far as to enlist organized crime leaders such as Semyon Terpetrosyan (an Armenian Bolshevik known as Kamo) to participate in his criminal and terrorist activities. Kamo and his organized crime family played a major part in enhancing the Bolshevik treasury through the use of robbery and other types of terrorist activities. Once the revolution ended, Stalin quickly eliminated his organized crime connections by killing them and therefore removing any type of stigma connecting the Bolsheviks to an organized criminal group's illegal activities (Chalidze, 1977).

We connected the earlier Communist government with organized crime; now we look at what kind of opportunity the downfall of that government created for organized crime in Russia. The change in political perspective created chaotic conditions throughout many parts of Russia especially in many of the states that were considered part of the USSR that became free states once again. Throughout many of these re-created new states, chaos took control, which gave members of various Russian ethnic organized crime groups the opportunity to steal any items that provided them with some type of profits. Banks were taken over, businesses were confiscated from legitimate owners, and military equipment (including nuclear devices and their energy/fuel sources as well as biological weapons) was stolen. This created a whole new black market option for terrorists throughout the world, an alternative flea market for terrorists such as Bin Laden. Of course, it is doubtful that Bin Laden was the only terrorist knocking on the door of Russian organized crime to buy nuclear weapons. We do know that the former government in the Soviet Union stockpiled over 30,000 nuclear weapons. The Soviet government also created what are known as suitcase nukes (small nuclear devices that fit in a backpack); no one knows how many of these devices were made in the USSR (Martin, 2003).

At this point, we do not truly know if the Russian gangs sold any of their illegally obtained nuclear devices, but there have been a number of accusations saying that they completed deals with unidentified terrorists. According to the *San Francisco Chronicle*, Bin Laden negotiated with members of Eastern European organized crime in an attempt to purchase anthrax, ebola virus, and high-grade uranium used for making weapons of destruction (*San Francisco Chronicle*, 2001). We have to remember that there is no such thing as an ethical issue to a member of any type of organized crime group; the only issues they understand are power and money. Another concern with the breakup of the old Soviet Union is that portions of the populations of these newly created nations are Muslims. In Uzbekistan, for example, there is a radical Islamic group known as the Islamic Movement of Uzbekistan (IMU) that has maintained an excellent relationship with both al-Qaeda and the Taliban and received financial support from both al-Qaeda and the Taliban. The IMU managed to take over control of heroin trafficking from Central Asia (U.S. Department of Justice, DEA, 2003). Uzbekistan is not the only new state in the old Soviet Republic that has a Muslim population; other areas of Eastern Europe have some al-Qaeda and Taliban sympathizers. These sympathizers could also conspire with members of Russian organized crime to obtain both biological and nuclear weapons.

NIGERIAN TERRORIST GANGS

Nigerian organized crime families managed to steal radioactive materials from oil companies in Nigeria. There seems to be no regulatory agency in Nigeria that attempted to control the illegal activities of any of the organized crime families in Nigeria. Thus far, there has been only a minimal amount of radioactive materials stolen, but due to the ability of the Nigerian gangs to manipulate government officials and to create scams for profit, there is no doubt that sometime in the near future they will have obtained a sufficient supply of radioactive materials to open their own business with Third World terrorists.

COLOMBIAN TERRORIST GANGS

The U.S. Drug Enforcement Agency (DEA) confirmed that 70 percent of the terrorist groups in the world are involved in drug-related activities. One of the first narcotics traffickers to get involved with terrorists was Pablo Escobar, the head of the Medellin cocaine cartel that controlled most of the cocaine traffic worldwide. He was able to use drug money to politically support terrorist groups to commit violent activities against governments and citizens with the intent to sway opinion. Escobar was as much a terrorist as he was a leader of an organized crime drug cartel. He put most of Colombia in a state of chaos by planning and ordering assassinations of politicians, judges, police officers, and civilians. Escobar also planned and carried out the bombing of an Avianca commercial airline in 1989; this terrorist act led to the creation of U.S.-Colombian police/military task force that ultimately led to the death of Escobar in 1993 (U.S. Department of Justice, DEA, 2003).

Escobar's terrorist activities led to other terrorist groups in Colombia becoming involved in drug activities. The Revolutionary Armed Forces of Colombia (FARC) was the first Colombian terrorist group to participate in the drug trade. Group members originally got involved as protectors of cocaine-processing plants in the jungles of Colombia, but it did not take them long to become more involved in the growing, processing, and selling of cocaine and heroin. To increase their participation in drug activities, FARC members used intimidation and instilled fear in the cocaine/heroin cartels, forcing the cartels to increase the monetary rewards to FARC. Remember that Colombia is a violent country where kidnapping and murder are everyday happenings. Two other Colombian terrorist groups quickly followed FARC into illegal drug activities: the United Self-Defense Groups of Colombia (AUC) and the National Liberation Army (ELN) (U.S. Department of Justice, DEA, 2003).

FARC set up close associations with international smuggling rings, including the Irish Republican Army (IRA) and the Basque Euskadi Ta Askatasuna-Basque Homeland and Liberty (ETA), and these relationships provided this terrorist organization with the ability to purchase high-tech military weaponry on the black market. This enhanced FARC's ability to continue its violent activities against the Colombian government and its people. In many cases, FARC used kilos of cocaine or heroin to purchase many of these weapons. Since early 2002, FARC has continuously shifted a majority of its terrorist actions from the countryside to the major cities in Colombia. On August 7, 2002 (the date Alvaro Uribe was being inaugurated as president of Colombia), FARC initiated a mortar attack on the presidential palace in Bogota, killing 21 people. Then on February 7, 2003, a car bomb planted by FARC exploded in front of Club El Nogel, a very popular social club in Bogota, killing 35 people. On May 5, 2003, members of FARC assassinated Antioquia Governor Guillermo Gaviria and Defense Minister Gilberto Echeverri as their car approached government headquarters in Antioquia, Colombia; the terrorist group also killed eight members of the Colombian military during this attack (U.S. Department of Justice, DEA, 2003).

AUC, on the other hand, is considered a paramilitary organization that is supported by influential citizens in Colombian society as well as by drug traffickers and local governments that lack the ability to police their communities. The usual outcome of letting AUC into a community is that AUC members take over total control of the town or village and use organized crime tactics to maintain their manipulative powers over the town or village. This terrorist gang has become adept at controlling people through the use of violence. During the first 10 months of 2000, members of AUC were involved in over 800 attempted assassinations, over 200 kidnappings, and 75 massacres, for a total of over 500 deaths. The major source of income for AUC is drug trafficking, but a second source of income is money earned by members who are for hire as assassins and terrorist bombers. All the Colombian terrorist gangs have expanded their operations throughout Mexico and Central America as well as the countries bordering Colombia without any intervention by any of those countries' governments or military forces. This has allowed these terrorist drug gangs to increase their ability to transport drugs throughout North America. The only government action taken against Colombian terrorist gangs took place in Panama on July 22, 2002, when a combined law enforcement task force seized 16 kilos of heroin, 300 kilos of cocaine, 260 kilos of marijuana, 139 AK-47s,

11 Dragonov sniper rifles, 2 submachine guns, and numerous amounts of ammunition clips and bullets (U.S. Department of Justice, DEA, 2003).

Since early 2002, investigations by the U.S. DEA resulted in a number of federal indictments being handed down against the leadership and membership of all three Colombian terrorist groups. A majority of these indictments involved both the distribution of drugs and weapons smuggling. This action by the U.S. government may be seen as too little too late.

OTHER SOUTH AMERICAN TERRORIST GANGS

Another problem that recently surfaced in South America (which has a population of over 6 million Muslims) is the increasing amount of activity by Hamas and Hizballah in the triborder area of Argentina, Brazil, and Paraguay. Members of these groups have been immigrating to this area of South America and setting up various businesses in order to cover their subversive activities. Thus far, these alleged merchants have managed to get involved in numerous legal as well as illegal behaviors. Some of these activities include drug trafficking, providing forged documents to other members of their groups, and selling weapons on the black market. These groups use Ciudad del Este in Paraguay and Foz do Iguacu in Brazil as their main bases of operation in South America. Thus far, these Arab terrorist gangs have set up profitable businesses throughout the triborder area. The revenues that both Hamas and Hizballah generated from cocaine and heroin trafficking have been used to provide monetary assistance to other members of these groups in the Middle East. Some of the profits have also been used to buy political influence through-out the triborder area (U.S. Department of Justice, DEA, 2003). Just being able to operate in this area indicates there is an ongoing conspiracy in place. Hamas and Hizballah members supply terrorist groups throughout South America with weapons in exchange for cocaine and heroin. A majority of the narcotics acquired in exchange for weapons is then smuggled into Europe and North America and sold to the highest bidder. One must remember that both of these organizations are made up of what would be considered street thugs who commit the same crimes as any organized criminal street gang. They fund their operations through the use of extortion, drug trafficking, robbery, and kidnap-ping. There is no justification for classifying any of these groups as just terrorists.

South American governments are very much aware of the growing problems with terrorist groups. Police in Paraguay located, arrested, and extradited Egyptian terrorist Said Hassan Mokhles in Ciudad del Este. Mokhles was the mastermind behind the terrorist attack and massacre of 58 tourists in Luxor, Egypt, in 1997. During an investiga-tion conducted by the FBI and Colombian police, Mohammed Enid Abdel Aai was captured as he was on route to a FARC guerilla camp in the jungles of Colombia. Abdel Aai was a member of the Egyptian terrorist gang known as Al Gama Al-Islamiya. Intelligence gathered by the Colombian police indicated that over 100 members of radical Islamic terrorist gangs (including al-Qaeda) are presently operating in South America. Colombian police reports showed that the wife of Mokhles, Sharar Abud Hamanra, is the South American contact for the al-Qaeda, Hamas, and Hizballah terrorist gangs (Martines, 2003).

Another growing organized crime/terrorist group is the Sendero Luminoso (SL), or Shining Path, which operates in the jungles of Peru. It seems to have lost some of its power in the past several years. The major source of income for the Shining Path gang was extortion of money from drug dealers. No one was allowed to either cultivate the coca plant or pass through any of the territories controlled by the Shinning Path without paying a fee to the gang. The money extorted from the drug gangs was used to purchase weapons and explosives to further the causes of this terrorist gang (U.S. Department of Justice, DEA, 2003).

AFGHAN TERRORIST GANGS

Another terrorist gang that is far more dangerous than the South American groups is the Taliban, rooted in Afghanistan. This group became noteworthy during the U.S. invasion and takeover of Afghanistan and is a highly radical and fanatical Muslim group. The Taliban ruled Afghanistan until the U.S. invasion; it ruled through the use of threat followed by acts of terror. Anyone who opposed this government was eliminated. One of their favorite tactics was the massacre; victims were then concealed through mass burials in shallow excavated graves (somewhat similar to the tactics of the Nazis during World War II). Like all other organized crime families the Taliban used members of the sect (whom we would consider thugs) to enforce their policies. During the time they ruled Afghanistan, they created their own source of income by placing a tax on traffickers who were illegally cultivating and processing opium. After they took over the country in the 1990s, the Taliban helped opium traffickers' production increase by more than 20 percent through the use of death threats. Once the Taliban, in cooperation with Bin Laden, used a profitable tactic. The Taliban forced heroin producers to cut back drastically on the opium crop, which, in turn, caused a seeming shortage in heroin supplies worldwide. The Taliban and al-Qaeda, however, had stored away a large amount of processed heroin; they sold their heroin after they had driven the price of heroin much higher. So what this tactic did for both the Taliban and al-Qaeda was to increase their profits in the drug-trafficking market (Jacoby, 2002). Afghanistan now produces over 70 percent of the world's supply of illegally produced opium. Through the use of fear and the threat of death, the Taliban has extorted a sufficient amount of money from opium traffickers to support its terrorist activities and to protect and help fund Bin Laden and his gang, al-Qaeda (U.S. Department of Justice, DEA, 2003). History shows us that Bin Laden modeled his organization after FARC, the terrorist organization that has taken control of the cocaine trade in Colombia in order to subsidize its terrorist activities against the Colombian government. The same thing was supposed to happen in Afghanistan, except that U.S. forces arrived in Afghanistan and Bin Laden and his terrorist gang went into hiding in the mountains of Afghanistan. Without a doubt, al-Qaeda has found a way to interlink drugs and terrorism, just like their counterparts in Colombia.

When the discussion mentions Bin Laden and al-Qaeda, remember that within a short time after his arrival in Afghanistan in 1996, Bin Laden and his al-Qaeda gangsters took control of a majority of the heroin growing and trafficking in Afghanistan. During the six-year period that Bin Laden's gang of terrorists operated in Afghanistan, they made a profit of over $1 billion by controlling the heroin market. The funds gathered by this narco-terrorist gang were used to support al-Qaeda's terrorist activities throughout the world (Blanchfield, 2002). Al-Qaeda still has a larger-than-life presence through-out Indonesia, Malaysia, and the Philippines, all places where narcotics are considered currency. According to retired Army Lieutenant Colonel Robert Maginnis, al-Qaeda "has dealings with nations in Southeast Asia, such as Vietnam, Laos and Cambodia. Drugs are, therefore, a currency that fuels terrorist groups everywhere" (Scarborough, 2003: 1). Representative Mark Steven Kirk (R-Ill.), who had just finished a fact-finding tour of Pakistan and Afghanistan, categorized Bin Laden as a "narco-terrorist." Then Kirk proceeded to state, "Heroin is the No. 1 financial asset of Osama bin Laden and there is a need for us to update our view on how terrorism is financed" (Scarborough, 2004: A7). Kirk added that "the view of Osama bin Laden relying on Wahhabi donations from abroad is outdated. And the view of him as one of the world's largest heroin dealers is the more accurate, up to date view" (Scarborough, 2004: A7). We must also remember that since mid-2003 U.S. military forces in both the Persian Gulf and the Arabian Sea have seized tons of hashish, heroin, and methamphetamines (with a total street value of over $100 million) that have been directly linked to the al-Qaeda narco-terrorist gang (Scarborough, 2003). In early January 2004, a U.S. A-10 jet fired rockets into and destroyed an al-Qaeda drug lab that contained 1.5 tons of opium plus the chemicals and production equipment used to refine the opium (Tyson, 2004). There is no reason in the world that Bin Laden and al-Qaeda cannot be considered a narco-terrorist gang: They are a highly organized gang, they commit numerous criminal acts, and they sell drugs for profit. This information certainly places Bin Laden and al-Qaeda into what we call an organized crime family.

UZBEKISTAN TERRORIST GANGS

Another radical terrorist gang that has increased its unsavory reputation since its creation in 1996 is the Islamic Movement of Uzbekistan. This organized terrorist gang has created havoc throughout Uzbekistan using robbery, kidnapping, and bombings in an attempt to intimidate the government. Like the incomes of all the other terrorist gangs, the major portion of this gang's income comes from drug trafficking. The Uzbekistan government openly credits this gang with controlling drug trafficking throughout Uzbekistan. Gang leadership is closely aligned with both the Taliban and al-Qaeda (U.S. Department of Justice, DEA, 2003).

ASIAN TERRORIST GANGS

A gang created in 1976 to oppose the government in Sri Lanka is known as the Liberation Tigers of Tamil Eelam (LTTE) (also known as the Tamil Tigers), but it wasn't until 1983 that this group started its open warfare with the Sri Lanka government. About this time, the Tamil Tiger members created cells within the gang to control all elements of the gang's activities. The notorious Black Tiger cell was created to be suicide bombers; a major portion of their activities included assassinations and bombings of government officials and government sites. There is also a strong association between this group, the Taliban, and al-Qaeda. Like all other terrorist drug gangs, this group also supports all its criminal activities through the use of robbery, extortion, and kidnapping, but their major source of income comes from drug trafficking. Gang members are drug couriers for all the major drug traffickers in both Southeast Asia and Southwest Asia (U.S. Department of Justice, DEA, 2003).

Abu Sayyaf (ASG) is a group that is now based in the Philippines but originated in Afghanistan. This gang of thugs surfaced as an Afghanistan guerilla group in the mid-1980s. In 1989, ASG moved its base of operations to the Philippines to join with other violent terrorist gangs to create their own separate Islamic state. ASG immediately joined forces with the Moro Islamic Liberation Front (MILF), but each gang remained a separate entity. Another group, the Moro National Liberation Front (MNLF), was highly active in the Philippines until 1991, when MNLF membership splintered and joined ASG, which resulted in the creation of a stronger ASG (U.S. Department of Justice, DEA, 2003).

ASG supports its causes through the use of kidnapping, extortion, robbery, drug and weapons smuggling, and any other type of criminal activity that is considered profitable. A recent kidnapping perpetrated by ASG involved the snatching of Gracias and David Burnham and the resulting death of David Burnham during the rescue mission. This was what government and law enforcement officials classify as a high-profile kidnapping and an example of the type of major crime members of this gang are participants in. Both MILF and ASG have connections to the Taliban and al-Qaeda through the Jemaah Islamiya gang, whose members were recently involved in the bombing in Bali, Indonesia, that killed over 200 people (U.S. Department of Justice, DEA, 2003). This group also was involved in an explosion at Davao City International Airport that killed 21 people and injured another 100 people in the southern part of the Philippines in March 2003 (Xinhua General News Agency, 2003).

Some of these terrorist gangs have formed an alliance known as Rabitatul Mujahidin (RM). This alliance was created in 1999, and its membership consists of Jemaah Islamiyah, Moro Islamic Liberation Front, Laskar Jandullah (Indonesia), Majelis Mujahidin Indonesia, Indonesian Mujahidin Council, Kumpulan Militan Malaysia, and other fanatical Muslim gangs in Burma and Thailand. Leaders of Jemaah Islamiyah formed this alliance in hopes of creating an Islamic province in this region by combining these groups' assets (money acquired from drug trafficking) and military forces (*Philippine Daily Inquirer*, 2003).

There is one other notorious terrorist gang in the Philippines that deserves some type of mention in this chapter. The New People's Army (NPA) that formed in 1969 as a Maoist group has been attempting to cause the downfall of the Philippine government through the use of guerilla terrorist tactics. This gang created its own base of income by cultivating, trafficking in, and distributing both hashish and marijuana; crystal methamphetamine has become NPA's newest source of income, and gang members are involved in the trafficking and distribution of this drug. NPA placed its marijuana plantations in areas they control, areas known to the Philippine government as "guerilla zones" (*Philippine Star*, 2003). Other sources of income are obtained by levying what the gang calls "taxes" on gambling casinos. This gang also provides protection for Chinese and Filipino narcotics traffickers and provides security for Philippine drug lords and their families and properties (U.S. Department of Justice, DEA, 2003).

MIDDLE EASTERN TERRORIST GANGS

Another organized criminal group that operates in the Middle East is a Turkish group originally known as Kurdistan Workers Party (PKK); it recently changed its name to the Freedom and Democracy Congress of Kurdistan (KADEK). (This group was discussed in more depth in Chapter 12.) Since 1984, this terrorist gang has increased the use of violent activities against military representatives of the Turkish government. Thus far, a total of over 30,000 deaths have resulted from this conflict, and the cost to the Turkish government has been over $140 million. It is estimated that the PKK produces over 60 tons of heroin yearly, with a profit of over $40 million; PKK controls a majority of the heroin market in Europe. PKK members set up a systematic drug-trafficking operation throughout Europe, basing their operations in Turkish communities in various countries in Europe (U.S. Department of Justice, DEA, 2003). A profile of PKK, its members and operations, classifies it as an organized crime operation with street gang tendencies.

The PKK-KADEK gang has been established as a terrorist organization by the United Nations. In January 2003, members of the U.S. diplomatic force in Turkey established contact with the PKK-KADEK; there were several meetings between high-ranking officials of the PKK-KADEK and American officials starting in early 2002. The Turkish newspaper *Milliyet* documented that these meetings took place; documentation included photos of PKK-KADEK as well as American diplomatic leaders in Turkey plus a letter sent to the U.S. State Department by Mustafa Karasu, a member of the PKK-KADEK presidency council (*Financial Times*, January 23, 2003). Once again the U.S. government is dealing with an illegal terrorist group while continually condemning terrorist groups worldwide. The question is whether this is going to backfire in our faces as our prior support for Bin Laden and Saddam Hussein did.

A Turkish group formed in 1994—the Revolutionary People's Liberation Party-Front (DHKP-C)—is renowned throughout Europe and the Middle East as a highly radical Marxist-Leninist gang that supports "violent, immediate, and total revolution" (Tudor, 2002). Many of this group's activities mirror the actions used by Palestinians in Israel. Members of the DHKP-C participated in bombings (especially suicide bombings) throughout Turkey. The Turkish government apprehended a number of these insurgents prior to their attempt to bomb locations in Turkey. In many cases, these apprehensions involved the seizure of large quantities of explosives. This group supports its terrorist activities by being involved in drug trafficking. DHKP-C has battled with PKK-KADEK since its inception in 1994. Like all the other terrorist gangs in the world, DHKP-C is another well-organized gang of drug-trafficking terrorists.

MEXICAN TERRORIST GANGS

Mexico has had problems with terrorist gangs. Mexican police intelligence indicated that al-Qaeda members have a working relationship with members of drug-trafficking Mexican organized crime groups. This affiliation not only involves drug trafficking but also includes smuggling members of al-Qaeda over the border into the United States to perform covert terrorist activities. Intelligence indicated a fire bombing attack on the Washington, D.C., metrorail system involving members of a Mexican terrorist gang was being planned (*Agence France Presse*, 2003). Investigators from both Spain and Mexico culminated a yearlong investigation in Mexico by arresting nine people; six of the people arrested were Spanish nationals who were active members of the Basque separatist/terrorist group known as ETA. During this investigation, a number of Mexican bank accounts were frozen. Investigators also confiscated a number of ETA operation manuals containing information of how to make chemical weapons. The six Spanish nationals were wanted in Spain for financing terrorist activities, forging documents, and being members of a terrorist organization. The three Mexican nationals arrested were members of a Mexican terrorist gang known as Refugiados (Grillo, 2003).

Mexico, like South America, has had continuous problems with narco-terrorist gangs. The People's Revolutionary Armed Forces (FARP), a splinter group of the Popular Revolutionary Army (EPR), seems to create the biggest terrorist problems for the Mexican government. Four members of FARP were convicted in 2002 for bombing three Banamex banks in Mexico; a reason given for bombing the banks was the sale of Banamex to U.S.-owned Citicorp (*Financial Times*, December 22, 2002). Organized crime, whether drug, street, prison, or narco-terrorist gangs, has given the Mexican government continual problems, but with a new administration in place, the Mexican government is making an attempt to eradicate these problems. (Chapter 10 of this book has more extensive coverage of the Mexican gang topic.)

IRISH TERRORIST GANGS

Another noteworthy organized terrorist gang is the Irish Republican Army (IRA). This terrorist gang has been around for over 80 years and blames its existence on Oliver Cromwell and William of Orange, who conquered Ireland in 1690. After the overthrow of the British government in the south of Ireland in the 1920s, the IRA lost its bid for control of southern Ireland when it lost an unpleasant guerilla war against the newly elected democratic Irish government. Since the mid-1920s, the IRA has held a great deal of political power through its political organization Sinn Fein. Members of Sinn Fein have participated in many illegal terrorist activities of the IRA, and leaders of Sinn Fein are active contributors to all decisions made by IRA leaders.

The intent of this group is to reunite Ulster with the 26 free counties in the south of Ireland. They have attempted to do this through the use of terrorist tactics that involve killing police officers and blowing up department stores full of shoppers. A great deal of their support comes from outside Ireland; there is minimal support for the IRA in Ireland (outside of its gang membership). Irish-Americans have become the mainstay of support for these terrorists. Every time a member of the IRA is imprisoned or visits the United States, some type of fund-raising is done by an Irish-American group to support these terrorists.

In addition to its American support, the IRA joined forces with Libyan and other Muslim extremist gangs. The IRA has had joint ventures with the Baasder-Meinhof gang, the Basque ETA group, PFLP, and FARC. In fact, members of the IRA supplied the Basque ETA group with the car bomb that killed Spanish Prime Minister Luis Carrero Blanco in Spain in 1973 (Currie, 1994).

As recently as September 2001, three members of the IRA were arrested in Bogota on charges they were in Colombia training members of FARC in weapons handling (Gardiner, 2002). The three Irish terrorists, James Monaghan, Martin McCauley, and Niall Connolly, were active members of the IRA and were charged with supplying instructions on weapons handling and preparation of explosives to members of FARC. Connolly is the Sinn Fein representative in Havana. This association indicates a definite connection between Irish and Colombian terrorist gangs. Apparently this connection between the IRA and FARC was initiated by the Basque ETA group, which had been working with the Colombian terrorists since they got together in Havana in 1966. ETA has been an active accomplice of the IRA since 1972, so it was not long before they connected the IRA with FARC (Thompson, 2002). A United Press International report indicated that the IRA was responsible for over 1,800 killings in Ireland and over 120 deaths in Colombia (Gallagher, 2002).

Colombian terrorist gangs use drugs and drug money to pay for this specialized training, knowing that the IRA (like many other terrorist gangs) has turned to drug sales to enhance its treasury. The drug angle has become a major issue within terrorist gang circles throughout Ireland. In Northern Ireland, the Catholic groups—the IRA and the Irish Peoples Liberation Organization (IPLO)—as well as the Protestant groups—the Ulster Defense Association (UDA) and the Ulster Volunteer Force (UVF)—have become heavily involved in drug trafficking. Drug activity has become so intense over the past several years that there has been an increase in the number of shootings involving members of both the Catholic and Protestant terrorist gangs (Sharrock, 1992). In July 2002, it was reported that the IRA collected somewhere between $7.7 million and $12.2 million a year from its organized criminal activities while the Catholic IPLO amassed $2.3 million from its illegal activities. The Protestant terrorist group UVF accumulated over $2.3 through its criminal activities, and UDA accrued $1.5 million illegally during 2001 (Associated Press, 2002).

In 2003, it was discovered that the IRA was trading guns for drugs in inner-city areas of Birmingham, Bristol, Manchester, and Nottingham in England (*Financial Times*, 2003). An open street war continues in Northern Ireland between the UDA and the UVA over control of drugs in Protestant areas of the north (Hennessy, 2003). Drug trafficking increased the income of the IRA to somewhere between $17 and $21 million in 2002 (Pogatchnik, 2003). One IRA terrorist, Tommy Savage, was reported by the Irish police to be one of the biggest drug suppliers in all Ireland. Greek police issued a warrant for Savage's arrest for importing four tons of marijuana into Greece in early 1997. He was also involved in the importation of large amounts of cocaine and amphetamines that were seized by Irish police in 1997. Savage was also a suspect in the importation of thousands of ecstasy pills into Amsterdam in 2000 (*Financial Times*, 2004). In May 2003 during a U.S. Senate judiciary hearing on narco-terrorism, the IRA was implicated as drug traffickers, as was the Basque ETA (Federal Document Clearing House, 2003).

A report in the *Irish Times* showed that other Irish terrorist splinter gangs (specifically the Irish National Liberation Army [INLA] and the Irish Republican Socialist Party [IRSP]) have become involved in drug trafficking to increase their earnings (*Irish Times*, 2004). Another report indicated that a recently murdered Irish drug dealer had handed over a great deal of his drug profits to the IRA for protection. This report also stated that this murdered drug dealer was killed because of his involvement in the killing of a relative of Sinn Fein leader Gerry Adams (Oliver, 2004).

SPANISH TERRORIST GANGS

Another highly visible terrorist group is the Basque ETA (Euskadi Ta Askatasuna-Basque Homeland and Liberty), which has been involved in the murders of over 800 people since its inception in 1959 (Woodworth, 2001). The formation of this organized criminal gang was due to the atrocities committed by General Francisco Franco against the Basque people during the Spanish Civil War in 1936–1939. Basque country extends from Bilbao to Bayonne on the coast; the southern inland territory borders the Elbro River to Tudela on the Spanish side and continues up to Pic d' Anie in the Pyrenees Mountains and across to Mauleon in France; the total population of this area is a little over 3 million residents. The Basque ETA movement has not received the support of a majority of residents in Basque country; in fact, the ETA gang is not appreciated in many sections of the Basque community. A good deal of this lack of support is due to the violent acts involving members of the ETA (Woodworth, 2001). Since 1968, ETA has supported 3,761 acts of street-level violence, including 3,391 attacks killing 836 people and injuring another 2,367 (Roman, 2002).

ETA didn't start killing people until 1968; in 1973 ETA members murdered dictator Franco's prime minister Luis Carrero Blanco. In 1975, Francisco Franco, the dictator despised by the ETA, died and was succeeded by King Juan Carlos, who was groomed by Franco. Juan Carlos immediately got his government working on a democratic constitution that would guarantee civil and political liberties to the people of Spain. This attempt at peace in all parts of Spain did not succeed, as the ETA killed 16 people during 1975 and another 91 in 1980. A majority of the people murdered by the ETA were senior members of the Spanish military. Then in 1981 Lieutenant Colonel Antonia Tejero failed in his attempt to seize the Spanish parliament. After 1981, the number of murders involving the ETA decreased, but violent attacks continued as the ETA's new weapon, the car bomb, killed as many civilians as military people (Woodworth, 2001).

ETA members received their training in the use of car bombs from members of the IRA. In 1989, a former member of the Basque ETA was named as a participant in a bombing in Bogota, Colombia, that killed 52 people and wounded another 1,000. The ETA member had trained members of the Medellin drug gangs in how to carry out the bombing of both private and public buildings in Colombia (*Houston Chronicle*, 1989). In another incident that took place in 2003, ETA members were named as coconspirators along with members of the IRA and FARC after a terrorist bomb blast in Bogota, Colombia, killed 30 and wounded another 162 people (Hennessy, 2003).

The ETA connection to drugs has been apparent since its association with Cuban and Colombian drug traffickers in the late 1960s. Terrorist groups are known to look for easy ways to support their terrorist activities, and drugs are one of the most effortless ways to provide financial support for a revolutionary cause; it is also a way to obtain untraceable cash without public knowledge. In 2002, a member of the Neapolitan Genovese organized crime family testified that the ETA supplied this Italian mafia group with drugs. The mafia informant, known only as RS, told police that he was a courier for the Neapolitan Genovese mafia family, and he further stated that he had received 8 kilos of cocaine from members of the ETA (packaged in 16 half-kilo packages) in Milan. According to the informer, ETA suppliers shipped cocaine and hashish each week to Genoa for delivery to members of the Neapolitan Genovese mafia group. In exchange for the cocaine, the Italian mafia supplied the ETA with antitank and ground-to-air missiles that were purchased in Eastern Europe by mafia members (Arostegui, 2002). The informer maintained that he was present during some of the meetings in Milan that were attended by a woman named Maria, two bodyguards representing the ETA, and Felice Bonetti, the mafia crime family representative (Arostegui, 2002).

Trading drugs for guns has become a common practice involving terrorist gangs and arms suppliers. Terrorist gangs first make a connection with drug traffickers, who in many cases are also connected to some type of armed gang that supplies protection to the drug traffickers. In many cases, the terrorist gang supplies the armed gang with specialized sniper training and techniques for making bombs and planting car bombs. The arrangement may even involve participating in some type of violent act to ensure it is carried out correctly. A joint trust between groups is formed, with some type of compensation supplied by the armed gang or as a show of appreciation for the training supplied by the terrorists. In the case of the ETA and the IRA, the compensation from Colombian drug traffickers or FARC has been drugs. The ETA has a very close relationship with both Colombian drug traffickers and FARC, which is the main reason why most European law enforcement agencies (including Europol) believe that Spain is the major entry point for Colombian drugs into Europe.

The drug involvement of the ETA is no surprise to members of the Spanish police intelligence units. According to Spanish government sources, the ETA has been involved in drug trafficking since the late 1970s. During 1984, three members of the ETA were apprehended in the Hague, the Netherlands, with a very large quantity of cocaine. In 1988, the French police apprehended and detained a notorious Colombian drug trafficker who was meeting with ETA members. Then in 1996, Jose Luis Filgueras, an ETA member, was apprehended in southern Spain with over 150 kilos of cocaine. Police in Spain also claimed that various ETA gangs have been involved in turf wars in order to decide who would control the drug trade in Spain (Arostegui, 2002; Dombroski, 2003).

This information showed that ETA members formed an early alliance with FARC to further their ability to control the cocaine trade in Europe. ETA members have managed to gain significant financial status for their gang by getting involved in drug trafficking. We know that the ETA supplies a number of Italy's mafia with drugs in exchange for arms; it has also become apparent that the ETA is one of the major suppliers of cocaine to most organized crime gangs throughout Europe.

CONCLUSIONS

What all the information in this chapter indicates is that terrorist gangs that claim they have a political cause and want to save their countries are speaking lies. Terrorist gangs are no different from organized crime gangs or street gangs. The only "just" cause of these terrorist gangs is to gain more financial status so that their leaders can lead the same type of life as the people they condemn—the rich. Even if terrorist gangs gain power in the country they are allegedly attempting to save, it is not long before that power leads to a dictatorship such as that in Cuba; it does not result in freedom and equal rights for all. Idealists, such as the narco-terrorists, who use any method possible to gain power have a cause, but it is not freedom for their people but rather self-gratification and power for themselves.

REFERENCES

Abadinsky, Howard (1981). *The Mafia in America: An Oral History*. New York: Praeger.

Adams, David. "The Organ Theft Scandal." *London Times*, November 18, 1993, p. 18.

Adams, Nathan. "Menace of the Russian Mafia." *Reader's Digest*, August 1992, pp. 33–40.

Agence France Presse. "Germans, Swiss Break Drug Ring, Seize Heroin." July 7, 1994, p. 4.

———. "Billion Dollar Jewish-Moslem Money Laundering Ring Cracked." February 19, 1995, pp. 3, 11.

Agence France Presse. "Terrorist Try to Enter US via Mexican Border." April 7, 2003, pp. 2, 3.

Agres, Ted, and Seper, Jerry. "Nigerian Nationals Are New Syndicate Plaguing the U.S." *Washington Times*, January 27, 1986, pp. 1, 7.

Albini, Joseph L. (1991). *The American Mafia: Genesis of a Legend*. New York: Appleton-Century Crofts.

Alcohol, Tobacco and Firearms Bulletin. Jamaican ORCR, 1993.

Alexander, Shana (1988). *The Pizza Connection: Lawyers, Money, Drugs, Mafia*. New York: Weidenfeld and Nicolson.

Aizlewood, John (2001). "Angels at Dawn." *Guardian*, 2: www.lexis-nexis.com. Last accessed March 10, 2002.

Akers, R. (1973). *Deviant Behavior: A Social Learning Approach*. Belmont, CA: Wadsworth Publishing.

American Psychiatric Association (1987). *Diagnostics and Statistical Manual of Mental Disorders*, 3rd ed., New York.

Anastasia, George (1991). *Blood and Honor: Inside the Scarfo Mob—The Mafia's Most Violent Family*. New York: William Morrow and Company, Inc.

Anderson, John Ward, and Khan, Kamran. "Heroin Plan by Pakistanis Alleged." *Washington Post*, September 12, 1994, p. A13.

Anslinger, Harry J., and Ousler, Will (1961). *The Murderers: The Story of Narcotics Gangs*. New York: American Book-Stratford Press.

Applebaum, Anne. "Some Former Terrorists Are Changing Their Ways: A Few Have Gone into Politics, While Others Smuggle Drugs, Cigarettes." *Washington Post*, March 25, 2004, p. A8.

Arlacchi, Pino (1986). *The Mafia Business: The Mafia Ethnic and the Spirit of Capitalism*. Great Britain: Biddles Ltd.

Arostegui, Martin. "Castro's Scapegoats." *National Review*, December 28, 1992, pp. 33–35.

———. "ETA Has Drugs for Weapons Deal with Mafia." *United Press International*, October 3, 2002, pp. 21–23.

Asbury, Herbert (1928). *The Gangs of New York*. New York: Alfred A. Knopf.

Associated Press. "Robbery in Nablus Raises Fear New Gang Forming." March 12, 1990, p. 6.

———. "Authorities Seize 1,422 Kilograms of Hashish." January 19, 1994, p. 4.

———. "Ulster Paramilitaries Raising Millions Through Crime," July 3, 2002, p. 3.

Australian Intelligence Journal. "The Development of the Triads in Hong Kong." Edition 1, 1993, pp. 3, 5.

Bagnall, Janet. "The Gangs Are Here! Ontarians Who Hailed the Visit of Outlaw Bikers Could Learn from Quebec." *Gazette*, January 17, 2002, p. B3.

Balagoon, K. et al. (1971). *Look for Me in the Whirlwind: The Collective Autobiography of New York 21*. New York: Random House.

Ball, Karen. "Suspect Tells 'My Side of Story.'" *New York Daily News*, June 9, 1995, pp. 4, 34.

———. "He Swipes at Extort Rap." *New York Daily News*, June 11, 1995, p. 13.

Balsamini, Dean C., and Duga, Amanita. "The New Mob: Nigerian Mafia Digs into Nation." *Staten Island Advance*, February 6, 1990, pp. A1, A17.

Baltimore Sun. "Probe Uncovers Links of Drug Cartel, Mafia." December 17, 1994, p. 4.

Barboza, Joe, and Messick, Hank (1975). *Barboza*. New York: Dell Publishers.

Barger, Ralph Sonny, Zimmerman, Keith, and Zimmerman, Ken (2001). *Hells Angels*. New York: HarperCollins.

Barker, Anthony. "New Polish Premier Declares War on Gangsters." *Reuters*, March 7, 1995.

Barr, Cameron W. "Japanese Extortionists Target Corporate Meetings." *Christian Science Monitor*, July 6, 1994, p. 2.

Barrett, Amy. "From Thefts of Art to Toilet Paper, Czechoslovakia Crime Wave Spreads." *Wall Street Journal*, November 6, 1992, p. 11.

Barzini, Luigi (1972). *The Italians*. New York: Bantam.

Beacon, Bill. "Report Says Russians Forced to Pay Protection Money." *Times Colonist*, December 24, 1993, p. F2.

Beck, Simon. "Chinatown Godfather." *Sunday Morning Post*, August 21, 1994, p. 12.

Bell, D. "Crime as an American Way of Life." *Antioch Reviews*, 13, Summer 1993: 131–154.

Bell, David. "IRA Trades Guns for Drugs." *Birmingham Post and Mail Ltd.*, January 3, 2003, p. 2.

Bell, Kenneth. "Insight" presentation. September 25, 1989.

Bent, Grahame. "Who Killed Biggie? The Plot Thickens." *PlayLouder News*. http://www.playlouder .com/news/+whokilledbiggie. Last accessed July 15, 2004.

Bergen Record. "Bumpy Road to Peace Talks Toll on Israelis." October 19, 1994, p. A22.

Berke, Richard L. "Bennett's Two Problems: Supply and Demand." *New York Times*, April 16, 1989, p. E2.

Bidi, Rahal. "Main Suspect in India Bombings Held at Station." *New Delhi Daily Telegraph*, August 6, 1994, p. 15.

Blanchfield, Mike. "Sweet Revenge of the Poppy Growers." *Southam News*, May 26, 2002, pp. 12–14.

Blee, Kathleen (2002). *Inside Organized Racism: Women in the Hate Movement*. Berkeley, CA: University of California Press.

Block, Alan A. (1994). *Space, Time and Organized Crime*. New Brunswick, NJ: Transaction Publishers.

Block, Alan, and Scarpitti, Frank (1985). *Poisoning for Profit: The Mafia and Toxic Waste*. New York: William Morrow and Company.

Blok, A. (1974). *The Mafia of a Sicilian Village 1860–1960*. New York: Harper and Row.

Blum, Patrick. "Crime Claims Anger Czechs." *Financial Times*, August 25, 1993, p. 2.

Blum, Howard (1993). *Gangland: How the FBI Broke the Mob*. New York: Pocketbooks.

Blumenthal, Ralph, and Bohlen, Celestine. "Soviet Émigrés in U.S. Fusing into a New Mob." *New York Times*, June 4, 1989, pp. 1, 38.

Bohlen, Celestine. "Russia Mobsters Grow More Violent and Pervasive." *New York Times*, August 16, 1993, pp. A1, A6.

Bonavolonta, Jules, and Duffy, Brian (1996). *The Good Guys*. New York: Simon and Schuster.

Bonanno, Joseph, and Lalli, Sergio (1983). *A Man of Honor: The Autobiography of Joseph Bonanno*. New York: Simon and Schuster.

Bonner, Raymond. "Poland Becomes a Major Conduit for Drug Traffic." *New York Times*, December 30, 1993, p. 3.

Borger, Julian. "The Spies Who Thumped Back in from the Cold," *Guardian*, February 19, 1994, p. 11.

Bosarge, Betty B. "White Heroin Pouring In: DEA, Police Trying to Cope, But Can't Stop the Flood." *Organized Crime Digest*, June 1980, Vol. 1, No. 6, pp. 1–3.

Boshra, Basem, "Biker Denied Bail as Judge Raps Lawyer." *Gazette*. June 22, 2001, p. A4.

Booth, Martin (1991). *The Triads*. New York: St. Martin's Press.

Brooke, James. "At Home (That's Prison) with Medellin's Ochoas." *New York Times*, February 28, 1995, p. A10.

———. "Kidnappings Soar in Latin America." *New York Times*, April 7, 1995, p. A8.

———. "Columbia Marvels at Drug Kingpin: A Chain-Saw Killer Too?" *New York Times*, June 21, 1995, p. A8.

Builta, Jeff. "Current Middle East Narcotics Activity." *Criminal Organizations*, Summer 1994, Vol. 9, No. 2, pp. 189–201.

Burgonio, T. J. "Filipino Police: Rabitatul Mujahiden—Islamic Militant Group 'Bigger' Than JI." *Inquirer News Service*, April 9, 2003, pp. 3, 9.

Burke, Dan. "Close-Up of an Asian Gang Lord." *Gazette, Montreal*, March 30, 1991, pp. B1, B6.

Burns, John F. "India Pressing Bombing Case Against Pakistan." *New York Times*, August 11, 1994, p. A6.

———. "Heroin Scourges Million Pakistanis." *New York Times*, April 1, 1995, p. 3.

Burns, Haywood. "Racism and American Law." *Law Against People*, Robert Lefcourt (ed.), New York: Bintae Books, 1971.

Bushart, Howard L., Craig, John R., and Barnes, Myra (1998). *Soldiers of God: White Supremacists and Their Holy War for America*. New York: Kensington Publishing.

Butler, Mark, Anderson, Paul, and Wallace, Rick (2002). "Gangs Linked to 23 Killings." www.lexis-nexis.com. Last accessed March 20, 2002.

California Department of Justice. "Russian Organized Crime," October 1993.

Capeci, Jerry, and Sennott, Charles M. "Snake Slithers to China." *New York Daily News*, June 20, 1993, p. 21.

Carroll, Dennis. "West African Fraud Activities." *International Association of Credit Card Investigators*, May, 1992, Vol. 10, No. 3, pp. 7–15.

CBS News (West 57th). "The Palestinian Connection: Dirty Business." June 27, 1989.

Chakravarty, Pratop. "Key Suspect in Bombay Blasts Arrested: Pakistani Involvement Alleged." *Agence France Presse*, August 5, 1994, p. 2.

Chalidze, Valery (1977). *Criminal Russia: Essays on Crime in the Soviet Union*. New York: Random House.

Chalmers, D.M. (1965). *Hooded Americanism: The History of the Ku Klux Klan*. New York: Doubleday and Company.

Chan, Ying. "Crackdown Traps Asian Prostitutes." *New York Daily News*, May 17, 1993, p. 7.

———. "Chinatown Tong Tied to Scam," *New York Daily News*, June 25, 1994, p. 9.

———. "Grand Good-bye to a Godfather." *New York Daily News*, August 14, 1994, p. 10.

———. "Queen of Smuggling Is Fujian Hero." *New York Daily News*, June 17, 1993, p. 7.

Chan, Ying, and Dao, James. "Crime Rings Snaking into a New Biz." *New York Daily News*, September 23, 1990, pp. 32–33.

Chan, Ying, and Merzler-Lavan, Rosemary. "Global Mob Ran Scam." *New York Daily News*, August 30, 1994, p. 7.

Chan, Ying, and Ross, Barbara. "Chinatown Big Dead." *New York Daily News*, August 7, 1994, p. 4.

Chicago Crime Commission (1990). *Organized Crime in Chicago*. Chicago.

Chicago Police Department. "Street Gangs." October 1993.

———. "Auto Theft Gangs." November 1994.

Chin, James. "Crime and the Asian American Community: The Los Angeles Response to Koreatown." *Journal of California Law Enforcement*, Vol. 19, No. 2, pp. 52–61.

Chin, Ko-lin (1990). *Chinese Subculture and Criminality: Nontraditional Crime Groups in America*. Westport, CT: Greenwood Press.

Chin, Steven A. "Viet Youths Find a Niche in Crime." *San Francisco Examiner*, April 29, 1991, pp. A1, A6.

———. "Scams Target Immigrant Investors." *San Francisco Examiner*, April 19, 1992, pp. A1, A8.

Christian, Paula. "Gang Defectors Get Lightened Terms." *Tampa Tribune*, September 1, 2001, p. 7.

Christian, Shirley. "Central America: A New Drug Focus." *New York Times*, December 16, 1991, p. A10.

Clerc, Herve. "Government Announces Spectacular Drug Seizures." *Agence France Presse*, March 25, 1995; *International News*, pp. 1, 2, 12.

Cleu Line. "Crime Is Out of Control." *Coordinated Law Enforcement Unit*, May 1994, pp. 1–10.

Cleu Line Policy Analysis Division. "People Trade and Other Scams." November 1992, pp. 12–13.

Cleu Line Policy Analysis Division. "People Slavery." November 1991, p. 9.

Cleu Line Police Analysis Division. "Transporting People a Scam." August 1993, pp. 9–11.

Clines, Francis X. "Cops and Robbers, Gangs and Vice; Moscow Finds Out It Has Them All." *New York Times*, December 6, 1990, p. A20.

Coffey, Thomas A. (1975). *The Long Thirst: Prohibition in America*. New York: Norton.

Cohon, Mary Ellen. "New Mafia Bilks Credit System." *Northtown News*, December 30, 1985, pp. 1, 8.

Cole, Richard. "Asian Gangs Like a Giant Spider Web Spread Across the World." *Seattle Times World*, July 17, 1994, p. A13.

Combined Agency Border Intelligence Network. "Nigerian Heroin Smuggling: An Overview 1989." Cabinet 1989.

———. "West African Narcotics Trafficking System." Cabinet 1989.

Committee on Governmental Affairs: United States Senate (1992). *Asian Organized Crime: The New International Criminal*. Washington, DC: U.S. Printing Office.

——— (1992). *The New International Criminal and Asian Organized Crime*. Washington, DC: U.S. Printing Office.

Conly, C.H. (1993). *Street Gangs: Current Knowledge and Strategies*. Washington, DC: National Institute of Justice.

Connecticut State Police. "Prison and Street Gangs in Connecticut." December 1992.

Connolly John. "The People Collectors." *New York Magazine*, January 16, 1995, Vol. 28, No. 3, 15(2).

Constantine, Thomas A. "Report to Subcommittee on Crime and Criminal Justice: Heroin Production and Trafficking Trends." U.S. House of Representatives, September 29, 1994.

Cooper, Michael. "U.S. Indicts a Fugitive over Drugs." *New York Times*, June 8, 1995, p. B3.

Copeland, Peter. "Drug Submarines Sneak Through Caribbean Waters." *San Francisco Examiner*, February 18, 1994, p. A17.

Cowell, Alan. "Heroin Pouring Through Porous European Borders." *New York Times*, February 9, 1993, p. 3.

Cressey, Donald R. (1969). *Theft of a Nation: The Structure and Operations of Organized Crime in America*. New York: Harper and Row.

Criminal Justice Institute: South Salem, New York (1985). *Prison Gangs Their Extent, Nature and Impact on Prisons*. Washington, DC: U.S. Government Printing Office.

CTK National News Wire. "Seminar on Organized Crime Held." March 31, 1994.

Cullen, Kevin (2001). "In Sicily, Don Leads Comeback of Mafia." *Boston Globe*. Al: www.lexis-nexis.com. Last accessed January 24, 2004.

Cullen, Robert. "Comrades in Crime." *Playboy*, October 1993, pp. 70–72, 130, 160–163.

Cummings, John, and Volkman, Ernest (1990). *Goombata: The Improbable Rise and Fall of John Gotti and His Gang*. Toronto: Little, Brown and Co.

Currie, Robin. "The Irish Republican Army: A Closer Look." *Journal of Social, Political and Economic Studies*, Fall 1994, Vol. 19, No. 3, p. 287.

Dade County Sheriff's Department. "Mariwlitos: A Religious Rite." August 1991.

Dahlberg, John-Thor. "Tracking the Russian Connection." *Los Angeles Times*, June 6, 1993, pp. A1, A12–A13.

Dao, James. "Asian Street Gangs Emerging as New Underworld." *New York Times*, April 1, 1992, pp. A1, B2.

David, John J. "Outlaw Motorcycle Gangs: A Transnational Problem." Paper presented at the annual meetings of the conference on Terrorism and Transnational Crime, Chicago, August 1988.

Davies, Andrew. "Street Gangs, Crime and Policing in Glasgow During 1930's: Case of the Beehive Boys." *Social History*, 1998, 23(2): 251–267.

Davis, R.H. "Cruising for Trouble: Gang-Related Drive-By Shootings." *FBI Law Enforcement Bulletin*, 1995, 64, 16–22.

Decker, S.H. "Collective and Normative Features of Gang Violence." *Justice Quarterly*, 1996, 13, 243–264.

Decker, S.H., and Kempf-Leonard, K. "Constructing Gangs: The Social Definition of Youth Activities." *Criminal Justice Policy Review*, 1991, 5, 271–291.

De Cordoba, Jose. "End of Pablo Escobar May Slow Violence, But Not Cocaine Trade." *Wall Street Journal*, December 3, 1993, pp. A1, A4.

Dees, M. (1996). *Gathering Storm: America's Militia Threat*. New York: HarperCollins.

Dees, M., and Filler, S. (1991). *A Season for Justice: The Life and Times of Civil Rights Lawyer Morris Dees*. New York: Mcmillan Publishing Company.

Demaris, Ovid. (1975). *The Last Mafioso: The Treacherous World of Jimmy Fratianno*. New York: Avon Books.

Department of Justice: Drug Enforcement Agency. "Narco-Terrorism." May 2003.

Department of Justice: National Drug Intelligence Center. "Russian Organized Crime— A Baseline Perspective." November 1993.

———. "Northwest Passage: Prospects for Russian Drug Trafficking to the U.S. Pacific North-west." May 1995.

Department of Treasury: Bureau of Alcohol, Tobacco and Firearms. "Overview of Asian Crime in the United States." March 1995.

Department of Treasury: Federal Law Enforcement Training Center. "Organized Crime." October 1989.

Department of Treasury: United States Customs Service. "Nigerian Drug and Money Launder-ing Activities." September 26, 1989.

———. "Asian Organized Crime Organizations." June 1993.

———. "Asian Organized Crime: Korean Groups." January 1994.

Derfner, Larry. "Israeli Mafia 'Reaches All over U.S." *Jerusalem Post Reporter*, September 9, 1990, p. 3.

DeStefano, Anthony. "Asian Gangs Preying on Garment Factories." *New York Newsday*, June 2, 1991, p. 18.

Deukmajian, G. (1981). *Report on Youth Gang Violence in California*. Department of Justice, State of California.

Dicker, Fredric. "On the Cocaine Trail." *New York Post*, January 7, 1987, pp. 4–6.

Dimmock, Gary. "Police Admit Biker War Has Spilled into Ontario." *Ottawa Citizen*, December 6, 2001, p. A1.

Dobson, Chris. "Fears of Triad-Led War Hit New York." *South African: Sunday Morning Post*, July 26, 1992, pp. 12–13.

———. "Triads Bid for World Link-Up." *South African: Sunday Morning Post*, September 6, 1992, p. 18.

———. "China's Police Chief Met Top Triad Bosses." *South China Morning Post*, April 11, 1993, pp. 1–2.

———. "Sun Yee on Incorporated." *South African: Sunday Morning Post Magazine*, October 3, 1993, pp. 6–9.

———. "The Shark's Fin War," *South African: Sunday Morning Post*. July 10, 1994, p. 14.

Dobson, Chris and Chan, Quinton. "Beijing Chief's Triad Remarks Distorted." *South African: Sunday Morning Post*, April 18, 1993, p. 17.

Dombrink, John, and Song, John Huey-Long. "Hong Kong After 1997: Transnational Organized Crime in a Shrinking World." *Journal of Contemporary Criminal Justice*, Vol. 12, No. 4, December 1996, pp. 329–339.

Dombroski, Joseph. "Narco-Terrorism Menaces the World." *Richmond Times Dispatch*, May 18, 2003, p. E6.

Drohan, Madelaine. "Russian Mafia Haunts Sweden." *Toronto Globe*, September 27, 1993, p. B7.

Drug Enforcement Administration. "Cocaine Trafficking Trends in Europe." Fall 1982, pp. 21–24.

———. "International Initiatives to Control Coca Production and Cocaine Trafficking." Fall 1982, pp. 6–9.

———. "Casinos and Drug Money: A Laundering Loophole." Summer 1984, pp. 22–24.

———. "Drug Trafficking by Nigerians." 1984–1985, 4(8), pp. 13–14.

———. "Heroin Trafficking: The Nigerian Connection." February 1985.

———. "Colombia." July 1985, pp. 1–17.

———. "Israeli Organized Crime." April 28, 1986.

———. "Heroin Trafficking by Israeli Nationals." October 1986.

———. "Mexican Organized Crime Groups." May 1987.

———. "Update on Pakistani Traffickers in the United States." March 18, 1987.

———. "Cocaine Trafficking by Colombian Organizations." April 22, 1987, pp. 1–14.

———. "Intelligence on Nigerian Heroin Traffickers." May 5, 1987.

———. "Statement by Robert Stuzman Concerning Emerging Groups in Heroin Trafficking." July 10, 1987.

———. "Cuban Drug Activities." December 1990.

———. "Dominican Narco-Traffickers." February 1992.

———. "Special Intelligence Report: Dominican Criminal Activity—A New York Perspective." February 1993.

———. "Trends in Traffic." May 1993.

Drug Enforcement Report. "Asian Criminal Organizations Move into Heroin and Ice Trafficking." October 8, 1991, p. 8.

Duffy, Brian, and Trimble, Jeff. "The Looting of Russia." *U.S. News and World Report*, March 7, 1994, pp. 36–47.

Duffy, John. "Nigerian Fraud." *IACCI News*, March/April 1986, Vol. 91, pp. 1–2.

———. "Fraudulent Applications." *IACCI News*, May/June 1986, Vol. 92, pp. 1–8.

Duga, Amanita, "The New Mob: Nigerian Mafia Feeding N.Y.'s Heroin Habit." *Staten Island Advance*, February 5, 1990, pp. A1, A6.

Duga, Amanita, and Balsami, Dean C. "The New Mob: $$ Scam-Island Banks Have Lost Millions to Nigerian Mafia Schemes." *Staten Island Advance*, February 4, 1990, p. A5.

Duga, Amanita and Balsami, Dean C. "The New Mob: Nigerian Mafia Digs into Nation." *Staten Island Advance*. February 6, 1990, pp. A1, A6.

Dunn, Ashley. "After Crackdown, Smugglers of Chinese Find New Routes." *New York Times*, November 1, 1994, pp. A1, A24.

Ebron, Betty Liu, and Mustain, Gene. "Cartels Cook Up Pipeline to U.S." *New York Daily News*, May 23, 1993, p. 20.

Economist. "Cuba and Drugs: Spot the Dots." April 18, 1992, pp. 23–24.

———. "Free to Cheat in Eastern Europe." March 11, 1995, p. 54.

Edgerton, R. (1989). Forward. "In 'J.D. Vigil,' (Ed.), *Barrio Gangs: Street Life and Identity in Southern California*." Austin: University of Texas Press.

Efron, Sonni. "Vietnamese Girl Gangs Become Armed, Violent." *Los Angeles Times*, December 10, 1989, pp. A1, A53.

Ehrenfeld, Rachel. *Evil Money: Encounters Along the Money Trail*. New York: Harper Business, 1992.

Eisner, Peter. "Godfather and the Witch Key Cult Slaying Suspects." *New York Newsday*, April 14, 1989, pp. 5, 33.

———. "Seeks Amnesty in Return for Fighting Communism." *Newsday*, September 10, 1989, pp. 7, 29.

Elliott, Dorinda. "Russia's Goodfellas: The Mafia on the Neva." *Newsweek*, October 12, 1992, pp. 50–52.

Energy Intelligence Group, Inc. "Latin America: Driven by Fear." March 25, 2004.

Erlanger, Steven. "Images of Lawlessness Twist Russian Reality." *New York Times*, June 7, 1995, p. A10.

Executive Crown Authority. "Charter of the Almighty Latin King Nation." January 1, 1991.

Fagan, J. (1993). "Interview with Conly." In C.H. Conly, (Ed.) *Street Gangs: Current Knowledge and Strategies*. Washington, DC: National Institute of Justice.

Faison, Seth. "Head of Chinese Gang Re-entered the U.S. After Deportation." *New York Times*, June 10, 1993, pp. A1, B4.

———. "More Sought After Raid on Smugglers." *New York Times*, August 30, 1993, p. B1.

———. "Asian Gang Members Arrested in Kidnapping." *New York Times*, March 22, 1994, p. B3.

———. "Dominican Officers Arrest 2 Linked to Violent Drug Gang." *New York Times*, April 4, 1994, p. B7.

———. "U.S. Says 17 Ran Murder Gang That Ruled Heroin Sales in the Bronx." *New York Times*, May 27, 1994, pp. A1, B2.

———. "Charges Against Tong President Threaten a Chinatown Institution." *New York Times*, June 1, 1994, pp. A1, B5.

———. "Arrests in New York Are Said to Cripple a Huge Drug Gang." *New York Times*, September 9, 1994, pp. A1, B4.

———. "U.S. Indicts 2 Businessmen as Chinatown Gang Lords." *New York Times*, September 10, 1994, p. A23.

Farley, Maggie. "Turning a Profit on Human Cargo." *New York Newsday*, June 7, 1993, p. 19.

Federal Bureau of Investigation. "Oriental Organized Crime." January 1985.

———. "Asian Organized Crime in the United States." March 1987.

———. "An Analysis of the Threat of Japanese Organized Crime to the United States and Its Territories." July 1992.

———. "Organized Crime in the Americas." October 1993.

———. "Vietnamese Criminal Activity in the United States: A National Perspective." March 1993.

———. "An Introduction to Organized Crime in the United States." July 1996.

Federal Document Clearinghouse Senate Judiciary Committee Hearings. "Narco-Terrorism." US Senate, Washington, DC, May 20, 2003.

Financial Crimes Enforcement Network. "Jamaican Organized Crime." August 1992. p. 7.

———. "DSP: 36 Years Imprisonment for Ocalan Instead of Execution." June 19, 2002, pp. 3, 4.

———. "Mexico-Terrorism: Mexican Guerrillas Sentenced for Banamex Bombings." December 22, 2002, pp. 4–6.

———. "US and Milliyet Battle over Alleged Contacts with PKK." January 23, 2003, p. 4.

Financial Times. "Castro's Executions Send Shocks Through Region." July 22, 1989, p. 12.

Financial Times Information. "Greeks Seek to Question Ex-IRA Man on DRUGS Haul." January 16, 2004.

Fisher, Ian. "A Window on Immigrant Crime." *New York Times*, June 17, 1993, pp. B1, B8.

Fopiano, W., and Harvey, John (1993). *The Godson*. New York: St. Martin's Press.

Foner, Philip S. (1995). *The Black Panthers Speak*. New York: DeCapo Press.

Foreman, James (1997). *The Making of Black Revolutionaries*. Washington: University of Washington Press, p. 58.

Franzese, Michael, and Matera, Dary (1992). *Quitting the Mob*. New York: Harper.

Freed, D. (1971). *Agony in New Haven: The Trial of Bobby Seale, Ericka Higgins and the Black Panther Party*. New York: Simon and Schuster.

Freedman, Maurice (1966). *Chinese Lineage and Society: Fukien and Kwangtung*. New York: Humanities Press, Inc.

Freedman, Robert. "The Organizatsiya." *New York Magazine*, November 7, 1994, pp. 50–58.

Fried, Joseph P. "2 Businesses Indicted as Heads of a Crime Gang in Chinatown." *New York Times*, December 10, 1993, p. B7.

Friedland, Jonathan. "Traffic Problem: Rising Tide of Chinese Illegal Immigrants Worries Japan." *Far Eastern Economic Review*, August 4, 1994, p. 20.

Gallagher, Mike. "Analysis: The IRA's Idea of Non-Combatants." *United Press International*, July 17, 2002, pp. 2–3.

Gannon, Kathy. "Pakistan's Thriving Drug Trade Earns Dealers 2.5 Billion Each Year."Associated Press, March 31, 1994.

Gardiner, Beth. "Panel Says Northern Ireland Paramilitary Crime Rings Raise Millions." Associated Press International, July 2, 2002. pp. 11–14.

Garfinkel, Harold (1967). *Studies in Ethnomethodology*. Englewood Cliffs, NJ: Prentice Hall.

Gargan, Edward A. "2 Suspects Held and 2 Flee in Fatal Bombay Blasts." *New York Times*, March 16, 1993, p. A3.

———. "India Bombings: Gangs Involved, But Who Else." *New York Times*, May 16, 1993, p. 1.

George, J. and Wilcox, L. (1992). *Nazis, Communists, Klansmen, and Others on the Fringe: Political Extremism in America*. Buffalo, NY: Prometheus Books.

Gerth, Jeff. "Israeli Arms, Ticketed to Antigua, Now in Colombian Drug Arsenal." *New York Times*, May 6, 1990, pp. 1, 23.

Ghazi, Katayou. "Drug Trafficking in Thriving Iran." *New York Times*, May 6, 1990, pp. 1, 23.

Ghosh, S.K. (1991). *The Indian Mafia*. New Delhi, India: Ashish Publishing House.

Giancana, Sam, and Giancana, Chuck (1992). *Double Cross: Inside Story of the Mobster Who Controlled America*. New York: Warner Books.

Gilbert, Andy. "Triads Flourish in an Industry Powerless to Act." *South China Morning Post*, November 30, 1993, p. 3.

Golden, Tim. "Violently, Drug Trafficking in Mexico Rebounds." *New York Times*, March 8, 1993, p. 3.

———. "Cardinal in Mexico Killed in Cross-Fire by Drug Traffickers." *New York Times*, May 25, 1993, pp. A1, A8.

———. "Mexican's Capture Drug Cartel Chief in Prelate's Death." *New York Times*, June 11, 1993, p. 1.

———. "Mexico's Drug Fight Lagging, with Graft Given as Cause." *New York Times*, August 7, 1994, p. 16.

———. "Tons of Cocaine Reaching Mexico in Old Jets." *New York Times*, January 10, 1995, p. 1.

Goldman, P. (1973). *The Life and Death of Malcolm X*. New York: Harper and Row.

Goldstein, A.P. (1991). *Delinquent Gangs: A Psychological Perspective*. Champaign, IL: Research Press.

Gonzalez, David. "Just Boys Being Boys, or Vicious Gangs." *New York Times*, January 16, 1992, p. B1.

Goodspeed, Peter. "The Curse of the Triads." *The Toronto Star*, February 2, 1992, pp. F1, F3.

———. "Asian Gang Members Enroll in Scam School." *Toronto Star*, August 7, 1994, p. E6.

Gosch, Martin A., and Hammer, Richard (1975). *The Last Testament of Lucky Luciano*. Boston: Little, Brown and Co.

Governor's Organized Crime Prevention Commission. "New Mexico Street Gangs." July 1990.

———. "New Mexico Street Gangs." May 1991.

Gray, Malcolm. "Capitalist Crimes." *Maclean's*, January 10, 1994, p. 17.

———. "Mob Rule." *Maclean's*, May 30, 1994, pp. 16–17.

Grennan, Sean A. "The Threatening Issue of Oriental Organized Crime." *IALEIA Journal*, Vol. 7, No. 1, Fall 1992, pp. 1–17.

Grennan, Sean A., Britz, Margie, Rush, Jeffrey, and Barker, Thomas (2000). *Gangs: An International Approach*. Upper Saddle River, NJ: Prentice Hall.

Grillo, Joan. "Mexican Authorities Make Arrests in Crackdown of Basque Group ETA." Associated Press. July 19, 2003, pp. 17–19.

Gross, Jane. "6 Are Killed as 8 Hour Siege by Gang Ends in California." *New York Times*, April 6, 1991, p. 6.

Guart, Al. "Drug Bigs Wired to Launder Cash." *New York Post*, February 6, 1995, p. 8.

Gurr, T.A. (1989). *Violence in America: Protest and Rebellion*. Newbury Park, CA: Sage.

Hagedorn, John. "Gangs, Neighborhoods, and Public Policy." *Social Problems*, 38, 1991, pp. 529–541.

Hamad, Haitham. "Palestinian Gangs Blamed for Murders." *Associated Press*, October 24, 1989, pp. 4–5.

Hamm, M.S. (1993). *American Skinheads: The Criminology and Control of Hate Crime*. Westport, CT: Praeger.

Handelman, Stephen. "The Russian Mafiya." *Foreign Affairs*, March/April 1994, Vol. 73, No. 2, pp. 7–9.

Hanley, Robert. "Teaneck Killings Laid to Chinese Gang's Power Struggle." *New York Times*, May 26, 1993, p. B5.

Hardman, Dale G. "Historical Perspective of Gang Research." *Journal of Research in Crime and Delinquency*, 1967, Vol. 4, No. 1, pp. 5–27.

Harris County Sheriff's Department. "Nigerian Check and Credit Card Schemes." 1986.

Harrison, Eric. "Jamaicans New Faces in U.S. Crime." *New York Times*, January 17, 1989, pp. A1, A23.

Hazarika, Sanjoy. "Indian Heroin Smugglers Turn to New Cargo." *New York Times*, February 21, 1993, p. 11.

Hennessy, Mark. "Colombia Links IRA to Atrocity." *Irish Times*, February 14, 2003, p. 11.

Hersh, Seymour M. "The Wild East." *Atlantic Monthly*, June 1994, Vol. 273, No. 8, pp. 7–8.

Hirschi, Travis (1969). *Causes of Delinquency*. Berkeley: University of California Press.

Hockstader, Lee. "Russia's Criminal Condition: Gangsters Spreading Web from Moscow to the West." *Washington Post*, February 26, 1995, pp. 1, 2.

Hockstader, Lee. "A Time of Thieves: Organized Crime in Post Soviet Russia." *Washington Post*, February 27, 1995, p. 2.

Hodgson, Liz. "Triads Linked to LA Car Thefts." *Sunday Morning Post*, August 22, 1993, p. 3.

Hoge, Warren. "Sinn Fein Spurns US over Arrests in Colombia." *New York Times*, September 19, 2001, p. A7.

Hogben, David. "Expert Puzzled by Home Purchase." *Vancouver Sun*, August 6, 1992, pp. B1, B5.

———. "Japanese Gangsters Smuggled Heroin into B.C., Police Say." *Vancouver Sun*, August 28, 1992, p. B7.

———. "Crime Boss Entered Canada Before Buying Home." *Vancouver Sun*, March 20, 1993, p. A5.

———. "Crime Chief Linked to Two City Companies." *Vancouver Sun*, March 20, 1993, p. A1.

Holmes, Stanley. "Getting a Line on Phone Fraud." *Rocky Mountain News*, September 27, 1994, p. 30A.

Horn, Daniel. "Youth Resistance in the 3rd Reich: A Social Portrait." *Journal of Social History*, 1995, Vol. 37, No. 3, pp. 190–207.

Horowitz, R. (1983). *Honor and the American Dream: Culture and Identity in a Chicago Community*. New Brunswick, NJ: Rutgers University Press.

———. (1990). "Sociological Perspectives on Gangs: Conflicting Definitions." In C. Ronald Huff, *Gangs in America*. Newbury Park, CA: Sage.

Houston Chronicle. "Former Basque Separatist Linked to Colombian Blast." December 8, 1989, p. 26.

Howell, Ron. "U.S. Denies Posses Linked to Politics." *New York Newsday*, March 12, 1989, pp. 5, 21.

Huff, C. Ronald (1990). "Denial, Overreaction and Misidentification: A Postscript on Public Policy." In C. Ronald Huff, *Gangs in America*. Newbury Park, CA: Sage.

Hughes, Mark. "Police Hold Mr. Big over Canada Drug Trafficking." *South China Morning Post*, September 16, 1993, p. 3.

Hughes, Mark, and Li, Angela. "Suspected Drug King Extradited." *South China Morning Post*, November 30, 1993, p. 2.

Humphreys, Adrian. "The Mafia's War of Independence: Ontario's Second High Profile Mob Killing This Summer Severs the Ties Between Canada and La Cosa Nostra." *Hamilton Spectation*. July 25, 1997, pp. 1–4.

Humphries, Stephen (1981). *Hooligans or Rebels? An Oral History of Working Class Children and Youth, 1889–1939*, New York: Random House.

Hundley, Tom. "Uprising Get a New Front Line as Protests Die Down, Palestinian Gangs Gain Prominence." *Chicago Tribune*, May 5, 1992, p. 14.

———. "Violent Turf War Hits Belfast; Paramilitary Groups Fight for Control of Drugs and Prostitution." *Chicago Tribune*, January 21, 2003, p. D5.

Hunter-Hodge, Karen. "Rape and Rob Gang on Prowl." *New York Daily News*, February 26, 1992, p, QLI 2.

Illinois State Police. *Criminal Intelligence Bulletin*, No. 42, January 1989.

Iloegbunam, Chuks. "Run of Pot Luck." *Newswatch*, July 11, 1988, p. 25.

Imasa, Peter. "Business Fraud Surges." *Nigerian Economist*, October 14, 1991, pp. 9–10.

Inciardi, James A. (1975). *Careers in Crime*. Chicago: Rand McNally.

International Association of Asian Crime Investigators. Eastern Region: Asian Crime Conference, December 11–13, 1991.

International Association of Asian Crime Investigators. "Korean Gang Problems: A Proactive Approach I." January 1992, Vol. 6, No. 1, pp. 1, 3.

———. "Korean Gang Problems: A Proactive Approach II." March 1992, Vol. 6, No. 2, pp. 2, 6.

International Association of Credit Card Investigators. "Nigerian Fraud Groups." 1984, pp. 1–8.

Internet. "The Formation of PKK." Accessed December 17, 1995.

———. "Jails: The Source for PKK's Personnel." Accessed December 17, 1995.

———. "PKK in Lebanon." Accessed December 17, 1995.

———. "PKK's Involvement in Drug Trafficking." Accessed December 17, 1995.

———. "PKK and Terrorism." Accessed December 17, 1995.

———. "The Media vs. the Mafia: A Country by Country Perspective on the Problem." Accessed January 9, 1996.

Interpol. "Asian Organized Crime Activities in Europe and the United States." December 1993.

———. "Worldwide Organized Crime." September 1998.

Iqbal, Anwar. "Pakistani Arrests Hundreds in the Southern Province." United Press International, June 20, 1992.

Irish Times. "Activities and Structure of the Paramilitaries." April 22, 2004, p. 10.

Irwin, Julie. "Just the Tip of the Iceberg: Bridal Shop Heist Part of Something Bigger." *Chicago Tribune*, August 31, 1994, p. 1.

Italiano, Laura, Fermino, Jennifer, and Miller, Adam. "ATM Scam Nets 225G in a Day." *New York Post*, December 3, 2003, pp. 1, 4.

Jackson, Pamela Irving. "Crime, Youth Gangs and Urban Transition: The Social Dislocations of Postindustrial Economic Development." *Justice Quarterly*, June 8, 1991, pp. 379–397.

Jacoby, Mary (2002). *Fighting Terror: War's New Target: Drugs*. New York Times Publishing Company.

Jamaican Information Service. January 1998.

James, George. "33 Suspected Chinatown Gang Members Are Indicted." *New York Times*, November 22, 1995, pp. B1, B3.

Jamieson, Allison. (1989). *The Modern Mafia: Its Role and Record*. London: Eastern Press Limited.

Janofsky, Michael. "Fake Bank Set Up by U.S. Agents Snares Drug Money Launderers." *New York Times*, December 17, 1994, pp. 1, 8.

Japan Times Weekly (International Edition). "Yamaguchi-Gumi Opposes Anti-Gang Law." April 20–26, 1992.

———. "Australian Embay Blocks Sale of Property in Kobe to Yakuza." August 10–16, 1992, p. 18.

———. "Yakuza Muscle Their Way into China." September 19–25, 1994, p. 17.

Johnson, Elmer H. "Yakuza Characteristics and Management in Prison." *Criminal Gangs*, January–February 1991, Vol. 7, No. 1, pp. 11–18.

Johnson, Richard (1979). *Juvenile Delinquency and Its Origins*. Cambridge, England: Cambridge University Press.

Johnston, J.W. "Recruitment to a Youth Gang." *Pacific Sociological Review*, June 24, 1983, pp. 355–375.

Jones, Clayton. "After Yakuza Threat Japanese Businesses Breathe a Sigh of Relief." *Christian Science Monitor*, July 1, 1993, pp. 1, 9.

Jones, Thomas L. (1982). *The Bonanno Family: Men of Honor*. New York: Macmillan.

Judson, George, "16 Charged as Members of Drug Ring." *New York Times*, June 30, 1994, p. B7.

Kaplan, David E. and Dubro, Alec (1986). *Yakuza: The Exolosive Account of Japan's Criminal Underworld*. Reading, MA: Addison-Wesley.

Kata, Koji (1964). *Japanese Yakuza*. Toyko: Daiwa Shobu.

Katz, Jesse. "Reputed Mexican Mafia Leader Dies in Prison." *Los Angeles Times*, November 10, 1993, pp. B1, B4.

Kehinde, Seye. "Nigeria: The Cocaine Epidemic." *African Concord*, May 13, 1991, pp. 31–37.

Kelly, Robert J., Chin, Ko-lin, and Fagan, Jeffrey. "The Structure, Activity, and Control of Chinese Gangs: Law Enforcement Perspectives." *Journal of Contemporary Criminal Justice*.

Kessel, Jerrold. "Israeli Raid on PLO Cell Condemned." *Guardian Foreign*, September 30, 1993, p. 12.

Kessel, Jochen. "Chinatown Crime Wave." *Ottawa Citizen*, March 16, 1991, p. B5.

Kessler, Robert E. "From Car Thief to Cocaine Kingpin." *New York Newsday*, February 15, 1987, pp. 6, 17.

———. "Agents Arrest 3, Seize Heroin in Hauppauge: Tip on Couriers from Pakistan." *New York Newsday*, November 8, 1991, p. 26.

Kiefer, Francine S. "Poland Is Now Key Link in Europe's Expanding Traffic in Stolen Cars." *Christian Science Monitor*, April 13, 1992, pp. 1, 4.

Kifner, John. "New Immigrant Wave from Asia Gives the Underworld New Faces." *New York Times*, January 6, 1991, pp. A1, A20.

Kirtzman, Andrew. "Chinatown on Gang War Alert." *New York Daily News*, July 9, 1990, p. 5.

Klebnikov, Paul. "Joe Stalin's Heirs." *Forbes*, September 27, 1993, pp. 124–134.

Klein, M.W. "Street Gang Violence." In N.A. Weiner and N.W. Wolfgang (Eds.), *Gang Delinquency and Delinquent Subcultures*. New York: Harper and Row, 1968.

Kleinfield, N.R. "Five Charged With Holding Thai Women Captive for Prostitution." *New York Times*, January 5, 1995, p. B1.

Kleinknecht, William, Sennott, Charles M., and Chang, Dean. "Empire of Terror." *New York Daily News*, June 20, 1993, pp. 6–7, 20.

Koleniak, Mike. "The Mob's Crashing in with Scams." *New York Daily News*, February 28, 1995, p. 28.

Korean National Police. "Report on Organized Gang Activity in South Korea." July 1994.

Kraft, Scott. "A Gaping Gateway for Drugs." *Los Angeles Times*, February 17, 1994, pp. A1, A8–A9.

Kronenwetter, Michael (1992). *United They Hate: White Supremacist Groups in America*. New York: Walker and Co.

Labate, John (2000). "Securities Fraud Crackdown Nets 98." *Financial Times*, World News: U.S. and Canada: 4: www.lexis-nexis.com. Last accessed March 10, 2002.

Laub, Karen. "Palestinian Gangs." *Associated Press Worldstream*, October 18, 1994.

Lavigne, Yves (1987). *Hell's Angels: Three can Keep a Secret If Two Are Dead*. New York: Kensington.

———. (1996). *Hell's Angels*. Toronto: Deneua and Wayne.

Law Enforcement News. "Growing in Power and Viciousness, Vietnamese Gangs Flex Their Muscles." May 15/31, 1991, Vol. 17, No. 336–337, pp. 1, 3.

Lawlor, Julia. "Quality Is Matter of Teamwork, Service: New York Telephone: Fraud Crackdown Rings Up Savings." *USA Today*, April 2, 1993, p. 4B.

Lehmann, John. "Crash for Cash Con." *New York Post*, December 1, 2003, p. 2.

Leitzel, Jim, Gaddy, Clifford, and Alexeev, Michael. "Mafiosi and Matrioshki: Organized Crime and Russian Reform." *Brookings Review*, Winter 1995, Vol. 13, No. 1.

Leusner, Jim. "2 Accused of Using Florida for Mideast Call Forwarding." *Orlando Sentinel Tribune*, August 11, 1992, p. A1.

Levitsky, Melvyn. "Drug Trafficking in China." *U.S. Department of State Dispatch*, May 25, 1992, pp. 415–416.

Levitt, Matthew A. "U.S. Policy Toward Syria." Federal Document Clearinghouse Congressional Testimony. Washington, DC, September 18, 2002.

Levy, Clifford J. "Russian Emigres Are Among 25 Named in Tax Fraud in Newark." *New York Times*, August 8, 1995, pp. A1, B5.

Lewerenz, Dan. "Aryan Nations Looking to Move to PA." Associated Press, November 17, 2001.

Lewin, K. *Field Theory in Social Science*. Selected theoretical papers. D. Cartwright (ed.), New York: Harper & Row, 1951.

Lillyquist, Michael J. (1982). *Understanding and Changing Criminal Behavior*. Englewood Cliffs, NJ: Prentice Hall.

Limb, Julia. "Colombians Here: Soccer Star Was Hit By Gamblers." *New York Post*, July 4, 1994, p. 4.

Lin, Wendy, and Tyre, Peg. "A Gamble All the Way." *New York Newsday*, June 8, 1993, pp. 7, 32.

Lintner, Bert. "The Volatile Yunnan Frontier." *Jane's Intelligence Review*, February 1, 1994, Vol. 6, No. 2.

Lintner, Bert, and Mai, Chiang. "Opium Wars." *Far Eastern Economic Review*, January 20, 1994, pp. 1, 9–10.

Linzer, Dafna. "Police Chief: Israel Becoming Major Russian Mafia Center." Associated Press, June 28, 1995, pp. 34–36.

Lipset, S.M., and Raab, E. *The Politics of Unreason: Right-Wing Extremism in America, 1709–1970*. New York: Harper and Row, 1970.

Lorch, Donatella. "Hong Kong Boy: A College Student, and a Ghost Shadow." *New York Times*, January 6, 1991, p. A20.

Los Angeles County Sheriff's Department. "L.A. Style: A Street Gang Manual of the Los Angeles County Sheriff's Department." April 1992.

Los Angeles Police Department. "Asian Gangs in Southern California," October 1982.

Los Angeles Times. "Troops Kill 4 in West Bank's 'Black Panther' Gang." December 2, 1989, p. 19.

———. "The Shadows." August 8, 1992, pp. 28–30.

———. "Who Killed Tupac Shakur? Death Row-Bas Boy Feud." September 7, 2002, p. A14.

Lupsha, Peter A. (1991). "Cuba's Recent Involvement in Drug Trafficking: The Ochoa-LaGuardia Cases." In Susan Flood (Ed.), *International Terrorism: Policy Implications.* Chicago: Office of International Criminal Justice.

Lyle, John P. "Southwest Asian Heroin: Pakistan, Afghanistan and Iran." *Drug Enforcement,* Summer 1981, pp. 2–6.

Lyman, Michael D., and Potter, Gary W. (2000). *Organized Crime* (2nd ed.). Upper Saddle River, NJ: Prentice Hall.

Maas, Peter (1968). *The Valachi Papers.* New York: J. P. Putnam.

MacFarquhar, Neil. "5 Held in Ring of Shoplifters at L.I. Mall." *New York Times,* March 11, 1995, pp. 25–26.

MacIntyre, Iain. "Bure Has Made No Payments to Russian Mobsters, Say Agent Salcer." *Vancouver Sun,* December 29, 1993, p. D7.

Magloclen. "Jamaican Criminal Activities." March 16, 1990.

———. "Special Report: Nigerian Organized Crime." January 1991.

———. "Asian Organized Crime Conference." December 5, 1991.

———. "2nd Quarterly Asian Organized Crime Regional Information Sharing Conference." February 26, 1992.

———. "Jamaican Gangs." June 1993, pp. 30–32.

———. "Dominican Gangs." June 23, 1993, pp. 28–29.

———. "Almighty Latin King Nation." January 14, 1994, pp. 27–29.

Mallory, Stephen J. "The Risks of Toll Fraud: Telephone Service Theft." *Risk Management,* August 1994, Vol. 41, No. 8, p. 23.

Maloney, Eddy, and Hoffman, William (1995). *Tough Guy.* New York: Kensington Publishing Co.

Manchester Guardian, "The Peace Process: Colombia: Trio's Trip to Jungle Costs IRA Dear: Link to Drug Funded Marxist Rebels Angers Sinn Fein's US Backers." August 18, 2001, p. 5.

Markham-Smith, Ian. "Police Smash Hong Kong Ransom Gang." *Sunday Morning Post,* March 22, 1992, p. 4.

Marshall, Jonathan. "New Israeli Cabinet Member Linked to Suspected Criminals." *San Francisco Chronicle,* April 30, 1991, p. 8.

Martin, Keith. "The Russian Mafia Is Bidding for Control of the U.S.S.R.'s 'Lost' Weaponry to Supply Terrorists with Atomic Clout." *Times Colonist (Victoria),* April 28, 2003, p. A11.

Martin, M.L. "Asian Gang Activity." *Garden Grove Police Department* (3rd Ed.), 1993.

Martines, Lawrence J. "TRES FRONTERAS (Three Borders): The Nexes of Islamic Terrorism in Latin America." *Journal of Counterterrorism and Homeland Security International,* Winter 2003, Vol. 9, No. 1, pp. 1–3.

Mascoll, Philip, and Pron, Nick. "Drug Posse Leaders Rule with Terror." *Toronto Star,* July 17, 1991, p. 2.

Maysilles, Jean. "Abe Buzzard and the Welsh Mountain Gang." *Journal of the Lancaster County Historical Society,* 1999, 101(2): 64–71.

McCormick, Erin. "Did bin Laden Buy Bioterror?" *San Francisco Chronicle,* October 21, 2001, p. A1.

McCoy, Kevin. "Really Hot Mags: Newsstand Raids Net 13 in Scam." *New York Newsday,* December 15, 1994, p. A33.

McFadden, Robert D. "Drug Trafficker Convicted of Blowing Up Jetliner." *New York Times*, December 21, 1994, p. B3.

McGee, Jim. "The Cocaine Connection: The Cali Cartel in America." *Washington Post*, March 26, 1995, pp. A1, A20.

———. "The Cocaine Connection: Murder as a Management Tool." *Washington Post*, March 27, 1995, pp. A1, A12.

———. "The Cocaine Connection: Lawyers Under Scrutiny." *Washington Post*, March 28, 1995, pp. A1, A8.

McGregor, Richard. "Police Links to Japan Garner Drug Arrests." *Australian*, August 11, 1992, p. 8.

McGuire, Phillip C. "Jamaican Posses: A Call for Cooperation Among Law Enforcement Agencies." *Police Chief*, October 1987.

McIllwain, Jeffrey Scott. "From Tong War to Organized Crime: Revising the Historical Perception of Violence in Chinatown." *Justice Quarterly*, March 1997, Vol. 14, No. 1, pp. 25–51.

McKenna, James J., "Organized Crime in the Royal Colony of Hong Kong." *Journal of Contemporary Criminal Justice*, December 1996, Vol. 12, No. 4, pp. 316–328.

McKenzie, Scott. "Australia Targets HK Triads in Drugs War." *South China Morning Post*, April 6, 1994, p. 5.

McKinley, James C. "Bronx Ring Stole 100 Luxury Cars a Month, Officials Say." *New York Times*, February 1, 1995, p. B3.

———. "U.S. Agents Seize 17 in Raids to Dismantle Jamaican Drug Ring." *New York Times*, December 8, 1990, p. 1.

McKinsey, Kitty. "Spate of Spectacular Raids Show Poland Is Now Drug Gateway to Europe." *Ottawa Citizen*, May 27, 1994, p. D14.

———. "Changing Lifestyles: Poland Fights an Influx of Illegal Drugs from Abroad." *Los Angeles Times*, July 19, 1994, p. 6.

Meier, Barry. "Drug Trade's Army of Crack Gunmen." *New York Newsday*, March 12, 1989, pp. 5, 20.

Mercer, Pamela. "Colombian Who Made World Cup Error Is Slain." *New York Times*, July 3, 1994, pp. A1, A13.

Merton, Robert K. "Social Structure and Anomie," *American Sociological Review* 1938, 3, 672–682.

Meskil, Paul S. (1972). *The Luparelli Tapes*. Chicago, IL: Playboy Press.

Messing, Philip, and Celona, Larry. "Ivankov the Terrible Reigns as City's New Czar of Crime." *New York Post*, March 20, 1995, p. 14.

Meyer, Josh. "Glasnost Gangsters in L.A." *Los Angeles Times*, April 10, 1992, pp. A1, A30–A31.

Michelini, Alex. "8 Charged in Slaying of Drug Dealers." *New York Daily News*, March 25, 1993, p. 7.

Middleton, Greg. "Bure 'Mafia' Target." *Province*, December 23, 1993, pp. A82, A84.

Miller, W.B. (1974). "American Youth Gangs: Past and Present." In A. Blumberg (Ed.), *Current Perspectives in Criminal Behavior*. New York: Knopf.

———. (1975). *Violence by Youth Gangs and Youth Groups as a Crime Problem in Major American Cities*. Washington, DC: National Institute for Juvenile Justice and Delinquency Prevention.

———. (1980). "Gangs, Groups and Serious Youth Crime." In D. Schicker and D.H. Kelly (Eds.), *Critical Issues in Juvenile Delinquency*. Lexington, MA: Lexington.

———. (1982). *Crime by Youth Gangs and Groups in the United States*. Washington, DC: National Institute for Juvenile Justice and Delinquency Prevention.

Miner, Colin. "Bad Heart Earns Murder Suspect Flee Bargain." *New York Post*, August 3, 1994, p. 8.

Mitchell, Alison. "Russian Emigres Importing Thugs to Commit Contract Crimes in U.S." *New York Times*, April 11, 1992, pp. 1, 28.

Mitchell, Chris, and Marzulli, John. "Terror Ordeal." *New York Daily News*, June 9, 1993, p. 7.

Moneyclips, Ltd. "Crime on the Rise in UAE." *Arab Times*, May 15, 1993, pp. 4–6.

Moody, John. "A Day with the Chess Player." *Time*, July 1, 1991, pp. 32–38.

Moore, Jack. "Gangster's Murder No Surprise to Police." *Vancouver Courier*, December 1, 1993, p. 4.

———. (1993). Interview with Conly and Conly. In C.H. Conly (Ed.), *Street Gangs: Current Knowledge and Strategies*. Washington, DC: National Institute of Justice.

———. (1993). *Skinheads Shaved for Battle: A Cultural History If American Skinheads*. Bowling Green, OH: Bowling Green State University Popular Press.

Morgan, W.P. (1964). *Triad Societies in Hong Kong*. Washington, DC: The Government Printer.

Moses, Peter. "Asian Youth Gangs Are Setting Up Shop in the Sun Belt." *New York Post*, July 29, 1990, p. 15.

———. "Ghost Shadows Blamed for Cemetery Shoot-Up." *New York Post*, July 30, 1990, p. 15.

Moses, Peter, and Furse, Jane. "Dominicans Prey on Dominicans." *New York Post*, November 21, 1991, p. 18.

Moses, Peter, and Pelleck, Carl J. "Kosher Nostra." *New York Post*, August 27, 1986, p. 7.

Mustain, Gene, and Robbins, Tom. "The Return of a Killer." *New York Daily News*, May 23, 1993, pp. 4, 20.

Mydans, Seth. "For Vietnamese, a Wave of Gang Terror." *New York Times*, April 8, 1991, p. A11.

———. "Racial Tensions in Los Angeles Jails Ignite Inmate Violence." *New York Times*, February 6, 1995, p. A13.

Myers, Steven Lee. "Life Sentence for Scourge of Chinatown." *New York Times*, October 24, 1992, p. 27.

Narcotics Control Digest. "Feds Indict 89 in Largest Case to Date Against Global Money Launderers." October 12, 1988, pp. 3–5.

———. "State Department Says Worldwide Drug Abuse Levels Continue to Increase." March 15, 1989, pp. 2–9.

———. "Nine Arrested in Reputed International Drug Ring." August 2, 1989, p. 2.

———. "Andean Drug Summit to be Held in Colombia, Despite Secret Service Worries." November 22, 1989, p. 5.

———. "Evidence Links Medellin Cartel to Members of Sicilian Mafia." November 22, 1989, p. 4.

———. "Italians Seize Pure Heroin, Crack Coke Smuggling Ring." February 28, 1990, pp. 8–9.

———. "Two Year Probe Leads to East Coast Heroin Bust Involving Colombians, Italians." April 28, 1993, pp. 2–3.

———. "Cocaine Interception Uncovers Russian-Colombian Links." May 26, 1993, pp. 1, 4–6.

National Police Agency of Japan. "Report on Sokaiya Activities." June 1993.

———. "Report on Japanese Organized Crime." June 1994.

Nelli, Humbert (1976). *The Business of Crimes: Italians and Syndicate Crime in the United States*. New York: Oxford University Press.

New African. "Shame of Nigerian Fraudsters." April 1992, pp. 30–31.

New Jersey State Police: Intelligence Services Section. "Asian Criminal Groups." April 1990.

New York City Housing Authority Police Department. "Gang Activity Briefing." July 15, 1994.

New York City Police Department. "Dominican Gangs in New York City." November 1991.

———. "Asian Gang Activities." January 27, 1993.

———. "Nigerian/West African Narcotic Trafficking Organizations." April 8, 1994.

———. "Gang Intelligence." July 15, 1994.

New York City Police Department: Office of the Deputy Commissioner of Community Affairs. "Information on Jamaican Gang Activities." March 8, 1988.

New York Drug Enforcement Task Force. "Dominican Drug Activity in the Northeast." October 1992.

New York Magazine. "The People Collectors." January 16, 1995, pp. 15–16.

New York Post. "The Queens Connection." September 7, 1989, p. 13.

New York Times. "Drug Smugglers Use Cuban Base for U.S. Shipment, Jury Charges." February 27, 1988, p. 17.

———. "Torrent of Violence." April 17, 1989, p. 14.

———. "F.B.I. Says Los Angeles Gang Has Drug Cartel Ties." *New York Times.* January 10, 1992, p. A12.

———. "Warsaw Tourist Shops Close in Protest Against Crime." August 7, 1994, p. 11.

———. "Police Forces Have Their Hands Full: Poland Purges Corrupt to Cops." August 14, 1994, p. 32.

———. "Asian Gang Leader Held in Plot to Kill 3." August 20, 1994, p. B7.

———. "Mexico Arrests 2 in Drug Cartel." September 3, 1994, p. 4.

———. "Russian Gang Chief Indicted in Slaying." March 9, 1995, p. B4.

———. "Colombia Drug Lord Is Captured in Police Raid in His Hometown." June 10, 1995, pp. 1, 3.

Newsweek. "Cocaine's Dirty 300." November 13, 1989, pp. 36–41.

———. "The Nigerian Connection." October 7, 1991, p. 43.

———. "Global Mafia." December 13, 1993, pp. 41–48.

———. "Deals Too Good to be True." September 26, 1994, p. 28.

Noble, Kenneth. "A Nigerian Racket Lures Foreigners." *New York Times*, April 5, 1992, p. 11.

Oakley, Robert B. "Combatting International Terrorism." *Drug Enforcement*, Summer 1985, pp. 25–32.

O'Brien, Joseph H., and Kurins, Andris (1991). *Boss of Bosses*. New York: Island Books.

O'Connell, Richard J. "California Reports on Rise of Israeli, Vietnamese, Japanese Organized Crime Activities." *Organized Crime Digest*, June 1982, pp. 1, 2–7.

O'Connor, Anne-Marie. "Empire of Norcotecture." *Gazette Montreal*, April 6, 1992, pp. A1, A11.

O'Connor, Eileen, "The Wild, Wild East, the Battle for Russia." Cable News Network, March 12 and 13, 1995, Transcript 467-1 through 5.

Office of Attorney General of California: Bureau of Organized Crime and Criminal Intelligence. "Criminal Information Bulletin." January–March 1991.

Ogar, Maurice. "Nigerians Abroad: The Bad, the Good, and the Ugly." *Times International*, August 7, 1989, pp. 12–16.

Oliver, Joe. "Baron was Killed over 'Adams Murder.'" *Financial Times Information*, May 23, 2004, pp. 31–36.

Omotunde, Dele. "War Against Junkies." *Newswatch*, August 20, 1990, pp. 10–12, 15, 18.

Onishi, Norimitsu. "Heroin Trail: A Record Deal for an Agent." *New York Times*, April 20, 1994, p. B4.

Organized Crime Digest. "Israeli Nationals Suspected in New Credit Card Scheme." July 1981, p. 8.

———. "L.A. Police: Russian Mob at Work." February 26, 1982, p. 12.

———. "Ten Soviet Emigres Arrested in Counterfeiting Scheme." September 1984, p. 4.

———. "Organized Crime Commission Exploring Role/Structures of International Cocaine Cartels." November 1984, pp. 1, 9–12.

———. "The Mariel Boatlift." March 1985.

———. "Germany Alarmed by Ruse of Chinese Crime Syndicate." February 9, 1994, p. 7.

O'Shaughnessy, Patrice. "Midtown Korean Extortion Ring Smashed." *New York Daily News*, May 9, 1993, p. 7.

———. "The Kings Empire Grows." *New York Daily News*, April 17, 1994, pp. 32–33.

Ostrow, Ronald J., and Montalbano, William D. "Drug Agents Break Global Money Laundering System." *Los Angeles Times*, September 29, 1992, pp. A1, A6.

Parascandola, Rocco. "Bx Man Ran Killer Gang from Wheelchair: Cops." *New York Post*, December 21, 1994, p. 8.

———. "Mobsters Unite to Wreak Havoc: Italian-Colombian Link in Brooklyn." *New York Post*, May 17, 1995, p. 18.

Parente, Michele. "Cops Grab 11 in Kidnapping Ring." *New York Newsday*, November 29, 1991, p. 23.

Parker L. Craig Jr. "Rising Crime Rates and the Role of Police in the Czech Republic." *Police Studies*, Summer 1993, Vol. 16, No. 2, pp. 39–42.

Paxton, John. "Federal Republic of Nigeria." *The Statesman's Year Book 1984–1985*, 121st Edition, 1986, pp. 922–927.

Pear, Robert. "Cuban General and Three Others Executed." *New York Times*, July 14, 1989, p. 3.

Pearson, H. (1994). The Shadow of the Panther: Huey Newton and the Price of Black Power in America. New York: Addison-Wesley.

Penn, Nigel. "Droster Gangs of the Bokkeveld and the Roggeveld, 1770–1800." *South African Historical Journal*, 1990, 23: 15–40.

Penn, Stanley. "Con Artists: Nigerians in U.S. Earn a Reputation for Ingenious Scams." *Wall Street Journal*, June 5, 1985, pp. 1, 18.

Pennsylvania Crime Commission. "Organized Crime in Pennsylvania: A Decade of Change." 1990.

Perez-Pena. Richard. "35 Are Indicted as Members of a Hyper-Violent Drug Gang." *New York Times*, September 16, 1993, p. B3.

———. "From Afghanistan to the Bronx, Immigrant's Journey Ends in Gun-Trafficking Charges." *New York Times*, November 29, 1993, p. B3.

———. "U.S. Indictment Charges 26 in Huge Drug Ring in Bronx." *New York Times*, December 21, 1994, p. B10.

Perlez, Jane. "Rogue Wrestlers Have an Armlock on Bulgaria." *New York Times*, January 12, 1995, p. A4.

Philippine Daily Inquirer. "Philippine Intelligence Warns of Militant Group 'Bigger' Than Jemaah Islamiyah." April 9, 2003.

Philippine Star. "Philippines: Communist Rebel Spokesman Denies Drug Trade Accusation." July 7, 2003.

Philips, Chuck. "Who Killed Tupac Shakur?; How a Fight Between Rival Compton Gangs Turns into a Plot of Retaliation and Murder." *Los Angeles Times*, September 9, 2002, p. A1, Part one.

———. "Who Killed Tupac Shakur?; How Vegas Police Probe Foundered," *Los Angeles Times*, September 7, 2004, p. A1, Part two.

Pierce, S.M. "Asian Crime in Victoria." *Victoria Police—Asian Division*, November 1992.

Pierre-Pierre, Garry. "4 Reputed Gang Members Face Drug Charges." *New York Times*, September 2, 1995, p. 23.

Pierson, Ransdell. "Colombians in Big Heroin Push Here." *New York Post*, May 7, 1993, p. 3.

Pileggi, Nicholas (1985). *Wise Guy: Life in a Mafia Family*. New York: Pocket Books.

Pinscomb, Ronald, and Everett, Ernest M. "Hong Kong's Triads Move into Australia." *Criminal Organizations*, Fall 1991, Vol. 6, No. 2.

Pistone, Joseph, and Woodley, Richard (1987). *Donnie Brasco*. New York: New American Library.

Pletka, Danielle. "Heroin Inc.: The Nigerian Connection." *Insight*, September 30, 1991, pp. 22–24.

Pogatchnik, Shawn. "Crime Gangs Dominate N. Ireland: Protestant Extremist, IRA Making Millions." *Gazette Montreal*, June 12, 2003, p. A24.

Polyak, Vladimir. "The Russian Mafia Pushes into Tel-Aviv." *Moscow News*, December 16, 1994, p. 12.

Porter, Bruce. "California Prison Gangs: The Price of Control." *Corrections Magazine*, December 1982, Vol. 8, No. 6, pp. 6–19.

Posner, Gerald, L. (1988). *Warlords of Crime*. New York: Penguin Books.

Potekhina, Irina. "The Rise of Russia's Crime Commissars." *World Press Review*, June 1994, p. 13.

President's Commission on Organized Crime (1985). *The Impact: Organized Crime Today*. Washington, DC: U.S. Government Printing Office.

——— (1986). *America's Habit: Drug Abuse, Drug Trafficking, and Organized Crime*. Washington, DC: U.S. Government Printing Office.

Project North Star: Joint Coordination Groups. "1993 Drug Threat Assessment to the United States and Canada." 1993.

Puffer, J.A. (1912). *The Boy and His Gang*. Boston: Houghton Mifflin.

Purdy, Matthew. "New Way to Battle Gangs: Federal Racketeering Laws." *New York Times*, October 19, 1994, pp. A1, B5.

———. "Police Say Albanian Gangs Are Making Burglary an Art." *New York Times*, December 17, 1994, p. 1.

Queens District Attorney's Office. "Asian Youth Gangs: Queens." January 9, 1992.

Raab, Selwyn. "Influx of Russian Gangsters Troubles F.B.I. in Brooklyn." *New York Times*, August 23, 1994, pp. A1, B2.

———. "Reputed Russian Crime Chief Arrested." *New York Times*, June 9, 1995, p. B3.

Reckless, Walter (1969). *Vice in Chicago*. New Jersey: Patterson-Smith.

Reuters World News Service. "Motorbike Gang Kills Watchman in UAE." March 29, 1994.

———. "Turkey, Israel to Jointly Fight Terrrorism." October 6, 1994.

———. "Middle East Drug Trafficking." September 18, 1995.

Riverside County District Attorney: Gang Prosecution Program. "Asian Gangs." June 1992.

Robbins, Tom. "The Bizman and the Thugs." *New York Daily News*, June 20, 1993, p. 21.

Roberts, Greg. "Yakuza Link with Casino Tender Feared." *Sydney Morning Herald*, September 18, 1992, p. 6.

Rohter, Larry. "Mexicans Arrest Top Drug Figure and 80 Policemen." *New York Times*, April 11, 1989, pp. A1, A8.

———. "As Mexico Moves on Drug Dealers, More Move In." *New York Times*, April 16, 1989, p. E2.

———. "In Mexico, Drug Roots Run Deep." *New York Times*, April 16, 1989, p. 14.

Roman, Mar. "Spanish Parliament Takes Steps to Outlaw Basque Party Accused of Links to Armed Separatists." Associated Press, August 26, 2002, pp. 1, 10–12.

Rosario, Ruben. "FBI Has Dragons by Tail." *New York Daily News*, May 19, 1991, p. 13.

Rosenbaum, D.P., and Grant, J.A. (1983). *Gang and Youth Problems in Evanston: Research Findings and Policy Options*. Evanston, IL: Center for Urban Affairs and Policy Research, Northwestern University.

Rosenberg, Howard. "Palestinian Network: A Full Report." *Los Angeles Times*, June 1, 1989, p. 6.

Rosenfeld, Seth. "U.S. Says It's Broken Key Asian Mafia Gang." *San Francisco Examiner*, October 13, 1993, p. 11.

Rosenthal, A.M. "In Eight Words, Bush Absolves Syria." *San Francisco Chronicle*, November 26, 1991, p. A16.

———. "The Syrian Sanctuary." *Sacramento Bee*, March 13, 1993, p. B6.

Ross, Barbara, and Gonzalez, Juan. "Multi-Ethnic Group Invades Drug Biz." *New York Daily News*, April 27, 1994, pp. 2, 20–21.

———. "The Money Launderer Sang." *New York Daily News*, April 28, 1994, pp. 24, 44.

———. "Rabbis Laundered Money." *New York Daily News*, April 29, 1994, pp. 16, 33.

Rowan, C.T. (1996). *The Coming Race Wars in America*. New York: Little, Brown and Company.

Rowan, Roy. "Pan Am 103: Why Did They Die?" *Time Magazine*, April 27, 1992.

Royal Canadian Mounted Police. "Organized Crime in Canada." December 1992.

Royal Hong Kong Police. "Triads in Hong Kong: Past and Present." 1994.

Royce, Knut. "Country Run on Drugs." *New York Newsday*, February 23, 1993, p. 6.

Rudge, David. "Crackdown by Police Nabs Ring of 'Drug Baron.'" *Jerusalem Post*, March 16, 1992.

Ryan, P. Personal communication, March 1998.

Sachs, Susan. "West Bank's New Kind of Intifada: Palestinian Gangs on the Prowl." *New York Newsday*, May 12, 1992, p. 4.

Sanchez-Jankowski, M.S. (1991). *Islands in the Street: Gangs and American Urban Society*. Berkeley: University of California Press.

Sanders, W. (1994). *Gangbangs and Drive-bys: Grounded Culture and Juvenile Gang Violence*. New York: Aldine de Gruyter.

Sanders, Wiley (1970). *Juvenile Offenders for a Thousand Years*. Chapel Hill, NC: University of North Carolina Press.

San Francisco Examiner. "Witness Ties Pebble Deal, Mob." August 11, 1993, pp. D1, D3.

Sanger, David E. "Top Japanese Party Leaders Accused of Links to Mobsters." September 23, 1992, pp. A1, A5.

———. "$50 Million Discovered in Raids on Arrested Japanese Politician." *New York Times*, March 10, 1993, pp. A1, A11.

Sarnecki, J. (1986). *Delinquent Networks*. Stockholm: Research Division, National Swedish Council for Crime Prevention.

Savitz, L.D., Rosen, L., and Lalli, M. "Delinquency and Gang Membership as Related to Victimization." *Victimology*, 1980, 5, pp. 152–160.

Savona, Dave. "Waging War on Pirates." *International Business*, January 1995, pp. 42–47.

Scammell, Michael. "Russia's Robber Barons." *Weekend Sun*, December 31, 1993, p. B5.

Scarborough, Rowan. "Drug Money Sustains Al-Qaeda; Cutoff Needed to Strangle Cells." *Washington Times*, December 29, 2003, p. 1.

————. "Osama bin Laden a 'Narco-Terrorist'; Legislator Cites Heroin Trade Link." *Washington Times*, January 22, 2004, p. 7.

Schoenberger, Karl. "U.S. Probes How Japanese Bought Riviera Club." *Los Angeles Times*, May 2, 1993, pp. A1, A28, A30–A31.

————. "Japanese Firm Agrees to Forfeiture." *Los Angeles Times*, October 3, 1993, p. D3.

Schut, Jan H. "Russian Roulette." *Corporation*, March 1995, p. 26.

Sciolino, Elaine. "State Department Report Labels Nigeria Major Trafficker of Drugs to U.S." *New York Times*, April 5, 1994, pp. A1, A11.

Scott, K. (1994). *Monster*. New York: Penguin.

Seagrave, Sterling (1985). *The Song Dynasty*. New York: Harper and Row.

Sebastian, Tim. "Carry on Drug Smugglers: Night and Day." *Mail on Sunday*, February 19, 1995, pp. 10–12.

Sennott, Charles. "Colombia: Days of Death and Drugs." *New York Post*, September 5, 1989, pp. 4, 19.

————. "Godfather of the Coke Clan." *New York Post*, September 6, 1989, pp. 3, 20.

Sennott, Charles, Robbins, Tom, Rosen, James, and Chan, Ying. "Wait in the Wings: Russian, Jamaican, Asian Syndicates Already Muscling In." *New York Daily News*, November 17, 1991, p. 33.

Sennott, Charles M. "Anatomy of a Drug Gang." *New York Daily News*, February 14, 1993, p. 30.

————. "Chinatown Gang Linked to Voyage." *New York Daily News*, June 8, 1993, p. 4.

————. "Gang Has Global Reach." *New York Daily News*, June 9, 1993, p. 23.

Serio, Joseph (1992). "The Soviet Union: Disorganization and Organized Crime." In Ann Lodl and Zhang Longguan (Eds.), *Enterprise Crime: Asian and Global Perspective*. Chicago: Office of International Criminal Justice, pp. 341–372.

Sexton, William. "Mob Links: How Organized Crime Took Up Golf in Japan." *New York Newsday*, January 11, 1988, p. 66.

Shannon, Elaine. "New Kings of Coke." *Time*, July 1, 1991, pp. 29–33.

Sharrock, David. "Drugs Split Terror Faction's Blood Feud: Three Shot Dead and More Killings Feared as Republican Splinter Group Forgets Politics in Dispute over Ecstasy Trafficking Profits." *Manchester Guardian*, September 22, 1992, p. Nopgcit.

Shenon, Philip. "Saudi Envoy Helps Expose Thai Crime Group: Thai Police." *New York Times*, September 19, 1994, p. A5.

————. "Burmese Military Steps Up Drive Against Major Drug Trafficker." *New York Times*, April 10, 1996, p. A5.

Sherman, William, and Goldfarb, Daniel. "Albanian Gangs Breaking into the Big Leagues." *New York Post*, January 11, 1996, p. 16.

Shigemasa, Kimikazu. "Land Boom Fallout Handicapped Ibaraki Club Members." *Japan Times Weekly* (International Edition), September 21–27, 1994, p. 17.

Shimbun, Yomiuri. "Bogus Pakistani Money Found at Factory." *Daily Yomiuri*, November 27, 1994, p. 2.

Sik, Barkin. "Turkey: Report Lists 450 PKK-KADEK Organizations in EU, Neighboring Countries." *Financial Times*, November 3, 2002, pp. 7–8.

Skonie, Sharon. "Hegewisch Cop Stings Polish Auto Theft Ring." *Times*, August 28, 1991, pp. A1, A7.

SLED. Personal correspondence with a variety of officers, 1997.

————. Gang training manual, 1997.

Smilon, Marvin. "Yellow Bird Caged for 20 Years in Bamboo Gang Trial." *New York Post*, January 4, 1987, p. 18.

Smith, Greg (2001). "Chin Is the Head." *Gazette*, www.lexix-nexis.com. Last accessed January 24, 2001.

Smith, Greg B. "Russians Face Gold-Smuggle Raps." *New York Daily News*, September 13, 1995, p. 10.

Smith, Greg B., and Chan, Ying. "Suspected Scam Firm Reopening." *New York Newsday*, August 31, 1994, p. 10.

Smith, Greg B., and Chan, Ying. "Chinatown Mob Bigs Arrested." *New York Daily News*, September 10, 1994, p. 5.

South China Morning Post. Chinatown Tells Its Secrets." March 7, 1991, p. 15.

———. "The Nasty Business of Being Stung by the African Mafia." February 2, 1992, p. 10.

———. "Trio Face Yakuza Charges." June 2, 1992, p. 12.

———. "Turning Up the Heat on the Yakuza." August 15, 1992, p. 13.

———. "Sun Yee on Branching Out." October 5, 1992, pp. 1–2.

———. "Confessions of a Hitman." September 19, 1992, p. 4.

———. "Three Die as Gang Wars Flare over Control of Tokyo." July 22, 1993, p. 12.

———. "Sun Yee on Membership Put at 56,000." January 29, 1994, p. 6.

Southern Cross. "Mafia Boss Hits Gold Coast." May 12, 1993, pp. 1–2.

Southern Poverty Law Center. "Skinhead Violence: It's Come Back Again." *Face of Terrorism*, 1997, 85, pp. 1–2.

Soyinka, Kayode. "A Fork on the Road." *Newswatch*, July 11, 1988, pp. 21–24, 26.

Speden, Graeme. "Kiwis Catch Up with Asian Crime." *South China Morning Post*, February 25, 1994, p. 31, 20(2): 179–199.

Spergel, I.A. "Youth Gangs: An Essay Review." *Social Service Review*, 1992, 66, pp. 121–140.

Spergel, L.A. (1993). Interview. In C.H. Conly (Ed.), *Street Gangs: Current Knowledge and Strategies*. Washington, DC: National Institute of Justice.

———. Testimony Before U.S. House Subcommittee on Juvenile Justice. C-Span, December 19, 1994.

Spergel, L.A., Curry, G.D., Ross, R.E., and Chance, R.L. (1990). *Survey of Gang Problems in 45 Cities and Six Sites*. Chicago: University of Chicago, School of Social Service Administration.

Spolar, Christine. "Rogue Explosions Shake Warsaw as Gangs Vie for Power." *International Herald Tribune*, March 14, 1995.

Stallworth, Ron. "Music, Culture and Politics of Gangsta Rap." Presented at the Second Annual Gang School, National Gang Crime Research Center, Chicago, July 10, 1998.

Statesman. "Pakistani Drug Money Aiding Militants in India, Says CIA." February 25, 1993.

Statt, Daniel. "The Case of the Mohocks: Rake Violence in Augustan London." *Social History*, 1995, 37, pp. 161–175.

Sterling, Claire (1990). *Octopus: The Long Reach of the Sicilian Mafia*. New York: Simon and Schuster.

———. (1994). *Thieves World: The Threat of the New Global Network of Organized Crime*. New York: Simon and Schuster.

Stovern, L.D. (1993). "Japanese Organized Crime." 15th Annual International Asian Organized Crime Conference. Neveda: Las Vegas.

Strom, Charles. "13 Indicted in Oil Scheme Laid to Mob." *New York Times*, May 6, 1993, p. B6.

Sullivan, Randall. "The Murder of Notorious B.I.G." *Rolling Stone*, June 7, 2001, pp. 80–106, 124–125.

————. "In Harms Way: It's Five Years Since Rap Superstars Biggie Smalls and Tupac Shakur Were Shot Dead, Yet No One Has Been Charged with Their Murders. Etc. *Guardian*, April 26, 2002, p. 2.

Sullivan, Ronald. "Five Indicted in a Robbery at a Church." *New York Times*, December 31, 1992, p. B3.

Sunday Morning Post. "Hong Kong Triads Take Root in U.S." November 24, 1991, p. 21.

————. "The Confessions of a Heroin Smuggler." August 3, 1992, p. 3.

————. "The Confessions of a Heroin Smuggler." August 9, 1992, pp. 2–5.

————. "Japan's Murky Revelations of Big Business and the Mob." December 13, 1992, p. 6.

————. "Wan Chai Sting Sheds Light on Dark World of HK Triads." November 28, 1993, p. 13.

————. "The North Korean Cash Connection." July 17, 1994, p. 15.

Sutherland, Edwin, H. (1973). *Principle of Criminology*. Dix Hills, NY: General Hall.

Sydney Morning Herald. "Heat Turned Up on Lawless Bike Gangs." www.lexis-nexis.com. Last accessed on February 9, 2002.

Tabor, Mary. "200 Members of Hispanic Gang Indicted in Multiple Killings." *New York Times*, June 22, 1994, p. B1.

Talese, Gay (1971). *Honor Thy Father*. New York: Dell Books.

Thompson, Bernard. "Drug Lords and Terrorists." *San Diego Union-Tribune*, October 17, 2002, pp. B7, B13, B15.

Thrasher, F.M. (1963). *The Gang*. Chicago: University of Chicago Press.

Tierney, Ben. "Passport to Crime." *Ottawa Citizen*, November 8, 1992, p. B5.

————. "Police Call the Big Circle Boys—Chinese Gangs—the Most Significant Development in Canadian Crime. All Came Here as Refugee Claimants." *Ottawa Citizen*, November 8, 1992, p. B5.

Time. "The Drug Thugs." March 7, 1988, pp. 28–37.

————. "Nigeria: Uncivil Disobedience." August 15, 1994, p. 27.

Torode, Greg. "Sun Yee on Move into Shenzhen." *South China Morning Post*, August 2, 1993, p. 3.

Toronto Star. "Gangsters Deliver Chilling Message with Slaying of Fuji Film Executive." March 3, 1994, p. F4.

Torres, D.M. "Chicano Gangs in the East Los Angeles Barrio." *California Youth Authority Querterly*, 1979, 32, pp. 5–13.

Trachtman, Paul (1974). *The Gunfighters*. New York: Time Life.

Train, Arthur (1922). *Courts and Criminals*. New York: Scribner's Press.

Treaster, Joseph B. "Colombia's Drug Lords Add New Product: Heroin for U.S." *New York Times*. January 14, 1992, pp. A1, B2.

————. "Nigerian Connection Floods U.S. Airports with Asian Heroin." *New York Times*, February 15, 1992, pp. 1, 29.

————. "U.S. Links Trail of Heroin to a 'Soviet Connection.'" *New York Times*, April 15, 1992, p. B3.

————. "Behind Immigrants' Voyage, Long Reach of Chinese Gangs." *New York Times*, June 9, 1993, pp. A1, B2.

————. "End to Gang Chief's Lavish Life on Run." *New York Times*, September 3, 1993, p. B4.

————. "3 Arrested in Smuggling Cocaine Found in Newark Cargo." *New York Times*, July 15, 1994, p. B3.

————. "U.S. Says It Uncovered $100 Million Drug Money Laundry." *New York Times*, December 1, 1994, pp. B1, B8.

Treaster, Joseph B., and Myers, Steven Lee. "A Dozen Killings Tied to Colombia." *New York Times*, May 16, 1993, pp. 1, 38.

Turek, Bogdan. "Poland Blames Gangs for Bombings." United Press International, March 14, 1995, p. 2.

Turkus, Burton, and Feder, Sid. (1951). *Murder Inc.: The Story of the Syndicate*. New York: Farrar, Straus and Young.

Tudor, Radu. "Report Details Turkish Terrorist Organizations with Branches in Romania." *Financial Times*, December 19, 2002, pp. 3, 9.

Tyson, Ann Scott. "War on Terror Is Also a War on Drugs." *Christian Science Monitor*, February 18, 2004, p. 1.

Uhlig, Mark A. "Raul Castro Adds Spark to Cuban Trial." *New York Times*, June 22, 1989, p. A3.

U.S. Customs Service. "Heroin Smuggling from Nigeria Strategy." August 1989.

———. "Nigerian Drug and Money Laundering Activities." September 26, 1989.

———. "Asian Organized Crime: New York City Street Gangs." May 1993.

———. "Asian Organized Crime Organizations." June 1993.

———. "Asian Organized Crime: Korean Groups." September 1994.

U.S. Department of Justice: Bureau of Justice Assistance. "Developing and Managing Asian Informants." January 20–22, 1993.

U.S. Department of Justice: Drug Enforcement Administration-Noform. "Drug Trafficking by Nigerians." 1984–1985, Vol. 4, No. 8, pp. 13–14.

———. "Heroin Trafficking: The Nigerian Connection." February 1985.

U.S. Department of Justice: Drug Enforcement Administration. "Statement to Robert M. Stutman Concerning Emerging Groups in Heroin Trafficking." July 10, 1987.

U.S. Department of Justice: Drug Enforcement Administration-Office of Intelligence. "Nigerian Heroin Smuggling Methods." May 12, 1987.

U.S. Department of Justice: Federal Bureau of Investigation. "Oriental Organized Crime." January 1985.

———. "Asian Organized Crime in the United States." 1987.

———. "Vietnamese Criminal Activity in the United States: A National Perspective." March 1993.

U.S. Department of Justice: Office of the Attorney General. "Drug Trafficking: A Report to the President of the United States." August 3, 1989, pp. 17–22.

U.S. News and World Report. "Narcotics: Terror's New Ally." May 4, 1987, pp. 31–38.

———. "The Men Who Created Crack." August 19, 1991, pp. 44–53.

———. "Coming to America." June 21, 1993, pp. 26–29, 31.

———. "Immigration Crackdown." June 21, 1993, pp. 34, 38–39.

United Press International. "Israeli Troops Kill Arab Ax Gang Leader." November 9, 1989, p. 12.

———. "Head of Palestinian Gang Killed by Israeli Soldiers." December 1, 1989, p. 6.

———. "Death Toll Crosses 200 in Sectarian Riots in India." January 10, 1993, p. 7.

———. "Poland Second Largest Producer of Synthetic Drugs." July 22, 1994, p. 17.

United States Department of State: Bureau of Public Affairs. "Cuban Involvement in Narcotics Trafficking. April 30, 1983.

———. "Nigeria." August 1992.

United States Department of Treasury: Bureau of Alcohol, Tobacco and Firearms. "ATF Overview of Asian Organized Crime 1993." 1993.

———. "Overview of Asian Organized Crime in the United States." March 1995.

United States Department of Treasury: United States Customs Service. "Asian Organized Crime: New York City Street Gangs." May 1993.

United States Drug Enforcement Administration: Drug Enforcement Task Force. "Dominican Narco-Traffickers." February 18, 1992.

United States Drug Enforcement Administration. "Israeli Organized Crime." April 28, 1986.

———. "Heroin Trafficking by Israeli Nationals." October 1986.

———. "Update on Pakistani Traffickers in the U.S." March 18, 1987.

———. "Trends in Traffic." May 1993.

United States Drug Enforcement Administration: Unified Intelligence Division. "Intelligence on Nigerian Heroin Traffickers." May 5, 1987.

———. "Special Intelligence Report Dominican Criminal Activity: A New York Perspective." February 1993.

United States Senate (1991). *U.S. International Drug Policy: Allegations of Increased Cuban Involvement in International Drug Trafficking*. Washington, DC: U.S. Government Printing Office.

United States Senate Committee on Foreign Affairs: House of Representatives (1989). *Cuban Involvement in International Narcotics Trafficking*. Washington, DC: U.S. Government Printing Office.

United States Senate Minority Staff of the Permanent Subcommittee on Investigations. "Asian Organized Crime Groups." November 5, 1991.

Vancouver Sun. "Big Circle Operating in Canada." September 16, 1993, p. A1.

———. "Crime Bosses from Russia Linking with Italy's Mafia." October 12, 1993, p. A13.

———. "Zhitnik Admits He's Been Target of Extortionists," December 27,1993, p. D1.

Vick, David. "International Alert Goes Out for Nigerian Fraudsters." *African Business*, May 1992, pp. 10–11.

Victoria Police: Asian Division. "Asian Crime in Victoria 1992." June 1, 1992, pp. 9–12.

Victoria Times. "Asia Based Gangs Wave of Future in Organized Crime." July 18, 1994, p. B15.

Viviano, Frank. "Eastern Europe's Lost Generation." *San Francisco Chronicle*, September 19, 1994, p. A1.

Volkman, Ernest (1998). *Gangbusters: The Destruction of America's Last Great Mafia Dynasty*. New York: HarperCollins Publishing.

Volsky, George. "Jamaican Drug Gangs Thriving in U.S. Cities." *New York Times*, July 19, 1987, p. 17.

Wade, B. (1993). Interview with Conly. In C.H Conly (Ed.), *Street Gangs: Current Knowledge and Strategies*. Washington, DC: National Institute of Justice.

Walker, Christopher. "Murders in Israel Blamed on Gangsters." *Times*, June 19, 1995.

Walsh, Anthony. "Behavior Genetics and Anomic/Strain Theory." *Criminology*, 2000, 38: 1075–1107.

Waxman, Sharon. "Rap Mogul Linked to 1997 Slaying; Death Row Label's Suge Knight Implicated in Star's Killing." *Washington Post*, April 21, 1999, p. C01.

Weekend Australian. "Asian Crime Gangs Lead Heroin Imports." November 20, 1993, p. 3.

Wells, Roger. "Popular Protest and Social Crime: The Evidence of Criminal Gangs in Southern England 1790–1860." 1997.

Wels, Saron (2000). "120 Charged in Probe of Mob on Wall Street." *Washington Post*, Last accessed on March 10, 2002.

West 57th Street. "The Palestinian Connection: Dirty Business," June 27, 1989.

Westrate, David L. "Drug Trafficking and Terrorism." *Drug Enforcement*, Summer 1985, pp. 19–24.

Wethern, George and Colnett, Vincent. (1978). *Wayward Angel*. New York: Marek Publishers.

Widlanski, Michael. "Assad Case." *New Republic*, February 3, 1992, pp. 8–10.

Wilkinson, Tracy. "Colombia's New Era of Traffickers." *Los Angeles Times*, February 12, 1994, pp. A1, A13–A14.

Williams, Laurie. "Alarm Grows over Similar Bankruptcies." *Tri-City Herald*, April 16, 1989, pp. A1, A2, A6–A8.

Williams, Phil. "Transnational Criminal Organizations and International Security." *Survival*, Spring 1994, Vol. 36, No. 1, pp. 96–113.

———. "The New Threat: Transnational Criminal Organizations and International Security." *Criminal Organizations*, Summer 1995, Vol. 9, Nos. 3, 4, pp. 63–76.

Wilson James Q. (1978). *The Investigators*. New York: Basic Books.

Wilson, Tracy. "Friends Helping Bail Out Christie." *Los Angeles Times*, October 5, 2001, Part 2, p. 3.

Witkin, Gordon, and Griffin, Jennifer. "The New Opium Wars." *U.S. News and World Report*, October 10, 1994, Vol. 117, No. 14, pp. 35–41.

Williams, Carolyn L., and Uchiyama, Craig. "Assessment of Life Events During Adolescence: The Use of Self Report Inventories." *Adolescence*, 1991, 24, pp. 95–118.

Woodworth, Paddy. "Why Do They Kill? The Basque Conflict in Spain." *World Policy Journal*, Spring 2001, Vol. 18, No. 1, pp. 1–12.

Wolf, Daniel (1991). *The Rebels: A Brotherhood of Outlaw Bikers*. Toronto: University of Toronto Press.

Woodiwis, Michael (1988). *Crime, Crusades and Corruption: Prohibition in the United States, 1900–1987*. New Jersey: Barnes and Noble.

Woolrich, Peter. "Chinese City Sells Its Citizens for 15G a Person." *New York Post*, June 9, 1993, p. 19.

———. "The Thai Connection." *Sunday Morning Post Magazine*, September 26, 1993, pp. 7–9.

X, Malcolm (1970). "By Any Means Necessary: Speeches, Interviews, and a Letter by Malcolm X." In G. Breitman (Ed.), *Malcolm X Speaks*. New York: Pathfinder.

X, Malcolm, and Haley, Alex (1964). *The Autobiography of Malcolm X*. New York: Grove Press.

Xinhua General Overseas News Service. "80 Tons of Drugs Destroyed in Syria." March 23, 1991, p. 9.

———. "Suspected Drug Smuggler Arrested." March 7, 1992, pp. 1, 6.

———. "Jamaah Islamiya Suspected Links to Philippine Airport Blast." May 12, 2003, p. 3.

Yablonsky, L. (1962). *The Violent Gang*. New York: Macmillan.

Yablonsky, Lewis (1997). *Gangsters*. New York: New York University Press.

Yglesias, Linda. "The Lust Roundup." *New York Daily News*, July 28, 1991, p. 21.

———. "Vice Grip." *New York Daily News*, July 28, 1991, pp. 4, 5, 21.

———. "Baby-Faced Boy, 13, Called Chinatown Thug." *New York Daily News*, November 28, 1994, pp. 4, 25.

Yunis, Khan. "PLO's Ability to Police Self Is Questioned: Arabs Fear Past Fighting Will Lead to Future Strife." *Dallas Morning News*, December 27, 1993, p. 1A.

Zatz, Marjorie. "The Changing Forms of Racial/Ethnic Basis Is Sentencing." *Crime and Delinquency*, 1985, 24, 69–92.

Zellner, W.W. (1995). *Counter Cultures: A Sociological Analysis*. New York: St. Martin's Press.

INDEX